COINAGE AND CURRENCY IN
EIGHTEENTH-CENTURY BRITAIN

THE PROVINCIAL COINAGE

IN MEMORY OF
MISS SARAH SOPHIA BANKS
1744-1818

VIRTUOSO, CONNOISSEUR AND
COLLECTOR OF PROVINCIAL COINS

Frontispiece: Sarah Sophia Banks, aged 44. Pastel drawing by John Russell, 1788.

COINAGE AND CURRENCY IN EIGHTEENTH-CENTURY BRITAIN

THE PROVINCIAL COINAGE

DAVID WILMER DYKES

SPINK

2011

First published 2011 by Spink & Son Ltd.
69 Southampton Row, London WC1B 4ET

ISBN 978-1-907427-16-9

Copyright ©2011 David Wilmer Dykes

All rights reserved. No part of this publication may be reproduced, stored in a retrieval system, or transmitted in any form or by any means, electronic, mechanical, photocopying, recording or otherwise, without the prior written permission of the author.

Typeset by Russell Whittle

Printed and bound in Malta
by Gutenberg Press Ltd.

PREFACE

POSTERITY will look with astonishment at the number and variety of provincial coins struck by various descriptions of men in the present century, and so far exceeding in design and workmanship the little towns-pieces and tokens issued about 100 years ago as a temporary supply to the circulation of copper money.

From a review of Samuel Birchall's *A Descriptive List of the Provincial Copper Coins or Tokens. The Gentleman's Magazine*, December 1797, 1034-35.

TOKEN, *s*. A small coin, struck by private individuals, to pass for a farthing, before the government struck such pieces. We, who have lately seen local and private tokens, as substitutes for silver coins, and before that in copper for pence, and two pences, cannot wonder at the practice.

Robert Nares, *A Glossary; or, Collection of Words, Phrases, Names, and Allusions to Customs, Proverbs, &c...* (1822).

Doctor Johnson defined the word 'token' as a 'sign', a 'mark' or, more to our purpose, as 'a piece of money current by sufferance, not coined by authority, formerly of very small value: in modern times, for the convenience of change...'. In effect, a currency substitute, something which was not normally official tender but which passed as an acceptable alternative in petty retail transactions, particularly when there was an absence or a shortage of the real thing.

Very much in Johnson's mind would have been the farthings issued under patent of the early Stuarts and, even more, the astonishing array of private tradesmen's pieces that took their place in the middle years of the seventeenth century. By Johnson's time, however, such tokens were, except in some remote parts of the country, things of the past occupying the scholarly attention of antiquaries and the curiosity of readers of the monthly magazines.

Johnson's *Dictionary* was published in 1755 and for most of his adulthood a regal copper coinage had been, by and large, the acknowledged medium for small change. Yet this regal copper money was itself regarded by authority as 'token'. Silver was still in the minds of most people, as it had been for centuries, the measure of value in the market place but, as Joseph Harris, the king's assay master, put it in the first part of his influential *Essay upon Money and Coins*,

> Silver is too dear to be coined into specie of the lowest denominations ... [and] ... a silver penny is too small for common use... To supply the want of very small silver coins, a kind of TOKENS or substitutes have been instituted; these, are now with us, all made of copper, and of two species only, called

halfpence, and *farthings*; and these are a legal tender in all sums below six-pence, which now is our smallest current silver coin.[1]

But the copper coinage was not considered as properly belonging to the Mint, it was struck intermittently and not effectively distributed over the country as a whole resulting in gluts in some parts and shortages in others. The full metal weight of the coinage also meant that it was prone to counterfeiting and by 1787 the Mint itself calculated that the forgeries in circulation exceeded its own regal issues. It was with the deplorable state of the coinage in mind and, partly to meet the needs of the workforce of his far-flung industrial empire, but with his eye mainly on capturing a national coinage contract that the copper magnate Thomas Williams issued his own 'Druid' pennies. In doing so he established the token or provincial coin, as it became known, as an increasingly familiar substitute for more regular currency in the last decade or so of the eighteenth century.

It is perhaps natural that someone coming from a town whose industrial foundations were built on the burgeoning copper trade of the eighteenth and early nineteenth centuries should have been attracted by this provincial coinage. In the 1940s Swansea – 'Copperopolis' – still had vestiges of the great days of its prime industry. John Vivian's gothic mansion overlooked Swansea Bay, as it still does today, the derelict 'moon land' of the long defunct smelting works[2] greeted the visitor by train from the east, while a drapery business continued to occupy the site of John Voss's shop and bank and was proud to display an image of his halfpenny on the back of its invoices[3].

What I have tried to do in this book is to set the eighteenth-century token into the context of the currency problems of the time, to say something about its manufacturers and issuers and their intentions, and thus to give a living dimension to a bygone monetary phenomenon. In this endeavour I have also attempted to do some justice to John Westwood whose key role in the establishment of the provincial coin has been ignored since the earliest days. For all his failings – and they were many – he is someone who deserves far more attention than he has been given. My focus has been on 'provincial coins' although I have not neglected political pieces or the collecting phenomenon, especially the contemporary publications that fostered it. What I have not attempted in any way has been to provide a catalogue of tokens, a task achieved a century ago by Dalton and Hamer in their irreplaceable, if at times overgenerous, conspectus and ably digested by Paul and Bente Withers in their recent handbook.

My obligations in writing the book have been many. First and foremost my thanks must go to the late William Hanna, Honorary

---

1 Harris (1757), 65.

2 Most of them owned by companies issuing eighteenth- or early nineteenth-century copper tokens: Williams's 'Upper Bank' and Vivian's 'Havod' works and the smelteries of the 'Birmingham', 'Bristol', 'Rose', 'Crown' and 'British' companies.

3 And to show the curious the old bank strong room, the scene of the skilful robbery of £24,000 in 1828 when the partners were at church and where the burglers left a chalked message 'Watch as well as Pray'.

PREFACE

Secretary of the Royal Institution of South Wales – in those days still a wonderful Victorian repository of books and artefacts – and to the late Anthony Thompson of the Ashmolean Museum who both did much to foster my youthful numismatic understanding as a schoolboy and as an undergraduate. More directly in the preparation of this book my thanks are due to Philip Attwood, Edward Besly, the late George Boon, David Brooke, the late Professor W. H. Chaloner, Kevin Clancy, Alan and Noel Cox, Graham Dyer, Catherine Eagleton, Ken Elks, Virginia Hewitt, Stephen Hill, Harrington E. Manville, Philip Mernick, Hugh Pagan, May Sinclair, Keith Sugden, David Symons, Susan Walker, Caroline Wilkinson, the late Kyffin Williams, and especially Paul and Bente Withers, Michael Dickinson, Peter Preston-Morley and Robert Thompson. Michael Dickinson, Peter Preston-Morley and Robert Thompson also very kindly read the text of an earlier version of the book and made invaluable comments.

It will be obvious from my footnotes that the book could not have been written without the help and courtesy of the staff of a number of institutions. I hope, however, that they will accept a collective expression of thanks here. Nevertheless, it would be ungenerous of me not to mention the British Library, those havens, the Athenæum and London Libraries, and the Royal Mint Library made especially memorable also for the hospitality of Graham Dyer and Kevin Clancy and the profitable discussions I have had with them. My deepest obligation is, however, to the staff of the Birmingham Archives and Heritage Service who have been unstinting in their search and provision of documents from the 'Archive of Soho'. Since my original researches in Birmingham the references of material in the Matthew Boulton and associated papers have changed and the Service has been very accommodating in providing me with new references where appropriate and where this was impractical David Symons helpfully stepped into the breach despite the burdens of the Matthew Boulton Bicentenary Exhibition and the discovery of the Staffordshire Hoard. Where it has not been possible to specify current references former references have been given from which the documents concerned may still be identified.

The following illustrations are reproduced by courtesy and kind permission of the individuals and institutions listed: Angela Archer and Brewin Dolphin: 61c; A. H. Baldwin and Sons: 105; Beazley Archive, Oxford University: 344b; Birmingham Libraries and Archives: 45, 53, 96, 101, 108, 110, 147, 161, 196, 201, 207, 210, 249, 374; Birmingham Museums and Art Gallery: 75, 77, 252; Bodleian Library, University of Oxford (John Johnson Coll. Trade Cards 20 (54)): 297; Carmarthenshire Museums Service: 150c; Coram held at the London Metropolitan Archives: 170; Dix Noonan Web: 70, 138a, 150a and b, 157, 180, 182, 205, 235, 257, 267, 269, 284, 307, 308, 309, 314, 316, 317, 324, 325, 360, 378, 382; Dundee Art Galleries and Museum (Dundee City Council): 123; East Sussex County Council Library & Information Service: 261; Christopher Eimer: 23a, 80; Fitzwilliam Museum, Cambridge: 155, 159, 203, 204, 224, 240, 244, 255c, 257, 271, 334; Lorna Freeman. Source English Heritage. NMR: 168; Glamorgan Archives and Royal Institution of South Wales, Swansea: 120; Hastings Museum and Art Gallery: 171; Herbert Art Gallery and Museum, Coventry: 194; The Hunterian, University of Glasgow: 3a; A representative of the Knatchbull Collection; photograph, Photographic Survey, Courtauld Institute of Art: Frontispiece; Lancaster City Collections (LANLM.1926.10.1): 158; Lewis Walpole Library, Yale University, 327; London Metropolitan Archives: 117, 328; Philip Mernick: 2, 3c, 5, 6; National Gallery of Scotland: 44; National Library of Australia: 127; National Library of Wales: 151; National Museum of Wales: 61a, 62, 149; National Portrait Gallery, London: 17, 28, 40, 71, 78, 125, 242, 323; Norfolk Museums and Archaeology Service (Norwich Castle Museum & Art Gallery): 153, 220; Royal Academy of Arts: 66; Royal Bank of Scotland Group: 175; Royal Mint Museum: 212, 290b, 293, 321, 361, 363, 365, 368, 371, 372, 377, 380, 383; Scottish National Portrait Gallery: 98, 272, 344a, 345; Senate House Library, University of London: 318; Sherborne Museum: 174; Smithsonian Institution, Washington, DC: 162a and b; Society of Antiquaries of London: 16, 65; Southampton City Council: 93; Spink and Son Ltd: 7, 9c, 14, 19a, 27, 39, 49, 106, 255a, 393; The Museum in the Park, Stroud, Gloucestershire: 166; Suffolk Record Office: 259 (Lowestoft Branch: 193/2/1), 387 (Ipswich Branch: PR/C/31); City and County of Swansea: Glynn Vivian Art Gallery Collection: 262; Trustees of the British Museum: 1, 12, 19b, 19c, 19e-19j, 19l, 42a, 42b, 79a, 79b, 82, 116, 134, 148, 198, 216, 218, 227, 246, 266, 290a, 332; Trustees of the National Library of Scotland: 277; Trustees of the William Salt Library, Stafford: 76; Victoria and Albert Museum, London: 233; Wellcome Library, London: 231a and b; Paul and Bente Withers: 48b, 214a, 241 and for their photographs of tokens in the British Museum and Fitzwilliam Museum. The remaining images are from the author's collection and library.[4]

I owe much to the encouragement of Douglas Saville who first suggested the writing of this book and to Philip Skingley who has so skilfully seen it through to publication. My deepest debt, though, as always, is to my wife, Margaret, for her constant support.

D. W. D.

Dorchester.
2011

---

[4] Every effort has been made to trace image copyright holders. Where unsuccessful the publishers would appreciate any information that would enable them to do so.

CONTENTS

LIST OF TABLES		x
ABBREVIATIONS		xi
PROLOGUE		1
I	THE STATE OF THE COINAGE	35
II	THE GREAT CONTENTION	71
III	A MOST SATISFYING ADVENTURE	115
IV	A BIRMINGHAM TOKEN CONSORTIUM: AN INGENIOUS MECHANIC AND AN ADMIRED ARTIST	157
V	THE NEW MEN	203
VI	COLLECTORS, DEALERS AND RADICALS	261
VII	LAST THINGS	295

APPENDICES:

I	Schedule of Provincial Coins Issued between 1791 and 1798	311
II	Biographical Notes on Artists, Engravers and Die Sinkers	323
III	The Contemporary Catalogues	329

BIBLIOGRAPHY

INDEX

LIST OF TABLES

1	Matthew Boulton's Provincial Coin Contracts	121
2	Westwood/Hancock Provincial Coin Contracts	167
3	Obadiah Westwood/Hancock Provincial Coin Contracts	178
4	Birmingham Manufacturers of Provincial Coins 1787-1804	211
5	Birmingham Token Manufacturers and Provincial Coin Commissions 1792-1798	213
6	Average Manufactured Copper Prices in £s per ton 1792-1799	214

ABBREVIATIONS

ABG – *Aris's Birmingham Gazette*

BAH – Birmingham Archives and Heritage Service, Birmingham Central Library

BHM – *British Historical Medals*

BL – British Library

BM – British Museum

BNJ – *British Numismatic Journal*

CRO – Cornwall Record Office

CSP – *Calendar of State Papers*

CTCJ – *The 'Conder' Token Collector's Journal* (1998-)

CTCN – *The 'Conder' Token Collector's Newsletter* (1996-98)

D&H – R Dalton and S H Hamer, *The Provincial Token-Coinage of the Eighteenth Century* ([Bristol], privately printed in 14 parts 1910-1918)

DNW – Dix Noonan Webb, Auctioneers and Valuers

DRO – Dorset Record Office

EconHR – *Economic History Review*

EETS – Early English Text Society

Eimer – Eimer, Christopher (2010), *British Commemorative Medals and their Values* (London)

GM – *The Gentleman's Magazine*

HMC – Historical Manuscripts Commission

LC – Library of Congress

LG – *The London Gazette*

MBP – Matthew Boulton Papers, Birmingham Archives and Heritage Service, Birmingham Central Library

NC – *The Numismatic Chronicle*

N&Q – *Notes and Queries*

NHM – Natural History Museum

NLS – National Library of Scotland

NMS – National Museum of Scotland

NMW – National Museum of Wales

OED – *Oxford English Dictionary*

ODNB – *Oxford Dictionary of National Biography*

P&P – *Past and Present*

Peck – Peck, C. W. (1960), *English Copper, Tin and Bronze Coins in the British Museum 1558-1958* (London)

Pridmore – Pridmore, F. (1975), *The Coins of the British Commonwealth of Nations: Part 4. India, Volume 1, East India Company Presidency Series c.1642-1835* (London)

PRO – Public Record Office

SAS – Society of Antiquaries of Scotland

SCMB – *Seaby's Coin and Medal Bulletin*

SNC – *Spink's Numismatic Circular*

TCSB – Token Corresponding Society Bulletin

UBD – *Universal British Directory*

Trans Cymmr – *Transactions of the Honourable Society of Cymmrodorian*

WRO – Warwick County Record Office

PROLOGUE

> In all well regulated governments it is found to be as requisite, that there should be money of small value for the use of the market and the poorer sort of subjects, as of the larger species for the other purposes of trade and commutation; and what the value of the smallest piece should be, is pointed out by the proportion the price of provisions bears to that of labour, and to the abilities of the lower class of people to purchase them.
>
> Thomas Snelling,
> *A View of the Copper Coin and Coinage of England*
> (1766), Preface [I].

On Thursday 7 May 1795 Miss Sarah Sophia Banks bought from John Hammond, a printer in London's St Martin's Lane, a few doors up from Charing Cross, a sixpenny pamphlet that he had just brought out. Hammond was well placed to promote what he called *A Descriptive List of Provincial Coins* since he dealt in such modern trivia as a profitable sideline to his printing work and was hand-in-glove with the seamier – and now burgeoning – end of metropolitan token production. And Miss Banks, in her anxiety to acquire what was the first of its kind, took care to take home to her library at 32 Soho Square two copies of his new catalogue.[1]

Miss Banks – 'Sophy' to her immediate family – was the formidable sister of an even more formidable brother, the distinguished botanist, Sir Joseph Banks, confidant of the king, scientific adviser to government and, already for more than sixteen years, President of the Royal Society. In scientific matters she was as much her brother's hostess as his wife, Dorothea, sharing to the full the Georgian luminary's 'zeal for science and the study of natural history', advancing her brother's interests, and taking as great a delight as he in the collection of the novel and the curious.[2] Equally, Sir Joseph's standing at the pinnacle of British scientific scholarship and his good offices with like-minded associates enabled Sophia Banks to achieve a cultural recognition denied to most

---

[1] Miss Banks's copies of Hammond's Descriptive List are both personally inscribed with her date of acquisition: 'May 7. 1795'. One copy is in the Royal Mint Library; the other (marked 'duplicate' by Miss Banks) was disposed of by the Royal Mint in 1985 (Spink Coin Auctions, 47 (10 October 1985), lot 1320) and auctioned again by DNW (Sale T9, 6 October, 2010, lot 4290). A third copy of the catalogue was sold by Glendining & Co. on 4 June 1992 (Sale 5/1992, lot 369). Hammond's shop was on the right hand side when going from Charing Cross into St. Martin's Lane.

[2] A biographical study of Miss Banks (1744-1818) is long overdue but for a contemporary, if capricious, vignette, see Smith (1905), 229-31, and for an all too brief, if appreciative, obituary, *GM*, November 1818, 472. See also *ODNB*; and Gascoigne (1994), esp. 23-27 and 66-67. Sir Joseph Banks's interest to the numismatist arises from his close friendship with Matthew Boulton (1728-1809) and Charles Jenkinson, Lord Hawkesbury and later 1st earl of Liverpool (1727-1808), which drew him to the reform of the coinage and, as a Privy Councillor from 1797, his active membership of the Council Committee on Coin. Banks's coin collection and numismatic library were presented to the Royal Mint in 1818 to form the nucleus of its museum and library. For Banks (1743-1820), see *ODNB*; Gascoigne (1994), especially 229-32; Carter (1988), especially 312-13 and 520; and Smith (1911).

women even of her class and intellect. And her own painstakingly annotated collections, among the largest and finest of their kind in Europe, echoed, albeit on a more limited scale, her brother's broader, global enthusiasms.

Sophia Banks was no mere dilettante virtuoso restricting herself to the typically feminine pursuits of shell and fossil collection for drawing room display – although such objects naturally came within her compass – or amassing an eclectic, indiscriminate cache of curios. She set out to create in her collections, if not an 'ethnography of Britain' as has been rather pretentiously claimed, at least something of a microcosmic reflection of the social world around her. So, from a meagre allowance, she brought together, purposefully and systematically, a remarkable array of collectables, past and present, from the rare to the rattletrap. Caricatures, playbills, trade cards, and all sorts of printed and engraved ephemera, were snapped up by this insatiable, but focussed magpie, preserving for future generations a wealth of fugitive material of the greatest historical value for an understanding of eighteenth-century social and commercial life.[3] It was, though, an attention not directed solely to the transient minutiae of urban life for she immersed herself, too, in the rural folk customs of her home county, and, as one of the country's earliest amateur philologists, compiled a not inconsequential 'glossary' of Lincolnshire dialect words.[4]

Nor did Sophia Banks lack practicality. In her younger days she had been quite a fashionable whip driving a four-in-hand with style, had been an accomplished archer and at Spring Grove, Banks's country retreat at Isleworth, where he maintained something akin to an experimental out-station in plant and animal breeding, she had charge of the hot houses and conservatories while her sister-in-law looked after the dairy.[5] Many saw in her the true eccentric and, although she enjoyed the close friendship of the king's third daughter, Princess Elizabeth,[6] she was outspoken, abrupt, lacked many of the graces of the drawing room, and adopted such a peculiar outdoor dress that she was on at least one occasion mistaken for a street ballad-singer. According to the printmaker and raconteur, John Thomas 'Antiquity' Smith, who was well acquainted with her as a Soho neighbour,

---

[3] The importance Sarah Banks attached to her pioneering collections is reflected in their bequest to Lady Banks who in turn presented the printed and engraved ephemera to the British Museum in 1818 (now divided between the Museum's Department of Prints and Drawings (about 19,000 items) and the British Library (nine volumes of broadsides, newspaper cuttings and other prints – BL: LR. 301. h.3-11)): Griffiths and Williams (1987), 82-84.

[4] Matthews (1935), 398-404.

[5] Smith (1911), 307 and 317.

[6] Cf. the dedication in an album of silhouettes given by Princess Elizabeth to Miss Banks in 1808 (Roberts (2004), 87): 'Sophia Zarah Banks – Genius, good sense, and Friendship kind, Must ever bring you to my mind. Eliza.'

PROLOGUE

> Miss Banks ... was looked after by the eye of astonishment wherever she went, and in whatever situation she appeared. Her dress was that of the *Old School*; her Barcelona quilted petticoat had a hole on either side for the convenience of rummaging two immense pockets, stuffed with books of all sizes. The petticoat was covered with a deep stomachered gown, sometimes drawn through the pocket-holes... In this dress I have frequently seen her walk, followed by a six-foot servant with a cane almost as tall as himself.[7]

It may be this form of apparel that she is shown wearing in James Gillray's cartoon, *An Old Maid on a Journey* [1] or perhaps one of the habits, made of her brother's Merino wool from Spring Grove, that she and her sister-in-law for a time sported regularly and in the most incongruous situations.[8] It is a not implausible identification although it carries no contemporary authority but, if it is Miss Banks that is caricatured, it was a cruel satire to put a person who, like her mother, was a deeply devout woman in the suggestive setting of a libidinous inn. As her obituarist in the *Gentleman's Magazine* observed, Miss Banks was someone whose 'moral worth, even more than her talents and knowledge, rendered her the object of esteem and regard'.[9]

1   *An Old Maid on a Journey*. From an engraving by James Gillray, published 20 November 1804 by Hannah Humphrey from her print shop at 27 St. James's Street, London: George (1947), 10300.

7   Smith (1905), 229. John Thomas Smith (1766-1833) was Keeper of Prints and Drawings at the British Museum, 1816-33. For Smith, described as 'a Rowlandson of the word', see *ODNB* and Owen (1994), 34-36.

8   For the supposed identification of the 'old maid' with Miss Banks see Wright and Evans (1851), 473 and Wright (1873), 31. Miss Banks is said to have ordered her woollen habits three at a time, one for best (Hightum), one for second best (Tightum), and one for everyday wear (Scrub): Smith (1905), 230. Smith, significantly, makes no reference to the cartoon

9   *GM*, November 1818, 472

However singular Miss Banks may have appeared to some contemporaries her reputation today is firmly founded on the exceptional collections that she built up and for which she was acknowledged even in her own day, especially among the wide circle of her brother's influential friends many of whom helped to sustain her appetite, particularly in the creation of her coin and medal collection. Here, she gathered together an outstanding numismatic cabinet of British and European coins, coins of Africa, Asia and the Americas, including the newly independent United States, and seventeenth and eighteenth-century trade tokens.[10] In such things, she was, as Sir Joseph admitted to his friend Matthew Boulton, 'a great pusher'. And over Sophia Banks's anxiety to secure a specimen of Soho's five-sol piece, newly struck for the French merchant house of Monneron [92], even the great panjandrum of late Georgian scientific endeavour had had to abase himself, if only half-jokingly, to the Birmingham entrepreneur: 'if you fear a lady's resentment or wish to court her Favour I would advise you to Furnish her with one as spedily [*sic*] as convenient and if you add to it any other new tokens it may be well, as the sight of them will certainly work favourably in her eyes'.[11]

That was in December 1791. Miss Banks had already caught the bug for the private coinages being put out in increasing numbers by industrialists and trades people as a substitute for small change towards the close of the eighteenth century and which, because of their originality of design and their being 'neatly executed', were beginning to find a niche in the collector's cabinet.[12] She built up an extensive collection much to the disappointment of 'Antiquity' Smith. Ever financially embarrassed, Smith years later recalled that possessing 'an immense number of tradesmen's tokens' he left them at Soho Square for Miss Banks who, after a few hours, returned them to him in person, 'holding up the front of her riding-habit with both hands, the contents of which she delivered upon the table, at the same time observing "that she considered herself extremely obliged to me for my politeness, but that, extraordinary as it might appear, out of so many hundred there was not one that she wanted"'.[13] Her reaction is not all that difficult to understand; when she died in September 1818 Miss Banks's numismatic collection as a whole – coins, tokens and medals – has been calculated as comprising in the region of nine to ten thousand

10 Miss Banks's numismatic collection (catalogued in eight MS volumes written up initially about 1810 and now in the British Museum, Department of Coins and Medals [Arc R 19]), also bequeathed to Lady Banks, was presented by the latter to the Mint subject to the selection by the British Museum of such specimens as were wanting in its collections. The bulk of the collection (more than six thousand coins, tokens and medals) went to the Museum, the remainder, well over two thousand objects together with Miss Banks's numismatic library, going to the Mint: Carter (1988), 520: information from Catherine Eagleton and Kevin Clancy.

11 BAH: MBP 272/36: Sir Joseph Banks to Matthew Boulton, 19 December 1791.

12 Leake (1793), Appendix, 7.

13 Smith (1905), 230-31.

PROLOGUE

items. And even then she had given away at least 3,800 British tokens and had a separate duplicates cabinet that she kept expressly for the purposes of exchange with other collectors. For, by the time she was patronising Hammond, Sophia Banks was far from alone in her enthusiasm; by then the quest for these provincial coins or tokens had become something of a fad which publications like Hammond's both fostered and fed upon.

But tokens, as a substitute for small change, were no novelty. They are known to have existed in the fifteenth century and it may well be that they functioned as a form of sub-coinage even earlier. Archaeological evidence for this, though, is meagre and documentary sources are wanting so that the true purpose of the coin-like lead or pewter 'pictorial' pieces [2] that are thought to have survived from as far back as the late thirteenth century must remain an open question.[14] These are more likely to have been used as redeemable vouchers for liturgical or charitable purposes with little or no cash value in themselves but it would be foolhardy to rule out any derivative circulatory role for them completely.[15] By the latter part of the fourteenth century, following continental precedents, such tokens do seem to have been developing a very low level monetary function in London. But it must still have been on a comparatively small scale and one must not necessarily read the existence of real coin or coin substitute into the occurrence of fractional sums below the farthing – the lowest value official coin minted – in contemporary accounting records; they are probably as much 'ghost money' as the equally abstract pounds and shillings of account.[16]

Nevertheless, the numbers of lead pieces seem to have increased as the Mint's minor silver became scarcer following a cut-back in the costly production of halfpennies and especially farthings after 1351 in the midst of the 'silver bullion famine' of the time. The dearth of these coins, said to be hampering the purchase by the poor of 'small quantities of bread and beer ... all over England' and inhibiting payments 'for God and for works of charity', was a repeated complaint

2 English pewter token, 13th. century.

---

14 Cf. Dolley and Seaby (1971), 446-48, describing the Winetavern Street, Dublin Hoard of tokens that the authors dated 'to the period immediately preceding the introduction of the round farthing by Edward I in 1279'.

15 Grierson (1971), 50-51; Mitchiner and Skinner (1983), 29-77. See also the valuable study of medieval token 'coinage' in its continental context by Courtenay (1972-73), 275-95.

16 There are, however, literary hints that halfpennies were cut into quarters although not unnaturally no examples of such miniscule pieces have come down to us and the word 'mite' seems to have referred to half a farthing: Spufford (1988), 331; Rogers (1995), 7.

3a Scottish (Perth) silver halfpenny of Robert III, 1390-1403.

3b Venetian *soldino* ('*Galey-Halpeny*') of Doge Francesco Dandolo, 1329-1339.

3c English lead token, late 14th.- early 15th. centuries.

4 Edward I silver farthing (Lincoln).

of a parliament alarmed at its social consequences.[17] But it was not until 1402 that the earliest documentary reference to lead tokens as currency was recorded. In that year a Commons petition alleged that for want of halfpennies and farthings poor people 'of great necessity' were being obliged to make use not only of base foreign coin such as Scottish halfpennies [3a] and Venetian *soldini* ['*Galey-Halpenys*'] [3b], but in some parts 'halfpennies divided' and in others lead tokens ['diverses signes de Plombe'] [3c] to meet their everyday needs.[18] Concern about the circulation of foreign currency and cut coinage was of long standing but this was the first positive reference to the circulation of lead tokens as small change. It was a solitary instance, however, and we hear no more about tokens until Tudor times.

England, unlike Scotland and many other European states, had traditionally turned its face against any official 'white' or 'black' billon money.[19] Sterling silver, with a face value close to the metal's intrinsic value, had been the general rule for its circulating currency and since Edward I's reign (1279) had been minted as low as the farthing [4].[20] Over time, however, rises in the value of bullion saw considerable reductions in the size and weight of fractional money so that by the fifteenth century the farthing, never more than 14 mm in diameter, had become impractically small. Still of good silver it was by now a tiny coin only about 9 mm in diameter and weighing less than a quarter of a gram. Time-consuming and disproportionately costly to produce, from mid-century it was never struck in sufficient numbers to be freely available, and, inconvenient to handle, it was easily lost.

Over most of the country the perennial scarcity of a fractional coinage in the later Middle Ages presented few problems. For in the subsistence economy of the essentially agricultural society that Britain was to remain in large measure until the nineteenth century

17 Rogers (1995), 7; Ruding (1840), I, 237-38, quoting parliamentary petitions of 1378 or 1379 and 1380. A further parliamentary petition of 1393 complained that 'the sustenance of poor beggars' was compromised by the shortage of halfpence and farthings, for 'worthy persons' were unwilling to disburse as a much as a whole penny in charity if there was no hope of receiving change. It also alleged that 'when a poor man would buy his victuals, and other necessaries convenient for him, and had only a penny, for which he ought to receive a halfpenny in change, he many times did spoil his penny in order to make one halfpenny': Ruding (1840), I, 245. Cut halfpennies and farthings may have been a feature of charitable giving. Cf. the Dunwich Hoard that contained an appreciable number of cut Short Cross/Long Cross fractions, perhaps the contents of a monastic offertory box: Hancox (1908), 125-26; Seaman (1972), 27-28.

18 'La Monoie d'estranges Terres, come Mill' d'Escoce, & autres appellez Galey-Halpenys, & es aucuns parties Demy-deniers coupes: ... & es aucuns lieuz diverses signes de Plombe': Rotuli Parliamentorum, III, 498. For an English version see Ruding (1840), I, 250. For the circulation of foreign coin in late medieval England see Spufford, (1963), 127-39 and Cook (1999), 231-84. Scottish coins circulated freely in the northern counties. For Scottish coins found on Anglesey, see Besly (1995), 75-76.

19 Debased coinage of half silver or less than 10% silver respectively.

20 The original farthings of 1279 were struck at an average weight of 0.43g alloyed and from 1280 at 0.36g sterling: Withers (2001), 6.

PROLOGUE

5   English sterling-type jetton, early 14th. century.

with its complex network of kin and co-operative neighbourliness cash was not the primary medium of exchange and even trifling transactions would be carried out by credit arrangements, 'reckoning' or off-setting reciprocal debts or, by settlements in kind or through barter. Shortages of ready money, especially in the middle years of the fifteenth century, encouraged such practices and although goods or labour would be measured by monetary prices this did not necessarily mean that actual coin changed hands more than it had to although more substantial payments for taxes and rents were a different matter and, in England, were normally required in cash. This is not to say that the lowest-value cash was never used in the countryside but such documentary and archaeological evidence as exists is sparse and not very informative although even Roman finds seem on occasion to have been pressed into service as small change.[21] It was in the less static, more anonymous milieu of the towns, especially metropolitan London (with perhaps 50,000 inhabitants in 1500 and growing rapidly), that such money was becoming more imperative for the myriad of small purchases that had to be made for everyday living. Although, even in the towns, many commodities would be supplied 'on the slate' for later cumulative settlement, growing migratory influx and developing commercialisation meant that impersonal contacts increasingly replaced the 'face-to-face' relationships and familiar trust of established communities. There was a heightening need for a minimal circulating currency to provide, in Adam Smith's words, the convenience of purchasing 'subsistence from day to day, or even from hour to hour'.[22] And, bearing in mind the purchasing value of the elusive farthing in the later middle ages – it would buy a standard loaf of the finest bread, a quart of ale or two red herrings – the popular reception given to base foreign money – *galyhalpenys* ('three or four' being 'hardly worth a sterling'), Dutch *seskyns*, *dodekins* and the like – is thus hardly surprising. It seems that almost any coin-like object – even perhaps jettons or reckoning counters intended for purposes of accountancy [5] – could slip into the currency and fulfil the function of small change.[23] And *galyhalpenys*, which had been effectively rooted out by the 1420s, made a brief resurgence in the early sixteenth

---

21 Muldrew (1998), 101-103; Wrightson (2000), 52. Cf. Dyer (1994), 276-77; Dyer (2005), 175-76; Dyer (1997), 38-40. Comparison might be drawn with Gilbert White's graphic description of how in the 1740s Roman coins found in the Selborne area of Hampshire 'passed for farthings at the petty shops': White (1813), 305-306.

22 Smith (1789) [1994], 391.

23 *Zeskins* have been identified by Professor Spufford as Flemish six-mite pieces or quarter-groats and *duitkins* as deniers of Holland worth roughly a farthing and half a farthing respectively. They seem to have been imported in only very small quantities: Spufford (1963), 136. Berry (1974), 28 points out that English jettons are almost invariably pierced or indented as a precaution against their use as coinage. On the possible use of jettons as coinage Barnard (1916), 78-80 has little conclusive to say other than in a fraudulent context while Snelling (1769), 7 is concerned only with their inappropriate designation as 'black money'.

century and were sufficiently common to enter common parlance as a symbol of worthlessness.[24]

The continuing need in the early Tudor period for an everyday currency below the level of the official coinage is exemplified by the tariffs set by local authorities and the government in the face of rapidly rising food costs. In 1533, for example, government statute stipulated that the retail price of mutton and veal should not exceed 'one halfpenny and half farthing' (⅝d) a pound, and, as late as 1551, that 'great, thick Essex cheese' should be pegged at the same amount while the comparable price for raw beef and pork was to be 1⅛d.[25] In practice, of course, foodstuffs would often have been bought in greater amounts than those quantified in the tariffs and on credit, so that actual use of any substitute half-farthing must not be exaggerated. Even so, many poorer townsfolk – an increasing element in a mobile population – would have chosen or been able to buy their basics only in small quantities and thus meat would no doubt have been frequently sold by less than the pound weight. And, at the local tavern, ale would manifestly have been sold in daily quantities less than the penny gallon. Much of this trade would have been 'on tick' and unofficial tokens therefore would have fulfilled a practical need as petty credit tallies specific to an individual tradesman, perhaps broadening out into a minimal medium of exchange if a more general acceptability could be assured in the locality. By this time literary evidence begins to accumulate for such usage though it is still sketchy and ambiguous. Erasmus, for instance, in a vague passage much cherished by numismatists, recalled the existence of lead 'coins' ['*nummos ... plumbeos*'] during his stay in England between 1509 and 1514 while at about the same time a Venetian diplomat mentioned in a letter home what were probably credit tallies ['*tessara*'] used for the purchase of everyday necessities.[26] These tallies no doubt seeped into the currency but tokens, of whatever kind, seem to have remained a largely London phenomenon until the mid-sixteenth century.[27] Nicholas Tyery, a minter petitioning Henry VIII for the right to undertake a coinage for Ireland, condemned, amongst other wrongs, the 'sufferaunce' of 'tokyns ... curraunt within your citie of london in deression of your coyne'. Such 'sufferaunce', he was persuaded, 'causyth ... grett

---

24 Spufford (1963), 137-38; *OED* s.v. 'galley-halfpenny': 'My riches are not worth a Gally halfe peny' [Thomas Becon ['Theodore Basil'], *The New Poleceye of Warre* (1542)].

25 Myers (1969), 958-59 (no 146, iv (a)); Hughes and Larkin (1964-69), I (1964), (no. 231), 531 (no. 380). For the pricing of meat in Henry VIII's reign see Heinze (1969), 583-95.

26 'Aereos nummos et hodie novit Flandria, plumbeos Anglia' ['Nowadays Flanders is familiar with copper coins, England with lead ones']: Desidarius Erasmus, *Adagiorum Opus* (Basel, 1533), 1051, no. 5109. Grierson ((1972), 85-87) identified the 1533 edition of Erasmus's 'Adages' as the first in which this passage occurred and argued that it probably related to a recollection of his stay in England in the years 1508-13 [*recte* 1509-14]. Letter of Nicolo di Favri, calendared in *CSP Venice* (1867), 90 (no. 219): 23 January 1513.

27 Cf. Dolley and Hocking (1963), 206-7.

PROLOGUE

6   English tin token, early 16th. century.

7   Edward VI silver farthing.

8   Elizabeth I pattern copper halfpenny 'pledge', c. 1578.

9a Elizabeth I silver three-farthings, 1561.

mysere' [6].[28]

If it did cause 'great misery' such 'sufferance' was, it seemed, not to be purged by government. By Elizabeth's reign, as the country's market economy developed, the shortage of regal small coin had become much worse. The silver farthing, a more workaday coin than its predecessor of the fifteenth-century though by now minute and a nuisance, had been discreetly abandoned by Edward VI [7] but nothing had been put in its place and, sparse and exiguous as it had become,[29] it left a void that was not to be successfully bridged for more than a century. An official billon or copper coinage such as had long been current in Scotland and on the continent, if adequately controlled, would have eased the situation but the state hesitated to experiment with what would have been of necessity a non-intrinsic token coinage and one prone to counterfeiting.[30] This was not for want of proposals for base or copper alternatives for a coin that, in the words of Christopher Bumpstead, a projector at the outset of Elizabeth's reign, was as 'necessarie … [as] … water is for the Thames' but in silver was not 'handable', weighed scarcely 0.19 g, and, as it was later said, could 'be blown away, with the breath of a man's mouth'.[31] Some schemes were even put forward by officials of the Mint itself, but the Queen, mindful of her own strenuous restoration of the coinage from the 'dross and base matter' of her predecessors, is said to have been adamant in her opposition and she remained so throughout her reign. 'Coarse and base alloy, to the slander and discredit of our fine silver moneys now being', the Queen announced c. 1601, 'we have clearly rejected'.[32] One scheme for copper halfpenny and farthing 'pledges' of payment in 'real' currency did apparently make some headway about the year 1576 but, although a draft proclamation was prepared and a pattern halfpenny eventually struck [8], the scheme was never endorsed by the Queen.[33]

Nothing was done beyond the striking of silver three-halfpence and three-farthing coins [9a], which in combination with the issue of

28 Lamond (1893), 184. Echoing the parliamentary concerns of a century before, Tyery also condemned the 'strange coynes … curraunt within your Reame' and 'the kyng of skottys copper coyne … curraunt in your towne of barwycke and the contray invyround'.

29 The physician and traveller, Andrew Bo[o]rde, noted the scarcity of farthings in 1542: 'The sylver of England is 'Grotes, halfe grotes, Pens, halfe pens, and there be some Fardynges': Furnivall (1870),121.

30 Snelling (1766a), 3-4. Sir Richard Martin, then warden of the Mint and later himself a sponsor of a base silver coinage pointed out apropos of a 1576 scheme that to accord with its intrinsic value a copper halfpenny would have to weigh an ounce – the weight of Boulton's 1797 penny. The first European *copper* coin was the *cavallo* introduced in Naples in 1472: Porteous (1969), 146 and 149.

31 *Christopher Bumpstead … to the Q: … re ye presidents for making of small moneys*: PRO: SP 12/20, 56, f.124; *Reasons to prove the Necessaryness for the making of Pence, Halfpence and Farthings of Copper…*: BL: Additional MSS 10113, f. 31(28 September 1607).

32 Hughes and Larkin (1964-69), III (1969), 22-23 (no. 805). For the various projects and presumptive patterns see *Peck* (1960), 9-18.

33 *Peck* (1960), 13-14. Official disdain for base coin was an insuperable barrier to the minting of an effective small currency, Sweden and Spain often being quoted as economies ruined by non-precious coin: Gaskill (2000), 162.

9b   Elizabeth I silver penny, 1567-70.

9c   Elizabeth I silver halfpenny, 1592-95.

10   Elizabeth I copper Irish penny, 1602.

twopenny pieces and pennies [9b], were intended, by 'juggling' (Sir John Craig's word) with one's change, to facilitate the making of halfpenny and farthing purchases. What has been described as an 'ingenious and rather intellectual experiment' was no more than an awkward palliative measure and was discontinued in 1583. The silver halfpennies [9c] that were subsequently reintroduced, though plentiful in their supply, were again 'inconvenient and troublesome in their use' ... 'so small and thin, that many cannot feele them between their fingers' – they now weighed little more than a fifteenth-century farthing – and did little to relieve the demand for small change.[34] As a result the flow of private tokens quickened, and augmented with the ever-present Scottish and continental base money, and after 1601 stray Irish copper pennies and halfpennies [10], they were increasingly the mainstay of the nation's petty currency.

Private tokens were, however, a mixed blessing; their shortcomings punctuated by Bumpstead, a London mercer. 'In these p[ar]ts', he declared, stressing his local concern, 'both vintners, grocers, chandlers, tipplers and other retailers do quoine in their houses several tokens of leade and do cause them to goe instead of pence, half pence and farthings to the great dishonor of the realme, and like hinderance to her ma[jes]ty's subjects for that the said leaden tokens are current in no place but in the several houses where they are quoined'.[35] While this hostile comment came from no disinterested observer Bumpstead was addressing the private tokens' cardinal weaknesses – their currency over a limited area and even within it the uncertainty of their exchange – charges to be echoed repeatedly down to Miss Banks's time.

Sometimes lead tokens seem to have passed at still lower values than the penny, halfpenny or farthing that Bumpstead and others identified. The young Swiss traveller, Thomas Platter, when he visited London in 1599, claimed to have come across tradesmen issuing lead or copper tokens worth as little as a quarter or a sixth of a halfpenny. These, he said, were saved up by the shopman's apprentices and exchanged for halfpennies when they had gathered enough together 'so that nobody loses'.[36] No doubt Platter's tokens were in reality credit tallies like those referred to by the Venetian diplomat, Nicolo di Favri, over eighty years before. But tokens, whatever their prime purpose and value, were no

---

34   Craig (1953), 123; Kent (2005), 53; Snelling (1766a), 3-4; Anonymous (1644), 5.

35   BL: Additional MSS 48020, f. 231. Thomas Snelling records that in Elizabeth's reign 'there were frequent complaints made of private persons, such as grocers, vintners, chandlers, ale-house keepers and others stamping and using tokens of lead, tin, lattern and even of leather for farthings and halfpence, to the great derogation of the princely honour and dignity, and as great loss to the poor, since they were only to be repaid to the same shop from whence they were first received, and no where else': Snelling (1766a), 2.

36   'Wann einer weniger dann für ein halben pfenning kaufet, ist yeglichem erlaubet, in seinem hau von bley oder kupfer zeichen zemachen oder zemüntzen, ettwan 4 oder 6 für ein halben pfenning; dieselbigen zeichen gibt er seinen handtwercksleüten; wann sie für ein halben pfenning oder mehr haben, wegslen undt rechnen sie undereinander, damit keinem unrecht beschehe': Keiser (1968), 825. For English translations see Williams (1937), 190 and Razzell (1995), 55-56.

PROLOGUE

11   Lead farthing token of John Brown of Bristol, 1567.

12   Bristol civic farthing token, 1578-83.

longer restricted to the metropolis. They had already spread to other parts of the country and possibly even to the little Devon wool town of Chudleigh where in the fifteen-sixties a marketman, Nicholas Ball, casting up his accounts, included on several occasions expenditure on lead and 'for smytyng of my tokenes'.[37] None of these are known today but, if they were monetary pieces, and it must be stressed that there is no evidence that they were anything more than seals for bales of cloth or other merchandise, they were perhaps not dissimilar to the surviving token of John Brown, a Bristol grocer, which it is not unreasonable to assume was dated 1567 [11].[38]

Bristol is of some significance in the story of the English token because from the 1570s the city corporation not only issued its own brass or copper farthings but did so under the direct authority of the Privy Council. Concern about the glut of private tokens that was plaguing the city and its surrounding neighbourhood – and the nuisance generated by their issuers, innkeepers, brewers, bakers and the like, who were refusing to honour them on the ground that they were being presented with forgeries – resulted in a warrant of January 1578 authorising the city to strike its own farthings [12].[39] These farthings, the earliest English brass or copper change issued with government approval, circulated far beyond the stipulated ten-mile radius of the city even crossing the Severn into south Wales. Over 86,000 of them, on somewhat crudely stamped squarish-shaped flans, had been struck by 1583 and demand was such that further issues appeared spasmodically from 1594 until the end of Elizabeth's reign. But the profits accruing to their manufacture was such – in 1594 the city itself made £22 16s 8d on £40 worth of farthings – that the tokens were massively counterfeited, so much so that the corporation was obliged to buy up 12,600 forgeries in 1587 at a cost of £13 2s 11d. It was a salutary lesson but it was one that was not taken on board for over three hundred years: that token money would always be prone to counterfeiting unless it was tightly controlled and limited in quantity to no more than was absolutely necessary for public use. In a sense, though, the very existence of the counterfeits demonstrated the demand for the tokens and their popularity. Nevertheless, Bristol's lead was not followed by other corporations; not by Norwich, the country's largest provincial city, whose supposed lead farthings and halfpennies are now thought to have been cloth seals, nor by London, whose size – by now approaching 200,000 inhabitants overall – precluded any 'city'

37   24 January 1562, 23 February 1566 and 23 February 1567: Burn (1855), xxxiii.

38   The date on Brown's tokens may be 1567 with the 6 reversed or 1597 with the 9 inverted. In either case the issuer may have been the 'John Browne' who was mayor of Bristol in 1572: Grinsell (1962), 20; Grinsell (1972), 15-16; and Grinsell, Blunt and Dolley (1973), 24 and pl. XII [Bristol].

39   Pritchard's association of certain thin brass bracteates bearing the city arms with the pre-1578 unauthorised tokens ((1899), 356 and pl. XVII, 1) has been disputed by Grinsell who dated them to the early seventeenth century ((1962), 20). But cf. Bird (1998), 262 where an earlier (pre-1569) dating has been postulated.

13 Elizabeth I pattern copper halfpenny 'pledge', 1601.

14 Scottish copper two-pence or turner of James VI, 1597.

15 French copper *double tournois* of Louis XIII, 1643.

16 Sir Robert Cotton (1571-1631).

bridling of its metropolitan plethora of private tokens.[40]

The contrast between an officially sponsored, if locally administered, token coinage, however maladroit, with the totally uncontrolled free-for-all nearer to home in London perhaps played some part in the government's resumed consideration of a national approach to the problem of small change. There seems to have been some movement towards this at the time the Irish copper coinage was introduced towards the end of Elizabeth's reign and pattern 'pledges' for pennies and halfpennies exist dated 1601 [13].[41] Again, nothing practical came of this and the new king, James I, though accustomed to billon placks, bawbees, and hardheads in Scotland and having himself introduced the copper turner or twopenny piece Scots [14] there in 1597, distanced himself from initiating a similar currency in his new realm.

Foreign coins, James's own Scottish turners in the northern counties and French *double tournois* [15] in the south, provided much of England's small change but private lead tokens still prevailed in London although they were increasingly spreading over the rest of the country.[42] The new reign did not lack schemes for replacing them with officially promoted copper tokens put out on a nation-wide scale. In 1611 the politician, Sir Robert Cotton [16], not for the first time employing his antiquarian knowledge for political ends, pressed James I, in a major advisory paper on ways and means of increasing the royal revenues, to 'restrain retailers of victual and small wares from using their own tokens'. He reckoned that 'in and about London, there are above three thousand who, one with another, cast yearly five pounds apiece of leaden tokens, whereof the tenth remaineth not to them at the year's end, and when they renew their store that amounteth to above 15,000*L*; and all the rest of this realme cannot be inferior to the city in proportion'.[43]

Cotton advised the coining of copper tokens under royal authority itself, thus at one stroke eliminating the need for private issues and, music to the king's ears, augmenting James's permanently depleted coffers from the profits of an enterprise 'whereby the advantage made by the retailers might accrue to the crown'. The upshot was that two years later, in April 1613, by a means that had already become a national scandal in Elizabeth's day but had been developed into a fine art by her successor, a monopoly was granted to a court favourite, Cotton's

---

40 Pritchard (1899), 350-55; Challis (1978), 208-10; Latimer (1908), Chapter 7; Caldecott (1943), 105-6; Thompson (2003), 163. 'Metropolitan London' is construed to include the City, Westminster, Southwark and the eastern suburbs without the walls.

41 *Peck* (1960), 10-12 and 14-15.

42 The Jacobean wit, William Fennor, sardonically compared London chandlers' cashboxes containing 'nothing but twopences, pence, halfpence and leaden tokens in them' with the meagre purses of many swaggering gallants: Fennor (1617), 450.

43 From *The Manner and Meanes How the Kings of England have from time to time Supported and Repaired their Estate*, quoted by Burn (1855), xxxviii. See also Ruding (1840), I, 369, note 4. Cotton's purpose was to provide historical precedents to support expansion of the royal revenues: Sharpe (1979), 122-23.

PROLOGUE

17   Lord Harington of Exton (1539/40-1613).

18a Copper Harington farthing of James I, 1614-16.

18b Copper Lennox farthing of James I, *c*.1616-*c*.1622/23.

18c Copper Richmond farthing (Uncut single flan) of Charles I, *c*.1633.

18d Copper Maltravers farthing of Charles I, *c*.1634-36.

cousin, John, Lord Harington of Exton [17], 'to make such a competent quantity of farthing tokens of copper, as might be conveniently issued amongst his subjects within the realms of England and Ireland, and the dominion of Wales' for a period of three years 'with the liking and consent of his loving subjects'.[44] The patent, it was calculated, would generate rich pickings for the crown and, at no cost to the king, would serve to compensate a loyal subject who had incurred great personal expenditure as guardian of the king's daughter, the Princess Elizabeth. At the same time the scheme, not untypical of Stuart ways of making money, had its paternalistic element which the king was at pains to make clear in his typically sententious proclamation of May 1613:

> Whereas there hath bene in times past some toleration in this our Realme, of Tokens of lead, commonly knowne by the name of Farthing Tokens, to passe betweene Vintners, Tapsters, Chaundlers, Bakers, and other the like Tradesmen, and their Customers, whereby such small portions, and quantities of things vendible, as the necessitie, and use specially of the poorer sort of People, doeth oftentimes require, may be conveniently bought, and sold without enforcing men to buy more ware than will serve for their use and occasions: Forasmuch therefore as the use of Farthing Tokens hath in it selfe a good end, tending to parsimonie, and to the avoyding of wast in pettie contracts, and pennie-worths; In which respect it cannot be but a great comfort to the poorer sort of the People.[45]

The new farthings 'made exactly and artificially of copper, by engines and instrument' were to be distributed by Harington at a discounted rate of 21/- worth of farthings for 20/- sterling [18a]. But they immediately ran into difficulties and before long became another byword for paltriness as 'not worth a brass farthing' passed into everyday idiom.[46] Initial demand for the tokens was sluggish and in a number of counties – Derbyshire, Staffordshire, Flintshire and Denbighshire are mentioned by Thomas Snelling – it was said that they were 'absolutely refused … although … countenanced by the magistrates'.[47] Harington died in August 1613 and, although the early returns on the scheme proved to be well below expectations, the monopoly was continued into Charles I's reign by a succession of patentees – dismissed by a contemporary polemicist as 'very Caterpillers of this Kingdome' – whose names are linked to their various issues: Lennox 'rounds', Richmond 'ovals', Maltravers 'rose' farthings *et alii* [18b-e].[48] They were small and flimsy, never more than 18 mm in diameter or half

---

44   Leake (1793), 290; Craig (1953), 140; *Peck* (1960), 19.

45   Larkin and Hughes (1973), 287 (no. 128).

46   Snelling (1766a), 8; *OED* s. v. 'brass': 'As bare and beggarly as if he had not one brasse farthing' [Daniel Rogers, *Naaman the Syrian* (1642)].

47   Ruding (1840), I, 369.

48   Anonymous (1644), 1. See also Ruding (1840), I, 402-403, note 5. The royal farthing tokens are surveyed in depth by Everson (2007).

13

a gram or so in average weight, perhaps reflecting the module of the smallest silver coins – some were even tinned to make them look more like silver – and of shabby workmanship. Despite their official image – they bore the king's name and regalia – they were of no intrinsic value. Plagued by the perception that they were merely an exploitative ploy – it was alleged with some degree of exaggeration that the 'profit for the makers of them was so great, as never was known the like: they could make out of an ounce of copper, which cost them not a full penny, the quantity of twenty pence in Tokens' – the farthings were at first only grudgingly accepted by a public to whom the distinction between a 'real' coin and a token coin substitute was unfathomable. Nevertheless, the banning of the private tokens and strenuous efforts to promote the 'royal farthings' resulted in the latter gradually gaining some degree of acceptability. After all, in the end there was nothing else and by 1644 when parliament discontinued the patent it was said that £100,000 worth (i.e. 96,000,000 tokens) of the 'rose' farthings alone had been put into circulation.[49]

But the royal-token plan was both ill-conceived and badly executed. As in later copper coinages there was no control of the volume or thought of distribution of the farthings to areas where they were really needed so that while some parts of the country ended up with an indigestible surfeit other localities faced a shortage. The tokens were open to other, private, abuses. Employers 'of the skinflint class', it was said, taking advantage of the discount available for bulk purchases, bought up vast quantities of the tokens to pay their 'handicraftsmen for their labour at the Week's end'.[50] The farthings, moreover, were widely copied, both at home and abroad, by counterfeiters even more unscrupulous than the patentees. Counterfeits swarmed especially during the reign of Charles I, a Suffolk clergyman and magistrate declaring by 1634 that the country was 'abused with whole barrels of false farthings',[51] and the frauds were not checked by the device adopted two years later of inserting a brass wedge – 'a little yellow spot in the copper' – into each 'rose' farthing [18e]. Counterfeiting led, too, to patentees attempting to evade their liability for redemption by refusing to accept even legitimate farthings on the grounds that they were bogus. Pressing 'sore upon many', it was said,

> it caused many teares to be shed by many poore women, and children, who lost all they had, as by many examples then were seen: for many poore women who got their living with selling of Fruit, Herbs, Fish, and other commodities, had all their stock in Farthings; some 6, 8, 10, to 20. shillings: this poor stock did maintaine them and their children, but upon a sudden this was all lost, to their utter undoing.[52]

18e Copper Rose farthing (with brass insert) of Charles I, 1636.

49 Snelling (1766a), 10; Anonymous (1644), 2 and 4.
50 Oman (1931), 299; Larkin (1983), II, no. 213.
51 Green (1861), 77.
52 Anonymous (1644), 3.

PROLOGUE

Parliament, although it self-righteously revoked the monopoly in 1644, did not see fit to replace the 'royal farthings' with any other fractional currency. Patterns for national coinages were produced from time to time and concern was expressed for the needs of 'the poorer sort' [53] but the dislocation of the next few years – the 'badness of the times' – and the sapped spirit of the Interregnum Mint did not accommodate such schemes and none was put into effect; the provision of small change was thus, once again, left to the public's own devices.[54] Despite their apparent early unpopularity the farthings had obviously afforded some relief to the need for small coin, and this must have been so in London, where 'some hundreds of Retaylers, who have Sparkes of Charity, and Reason in them' petitioned the Commons for their resumption.[55] Any void created by their suppression, however, was quickly occupied by a resurgence of private tokens, but the traditionally crude productions that emerged were a stopgap only for a few years. It may be that the execution of the king on 30 January 1649 and the abolition of the monarchy five weeks later were seen as a release from regal control of the coinage for by then a series of well-choreographed and professionally produced brass and copper issues had begun to appear.[56] The first of these new tokens, dated 1648 and issued in and about London, may have been struck before the king's death or, more likely, after his execution during the last two months of the 'old style' year, February and March 1648-49. The earliest, it was said by the antiquary, Browne Willis, was that struck for the King's Head tavern, near London's Tower Hill and significantly close to the Mint [19a].[57]

19a The King's Head, Tower Street, London, farthing token, 1648. 'The first [tradesman's token] ever coined'.

At first the quantity of tokens issued was comparatively small probably because a large proportion of the 'royal farthings' still remained in circulation in the country as a whole. But, spreading out from London,

---

53 'Many aged and impotent poor and others that would work and cannot get employment are deprived of many alms for want of farthings and half-farthings, for many would give a farthing or half-farthing who are not disposed to give a penny or twopence, or to lose time in staying to change money, "whereby they may contract a noisome smell or the disease of the poor"': 'Reasons submitted by Thomas Violet to the Mint Committee to prove the necessity of making farthing tokens and half-farthings', 10 August 1651: *CSP Domestic 1651* (1877): 313-315, at 314. Violet's argument is reminiscent of the parliamentary petition of 1393 quoted in note 17 above.

54 See *Peck* (1960), 82-103.

55 For *The Humble Petition and Remonstrance of some hundreds of Retaylers, who have Sparkes of Charity, and Reason in them. And of Country Chap-men of the Associated Counties, and of thousands of poore people besides: For the restoring of Farthing Tokens; who are extremely damnified, and are like to perish by the suppression of them ...1644*, see Barnard (1915), 169-81. The pamphlet argued, *inter alia*, that opposition to the 'royal farthings' was based upon the selfish interests of private token issuers.

56 The assumption by Parliament of such regulatory powers over the coinage in April 1649, however, did nothing to stem the issue of tokens and neither did the restoration of Charles II in 1660.

57 Heal (1928), 4; Milne (1951), 334; Thompson (2007), xi.

19b The Great Turk Coffee House, Exchange Alley, London, penny token.

19c Ridgley Hatfeild, merchant, Dublin, penny token, 1654.

19d Bristol civic farthing token, 1662. The letter 'R' beneath the date stands for David Ramage, the Royal Mint engraver responsible for many token dies until his death in 1662.

the new tokens mushroomed in number from the late fifties and despite a sharp decline about the time of the Restoration because of rumours of a new small-value regal coinage being introduced they re-gathered momentum to reach a climax in 1666-67. They then gradually tailed off until they eventually disappeared in England and Wales some years after their official suppression in 1672 when the first truly regal copper coinage was introduced by Charles II. Initially the tokens were restricted to farthings but with the abandonment of the silver halfpenny following the demonetization of the Commonwealth coinage in 1661, halfpence became the commonest token denomination. Penny tokens, too, began to appear in the 1660s in London, where coffee houses in particular found their issue worth their while [19b], and in some of the remoter parts of the kingdom. In Ireland pennies are known from as early as 1654 [19c] but were often no bigger in size than a halfpenny or farthing token. No satisfactory explanation has been given for what was a later development common in north Wales[58] and Cheshire but also occurring, though on a lesser scale, in Shropshire, Lancashire and Yorkshire except that the early Restoration striking of silver pence and twopences may not have penetrated in useful quantities to these outlying areas and, perhaps, that commodity prices there were inflated by higher distribution costs.[59]

Whatever their expressed value their generic description 'tradesmen's tokens' – sometimes, it seems, known as 'Traders' by contemporaries[60] – defined their stronghold as the 'standing' retail shop, now proliferating as a permanent urban feature, though, the role of the local inn or alehouse must not be underestimated; after all it was the 'Tavern and Tippling-House' that Evelyn singled out as the issuer of these 'arrant trifles' and it may well have been a tavern keeper who initiated the whole series.[61] But they were also put out in great numbers by civic authorities and other public bodies especially those concerned with poor relief, the 'Overseers of the Poor' in Biggleswade, Bedfordshire, for example. Bristol, again, was to the fore. Its city farthings [19d], first issued about 1651 and continued sporadically until 1670, were a model for others and were followed by over ninety authorities in England and one in Wales (Brecon). Generally the municipal pieces seem to have been well managed and were frequently intended to stifle the issue of private tokens in their area. Only five private issues are known, for instance, in Bristol despite its being the third largest city in the kingdom with some 15,000 inhabitants. Salisbury put out its borough farthing in 1659 to counter the sharp practices of its tradesmen issuers, Worcester and Norwich replaced all their private tradesmen's tokens with a city issue in 1667 and the same seems to

---

58 The earliest penny token issued in mainland Britain was that of John Davies, a Llanrwst mercer, in 1663.

59 Boon (1973), 22-23. A few extremely rare tokens of denominations higher than the penny are known in London and Southwark.

60 Milne (1951), 334, quoting Ashmolean Museum MS Willis 63; [Hill] (1751), 189.

61 Evelyn (1697), 16-17. Cf. text at note 57 above.

PROLOGUE

19e   Lincoln civic halfpenny token, 1669.

19f   Sherborne civic farthing token, 1669.

19g   Richard Rich, farthing changer, Drury Lane, London, halfpenny token.

19h   Richard Ballard, innkeeper, Monmouth, halfpenny token, 1668.

have happened in Sherborne in Dorset where a consortium of traders put out a 'town' farthing two years later. Lincoln, also in 1669, issued a 'Citty halfepenny' of 'good yellow brass' to relieve its 'citizens and inhabitants' from the 'loss and trouble by their receiving halfpence and farthings of so many several stamps that they cannot without much trouble distinguish the owners … and sometimes the owners do absolutely refuse to change the same' [19e]. Farthings followed and then more halfpennies, all pledged to be convertible, effectively ending the confusion and rancour occasioned by the plethora of private issues. As with Salisbury and Sherborne, though, a major incentive seems to have been to divert private profit to the corporation to ease the charge of the poor rate 'that is so heavy a burden to the inhabitants' [19f].[62]

Never before had tokens appeared in such large numbers and over such wide areas of the country. Over 12,000 issuers put them out over the British Isles – though there were few in Scotland because of that country's regal copper – and many thousands of different varieties are known today. As might be expected, London and Southwark between them – with a population of some 350,000 and a profusion of shops, taverns and alehouses – accounted for roughly one third of the overall output but tokens were issued in over 1,500 towns and villages of provincial England and Wales, 'nearly twice as many places as there were market towns in 1640'.[63]

Virtually every known trade is represented on the tokens, including, in London, one that they had themselves brought into existence – that of 'Changer of Farthings' [19g]. The majority of the issuers came from the wealthiest rung of shopkeepers: mercers, grocers, chandlers and apothecaries and, naturally, innkeepers too. Yet, although token issuers were frequently leading figures in their communities – the Cromwellian Mathew Davies of Swansea and the royalist innkeeper Richard Ballard of Monmouth [19h and 20], for example, were just two of very many who served as a town's portreeve or mayor[64] – the fact that a tradesman issued tokens need not by itself be taken as a mark of affluence. The cost of producing the trade tokens probably did not amount to much. For even the most prolific individual tradesman, it is likely that the outlay of no more than a pound or so would have been required to meet his needs and in many cases it would have been even less. Town tokens tended to be weightier but in 1667 Poole in Dorset obtained £19 4*s* worth of farthings for £10. Such a figure would suggest that the gross profit on a tradesman's outlay on tokens could have approached 100%, more than readily attainable if like some Norwich or Lincoln shopkeepers he refused to take them back.[65]

62   Grinsell (1962), 21; Thompson (1988), ix- xxxiii; Rowe (1966), 17; Williamson (1967), III, 1287; HMC, *Lincoln* (1895), 105-107; Weinstock (1953), 62.

63   Willan (1976), 85. The population of England at the time has been computed at about five million: Wrigley and Schofield (1981), 532.

64   Dykes (1961), 64-65; Boon (1973), 120-121.

65   Snelling (1766a), 12 and 'Appendix', 6; Williamson (1967), I, 184 and II, 867; HMC, *Lincoln* (1895), 105.

COINAGE AND CURRENCY IN EIGHTEENTH-CENTURY BRITAIN

20   Plaster overmantel in the King's Head, Monmouth, bearing the effigy of Charles I. Reputedly installed by the innkeeper Richard Ballard.

19i   Henry Munday, chandler, Swindon, halfpenny token, 1669.

The trade or following acknowledged on the token should not be over readily accepted as the issuer's only means of livelihood. Edward Steavens of Henley, for instance, was not only the barber-surgeon whose arms he displays but a haberdasher and grocer too while Thomas Harwick of King's Lynn, a mercer, was also a bookseller, a comparatively rare trade even in the 1660s.[66] The pursuit of two callings in the seventeenth century was not uncommon, and there must have been many 'urbanised' traders, with time on their hands, who had some interest, great or small, in the land. William Adkens, landlord of the Black Lion in Thame, was one such.[67] Neither should a tradesman describing himself as a 'mercer', 'grocer' or 'chandler' on his token be regarded necessarily as a specialist tradesman. There would have been many, especially in smaller localities, who had developed into more general shopkeepers. This is hinted at on a number of tokens. Henry Munday of Swindon in Wiltshire, for example, described himself as a chandler on his halfpenny of 1669 but combined the Grocers' arms with those of the Tallowchandlers in a novel heraldic display [19i]; no doubt he ran something akin to a general store. Similarly, Thomas Allen of Brigstock in Northamptonshire described himself as a chandler on his farthing but adopted the Grocers' not the Tallow Chandlers' arms.

Nor should the use of the arms of one of the London livery companies on a token necessarily be taken as indicating the issuer's actual membership of the company concerned. The London companies did maintain provincial connections and had local members but the use of their arms on tokens is too prevalent to be anything more than a symbolic indication of an occupation. It was simply a conceit,

---

66   Milne (1935), x and 12; Williamson (1967), II, 849.
67   Milne (1935), x and 14.

PROLOGUE

devised by the die-engraver, to display what he understood to be the tradesman's main calling and points more to a London origin of the token dies than it does to an individual's livery membership. Care must be taken, too, over what might be thought to be inn signs on tokens thus all too readily attributed to innkeepers; in reality they may simply be shop signs bearing devices unrelated either to inn keeping or to a tradesman's actual calling as in the case of the 'pheasant' farthing of Ellis Jones, a Caernarvon mercer. On the other hand inns and taverns – the commonest interface between retailer and customer [68] – were probably, as Evelyn implied, the stronghold of the token and many a tradesman would have run an alehouse as a secondary business.

The tokens are not of exceptional artistic merit. While, overall, the craftsmanship is competent and occasionally not unaccomplished, in most cases the designs are simple. The tokens are generally circular but, after 1667, octagonal or, more rarely, squarish (sometimes fashioned as a lozenge) or 'harty'-shaped pieces appear. In most cases they bear the name of the issuer (occasionally a widow or a partnership), his or her trade or occupation, and the town or village where the business was carried on. There are also often the mark of value of the coin, the date (which is not necessarily the date of actual issue), the initials of the tradesman (and perhaps that of the Christian name of his wife), together with a device, usually, as already mentioned, the arms of a London livery company, a business sign, a merchant's mark, a motif denoting his occupation or a representation of the issuer's family arms, sometimes fictitious but often authentic. Normally the tokens are painfully unimaginative in concept, but some are quaint. Thomas Juxson's striking octagonal Brecon token, for instance, carries the design of a pair of shears and a gauntlet [19j], while that of the Quaker, Thomas Wynne, 'Chyrurgeon' of Caerwys in Flintshire, teeth and a forceps. Some bear naively simple and direct legends: the invitation of Sam Endon's Macclesfield token **WELCOM YOU BE TO TRADE WITH ME** or the anonymous Staffordshire halfpenny's request to **SEND MEE TO THE MERCER OF GNOSHALL**, for instance. Francis Swindell of Macclesfield countered the possible ill effect of his surname by inscribing **SQUARE DEALING IS BEST** on a *square* token [19k]. Or it may be that he was a Quaker setting a firm price on principle and sticking to it.

The tokens, of course, would bring some commercial advantage to the tradesman. Not so much as advertisements (although this might have been a consideration 'sold' by a token-maker's agent) since, limited geographically, their recipients would be knowledgeable locals

19j   Thomas Juxson, glover, Brecon, halfpenny token, 1669.

19k   Francis Swindell, Macclesfield, halfpenny Token, 1669.

---

68   The phrase is Robert Thompson's who also makes the interesting point that – if Browne Willis is to be trusted – the location of the token 'first ever coined', a tavern near the Mint, may have arisen from a moneyer or his acquaintance taking refreshment there and suggesting tokens as a solution to the landlord's problems over small change: personal communication.

– on average people travelled little more than seven miles to market.[69] But rather because, as they would normally be redeemable only at the issuer's place of business, holders would be encouraged to return to exchange them for further goods and additional purchases, or provide even more financial advantage to the retailer by not returning them at all. Because of the difficulty of redeeming them elsewhere, the tokens tended not to wander too far from home although the authority of town pieces – such as those of Bristol, the 'great emporium of the west' – would have given them a more trusted remit beyond municipal boundaries.[70] This limited circulation coupled with the issuer's hold over the quantity put out meant that by and large their use, outside the greater towns at any rate, could be controlled through the interpersonal trust of the community and unlike the royal farthing tokens, counterfeits could be quickly spotted and eliminated.[71]

Nevertheless, the very localism of tokens had considerable drawbacks for the public as Albert Jouvin, a French visitor, was drawn to remark in 1672:

> It is a remarkable thing in England, that in the cities and towns, and even in every street of the villages, they strike a particular small piece of copper or brass money called a *fardin*, which will not pass beyond the street or quarter wherein it was coined. These are generally marked with the name of some citizen or of some shopkeeper, such as a grocer, a chandler or a mercer, who buys that permission from the king. So that it is a great inconvenience to travellers since, on quitting a town or village, or any city, all this small money ceases to be current. But that is not the case of the silver coin, which is received every where at the same price: of these there are so many of different values, that one may change a large piece, and receive this small coin without any of those farthings.[72]

---

69 Everitt (1967), 498-99. This average distance, of course, hides a wide variation across the country. Distances were greater in the north and west where shops were fewer and more scattered.

70 Strays, especially municipal issues, are sometimes found a long way from home – Bristol farthings, like their sixteenth-century predecessors, in south Wales, for example, no doubt as a result of the coastal trading connections between the city and local ports. For some unexplained reason Surrey tokens evidently had considerable compass outside the county. While tokens from the south of England are sometimes found in the north very few from the north found their way southwards: Williamson (1967), I, xxiii.

71 Muldrew (2001), 102-103. That tokens did circulate, albeit within a limited area, is indicated by the existence of a sorting box for tokens kept by a Rochester tradesman to facilitate exchange with his fellow traders: S[amuel] Pegge, *GM*, November 1757, 498-99.

72 From *Voyageur d'Europe* (1672-76), IV, 17, quoted in translation in Grose and Astle (1809), IV, 562-63 where the author's name is given as 'Jorevin de Rochford'. For a French text see Snelling (1766a), Preface, [ii], note *. I am indebted to Robert Thompson for the correct identification of the author.
As Snelling pointed out, of course, Jouvin erred in saying that permission to strike tokens was bought from the king.

Moreover, as the political economist, Sir William Petty – no stranger to tokens as a promoter of them himself in Ireland – insisted, tokens were acceptable as change only if their issuers were 'responsible and able to take them back, and give Silver for them'.[73] But all too commonly the issuers were not responsible, would oblige customers to take tokens in change and then redeem them only for further goods often at a cost greater than they would charge for coin of the realm. It was a practice that the inventor – and promoter of a national tin coinage – Sir Edward Ford, echoing Bumpstead's censure of a century earlier, was only too ready to enlarge upon in a petition of 1665:

> That the use of Farthings or Tokens is necessary for ye Exchange of Money in all Retailing-Trades, is most apparent by the universal practise of all Retailers, who do cause Tokens of Brass, Copper, and other Metals to be stamped for their Exchange with their Customers; And though he y^t takes them, cannot make any thing of them, unless he return y^m to ye same Person of whom he had them, yet the Necessity of his taking y^m or nothing in Exchange, makes him submit to it: And by that means ye Receivers sustain a great Loss, & ye first Deliverer of y^m an unjust & great Profit; For he issues that for twenty shillings, which cost him but three, or four at most, & so gains sixteen or seventeen shillings in ye Pound by as many as are not returned to him. Besides, ye Poor are great Losers by this Trade; for ye Farthings y^t are given them they have no use, unless they finde out ye particular shop of ye first Deliverer, & if they do, they are enforced to give them six Farthings for one Penny-worth of ware.[74]

Ford's emphasis upon the poor brings out the underlying *raison d'être* of the token and explains the paucity of references to it in the diaries and reminiscences of the day; Pepys, for example, although he frequented many London inns and taverns that issued tokens never mentions them once. Middling folk and their betters still functioned on a system of credit and bulk purchase, had little recourse to small change and, like Evelyn, probably saw tokens as no more than curiosities.[75] The respectable craftsman household with annual earnings of perhaps £40 a year would not have had much need for tokens except perhaps in the local alehouse but even there the slate was readily available for the regular and reputable. The necessity for tokens in retail trading can, therefore, be overestimated. But, as George Boon pointed out, there was 'one large and growing class

---

73 Burn (1855), lxvi, quoting Petty, *Treatise of Taxes and Contributions* (1662). For Petty see *ODNB* and Thompson (1999), xi-xviii.

74 From a MS petition of Sir Richard [*recte* Edward] Ford and others about the coining of tin farthings, 1665, quoted in Rannie (1898), 261. The bibliographer Myles Davies (1662-c.1719) in his *Athenæ Britannicæ* (1716-19) noted that 'Traders were not obliged to take one another's Coyns, or such like Token-Propriums, no more than they were obliged to take one another's words': Heal (1928), 5.

75 Evelyn (1697), 16-17.

of the population which could not stock up at home, nor expect credit, nor think beyond the purchase of the smallest necessities' to whom tokens would have been a staple: the poorest labouring families earning no more than £15 a year and in many instances much less and, it is said, accounting for 50% of the population.[76] Over the centuries, as we have seen, stress had been put on the need for small change for the benefit of the poor, a theme embodied by James I in his proclamation of the Harington farthings in 1613 and encapsulated in the legends of many tradesmen's' tokens, especially those issued in the name of some municipal authority: **THE POORE'S HALFPENNY, REMEMBER THE POOR,** and **FOR THE USE OF THE POORE [191]**.

191   Wimborne civic halfpenny token, 1669.

For many years the questions of who made these tokens and where have exercised numismatists, debate focussing on whether they were manufactured centrally (in London) or in the localities of their issue. Long ago it was established that most of the dies were produced in London with David Ramage, a Mint engraver, being responsible for at least some of them until his death in 1662 – his initial 'R' appears on the Bristol [19d] and Oxford municipal issues, for instance – but obviously with others being involved.[77] The existence of a small number of locally-found dies, though, muddied the waters and inspired at least one distinguished authority to conclude that while most dies might have been engraved in London the tokens themselves *must* have been produced locally. Documentary evidence, however, makes it clear that a number of municipal authorities ordered their *tokens* in bulk from London (Lincoln, Grantham and Norwich, for instance) and recent research by Robert Thompson has shown fairly conclusively that tokens generally were struck by screw press in London and at the Tower Mint itself, locally found dies being explained by their dispatch to the issuers who had asked for them with their consignments of tokens.[78] There *are* tokens of inferior style which may be of purely local origin as are many Irish issues but the hand of Mint employees is clearly seen in the production of the majority of tokens and was the subject of criticism as early as 1651:

> And we hear – I pray enquire the truth of it – that your mint in the Tower of London is come to such contempt, where you were wont to coin forty thousand pounds a week and above twenty thousand pounds a week constantly in gold and silver, there is not so much coined in a year as was within this five year coined in a week, and that now your coin in your mint [is] nothing almost but counters and farthings. If it should be true, which I pray enquire the thing out, it is a high dishonour to the nation

---

76   Boon (1973), 29; Muldrew (2001), 104. Especially, of course, in the urban context.

77   Milne (1935), xiv-xvi.

78   HMC, *Lincoln* (1895), 106; Thompson (1989), 198-211. See also Thompson (2003), 166-67. A local press from Chesterfield is described by S[amuel] Pegge, *GM*, November 1757, 498-99.

PROLOGUE

in so sacred a place as the mint is, to coin nothing but counters and farthings and in so famous a mint as the Tower of London. For the honour of the nation, use your interest to let their mint not be employed rather than suffer such trumpery as counters or farthings to be made within the walls.[79]

At a time when Mint production was at a low ebb and individual enterprise at a premium it seems that mint employees set out to corner the market and brook no competitors. The aim of 'one *Rammage*', it was claimed in 1660, 'in all this business is, To suppress all Tools for making Farthings but his own; the said *Rammage* having proffered a large weekly Sum to be paid to one party, if all the Presses for making Farthings may be but taken away about *London* but only his, so that he may have the sole Trade in his hands'.[80]

21a Charles II pattern copper halfpenny, *c.*1665-72.

Another mystery and one still to be elucidated is the mechanics by which the tokens were ordered and the orders transmitted to the Mint. The nation's road system, though improving, was far from adequate off the main highways – the first turnpikes did not appear until the 1690s – and the fact that in provincial England and Wales alone nearly 8,000 distinct varieties of token were issued by over 6,500 tradesmen and municipal authorities in more than 1,500 places many of which were comparatively insignificant and out of the way speaks volumes for an efficient organisation of itinerant agents and riders drumming up business across the country. As Boon put it the 'tentacles' of a 'considerable industry' extended 'into the furthest corners of the realm' – a process more effective than anything government itself was to achieve for another one hundred and fifty years. And the coincidence of date and sometimes of device on many if not most of the tokens of particular areas bears out the concentrated and persuasive sales campaigns that underlay it; it is of more than passing interest that seven out of the eight town pieces issued in Dorset, for instance, are dated 1669.[81]

21b Charles II pattern copper farthing, 1662. The ship depicted on the reverse is said to be the *Sovereign of the Seas*.

The issue of a regal copper coinage that would have put an end to the problem of small change was long in gestation. Pattern halfpennies and farthings, both official and unofficial, were made during the first decade of the Restoration, some, it is said, even being submitted to the king himself who apparently took a personal interest in the schemes [21a, b and 22a].[82] But it was not for twelve years that anything positive was done. Eventually, on 16 August 1672 the King, declaring that his 'subjects would not easily be wrought upon to accept the Farthings and Halfpence of ... private stampers, if there were not

---

79 James Yard (?) to Sir Robert Stone, 26 May 1652: Thirsk and Cooper (1972), 644-45.

80 From a contemporary tract, quoted by *Peck* (1960), 98.

81 Boon (1973), 18; Dickinson (1986), 11. The exceptional Dorset town piece is that of Poole (1667).

82 The farthings with the reverse legend **QVATVOR . MARIA . VINDICO** . ('I protect the four seas') were for generations known as 'Lucas Farthings' following Lord Lucas's dismissal of the legend as grandiloquent for a copper coin in a parliamentary debate of 1670: Cobbett, IV (1808), col. 474.

23

22a Charles II official silver pattern farthing, 1665.

22b The regular copper farthings of 1672 onwards have the reverse legend replaced by 'BRITANNIA' and the date moved to the reverse exergue as seen on a currency farthing of 1679.

some kind of necessity for such small coynes to be made for publique use, which cannot well be done in silver, nor safely in any other metal, unless the intrinsic value of the coyn be equal or near to that value for which it is made currant,' proclaimed the issue of a regal coinage of copper halfpence and farthings [22b] which were to be made current for all transactions under the value of sixpence.[83] Despite the caution that all those who should, after 1 September 1672, 'make, vend or utter' any coins other than those authorised would be 'chastised with exemplary severity', the use of private tokens continued for a few more years until gradually, after a number of further warnings, they disappeared from the local scene, although Chester and Norwich had to be threatened with legal proceedings to bring them into line.[84]

Most seventeenth-century tokens, sooner or later, went for scrap metal but, even within a decade or so, those that were left were becoming the quarry of some numismatists, especially those with an interest in local history and antiquities, like Ralph Thoresby, the Leeds antiquary and topographer (1658-1725), who seems to have begun to include a small collection of tokens in his cabinet well before the century's end.[85] When Thoresby's one hundred and forty four 'Town pieces and Tradesmen's Tokens' were eventually sold in 1764 they fetched 56s; a remarkable price for objects that Evelyn had derided as 'arrant trifles' half a century earlier though he had had the prescience to remark that they might 'happily in after times, come to exercise and busie the learned *Critic*, what they should signifie, and fill whole Volumes with their Conjectures'.[86] By 1741 the antiquary Browne Willis (1682-1760), said by Snelling to have been the 'first person that appears to have made a collection of these pieces', had been able to present a collection of over 1,100 specimens to the Bodleian Library and could record in his papers the names of some sixteen other collectors who had built up significant cabinets. One of these was the herald Stephen Martin Leake (1702-1773), who had already included a brief description of tradesmen's tokens in his *Nummi Britannici Historia*, anonymously published in 1726.[87] It was to be another forty years, however, before the first extended and scholarly account of the series was given by Thomas Snelling [23a] in the

23a Thomas Snelling (1712-1773), author of *A View of the Copper Coin and Coinage of England* (1766), the first serious review of seventeenth-century tokens. Medal engraved by Lewis Pingo.

83 For the text of the proclamation see *Peck* (1960), 603.

84 In Ireland the issue of tokens continued until 1679.

85 Heal (1928), 3: according to Thomas Hearne Thoresby's collection of coins and medals was well known by 1682. It was auctioned by Whiston Bristow (not Sotheby as in Heal) on 5-7 March 1764: Manville and Robertson (1986), 17.

86 Evelyn (1697), 17-18. In recording an Oxford token in 1713 Thomas Hearne said he did so 'that hereafter it may be known that there were such kind of Farthings. For they will in time grow very rare, and 'twill be forgot that there were any such': Rannie (1898), IV, 207.

87 Heal (1928), 3; Milne (1952), 333-34; Snelling (1766a), 'Preface' [2]; [Leake] (1726), 117-18. Leake published a much expanded second edition of his work 'with great additions and improvements', under his name and with its English title only, in 1745. A reprint of this with an appendix was published as a third posthumous edition in 1793. The seventeenth-century tokens are treated on pp. 368-71 of both these editions.

course of his *View of the Copper Coin and Coinage of England* (1766), a work that, as Robert Thompson makes clear, was notable for its thorough documentation and its painstaking survey of tradesmen's tokens [23b].[88] With his lists of issuers' names and of places where the tokens had been put out, Snelling provided a pioneering overview for collectors that went far beyond the simple explanation of his five excellent plates that might have been expected in such a publication.

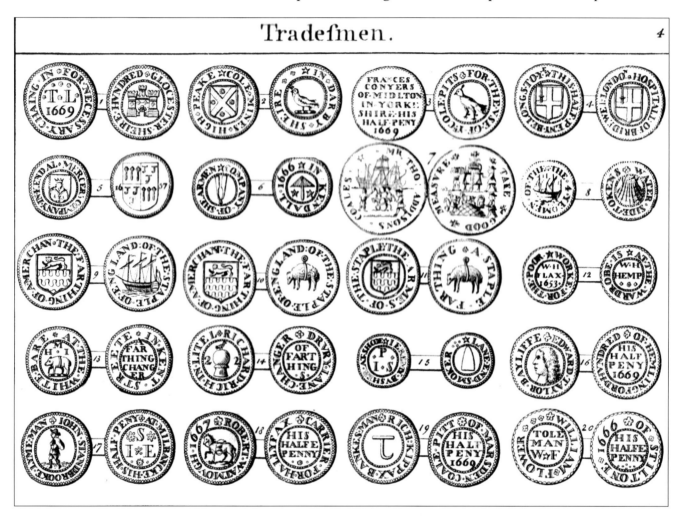

23b Plate 4 of Thomas Snelling's *A View of the Copper Coin and Coinage of England* (1766).

The new coppers were, for the first time, coins of the realm and, though they were never admitted to be 'real' money but only 'tokens', they were of a weighty, well-made character. The farthings averaged 5.8 g, considerably heavier than anything that had gone before with the exception of the remarkable 8.5g weight token of the London brazier,

88   Snelling (1766a), 11-32. For Snelling see Robert Thompson's biography in *ODNB*.

COINAGE AND CURRENCY IN EIGHTEENTH-CENTURY BRITAIN

24 Edward Nourse, brazier, Bishopsgate Street, London, farthing token, 1666.

Edward Nourse [24].[89] Initial problems of production – the Mint had little experience of striking copper and no preparatory facilities so that the coins had to be struck from imported Swedish blanks – and of distribution delayed a speedy and widespread circulation that was also hindered by the continuing use of tradesmen's tokens. Petty suggested, too, that John Roettier's appealing reverse image of Britannia, harking back over fifteen hundred years to the Roman emperor Antoninus Pius, was an impediment to the coins' circulation since 'upon the account of Beauty' they 'were almost all hoarded as Medals till they grew common'.[90] And the anomaly of the king's effigy facing left rather than the right of the current gold and silver coinage with the curious legend **CAROLUS A CAROLO** ('Charles from Charles', i.e. Charles II) only served to enhance the initial singularity of the halfpennies.

Nevertheless by 1675 the situation was well in hand and production of the halfpennies came to an end early that year and that of farthings in 1679. Unfortunately the coppers were apparently counterfeited and in an effort to counter this, to reduce costs, stimulate the Cornish tin industry and thus enhance the profits of the crown, tin halfpence and farthings were introduced, under patent, in 1684.[91] Despite the precautions of plugging them with a square of copper and stamping their edges with the date and the legend **NUMMORUM FAMULUS** their very cheapness rendered them even more prone to counterfeiting than the copper they replaced.[92] Subject to oxidisation the tin coins were, moreover, a less durable substitute and, deeply unpopular, they were finally abandoned in 1693 [25]. It was the end of experimentation and in the following year a return was made to copper, using British metal. A chapter in the story of the British token had closed. A regal copper coinage, if often of low quality, varying weights and indifferently produced by the Mint, was now to be the norm for small change and, with some breaks in production, was to remain so until the reign of George III. But it was to be a currency without any recoinage or recall of worn specimens, so that even as late as the year of the '45 barely decipherable remnants of the original halfpennies and farthings of Charles II were still in circulation; and as the currency deteriorated

25 William & Mary tin farthing (with insert of copper), 1691.

89 Eighty-five years later Joseph Harris, the King's Assay Master at the Mint, still maintained that 'Copper coins with us are properly not money, but a kind of *tokens* passing by way of exchange instead of parts of the smallest pieces of silver coin': Harris (1757), 45, note. The minting of copper was never included in a Mint indenture: Craig (1953), 174. For the new copper coinage see Challis (1992), 365-70 and for Nourse see Thompson (2000), 147-50.

90 Petty (1695) [1856], 8 [162]. For the numismatic use of the Britannia image see Eustace (2006), 323-36 and plates 42-48.

91 Counterfeit halfpence and farthings of Charles II are, however, hardly ever met with today: personal communication from Peter Preston-Morley.
The legend 'Nummorum Famulus' ('Servant of the Coinage') was adopted to indicate that the coins were not of true intrinsic value or 'real' money. For the episode of the tin coinage see Horsefield (1982), 161-80 and Challis (1992), 370-73.

92 Some of the 'tin' forgeries were 'so crude that no one in his right mind could have mistaken them for regal coinage': Mitchiner and Skinner (1986), 181.

PROLOGUE

26 Charles II milled silver penny, undated but prior to 1670.

over the years so the abiding merchandise of the counterfeiter became a plague.[93]

But if copper deteriorated the silver coinage did so to a far more damaging degree. Milled coinage had been introduced to the Tower in 1662/63 [26] but the old hammered money, except for that of the Interregnum, had not been called in and continued to exist side by side with the new. Yet, however worn and defective it was, on the whole it retained its face value in ordinary use and it quickly began to drive the milled money out of circulation. Since the market price of silver was usually above the Mint price – 5s 2d an ounce since 1666 when mint charges had been abolished – the greater part of the £3.75 million of machine-struck silver produced over the next thirty or so years was either hoarded or more often melted for bullion and shipped off to France and Holland. And after 1689 the war effort in the Low Countries took even more silver out of the country, some £938,000 in bullion being sent to Europe by 1695. What was left in circulation was a wasting coinage reaching back to Elizabeth's reign and beyond, a coinage drastically eroded by wear, and more latterly by an excess of 'rounding' and clipping 'even to the quick' as the enterprising discovered that their whittling could be converted into profitable exportable bullion or go towards the making of counterfeits.[94] An amazed reaction greeted William Stout, a Lancaster grocer and ironmonger, on a journey south to London in 1693, when, paying for books and household goods with good broad silver, he was asked 'where I came from and whether we had such large money, and not diminished in our country'. Of milled silver, the honest Quaker agonised, 'there was scarce any of it to be seen'. The following year John Evelyn noted that 'there was hardly any mony stiring that was intrinsic[c]aly worth above halfe the value, to such a strange exorbitance things were arrived, beyond that any age can shew example'; the evidence of money received at the Exchequer between 1686 and 1695 suggests that the diarist was very close to the mark.[95]

Although the battered silver had at times been taken by prudent tradesmen only by weight – as early as 1647 the Yorkshire yeoman Adam Eyre had to face a loss of 4s 6d in exchanging 23s of light money for good – more often than not, even as late as the early 1690s because

---

93 Leake (1793), 371. A comparison may be made with Boulton's 'cartwheel' pennies, which were to survive until the introduction of a bronze coinage in 1860. A sample survey of the nation's copper coinage instituted by Thomas Graham, the Master of the Mint, in 1857 suggested that they constituted some 28% of the penny currency: Dyer (1996), 63. The Victorian 'Bun' pennies that replaced the copper remained in circulation in their turn until decimalisation.

94 Milled silver accounted for probably less than one-half per cent of the total silver circulation immediately prior to the Recoinage: cf. Feaveayear (1963), 124; Craig (1953), 193.

95 Marshall (1967), 108; Beer (1955), V, 186: 15 July 1694; Lowndes (1695) [1856], 60-61 [228-29] and 90 [258]; Haynes (1700), 75-76. Cf. also the evidence of the Bristol 'Welsh Back' Hoard (1688) which contained only 181 milled pieces among 5,267 silver coins over 52% of the hammered being clipped: Malcolm (1925), 236-64 and 402.

of the shortage of good silver, it still tended to pass freely from hand to hand at its nominal face value especially among wage earners and the poor who had little recourse but to accept it. The Mint official Hopton Haynes later recollected that clipped shillings and halfcrowns 'were received and pass'd as current, as when they were full of weight and value'. But by 1695 the situation was changing dramatically and fast. Reform was in the air. And as rumours that a recoinage was imminent and that the value of the old coin would be called down became rife clippers increased in 'their numbers and their diligence, and vended the money they had clipd in all places without any cheque or fear from the Laws'. The door opened, too, to a flood of counterfeits and the currency became even more deranged. But, as Haynes argued, the counterfeiters needed no 'exactness for the people were extremely Supine and seemed not altogether unwilling to be imposed upon at that time: and continued in that humour, til the begin^g. of the year 1695 which was the greatest encouragem^t. that could be given so pernicious a practice'. At least the poet Dryden when he received forty brass shillings besides clipped money from his publisher, Jacob Tonson, was far from supine: he returned the lot and demanded guineas in their place.[96]

It was an 'evil', Martin Folkes later fulminated, 'which rendered all trade and dealing between man and man precarious, and at last threatened no less than the total destruction of all our silver coin'. From his personal experience William Stout could bemoan the 'great confusion in trade' that arose from the state of the silver coinage, 'people being cautious in setting a price of their goods without knowing in what money they should be paid'; 'it was feared', he added, that 'the distraction about the coyne would be more fatal than the war with France'. Haynes, at the Mint, echoed the Lancastrian's anxiety:

> The whole Kingdom was in a general distraction by the Badness of the Silver coin and the Rise of Guineas, for no body knew what to trust to, the Landlord knew not in what to receive his Rents, nor the Tenant in what to pay 'em. Neither of them could foretell the value of his moneys tomorrow. The Marchand could not forsee [*sic*] the worth of his Wares at 2 or 3 days distance, and was at a loss to set a price upon his Goods. Every Body was afraid to engage in any new Contracts, and as shy in performing old ones.[97]

With good silver virtually non-existent the gold guinea had became more familiar as day-to-day money. For Stout it was the coin 'which most payments were made in', William Lowndes noting that 'the present Badness of our Silver Coins, which are so exceedingly

---

96   Eyre (1877), 66; Haynes (1700), 71 and 79; Ward (1942), 75.

97   Folkes (1763), 117; Marshall (1967), 109-110; Haynes (1700), 94. Cf. Evelyn (1697), 228: '*Nor is there a more fatal Symptom of Consumption in a State, than the Corruption and Diminution of the Coin*'. See Macaulay (1849-61), IV (1855), 626-27 [chapter XXI] for a vivid portrayal of the havoc of the time.

PROLOGUE

27 Charles II guinea, 1663. The elephant below the king's bust represents gold supplied by the Africa Company trading along the West African 'Guinea Coast' which gave the name 'guinea' to the new coinage, whatever the source of its gold content.

Counterfeited, and Clipt, that the Common People will take Guineas almost at any Rate, rather than stand the hazard and vexation of such Silver Moneys as are now Currant amongst them'.[98] Although introduced as a milled coin in 1663 [27] with a theoretical value of 20s, it was allowed to find its own level and it eventually settled at 21s 6d, a rating it held until the last decade of the century. By the mid-1690s, however, the guinea began to soar to unprecedented heights. It had reached 30s in London by June 1695 as Stout discovered when he visited the capital and happily returned home having made a handsome profit through the exchange of guineas originally gathered together in Lancaster for 22 or 23s apiece.[99]

At the heart of this spectacular leap in the value of the guinea, some 35% in six months, was undoubtedly the scarcity and poor quality of the silver currency. But it was by no means the only factor. Clipping, after all, had been going on for half a century and more.[100] Now, though more serious than ever before, it was just one element in a complex and tangled web of determinants: the large-scale government borrowing and excessive issue of paper money embarked on to meet the enormous costs of 'King William's War' and, ultimately as the price of the guinea spiralled upward, a wild spree of speculation in gold; each played its part in the dislocation of the currency. Nevertheless, for most people the clipper was the villain of the piece and in the heightened inflationary crisis a drastic reform of the silver coinage came to be seen as imperative. While the solution of the problem seemed obvious, however, the method of achieving it was far from clear. Opinion was sharply divided as to whether any new coinage should be minted at the traditional standards of weight and fineness enjoyed for almost a century or whether they should be reduced to bring its nominal value more into line with the current market price of bullion.[101]

As the monetary situation deteriorated the Treasury came to the view that the currency should be stabilized at its depreciated value and called upon its Secretary, William Lowndes, to prepare a detailed

---

98 Marshall (1967), 108; Lowndes (1695) [1856], 50 [218].

99 Marshall (1967), 113-14.

100 Clipping, although endemic to the silver coinage, seems to have become especially severe from the 1670s onwards. Hopton Haynes recollected that 'the clipping of our coins began to be discoverable in great recipts [sic] a little after the Dutch war in 1672, but it made no great progress at first for some years... But from the year 1689 ... the clipping was mightily advanced every year till the recoynage, in so much that the nation lost yearly between 2 & 3 hundred thousand pounds by clip'd money and the like Counterfeit pieces': Haynes (1700), 74 and 77.

101 For valuable discussions of the Recoinage see Kelly (1991), I, 1-121; Feavearyear (1963), 121-37 and, for the debate surrounding it, Horsefield (1960), 23-70; Fay (1933), 143-55; and Appleby (1976), 43-69. See also Ruding (1840), II, 35-58.

28 John Locke (1632-1704).

statement on the issue.[102] Lowndes' *Report*, a model of monetary analysis, recommended a devaluation of some 20 to 25% to bring the currency into broad parity with the market price which had now risen to the equivalent of 6*s* 5*d* an ounce on the continent. The nub of his argument was that the mint price for silver was too low and as long as bullion was worth more by weight than coin it would never be brought to the Mint for coining but would always be melted down and exported. The solution to the problem, he explained, was to follow precedent and, since the King 'Solely and Inherently' possessed the 'Power of Coining Money and Determining the Weight, Fineness, Denomination and Extrinsick Value thereof', such authority should be exercised to reduce the nominal weight of the coinage to something approaching its actual weight. After all, as he showed in his exemplary historical review of the currency, similar adjustments had been successfully carried out 'from time to time as any Exigence or Occasion required'.[103]

Lowndes' arguments proved unpalatable to the government, however, and particularly to William III who was wedded to maintaining the existing standard, and, having sought advice from a number of authorities, it persuaded John Locke [28], a dominant influence in the political thinking of the age and regarded in Whig government circles as an expert on trade and coinage, to produce a response that might be used to convince Parliament of the king's view.[104] Locke's *Further Considerations Concerning Raising the Value of Money*, a treatise rooted firmly in his political philosophy, was decisive and although not all his arguments were ultimately accepted Parliament adopted his view that the Recoinage should be undertaken at the existing legal weight standard.

Central to Locke's scheme of things was his belief that the natural property rights of the individual preceded and transcended any sovereign authority and that money was a key element in such rights. Money, he thus asserted, had an immutable, intrinsic value and could not be changed by king or parliament – although this simply meant confirming the silver weight standard set in 1601 since going back

102 Lowndes (1695) [1856], 1 [169]-90 [258]. For William Lowndes (1652-1724) see *ODNB*. Lowndes, a Treasury official by 1675 and its Secretary from 1695 until his death, was credited by Lord Chesterfield with the maxim 'Take care of the pence and the pounds will take care of themselves': Chesterfield (1932), III, 1051: 6 November 1747; IV, 1500: 5 February 1750.

103 Lowndes (1695) [1856], 38 [206], 46 [214], 7 [175] and 31 [199].

104 Locke had earlier (*c*.1691) published a paper opposing devaluation *Some Considerations of the consequence of the lowering of Interest, and raising the value of Money* (London, 2nd Ed. Corrected 1696), reprinted in Kelly (1991), I, 207-342. What has traditionally been known as the 'Locke-Lowndes Controversy' is now thought to be something of a misnomer. It is not clear, for example, to what extent Lowndes was personally attached to the Treasury's promotion of devaluation and he seems to have encouraged Locke in his opposition to it. Lowndes, moreover, was not the only exponent of devaluation for there were more than two hundred and fifty contributions to the very public debate. See Kelly (1991), I, 106-109 and, for a list of the publications in the pamphlet war, the comprehensive bibliography in Horsefield (1960), 289-311.

beyond the 43rd year of Elizabeth was patently impractical. Only 'Harm', Locke insisted, would come by 'Change' which with 'a thousand other inconveniences' 'unreasonably and unjustly gives away and transfers Mens properties'. He might ridicule Lowndes's proposals as an operation comparable to lengthening 'a foot by dividing it into Fifteen parts, instead of Twelve; and calling them Inches' but the preservation of individual rights was the essence of his argument: 'lessening our coin', he claimed, 'will, without any Reason, deprive great Numbers of blameless Men of a Fifth Part of their Estates beyond the Relief of *Chancery*'.[105] It was less Locke's subtle philosophy than his argument that devaluation would rob creditors of their debts and landlords of their rents that persuaded a Parliament representative of the landed interest. A Parliament, too, apprehensive of change and motivated by a dread that devaluation would be a slippery slope leading in the future to further 'resolutions for falling it again'; a fear not diminished by Lowndes' intended but double-edged reassurance that there need be nothing permanent about his proposed devaluation.[106]

As it turned out the Recoinage, promulgated by Parliament in January 1696, was badly mismanaged and caused considerable disruption. For a limited period of five months clipped coin was accepted at face value for the payment of taxes and government loans which in practice meant that only those with large tax liabilities or the means of advancing loans to the government could be sure of recouping the nominal value of their specie in new coin. For the rest, the majority of people, there was little chance of securing such an advantage and when the deadline came in June 1696 and the old coinage was demonetised there was still something approaching £5 million of defective coin in the hands of the public which could only be redeemed by weight, entailing a loss of at least £1 million on its holders, mostly the poorer element of the population.[107]

The process of recoinage was very slow in its first two years. By the close of 1696 £4.7 million of clipped coin had been converted into £2.5 worth of new money so that something in the region of £2.3 million nominal value was actually lost to circulation and as much may have been lost again in the following year. Wage-earners and shopkeepers found themselves desperate for cash. Evelyn, even in May 1696, was bemoaning the scarcity of money 'so as none was either payed or received, but on Trust, the mint not supplying sufficient for common necessities'. Lowndes' concerns about the effects of a restoration of the old standard were almost immediately fulfilled as the scarce new coinage quickly began to disappear from circulation, most of it, as in the past, vanishing overseas. For although a ceiling of 22*s* had been put on the value of the guinea it was still overvalued in relation to silver, the mint price of which – pegged at 5*s* 2*d* an ounce – remained below

---

105 Kelly (1991), II, 463, 417 and 404 [Dedication].
106 Horsefield (1960), 68; Lowndes (1695) [1856], 31 [199] and 49 [217].
107 Feaveayear (1963), 139 and 142.

29　William III shilling, 1696. The 'B' under the king's bust representing the Bristol mint, one of five provincial mints set up to assist in the silver recoinage of 1696-98.

the market value of the metal. Evelyn was soon complaining not only about the 'Want of current money to carry on not onely the smalest concernes' but also the 'greate summs daily transported into Holland, where it yields more'.

> [N]othing considerable coined of the new [he observed] & onely current stamp, breeding such a scarsity, that tumults are everyday feared; no body either paying or receiving any mony; so Imprudent was the late Parliament, to damne the old (tho clip't & corrupted) 'til they had provided supplies.[108]

Things looked 'very black' in the early summer of 1696, especially in the poorest parts of the country, the north. In Manchester it was reported that so great was the 'danger of distresse for want of current money, that without some speedy supply, all traffick will cease. Our markets cannot be continued. The poor have been, in severall markets, tumultuously murmuring; and we are, I think, in great danger of greater unquietness'.[109] Rioting did break out in Kendal and Halifax; rumours of Jacobites exploiting the situation were rife in Newcastle and Shropshire; the atmosphere in Sheffield was 'near puncheable'; there was a fear of insurrection among the miners of Derbyshire and of disturbances in Liverpool, Bristol and Staffordshire; there was a run on the recently established Bank of England; people had difficulty in buying bread and the government in paying the military.[110]

While the 'tumults' proved to be temporary and the creation of five provincial mints eased concern about local distribution of the new coin it took three years for a full-weight silver currency to be established [29]. But it was a currency that had been severely reduced in quantity – from the £11 million in circulation prior to the Recoinage to some £6.8 million of new coin and silver was never to regain its dominance as the country's effective standard of value. The official overvaluation of gold continued, good silver coin progressively fled abroad and the country was left with an increasingly scarce and worn silver currency that had been counterfeited from the earliest days of the Recoinage.[111] Gold on the other hand was thought to have increased from £6 million to something in the region of £9.25 million by 1701 and was augmented after the Methuen Treaty of 1703 by the import of considerable quantities of Portuguese and Brazilian coin.[112] Silver that had been the standard of value and the normal medium of

---

108　Beer (1955), V, 242: 24 May 1696 and 245: 11 June 1696.

109　HMC, *Kenyon* (1894), 409 (No. 1018).

110　For an account of the discontent see Beloff (1938), 100-106 and Gaskill (2000), 194-97.

111　By 1717 Sir John Craig estimated that barely a couple of million pounds worth of the reformed coinage remained in circulation: Craig (1953), 194. Gaskill (2000), 127, records that the new coinage was less than a month old when a Derby man was apprehended with £700 of newly minted counterfeits in his possession.

112　For the importance of Portuguese gold in effecting the transition from a silver to a gold standard see Vilar (1984), 227-30.

exchange for centuries had begun a rapid descent almost to the status of a subsidiary currency while gold, once useful for major purchases only, was of necessity becoming a recognised tool for ordinary business transactions. The sacred mantra of Locke's creed of the immutability of Mint weights was to have considerable repercussions for the country's growing economy and its coinage over the next century as Britain blindly but remorselessly stumbled to a gold standard and a token silver coinage.

I

THE STATE OF THE COINAGE

When your Money is richer in substance and lower in price than that of your Neighbour Nations, as our Silver is than the Silver in the *Low-Countries*, how can you expect that the Merchant, who only seeketh his profit, will ever bring hither any Silver when he can sell it in the *Low-Countries* at a higher Rate, and make more money of it here by returning of it from thence hither, or by Exchange, or by Commodities? Or, if any Merchant do bring Silver hither, it is to sell it to such who will give a higher rate for it, than can be produced at the Mint, as the price of our Silver Coins now stands...

Rice Vaughan, A Discourse of Coin and Coinage
(1675) [1856], 76 [76].

Copper serves only for the meaner Sort
Of People; *Copper* never goes at Court.
And since one Shilling can full Twelve Pence weigh,
Silver is better far in *Germany*.
Tis true the Vulgar seek it, What of that?
They are not Statesmen, — let the Vulgar wait.

[Charles Leslie], On the SCARCITY of the Copper Coin.
A SATYR (1739), 6.

The tokens that so absorbed the energies of collectors like Miss Banks were occasioned by the wretched state of Britain's domestic money supply, not just of the copper coin they directly represented but, implicitly, of the silver that was traditionally the medium for everyday exchange – 'the pale and common drudge 'tween man and man'[1] – for, as we shall see, the condition of the one had more than a passing influence on the other.

Over decades *good* silver coin had effectively disappeared from the circulating currency, an unavoidable consequence of the rigid application of the monetary principles that had been embraced at the time of the Great Recoinage. These had stabilised the hitherto fluctuating value of the gold guinea in relation to silver at a maximum of 22*s* for fiscal purposes (later brought down further to 21*s* 6*d*); in practice fixing its commercial value at this level and setting a course to a gradual and unconscious redefinition of the nation's currency in terms of gold rather than the time-honoured sterling silver standard. At the same time the coined value of silver – and, since no charge was made for its coining, the Mint price of silver – had been confirmed at

[1] *The Merchant of Venice*, I, Scene ii.

62s the troy pound (or 5s 2d the troy ounce), the standard operative since 1601. In terms of the market this was an unrealistic price resulting in an ingrained undervaluation of silver coin in relation to gold that was out of step with much of Europe outside the Iberian peninsula and even more so with the Far East where silver was much in demand. The commercial price commanded by exportable silver bullion, thus, relentlessly outstripped the Mint price spawning a persistent exodus of silver from the country. And from the currency; for while the export of precious metals was, by law, restricted to bullion and foreign coin, and the conversion of coin of the realm into bullion for export was illegal, such a prohibition was winked at by the money jobber or exchange dealer prepared to perjure himself, have his coin melted down and then shipped abroad. The law was unenforceable; the profit substantial and good silver simply took flight. It was a truth that the lawyer Rice Vaughan had tried to drive home years before [2] and now the ballad-monger in the guise of an honest turnip man lamented its disappearance abroad:

> 'O Yes! O Yes! Can any say', the honest turnip man lamented,
> 'Where all the Money's run away ...
> Was it by Night, or yet by Day,
> That Money fled from hence away?
> Or has it taken pray its flight,
> To *Antwerp* unto Mr Knight?
> Or is it fled to France or Spain
> Or in another Place remain...' [3]

Sir John Craig estimated that by 1717 barely a couple of million pounds' worth of the £6.8 million recoined in 1696-98 remained in circulation and although that year the guinea was written down to 21s on the advice of Isaac Newton, the Master of the Mint, it was a half-hearted gesture that – as Newton himself recognized – could do little and, in the event, *did* little to stem the flow abroad.[4] Even under the new dispensation the British ratio of silver to gold, now reduced to about 15.2:1, was still far too high, a point that the economist George Whatley, among many other observers, was at pains to point out:

---

[2] Vaughan (1675) [1856], chapter 13. Vaughan's treatise, the most noteworthy on currency prior to the 1690s, was probably written in the 1630s although not published (posthumously) until 1675.

[3] From *THE OLD TURN-P [TURNIP] MAN'S HUE-AND-CRY After More MONEY, OR Two Bunches of TURNIPS for a Penny* (London, 1721): PRO: SP 35/28109. 'Mr. Knight' was Robert Knight, a founder of the South Sea Company who fled to the Low Countries in January 1721: *ODNB*.

[4] Craig (1953), 193-94; Newton (1701-25) [1967], 170; Conduitt (1774) [1967], 195; Merrey (1789), 54.
The reduction of the value of the guinea caused so much public concern and hoarding of silver in the expectation of further revaluations that both Commons and Lords resolved early in 1718 that they would not again alter the standard of gold and silver coins 'in fineness, weight, or denomination': Ruding (1840), II, 66, note 6.

THE STATE OF THE COINAGE

> For so long as 15 *Ounces and about* $1/5$ of *pure Silver* in *Great-Britain*, are ordained, and deemed to be equal to *one Ounce of pure Gold*, whilst in neighbouring States, as *France* and *Holland*, the proportion is fixed *only* $14\frac{1}{2}$ *Ounces of pure Silver*, to *one Ounce of pure Gold*, it is very evident, that our Silver when *coined*, will always be the most acceptable Merchandize by near five in the Hundred, and consequently more liable to be taken away, or melted down, than before it received the Impression at the Mint.[5]

What Whatley failed to stress was that in the Far East the ratio was considerably lower even than that in Europe: in the Indies about 12:1 and in China and Japan only 9 or 10:1.[6] The incentive for export to the Orient was, thus, immense and virtually irreversible. Between 1700 and 1717 the East India Company alone shipped out enough silver to have furnished a coinage of £5,730,000; and over the subsequent four decades this had escalated to an amount sufficient to provide for an annual coinage of £500, 000.[7]

The undervaluation of silver not only led to its export but also inhibited its import and its coining. Although there was no shortage of silver bullion in the country – and good coins were hoarded and plate manufactured in abundance – there was no incentive for the metal to be brought spontaneously to the Mint by private individuals in quantities sufficient for coining under its reactively bespoke minting arrangements. With the market price of silver seldom less than $1\frac{1}{2}d$ above the immutable Mint price of 5s 2d the troy ounce and on occasion reaching as much as 5s 11d it was impossible for the Mint either to provide or to maintain an adequate supply of good silver coinage except at a loss, under impress from the mining companies or from the fortuitous bounty of the spoils of war. As John Conduitt, Newton's successor at the Mint, explained in 1730 'no silver' had 'been imported to the mint' in twenty-six years 'but what was forced thither' and by mid-century even the small deposits required from the mining companies had ceased to be forthcoming [30].[8]

It was for these reasons rather than, as too many commentators have suggested, any inefficiency on its own part that for most of the second half of the century the Mint was effectively closed to any large-

30 George II sixpence, 1728. The reverse plumes denote the use of Welsh silver in the melt of metal for the coin.

---

5 [Whatley] (1762), 8. As Whatley stressed 'By law, 62 shillings are to be coined out of One pound, or 12 Ounces of Standard Silver. – This is 62 pence an Ounce. Melt these 62 shillings, and in a Bar this Pound Weight *at Market*, will fetch 68 pence an ounce, or 68 Shillings. The Difference therefore between coined and uncoined Silver in *Great-Britain is now* $9\ 2/3$ per Cent' (pp. 9-10). Cf. *Leeds Intelligencer*, 6 March 1769, quoted in Marsh (1971), 30.

William Stout was able, in 1701, to export £40 worth of crown pieces to purchase 'tarr (*sic*) and dales [deal]' in Bergen that yielded him 'above ten pounds clear ganes [gain]': Marshall (1967), 136.

6 Newton (1701-25) [1967], 168; Ashton (1955), 168 (and note 3) -69 and 171.

7 Craig (1953), 215 and 219.

8 Snelling (1762), 50, note (*k*); Anonymous (1771), 4; Craig (1953), 246-7; Conduitt (1774) [1967], 195 and 191; Dyer and Gaspar (1992), 433.

37

COINAGE AND CURRENCY IN EIGHTEENTH-CENTURY BRITAIN

31   George II shilling, 1758.

32   George III shilling, 1787.

scale production of silver and was confined mainly to the minting of exiguous issues of Maundy money. No crowns or halfcrowns were struck after 1751, for these weighty denominations were perceived as being the most attractive for conversion into bullion, and few shillings or sixpences were produced for public consumption after 1758. Even the now common silver coins of 1757-58 [31] and the equally familiar shillings and sixpences of 1787 [32] were produced at a loss chiefly to the order of the Bank of England; in the former case largely to meet 'the Discharge of Seamen's Wages' during the Seven Years War, and in the latter not for ordinary currency but for issue 'in small quantities' to the Bank's customers at Christmas and stockpiled by Threadneedle Street for years to come.[9] But their very paucity as ordinary currency only served to promote their forgery. As the *Daily Universal Register* grumbled in the April of 1787 although the coins of that year were still 'only handed about as curiosities' in the London area '*fac similes*' were already being forged by '*ingenious*' artists' in Birmingham; no doubt, it sniffed sardonically 'we shall soon have *striking likenesses* of them in plentiful circulation'.[10]

Some serious thought does seem to have been given to an issue of silver for general circulation in the early 1760s following the taking of Spanish treasure at Havana and Manila. It resulted in the minting of £10,000 worth of threepenny pieces specifically for small change in 1762 and 1763 [33] but they probably made little impact on the currency, their scarcity provoking one observer to deride them as curios 'for children to admire'.[11] And what appears to have been projected as a companion issue of shillings saw only the minimal production of the

33   George III threepenny piece, 1763.

34   George III 'Northumberland' shilling, 1763.

9   [Morris] (1757), 4; Leake (1793), Appendix, 5; Bank of England Archive: M695: 'Questions asked by the Privy Council's Committee on Coin on the 21st February 1798 and the Answers given by the Bank', A. 38. The Bank indicated in its return of 1798 that £22,800 of the £55,280 worth of shillings and sixpences coined in 1787 was still being held in its vaults. See also Kelly (1976), 7 and 136.

The presence of an uncirculated shilling of 1758 and one of 1787 among fifty-seven guineas in the Westmancote hoard (*c.* 1794) is symptomatic of the curiosity value of these coins. For the hoard see Kent (1969), 166.

10   *The Daily Universal Register*, 9 April 1787.

11   Merrey (1789), 18. Merrey adds that 'not one person in ten thousand had ever seen the present King's face upon any other coins' until the shillings and sixpences of 1787. Snelling makes no mention of them in 1766: Snelling (1766b), 1.

The Daily Universal Register, in 1785, called for the coining of fourpenny and twopenny pieces to 'answer the intermediate purposes and convenience of change' while the London magistrate, Patrick Colquhoun (1745-1820), advocated the issue of 'an extensive coinage' of silver threepences in the 1790s to 'remedy some of the abuses and pressures which arise from the vast quantity of base copper now in circulation': *The Daily Universal Register*, 1 November 1785; [Colquhoun] (1796), 139-40 and 463.

THE STATE OF THE COINAGE

35a Spanish dollar of Carlos IV (1792) countermarked with head of George III, 1797.

35b Spanish half dollar of Carlos IV (1796) countermarked with head of George III, 1797.

36 George III third guinea, 1797.

so-called 'Northumberland' shillings of 1763 [34].[12] A pattern shilling was commissioned the following year but if any reformation of the coinage was contemplated at that time it came to nothing.[13]

The shillings and sixpences of 1787 marked the end of silver currency production by the Mint for the remainder of the century and although the need for a new coinage was recognised in the ensuing decade or so little was done apart from the issue of countermarked Spanish dollars from the Bank of England's holdings in the emergency of March 1797 [35a and b]. It was an unsuccessful experiment, the stamp was widely counterfeited and the dollars were quickly called in to relieve the Bank of too great a loss to be replaced by gold seven-shilling pieces before the end of the year [36].[14] A coinage of shillings and sixpences was projected by a consortium of bankers in 1798 when a temporary fall in the price of silver made minting a feasible proposition. Striking seems, however, to have been halted on the advice of the Privy Council Committee on Coin that had been reconstituted a few months earlier to carry out a fundamental review of the coinage. The bulk of the proposed issue was melted down but a few of the shillings, struck to the design of the 1787 coins – the miscalled 'Dorrien and Magens' shillings – did find their way into the hands of the public.[15]

Such new coin as did enter the public domain quickly disappeared either into the hoarder's cache, the goldsmith's crucible for the manufacture of fashionable plate, or, more likely, into the speculator's melting pot for export. It was an age-old story that Peter Vallavine, a Kent clergyman and crusader against coinage abuse, echoing Vaughan, had raged about in 1742: while 'the Market Price of Silver in Bullion is above the Value of Silver in Coin'… 'not only no Silver will be brought to the Mint to be coined: But of all that which is already coined, all the weighty which can be pick'd up by those who know how to make their Advantage of it, will be melted and converted into Bullion, for the Profit that is to be made by so doing'.[16] The upshot was, in Professor Ashton's words, that 'only the old worn or clipped pieces …were left

---

12 The association of these shillings with the duke of Northumberland as Lord Lieutenant of Ireland has obscured their intended, but quickly abandoned, striking for general currency. Few could have found their way into circulation and, even two decades later, they were being 'sold for several guineas a piece, to deposit in the cabinets of the curious': Merrey (1789), 18. The striking of '1758' shillings seems to have continued on a limited scale into the early years of George III's reign and a small number of sixpences, presumably struck from 1758 dies, was delivered to the Bank of England in November 1762.

13 Pattern shillings were also produced in 1775 and 1778 again presumably with a currency issue in mind.

14 Kelly (1976), 17-35 and Manville (2001), 3-4.

15 Dyer and Gaspar (1982), 198-214.

16 Vallavine (1742), 31-32. See also Vallavine's 'To prevent the Diminishing of the Current Coin' (1752): PRO: MINT 1/11; *GM*, November 1754, 507: 'Most of our crown and half crown pieces have, it is thought, been melted down, or conveyed abroad. Many of our old shillings, and most of our old six-pences, are greatly defective in weight. This, indeed, is chiefly owing to the wear, and not to fraud'.

39

COINAGE AND CURRENCY IN EIGHTEENTH-CENTURY BRITAIN

37   French *demi-écu* of Louis XVI, 1791.

in circulation: the rest had gone to grace the bodies of women in India, to provide votive offerings in the temples of China, or simply to swell hoards in these far-off places'; or, as the *Daily Universal Register* grumbled about the home country itself, 'to supply the increased luxury of the present times in the articles of wrought plate'.[17]

Scarce as it was silver was the coin most needed for wage payments and for the bulk of retail transactions. It was, as the Privy Council Committee on Coin was to grasp all too tardily at the end of the century, 'the Coin which the Poor principally use' …'much wanted for change, particularly among the lower Ranks of People'.[18] And for most of George III's reign the public inevitably had to make do with an abraded silver currency stretching back to King William's reign, swollen with forgeries, and, in London and the seaports especially, augmented with over-valued foreign coin.[19] French *demi-écus* [37] were readily passing at 2s 7½d in the metropolis in 1766 and remained popular until the end of the century. Indeed, in 1785, the *Daily Universal Register* was urging 'a general agreement to take all foreign coin, and especially that of Spain, Portugal, and France, in every purpose of trade and commerce' until an effectual remedy for the state of the coinage could be devised.[20] But the very acceptability of such coin was a further temptation to the counterfeiter, emboldened by the uncertain application of the Elizabethan laws respecting its forgery. Prior to Romilly's act of July 1797 'coinages of *Louis d'Ors, Half Johannes, French Crowns, Half Crowns*, and *Shillings*, as well as several Coins of Flanders, Germany, and other Countries' were 'going forward without

---

17   Ashton (1955), 169; *The Daily Universal Register*, 1 November 1785.

18   PRO: BT 6/127, 10 February 1798, quoted in Peter Mathias (1962), 26 and (1979), 204 and 208, note 25; Bank of England Archive: M695: 'Questions asked by the Privy Council's Committee on Coin on the 21st February 1798 and the Answers given by the Bank', A. 38. See also Kelly (1976), 134. Cf. Harris, Part II (1758) [1856], 62 [492].

19   Reference was made in the Prologue to the circulation of minor foreign coin as small change in England but for generations high value silver had also circulated. In 1644, for instance, the author of *A Remedie* … complained about such coin especially along 'most our Sea-coast of Kent, Sussex, Hampshire, and generally all the West Country, and this is divers sorts of forraigne coyne, which the people thorow ignorance take, much above its value: as divers sorts of Dollers, which are two pence a piece worse then the right sort of Rixdollers: also a sort of Spanish money commonly called Peeces of Eight, which go current at foure shillings and four pence amongst them: it is true, the right sort, or the Sivill coyne, are worth so much: but amongst these are very many which are very light, and want much of their weight … and instead of bringing them to the Mint to reduce them to our owne coyne and value, they will be prest upon the Subject, to their great prejudice': Anonymous (1644), 6.

20   Snelling (1766b), 1; *The Daily Universal Register*, 1 November 1785.

any dread of punishment on the part of those concerned'.[21]

Even by the 1760s the currency had become so degenerate that, for Charles Jenkinson, it was already a token coinage comprising 'mere Counters, without any impression on the face or reverse, or any graining on the edges, or indeed any exterior mark by which they can be distinguished as Coins'. As Laurence Sterne could fret at Versailles in 1768, he had in his pocket a 'few king William's shillings as smooth as glass' that had 'become so much alike, you can scarce distinguish one shilling from another'. It was an open sesame for forgers who 'by putting only a faint King William's Head on one Side, and [leaving] the other ... quite plain ... if they were taken up ... could say they were made for Buttons, but was [sic] not yet shanked'.[22]

As early as 1742 Vallavine had calculated that a sample of shillings then in circulation was on average 8½ per cent under weight and sixpences 16 per cent. By the time of the king's accession in 1760 Jenkinson estimated that shillings were 16 per cent under weight and sixpences at least 25 per cent. A generation later the Mint itself was computing that half-crowns were about 8 per cent under weight, shillings 20 per cent and sixpences 35 per cent. Eleven years on these denominations were thought to have been diminished by about 10, 25 and 38 per cent respectively.[23] These were analyses borne out by practical experience on the street which correspondents to the *Gentleman's Magazine* were eager to report. Rowland Rouse, a Market Harborough draper and auctioneer, concluded in 1786 that, having sampled 1,200 sixpences and 1,400 shillings, the former were intrinsically worth only 4¼*d* each and the latter, 10*d*. Three years later he argued that 'Great numbers of *sixpences*', were 'received and paid away without the least scruple or difficulty, which weigh only 22 grains [1.43 g], and whose intrinsic value, consequently, is not quite three pence'. In 1795, silver was 'so worn and defaced as to be much below its standard value (a shilling being intrinsically worth little more than 8*d*)'.[24] Yet when good coin

---

21 [Colquhoun] (1795), 4-5; Anonymous (1771), 19. The 1572 act, 14 Elizabeth cap. 3, making it misprision of treason to clip or counterfeit gold and silver coin of other realms not current in this realm (punishable by life imprisonment, forfeiture of goods and loss of profits of and during life) was still on the statute book but, according to Colquhoun, had not been effective for many years. This situation was remedied by Romilly's act (37 George III cap126) which made it a felony to counterfeit such coin. Technically, John Milton the Mint engraver dismissed in March 1797 for supplying dies for the counterfeiting of foreign gold could have been arraigned as an accessory under the Elizabethan act had this been proceeded with against the forgers: see Stainton (1983), 135.

22 Liverpool (1805), 2 and 168; Sterne (1768) [1984], 90; Anonymous (1771), 6. Even in 1745 Leake could say that William III shillings and sixpences were 'the bulk of our silver Money' and many of these had been 'reduced to blanks': Leake (1793), 427-28; Merrey (1789), 83.

23 Vallavine (1742), 28-29; Liverpool (1805), 187-88.

24 *GM*, January 1786, 27 and July 1789, 608: Rouse (1739-1823) was an eminent local historian and antiquary; *GM*, January 1795, 14. Cf. Leake (1793), 427: 'Our Sixpences are, many of them, worn to Groats, and some Shillings not much better in proportion'.

was short any sort of money would pass and with the livelihood, even the existence, of so many dependent on its free exchange it would be tolerated at its nominal value. The silver coinage had simply been allowed to decay into a token currency. And, there were times when even the most decrepit could command a premium. 'It is well known', declared Sir John Barnard, the City merchant, in 1759, that bankers 'generally give a Premium for silver Coin, to supply their Customers', a practice especially prevalent at harvest time and other occasions when large wage payments were critical. 'Most of our Tax-Gatherers give a Premium for Change', alleged a commentator in 1771, and although it was 'a scandalous and base Trade … strictly forbidden by Law' clerks in the public offices were said to hope that silver 'would never be plenty' to diminish their profits from the practice.[25]

The deplorable condition of the silver currency could have been remedied only by a fundamental recoinage recognising that in practical usage its place as the standard measure of value had been taken by gold. This could have been achieved in one of two ways; either, as was suggested by the Board of the Mint to the Privy Council Committee on Coin in 1787, by debasing the fineness of the coinage from 925 to 883.5 parts pure silver or alternatively by depreciating the weight standard from 62*s* to 65*s* to the troy pound. Either revision would have had the effect of bringing the British silver/gold ratio (15.21) more into line with that of Europe, especially the contemporary French standard of 14.47, but neither solution captured the imagination of the Committee on Coin.[26] And, in any case, government for years had shown itself implacably opposed to upsetting the monetary principles of the Great Recoinage.

While debasement, with its notorious Tudor precedents much in mind, could never have been an acceptable answer – Adam Smith was not alone in regarding it 'a concealed operation … an injustice of treacherous fraud' – a reduction in the *weight* of the coinage to permit it to pass for more than its worth in bullion had been canvassed frequently.[27] As we saw earlier Lowndes, basing his argument on historical precedent, had championed this solution in the acrimonious debate leading up the Great Recoinage but had lost out to the tendentious philosophy of Locke. In 1730 John Conduitt had advocated striking silver at the rate of 64*s* 6*d* to the troy pound, the market price the metal had averaged for the previous decade.[28] Smith, himself, in the aftermath of the Gold Recoinage of 1774, rather

25 Liverpool (1805), 188; *GM*, March 1759, 123; Merrey (1789), 56; Sutherland (1933), 33, note 1. Cf. Bank of England Archive: M695: 'Questions asked by the Privy Council's Committee on Coin on the 21st February 1798 and the Answers given by the Bank', A. 38; Anonymous (1771), 4-5.

26 Craig (1953), 257.

27 Smith (1789) [1994], 1011-12.

28 Conduitt (1774) [1967], 212. In 1752 Vallavine had suggested lowering the silver standard by a shilling to the troy pound and the gold by about threepence to achieve a more equitable ratio with European countries: 'To prevent the Diminishing …': PRO: MINT 1/11.

THE STATE OF THE COINAGE

38 Samuel Garbett (1717-1803). Pattern medalet by John Gregory Hancock.

haltingly suggested a similar reduction tied to a legal tender limit for silver coin up to a guinea.[29] A much more radical proposal was that of the Birmingham entrepreneur Samuel Garbett [38] and his son Francis in their report on the workings of the Mint undertaken at the request of Lord Shelburne, the Prime Minister, in 1782. They had established that 15 lb of shillings 'taken promiscuously from the heap at a banker's' on average comprised 76 shillings or 190 sixpences in tale to the lb: that if a pound of silver of the obtaining legal standard 'was coined into 76 shillings or 152 sixpences [as opposed to 62 shillings or 124 sixpences], it would be a great accommodation to the public by distributing a better coin than is at present in circulation, and which would probably continue there, as its value in money would be superior to the bullion it contained'.[30]

Such a reduction – of something like 22% – was far beyond anything the Mint could contemplate. William Chamberlayne, the Mint solicitor, asked for his opinion of the Garbetts' proposals, expressed his surprise at their adoption of 'Mr. Lowndes's Scheme of 1695 of lowering the standard weight [of the silver coin]; a measure which has been so often exploded by the wisest men from Queen Elizabeth's time to the present.' His concern – and he had considerable experience of the problem [31] – was that a currency devalued on the scale that the Garbetts proposed, would, despite their caveat that it should pass as tender for no more than 10s 6d, create an untold opportunity for the counterfeiter. It was, as Chamberlayne was at pains to stress, just what had happened to the copper coinage the metal value of which was much less than its face value, but its social consequences would be much more serious.

> No one would exchange Gold for them [the Garbett's proposed silver coin] but in cases of necessity all retail Dealers would be obliged to take them [and] their wholesale Dealers possibly must take them or nothing. The Bankers would naturally refuse them and the last Receiver must keep them a Dead weight by him or sell them for old Silver for their intrinsic worth. But that would not be all. The profit would soon tempt counterfeiters to imitate them until such a Quantity should exist as to Cause universal distress among the trading part of the nation who could only be relieved by a General Recoinage of Standard money and having the loss of each Individual made good by the public even as to the Counterfeit money which would then be in circulation.[32]

29 Smith (1789) [1994], 49-50.

30 Garbett and Garbett (1837), 221.

31 William Chamberlayne (1728-99), a friend of George Rose, Pitt's influential Secretary of the Treasury, was successively solicitor to the Mint (1755-75), to the Treasury (1775-95) and, until his death, a commissioner of public accounts. As solicitor to the Mint he had been principally concerned with combating the activities of coiners. See, for example, Styles (1980), *passim*.

32 PRO: SP 37/27/427-28: 'Copy of Mr Chamberlayne's Letter to Lord Shelburne with observations on Messrs. Garbett's Report'.

43

COINAGE AND CURRENCY IN EIGHTEENTH-CENTURY BRITAIN

39 'Mr. Garbett's Pattern Sixpence', produced by Matthew Boulton to impress William Pitt, the Prime Minister, 1787.

40 Charles Jenkinson, Lord Hawkesbury, later 1st Earl of Liverpool (1729-1808), 1786.

Samuel Garbett, in the event, was not to be put off and five years later when the Committee on Coin was set up he was still lobbying for a silver recoinage at the rate of seventy-six shillings to the troy pound and trying to convince his friend Matthew Boulton to bend his energies to the minting of silver rather than of copper. He persuaded Boulton to produce a few pattern sixpences [39] at his favoured weight-rate to impress Pitt, the Prime Minister, of the desirability of such a small-denomination silver coinage. But even Garbett's persistent promotion of a purely palliative measure failed to win the support of an administration that shared Chamberlayne's fear of the spur it would give to the counterfeiter.[33]

A key figure in the government's consideration of the state of the coinage was Charles Jenkinson, ennobled as Viscount Hawkesbury and appointed President of the Board of Trade in 1786 [40].[34] 'Jenky', whose ear Garbett constantly bent, had made a close study of coinage matters for many years and had been the inspiration behind the gold recoinage of 1773-75. As his views developed he came firmly to the conclusion that gold should be formally recognised as the country's monetary standard and, somewhat more nebulously, that silver, occupying a purely supplemental role, should be reduced to a token coinage by taking into account the cost of its production in establishing its face value. The slight weight reduction that would ensue coupled with a limit on the legal-tender value of silver coin only for small sums would, he hoped, deter the counterfeiter and protect the coin from the crucible and the money-jobber. These were ideas Jenkinson floated before the Committee on Coin when it was reconstituted in 1798 and later published in his *Treatise on the Coins of the Realm* of 1805.[35] It was to be long after his death, nevertheless, before his proposals were to come to fruition in the Coinage Act of 1816 promoted by the government of his son, the second Lord Liverpool. Then, with the market price of silver standing at 5s 1½d the troy ounce, a new silver coinage was promulgated with its weight reduced to 5s 6d to the pound. With its legal tender status, too, restricted to amounts only up to two guineas it had at last officially become the token coinage for which the public's toleration of the old degenerate currency had paved the way.[36]

---

33 Dykes (2005a), 169-172.

34 Jenkinson was President of the Board of Trade for eighteen years until 1804. A confidant of the king and regarded as something of an *éminence grise* he was not altogether trusted by his colleagues and always viewed with some suspicion by Pitt whose more liberal, free-trade views he did not wholly share. He was raised to the earldom of Liverpool in 1798. For Jenkinson's career see *ODNB*. See also Gash (1984), 8-10.

35 According to Ruding (1840), II, 97 Liverpool's proposals were supposedly obstructed by the opposition of the Chief Justice of the Common Pleas (Sir James Eyre). The *Treatise* bears strong evidence of the influence of Garbett who maintained a lengthy and detailed correspondence with Jenkinson on coinage matters but Garbett is acknowledged only in reference to the price of bullion: Liverpool (1805), 150-51.

36 Dyer and Gaspar (1992), 481; Carlile (1901), 19-20.

THE STATE OF THE COINAGE

41a George I quarter guinea, 1718.

Many factors militated against any major recoinage in the 1780s and 90s and deterred the naturally cautious Pitt – a man whom Garbett considered would 'hear a talk' but lacked administrative decision – from embarking on such a course. It would have been costly; it would have been disruptive to trade; and, more significant in the eyes of government, it would have been a likely cause of popular unrest. Memories were long and the dislocation, expense and civil discord attendant upon the Great Recoinage had been a lesson not easily forgotten. Government therefore did nothing while the Mint, having no obligation to correct even the normal ravages of the wear and tear to which the coinage was subjected, did nothing either.

For greater hand-to-hand business the currency gap was filled by gold or by the increasing use of paper currency – promissory notes and negotiable drafts – as the country's nascent banking system developed. Generally – but by no means invariably, especially in Scotland – provincial bank notes were of too high a denomination for most ordinary everyday purposes particularly after the Saville Act of 1775 banned the issue of such notes below a value of £1.[37] For most people money meant coin. The guinea, as was mentioned earlier, had begun to achieve a degree of familiarity as a medium of exchange even before the Great Recoinage when good silver had earlier been in short supply. In 1717 it had been recognized as legal tender for all transactions and in the following year a quarter guinea was introduced as a palliative for the shortage of silver [41a]. Tariffed at the awkward sum of 5s 3d it was quickly discontinued since it proved difficult and expensive to make, inconvenient to use and unpopular with the public. Nevertheless, over the ensuing century, gold coin inexorably supplanted silver as the *de facto* measure of value. With a plenitude of gold coin and a scarcity of respectable silver it was a not unnatural process – brought about, in Lord Liverpool's words, 'by the disposition of the people' – but it was an almost unconscious one that contemporaries failed to appreciate for many years. Although by 1730 Conduitt could express the view that 'nine parts in ten, or more, of all payments in England, are now made in gold', the sanctity of silver as the country's standard of value remained unquestioned. A generation later Joseph Harris, the Mint's influential Assayer, while recognising that 'more payments, or of greater value, are made in gold than in silver coins' still insisted that 'there can be but one standard of money, and silver is and ought to be that standard'. It was a principle still being maintained by as perceptive a commentator as Adam Smith in 1789.[38]

---

37 See pp. 66-67 below. In 1777 the minimum value for private bank notes was raised to £5. Bank of England notes – restricted to the high denomination of £10 until 1793 when £5 notes began to be issued – being payable only in London tended to have a limited circulation much beyond the capital and were treated with great suspicion because they were easily forged: Pressnell (1956), 15-16 and 138.

38 Dyer, G. P. (1997), 73; Liverpool (1805), 85; Conduitt (1774) [1967], 203 and 193; Harris, Part I (1757), 59 and 64, note; Harris, Part II (1758) [1856], 57-58 [487-88]; Smith (1789) [1994], 44-47; Carlile (1901), 19-21.

45

41b George III quarter guinea, 1762.

The Bank of England, perhaps, was more attuned to the needs of ordinary commerce than the Mint and in 1758 pressed for the introduction of a gold third guinea or 7s piece in an attempt to provide an alternative small denomination to the absent silver. The proposal was given short shrift by Harris, who, probably harking back to the luckless quarter guinea, condemned the introduction of another denomination: 'new coins', he declared, 'might palliate and amuse for a short time yet … they could not supply the place of silver'. The Bank made another approach three years later but it proved equally abortive.[39] Eventually, in 1762, the Mint to an extent gave way, but perhaps with failure in mind, it once more put out a 5s 3d piece [41b]. Again impractical and easily lost, the 'whore's curse' was even smaller than the threepenny piece that accompanied it.[40] Like its ill-fated predecessor, seems to have been largely 'laid by as a curiosity' and proved to be as short-lived, being 'silently annihilated' during the gold recoinage of the 1770s. Yet its cessation was due more to the cost of its production than any presumed public antipathy. Although it was criticised as being too close in size to the half and quarter moidores and troublesome for change – seven or fourteen shilling pieces, it was thought, would have been far more convenient – it did have its defenders. Walter Merrey, a Nottingham master hosier widely experienced in the practical problems of the currency, could declare, for instance, that it had been 'of great service for change'; if the guinea had been divided into other parts when quantities of gold were coined annually, he added, 'it would have shewn some consideration for the public'.[41]

The critical role of gold in the currency is vividly demonstrated by the fact that by the early 1770s its circulating value exceeded that of silver by well over 25:1. Just as with the silver there was, though, no provision for the calling in and replacement of worn gold and while the old pre-1663 hammered coin had been withdrawn in 1733-34 milled guineas and half-guineas already up to seventy years old continued in circulation and remained so. Three decades on the domestic gold coinage was becoming almost as decayed as the silver. Good coin –

---

39 Craig (1953), 241 and 261; Kelly (1976), 5; Challis (1992b), 432. The Bank again unsuccessfully petitioned for the issue of a third guinea in 1773. As we have seen the denomination was eventually issued in 1797 [36] following the failure of the countermarked dollar scheme and its utility was such that it thereafter continued to be struck in most years down to 1813.

40 The quarter guinea derived its nickname from its being said to have been 'frequently given to women of the town by such as professed always to give gold, and who before the introduction of those pieces, always gave half a guinea': Grose (1796) [1931], 369.

41 [Morris] (1757), 14-15; Snelling (1763), 32, note n; Ruding (1840), II,124; Kenyon (1884), 187; Anonymous (1771), 14; Leake (1793), Appendix, 3; *GM*, Supplement 1761, 616 and *GM*, December 1791, 1103; Merrey (1789), 64 and 66; Dyer, G. P. (1997), 74. Merrey (1789) is reviewed and quoted in *GM*, August 1789, 728-29. Merrey (c. 1723-99) is said to have owned 'an immense collection' of coins, many discovered in the Nottingham area, but its fate, after his death, is unknown: *ODNB*.

THE STATE OF THE COINAGE

42a Portuguese *moidore* of João V, 1712, current in England for 27s.

and such new gold as was struck was produced mainly for the Bank of England to sustain the convertibility of its note issue – quickly disappeared into the melting pot since, as in the case of silver, the exportable market price of gold bullion, for much of the 1760s, exceeded that of its Mint price. In 1763, at the end of the Seven Years War, it was declared that 'the demand for gold in coin is so great that the Jews now give 4 guineas an ounce [as opposed to the legal rate of £3 17s 10½d], so that we may soon expect to have that as scarce as silver. The reason is, the Dutch are drawing their money from our funds, in order to accommodate the French, who give 8 per cent'.[42] By 1773, according to Jenkinson,

> the deficiency in weight, of the Gold Coins then in circulation, was become very considerable; so that, as soon as any new Gold Coin was brought from the Mint, these perfect pieces were exchanged, or bought up, for the old deficient Coins, and immediately melted down or exported … and such was, at that time, the state of the currency of this country, that there was very little of good or perfect Coin of any metal circulating in it.[43]

What remained in the country was again a dross made up of 'shortened'[44] coins that to an indiscriminate public were often indistinguishable from the underweight fruit of normal wear, plain forgeries and freely circulating and overvalued Portuguese specie. 'Moidores' [*moedas de ouro*], supplemented after 1722 by the *escudo* series of João V (1706-50) and José I (1750-77) popularly known as 'joes' in England, and passing as currency 'by courtesy, and not by law' as Snelling put it, were imported on a vast scale for more than the first half of the century in settlement of England's trading surplus with Portugal [42a, b and c].[45]

42b Portuguese *dobra de quatro escudos* ('Joe') of José I, 1753, current in England for 36s.

---

42   *GM*, May 1763, 256.

43   Liverpool (1805), 3-4.

44   Coins diminished through filing or sweating [garnering metal dust by shaking coins together in a container or by precipitating a residue from them in a solvent such as aqua fortis (nitric acid)]: cf. Borrow (1857), 124-25. It was said that much 'shortening' of British coin was done in Holland and especially France to avoid the exigencies of the law and then re-imported: Anonymous (1771), 5.

45   A partial consequence of the Methuen Treaty of 1703: Smith (1789) [1994], 587-88; Snelling (1766c), 69; Vilar (1984), 227-30.

47

COINAGE AND CURRENCY IN EIGHTEENTH-CENTURY BRITAIN

42c   Plate (13) of Portuguese Coins from Thomas Snelling's *View of the Coins at this time current throughout Europe* (1766), nos. 7, a 'moidore' (27s), 8, a ¼ 'moidore' (6s 9d), 9, a ¹/₁₆ 'joe' (2s 3d) and 10, a 'joe' (*dobra de quarto escudos*) (36s).

It is thought that some £25,000,000 worth of Portuguese bullion, chiefly in gold coin from Brazil, reached Britain between 1700 and 1760 and even the Bank of England seems to have had something like one-sixth of its gold reserve in such coin in 1739.[46] As currency the Portuguese coins had the virtue of ranging over some eleven values as opposed to the guinea's three (if one included the quarter). For Merrey it was a useful substitute for the country's attenuated silver in its smaller values of 9s [¼ 'joe'], 6s 9d [¼ 'moidore'], 4s 6d [¹/₈ 'joe'] [43a] and 2s 3d [¹/₁₆ 'joe'] [43b] since such 'parts' allowed him to 'make up any payments with very little silver'.[47] In the early forties Peter Vallavine described the Portuguese imports as being 'in great

---

46   Fisher (1971), 136; Clapham (1944), I, 232. Foreign coin, though readily passing in exchange, was not accepted for the payment of taxes: Leake (1793), 426.

47   Conduitt ((1774) [1967]), 188; Merrey (1789), 65.
    On the subject of the Portuguese bullion trade and the circulation of Portuguese coin in Britain see Fisher (1971); Sutherland (1933), Chapter II. There is no comprehensive study of the circulation of Portuguese coin in Britain but see the valuable overview by Kent (1985), 389–405.

THE STATE OF THE COINAGE

43a Portuguese ⅛ escudo of João V, 1726, current in England for 4s 6d.

43b Portuguese ¹⁄₁₆ escudo of João V, 1734, current in England for 2s 3d.

44 Sarah Malcolm in Newgate. A portrait by William Hogarth, 1733.

Measure the current Money of the Nation' – though counterfeits, whose makers, as we have seen, were not subject to the ultimate penalty exacted for forging gold coins of the realm, were abundant 'and not so easily discovered as in our own Money'.[48]

Contemporary literature abounds with references to Portuguese coin. Tobias Smollett's highwayman, Rifle, for instance, was chagrined to find only 'ten Portugal pieces in the shoes of a Quaker' when he robbed a coach while Roderick Random, the eponymous hero of Smollett's novel, was equally mortified to discover that it was the custom to pay the secretary of the navy board a 'three pound twelve piece' [double 'joe'] as a bribe for a surgeon's mate's warrant.[49] Such a practice was no doubt Smollett's own real-life experience in 1740. Much more serious, however, was the grisly cause célèbre of seven years earlier when the murderess, Sarah Malcolm [44], was found with twenty 'moidores' from a cache of gold coin and other valuables she had stolen from her employer after strangling the latter and her elderly lady companion and cutting the throat of their maid.[50]

By the 1760s the influx of Portuguese gold had considerably diminished due to England's declining export surplus and the quantity of *moedas* in circulation began to fall sharply. Even in the West Country, where they had been particularly prevalent owing to their entry to the country through Falmouth, the port of arrival for the Lisbon packets, *moedas* were petering out. In rural Somerset they had already become curiosities by the time the young James Woodforde bought two 'double joes' from a neighbour at Ansford for 'Seven new guineas' in 1769.[51] By the early 1770s the poor state of the gold currency began to be reflected in a reluctance to take foreign coin resulting in shopkeepers in different parts of the country stipulating that they would accept authentic Portuguese gold only if it commanded a reasonable weight [45]. In 1774 the international financier, Isaac de Pinto, remarked that since 'the profits of [the Portugal] trade have declined rapidly within these fifteen years ... we see no more [Portuguese] gold in circulation'. Pinto exaggerated somewhat for in the north of England Portuguese coins – and their counterfeits [46] – were still relatively plentiful. And, even after the gold recoinage of the middle seventies which might have been expected to give the foreign money the *coup*

---

48 Vallavine (1742), 37. Leake (1793), 426. The rifeness of the forgery of Portuguese gold in Britain, especially between 1752 and 1769, is reflected in the *Gentleman's Magazine*, e.g. *GM*, April 1765, 193: 'Several pieces of counterfeit gold coin have lately been discovered at Birmingham, so nicely finished as hardly to be discovered; they are chiefly 36s. pieces of a pale colour, and the date 1750'.

49 Smollett (1748) [1995], 41 and 82.

50 The Portuguese coin furnished the bulk of Malcolm's haul which, in addition to the 'moidores' contained eighteen guineas, a few 'broad pieces' and 25s in silver: Proceedings of the Old Bailey: t17330221-52.

51 Winstanley (1986), 46 and 263 (18 July 1769). Portuguese coins are not mentioned by Parson Woodforde during his long years in Norfolk from 1776 to 1803.

49

de grâce, the continued manufacture of Portuguese-value coin weights in Birmingham suggests that *moedas* and their imitations persisted in some measure and probably remained so for some time.[52] By the year of the French Revolution, however, the 'Portuguese phenomenon' had become little more than a memory for one observer and three years later Pitt could be told by the Treasury that 'the usual supply of gold from Portugal ... [had] ceased some time past'.[53] Portuguese coin was still counterfeited but 'as articles of commerce for the purpose of being fraudulently circulated in the British Colonies or in Foreign Countries'.[54]

45   Advertisement in *Aris's Birmingham Gazette*, 13 September 1773.

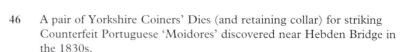

46   A pair of Yorkshire Coiners' Dies (and retaining collar) for striking Counterfeit Portuguese 'Moidores' discovered near Hebden Bridge in the 1830s.

47   Commemorative medal of the gold recoinage, 1775, by John Kirk.

It was left to Lord North's government, spurred on by Jenkinson, now a privy councillor, to grasp the nettle in 1773 and embark on a major gold recoinage [47]. Over the years from 1773 to 1778 some £16.5 million worth of worn or clipped coin, and Portuguese imports

52   Fisher (1971), 137; Phillips (1894), 229-30; Biggs (2004), 106-107.

53   Fisher (1971), 137; Phillips (1894), 229-30; Merrey (1789), 65: 'now that we have no Portugal money and the light half-guineas will not pass, our distress is doubled'; Clapham (1944), I, 220 and 258.

54   Colquhoun (1800), 172-73.

THE STATE OF THE COINAGE

– estimated at seventy-five per cent of the total gold currency – was surrendered for recoining.[55] The exercise cost the Exchequer over £750,000 and the public perhaps an even greater sum but it resulted in a new and highly esteemed coinage, the integrity of which was secured if only for a time by a strict enforcement of prescribed weight standards – the concept of Chamberlayne – and a more general use of scales by the public such as those manufactured by the Westwood brothers of Birmingham [48]. The heightened awareness of sub-standard coins, though, was no comfort to the Honourable John Byng when a half-guinea he had taken one morning in 1792 was refused in Manchester – 'a dog hole' – 'because it was a light one'; as he splenetically mused, 'One cannot travel about, like Shylock, with a pair of scales'.[56]

48   A boxed set of coin-weights produced by John and Obadiah Westwood in the 1770s. Although the label inside its japanned metal box lid implies that it comprised a 'long set' of eleven weights for British and Portuguese coins it actually contained only the three weights of the guinea series.[57]

49   George III 'recoinage' guinea, 1774.

But the very quality of the new gold worked to its disadvantage and it was not long before it again began to be siphoned abroad. By 1779 money in London 'was scarce beyond conception'. The writer Philip Thicknesse was made aware of this immediately on arriving at Calais at the start of a continental tour three years earlier. Having made his bow, and 'given ... a side look, as a cock does at a barley-corn', the first question his French innkeeper put to the traveller was whether he had any guineas [49] to change? On his eventual return to Calais Thicknesse found that he could not get the innkeeper to convert his accumulated *Louis d'ors* back into guineas but that, 'in lieu thereof', he had to accept a bagful of *Birmingham Shillings*. As he ruefully put it,

---

55   Craig (1953), 244; Dyer and Gaspar (1992), 440.

56   Andrews (1934-38), III (1936), 117.

57   The weights are illustrated by courtesy of Paul and Bente Withers.

51

COINAGE AND CURRENCY IN EIGHTEENTH-CENTURY BRITAIN

50 George II halfpenny, 1753.

I am afraid, when Lord North took into consideration the state of the gold coin, he did not know, that the better state it is put into in England, is the surest means of transporting it into France, and other countries; and that scarce a single guinea which travellers carry with them to France (and many hundred go every week) ever returns to England.[58]

Whatever problems attended the gold coinage, soon to be exacerbated by the drain of specie for the American war, they paled into insignificance with the continuing calamity of the silver. The silver coinage had been untouched by the recoinage of gold so that by 1778 although some £18 million worth of new guineas and half-guineas had been put into circulation little more than £800,000 in decayed silver remained by their side.[59] The supremacy of gold as the standard of value for internal monetary exchange was thus, if only for a fleeting moment, reinforced by quality and quantity while silver was further humiliated to a subsidiary role by its legal tender being restricted, by tale, to payments not exceeding £25.[60] North's reforms, in effect, endorsed the country's century-long unconscious progression to a gold standard and relegated silver to a token coinage forty years before the actuality of the Coinage Act of 1816.

For most of the century the limited availability of silver specie was such that, even augmented, as it was, with foreign coin and forgeries,[61] it had, of necessity, to be topped up by copper halfpence and farthings despite their legal-tender limit of sixpence. It was a telling commentary on the currency shortage and the abnormal role of copper that when Walter Merrey, the Nottingham hosiery manufacturer, decided with other local employers to offer no more than 6*d* worth of copper in their out-workers' wage packets their action only served to create problems for the workpeople in finding change for small purchases themselves.[62] Yet, if the silver coinage was in a blighted condition that of copper was even more ramshackle. Between 1729 and 1754 a total of more than £175,000 (800 tons+) of copper coin, chiefly in halfpennies [50], was struck by the Mint. Much of this was obviously intended as a gap-filler for the attenuated silver coinage but, as we will

---

58 Sancho (1803), 181; Thicknesse (1777), I, 9-11. By the 1780s the nation's stock of gold currency was steadily deteriorating as the best was profitably exported and as old, lightweight coin designedly sent to America 'as prompt payment' for imports at the time of the Recoinage drifted back home, a situation compounded by a renewal of counterfeiting: *ABG*, 2 August 1784. Cf. Craig (1953), 246 and Dyer and Gaspar (1992), 441.

59 One consequence of the Recoinage, according to Merrey, was that 'such numbers of half-crowns appeared as had not been seen for twenty or thirty years preceding ... but ... *they* generally want about three-pence of the standard weight, or near ten per cent': Merrey (1789), 56.

60 Ruding (1840), II, 85 and 92.

61 Leake's continuator (Leake (1793), Appendix, 5) exaggerated when he suggested that 'few, very few indeed, of the shillings and sixpences now in use, appear ever to have been legally coined' but his remark emphasizes the degenerate state of the coinage.

62 Merrey (1789), 67.

THE STATE OF THE COINAGE

51 George III halfpenny, 1770.

52 Counterfeit George III halfpenny dated 1774.

see, the quantity produced, swollen by the counterfeits it spawned, only served to encumber the urban and metropolitan retail outlets it primarily supplied. As a result copper production was halted after 1754 – apart from a very small issue of farthings in 1762-63 (still struck from dies of 1754) produced, it was said, to accommodate the London brewers who had raised the price of beer to 1¾d a pint – until, in the wake of a petition from London tradesmen for a resumption of coining, a larger issue of halfpence and farthings was put out between 1770 and 1775 'as an Experiment of a Temporary relief to the Public' [51]. How much relief the new coins themselves actually did give to the public is questionable for far too many were promptly and remorselessly converted into counterfeits [52]; thereafter no regal copper was produced for currency until Matthew Boulton's Soho 'cartwheels' of 1797.[63]

Although the face value of the 'Tower' halfpenny was supposed to be roughly equal to its metal value (plus the cost of manufacture) in practice it rarely met this standard. All too often it was made too light – often well below the notional standard of 9.86g – and, like its silver cousins, to all intents and purposes it had become a token. Moreover, its paltry weight coupled with its unsophisticated design and indifferent execution furnished an irresistible temptation to counterfeiters, barely constrained by the law, to relieve the demand for small-denomination coin with a flood of still lower-weight forgeries.[64] 'If it were intended to tempt the unwary to commit the crime of counterfeiting', commented Rogers Ruding, 'a more effectual mode could not have been devised, than that of making the workmanship of the money rude, and consequently easy of imitation. The effect of this is, that almost every worker of iron can sink a die to imitate the present coinage'.[65] Their task was made that much easier, too, since with well-worn copper reaching back to the previous century still in ready circulation there was often little to identify the genuine article from the counterfeiter's judiciously 'aged' fraud.[66] Particularly prone to forgery were the issues of William III and the early pieces of George I; both had been so 'badly and variably struck' that imitations were easy to pass, especially from the 1750s when, 'publish'd … in a new edition', counterfeits began to

---

63 The amounts in 1762/63 and 1770-75 were approximately £3,800 and £46,000 respectively: Dyer and Gaspar (1992), 435-36; Anonymous (1771), 7-10.

64 Until 1742 the counterfeiting of copper was treated as a misdemeanour incurring only slight penalties. The crime then became punishable by two years' imprisonment but, in practice, continued to be treated lightly. Even after 1771 when it was made a felony, according to Patrick Colquhoun, it normally attracted no more than a year's imprisonment and the new law had little effect: [Colquhoun] (1796), 135.

65 Ruding (1840), II, 126.

66 In his *Letters from England by Don Manuel Alvarez Espriella* Robert Southey ([Southey] (1807), II, 121-22) tells us that counterfeiters fried their products 'every night after supper for the next day's delivery, thus darkening them, to make them look as if they had been in circulation'.

be stamped rather than cast.[67] Even the Mint could be nonplussed. A parcel of halfpennies sent to its 'officers … for inspection' in 1787 was admitted to be 'not without suspicion, though they believed [the coins] to be good; that they had lost the nicer marks by which the question might be determined with certainty; but that, after examining them attentively, and consulting with the assay-masters, gravers, and other moneyers of that office, they had good reason to believe the said six halfpence to be all genuine coins, and not counterfeits'.[68]

Part of the Mint's reluctance to embark on a minting of new copper coin in the latter part of the eighteenth century was due to the rapidity with which it was re-fabricated. The George II 'Old Head' halfpennies of the 1750s, for example, were quickly transmuted into 'worn' imitations 'of the old King *William's* Halfpence'.

> These being observed to want about one in four of the Weight of new ones, gave a hint to the ingenious to melt down the New and re-coin them after the old … consequently the Artist gained clear an Half-penny in Two-pence, or Three-pence in a Shilling by the Operation.[69]

And, as the Mint feared, the new coinage of 1770-75 was also systematically melted down to re-emerge in a lighter-weight, apparently well-worn, edition. Few of the new coins seem to have lasted long as small change in the public's hands, many being hoarded because of constant fear that the issue would be abruptly discontinued as in 1754 and the rest 'being destroyed by the makers of counterfeit halfpence, who have but little prospect of putting off theirs while there is plenty of good coin'. By the beginning of 1776 the 'Circulation of Counterfeit Copper Money' had risen to 'such an enormous height', in London especially, that production of the legitimate coin was ended but, despite vocal pressure from the City's 'most respectable and opulent Traders', any hope of successfully suppressing the 'alarming and increasing Evil' itself proved to be of no avail.[70]

---

67 Craig (1953), 253; *GM*, November 1752, 500.

68 *GM*, January 1788, 75-76. The coins emanated from Scotland where 'for what reason cannot be accounted for the common people would not receive the half-pence of King George III': *GM*, May 1789, 464. James Lawson, one of Matthew Boulton's technical managers, reported in 1791 that in Glasgow 'not a Halfpenny of Geo 3^d will pass as they are all reckoned counterfeit [;] a plain piece of copper with a wore [*sic*] appearance passes but tho' ever so good with the Head of Geo 3d is not passable': BAH: MS 3782/12/66/19: James Lawson to Matthew Boulton, 5 September 1791.

69 Anonymous (1753), 2-3.
    Patrick Colquhoun pointed out in 1796 that even 'the legal coinage of copper must produce an immense profit, seeing that *one pound* of copper estimated at 15 *pence* will make as many half-pence of the legal coinage as pass for *two shillings*.' [Colquhoun] (1796), 127. A few years earlier, he tells us, sheet copper had been as low as 11½d a pound. This had been in 1793; in earlier years it had been appreciably cheaper: cf. *Copper Report* (1803), Appendix 9, 702 and Hamilton (1967), Appendix XI, 366.

70 Anonymous (1771), 9; *The Monthly Review*, September 1771, 231; *ABG*, 12 February 1776.

News of this metropolitan reaction 'to a Practice, in itself highly illegal and infamous, and materially injurious to the honest upright Trader' was immediately sent off to Birmingham for publication in the local newspaper.[71] Intentionally so, for Birmingham, long a centre specialising in metal work, much of it cheap and tawdry, had for a century and more earned the direst of reputations for illicit coining. 'Birmingham' or 'Brummagem ha'pence', like 'Brummagem shillings', had become a byname for false coin, excoriated at a public meeting of protest against counterfeit copper in Abingdon in 1752 and declaimed against by *The Gentleman's Magazine* five years later:

Upon a BIRMINGHAM HALFPENNY

Hence! False, designing cheat, from garret vile
Or murky cellar sprung! Thy spurious birth
And mix'd embrace thy pallid hue proclaims.
Thrust thou 'mongst those of pure and generous stamp,
To pass unknown, and by dissembling face
And mimic form, to gull me, credulous.
I mark'd thee midst thy betters, and with eye
Distinguishing arrested thy deceit! ...
Nought will avail thy name and face assumed
And regal head with *George's* laurel bound:
Thy telltale paleness speaks thee counterfeit.
Lives there a beggar wretch, with hunger prest,
Would take thee offer'd? Thou art known so well,
The honest tradesman will not sell thee wares...
I've got thee safe; no more expect to thrive
By cheating innocence; in durance firm
I'll fix thee, to deter thy bastard race. [72]

Even the unscrupulous industrial spy, Thomas Attwood Digges, in Birmingham in 1793 seeking out artisans and machinery to smuggle to America determined that 'no Artist in the diesinking way, goes from this quarter, for the genius & wickedness of the place would soon lead to counterfeit the American moneys'.[73]

But counterfeit copper did not only emanate from Birmingham.

---

71 *ABG*, 12 February 1776.

72 *GM*, November 1752, 500; *GM*, July 1757, 325. But Birmingham's ill-favoured reputation for coining reached back far earlier to the seventeenth century; see, for example Rollins (1931), 173 for *The Royal Regulation* a ballad of 1696: '... Their money for food would not pass, 'twas either Clipp'd, Burmige or Brass ...'

A century or so later the comment was made of Boulton's 'cartwheel' coinage that it 'strangely confused the ideas of the lower orders of people, who could not readily apply the term Birmingham, which had so long been the designation of base Money, to the lawful Coins of the Realm': Ruding(1817), II, 500, note i and (1840), II, 94, note 4.

73 LC: Thomas Jefferson Papers, Th[omas] A[ttwood] Digges to Thomas Pinckney [the American Minister in London], 6 April 1793. This letter also contains Digges's impressions of the extent of counterfeiting in Birmingham. See also Elias and Finch (1982), 452-56.

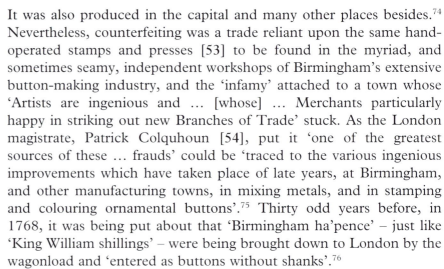

It was also produced in the capital and many other places besides.[74] Nevertheless, counterfeiting was a trade reliant upon the same hand-operated stamps and presses [53] to be found in the myriad, and sometimes seamy, independent workshops of Birmingham's extensive button-making industry, and the 'infamy' attached to a town whose 'Artists are ingenious and … [whose] … Merchants particularly happy in striking out new Branches of Trade' stuck. As the London magistrate, Patrick Colquhoun [54], put it 'one of the greatest sources of these … frauds' could be 'traced to the various ingenious improvements which have taken place of late years, at Birmingham, and other manufacturing towns, in mixing metals, and in stamping and colouring ornamental buttons'.[75] Thirty odd years before, in 1768, it was being put about that 'Birmingham ha'pence' – just like 'King William shillings' – were being brought down to London by the wagonload and 'entered as buttons without shanks'.[76]

Counterfeiting of copper, treated tenderly by the law and tolerated by the public, was ubiquitous and was frequently a more open business than Rudolf Erich Raspe's oft-quoted reference to 'shabby, dishonest button-makers in the dark lanes of Birmingham and London' might lead one to believe. In Birmingham itself rigorous efforts on the part of the authorities to put a stop to the town's all too conspicuous trade were completely nugatory. In 1780 the local newspaper railed, not for the first time, against the 'amazing Quantity of Counterfeit Halfpence now in Circulation, and the great Effrontery with which they are given in Payment, in open Contempt, or Defiance of the Laws for their Suppression'. It was to no avail, the coiners even having 'the audacity to hang up Signs in the Street **All sort of Copper Coins made here**' as Matthew Boulton later discovered to his chagrin.[77] Colquhoun declared in 1795 that he had

53   J. Bisset, *A Poetic Survey Round Birmingham* … (1800), Plate R, showing a button maker's lathe, fly-press (extreme left) and stamp.

54   Patrick Colquhoun (1745-1820).

74   Colquhoun cites the Black Country towns of Bilston, Wednesbury ['Wedgbury'], and Wolverhampton in addition to Birmingham as centres of counterfeiting: [Colquhoun] (1796), 120. Years later an 'aged and intelligent mechanic' recalled that Birmingham had a bad character for false money… Wolverhampton was, perhaps, still worse… but Bilston was the worst place of all, and actually swarmed with coiners of bad money': From *The Morning Chronicle*, 10 February 1851, quoted in Razzell and Wainwright (1973), 311.

75   In 1788 there were at least 188 button makers in Birmingham, many of them operative in back-street garrets: Hamilton (1967), 266. Anonymous (1753), 2; Colquhoun (1800), 172. In 1769 Matthew Boulton recorded in his notebook that 'all our ornaments may be stamped or may be press[ed] in the fly press or may be formed in the Leviathan': quoted in Goodison (2002), 130. For the operation of the fly or screw press see Cooper (1988), 51 and Quickenden (1989), 108-9. Cf. Michaelis-Jena and Merson (1988), 17 on Birmingham coiners 'parading as makers of buttons'.

76   *The Manchester Mercury*, 27 September 1768, quoted in Wadsworth and Mann (1931), 400, note 4.

77   Raspe (1791), xlii; *ABG*, 17 January 1780; BAH: MS 3782/12/42/84, Matthew Boulton to Sir George Shuckburgh-Evelyn. [Draft, endorsed in pencil 'March 1797'].
Silver seems to have been more subject to clipping, filing and sweating than counterfeiting probably because the forging of gold and silver was a treasonable offence punishable by death.

an alphabetical list of more than fifty coiners in the metropolis and in Birmingham and the country around 'whose names and places of residence are generally known'. On his reckoning three people between them could stamp £200 to £300 worth of copper coin (at a nominal value of between 96,000 and 144,000 halfpennies) in the course of a six-day week – 'and when the number of known Coiners are [*sic*] taken into the calculation, the aggregate, in the course of a year, must be immense!' [78]

The business was also often more highly organised than Raspe's comment might suggest. Colquhoun, again, related how, in London, regular markets were held by the principal dealers where

> *Hawkers, Pedlars, fraudulent Horse-Dealers, Unlicenced Lottery-Office Keepers, Gamblers at Fairs, Itinerant Jews, Irish Labourers, Servants of Toll Gatherers and Hackney Coach Owners, fraudulent Publicans, Market Women, Rabbit Sellers, Fish Cryers, Barrow Women*, and many who would not be suspected, are regularly supplied with counterfeit Copper and Silver, with the advantage of nearly 100 per cent in their favour; and thus it happens, that through these various channels, immense quantities of base Money get into circulation.

'Scarce a wagon or coach', he added, 'departs from the metropolis, that does not carry boxes and parcels of base Coin to the camps, sea-ports and manufacturing towns, insomuch, that the country is deluged with counterfeit Money'.

> The trade of dealing in base money acquires its greatest vigour towards the end of March, for then the Lotteries are over, when *Swindlers, Gamblers, Pretended Dealers in Horses, Travellers with E. O. Tables*, [79] and *Hawkers* and *Pedlars* go into the country, carrying with them considerable quantities of counterfeit silver and copper coin, by which they are enabled in a great degree, to extend the circulation by cheating and defrauding ignorant country people.
>
> It is in the spring season too, that the dealers in base money begin to make up their orders for the different country towns, and it is supposed upon good grounds, that there is now scarce a place of any consequence all over the kingdom where they have not their correspondents ... [who] ... come regularly to the *metropolis*, and also go to Birmingham once or twice a year for the purpose of purchasing base money. [80]

---

78 [Colquhoun] (1795), 6-8. See also [Colquhoun] (1796), 22-23.

79 'E.O. tables' related to a game of chance 'Even or Odd', 'which was determined by the letters E and O being marked upon that compartment of a box into which a die or ball fell': Macquoid and Edwards (1954), iii. 192-3. I am grateful to Robert Thompson for this reference.

80 [Colquhoun] (1796), 19-20; 128-29.

Matthew Boulton had personal experience of such importuning but it was a trade that worked in the opposite direction too. With all the efficiency of a legitimate business coiners sent out their own commercial travellers to drum up trade, 'Knights of the Sadle [sic] Bag', as Boulton called them, who took out 'upon their Journeys pattern Cards of halfpence as regularly as they do of Buttons'.[81]

In the 1750s Thomas Snelling, in what one imagines was a fairly authoritative statement, declared that 'near $\frac{1}{2}$ (or $\frac{2}{5}$)' of the copper coinage was counterfeit, an estimate borne out by at least one of the very few copper hoards of the period.[82] Thirty or so years on Mint officials themselves were of the opinion that the quantity of counterfeit copper actually exceeded the legal coinage. A random sample of the coinage revealed that only 8% 'had some tolerable resemblance to the king's coin', 43% were blatantly inferior, 12% were blanks and the remainder were 'trash which would disgrace common sense to suppose it accepted for coins'. In 1789, Boulton, writing to Jenkinson, admittedly with an axe to grind, famously reckoned that in the course of his travels he received 'upon an average $\frac{2}{3}^{ds}$ counterfeit halfpence from Tolegates [sic] &c', an evil that he argued was 'daily increasing'. Already, two years earlier, he had mused that counterfeit coin was 'supported by Connections between Shopkeepers, Retailers of victuals, Drink, & Drams – Clerks of Manufacturers, Turnpike men &c'.[83] Turnpike tolls were generally charged in copper values providing ample opportunity for the passing of counterfeits [55]. Byng, for example, on one of his summer jaunts about the country, protested that 'whenever any person changes a note, a guinea, or a shilling, he is sure to have in change, bad money tender'd to him, as if it was part of the profit of inns, and turnpikes'. And according to one observer towards the end of the century counterfeit copper had 'increased ten-fold through the agency of turnpikemen, waiters, &c.' who operated a 'regular trade' in the coin. Colquhoun, who had an equally jaundiced view of 'Turnpike-men and others, who wilfully pass bad Halfpence at one gate which are refused at another', concluded in 1796 that counterfeits had risen to three-quarters of the whole. His assessment – in tune with John Pinkerton's conviction that 'not the fiftieth part' of the copper currency (Pinkerton almost certainly included tokens in his account) was legitimate – was probably not all that far out. At any rate such pronouncements expressed the public's perception

---

81 See Stainton (1983), 136, notes 14 and 15, for examples of such approaches to Boulton mainly for the production of French or Portuguese gold; BAH: MS 3782/12/42/84, Matthew Boulton to Sir George Shuckburgh-Evelyn. [Draft, endorsed in pencil 'March 1797'].

82 Snelling (1766a), 44. The Dunchurch Hoard (1961) of 89 halfpennies from William and Mary to George II (1751) of which at least 39 and probably more were forgeries: Robinson (1972), 147-58.

83 Liverpool (1805), 198; Craig (1953), 253; BAH: MS 3782/12/34/64, Matthew Boulton to Lord Hawkesbury, 14 April 1789; BAH: MS 3782/12/108/51, Notebook 3, p.14.

THE STATE OF THE COINAGE

of a situation that for Jenkinson himself was 'in truth beyond calculation'.[84]

55   *The Times*, 20 October 1788.

Nevertheless, as Sir John Craig emphasised, 'ordinary folk, if short of small change cared nothing about either intrinsic value, high quality of copper, pattern or limits of legal tender' and as long as counterfeits were countenanced and accepted by the public they at least helped to keep the wheels of retail business turning. In Sir Albert Feavearyear's words 'so long as the Government was unable to find a method of providing the country with a sound and adequate coinage … counterfeit [coinage] was a good thing… The counterfeiter tended to fill up the void, and he could do no harm to the standard'.[85]

A contemporary recalled, years later, that 'almost any kind of rubbish used to pass as copper money'. Foreign copper, French *liards* [56], even 'Wood's Halfpence', commonly passed for a farthing. 'And all this made the trade of the false coiner more easy'.[86] It was all very well for the Mint to adopt an over-righteous stance and blame the public for suffering 'themselves to be imposed upon by the most bungling imitations' or 'wilfully to neglect all endeavours for their own security' (whatever these might have been).[87] As long as government itself lacked the vigour to put down counterfeiting, the will to regulate the copper coinage effectively and the capacity to distribute the coin where it was needed, it was a state of affairs the public was bound to

56   French copper *liard* of Louis XVI, 1789.

---

84   Moritz (1795) [1924], 20; Andrews (1934-38), II (1935), 232; *GM*, December 1799, 1035 (see also *GM*, April 1797, 267); Colquhoun (1800), 198; [Colquhoun] (1796), 125; Pinkerton (1789), II, 85.
     One London gang of counterfeiters was caught red handed after 'they had sent a child for some beer, with new halfpence to pay for it; and the landlord observing to the child that they were warm, she innocently replied, that her daddy had just made them': *GM*, April 1774, 185.

85   Craig (1953), 253; Feavearyear (1963), 169.

86   From *The Morning Chronicle*, 10 February 1851, quoted in Razzell and Wainwright (1973), 311; Anonymous (1771), 15.

87   PRO: MINT 1/14, 30 (14 November 1787).

59

accept.[88] A correspondent to the local newspaper responding to one of the recurrent calls by Birmingham shopkeepers to outlaw counterfeits was drawn to express just such a view in September 1775:

> Yesterday I weighed three [counterfeit halfpennies], which weighed one Ounce Troy, and that is equal to the new ones delivered at the Mint, and the Impression is well executed; it is the Opinion of most of the Inhabitants of this Town that we should be much to blame to discountenance them amongst ourselves, until the Legislature should think fit by some Means to make the Stop general, as they are not now refused in other Places; and from a Sense of the Inhabitants here, which has been carefully taken, it appears they wish to act in Concert with neighbouring Towns, and will take them as usual, as is practised elsewhere.[89]

The whole situation was a self-perpetuating vicious circle as a London 'Tin Man' made plain to Lord Shelburne:

> The retailers are obliged to take them or nothing; for if one refuses, another will not, under the idea of getting rid of them by degrees & increasing their trade but those whose capital is small it distresses severely as they cannot afford so much money to lay dead & should a total prohibition of this kind of coin take place, numbers must inevitably be ruined.[90]

One brazen Bristol hawker during the 1750s' rash of forgeries, capitalizing on such competitive instincts, advertised his wares for purchase by counterfeit halfpennies. It was a trade that continued for much of the century and one that, incidentally, returned a good profit through the selling on of counterfeits north of the Border where, it was said, legal copper was spurned in favour of the spurious.[91] Counterfeit coins could prove their use, too, in paying off highwaymen, if with some apprehension, as Horace Walpole learned one dark night in 1781.[92]

88 As Professor Mathias has pointed out, however, the fluctuation in the price of copper required recoinages to be frequent with successive issues of varying weights and sizes: Mathias (1962), 12 and (1979), 192. In practice this would lead to confusion and public rancour as happened in 1799 over Boulton's 'reduced' weight halfpennies and farthings.

89 *ABG*, 11 September 1775 and 18 September 1775. The public expression of local Birmingham opinion on the subject of counterfeits brought to the fore the rift between sensitivity to the town's reputation on the one hand and concern for its trading interest in the need for and manufacture of small change on the other. Cf. Money (1977), 57-58.

90 BAH: Shelburne-Garbett Papers, R. House, junior to Lord Shelburne, quoted in Wager (1977), 19.

91 *ABG*, 4 November 1751; *GM*, November 1751, 520. Cf. *GM*, May 1789, 464 (see note 68 above). As late as 1799 a Bath draper was offering goods for 'half payment on bad halfpence, no Promissory, those who have quantities will find it worth their while': *Bath Journal*, 21 January 1799.

92 Horace Walpole to the Countess of Upper Ossory, 7 October 1781: Lewis and Wallace (1965), 295-96. Johann Wilhelm von Archenholz, a Prussian visitor to England, describes the common precaution of travellers carrying two purses, one hidden and one for surrender to a highwayman if circumstances demanded: Archenholz (1789), II, 80.

Yet, what was more critical than the rash of counterfeits was government's inability to distinguish those parts of the country where coin was most needed from those where it was over-abundant or to channel the coinage appropriately.[93]

The gathering momentum of contemporary industrial change meant that the demand for cash in localities close to the sources of raw materials or waterpower but often far removed from the old economic centres of the country was intensifying. So much so that while the brewers and shopkeepers of London and of many a market town could be 'greatly opprest' with 'vast quantities' of superfluous copper coin, outlying regions with isolated but developing communities reliant on a money wage, rootless, and dependent on shop-bought necessities could be starved of it.[94] It was a dichotomy of glut and dearth for which the times provided no solution.

There was no organization to redistribute the excess – the country's growing banking system did not normally handle coppers – and the government's only answer to urban surplus, of which they were made very conscious by the strength of metropolitan lobbying, was complete stoppage. This happened, as we have seen, in 1754 following mounting complaints from London's 'bakers, butchers and other dealers in provision and the necessaries of life' – especially, no doubt, its many brewers and publicans who bore the brunt of the problem – over the satiety of copper coin in the metropolis.[95] It was a stoppage that was to last for more than four decades, redeemed only by the brief and limited bursts of activity of the early 1760s and 1770s, and it was just at a time when the call for coin was becoming especially desperate in the newly-emergent mining and manufacturing districts of the country and little less so among more traditionally organised domestic out-workers in the remoter areas of the north and west.

Although, as Professor Mathias has pointed out, a sophisticated web of credit arrangements minimized the cash requirements of eighteenth-century industrial concerns in their day-to-day commercial dealings, actual coin was still required for the payment of wages for their employees' basic necessities. And it was the perennial shortage of this 'real' money that forced industrialists and manufacturers into a variety of stratagems for satisfying the monetary needs of workers and their

---

93 Craig (1953), 252. The Mint supplied copper coins only at the Tower so that what could be significant costs of carriage fell upon the customer: Dyer and Gaspar (1992), 448. An allowance for carriage costs for copper coin was introduced only in 1797.

94 A correspondent ['Obadiah'] to the *Gentleman's Magazine* in 1795 related that in the 1780s he knew of one tradesman 'who, though resident only in a market town, and that not very populous, has upwards of 100*L*. in copper halfpence' and asserted that shopkeepers' drawers were 'loaded with copper': *GM*, March 1795, 199.

95 Snelling (1766a), 44. The so-called 'Southwark Memorial' to the government in 1789 signed by '800 of the principal traders of the Borough' was inspired largely by the brewers and publicans of the area protesting against their vast accumulation of counterfeit coin: BAH: MS 3782/12/34/151, H. Thrale and Co, Brewers, Southwark to Matthew Boulton, 22 August 1789.

dependants living out their lives in the new industrial communities.

Group payment in gold of a guinea or more transferred the trial of finding change from the employer to the employee but often at a cost to the latter. Shopkeepers, and innkeepers in particular, were a source of change but any silver given was almost invariably accompanied by a demand that excess copper should be taken too. As 'AN ENEMY TO IMPOSITION' was drawn to complain to the *Birmingham Gazette* in 1776 'If Change for a Guinea be wanted, the Request is granted upon Condition of receiving Five or Seven Shillings in Half-pence, which are so bad in General, as cannot be circulated in any Place where this iniquitous practice is not carried on'. Walter Merrey made plain the difficulties involved:

> If the work of two men comes to near a guinea, or three men to near two guineas, we give them the gold and they must go together till they can get change by purchasing what they want. If they go to a grocer he will not give change unless the quantity of sugar, tea, &c. amounts to a certain sum, and then he stipulates for their taking a certain quantity of halfpence; if there be not above two shillings in goods he will offer four or five in half-pence... It very often happens that groceries are not wanted by poor men who come from villages around, who seldom care to take tea and sugar home; but they generally have a public house in the market town at which they call to refresh and to it these two or three poor fellows (though not all countrymen) go, with a good excuse to get their gold changed: if they find, after drinking a pint or two, that they cannot succeed, what can they do but go to another house, where one of them may be acquainted?... [W]hether they get change at the first or second attempt, they are not served without taking several shillings in copper, and this of the worst quality that can be forced into circulation. The reason of this is apparent; for if a person has a few bad halfpence that have been refused by shop-keepers he goes to an alehouse and drinks his liquor before he is asked for his money. Grocers frequently take their goods back if the halfpence do not please; but What can the publican do if he objects, and is answered I have no other? he must either trust or take bad ones; hence *their* copper is, in general, worse than that of the shops; and if it be objected to, the reply naturally is, I will take them again next time you come; and thus are the poor workmen drawn to go again to spend their bad money.[96]

Merrey himself as a 'considerable manufacturer' had some clout in Nottingham and could dictate terms in the town: 'I laid out five shillings with a druggist lately, and offered a guinea; the question was, Could I take a few halfpence? I replied, Yes, if good, and having took two shillings had the rest in silver'.[97] Ordinary workers had none of Merrey's advantages and, if paid in gold or paper currency at the local alehouse where employers often set up their pay-tables, they ran, in seeking change, the all too frequent hazard of being 'tempted to spend, in the purchase of liquors, a part of what they have gained by their

---

96   *ABG*, 29 January 1776; Merrey (1789), 67-68.
97   Merrey (1789), 67.

THE STATE OF THE COINAGE

industry, which ought to have been reserved for the sober maintenance of themselves and families'.[98] An alehouse pay-table could, moreover, be manipulated to the direct advantage of a close-fisted employer. By delaying the payment of wages until late on a Saturday night – the normal pay day – and arranging with a colluding landlord for workers to drink 'on the slate' while they waited he could limit his cash outlay by deducting their score from their earnings. The master thus trimmed his wage bill while the 'mechanic' went 'home drunk and empty-handed to his family, where distress begets words then blows'.[99]

'Long pay' periods were adopted to allow wages to be deferred, frequently for a month or two, although in the royal dockyards – the largest industrial units in the country – workers often had to wait for a year or more, giving money-lenders and credit merchants a field day.[100] In the 1780s shortage of coin forced the cotton manufacturer, Samuel Oldknow, to a fortnightly cash payment for his weavers at Anderton and Stockport while his more affluent spinners were obliged to accept their wages in two-month bills. Later, in building up his factory community at Mellor in the Derbyshire Peak, he adopted the expedient of providing his employees with houses, milk, coal, meat, and beds taking care to deduct the cost from their wages. It was an elaborate system of 'truck' combined with paper money [57] which virtually eliminated the use of cash from his wages bill at a time of financial crisis.

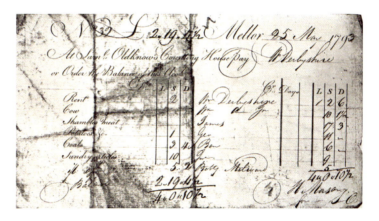

57 A two-week wages note for a family at Oldknow's Mellor factory showing deductions for 'Potatoes &c, Coals and Sundry articles' at the company shop. The reverse was endorsed with further deductions for, inter alia, bread, butter, cheese, flour and linen.

98 Liverpool (1805), 194.

99 Sir John Fielding quoted in George (1992), 287. On the iniquities of alehouse pay-tables see George (1992), 287-290.

100 Pay for the army and navy had always been notoriously in arrears. Samuel Pepys, for example, was complaining in 1665 that the lack of coin to meet wages long outstanding was causing severe problems for the naval dockyards: '[there was] disorder in the yard at Portsmouth, by workmen's going away of their own accord for lack of money, to get work of hay-making or anything else to earn themselfs bread ... we have not enough [money] to stop the mouths of the poor people and their hands from falling about our eares here, almost in the office': Latham and Mathews (1970-83), VI (1972), 144 and 149. By the 1770s the total labour force in naval dockyards had reached over 8,000: Brewer (1989), 36.

Oldknow was not unique in this. Settlement in kind or through customary perquisites was rife in every trade and a fine line often developed between 'benefits' and embezzlement with employees on 'long pay', especially, seeing to it, in Ashton's words, 'that the crumbs from the master's table were ample'. And, as Professor Rule makes clear, the recondite cant terms adopted by workers – bugging to hatters, cabbage to tailors, blue-pigeon flying to plumbers and glaziers, chippings to shipwrights, sweepings to porters, and flints and thrums to weavers – conferred a hallowed legitimacy to practices that while time-honoured often strayed into theft.[101]

As with Oldknow the operation of company shops and the issue of credit-notes with local tradesmen (often convertible only at a premium) were quite generally resorted to as ways of coping with local shortages of hard cash to meet an industrial worker's average pay of perhaps 15 to 20*s* a week.[102] Such expedients, of course, opened the door to exploitation and while the motives behind such contrivances may frequently have been rooted in an enlightened, albeit self-interested, concern for the needs of employees – as with Oldknow and the Crowleys in County Durham – the reality of their existence was a cause of resentment and bitterness and often bore heavily on the workers and their families. No more so than in the West Country woollen industry where 'truck' payments in various guises became a gross evil that a succession of statutes failed to curb.[103]

All too often coin had to be hunted down. In some parts of the west and the north the dearth of coin was such that masters were said to spend an inordinate amount of time riding about in search of cash to pay their workers.[104] Sometimes money could be borrowed from neighbours and even local 'carters, boatmen and sailors' might oblige with surplus cash but it was always at a premium. The Crowleys, for instance, willingly paid 20*s* 6*d* for a pound's worth of copper coin and on occasion their agent was authorised to offer up to as much as an 8*d* premium to shopkeepers in the Newcastle area to raise the necessary cash.[105] To find the weekly cash to pay his weavers Samuel Oldknow sought out 'anyone, however distant, whose business brought a regular supply of currency and who was prepared to give him credit'. In the financial crisis of 1793 Oldknow even

---

101 Unwin (1968), 70 and 181-93; Ashton (1955), 208; Rule (1992b), 182-185. 'Bugging' = the substitution of beaver fur with inferior material; 'cabbage' = purloined cloth; 'blue-pigeon flying' = stealing cut-offs of lead; 'thrums' = web ends of thread or yarn.

102 Unwin (1968), 70; Wadsworth and Mann (1931), 400; Ashton (1955), 207-8.
Because of the variables across the country a general computation of wages in these years is difficult. Professor Mathias has suggested, however, that unskilled labourers earned between 10 and 15*s* per week and skilled from perhaps 15 to 20*s* or more depending on their trades: Mathias (1962), 26 and (1979), 204. A valuable survey of eighteenth-century wages is given in Rule (1992a), Chapter 7, 166-195.

103 Hilton (1960), 47 and 71-79.

104 Fell (1908), 332.

105 Flinn (1962), 179.

> fitted up a light cart and sent a young man [106] with it, full of goods, to supply the retailers in every part of the country, and to bring home the specie every Saturday, whatever might be the loss. The expedient succeeded for about three weeks, but had now failed, and he had come to Liverpool to try if by any possible means he could raise a few hundred guineas, to get over another week and keep his people alive… They [the workers] had agreed to wait this young gentleman's return from Liverpool, and what money he was able to raise, they had consented should be laid out in oatmeal, which being boiled up with water, potatoes, and some of the coarser pieces of beef, should be shared out in fair proportions among them; and thus in the cheapest manner provide for their subsistence.

Despite the thousands of pounds that Oldknow had owing to him his emissary returned home empty-handed not knowing how he was to face 'the poor people … each of whom had four to six weeks' wages due'.[107]

The carriage of large sums from afar could present its own problems, not least of security. The ironmasters of Furness equipped their carriers with pistols while Oldknow would arrange for his regular cash supplies to be hidden in bales of goods; the latter precaution taken not only to counter the possible depredations of highwaymen and footpads but also to avoid the prying eyes of tax collectors who often had previous intelligence of the movement of money and would lie in wait for it.[108]

The wiles of conserving cash took many forms. One practice, iniquitous if really true, was alleged by campaigners against the licensing of a theatre in Birmingham in the 1770s as being rife in some industrial towns. In such places, it was asserted, the existence of theatres encouraged masters to force playhouse tickets on their workers in lieu of wages which the latter were then 'obliged to sell at a half or less price to buy bread'. The accusation was in large measure directed against Matthew Boulton, a major supporter of the theatre scheme, who was compelled to insist that he had frequently provided his designers and modellers with tickets for the playhouse on his own account but only in order that they should learn to capture 'an attitude or a passion' from the life.[109] How trustworthy this partisan charge was in more general terms must be open to question. A much more legitimate – and ingenious – expedient was adopted by a north-country cotton-spinner who, Professor Ashton tells us, staggered the payment of his wage bill:

> Early in the morning a third of the employees were paid and sent off to make their household purchases; within an hour or so the money had passed through the hands of the shop-

---

106 This was Peter Ewart (1767-1842), a partner of Oldknow. A former Soho engineer he subsequently became a distinguished applied scientist. For Ewart see *ODNB*.

107 Fitton and Wadsworth (1958), 240-41.

108 Fell (1908), 334-36; Unwin (1968), 176-77.

109 HMC 15, Appendix, I, *Dartmouth III* (1896), 232-35.

keepers and was back at the factory ready for a second group of workers to be paid and sent off; and in this way before the day was over all had received their wages and done their buying in.[110]

58   3s 6d promissory note of the mill firm, Gamwell Sutcliffe & Son, Heptonstall, c. 1775.

In Lancashire and Yorkshire, it was reported in 1773 in the aftermath of the recent financial crisis, that 'several very considerable manufacturers' had adopted the expedient of paying their out-workers with small denomination promissory notes that they then redeemed through 'badgers' [the manufacturers' agents or middlemen] or local shopkeepers [58]. It was a practice that went back decades and even as early as the turn of the century Sir Ambrose Crowley, the County Durham ironmaster, was said by Jonathan Swift to have circulated notes 'from *Two Pence* to *Twenty Shillings*' in the villages about his works where they 'passed current in all Shops and Markets, as well as in Houses, where Meat or Drink was sold'. These notes, though, were issued for discrete amounts as occasion demanded and not for the rounded sums that Swift implied – more like cheques today than banknotes. They were readily convertible and assignable and served as bills of exchange as well as for wages.[111] True low-value currency notes were put out by the West Midlands ironmaster, John Wilkinson, in 1773 and 1774 and by a number of provincial banks including that of Taylor and Lloyd of Birmingham whose notes for 5s 3d were the subject of a squib by the poetaster John Freeth in the local newspaper:

---

110   Ashton (1948), 99-100.
111   The *Manchester Journal*, 10 July 1773, quoted by Wadsworth and Mann (1931), 401. Cf. also Pressnell (1956), 16. Davis (1955), 58. See also *GM*, November 1803, 1004; Flinn (1962), 180-81.

> Light Gold is the Devil, good Silver is scarce,
> And Ports were rejected to keep up the Farce;
> But the Bank has reliev'd us in being replete,
> With Pieces the LIGHTEST yet quite the full Weight.[112]

Such notes were evidently sufficiently widespread and proved to be such a mischief that they were prohibited by the Savile Act in 1775.[113] The ban was not partially lifted until 1797 but it did nothing to prevent Wilkinson from issuing countersigned French *assignats* as currency substitutes for 3*s* 6*d* 'or some such trivial sums' at his Bersham works in 1792.[114] These, in turn, were quickly outlawed [in January 1793] but, undaunted, Wilkinson was issuing shilling, sixpenny and threepenny notes 'on cards' as soon as the 1775 prohibition was curtailed. No specimens of any of Wilkinson's promissory notes appear to have survived but examples of the paper money or orders on the shop issued by Samuel Oldknow to his workers at Mellor do exist as we saw earlier [57]. And, as with Wilkinson's promissory notes, they seem to have developed a life of their own as a form of currency passed from hand to hand in the locality.[115]

Quite a few employers, even when they could have bought in 'Tower' halfpence, faced with the crippling carriage costs involved – they had to buy the coin at face-value at the Mint itself – chose the far cheaper alternative of procuring light-weight counterfeit copper locally. In the early 1750s, when counterfeiting had reached an apogee, one observer was claiming that 'every Town and Village has it's [*sic*] Mint where many of our Master-Manufacturers get them [counterfeits] coined as cheap as they can for their Use to pay their Workmen with. Each endeavours to under-coin his Rival, in order to under-sell him in his Trade'. After all, even when the counterfeiting of copper or its sale below its denominational value had been made a felony, there was no penalty imposed on those who had *bought* it below par and then paid it to employees at face value.[116] Years later the Committee on Coin was forced to admit that 'an insuperable Difficulty has always occurred in getting them [regal copper coins] into Circulation in all parts of the

---

112 Chaloner (1948b), 550; 'On issuing Five and Threepenny Notes from the Birmingham Bank': *ABG*, 13 September 1773. A Sheffield Bank note for 10*s* 6*d* is illustrated in Hewitt and Keyworth (1987), 31.

113 Liverpool (1805), 226.

114 Kenyon (1873), 270-71. The *assignats* were endorsed by Gilbert Gilpin, Wilkinson's manager at Bersham from 1786 to 1796 and later the proprietor of chain works at Coalport and Dawley where he issued silver tokens in 1811 (Dalton (1922), 25). A local informant alleged that Wilkinson's Bersham workers were 'regularly paid every Saturday with assignats. The Presbyterian tradesmen receive them in payment for goods, by which intercourse they have frequent opportunities to corrupt the principles of that description of men, by infusing into their minds the pernicious tenets of Paine's Rights of Man': Kenyon (1873), 271; Chaloner (1948b), 552; Thompson (1981), 200-203.

115 Chaloner (1948b), 550-553; Unwin (1968), 179-193.

116 Anonymous (1753), 2; Merrey (1789), 64.

Kingdom. Those who live at a Distance will not send for them and it is probably to this circumstance that the Counterfeits have been made use of in preference to those hitherto coined at the Tower'.[117]

Walter Merrey, who operated a considerable 'putting-out' business with domestic stocking frame knitters, was well versed in the problem:

> Of late years, manufacturers have been obliged to apply to a baker, or publican, weekly, for a little change to pay their workmen with, which, if complied with, was always for the sake of getting a quantity of halfpence off his hands; when all sorts of base copper passed, it would mostly exceed the value of the silver; the workmen had these halfpence, tied up in papers of half a crown and five shillings, and were hardly ever paid without one or two of these papers. Those masters who were mean enough to procure them [i.e. counterfeits] from the maker, at a low price, having less silver than others to pay with, would frequently pay all in copper; especially if the wages did not amount to a piece of gold.[118]

But it was not a new problem. Almost a generation before 'An Enemy to Imposition' had protested to the local Birmingham newspaper that:

> An industrious Nailor ... who labours hard all the week for four or five Shillings, receives a Part even of this small Pittance in such base, unlawful Coin, which he takes with him into the Country, and offers for the Necessaries of Life; but there the Tradesman refuses them; they then either remain on the Poor Man's Hand, or are more injuriously employed at the Ale-house, to the manifest Destruction of his Health, and perhaps the Ruin of his Family. These are not mere suppositions. Facts of this Nature occur every Day. The Necessity then of putting a Stop to this Evil cannot but be obvious to Every Man. Policy and Humanity both recommend and enforce it.

Whatever 'Policy' and 'Humanity' recommended and despite the efforts of the town authorities, even to the extent of setting up a fund to reward informers against coiners, the problem remained ingrained and a decade later a correspondent to the same newspaper cried out again that:

> The advantage taken by certain individuals of poor workmen in this place, loudly calls for the interference of the officers to put a stop to the circulation of counterfeit copper coin. On Saturday night last, a poor workman, who, upon an average does not get more than 9s or 10s per week, had halfpence to the amount of 5s forced upon him, in part of his week's wages, which were not intrinsically worth more than 2s.[119]

---

117 PRO: BT 6/126, 1 August 1799. In the 1770s the traders and shopkeepers of Manchester raised a subscription to bring down silver and copper coin of the realm from London: Wadsworth and Mann (1931), 401, note 4.

118 Merrey (1789), 66-67.

119 *ABG*, 29 January 1776 and 30 January 1786.

THE STATE OF THE COINAGE

These were sentiments echoed by Boulton when he laid the increase in counterfeit coin at the door of the 'lowest Class of Manufacturers who pay a part of the wages of the poor people they employ, with them, & they purchase from these Subterranean Coiners 36 shillings worth (in nominal value) for 20s/'.[120] Yet it was not necessarily Merrey's 'mean' master or Boulton's 'lowest class' of manufacturer who resorted to counterfeit copper. Even the more respectable succumbed; and, despite some public clamour, people at large, if only on sufferance, seemed to have become inured to its general circulation as an ersatz currency. A workman, although legally entitled to be paid in silver for sums of sixpence or more, but compelled to accept counterfeit copper when the alternative was a delayed wage, recirculated it through alehouses – 'to the manifest Destruction of his Health, and perhaps the Ruin of his Family' as the 'Enemy to Imposition' claimed – and through small shops that otherwise might have to face the unwelcome burden of extended retail credit for petty items. It was not unnatural that when the tradesmen of Newcastle upon Tyne combined in 1784 to refuse, except at a discount, the counterfeit copper that employers had paid to their men at face value the mayor found himself with a 'very riotous' situation on his hands. 'The present complaint', John Vernon, the solicitor to the Mint, cursorily dismissed as 'only one of a vast number of similar ones'. In the event Newcastle's predicament was resolved by the supply of good copper from the Tower yet repeated attempts to discountenance counterfeits in Birmingham and other towns over the years proved totally ineffective either in suppression or relief.[121]

But it was also a state of affairs that eventually encouraged the more resourceful of a new breed of large-scale entrepreneur with access to the raw material necessary for minting to take the initiative and issue private coinages of their own. Although, as we have seen, steps had been taken to suppress the issue of the seventeenth-century series of private tokens in the 1670s with the introduction of a regal copper coinage the practice may well have been resumed towards the end of the century by industrialists who had to cope with shortages of small denomination money. But, if so, it had been sporadic and restricted to comparatively isolated industrial settlements huddled around some of the collieries and works of the north of England. The Crowleys, it was said, issued leather tokens for their ironworkers in the north east 'which from the great credit of the makers, gained a considerable currency'. Although they were called in at the time of the Great Recoinage and none seem to have survived to the present day they could still apparently be found in the cabinets of late eighteenth-century collectors. In 1725 tokens had been produced by the Mint for the Curwens' mines at Workington on the Cumberland coalfield while

---

120   BAH: MS 3782/12/34/64; BL: Additional MSS 38422, f.13, Matthew Boulton to Lord Hawkesbury, 14 April 1789. A draft version of this letter is to be found in Dickinson (1937), 138-39.

121   Cf. Styles (1980), 177; PRO: MINT 1/13, 178-79; *ABG*, 9 April 1750; 11 September 1775; 19 and 26 February 1776; 7 December 1778 and 17 January 1780. Cf. Davis (1895), xiii.

COINAGE AND CURRENCY IN EIGHTEENTH-CENTURY BRITAIN

59   Lowther coal token for the Whitehaven Colliery, Cumberland, *c*.1700.

the Lowther collieries nearby were using tokens even earlier [59]; and although apparently intended as carriers' receipts or colliers' vouchers it is likely that they found some circulatory value possibly through an early form of 'truck' payment. [122]

One such issue – for payment to the employees of Colonel Charles Mordaunt's cotton mill, a small spinning factory at Halsall near Ormskirk – seems to have achieved, for a few years in the 1780s, a more general acceptance in Lancashire, especially in and about the port of Liverpool.[123] To avoid any perceptible breach of the royal prerogative Mordaunt's token was deliberately tariffed at the innovatory copper denomination of a penny with 'the Earl of Petersbourgh's (*sic*) Coat of Arms on one side; and the Word **Halsall** across the ba[ck]' [60].[124] Of good metal, a passable, if not generous, weight (on average about 17.5g approaching double that of a new regal halfpenny) and maybe struck from Soho dies, it set the stage for the token to become something of a substitute national currency, presaging a major breakthrough that was to take place, again in the north-west of the country, in the early spring of 1787, with the production of the 'Druid' pennies of the Parys Mine Company of Anglesey. Mordaunt's pennies were the swallow that made the summer and though by 1791 they seem to have been driven out of general circulation in Liverpool it was by the much heavier and more attractive Anglesey pennies and the halfpennies of Thomas Clarke, John Wilkinson and Roe and Company.

60   Halsall Mill, Ormskirk, penny token, *c*.1784.

122   Nathaniel Hillier to Horace Walpole, 1 May 1780: Lewis and Wallace (1952), 76-77; Flinn (1962), 178; Barnard (1921), 152-55; Davis & Waters (1922), 285-86. See also Kennett (n.d.), 247-51 and especially Finlay (2006), *passim*.

123   Chaloner (1972), 402-3; Anderson (1970), 88, note 1.

124   BAH: MS 3147/3/379/26, John Moon [the Halsall mill superintendent] to Matthew Boulton, 2 December 1783. Moon, in his letter, asked for dies for two-penny and one-penny pieces 'the weight of Four good Half Pence for the support in payment of the hands at his [Mordaunt's] Works'. No twopenny pieces are known.
Colonel Mordaunt (1729-1808), a former guards officer and 'gentleman of family but not much fortune' (he was a great-great-grandson of the 1st Earl of Peterborough – hence his token's armorial bearings), had opened his spinning factory at Halsall before the summer of 1778 when he was granted a patent for 'preparing cotton, sheep's wool and flax, for the loom; materials and necessary articles for manufacturing cotton and linen cloth': Patent Specification 1198, 11 August 1778: Woodcroft (1854) [1969], 386. He achieved some fame in 1782 in being the initial target of Richard Arkwright's assault against a number of Lancashire cotton spinners for infringing his carding patent. Arkwright's failure in the King's Bench case *Arkwright v. Mordaunt* effectively broke his monopoly: Fitton and Wadsworth ([1958]), 83.

70

II

THE GREAT CONTENTION

THE COPPER KING AND THE FIRST MANUFACTURER IN ENGLAND

> At no time during the present reign, has there been a greater necessity for the regulation of the current coin of the realm than the present. Gold, silver and copper, want reformation. The gold coin, from the great influx of it from America to our merchants here, is generally speaking about three parts standard weight to one light, and few guineas indeed will kick the beam; half guineas are not weight five in twenty. The silver that you receive in change, has not at any period seen his Majesty's mint, and as for the copper coin, the industrious mechanic, who is obliged at a pay table to take half his earnings on Saturday night in counterfeit halfpence, can best exemplify the bad effects the circulation of such trash has upon him individually, and the public collectively, who are obliged to take such money in payment for food, raiment and rent, or put up with receiving nothing at all! It is to be hoped this heavy grievance will be speedily remedied.
>
> *The Daily Universal Register*, 19 December 1786.

The copper magnate, Thomas Williams, managing partner of the Parys and Mona Mine Companies of Anglesey [61a], would have warmly endorsed the *Daily Universal Register*'s sentiments. With a mining, smelting and manufacturing empire stretching from Anglesey to Deeside and from Lancashire to South Wales, he was only too aware of the severe cash handicaps that saddled the industrial entrepreneur. But the final words of the critique would have been particular music to his ears for he was ready to remedy the 'heavy grievance' of the copper coinage and had already embarked on a scheme of reform, less for any altruistic reasons, although these were not totally absent from the mind of a man long remembered by his workforce in Anglesey as 'Twm Chwarae Teg' ['Tom Fair Play'], than to open up a new market for his copper.

The eldest son of an Anglesey yeoman family of some substance, Thomas Williams of Llanidan had by the late 1760s established himself as a successful local attorney and the man of business for several of the island's gentry.[1] In 1769 one of these, an obscure local

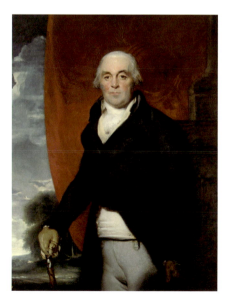

61a Thomas Williams (1737-1802). Portrait by Sir Thomas Lawrence, 1789.

1   For Thomas Williams see Llwyd (1833), 388; Harris (1964) and *ODNB*.

61b Rev. Edward Hughes (1738-1815).

clergyman, the Reverend Edward Hughes [61b], whose heiress wife (Mary Lewis) was a connection of Williams, asked him to act for the family in a dispute with a great Anglesey landowner, Sir Nicholas Bayly of Plas Newydd.[2] It was an instruction that was to set Williams's career in a new direction, transform his fortunes and introduce a new element into the nation's currency.

A year earlier a mass of easily worked copper ore had been discovered on Bayly land on the eastern (Cerrig y Bleiddia Farm) slopes of Mynydd Parys, a barren, hump-like hill a mile and a half south of the little port of Amlwch. Unfortunately, while Bayly owned this side of the upland outright, his possession of the western half (Parys Farm) was shared with the Lewis family in undefined moieties. It soon became clear that the vein of copper ore, being worked by the Macclesfield Copper Company under contract from Bayly,[3] ran through from Cerrig y Bleiddia into Parys Farm land and although Bayly had leased the Lewis portion of the latter since 1753 his rights to any mineral workings there were unclear.[4] When Bayly sought to extend the Macclesfield Company's activities into the Parys estate the Hughes family reacted by precipitating the lawsuit in which Williams acted for them. The dispute dragged on for seven years in the course of which Williams, in Welsh lawyer-like fashion, became increasingly enmeshed in the interests of his clients. Joint working was eventually ordered under a Chancery ruling in 1776 but within two years Bayly had leased his interest in the Parys workings to a London money-scrivener and broker, John Dawes [61c], who was promptly and skilfully cajoled by Williams into joining Edward Hughes and himself to form the Parys Mine Company, thus bringing the whole of the mineral capability of the Parys estate into one entity and creating 'a veritable El Dorado'.[5]

Thomas Pennant visited Anglesey in the 1770s and left a vivid description of what was then the largest copper mine in the world, 'the most considerable body of copper ore perhaps ever known' [62].

> The whole of this tract [Parys Mountain] has, by the mineral operations, assumed a most savage appearance. Suffocating fumes issue from the burning heaps of copper, and extend their baneful influence for miles around. In the adjacent parts vegetation is nearly destroyed; even the mosses and lichens of the rocks have perished: ...
>
> The ore is not got in the common manner of mining, but is cut out of the bed in the same manner as stone is out of a

61c John Dawes (c. 1724-1788).

2 Sir Nicholas Bayly (1707-82) was the grandfather of the 2nd Earl of Uxbridge (later 1st Marquess of Anglesey), commander of the cavalry at Waterloo.

3 Charles Roe's Macclesfield Copper Company had taken a twenty-one year lease of Bayly's own hitherto unproductive workings at Cerrig y Bleiddia in 1764.

4 As the result of a legal judgement of 1568 all minerals, except gold and silver, are held to belong to the owner of the soil in which they are found: Ashton and Sykes (1929), 1.

5 Apparently the original Parys Mine shareholding was one-half, Hughes; one-third, Williams and one-sixth, Dawes: Harris (1964), 151; Hamilton (1967), 153.

THE GREAT CONTENTION

62 *Watercolour Drawings of the Parys Mountain Mine* by Julius Caesar Ibbetson, 1792.

62a The view on the left shows the huge opencast pit on Parys Mountain – although the artist does not do justice to its spectacular depth or the dangers involved – with men and materials being raised and lowered by hand-operated winches mounted on flimsy-looking cantilevered platforms. A horse gin on the far side of the pit shows that alternative methods of haulage were also used.

62b The right-hand view depicts women labourers – the 'copper ladies' who with children were ordinarily employed in this work – breaking up the copper ore.

quarry. A hollow is now formed in the solid ore open to the day, and extends about an hundred yards in length, about forty yards in breadth, and twenty-four yards in depth. The ends are at present undermined, but supported by vast pillars and magnificent arches, all metallic; and these caverns meander far under ground. These will soon disappear, and thousands of tons of ore be gotten from both the columns and roofs. The sides of this vast hollow are mostly perpendicular, and access to the bottom is only to be had by small steps cut in the ore; and the curious visitor must trust to them and a rope, till he reaches some ladders, which will conduct him the rest of the descent. On the edges of the chasms are wooden platforms, which project far; on them are windlasses, by which the workmen are lowered to transact their business on the face of the precipice. There suspended, they work in mid air, pick a small space for a footing, cut out the ore in vast masses, and tumble it to the bottom with great noise. In such situations they form caverns, and there appear safely lodged, till the rope is lowered to convey them up again...[6]

Neither Hughes, the principal proprietor of the mine, nor Dawes ever seem to have been functionally involved in the mine's management or its associated activities.[7] Hughes was never more than a sleeping partner, in effect a *rentier*, over time stolidly drawing an immense fortune from the development of Parys Mountain, while Dawes who died in 1788, though a key figure in securing financial

---

6   Pennant (1810), III, 57-67.

7   Hughes' brother Michael (1752-1825) was, however, very active in the north Wales copper industry and its various offshoots and became a key figure in the industrial and financial development of the area: Harris (1950), 139-167.

backing for the project and an invaluable City intermediary in its early trading negotiations, was becoming increasingly remote from its innermost counsels.[8]

Direction was left very much to Williams, from the start the 'active' partner and driving force of the firm. In the early days of the new venture, however, it was difficult for him to maximise the profits of the business because of the long-standing stranglehold a closely-knit combination of the more important smelting companies had over the copper industry. For decades the so-called 'Associated Smelters' or 'Old Company' had monopolised the market for copper ore, controlling prices and profits, dominating the Cornish mines, the richest British source of the metal, and effectively preventing the entry of new concerns into the manufacturing side of the industry. Williams failed to reach any accommodation with the cartel and set about breaking its monopoly by setting up his own smelting, manufacturing and marketing operations. It was an immense undertaking, employing some fifteen-hundred workers on Anglesey with much the same number spread over his smelting works in Amlwch, the Swansea Valley and Lancashire and his rolling mills and battery plant in Flintshire, giving Williams a virtually unique control of all the production processes from extraction through to manufacture.[9]

But if these developments were in themselves a rude shock to the other copper companies worse was to follow. In the early eighties Williams succeeded in combining new processes of making copper bolts, patented by 'two ingenious artists of Birmingham', William Collins, a button and buckle manufacturer who Jeremy Bentham described as 'a mechanic of the gentleman class', and John Westwood, an experienced engraver turned button maker and copper-roller. 'Westwood and Collins's Patent Bolts' enabled Williams to solve the problem of fastening copper sheeting to ships' bottoms by eliminating the devastating corrosion caused through the galvanic action of the copper on the iron bolts which had previously secured the hull planking to the main timber frame.[10] The maritime market, naval and mercantile, for both bolts and sheathing, that he was able to exploit not only in Britain but in Europe as well, coupled with his capture of a hugely lucrative contract for the supply of copper to the East India Company, marked Williams's arrival as a major player in the industry. Even as early as 1785 Boulton was envying Williams's success in this

---

[8] There are no biographical studies of Hughes or Dawes but see Dodd (1951), 155 *et seqq.* for Hughes; and Dykes (1998a), 352-55 and Archer (2000), 37-39 for Dawes.

[9] The workings on Anglesey were largely opencast by this time and required little mining skill. The wages of the workforce reflected this, piece rates amounting from a shilling to 1*s* 8*d* a day, still comparing favourably with the 1*s* 4*d* paid to a skilled Caernarvonshire quarryman: Rowlands (1966), 100.

[10] *Copper Report* (1803), 668; Harris (1964), 47 *et seqq.* and (1966-67), 558-63. For Collins (*c.* 1751-1819) see *GM*, June 1819, 582-83, *Copper Report* (1803), 662 and Bowring (1843), X, 572-73.

area [11] and before the end of the century Williams could argue that his sheathing processes had given the Royal Navy an 'incalculable advantage' in the French wars; never, he told a House of Commons committee on the copper trade, had 'the fleets' been 'so well formed or so prompt for immediate service upon short notice'.[12]

At the same time his power base in Anglesey was consolidated by his entering into partnership with Nicholas Bayly's son, the 1st Earl of Uxbridge, to exploit the original workings on Cerrig y Bleiddia Farm when the Macclesfield Company's lease expired in 1785. And although he held only a quarter share in the Mona Mine Company, as the new venture was called, Williams was again the 'active' partner. He thus came into effective control of the whole potential of the Parys Mountain and through his conglomerates he was on the brink of establishing an industrial and commercial ascendancy over the entire copper trade. Within two years, by his effective take-over of the Cornish Metal Company, the commercial arm of the Cornish miners, and the marketing of its ores, Williams had achieved a practical monopoly of the metal at a time when Britain was the world's largest copper producer and exporter.[13] He had become, in Matthew Boulton's words, the ♀ 'Copper King', 'the dispotick Soveraign of the Copper Trade' who possessed through his Bayly alliance an effective parliamentary lobby that he had lacked before.[14]

Williams thus had the raw material, the capacity and the personal dynamism to solve the problem of the nation's copper coinage and, given a fair wind, the determination to make a profitable venture out of it. And coinage, as Matthew Boulton explained to James Watt, was an obvious candidate in Williams's constant search for 'new consumptions of ♀ [copper] that did not before exist'.[15] Even before the accommodation with Uxbridge Williams had floated the idea of his striking a regal copper coinage with the Master of the Mint, the Earl of Effingham. He had little experience of coining other than in the rolling and cutting of copper blanks for a Dutch East Indies Company coinage and he likely relied on the expertise of John Westwood, already closely associated with Williams over the manufacture of copper bolts

11 'They [the Anglesey Mines companies] have created many new uses of copper, particularly Forged Bolts and Nails which are used in all the dockyards and their Rolled bolts are sold to all the naval powers in Europe as well as their sheathing': Matthew Boulton to James Watt, 10 June 1785, quoted in Harris (1964), 49.

12 *Copper Report* (1803), 668 and 669.

13 The Cornish Metal Company had been set up in 1785 by the county's united miners as a marketing organisation to free themselves from the power of the Associated Smelters but its virtual failure by 1787 gave Williams the opportunity of controlling its sales for the ensuing five years: Hamilton (1967), 168-201; Rowe (1953), 82-91; Harris (1964), 63-68 and 84-87.

14 BAH: MS 3782/13/116, Matthew Boulton to Thomas Lack [Lord Liverpool's secretary], 4 December 1799; BAH: MS 3782/12/9/40, Matthew Boulton to Messrs Monneron, 26 December 1791; Harris (1964), 36-37.

15 BAH: MS 3147/3/9/8, Matthew Boulton to James Watt, 6 June 1785.

63 Thomas Williams: Pattern Parys Mine Company penny engraved by John Milton, 1786.

and with William Welch, the Anglesey companies' Birmingham agent, in metal dealing. A prime feature of the proposed coinage was that the edges would be lettered as a precaution against forgery, no doubt utilising a technique devised by Westwood and one sufficiently novel for Williams to agonise that his submission to Effingham might expose it to 'the Treachery of Workmen who, on any difference with us, might communicate ye same exact mode of stamping the Letters to those who ought by all means to be kept ignorant of it'.[16]

Williams's immediate discussions came to nothing but, undeterred, he decided to press on by producing a private token coinage as a practical demonstration of his capability as a coiner; a venture that in serving his own needs would if successfully marketed on a country-wide scale either prove a profitable speculation in itself or convince government of his fitness to manage a national coinage contract. As Boulton afterwards boasted to Jean-Pierre Droz, 'if our Government will not make a new Copper coinage we shall force them to it by coining for our selves such copper pennys'.[17] Again Williams turned to Westwood and with the aid of Collins, now living in Greenwich to pursue his maritime interests, and John Milton, then a young engraver of rising reputation and shortly to take up what would prove to be an ill-fated appointment at the Mint, he produced a prototype penny in the name of the Parys Mine Company [63].[18] The contemporary collector, William Robert Hay, tells us that this 'Monogram' penny 'was executed by Milton in the Tower, and after a very few were struck, the die of the monogram was broken'. A Tower provenance is hardly likely since Milton did not take up his Mint appointment until March 1787 and Pye's statement that the penny was struck by John Westwood is more convincing. If this was the case the penny was probably produced at the latter's metal-stamping workshops in Great Charles Street, Birmingham before the end of 1786 although at this time Westwood did not yet have any purpose-built coining presses.[19] It

---

16 PRO: MINT 8/1, Thomas Williams to Lord Effingham, April 1785.

17 BAH: MS 3782/12/15, Matthew Boulton to J-P. Droz [Transcribed English Version], 7 March 1787.

18 John Milton (1759-1805) was appointed an assistant engraver at the Mint in March 1787 and dismissed ten years later for supplying dies for counterfeit *Louis d'ors* and other foreign gold. Nothing is known of his early life but one wonders whether there was some close personal connection with Sir Joseph Banks who took a constant and protective interest in Milton's career. Interestingly, Milton's first medallic commission was for the Society of Industry, an organisation operating working schools in Lincolnshire, Banks's home county. For a study of Milton and his works see Stainton (1983), 133-59.

19 Hay's MS note is contained in his copy of Pye's *Provincial Copper Coins or Tokens* (now in the present writer's possession), interleaved at plate 28; Pye (1801), 5. A specimen of this token (Lot 72), included in the sale of Samuel Tyssen's collection (Leigh, Sotheby & Son, 12 April 1802), was described in the catalogue as 'The first Penny Piece struck by the Anglesey Copper Company in 1786, (no date) – engraved in London by John Milton'. It was bought by Young for £1 3s. There is no clear evidence that Westwood possessed a purpose-built coining press himself before October 1787: cf. Gould (1969), 274.

THE GREAT CONTENTION

64 Thomas Williams: Parys Mines Company 'D' Penny, 1787.

is a remarkable piece with a deeply cut and arresting obverse portrait, befitting a first-rate artist trained as a seal-engraver, and characterised by an eremitic face and piercing eye.[20] The reverse has a 'Rococo' PMC° cipher while most specimens, struck in a collar, have a lettered edge bearing the names of the partners of the Parys Mine Company: EDW. HUGHES . THO. WILLIAMS . JOHN . DAWES + PARIS LODGE . .[21]

Whether Milton's die was broken deliberately or failed because of the deep cutting of the image we do not know. In any event it was struck in comparatively limited numbers and the model was not used for the general run of Williams's 'Druid' coinage. It was probably never intended to be more than an essay and was quickly replaced by a new type – the 'D' penny [64] – with a lower-relief profile more suitable for large-scale production on the manual presses then available.

According to Hay, Collins is said to have furnished Williams with a preliminary drawing for the new penny as he may have done for Milton's prototype. This belief is not implausible for Collins was an amateur artist of no mean accomplishment. But Collins probably found his inspiration for the new profile in some already published source that expressed a more contemplative characterization than that of Milton's 'Druid'. The late George Boon suggested that this might have lain in William Stukeley's Stonehenge engraving of *A British Druid* [65].[22] Equally, and more modishly, Collins might have drawn on the placid hermit depicted in a Richard Wilson landscape inspired by James Thomson's descriptive poem *The Seasons* [66]. Outstandingly popular at the time in the form of *Solitude*, a mirror-image engraving by William Woollett published only a few years' earlier in 1778, it was redolent of a secluded Anglesey oak grove, a haunt of meditation, as Thomson described it in his *Summer*,

> where ancient Bards th'inspiring Breath,
> Extatic, felt; and, from this world retir'd.[23]

65 *A British Druid*, engraved by William Stukeley, 1740.

20 George Boon's suggestion that Milton's portrayal of the 'Druid' owes much to the windswept figure of Thomas Jones's *Bard* (1774, engraved by Thomas Ryder 1775) I find unconvincing: Boon (1983), 124-25.

21 Other specimens are found with plain edge (*D&H*: Anglesey 2a), sometimes struck without collar (*D&H*: Anglesey 2b).

22 Hay (as in note 19): 'Mr. Collins of Maize Hill, Greenwich, a Gentleman much employed by the Paris Mine Company, made a drawing of the D. Penny & sent the design to Hancock. This was the 2d. The Monogram was the first of all, which was probably designed by Mr. Collins'. See also Hamer (1903), cols. 6054. The suggestion that William Stukeley's engraving was the source of the token's image is made by Boon (1983), 124, the engraving having been published as Plate I of Stukeley's *Stonehenge, a temple restor'd to the British Druids* (1740).

23 From Thomson's *Summer*, lines 522-4, which appear in the caption to Woollett's engraving. Richard Wilson's original painting (1762) is in the Glyn Vivian Art Gallery, Swansea and is reproduced in Solkin (1982), 212.

66   Detail from *Solitude* engraved by William Woollett after the painting by Richard Wilson, 1778.

Wilson's hermit in its turn does seem to have owed much to Stukeley's *A British Druid* but whatever its ultimate source the obverse image of Williams's token was calculated to strike a chord with the romantic antiquarianism of the age. It was an evocative symbol of Anglesey's supposed importance as 'the metropolitan seat' of ancient British druidism now made famous again by Williams's mining exploits.[24]

Charles Pye tells us that the dies of the new penny were engraved by the Birmingham die-cutter, John Gregory Hancock, and that the token was struck in Birmingham at the Parys Mine Company's mint. Despite their near eye-witness testimony Pye and his collaborators were by no means infallible, however, and while a limited initial run, perhaps of presentation pieces, may well have been produced in Birmingham, by Westwood, for instance, on the type of fly press available, as we have seen, to most ornamental metal workers, neither he nor Williams at this time had any facility capable of large-scale quality currency production available in the town.[25]

24   Anglesey's 'druidical' significance – founded on the reference to *Druidae* by Tacitus in his vivid description of the storming of the island by Suetonius Paulinus in AD 60 (*Annals*, XIV, 30) – had been expounded earlier in the century in Henry Rowlands' pioneering study of the island's prehistory, *Mona Antiqua Restaurata*, the 1766 edition of which contained an equally pensive 'Chief Druid' (Plate XVIII, 3) from which Stukeley's druid was adapted. Rowlands, a former vicar of Llanidan, would have been well known by reputation to Thomas Williams, who would no doubt have had a copy of Rowlands' book in his library. Williams is said to have adopted an engraving of a druid's head as his personal seal: Vice (1989), 9, and Hawker (1996), 2.

25   As early as 1769 Boulton recorded that 'all our ornaments may be stamped or may be press[*sic*] in the fly press or may be formed in the Leviathan': BAH: Matthew Boulton's Notebook 6 (1768-75),108-109, quoted in Goodison (2002), 130

THE GREAT CONTENTION

What was actually happening is totally obfuscated by the dearth of credible archive material. Williams's personal and business records do not appear to have survived and we are largely dependent on the papers of Matthew Boulton, Williams's rival for a national coinage contract, and the rumours of the latter's intrigues that constantly assailed the Birmingham entrepreneur. And what we do have through the fog is often based on little more than hearsay or preconceived views. There is good reason to believe, nevertheless, that the initial production of Hancock's 'Druid' ('𝔻') tokens was begun not later than the beginning of 1787 and that, even if the very earliest were struck in Birmingham, from the evidence of Boulton's correspondence, the greater part of them was produced at one of the Anglesey companies' manufacturing plants in Flintshire where Williams had quickly installed a coining press alongside his rolling mills and cutting out presses.

On 24 February 1787 Boulton's friend, Samuel Garbett, was grudgingly reporting from London that, having seen 'the paris Mine Comp[y].'s Penny – the Head is tolerably executed'. No doubt it was a '𝔻' penny, for nine days earlier the virtuoso Daines Barrington had presented just such a specimen to the Society of Antiquaries. A full description of the penny is given in the Society's minute book, which, interestingly, concurs with the later Pye gloss in stating that it was coined in Birmingham.[26] The record gives the edge reading on this token as 'on Demand in London, Liverpool, & Anglesey', the legend (*recte* ON DEMAND IN LONDON LIVERPOOL & ANGLESEY) of a penny in Miss Banks's collection (SSB 184-16-1) that she describes in her register as 'the second dye' (in succession to the 'first dye' 'Monogram' tokens). It is a lightweight piece (20.16 g), not struck in a collar, and of the type listed by Dalton and Hamer in their catalogue (page 330) as 'Anglesey 9a'.[27] All pennies of this type seen by the writer are about 20g in weight – as are those of *D&H*: Anglesey 4 and 9 with the edge reading ON DEMAND IN LONDON LIVERPOOL *OR* [my italics] ANGLESEY – compared to the usual 28g or so of the general run of '𝔻' pennies with this latter edge-reading. It seems likely that these lightweight '𝔻' pennies, which approximate in weight to Milton's 'Monogram' tokens, are in fact the earliest Anglesey tokens (initially *D&H*: Anglesey 9a with the '&' edge reading, followed by *D&H*: Anglesey 9 and 4 with what became the standard '**OR**' edge reading) of this type. Why the weight standard was increased to *c.* 28g (or one ounce) is unlikely ever to be known; one can only speculate that having essayed the lightweight pieces, which approximated to the Tower standard of 23*d* to the lb, Williams came to the conclusion that a coin

---

26 BAH: MS 3782/12/62/35, Samuel Garbett to Matthew Boulton, 24 February 1787; Society of Antiquaries of London Minute Book, 15 February 1787. I am indebted to Hugh Pagan for this reference. Unfortunately the penny is no longer in the Society's collections and since it is not included in Albert Way's *Catalogue of Antiquities, Coins, Pictures and Miscellaneous Curiosities in the Society's Possession* (London, 1847) it must already have disappeared before the mid-nineteenth century.

27 Miss Banks's collection also contains a silver proof of *D&H*: Anglesey 9a.

weighing an ounce would be more acceptable to the public and, at the same time, would use up more of his copper.

By the end of March 1787 Boulton, in something of a panic, was telling Garbett that he had heard that Richard Ford, a rival Birmingham manufacturer, had introduced Westwood to King George III and had shown the king some Anglesey pennies: 'Westwood & Hancox the dye Graver', he added, 'speak publickly of their going to reside in the Tower very soon to manage the ♀ Coinage. Hence it appears that Williams seemd sure of the Contract ... Williams (I was told yesterday by Wilkinson [John Wilkinson, the ironmaster and an associate of Williams in some of the latter's concerns]) hath got several presses at work at Hollywell & is making pieces for himself and for Wilkinson'.[28] Specimens of the 'D' penny – with the 'OR' edge reading – had, in fact, already percolated beyond the confines of Somerset House and St. James's Palace and had become sought-after curios elsewhere in London. On the very same Wednesday that Boulton was writing to Garbett a news item in John Walter's *Daily Universal Register* – the forerunner of *The Times* – described the coinage:

> The new money, which, by permission of Government, the Anglesey Company has issued, is a species of promissory coin for one penny, struck upon copper, intended only for the convenience of paying their men. The die is most beautifully conceived and executed, and the intrinsic value of the copper is nearly a penny. A Druid, encircled with a wreath of oak, occupies one side. The reverse has a cipher, P. M. Co. *i. e.* ' Parry's Mine Company', over which are the letters (D) *Denarius*, encircled with the following words: "We promise to pay the bearer one penny" – on the outside of the rim, are the words, "On demand, in London, Liverpool, *or* [my italics] Anglesea". There are several of these pieces in town, but they are picked up with great avidity.[29]

It is hard to believe that the *Register*'s report was not based on a 'puff' put out by Thomas Williams himself to further his campaign for a national copper coinage. But, whatever Williams's intentions, his 'Druids' immediately caught the public's imagination; compared to the Tower halfpenny they were substantial pieces and they far surpassed the Tower halfpenny in the elegance of their design and the quality of their finish.[30] Moreover they broke new ground. They were promissory, that is – in theory at least – they could be exchanged for 'real' money and, even more remarkably, they were valued at the novel copper denomination of a penny; a feature that the *Register* had earlier remarked upon: a coinage

---

28 BAH: MS 3782/12/6/40, Matthew Boulton to Samuel Garbett, 28 March 1787. Boulton had already recorded in a notebook on 14 March that 'Wilkinsons head' was 'now cutting by Westwood for a Coin to be circulated': BAH: MS 3782/12/108/51, Notebook 3, 14.

29 *The Daily Universal Register*, 28 March 1787.

30 A discordant voice was that of Pitt who apparently thought the 'Druids' inconveniently heavy for the pocket though his experience of such a burden must have been minimal: Vice (1989), 3.

THE GREAT CONTENTION

67 Enlarged reverse of the 'D' penny, where the '1' within the 'D' - as in the date - is clearly shown to be a numerical value reference not a letter as in the 'I' of 'PROMISE'.

'of one penny pieces, not one halfpenny as heretofore'.[31]

This, of course, is the explanation of the 'D' device [67], as the *Register* and, indeed, the *Gentleman's Magazine* recognised: 'On the reverse, the cipher PMC° signifies the Paris Mountain Company; and the letter D, inclosing the numeral 1 over it, one penny'. In recent years the notion of reading 'D' as representing the initials of John Dawes has exercised numismatists but it is an untenable conceit at variance with the commonplace and contemporary interpretation of the mark.[32]

Its purpose was to stress the innovatory nature of the coinage, to distance Williams's tokens from the paltry Tower halfpence to which the public had become inured but not to displace them so that, in denomination and in design, there should be as little association as possible with the current coin of the realm, formally protected by statute (11 George III, cap. 40), and thus no perceived breach of the royal prerogative. At the same time the press reports craftily paraded not only the 'Druids'' denominational novelty but also called attention to their apparent local character while setting out to cultivate in people's minds the impression of a wider remit. 'By permission of Government' and 'contract with Government' were, characteristically, disingenuous statements calculated to convey an official imprimatur that did not exist. Thus, although he might protest in the public prints that his Parys Mine Company intended its new 'Druid pennies' to be a purely local expedient, 'only for the convenience of paying their men', Williams made it clear by implication that what he had in mind was something of far wider bearing and took care to circulate among members of parliament and other individuals of influence both pattern cards and proof samples of his pennies in copper and silver.[33]

In April 1787 Boulton was edgily telling Garbett that Williams had 'articled with Hancox and he is going to Hollywell'. But whatever garbled messages were being fed to Boulton Williams had already taken a decision to move his coinery from Flintshire to the Anglesey

---

31 *The Daily Universal Register*, 23 March 1787: 'There is a new coinage, by contract with Government, now going on in the Isle of Anglesea, at the great copper mines there. This coinage consists of one penny pieces, not one halfpenny, as heretofore. The die is, a Druid on one side, and the King's head on the other; and the size is about that of half-a-crown. One hundred tons are said to be the quantity agreed for; and forty shillings per ton is to be allowed for coining, the contractors finding their own copper. They are to be in London in about a month'.

32 *GM*, 'Supplement' 1787, 1160. The Society of Antiquaries Minute Book (note 26 above) also referred to the device as 'probably' standing for '<u>Denarius</u>, a Penny'. Perhaps the device owed something to seventeenth-century penny tokens such as that struck for Hugh Davis of Holyhead in 1666, illustrated with Anglesey pennies on Plate (Fig. 3), facing 1156, *GM*, 'Supplement' 1787: see p. 82 below. Cf. Dykes (1998a), 352-55.

33 *The Daily Universal Register*, 28 March 1787; 'Will[ms] is very busy in London ..., & his Birmingham Artist [Hancock] set out yesterday with a fine patt[n] Card of Copper & Silver Money which are intended to be distributed to every member in the House of Commons': CRO: AD1583/2/42/1, Matthew Boulton to Thomas Wilson, 10 April 1787; Harris (1964), 153, note 6. Miss Banks's silver version of *D&H*: Anglesey 9a is an example of a presentation proof (see note 27 above).

81

69 Thomas Williams: Parys Mine Company penny, 2nd. Type, 1787.

warehouse in Great Charles Street, Birmingham to take advantage of the better distribution potential of the midlands and to equip himself with machinery to cope with the large-scale production he had in mind.[34]

Coining at Holywell was short-lived, lasting no more than three months or so, and the transfer to Birmingham probably heralded the end of the 'D' pennies. Hay's belief that 'they were never put into circulation but were only given as presents' presumably reflects his knowledge of their initial issue as promotional pieces yet, even in the short time of their production, something in the region of three or four tons, approaching perhaps 145,000 tokens, must have been struck.[35] But, as the *Gentleman's Magazine* in the commentary to its plate [68] – as far as I am aware the first contemporary illustration of eighteenth century tokens – made plain, they had been 'scarcely issued' when they were superseded by a new type where the 'D' device was replaced by the date [69].[36]

68 *The Gentleman's Magazine*, 'Supplement' Plate, 1787.

34 BAH: MS 3872/12/6/63, Matthew Boulton to Samuel Garbett, 22 April 1787. As far as Boulton was aware Williams had only '4 small Presses for cutting out blanks, but I believe he hath not more than one Coining Press': BAH: MS 3782/12/6/80, Matthew Boulton to John Vivian, 5 May 1787.

35 Hay (as in note 19), interleaved at plate 28; Pye ((1801), 5, Plate 1, nos. 2 and 4) indicates rarities of 'rrrr' and 'rrr' for the varieties of the 'D' penny.

36 *GM*, 'Supplement' 1787, Plate facing 1156. *The Gentleman's Magazine* concluded erroneously that the new type [69] was counterfeit.

THE GREAT CONTENTION

We do not know when the move actually took place but by the beginning of May 1787 Boulton had heard a rumour that Williams was now employing a coining press belonging to a person in Birmingham.[37] What this tittle-tattle meant, if true, is far from obvious but it may suggest that the press employed at Holywell had been brought down by Westwood to the Great Charles Street warehouse. Whatever the immediate logistics of the relocation were, however, Westwood was not to run the new coinery for long although he was to supply it with rolled Anglesey copper for another two years.

By June Williams's mint was definitely up and running in Great Charles Street under the management of Charles Wyatt, an erstwhile Boulton employee who had left Soho under a cloud in 1777; new presses had been acquired from specialist Birmingham manufacturers such as William Whitmore, the Newhall Street engineer and machine-manufacturer; Hancock had engraved dies for the new series of 'Druid' coins; and Williams had started coining for Wilkinson as well as for himself.[38] In August Boulton might exult that initial production was slow, that 'though they have boasted in the newspapers of their superior skill, though they offered to Mr. Pitt to coin 25 ton per week, yet the fact is they have been very busy coining for a month past and have not coined 1 ton'.[39] Nevertheless, whatever natural teething troubles Williams had to face in his first few weeks in Birmingham he had succeeded in striking, even on Boulton's figures, a not insignificant number of tokens on traditional manual presses and in a collar. Over the next two years he was to go on to produce, if Pye's figures are a true guide, 250 tons of 'Druid' pennies and, from about April 1788, fifty tons of 'Druid' halfpennies [70], as well as several tons of tokens for John Wilkinson.[40]

Although this was small beer in terms of Anglesey's annual output of 4,000 tons of pure copper at the time it was a remarkable accomplishment for Wyatt in Great Charles Street and amounted to an injection of some fifteen million coins into the nation's currency. Moreover, the quality of the Anglesey tokens, their remarkable weight, fine artistry and their coordinated distribution gave them an acceptance and a geographical reach that the Mint had never striven for. From the start Williams's own tokens and those he produced for Wilkinson were sold on to other industrialists and found a ready passage in the manufacturing districts of the northwest. In April

70 Thomas Williams: Parys Mine Company halfpenny, 1787.

---

37 BAH: MS 3782/12/6/80, Matthew Boulton to John Vivian, 5 May 1787.

38 Charles Wyatt, son of the inventor John Wyatt, replaced William Welch (d. April 1787) as the Anglesey companies' Birmingham agent on 13 June 1787: Selgin (2005), 113-20, esp. 118. Rolled copper was also supplied by Wyatt's brother-in-law, Thomas Dobbs, another Birmingham metal roller and dealer. For Whitmore's presses, 'one or two': BAH: MS 3782/12/73/83, Thomas Williams to Matthew Boulton, 8 June 1789. Both Dobbs and Whitmore were later to manufacture tokens.

39 BAH: MS 3782/12/6/107, Matthew Boulton to John Vivian, 13 August 1787.

40 Pye (1801), 5 and 18. Pye erroneously attributes the manufacture of the Wilkinson tokens struck by Williams – and later Westwood – to Hancock.

1789 the Manchester judge and Unitarian philanthropist, Thomas Butterworth Bayley, could inform Lord Hawkesbury that:

> One Gentleman, from Compassion to the Poor grievously injured by the bad halfpence, has lately introduced into a neighbouring Town, one hundred & seventy five thousand of these Druids. And as no new Coinage of half pence yet appears, it is proposed generally to adopt the Circulation of this Welch money. I own, [he concluded] I cannot approve of this measure, though it originates in Charity & Pity to the labouring Poor, as it appears to me, to be a Revival of the Tokens, which were formerly so prejudicial to Trade, & prohibited according[ly] and to be an improper Interference with the Executive Government, and his Majesty's royal Prerogative.[41]

No doubt Bayley's 'neighbouring Town' was Stockport where the magistrates and inhabitants had three months earlier come to 'a Resolution at a public meeting to take no other halfpence in future than those of the Anglesey C°'.[42] Whatever Bayley's own reservations the 'Druids'' solid respectability was already assured and their novel design, a *tour de force* for everyday currency, quickly captured the public's imagination to the extent that Hancock – if only cryptically – could even achieve recognition in a lampoon in the *General Magazine* for July 1792:

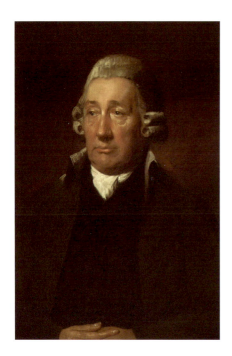

71   John Wilkinson (1728-1808). Portrait after Lemuel Francis Abbott, *c.* 1795.

EPIGRAM.
On Mr H—n—k, who struck the Die of the Anglesea Penny.
By George S. Carey.
The artist paus'd awhile in great suspense,
To make a penny of some consequence,
And having Stukely, or old Dugdale, read,
He stamp'd the pittance with a Druid's head;–
To make his *own* resemblance next he try'd,
And struck a *Cypher* on the counter-side.[43]

Production of Williams's tokens for John Wilkinson [71] may have begun at Holywell – our only evidence, Wilkinson's comment as retailed by Boulton, is ambiguous – but, if true, output must have been very limited until the move to Birmingham. Boulton, for one, does not seem to have obtained a specimen of Wilkinson's coinage much before 1 August 1787 (a few weeks after the move) when, as he told John Vivian, the Cornish mine adventurer and entrepreneur, it was 'now put into circulation'.[44] The token bore no statement of value or promise

---

41   BL: Additional MSS 38422, f.12, Thomas Butterworth Bayley to Lord Hawkesbury, 8 April, 1789. Cf. Dickinson (1937), 139.

42   BAH: MS 3782/12/34/64 and BL: Additional MSS. 38422, f.13, Matthew Boulton to Lord Hawkesbury, 14 April 1789.

43   *The General Magazine and Impartial Review*, July 1792, 316. For George Saville Carey (1743-1807) see *ODNB*.

44   BAH: MS 3782/12/6/101, Matthew Boulton to John Vivian, 1 August 1787.

THE GREAT CONTENTION

of repayment and while it was only half the weight of Williams's heavy penny and on a module approximating to that of the Tower halfpenny it was initially tariffed at a penny. On 12 August a peevish Boulton wrote to John Motteux, a London merchant, agent for Soho's plated and silver ware, and a key figure in Boulton's relations with the East India Company of which he was a director:

> I will send you a few of M^r. Wilkinson's Coin which he pays his workmen for pence. There is 32 of them to the pound; consequently he sells them at 2^s/8^d per lb whereas the Mint price is 1/11^d per lb – A rare profit & if Gov^t. doth not put a stop to ye trade every Manufacturer in Birm^{gm}. will coin his own copper money – When I consider the news paper puffs that have been pub^d. & the extraordinary price I do not think ye excellence & beauty of ye Coin equal to it. It is easy to make the letters indented but not so easy to make them in relief like ye French Crown [82].[45]

72 Thomas Williams: 'Forge' halfpenny for John Wilkinson, 1787.

Boulton's irritation was compounded by the realisation that Williams, with his 'Druids' and now Wilkinson's 'pennies', slow though their initial production might have proved to have been, had stolen a march on him. Public reaction might soon force Wilkinson to revalue his pieces as halfpennies but they were at least in the public domain. Technically imperfect as they might have seemed to Boulton's over-scrupulous eye he himself had so far failed to produce any practical result from his own time-consuming, expensive and frustrating coining experiments at Soho. Strangely, discomfited as Boulton was, he made no comment about the most obvious feature of Wilkinson's new coin [72]: its bold portrait, engraved by Hancock that, aping the regal coinage, typified the brash egotism of the greatest ironmaster of the age, his arrogance not diminished by the simplicity of its legend **JOHN WILKINSON IRON MASTER**; a presumption that did not fail to provoke a satirical reaction in the public prints.

EPIGRAM.

On Mr. WILKINSON'S Copper Money.

In Greece and Rome your men of parts,
Renown'd in arms, or form'd in arts,
On splendid coins and medals shone,
To make their deeds and persons known.
So, Wilkinson, from this example,
Gives of himself a matchless sample!

---

45 BAH: MS 3782/12/6/103, Matthew Boulton to John Motteux, 12 August 1787. Motteux, a Walbrook merchant, handled much of Boulton and Fothergill's European sales and patiently financed their Bill Account (an account similar to a modern banker's overdraft originating in the over-expenditure on the building of the Soho manufactory: Cule (1935), 10-11). Motteux was deputy chairman of the East India Company in 1786 and chairman the following year: Philips (1961), 337-38.

73 Thomas Williams: 'Ship' halfpenny for John Wilkinson, 1788.

74 Thomas Williams: Silver 3s 6d 'Ship' token for John Wilkinson, 1788.

> And bids the Iron Monarch pass,
> Like his own metal wrapt in brass!
> Which shews his modesty and sense,
> And how, and where he made his pence:
> As Iron, when 'tis brought in taction,
> Collects the copper by attraction.
> So, thus in him 'twas very proper,
> To stamp his brazen face --- on copper. [46]

Hancock's reverse image of a forge with its massive tilt hammer, dramatic in its austerity, was the design that formed the bulk of Wilkinson's issue until Williams gave up token manufacture in 1789. Some few halfpennies of 1788, however, have a reverse representation of a two-masted ship [73]. A brig or snow, it reflected Wilkinson's sea-borne trade particularly with France as the forge scene did his iron manufacture. What the clinker-built vessel depicted cannot credibly represent – as is sometimes suggested [47] – is his shallow-draft iron-hulled canal boat, *The Trial*, launched at Willey on 6 July 1787 and described in some detail in the *Gentleman's Magazine* on its arrival in Birmingham later that month, or even his later (October 1788) Severn barge from which the name 'Barge Halfpenny' was presumably derived by Samuel Birchall, the first of the early token cataloguers to use this designation.[48]

The ship motif, but from a different die, was also used on a silver token [74] again dated 1788. Wilkinson no doubt saw in this venture, initially tariffed at an excessive 3s 6d, a solution to his critical need for silver for wage payments.[49] As things turned out, just one hundred silver tokens were struck according to Pye – though this may well be something of an underestimate – and, if any did circulate, it was for only a short time; most must have been snapped up as curios, the wear evident on many survivors probably being due to their being kept as pocket pieces. It may be that Wilkinson was deterred from pursuing any serious consideration of striking silver at this juncture because of a presumed infringement of the royal prerogative or perhaps because there was a reluctance to accept as currency a coin that was so patently overvalued and which he may have been obliged to call down to 2s.

46 *The New London Magazine*, December 1787, 662. Another humourist using a Macclesfield edged blank produced an imitation 'Wilkinson token' with the inscription 'AND HE SAID LET US MAKE PENNYS AFTER MY OWN IMAGE': *D&H*: War. 334.

47 For example Stockdale (1872), 217 and 124: 'a representation *of the First Iron Ship ever built*, he [Wilkinson] being the *builder* and *inventor*, in 1787'. Stockdale was a nephew of John Wilkinson's brother William but his account of Wilkinson is useful more for his reproduction of family correspondence than its interpretation.

48 *GM*, August 1787, 732; Birchall (1796), 98: earlier 'Williams' [John Hammond] (1795), 5 and, following him, Spence (1795), 48 had referred to the vessel as a 'Ship'. For a description of Wilkinson's venture into iron-hulled boats, see Stockdale (1872), 217-18 and, subsequently, Dickinson (1914), 26-28 and Randall (1917), 17-19 although the evidence cited is confusing.

49 At an average weight of 15.5g it compared with the average 15g of the most recent regal half-crown but it was intended to be a *token* not a 'real' coin.

THE GREAT CONTENTION

Nevertheless, he seems to have toyed with the notion of a silver coinage again the following year and, as we have seen with his low-value notes, he was not necessarily a man to be put off by legal niceties.[50]

Pye tells us that the copper 'ship' tokens were produced by Boulton from dies engraved by Hancock. While there can be little doubt about the identity of the die-sinker it is most improbable that Boulton could have had any hand in their manufacture as early as 1788. It is much more likely that the halfpennies were struck by Thomas Williams at his Birmingham warehouse where he was already manufacturing Wilkinson's 'Forge' halfpennies. It is, of course, not inconceivable that they were among the batch of tokens that Boulton produced the following year when he took over Williams's coining enterprise but there seems to be no reference to them in the Soho archives. The silver pieces have been equally problematic for some numismatists have read into Pye's reference to them an attribution to Boulton. We know from Wilkinson's own testimony, however, that they *were* issued in 1788 – on Monday, 20 October to be precise [51] – and again the presumption must be that they were struck by Thomas Williams.

All Wilkinson's genuine tokens have the edge-reading **WILLEY SNEDSHILL BERSHAM BRADLEY**, the main sites of Wilkinson's iron works, the places where they were issued and where they were in theory redeemable: Willey, in Shropshire, near Broseley, close by Ironbridge and Coalbrookdale but south of the Severn; Snedshill, to the north in Oakengates but in the same area of Shropshire; Bersham, now a suburb of Wrexham, in Denbighshire; and Bradley near Bilston in Staffordshire. Conder, the first cataloguer to arrange eighteenth-century tokens under counties, unfortunately seems to have identified Willey with a small agricultural village of the same name in Warwickshire and Wilkinson's tokens have since been traditionally listed under that county although Wilkinson had no industrial undertakings there.[52] But, like Williams's 'Druids', Wilkinson's tokens soon achieved a geographical circulation far beyond their home areas, their acceptability as currency attracting an immense trade in counterfeits.

While Williams's underlying aim all along had been the winning of a national coinage contract what he had perversely achieved by the very success of his flirtation with his own and Wilkinson's tokens was the creation of something approaching an acceptable *substitute* for the regal coinage. His output in two years had eclipsed the Mint's total production of copper coin in the 1770s and proved to be an incentive to other manufacturers, like his own protégé, John Westwood, to follow in his footsteps with a plethora of other tokens and to prompt an evasive government into yet further procrastination over a recoinage.

As Williams had schemed his way to control of the copper industry, his relationship with the Birmingham manufacturer, Matthew Boulton [75],

50   Pye (1801), 18; Stockdale (1872), 123-24; BAH: MS 3782/12/8/31, Matthew Boulton to Walter Taylor, 24 December 1789.

51   Stockdale (1872), 218 and Dickinson (1914), 28, quoting a Wilkinson letter of 20 October 1788: 'My silver coinage of 3s. 6d. issues this day'; Randall (1917), 19 (misdates this letter to 20 October 1787).

52   Conder (1798), 172-74.

COINAGE AND CURRENCY IN EIGHTEENTH-CENTURY BRITAIN

75 Matthew Boulton (1728-1809). Portrait by J. S. C. Schaak, 1770.

a substantial copper and brass user with crucial interests in the Cornish mines, had become increasingly fraught. By the late 1780s this had degenerated into a personal struggle, on the surface often superficially amicable but inherently wracked by suspicion and recrimination, and eventually focussing on the two men's ambitions to obtain the contract for a national coinage.

Matthew Boulton shared to the full the business drive of Thomas Williams and like the Anglesey attorney his family roots also lay among the minor country gentry, in Boulton's case apparently in the area around Lichfield.[53] According to Smiles it was Boulton's father (also Matthew) who had settled in Birmingham where, after apprenticeship to a stamper and button-maker, he had established himself as a toy maker[54] specialising in the manufacture of quality steel-based articles, particularly buckles, but operating, in the town's traditional way, from a clutch of small workshops surrounding the family home in what was then the relatively rural neighbourhood of Snow Hill.[55] It seems to have been a successful business and Matthew Boulton was brought up in comfortable circumstances. Surprisingly, little or nothing is known about this period of his life but about 1742 Boulton entered the business and appears to have taken to it readily. Even before he took it over on his father's death in 1759 Boulton – already a partner for nine years – had been effectively running the firm for some time and had begun to extend its range of products to meet the fashionable demands of the day and efface the tawdry name of 'Brummagem'. And, perhaps with visions of echoing the success of Birmingham's 'principal manufacturer', John Taylor, he had his eye on developing his business into something even bigger. As Lord Shelburne noted on a tour of the town's industries organised by Samuel Garbett in 1766, when he and his wife visited Taylor's impressive button works – among the scores of small foundries and metal-working shops in Birmingham exceptional in its size and organization – others were 'beginning to rival him in the extent of his trade'.[56]

Boulton, though, differed from his fellow toy makers not only in the extent of his ambition and his technical and commercial ability but in

---

53 Mason (2005), 197-212; Smiles (1865), 163; Delieb (1971), 17.

54 Sketchley (1767), 57 described 'toy makers', a staple trade of Birmingham, as makers of '*Trinkets, Seals, Tweezer and Tooth Pick cases, Smelling Bottles, Snuff Boxes, and Filligree Work, such as Toilets, Tea Chests, Inkstands, &c &c. The Tortoise[shell] Toy Maker, makes a beautiful variety of the above and other Articles; as does also the Steel; who make Cork Screws, Buckles, Draw and other Boxes: Snuffers, Watch Chains, Stay Hooks, Sugar Knippers, &c, and almost all these are likewise made in various Metals, and for cheapness, Beauty and Elegance no Place in the World can vie with them*'.

55 At the time of Matthew Boulton's birth the family lived in Steelhouse Lane (then called Whitehalls Lane) but moved to Snow Hill (close to the Garbetts' home) in 1731: Robinson (1957), 85-89.

56 Boulton always held Taylor (c. 1711-1775), 'the Esquire', 'our great manufacturer', in the highest regard. An entrepreneur of 'ingenuity in mechanical inventions' with a consummate flair for the organization, management and marketing of his products Taylor was an exemplar who Boulton strove to follow at Soho. He probably possessed greater business acumen than Boulton demonstrated in his foundation with Sampson Lloyd II of what eventually became Lloyds Bank: Skipp (1980), 54-56; Fitzmaurice (1912), I, 274-76; *ODNB*, s. v. John Taylor.

the depth of his 'pure' scientific understanding and knack of taking on board new ideas. He was, said his friend and rival, Josiah Wedgwood, 'very ingenious, Philosophical, & Agreeable'.[57] His enthusiasm for science and his awareness of the contribution such knowledge might make to manufacturing processes is exemplified by his many notebook jottings and his centrality to the activities of the self-styled Lunar Society. The latter, a small, lively – if loose and varying – circle of professional men, industrialists and gifted amateurs, through their meetings and, more importantly, their correspondence, not only indulged in a passion for gadgetry but more significantly explored a common concern for science and its practical application. It was, though, perhaps less the 'informal technological research organisation', discerned by its foremost historian, than an empirical network of like minds devoted to 'the uninhibited acquisition and transmission of natural knowledge' although the usefulness of their speculations was never altogether divorced from the thoughts of the industrialists among them: Boulton's experiences in the Paris of 1786-87 led him to conclude 'Science too much cultivated & the practice too little'.[58] As his fellow Lunar Society member, the chemist and industrialist James Keir, recollected in his personal memoir after Boulton's death:

> Mr. B ... had very correct notions of the several branches of natural philosophy, was master of every metallic art, and possessed all the chemistry that had any relation to the objects of his various manufactures. Electricity and astronomy were at one time among his favourite amusements. It cannot be doubted that he was indebted for much of his knowledge to the best preceptor, the conversation of eminent men.[59]

---

57   Josiah Wedgwood to Thomas Bentley, 23 May 1767: [Farrer] (1903), I, 142. See also Uglow (2002), 132; Dolan (2004), 227.

58   Schofield (1957), 411; Jones (2008), 82-94 and 230; BAH: MS 3782/12/108/49, Matthew Boulton, Diaries and Notebooks 1786-87: see also Jones (2008), 141. Most of the core members of the group, including Boulton, Erasmus Darwin, Keir, Joseph Priestley, James Watt and William Withering, also over the years became Fellows of the Royal Society.
    The name of the Society derived from the fact that the members usually met on a Monday (originally a Sunday but changed to accommodate Priestley) nearest the full moon to give them light for their journies home. For the Lunar Society, see Schofield (1963), Robinson (1962-63), Uglow (2002) and Jones (2008).

59   Keir (1809) [1947], 8.

COINAGE AND CURRENCY IN EIGHTEENTH-CENTURY BRITAIN

76 Soho House in 1801. Francis Eginton's aquatint engraving of Boulton's house (by now remodelled and extended) set in an idyllic landscape with the Hockley Pool shown as an ornamental lake and the manufactory discreetly hidden among the woods to the left.

Five years before the Shelburnes' trip to Birmingham Boulton, constricted by the Snow Hill site [60] and unable to tap any available sources of waterpower to foster his ambitions in Birmingham itself, had already moved many of his own operations to Handsworth Heath, leasing thirteen acres of scrubby land two miles north-west of the town. Here, at Soho, on the site of an existing rolling mill with a mill pool fed by an already canalised Hockley Brook and close to the high road from Wolverhampton and Wednesbury with its easy supply of Black Country iron and coal, he was able, in partnership with a Birmingham merchant, John Fothergill, to embark on a much larger-scale development.[61] Gradually 'collecting all our Manuf. together upon one spott', as Fothergill put it, the bulk of Boulton's production was concentrated in the complex of a new manufactory: 'one building that will hold 400 workmen', supervised, to Boulton's satisfaction, 'under our Eyes and immediate management ... every day and almost every hour' to achieve his ambition of promoting 'an artistic style and

60 And limited by the metal rolling facilities available at Sarehole Mill in Hall Green which had been leased by the Boultons since 1755.

61 After 1772 the Birmingham Canal provided Boulton not only with a still more convenient mode of cheapened local carriage but also access by water to Bristol, Liverpool and Hull.

90

finish not obtainable elsewhere'.[62]

On a rise above the manufactory Boulton refashioned (*c.*1766) Soho House [76], a classically designed villa, that with its elegant gardens and its landscaped grounds running down to the Hockley mill pool disguised as an ornamental lake, sought to emulate a country gentleman's seat. It was part and parcel of Boulton's ambition to be seen as 'an influential citizen in the new social order' of his time and his appetite for gentrification eventually to be formally recognised in 1794 with his appointment as High Sheriff of Staffordshire and a grant of arms. Jabez Maud Fisher, a young Quaker from Philadelphia, found the gardens in the summer of 1776 'beautiful, interspersed with Canals, which are nothing more than his Mill Damb [*sic*] and his Races, which he has ingeniously constructed to answer the *Dulce* as well as the Utile. Over these he has bridges, and other good objects which are not a little beautiful'.[63] James Bisset, a local artist, gazetteer and token issuer, was moved to verse by the transformed scene:

> On Yonder gentle slope, which shrubs adorn,
> Where grew, of late, "rank weeds," gorse, ling, and thorn,
> Now pendant woods, and shady groves are seen,
> And nature there assumes a nobler mien.
> There verdant lawns, cool grots, and peaceful bow'rs,
> Luxurient, now, are strew'd with sweetest flow'rs,
> Reflected by the lake, which spreads below,
> All Nature smiles around – there stands SOHO![64]

The manufactory [77], 'The Soho', as it became known to locals, the first stages of which were completed in 1767, was not a factory in the modern sense but a mesh of individual specialised workshops 'which like Bee hives are crowded with the Sons of Industry', men, women and children, supported by a rationalised system of project design, warehousing and marketing, and even providing accommodation for key workers, much of it under the one roof of a 'great and wonderful' building fronted by an English Palladian-manner facade. With motive power provided by a huge water wheel, 'The whole scene' was to Fisher

> a Theatre of Buisness [*sic*], all conducted like one piece of Mechanism, Men, Women and Children full of employment according to their Strength and Docility. The very Air buzzes with the Variety of Noises. All seems like one vast machine... Tis wonderful, astonishing, amazing.[65]

---

62 BAH: MS 3782/1/37, John Fothergill to John Lewis Baumgartner, 13 July 1765; Uglow (2002), 69. It had apparently not been Boulton's original intention to concentrate his workforce but he was persuaded to do so because of the losses he was incurring from relying on out-work.

63 Pierson (1949), 9; Mason (2005), 99 (where the Boulton family arms are illustrated); Morgan (1992), 253.

64 Bisset (1800), 12.

65 Pierson (1949), 9; Tann (*c.*1970), 153; Morgan (1992), 253.

77　The Soho Manufactory, *c.* 1766-75. This early view of Boulton's works busy with visitors was calculated to attract the interest of potential customers.

It was an enterprise producing intricate steel jewellery, clocks, Sheffield plate (Boulton was said to have been the first manufacturer in Birmingham to make what he called 'plated ware'), sterling silver ware, ormolu [66] and, for a short period, mechanically-copied paintings. He even contemplated starting a pottery to produce his own vases for the mountings he had hitherto supplied to Josiah Wedgwood, a potential rivalry that caused the potter to confess that it doubled his 'courage to have the first Manufacturer in England to encounter with … I like the Man, I like his spirit.– He will not be a mere snivelling copyist like the antagonists I have hitherto had'.[67] A 'SKETCH of the

---

66　Boulton's ormolu [*or moulou* = ground gold], objects decorated normally with brass or sometimes bronze or copper fittings, cast and chased, and gilt by a process of mercurial gilding, was regarded as the best produced in England: Goodison (2002).

67　Josiah Wedgwood to Thomas Bentley, 27 September 1769: [Farrer] (1903), I, 286. See also Schofield (1963), 84; Dolan (2004), 231.

THE GREAT CONTENTION

SOHO' in a directory of 1773 described its 'Thousand Workmen' [68] as excelling 'not only in the fabrication of Buttons, Buckles, Boxes, Trinkets, &c. in Gold, Silver, and a variety of Compositions; but in many other Arts, long predominant in France, which lose their Reputation on a Comparison with the product of this Place: ...Their excellent, ornamental Pieces, in Or-Moulu, have been admired by the Nobility and Gentry, not only of this Kingdom but of all Europe; and are allowed to surpass anything of the Kind made abroad'.[69] The irrepressible Bisset expressed his enthusiasm for the showpiece that 'Soho' had become in his grandiloquent way:

> SOHO! – where GENIUS and the ARTS preside
> EUROPA'S wonder and BRITANNIA'S pride;
> THY matchless works have rais'd Old England's fame,
> And future ages will record thy name;
> Each rival Nation shall to thee resign
> The PALM of TASTE, and own – 'tis justly thine;
> Whilst COMMERCE shall to thee an alter raise,
> And infant Genius learn to lisp thy praise:
> Whilst Art and Science reign, they'll still proclaim
> THINE! Ever blended, with a BOULTON'S name. [70]

Years earlier Erasmus Darwin, the founding spirit of the Lunar Society and later celebrated for his poetic panorama of nature and industry, had already enthused – if only in prose – over Soho's 'mechanic inventions ... superior in multitude, variety, and simplicity, to those of any manufactory (I suppose) in the known world. Toys and utensils of various kinds in gold, silver, steel, copper, tortoiseshell, enamels and many vitreous and metallic compositions, with gilded, plated and inlaid works, are wrought up to the highest elegance of taste and perfection of execution in this place. Mr. Boulton, who has established this great work, has joined taste and philosophy with manufacture and commerce'. [71]

For all this lyricism Boulton's overarching ambition to create 'the largest Hardware Manufactory in the World' soon precipitated grave financial problems for himself and Fothergill. The manufactory might

---

68 An exaggeration but a figure used by Boulton as in a letter to Lord Hawkesbury justifying his take-over of common land: 'I founded my manufactory upon one of the most barren commons in England, where there existed but a few miserable huts filled with idle beggarly people, who with the help of the common land and a little thieving made shift to live without working. The scene is now entirely changed. I have employed a thousand men, women and children, in my aforesaid manufactory, for nearly thirty years past': BAH: MS 3782/12/8/55, Matthew Boulton to Lord Hawkesbury, 17 April 1790. In March 1790 François de La Rochefoucauld described Soho, 'the biggest factory in the whole of Britain', as employing 'between five and six hundred workpeople': Scarfe (1995), 111.

69 Swinney (1773), 'Preface'.

70 Bisset (1800), 12.

71 Erasmus Darwin to the Rev. Thomas Feilde of Brewood, Staffordshire, 26 August 1768, quoted in Shaw (1798-1801), II (1801) 117.

mirror and even surpass John Taylor's hitherto unique concept but it grotesquely failed to generate the 'Esquire''s wealth. The pretentious central brick edifice, likened by some to the 'stately Palace of some Duke' or, with its clock cupola, dismissed by others as a grandiose stable block, exceeded its estimates almost five-fold.[72] Excessive investment in sophisticated machinery and over-production of fashionable goods that a fluctuating market could not sustain led to considerable and continuing losses, exacerbated early on by the economic recession of the 1770s. Although the partnership had every appearance of being prosperous it was far from sound and by 1777 its huge Bill Account – what we would see as an overdraft – amounted to little less than £25,000. As James Keir put it, several of its ventures, 'on which so much ingenuity, taste & capital' were expended, 'did not make suitable returns of profit, but were rather rewarded with the fragrant odours of Praise & admiration, than with more solid advantage'.[73]

'Whatever he did or attempted,' recalled Keir, 'his successes or failures were all on a large scale', for Boulton, 'a man of great vitality and diversified taste', was limitless in his ambitions and seemingly unable to restrict his business ventures. Even young Jabez Fisher on his fleeting visit to Soho caught something of Boulton's Achilles heel:

> He is a sensible, ingenious, and enterprizing Man, who plans and executes with equal Expedition, but like many other great Men he has his hobby horse. He is scheming and changeable, ever some new matter on the Anvil to divert his attention from a steady pursuit of some grand object. He is always inventing, and by the time he has brought his Scheme to Perfection, some new Affair offers itself. He deserts the old, follows the new, of which he is weary by the time he has arrived at it. This Volatility prevents him from becoming very rich.[74]

'Born promoter' that Boulton was, with an abiding 'love of a money-getting ingenious project', the very diversity of his activities, his proneness to sudden enthusiasms which in Eric Roll's words

---

72   BAH: MS 3782/12/1/42, Matthew Boulton to J. H. Ebbinghaus [of Iserlohn (North Rhine-Westphalia) and for a time a secret partner in Boulton and Fothergill], 2 March 1768; Morgan (1992), 253; Robinson (1979), 19. Boulton was not alone in building his manufactory on classical country house lines. Samuel Oldknow's 'handsome and imposing' Mellor cotton mill was 'beautifully situated' 'amidst grounds well laid out' but, like Boulton, his costs were high and he had to mortgage the estate almost immediately the mill was built: Unwin (1968), 124, 149 and 194.

73   Roll (1968), 98-100; Cule (1935), 74; Keir (1809) [1947], 6 and 9; The production of clocks was thus abandoned in 1770, Ormolu in 1775, japanned goods and mechanical paintings – in partnership with the decorative artist Francis Eginton – in 1780 and sterling silver manufacture was run down in favour of plated articles. Dickinson (1937), 58; Roll (1968), 99; Quickenden (1980), 288.

74   Morgan (1992), 255. This was likely to have been the received opinion of Fisher's fellow Quakers, Samuel Galton, junior (gun maker, banker and Lunar Society member) and Charles Lloyd (banker), who accompanied the American to Soho.

were 'often taken up in quite a casual way', prevented him from giving them the managerial care that they needed. Although most of Boulton's business adventures – apart from his coining activities which were throughout his own personal concern – were undertaken as partnerships his was always the dominant entrepreneurial spirit. The range of his enterprises, his frequent and often extended absences from Soho (in Cornwall on mine and steam engine business and in London lobbying for a Birmingham assay office or a coinage contract), his involvement in the General Chamber of Manufacturers and the promotion of canals, self-interested as they may have been, all dissipated Boulton's attention. Even the constant stream of visitors to his showcase manufactory, however much 'praise and admiration' resulted, occupied 'too many of those hours which could not be spared from his own concerns'.[75]

And he was in a relentless state of financial embarrassment, crippled by his ever-present Bill Account – 'the greatest drain of all others to our profits' – and pressurised by a fundamental lack of circulating capital for wages and materials. His own inheritance and sale of property, the financial support (mainly borrowed) – and eventual ruin – of the cautious Fothergill, plunder of the riches brought to him by his two heiress wives and their family, loans from friends like Thomas Day and Samuel Garbett, from London and Amsterdam banks and ultimately from security provided by the steam engine account just managed to keep his creditors at bay. For all 'the glittering façade provided by Boulton's activities' at his Soho emporium his reluctance to take costs into account created a constant and painfully fragile hand to mouth operation and, in the view of John Scale, Boulton's button-making partner after the shabby removal of Fothergill in 1781, an inefficiently run one. Not until he and James Watt succeeded in marketing the latter's rotative steam engine in 1784 was Boulton ever truly able even to begin to hold his head above water and in due time take his place as one of the country's most opulent manufacturers.[76] Boulton's incessant scrabble for funds never dampened his grasshopping enthusiasm for new, often financially disastrous, challenges even beyond Soho's enormously manifold production of ornamental articles and the more mundane brassware, bolts, taps, locks and rings he manufactured for industrial customers.[77] But any aspirations he may have had for yet further expansion at Soho were hampered early on by the fluctuating water supply from the Hockley Brook which affected the operation of his mill wheels especially during summer droughts. His quest for a reliable and relatively inexpensive power source to replace the horse-mill that he used to recycle the precious water of the mill pool turned

---

75 Schofield (1963), 18; Dickinson and Vowles (1943), 38; Roll (1968), 132; Keir (1809) [1947], 7.

76 Cule (1935), 136; Hopkins (1998), 86-87. For Scale's criticisms see Cule (1935), 39-43.

77 As with his hardware partnership with Fothergill most of Boulton's ventures cost him dear. 'He entered one partnership to work a silver mine, another to make spelter, subscribed to the Grand Trunk Canal, and in all these lost money': Cule (1935), 300.

his mind to steam power, seeking the advice of scientific friends such as Benjamin Franklin and Darwin and designing a model engine as early as 1765. It was, though, not until the arrival of Watt on the Birmingham scene that a solution was eventually found in the latter's experimental reciprocating engine brought down from Scotland and installed at Soho in 1774; the 'new kind of fire- or steam-engine' that Georg Christoph Lichtenberg, the German natural scientist, spied the following year although 'Mr. Bolton ... makes a secret of it'.[78] Partnership with its inventor, after a Parliamentary extension of his patent for twenty-five years had been obtained, followed in June 1775 and, despite all the uncertainty of the prospects ahead of him, Boulton characteristically threw himself into the development of steam power; to make engines, he pointedly made clear to the guarded Watt, 'for all the world'. His ambition, as the '*iron chieftain*' boasted to James Boswell when the biographer visited Soho only a year later, was to 'sell here, Sir, what all the world desires to have – POWER'.[79]

The steam engine, through the monopoly assured by the extension of Watt's patent, was ultimately to be Boulton's salvation. For the first decade or so its main market, indeed virtually its only market, lay in Cornwall and even as early as 1782, despite the competition of other engine makers, Boulton and Watt had twenty-one reciprocating engines at work pumping out the deep copper mines of the county ever prone to waterlogging. 'The profits arise every minute ... if I can keep the present Cornish Battery of 21 great guns going', Boulton hopefully excused himself to William Matthews, one of his London agents (a patiently loyal creditor and Boulton's banker from 1784), 'I have no doubt but I shall soon vanquish all my difficulties'.[80] To promote their sales and ensure the payment of the monthly premiums due on the use of their patent [81] both Boulton and Watt began investing directly in some of the mines they supplied despite their concern over what they saw as the inefficiency of the local mine adventurers; 'an army of

78 Mare and Quarrell (1938), 97-98. Steam power and its practical development were subjects of speculation among members of the Lunar Society long before Watt appeared on the Birmingham scene: Schofield (1963), 60-62; Pelham (1963), 83. Shaw (1798-1801), II (1801), 118, says that Boulton installed a Savery pumping-engine at Soho in 1767 but there is no other evidence of this and Shaw probably had in mind the Savery *model* engine that Boulton built about this time: cf. Lord (1923), 96-97.

79 Schofield (1963), 68-72; Goodison (2002), 367, note 48; March 1776: Boswell (1799) [1934], II, 459.

80 Matthew Boulton to William Matthews, 11 January 1782, quoted in Lord (1923), 160, note 1. William Matthews was a London merchant, shipowner and underwriter, and was the mainstay of Boulton's Bill Account; his young widow, Charlotte (d. 1802), successfully ran his banking business following his death in 1792.

81 As Watt's engines were patented users were required to pay premiums according to the savings they achieved. By the end of 1791 the partnership had received over £76,000 in premiums from the forty-two engines erected in Cornwall as well as income from the sale of machine parts: Rowe (1953), 79. Only twenty-six were actually at work in 1794 and it must be remembered that non-Watt engine makers accounted for more than half the engines in the county: Rowe (1953), 101; Harris (1967), 146.

old women' as Thomas Wilson, their Cornish agent and a mine owner himself, described them. Cornwall became vital to Boulton's credit worthiness and the ruin of its industry would have brought disaster to the partners; as Cule graphically put it 'If the beams ceased to rock in Cornwall, the bailiffs entered Soho'. But the mines there faced critical problems other than local mismanagement and drainage difficulties that limited their profitability and threatened their very existence: cut-throat competition from the cheaper, more easily worked, ores of Anglesey and the stranglehold the 'Associated Smelters' exerted over their sales.[82] Boulton's returns were thus compromised and he sought relief in the creation in 1785 of the Cornish Metal Company, a marketing organisation set up in uneasy concert with Thomas Williams to destroy the crippling economic power of the smelters.

In the event the Company proved to be a commercial failure; it made no attempt to match supply to demand and its marketing organisation bore no relation to that of the dynamic Williams.[83] Over the two years until its sales were taken over by the Anglesey entrepreneur increasingly large stocks of unsold copper were allowed to accumulate in the Company's warehouses as the mine adventurers – veritable 'drones' in Boulton's view – dredged up various bold but impracticable schemes to resolve their difficulties.

For Boulton at least a partial and perhaps, over time, a not insignificant route to Cornwall's deliverance – and his own – lay in a national copper coinage. As he confided to Wilson, 'I am so sensible of the importance it is ... to obtain a <u>speedy consumption of a large quantity</u> of their Copper [the Cornish Metal Company] that I have anxiously promoted it in many shapes... My anxiety for Cornwall hath caused me to neglect my own business & my own interest. It hath induced me to put my self to a considerable expence in makeing [sic] new Machines & Experiments to perfection the art of Coining ... I have always heartily had in view to promote the most speedy consumption & greatest quantity of Cornish Copper possible'.[84]

Watt's steam engine, if by unpremeditated steps, had led to Cornwall, to the partners' involvement in the county's mines, to the marketing of its copper and, through Boulton's anxiety to promote its consumption, ultimately from idle theorising about reform of the coinage to the addition of coin production to the gamut of his activities. 'Steam' and 'copper' were thus to combine to produce the ultimate 'hobby horse' – the Soho Mint, 'the favourite and nearly the sole object of the last

---

82   Allen (1923), 74-85; Cule (1935), 249; Rowe (1953), 71-72.

83   To be fair the situation the Company faced was difficult, compounded by the deviousness of Williams who violated the terms of his agreement with the Company, over production by the mines and the import of foreign ore and copper all of which depressed prices.

84   CRO: AD 1583/2/47, Matthew Boulton to Thomas Wilson, 6 May 1787.

twenty years' of Boulton's active life.[85]

Much has been made of Boulton's social concern and his anxiety – often self trumpeted – to eliminate counterfeiting through the production of 'more excellent coin than had ever been seen'. As he told Sir Joseph Banks 'I took up the subject because I thought it would be a publick good', adding somewhat ingenuously as things were to turn out, '& because Mr Pitt had expressd [sic] a Wish to me of seeing something done to put an end to Counterfeiting the Copper Coin'.[86] Nevertheless, while he might be regarded as a 'liberal, hospitable and benevolent' man, 'a father to his tribe' valuing and encouraging his craftsmen, instituting an insurance scheme for his workmen, Boulton's approach to coining, as indeed his approach to business generally, was that of an entrepreneur. It was a determined approach that, while tempered by taste and discrimination, was driven by an impulse for innovation and technological improvement; 'by the help of machinery', as Keir put it, for his products 'to be made with greater precision, & cheaper, than those commonly sold'. But underlying it always were financial, and, more often than not, desperate financial considerations. Boulton's methods were not always above criticism yet he was probably no worse and, perhaps, a great deal better than most business men in a self-seeking generation.[87]

Reform of the coinage, its management as well as its manufacture, had, it is said, interested him, at least in general terms, since the 1770s. In 1772, lobbying the local grandee Lord Dartmouth, newly appointed by his step-brother North as President of the Board of Trade, Boulton had expressed the view that 'the present state of Coinage was a proper subject for the consideration of it [the government] as well as the present State of Commercial Credit, there being neither coin or paper sufficient in the circle of Commerce from the present state of it'. But this was Boulton, the employer and manufacturer, speaking from his personal experience of having to accept from local bankers, taking advantage of his financial pressures, 'the most wretched coin and small guineas' to meet his wage bills. In April 1773 matters came to a head at Soho as an alarmed Fothergill reported to his absent partner: 'You would have been unhappy to have been witness of the clamour at your house and mine last Saturday night and Sunday morning; poor people brought guineas which they could not dispose of under 3/= or 4/= loss

---

85   William Murdock (1754-1839), the engineer and inventor (of the 'sun and planet' gear for rotary engines and of coal gas lighting among much else), and a linchpin of the firm of Boulton and Watt for sixty years, quoted in Smiles (1865), 390. In fact Boulton developed two separate mints at Soho, the first in 1788-89 to be replaced by a second in 1798-99: Doty (1998a), 23-63.

86   Keir (1809) [1947], 6; BAH: MS 3782/21/14/1, Matthew Boulton to Sir Joseph Banks, 2 September 1789. A similar sentiment was expressed to one of his London agents, James Woodmason, that his 'principal reason for turning coiner was to gratify Mr. Pitt in his wishes to put an end to the counterfeiting of money': BAH: MS 3782/12/8, Matthew Boulton to James Woodmason, 13 November 1789; Dickinson (1937), 137.

87   Watt (1809) [1943], [11]; Boswell (1799) [1934], II, 459; Keir (1809) [1947], 6.

THE GREAT CONTENTION

and seemed in the utmost want and several hands will be obliged to go to Taylors [John Taylor's bank established in 1765] on that account'.[88] There is no real hint that Boulton was personally edging towards any practical solution of the coinage problem at this time. Watt, in later years, is said to have recalled that he and Boulton had discussed coining by steam power as early as 1774 but even if Watt's recollection was accurate – and he was notoriously vague as to dates – it was probably no more than a typically Boultonian pipe-dream. As we have already seen Boulton had been actively interested in the development of a steam engine as early as 1765 but this had been essentially to cope with his need to maintain a water supply from his mill pool, a problem eventually relieved by the installation of Watt's archetype engine from Scotland.[89]

By the mid-1780s, however, matters began to take a more positive turn. As we saw earlier no regal copper had been produced at the Tower since 1775 but now it seemed that government was at last prepared to grasp the nettle of a radical recoinage. The hint – for so it was put about in political circles – that this might be done through the agency of a private contractor rather than directly through the Mint generated a frenetic flurrying of lobbying and added a new dimension to the confrontation between Williams and Boulton. The returns to be gained from a national coinage contract were undeniably exaggerated by the industry but the perceived profit and the additional outlet that would be created for a metal in surplus were the fundamental forces behind this rivalry, at its heart the bitter conflict between the mines of Cornwall and those of Anglesey.

Boulton had been close to his friends the Garbetts in their study of the Mint constantly plying them with advice even though Samuel Garbett was much the more expert in the matters in hand. Boulton was also well aware that the Garbetts had assumed, rightly or wrongly, that they would be compensated for the costs and energies they had expended by involvement in the implementation of some of their proposals. When in the autumn of 1786 rumour that government was seriously contemplating a new copper coinage reached Boulton's ears it was natural for him to alert Garbett.[90] Although, he understood that Thomas Williams was already 'in Treaty for it' he still thought he stood a good chance of obtaining the contract. But, he added,

---

88 From letters from Matthew Boulton to the Earl of Dartmouth (10 November 1772), quoted in Dickinson (1937), 135, and from John Fothergill to Matthew Boulton (27 April 1773), quoted in Cule (1935), 59-60. The incident at Soho may explain Watt's otherwise puzzling statement that 'When the new coinage of gold took place in 17[74], Mr B. was employed to receive & exchange the old coin, which served to revive his ideas on the subject of coinage which he had considered as capable of great improvement': Watt (1809) [1943], 7. I have found no other evidence to suggest that Boulton was an official receiver of old coin during the recoinage of the early 1770s.

89 Smiles (1865), 389.

90 Pollard (1968), 241-65; Dykes (2005a), 169.

78   William Petty, Marquess of Lansdowne (1737-1805). Portrait after Sir Joshua Reynolds, 1766.

After what has passed between you and me on this subject, I cannot think of it for myself, as I consider it a just debt owing to you from Government, therefore if you choose to apply for it, I will do the manufacturing for you, or I will go you halves in the undertaking. I can do it for less than ½ what the Tower pays, & make a far more elegant coin. Suppose you apply to the Marquis [Shelburne, since November 1784 Marquess of Lansdowne] [78] upon this head? [91]

Boulton's decision to involve the Garbetts in any bid for a contract is understandable. He had no experience of coining [92] and although well versed in lobbying techniques on local Birmingham issues he lacked Samuel Garbett's apparent ease of access to leading parliamentary figures especially in economic and monetary matters. Garbett had known Lansdowne, the former Prime Minister, since 1764 from his days as a principal partner in the great Carron ironworks and, as a promoter of Birmingham's manufacturing interests, had incessantly bombarded the politician with homilies on the needs of trade.[93] Boulton's impression, though, that Garbett still had such influence was ill founded. The Marquess of Lansdowne, for one, was no longer a figure of authority. The Garbetts' Report had been shelved in the wake of his fall from power in February 1783 and neither the short-lived Fox-North coalition that followed nor Pitt's succeeding administration displayed any real interest in their conclusions.[94] Nevertheless, implementation of the Report was a chimera that Garbett relentlessly pursued in these years, repeatedly complaining about the lack of government response to all who would listen. He had already, in April 1786, reiterated his thoughts on the Mint to Lansdowne, now adding the Burkean point that:

> The whole Business [of the Mint] ought to be carried on as a Trade by Persons of Knowledge in the subject, & that have had experience in great works, & to be stationed as Directors of the Mint; ... and our Idea is, that the directors should neither have a salary, nor a shilling in any shape, but from the savings or gain that may be made, & this Point should be settled in some distinct & permanent manner.[95]

91   BAH: MS 3782/12/6/225, Matthew Boulton to Samuel Garbett, 8 October 1786.

92   He had, it is true, dabbled in medal making but this had been on a small scale and he was, of course, a skilled button maker. See below p. 105.

93   Norris (1958), 450-60.

94   The report, Garbett and Garbett (1837), compiled by Samuel Garbett and his son Francis had been submitted to the Treasury in November 1782. Shelburne resigned in February 1783 and his administration, which included William Pitt as Chancellor of the Exchequer, was succeeded by the short-lived Fox-North coalition. This in turn was followed by Pitt's ministry in December 1783, a government that did not overcome an uncertain future until the general election of March 1784.

95   BL: Lansdowne B11 f. 188v, Samuel Garbett to Lord Lansdowne, 16 April 1786 (BL: Lansdowne B11 ff. 186-188v).
     Edmund Burke's demand that the Mint should be 'undertaken upon the principles of a manufacture; that is, for the best and cheapest execution, by a contract upon proper securities, and under proper regulations' was made in his famous Commons speech on economical reformation of the civil and other establishments on 11 February 1780: Burke (1854-56), II, 90.

Garbett, of course, saw himself as just such a knowledgeable person and one deserving a *quid pro quo* for his Mint exertions more substantial than the derisory sum of £500 he had been promised – but apparently not yet been paid – by Lansdowne's successors.[96] We do not know but it seems not unlikely that Lansdowne had intended to reward Garbett much more substantially; certainly the Garbetts seem to have thought so. Lansdowne, now, could do little more than suggest that Garbett make his representations to the current Prime Minister, Pitt, who, as Chancellor of the Exchequer in his own administration, had first-hand knowledge of the Report. Pitt, though, characteristically over a matter that did not capture his immediate interest, totally ignored Garbett's initial approaches but, following Boulton's prompting, Garbett tried again on 25 October 1786 asking whether it was true that offers were being solicited for 'the Execution of a new Copper Coinage'.

> We beg the Honour that you will permit us to know whether this is the case, for We are extremely desirous of supporting our Character and that the Opinion We gave [in relation to the Mint] should be carried into the most perfect and profitable Execution. As We know that We can execute a more perfect Coin than hath ever been done in this or any other Country far cheaper than the present Cost in the Tower and full as cheap as in the Power of any Person whomsoever. We trust therefore you will excuse the Liberty I take, and the more so when the Treasury Minute will shew that We were not paid for the Time and Attention We gave to the Elucidation of a subject which before had not been successfully attained and considering all the Circumstances We shall be allowed a Preference for the Execution of so beneficial a Measure to Government and which We ourselves pointed out.[97]

There was no mention of Boulton – and yet again no response from Pitt. So two weeks later Garbett tackled the Prime Minister once more, disclosing now that Boulton was to be included in a trio of manufacturers:

> The Quantity of Counterfeit Copper Coin brought daily into Circulation is incredible. I have reason to believe it amounts to much more than five hundred thousand Pounds Sterling, probably more than a Million, & the Profit of making it is so great as to afford a cruel temptation to many hundred Workmen. It is much the same in Silver Coin, both might be honourably

---

96 Garbett wrote to Shelburne in March 1783: 'As it is possible your Lordship's successors may suppose £500 a compensation for our trouble and knowledge, it may be proper to assure you that we spent more than £300 on the occasion, and that at this time we pay the manager of our works in Scotland [Carron] a salary of £500 a year, and did for some years pay the same salary to our agent in London ... your Lordship will see what idea we can have of £500 as a reward...': Samuel Garbett to Lord Shelburne, 20 March 1783, quoted in Bebbington (1938), 117.

97 BL: Additional MSS 38421, f. 127, Samuel Garbett to William Pitt, 25 October 1786. Garbett apparently first wrote to Pitt on 31 July 1786.

> profitably & effectually remedied if Administration would attend to the Subject by putting into circulation a coin which few Men in the World could so counterfeit as to impose on the Public & which Mr. Boulton, my Son & I could complete in a Manner that should excel any Coin that ever was made & thereby add to the Reputation of the Manufactures of Great Britain.
>
> I hope you will excuse my saying that I wait with great anxiety for the Information relative to the Offers made for executing a new Copper Coinage, when I trust that having pointed out the Improvement & offering to make it as cheap as any Offer that can have been made & better than has hitherto been done that I shall be allowed the Honour of executing it, for which Purpose I propose to apply to you through my Family Friends.[98]

Garbett's representations with his parting reference to undeclared influence not unnaturally received scant attention from someone whose general attitude to patronage was dismissive when political considerations were not paramount. When after some anxious weeks Garbett was at last able to have an audience with the Prime Minister and press his case in person, Pitt remained unmoved by his arguments. His recollection of Garbett was as a vocal lobbyist on behalf of the manufacturing interest against his proposed coal tax and Irish free-trade treaty only a year or so earlier. He now suspected Garbett of being self-seeking, something of an obsessive and too closely associated with his former leader Lansdowne from whom he wished to distance himself. He was also unconvinced that any new copper coinage would provide any significant relief to the Cornish mines and, in more general terms, saw the £10,000 that Garbett thought could be saved in the operation of the Mint as very small beer in relation to the government's schemes to reduce the country's overall budgetary problems. Garbett's plea that he himself was 'desirous only of a per centage upon the Profits or Savings' achieved served only to evoke the sharp rejoinder that Pitt would consider the problems of the Mint and of the copper coinage when he had more leisure.[99]

Garbett was not to be put off, however, and, with Lansdowne a declining asset he increasingly turned to Lord Hawkesbury as a key political contact, bombarding him with homilies as regular and voluminous as he had the former Prime Minister. Hawkesbury, now President of Pitt's reconstituted Board of Trade, shared many of Garbett's economic ideas and his views on the necessity of reforms in the Royal Mint, and Garbett was quick to impress on him the capability of his Birmingham group to mastermind a copper recoinage.[100]

---

98   BL: Additional MSS 38421, f. 129, Samuel Garbett to William Pitt, 6 November 1786.

99   Cf. Bebbington (1938), 118.

100 As Hawkesbury (by then 1st Earl of Liverpool) commented to John Robinson when his son was appointed Master of the Mint in 1799 'many reforms are to be made there, in which I have been and shall be principally employed': Aspinall (1967), III, 192, note 3. Liverpool's eventual *Treatise on the Coins of the Realm* (1805) owed much to Garbett though this was never to be sufficiently acknowledged: see p. 44, note 35 above.

By April 1787 it looked as though Garbett might be within an ace of securing a coinage contract – the public prints certainly seemed to think so – but at the last moment Pitt told him that he was 'too much hurried to do anything in Copper Coinage immediately'. The reality was that others were in the field and actively jockeying for the Prime Minister's favour. We have seen how Thomas Williams had made overtures to Effingham as early as 1785 and he was unceasing in his manoeuvres to win the supposed coinage contract. Garbett was only too well aware that Williams was still 'moving in many ways to have a Concern in the Copper Coinage ... if he attempts to Coin Money it will no doubt be in connexion with Westwood, who he is already concerned with in Ship's Bolts'.[101]

In May 1787 when Williams discovered that Boulton had engaged Jean-Pierre Droz he sought out the engraver in Paris and attempted to lure him into his own employment and when this manoeuvre failed he sought publicly to traduce Boulton's scheme in the national press:

> We hear from Birmingham, that Messrs. Garbett and Boulton, in hopes of obtaining a Contract for the intended Copper Coinage, are in Treaty with a Swiss at Paris to come to London to execute the Dyes. If they succeed what a Reproach will it be to the English Artists! That among them all Mr. Boulton could not find out one who could sink a Dye for a Half penny! And what a Triumph to Frenchmen, that one whose offered Services their Government rejected should be looked up to with Reverence in England; nor less perhaps will the patriotick spirit of Mr. Boulton triumph in the happy success of his secret Expedition to France.
>
> Let it not however be supposed that foreign Artists are wanted in England; Birmingham where the speculating Gentleman's better days were spent has Artists who will yield to none in Ingenuity, either of Invention or Execution. Witness the Anglesea Copper Medals, which excel all the Coins of Europe, and after such a specimen we hope the Government will not suffer Foreigners to be obtruded on us.[102]

Williams even tried, through Dawes and John Philip Marindin, a Birmingham merchant, to inveigle Garbett as an ally when Garbett was in the midst of his own negotiations with ministers. But Garbett was not to be seduced: 'M[r]. Williams' was 'a Welch Attorney', a byword for duplicity in Garbett's mind, who had 'supplied the Counterfeiters of halfpence with Rolled Copper – they are neither of them [Williams or Westwood] capable of conducting such a manufacture as the Mint ought to be'.[103] Now Garbett learnt from Pitt that 'wild' proposals

---

101 *The Times*, 23 April 1787 and 8 May 1787; Samuel Garbett to Matthew Boulton, 26 March 1787, quoted in Westwood (1926), 10.

102 12 June 1787: quoted in Westwood (1926), 10-11.

103 BAH: MS 3872/12/108/51, Notebook 3, 17 (26 March 1787): although understood to be Boulton's notebook pages 17 and 18 appear to be in Garbett's hand.

were also being put forward by the 'Cornwall Gentlemen' to produce 3,000 tons of copper coin in 20 months. It was a hare-brained scheme calculated to spite Boulton and 'next to impossible' to carry out when it was 'considered that the whole of yᵉ apparatus is yet to make'. More worryingly Garbett had found out that:

> Gentlemen in London are very sanguine to obtain a heavy and a cheap Copper Coinage, and don't consider either the Capital it will employ or the Profit that is necessary to induce respectable Persons to attend to the Manufacture or to the Sales, or to the Credit (or Equivalent) that must be given to Dispensers in every Town in the Kingdom. Somebody in London has sent for John Westwood from this Town, who has been an Associate with Counterfeiters of Foreign Coin. And I am told that he is to go to London on Saturday next. But he and all his Associates are incapable of making such a Coin as is proposed by Mr. Boulton… [T]his Westwood is the Person who engraved the Die for Mr. Williams of the Paris Mine Cº. to strike the Pennys now coining in Quantities at Holywell, surely Mr. Williams should have notice to stop that Coinage. [104]

79a John Westwood: Pattern halfpenny designed by Samuel More, 1788.

79b Royal Mint: Pattern halfpenny engraved by Lewis Pingo, 1788.

We do not know exactly what Garbett had heard or how true it might have been for Birmingham was rife with gossip over a national copper coinage. Only a week earlier Westwood and Hancock were said to be openly talking of their going to the Tower to manage the copper coinage and a dismayed Boulton had assumed from this rumour that Williams was on the brink of gaining the contract. Although Westwood was eventually to set himself up as a coin maker on his own account he was still very much in the Williams camp at this time. In June 1787 Boulton was to confess to the Paris-based Swiss engraver Jean-Pierre Droz, whom he was attempting to entice to Soho, that he had 'no Artist who is capable to engrave a head' since Williams had 'already hired the 2 best Die Engravers in England [Hancock and Westwood] in order to prevent other persons from benefit by their service'.[105] Westwood's journey to London, if it ever did take place, may have been connected with preliminary discussions with Samuel More, the secretary of the Society of Arts, which were to result in Westwood's production of the enigmatic pattern halfpenny for More dated 1788 [79a]. Little is known about this rare coin, said to have been engraved by Hancock, some fourteen specimens of which have been recorded in four edge varieties [*Peck* 928-933].[106] More was well known to Williams, it is believed that he had had a hand in the original concept of the 'Druid'

---

104 BAH: MS 3782/12/62/48, Samuel Garbett to Matthew Boulton, 21 April 1787; CRO: AD/1583/2/47, Matthew Boulton to Thomas Wilson, 6 May 1787; BL: Additional MSS 38421, ff. 134-135, Samuel Garbett to William Pitt, 5 April 1787.

105 Matthew Boulton to J-P. Droz (Draft), 12 June 1787, quoted in Hawker (1996), 10.

106 The style of portrait and the cable pattern edge of some specimens, as *Peck* plausibly suggests, seem to copy the design of the Droz patterns prepared for Boulton: *Peck* (1960), 238-39 and plate 15, 929.

THE GREAT CONTENTION

79c Matthew Boulton: Pattern halfpenny engraved by Jean-Pierre Droz, 1788.

80 Matthew Boulton: 'Otaheite' medal engraved by John Westwood, 1772.

design with his friend William Collins and it may be that the impetus behind the pattern came from Williams.

As Boulton recognised, these new approaches served only to delay further any decision on a coinage contract and, despite Garbett's persistent badgering of Hawkesbury and indeed of Pitt, the government took the not unnatural step of setting up a Privy Council committee to review the state of the currency in the November of 1787.[107] As far as the copper was concerned, it decided, in the light of the submissions it received, to call for the tender of pattern halfpence from the Mint [79b], from Boulton [79c], and, it is not unreasonable to think, from Williams too [79a].

Boulton, as a seasoned button maker, had some expertise akin to coining but little experience of the complexities of coin-die making and nothing in the way of the equipment necessary for a large-scale coinage other than the water-driven rolling mill and cutting-out plant for blanks at Soho. He had in the days of his partnership with Fothergill done some limited medallic work. He had, for instance, produced, at the behest of Joseph Banks, the 'Otaheite' medal for Captain Cook's second voyage to the Pacific in 1772 but this medal, from dies engraved by Westwood, had been struck by drop hammer at Soho [80]. Two years later Westwood had also cut the dies for some regimental medals for Sir Eyre Coote, a singularly unsuccessful assignment that had exposed the partnership's supervisory inadequacies and technical inexperience in medal making. Both had been small bespoke commissions although specimens of the 'Otaheite' medal had also been made for public consumption. A more commercial endeavour, intended to capitalise on the public euphoria arising from Admiral Rodney's seizure of the Dutch West Indies entrepôt of St. Eustatius in 1781, had been a commemorative medal but despite all the popular excitement it did not sell well.[108] There may have been other speculative ventures of the kind but Boulton had no specialist medal or coin press at Soho and when in the summer of 1786, through the good offices of John Motteux, he precipitated himself, ever the optimist, into the production of a copper trading coinage for the East India Company's Sumatran settlement at Bencoolen (now Bengkulu City) he had to set up a conventional manually operated mint from scratch and in London in a John Company warehouse.[109]

This had been a struggle against time, an operation that as John Scale who had had charge of it, was at pains to point out, 'was begun without tools, without experience, without either men or masters but such as were engaged in other Branches and could not pay their sole

107 The chairman of the committee was Lord Camden, the Lord President of the Council, not Hawkesbury as is often stated, although the latter was a member.

108 Westwood (1926); Smith (1985); Vice (1988), 2-4 and (1998), 3-9. Boulton's 'St. Eustatius' medal cannot be positively identified but it is most likely to be *BHM* 230.

109 Gould (1969), 270-77. The mint was equipped by Boulton – with at least some presses manufactured by Anthony Robinson of Birmingham – but paid for by the East India Company.

105

COINAGE AND CURRENCY IN EIGHTEENTH-CENTURY BRITAIN

81 Matthew Boulton: East India Company 1 keping for the Bencoolen settlement, Sumatra, 1787.

attention to it'. Divided between two sites a hundred miles and more apart, with coin being blanked at Soho from copper supplied by the Company and struck in London, it was an undertaking fraught with delays and transport problems. Some eighteen tons of coins dated 1786 were eventually completed, by degrees, in 1787 followed by perhaps another thirty tons of a 1787-dated issue a year later. The 'kepings' [81] were a crude production, an extension of Boulton's button-making process, using simple dies stamped merely 'with letters & figures or such things as are put in with punchions' and a far cry from Boulton's declared ambition of striking a 'more excellent coin than had ever been seen'.[110] But, perhaps because of all his difficulties with a project that Boulton had to admit even to Thomas Williams was nowhere near a resounding financial success, his mind was already turning to technological refinements in 'the art of coining' and to fully automated presses, harnessed to Watt's rotative steam engine, that might be exploited to his advantage in the competition for a national coinage. And traditional, even rudimentary, as Boulton's East India Company coining had been he had at least already achieved one critical improvement with the incorporation of an automated 'laying-in' and ejection device into the London presses.[111]

During a visit to Paris with Watt in the winter of 1786/87 at the invitation of the French government, Boulton, on Samuel Garbett's suggestion, took the opportunity of seeing something of the French Mint and its methods of coining.[112] There he met Jean-Pierre Droz, a Swiss engraver at the Mint, who showed him some refinements he had been making in coining techniques. These included a six-segmented collar that, enveloping a coin blank as it was struck, allowed the edge to be inscribed in the striking process and then, automatically opening, released the finished coin. The process facilitated the simultaneous production of a consistently round coin with an ornamented edge (which hitherto had been applied to the blank at the rolling stage) and, as examples of the fruit of Droz's contrivances, Boulton came away with some specimens of a pattern *écu* [82].[113] Droz claimed also to have designed an improved coining press to accept his collar and to have developed new methods of 'multiplying dies'. Boulton, impressed with Droz's artistry and technical expertise, took steps to invite him to Soho. He had, he hoped, found an engraver of rare distinction whose mechanical ingenuity would help him so to improve the steam-driven coin presses he was designing at Soho that there would be no doubt of

82 French pattern *écu* engraved by Jean-Pierre Droz, 1786. (Miss Banks's Collection, British Museum).

110 BAH: MS 3782/12/15, Matthew Boulton to J-P. Droz, 5 April 1787.

111 BAH: MS 3782/12/72/65, John Scale to Matthew Boulton, 21 April 1787; BAH: MS 3782/12/3/64, Matthew Boulton to Thomas Williams, 3 July 1788; BAH: MS 3782/12/6/142, Matthew Boulton to Thomas Jeffries, January [1788]; Gould (1969), 272-73; Vice (1997), 50-51.

112 BL: Additional MSS 38422, f. 116, Samuel Garbett to Lord Hawkesbury, 7 April 1790.

113 Known popularly as an *écu de Calonne* after Charles-Alexandre de Calonne, the French Controller General of Finance, of whom Droz was a client. Calonne's fall from power in 1787 was a factor in persuading Droz to come to Birmingham.

THE GREAT CONTENTION

his capturing a national coin contract.

It was an unhappy relationship. Droz did not live up to expectations. He was dilatory over the preparation of promised pattern coins, evasive over mechanical drawings he had agreed to supply and when, in October 1788, after prevarications of eighteen months he did at last come to Soho on an established basis his inventions proved to be impractical and he succeeded in discomfiting Boulton's senior technical staff. As Watt later recalled:

> Mr Droz was found to be of a troublesome disposition, several of his contrivances were found not to answer & were obliged to be better contrived or totally changed by Mr B. and his assistants. The split collar was found to be difficult of execution, & subject to wear very soon when in use, & in short very unfit for an extensive coinage. Other methods were therefore adopted & it was laid to rest. Mr Droz was dismissed after being liberally paid, and other engravers were procured. (It should be noticed here that Mr D's method of multiplying the Dies did not answer & that it appeared that he did not know so much on that subject as Mr B. himself did. That process was therefore brought to perfection by Mr B. himself and his assistants).[114]

The Droz saga and Boulton's difficulties with the temperamental Parisian artist – 'of all the men I ever had any concern with … the most Vain, humoursom[sic], troublesome, tedious & trifling; & the most unlike a man of business. His only excellence is He is a neat Engraver but no Mechanick' as Boulton eventually expostulated to Garbett – are well known. The story does not need retelling here although it must be stressed that the evidence we possess is one-sided, provided only by Boulton and his sympathisers with nothing in defence of Droz. As the late Graham Pollard pointed out Droz's association with Boulton was 'only a brief episode in a generally distinguished career' at the Paris Mint.[115]

Whatever the rights and wrongs underlying the relationship between the capricious, secretive Droz and the masterful Boulton, it cost the latter dear and Droz's eventual departure from Soho in 1790 left him with little to show for his money or his aggravation and nothing for public consumption other than Boulton's medal celebrating the king's recovery from illness in 1789 [83]. These were troubled times for Boulton for which insufficient record exists. But left to his own resources, with presses having to be adapted by his own staff and with few positive results from Droz's vaunted creativity, he continued to persevere with his technical innovations and to convince the authorities of his suitability to manage a national contract. It is clear that at the outset Boulton's intention had been that his scheme to better 'the art of moneying' 'should be conducted in the Tower &

83   Matthew Boulton: Silver medal celebrating George III's recovery from illness engraved by Jean-Pierre Droz, 1789.

---

114   Watt (1809) [1943], 8.

115   For details of the Droz episode see Pollard (1968), 241-65 and Doty (1998a), 26-45; BAH: MS 3782/12/62/83, Matthew Boulton to Samuel Garbett, 29 March 1790; Pollard (1968), 242; Forrer (1902-1930), I (Revised 1904), 621.

107

executed by machinery greatly improved, wch I will undertake'. As he explained to Thomas Wilson in May 1787 'there is no probability of obtaining leave to Coin halfpence & farthings at any other place than the Tower. Many material objections present, & amongst the rest, it hath been refused to Scotland where there is a Mint Establishment of officers, presses &c &c'. Within months, however, much to the chagrin of Garbett who had done so much to promote Boulton's case with ministers on the basis of his striking at the Tower, he had embarked on the construction of a full-scale mint at Soho itself. By February 1788 Boulton was announcing to his son, 'I am building a Mint and new Manufacture for it in our Farm Yard behind the Menagery at Soho'; well out of sight of prying eyes.[116]

It was to prove an arduous, costly, almost cavalier, operation which quickly became a severe drain on his finances, rapidly absorbing the profits accruing from Watt's rotative steam engine and the revitalised button making company under John Scale. Almost six months were to pass before he had a single press working efficiently by steam and it was not to be for more than a further twelvemonth that he had a battery of four presses fully functional and capable of producing anything like the thousand tons of coin a year that he had boasted to Hawkesbury could be feasible by the New Year of 1789. Even the initial pattern halfpennies (with a disappointing guilloche-patterned edge rather than a lettered one) submitted to the Privy Council Committee on Coin in the spring of 1788 [79c] had to be struck by Droz on the press he had constructed in Paris 'there being no one in England capable of striking such'.[117]

> **COPPER.**
> The plan which is said to be determined upon, by Government will totally stop the circulation of counterfeit copper. Each halfpenny is to contain as much metal as is intrinsically of the value of one halfpenny, and the expence of coinage, &c. is to be defrayed by Government. Upon calculating the expence of coining them at the Tower, and comparing that calculation with what the Birmingham people offer to do them for, it is found that a most considerable saving will be made by employing these old practitioners in the art of making money. They are accordingly to be employed.

84   *The Times*, 20 October 1788.

116   BAH: MS 3782/12/6/40, Matthew Boulton to Samuel Garbett, 28 March 1787; BAH: MS 3782/13/36/19 Matthew Boulton to Matthew Robinson Boulton, 8 February 1788; CRO: AD/1583/2/47, Matthew Boulton to Thomas Wilson, 6 May 1787.

117   Dickinson (1937), 137, quoting Boulton's submission to the Committee on Coin, 28 May 1790.

THE GREAT CONTENTION

The Committee on Coin, comprising, as did most Council committees, an assortment of ministers and notables with a sprinkling of more expert figures, probably found its task too technical and dithered its way through most of 1788. As Sir John Craig put it, the Committee 'continued to brood'. If the *Times* [84] is to be believed, by the autumn it seems to have been coming down in favour of the Tower on grounds of cost but, even if this was so, such a conclusion was never carried into effect. For within a few days of the *Times* news item it was becoming apparent that the King was seriously ill and by early November he was showing every sign of being insane. The shock of the King's breakdown over the next four months and the political turmoil it precipitated – with the looming probability of the Prince of Wales becoming Regent and the very survival of Pitt's administration at stake – put any question of a recoinage out of court. And even when the King was restored to health and the political situation returned to some semblance of normality at the end of February 1789 the government's other, weightier, concerns and the Committee's own increasing involvement in what it saw as the more pressing problems of the gold and silver coinages, coupled with the strident opposition of the Mint to any effective reform under its malleable Master, Effingham [85], put an end to any early solution of the problem of the country's everyday currency.

There was, from time to time over the ensuing years, the occasional hint that the Committee might shortly come to some decision and Boulton's hopes of securing a national contract rose but as quickly fell again as the reports proved to be unfounded. And Boulton's repeated pleas for consideration received little response. While the King was still afflicted Boulton, worried of the consequences if Pitt's administration should fall, had set out his case both to Hawkesbury and directly to the Committee. Without the *deus ex machina* of a contract his coining adventure was becoming an almost unsupportable financial burden. As he confessed to Hawkesbury in January 1789:

85 Lord Effingham, Master of the Mint 1784-89. Memorial medal by John Milton, 1791.

> I cannot help turning my thoughts to the loss I am likely to sustain by the probability by the Copper Coinage falling to the ground: My primary Motive for taking that Matter up arose from a full persuasion, that I could put a final stop to the counterfeiting of Money, and to the retrieving the honor of that branch of the Mechanick Arts, but after I had put myself to a considerable expense (which was necessary even to make the Specimens which the right honourable the Lords of the Privy Council ordered me to do): It was natural that I should then calculate not only upon the repayment of that expense, but likewise upon the gaining a small profit, and for this purpose I have remounted my Rolling Mill and made it the best in England, I have built a Building in my Garden detached from all other buildings or Manufactories for the purpose of carrying on the Coinage, I have erected two Fire Engines for that purpose and have contrived and executed such new machinery as is sufficient to Coin Gold, Silver & Copper for half Europe, similar to the specimen for a French

Crown which I had the honor to present to your Lordship: I have made an engagement with M‍r Droz the Engraver upon terms that will fall very heavy upon me, but without which I could not have attained that degree of perfection I have aimed at: I have neglected my other Persuits in a great measure, and have already expended several thousand Pounds in making preparations to execute the Coinage upon such terms and in such a manner as to put an end to the evils and inconveniences resulting from counterfeiting, and such as there is little probability of being accomplished by any Other Person. [118]

Hawkesbury, though, much as he paraded his personal sympathies for Boulton's predicament, sought to distance himself from the latter's ambitions.[119] For the truth was that his monetary concerns ran far wider than the copper coinage and its problems held a lesser place in his mind than those of gold and silver. Moreover, although he was himself a member of the Committee on Coin and a moving spirit in its deliberations, he was in a 'very teizing situation' as Garbett put it, unable to secure a concerted view among its members. At the same time, while an increasingly powerful figure in matters of trade and perhaps the most competent administrator in the government, he still at this time exerted only a limited effect on Pitt and could not necessarily rely on the support of a prime minister who lacked rapport with him and was in any case occupied by more fundamental policy issues.[120]

There was a further, more immediate, and for Boulton, a more personally awkward, factor, however: the influence of Samuel Garbett. Hawkesbury had great respect for Garbett, valuing his wide-ranging knowledge of industry, foreign trade and exchange and his more general grasp of economic matters. Their views on the Mint and 'the general Principles of Coin', he acknowledged, were very much in tune.[121] Indeed Hawkesbury owed a great deal to Garbett's expertise in formulating his own ideas on the problems of the nation's currency and now Garbett began to voice to the minister his long-held disquiet over Boulton's grandiose coining schemes at Soho. In April 1790 he explained that, since his visit to Paris, Boulton, his friend 'for more than 30 years', had 'inadvertently embarked his Passions, & since then

---

118   BAH: MS 3782/12/34/13, Matthew Boulton to Lord Hawkesbury [Copy], 12 January 1789.

119   After the King's recovery in early 1789 Hawkesbury tried unsuccessfully to deflect Boulton's badgering by stressing that 'the Pressure of Public Business has been so great that it has been impossible to resume that of the Copper Coin, & tho' I may have some share in this Transaction, yet it properly belongs to the Lord President [Earl Camden], who is at the Head of the Committee appointed for that Purpose': BL: Additional MSS 38422, f. 35, Lord Hawkesbury to Matthew Boulton, 13 April 1789.

120   Ehrman (1996), 14; Gash (1984), 8-9.

121   BL: Additional MSS 38422, f. 48, Lord Hawkesbury to Samuel Garbett, 25 January 1790. As Hawkesbury later told the King Garbett was 'a principal manufacturer at Birmingham and a Person of most influence in that Town, he is an honest man, and very ingenious, but very active, punctilious, and a little apt to be troublesome; Lord H. would recommend therefore, that some general attention should be paid to him': BL: Additional MSS 38422, f. 236, Lord Hawkesbury to George III, 6 October 1794.

THE GREAT CONTENTION

his Property, I believe to the amount of near 10,000£, upon Plans very contrary to my declared opinion'. Boulton's situation had become 'pitiable' yet Garbett stressed he 'never did & do not now approve of the Measures my Friend has inconsiderately adopted'.[122]

Since the time of his Enquiry in 1782 Garbett had always taken the view that, even with the Mint conducted 'as a Trade' under the direction of 'Persons of Knowledge in the subject … & … experience in great works', coining should still be maintained at the Tower 'in the same Rooms by the same manufacturers [i.e. artificers] & under the Conduct & Inspection & Checks of the very same Persons as heretofore'.[123] With regard to the circulating currency he had two practical proposals. For the silver, as we have seen, an issue of shillings and sixpences at the reduced weight standard of 76s to the Troy pound on the basis of which when the earliest overtures were being made to Droz he had persuaded Boulton to commission dies for pattern shillings and sixpences from the Paris engraver [86].[124] And for the copper, a new coinage 'executed at the Mint as expeditiously as possible from dies of a superior engraving, with a milled foliage round the edge'.[125] There was no suggestion that the new coinages should be struck at any place other than the Tower or that the copper should depart from the notional Mint weight standard of 46 halfpennies to the lb. Boulton's erection of a 'Mint to coin the whole Copper Coinage at Birmingham' and his 'Coining Halfpence heavier than formerly & heavier than is done by other States' were thus 'upon Plans very contrary to my declared opinion'.[126] In the latter respect it seems that Garbett's concern was that a new heavier coinage would drive the existing copper – regal as well as counterfeit – out of circulation, creating shortages and intolerable confusion. It was an expression of the same apprehension that was to persuade a later Committee on Coin to accede initially only to the issue of twopenny and penny 'cartwheels' in 1797.

Boulton in his desperation had expressed the wish that the government would allow him 'to make a small beginning if it was for no other use than to prove by a regular course of work whither [*sic*] all my apparatus is perfect as well as to enable me to judge whether I shall stand in any need of M[r] Droz further assistance'. Such a suggestion of a limited trial coinage Garbett found very dangerous for

86   Matthew Boulton: Pattern sixpence engraved by Jean-Pierre Droz, 1788.

---

122   BL: Additional MSS 38422, ff. 116-117, Samuel Garbett to Lord Hawkesbury, 7 April 1790.

123   BL: Lansdowne B11 f. 188v and 187, Samuel Garbett to Lord Lansdowne, 16 April 1786 (BL: Landsdowne B11 ff. 186-188v).

124   The smaller but thicker versions of Droz's 'Britannia' sixpence, dated 1790 and 1791, were struck to the same 'Garbett' weight standard. The pattern shillings never seem to have been produced.

125   Garbett and Garbett (1837), 223.

126   BL: Additional MSS 38422, ff. 116-117, Samuel Garbett to Lord Hawkesbury, 7 April 1790. Although in the latter respect the Mint itself had set a new standard of 24 to the lb with its patterns by Pingo [79b].

whenever it is known that Government is determined to suppress a <u>Part</u>, or, the <u>Whole</u> of the present Coin or, <u>That</u>, the public by any means <u>know with certainty</u> the determination of Government, great confusion & distress will be produced if <u>extreme caution</u> is not taken to secure to poor People a ready unquestionable Medium for their Marketings. I look upon this as a dreadful Circumstance, for the Transactions by the Medium of Copper Coin are prodigiously more numerous than <u>all other</u> Transactions in Coin, & most of them among a set of people who have no other means of daily obtaining the necessaries of Life.[127]

Garbett was in a cleft stick, his loyalty to Boulton compromised by the latter's typically headlong sally into an enthusiasm which he could not endorse and with which he did not wish to be publicly associated. But Boulton was now too far committed, and aware as he was of Garbett's reservations, he had little option except to retreat totally from coining at far greater cost than his earlier withdrawals from ormolu and mechanical paintings or to persevere in his efforts to convince the authorities of his suitability to manage a coinage contract. Although toying with the idea of selling his mint to the French he chose the latter course, continuing to spend 'much midnight oyl' in bringing the 'art of Coining' to a 'ne plus Ultra degree of perfection' with the ever-present fear 'of having his very ingenious Contrivances exposed' by the wayward Droz and other disaffected staff who though he paid them 'large Wages ... knowing that he has expended so much money on this Subject' treated him 'as being in their Power'; 'artists & workmen' who would 'be eagerly taken by our Birmingham Coiners, under the Idea of possessing themselves of my inventions, & rivaling [sic] me in the favour of Government'.[128] Garbett continually urged him to 'secure his secret' by taking out a patent. This he eventually did in July 1790 and, determined to maintain his coining plant, Boulton hunted around for private contracts to keep his staff employed and find ways of recovering at least some of the vast sums he had committed to his mint.[129]

Thomas Williams, in the meantime, with far less to lose, had already begun to appreciate that the government's equivocal attitude with its sensitivity to the Mint's pretensions was calculated to lead to nothing in the foreseeable future; a belief strengthened by the constitutional crisis brought about by the king's illness. Nearer to home, too, Williams was also struggling with delays and production problems at

127 BL: Additional MSS 38422, ff. 116-117, Samuel Garbett to Lord Hawkesbury, 7 April 1790; and f. 119, Matthew Boulton to Samuel Garbett, 29 March 1790 (BAH: MS 3782/12/62/83).

128 BAH: MS 3782/12/44/385, Matthew Boulton to Joseph Cotton [Draft], 25 November 1799; BL: Additional MSS 38422, ff. 116-117, Samuel Garbett to Lord Hawkesbury, 7 April 1790.

129 BL: Additional MSS 38422, ff.116-117, Samuel Garbett to Lord Hawkesbury, 7 April 1790; Patent Specification 1757, 8 July 1790: Woodcroft (1854) [1969], 59: 'Application of the powers of water-mills, cattle-mills, and steam engines, either simply or combined with the pressure of the atmosphere, and with weights and springs to the working of fly-presses or stamps'.

his Birmingham plant exacerbated by the demand for halfpenny tokens that he was finding were more expensive and troublesome to strike than the pennies he had originally embarked upon.[130] Increasingly secure in his dominance of the copper market following his virtual take-over of the Cornish Metal Company in November 1787 Williams was moreover confident that whatever agency was ultimately charged with the production of a regal coinage it would have to depend on his sources of metal supply, which in the interim the evident demand for tokens would also help to absorb. In the latter months of 1788 he gradually came to the conclusion that he should cut loose from an enterprise that for him was a needless expenditure and give up the manufacture of tokens. And, as things turned out, the whole undertaking, minting machinery and all was abandoned to Boulton.

It is not clear where the initiative lay, whether with Williams or with Boulton on hearing talk that the former's interest in coining was waning, but by March 1789 an agreement had been reached by which Williams's machinery should be transferred to Boulton on the understanding that Williams 'would give me all his Coinage & relinquish all opposition to me in the Governm^t Coinage'.[131] Boulton had little use for Williams's traditional presses, which were to him not worth 'more than so much old Iron' ... 'not in any degree applicable to my improved mode of Coining' but, as he stressed to Thomas Wilson he 'thought it prudent to Clip his Wings & to disarm him'. With a view to limiting his expenditure Boulton tried to unload them on Westwood, who, in concert with Hancock, was about to embark on large-scale coining himself. Westwood's forthright response was that the equipment he had himself used to produce the most elegant of coinage comprised 'the worst presses he ever saw' and that 'he could get new Presses twice as good at half the price'.[132]

The ostensible advantage of the deal to Boulton was the elimination of his rival from the contest for a national coinage contract. Williams, though, was to be a thorn in Boulton's flesh for years, both through his manipulation of the copper market and because of apprehensions that he was breaking the agreement by setting up a clandestine mint in London on Boulton's 'patent principles' – the source, maybe, of the Anglesey tokens attributed by Pye to William Williams of St. Martin's Lane.[133] It was obviously impossible, as Boulton had pontificated some

---

130   Vice (1989), 3.

131   CRO: AD 1583/4/116, Matthew Boulton to Thomas Wilson, 12 December 1791.

132   CRO: AD 1583/3/13, Matthew Boulton to Thomas Wilson, 10 March 1788; BAH: MSS 3782/12/8/3 and 3782/12/8/4, Matthew Boulton to Thomas Williams, 10 [?] May 1789 and 24 May 1789.

133   CRO: AD1583/4/116, Matthew Boulton to Thomas Wilson, 12 December 1791; Pye (1801), [5]: Plate II, 3 and 4. According to Pye the dies of these tokens (*D&H*: Anglesey 252, 385 and 398-410) were engraved by 'Wilson'. This was the London engraver William Wilson, an erstwhile Soho apprentice and journeyman die-sinker, who Boulton tried unsuccessfully to coax back to Soho as a replacement for Droz in March 1790. Cf. Quickenden (1995), 356 and Quickenden (2007), 56-57.

years before, 'for the Ethiopian to change his skin or the Leopard his spots'.[134] The practical and immediate effect of the agreement, however, was to propel Boulton into the manufacture of tokens which he had hitherto shunned partly because of his fear that their increasing public acceptance would persuade a prevaricating government into yet further delays over a national coinage but also because of his inability to execute large-scale private contracts on the coining equipment he had available. Now with his steam-driven presses coming on line he could take over the striking of Williams's 'Druids', cope with any outstanding commitment the latter had to Wilkinson and seek out private coinage contracts both at home and abroad.

Boulton was to take a personal interest in such commissions both in terms of production and design for they were to be a lifeline since a national coinage contract remained as remote as ever.[135] Yet his attitude to British tokens remained as equivocal as ever depending on who was manufacturing them and who he was addressing. Even as late as April 1789, having heard that John Westwood had won a contract from Roe and Company for halfpennies for its English concerns and for its associated mining company in Ireland, he could protest to Lord Hawkesbury

> I have just learnt from the parties themselves that the Macclesfield Copper Cº. after the example of the Anglesey Cº. and others have [sic] made a beginning of 40 Ton which are to be called Macclesfield halfpence. The said Compy also are going to coin a quantity for Ireland wth. St. patricks head on one side [the Cronebane pieces].
>
> I have reason to believe these examples will be followed by others, unless the growing mischief is put a stop to by the hand of power.[136]

87 Matthew Boulton's Medallic Scale Medal, 1803. Probably engraved by Conrad Heinrich Küchler (obverse) and Rambert Dumarest (reverse), Boulton's Medallic Scale Medal was produced for a French audience to counter claims made by Droz that he and not Boulton had been responsible for the coining improvements at Soho. Each reverse concentric ring represents the diameter of a coin and indicates the number that could be struck in one minute by eight children operating eight coining presses 'SANS FATIG[UE]'.

134 BAH: MS 3782/12/73/14, Matthew Boulton to John Vivian, 18 April 1787. It has to be said that many of Boulton's own actions were hardly creditable and, to be fair to Williams, Boulton was attempting to plead for a reduction in copper prices to cover his losses on purposely low coinage tenders intended to lead to more lucrative contracts: Harris (1964), 101.

135 Boulton's personal involvement and experimentation in his coining processes is illustrated by his comment to his friend Charles Dumergue, the royal family's dental surgeon, that he had hardened and tempered a die 'with my own hand': BAH: MS 3782/12/36, Matthew Boulton to Charles Dumergue, 10 August 1791.

136 BAH: MS 3782/12/34/64, Matthew Boulton to Lord Hawkesbury, 14 April 1789.

III

A MOST SATISFYING ADVENTURE

> Of all the mechanical subjects I ever entered upon there is none in which I ever engaged with so much ardour as that of bringing to perfection the art of coining in the reign of George III.
>
> Matthew Boulton to Samuel Garbett.[1]

> [H]ad Mr B. done nothing more in the world than what he has done in improving the coinage, his fame would have deserved to be immortalized, & if it is considered that this was done in the midst of various other important avocations, & at an enormous expense for which he could have no certainty of an adequate return, we shall be at a loss whether to admire most his ingenuity, his perseverance or his munificence.
>
> *Memoir of Matthew Boulton by James Watt* (1809).[2]

Although by the spring of 1789 Matthew Boulton might have hoped that he had removed Thomas Williams as a coining rival he was still left with a fledging mint, massive debts and an under-employed workforce. The prospect of a national coinage contract seemed more distant than ever but his complex deal with Williams at least gave him the expectation of some relief with the production of 'Druids' for the Parys Mines even if this meant his changing tack over provincial coinage and venturing into a territory to which his attitude in the past had been ambivalent if not hostile. In the event it was to be the autumn before Boulton could start striking Anglesey tokens, for Wyatt, only too aware that there was no place for him in the new regime, had hampered the dismantling of the Great Charles Street mint while Hancock had dragged out the production of new 'Druid' dies that for some reason were deemed necessary.[3]

In the meantime some comfort came from an unexpected source even if as things turned out it was to be a mixed blessing. In March 1789 John Westwood, about to embark on coining on his own account, had been commissioned by the Macclesfield Copper Company (Charles Roe and Company) to produce halfpennies for its works in Cheshire (Macclesfield and Congleton) and Liverpool and for

---

1   Quoted in Smiles (1865), 393.
2   Watt (1809) [1943], 9.
3   This was the gloss that Williams put on the delays in completing the transfer of the minting equipment to Boulton.

88 Matthew Boulton: Cronebane halfpenny for the Associated Irish Mine Company, 1789.

89 Westwood/Hancock: Macclesfield halfpenny for Roe and Company, 1789.

its associated mining concern at Cronebane in County Wicklow.[4] Westwood, however, was not yet geared up to strike tokens and in his embarrassment he turned to Boulton for help. Boulton agreed to act as Westwood's sub-contracting manufacturer or 'journeyman … a meer striker of Blanks' (as he described himself to Thomas Williams) from ready-milled and edged flans provided by Westwood and dies engraved by Hancock. It was an arrangement that Boulton justified as being undertaken 'out of regard' for Westwood, a man he thoroughly despised, but then the master of Soho was often economical with the truth when he thought a profitable commission was in the offing or verity about his finances had to be obfuscated.[5]

Although it seems that Roe and Company had wanted priority to be given to their Macclesfield halfpennies, problems in the production of the dies meant that the Cronebane issue was finished first. Hancock apparently charged three guineas a pair for the dies which depicted St. Patrick's mitred head on the obverse and the mine company arms on the reverse [88].[6] By the beginning of September 1789 Boulton had produced something over twenty tons of tokens for the Wicklow mine on a standard of 36 to the pound of copper (over 1.6 million halfpennies), the first coins struck from a steam-operated press but without a collar and from Westwood's traditionally edged blanks; what Richard Doty has called a 'hybrid' issue 'reflecting at once the technology of the past and the future'.[7] The Wicklow halfpennies were quickly circulating in Ireland [8] but the overall contract with Roe and Company was not to be completed at Soho. Difficulties with the Cheshire firm over the payment of the coinage bills and contractual complications arising from the financial failure of Westwood in December 1789 brought Soho's coining for the company to an abrupt stoppage and its abandonment of the manufacture of the projected Macclesfield halfpennies. Hancock had not yet been able to complete the dies for these tokens and rumour has it that Roe and Company redirected its Macclesfield commission to a coining firm in London.

If this story was true – and it was credited to John Hurd, Boulton's partner in a Birmingham copper warehouse and a major creditor of Westwood, who was in a position to know – it must relate to the Macclesfield 'Beehive' type tokens also dated 1789 [89]. The difficulty with the story is that Charles Pye in the 1801 edition of his *Provincial Coins and Tokens* attributed the die-sinking and production of the

4 For Boulton's involvement in the manufacture of the Cronebane tokens see Vice (1991a), 2-6, an essential study of the documentary evidence on which this and the following two paragraphs are based.

5 BAH: MS 3782/12/8/4, Matthew Boulton to Thomas Williams, 24 May 1789. For Boulton's ready business dissimulation both towards his partners and in regard to his products see Quickenden (1989), *passim*.

6 Vice (1991a), 6, note 9. The currency versions of the Cronebane halfpenny are listed by *D&H* as Wicklow 3-17 and 19-31.

7 Doty (1998a), 303.

8 *GM*, September 1789, 822 and Plate 3.

A MOST SATISFYING ADVENTURE

'Beehives' to Hancock, presumably on the latter's say-so and, as we will see later, this would point to their manufacture by Westwood. Westwood had from the start been the primary contractor to Roe and Company and, despite his bankruptcy, presumably remained so since he was to go on to produce the 'Charles Roe' portrait halfpennies for the Macclesfield company in 1790-92. The likely scenario, therefore, which would reconcile the apparent discrepancy between Hurd's and Pye's testimony, was that, since Westwood still did not yet have the presses to complete the 'Beehive' commission himself, he sub-contracted the actual striking of his own prepared blanks to a London coiner (perhaps William Williams) just as he had been obliged to do with Boulton. What we can be positive about is that the 'Beehive' halfpennies were not struck at Soho; unlike the Cronebane halfpennies they were never included in the 'collectors' sets of Soho provincial coins that Boulton produced in the 1790s or listed in the mint's later promotional literature and such evidence as has been adduced to suggest a Soho origin does not bear that conclusion.[9]

More problematical is the number of 'Beehive' tokens that were struck. Pye stated that this was one ton. From the evidence of the tokens this must again have been at a standard of 36 to the pound, but the 80,500 pieces Pye's reckoning suggests must be an underestimate. The token is relatively common and the number of dies listed by Dalton and Hamer implies a much larger issue than Pye would have us believe. Some recent commentators have suggested a mintage as high as 21 tons on the basis of a comment Boulton made to Samuel Garbett in March 1790: 'The Macclesfield Co have lately ordered of J. Westwood an addition of 25 Tons to the 21 tons lately issued by them (36 to ye lb) and those of the last order have the Head of old Roe upon them'.[10] It is, however, a bold step to conclude from this remark that Boulton was referring to the 'Beehives' rather than the Cronebane halfpennies he had himself struck in such a measure the summer before. While Pye may have been misinformed or he or his printer may have nodded one cannot conceive that the 'Beehive' production, large as it might have been, was anywhere as extensive as the Cronebanes or its successor with the 'Head of old Roe'.

What one can say is that Hancock's dies with the Roe family armorial device and company monogram as its obverse and the Genius of Industry as its reverse – based on Roe's memorial in Christ Church, Macclesfield [90] but modified to reflect the Britannia of the regal coinage – resulted in a coin of some elegance. Perhaps it was this Macclesfield token that along with an Anglesey halfpenny John Byng, morosely fleeing Buxton for the day on 11 June 1790 – 'a most uncomfortable, dreary place' he had decided – was 'surprised

90   Charles Roe's Monument in Christ Church, Macclesfield.

---

9   Dr. Doty's argument that the 'Beehive' halfpennies were struck by Boulton, based on a hazy account of a decade after the event, cannot be sustained: Doty (1998a), 302. Cf. Vice (1997), 42.

10 BAH: MS 3782/12/62/83, Matthew Boulton to Samuel Garbett, 29 March 1790. Cf. Vice (1997), 42.

to receive in change' at the Fairfield turnpike: they were 'a better coinage and of more beauty than that of the mint, and not so likely to be counterfeited'. So impressed was the normally dyspeptic Byng with the Macclesfield halfpenny that when he reached the town he sent to the copper works for sixpenny worth of the firm's 'new' coinage (presumably the portrait tokens) 'of much better make and value than Government can afford'.[11] For all Byng's confidence both the Macclesfield halfpennies – that he noted reached 'far and wide' – and those of Anglesey were heavily counterfeited, as were all the early industrial tokens that achieved a general circulation, although the 'Beehives' seem to have appealed less to the forger than either the Cronebanes or their sister portrait issues.

As the Cronebane contract came to a halt in early September 1789 Boulton at last received the necessary Anglesey dies from Hancock and the edged blanks from Wyatt at the Anglesey warehouse and began to strike halfpennies for Thomas Williams. Something in the region of 900,000 tokens dated 1789 were struck during the autumn and winter, two-thirds of them at 32 to the lb and the remainder at the lighter rate of 35 to the lb, all without a collar. As David Vice has pointed out the task of identifying which of these are the products of Soho as opposed to Wyatt's mint is one fraught with difficulty but he has suggested that Dalton and Hamer's Anglesey 357 to 364 are the most likely to be Soho productions.[12] In later days Boulton never publicly recognised them or the small quantity of halfpennies he struck for John Wilkinson at the close of the year from the residual 'Willey' blanks in the Anglesey warehouse and which, presumably dated 1788 since there are no '1789' Wilkinson halfpennies, cannot be distinguished from the tokens hitherto produced by Thomas Williams unless they are, but rather improbably, the 'Ship' halfpennies attributed to Boulton by Pye [73].[13]

In the spring of 1790 Thomas Williams ordered a further supply of halfpence from Boulton. Droz was to have been contracted to prepare the dies in a private arrangement but the project came to nothing and the task was given to the Parisian engraver Rambert Dumarest whom Boulton was enticing to Soho as Droz's replacement. Eventually, after months of disagreement with Williams – who complained at one point that the druid's beard on one of Dumarest's trials (*D&H*: Anglesey 380) resembled 'a run of Waters more [than] a man's beard' – Dumarest completed new dies adapted from those of Hancock for the Anglesey

---

11 Andrews (1934-38), II (1935), 167 and 171. It may, of course, have been a portrait halfpenny that Byng was passed at the Fairfield turnpike.
Two years later (27 June 1792) Byng returned to the copper works where he took 'an accurate, and gratifying survey, of their mixing, melting and flat'ning the copper; a most unwholesome employ, for which the workmen, I think, are meanly pay'd, as the best earn but 14s. per week': Andrews (1934-38), III (1936), 122.

12 Vice (1989), 5 and 8.

13 If Pye's attribution to Boulton is correct the 'Ship' halfpennies could hardly have been produced as early as 1788 their declared date. They, like the silver 'ship' pieces, were almost certainly struck by Williams.

A MOST SATISFYING ADVENTURE

91 Matthew Boulton: East India Company 2 pice piece for the Bombay settlement, 1791.

halfpence struck at Soho in 1789 and some sixteen tons of Anglesey tokens were struck in 1791 (*D&H*: Anglesey 386-391) alongside halfpennies for Taylor, Moody and Company of Southampton. With these tokens Soho was bringing coinage into a new era for not only were its coining presses operated by steam the tokens were at last struck with the collar/ejecting mechanism that Boulton had been attempting to perfect since his involvement with Droz: modern-looking coinage with a sharp vertical edge had at last made its appearance. [14]

By September the order had been completed but it was not to be the last Soho commission for Williams. One of the components of the batch of left-over blanks made over to Boulton with the closure of the Charles Street mint in 1789 had been some 19 cwt for Anglesey pennies. These seem to have been neglected until the autumn of 1791 when Williams apparently decided to have them struck. The resulting pennies (*D&H*: Anglesey 255), struck from an adapted Hancock obverse die but married to a new reverse (dated 1791), were completed at a standard of 16 to the lb by the July of 1792. This brought Boulton's involvement in the production of Anglesey tokens to a close. But Williams remained a trial and continued to take a perverse delight in provoking Boulton, both, as we have seen, in the comparatively trifling matter of striking Anglesey tokens in London and much more seriously over the supply of copper which he had monopolised since the collapse of the Cornish Metal Company.

As the prospect of a contract for a regal coinage seemed as far away as ever Boulton searched around for overseas contracts, from the nascent United States and even, through his old friend Motteux and one time European agent, from revolutionary France and as these schemes fell by the wayside he even contemplated selling off his 'coining mill with all its appurtenances' to the French government.[15] Then, as things seemed at their blackest, Boulton was suddenly presented with the opportunity of another East India contract, this time of coppers for the Company's Bombay Presidency. What seemed at first to be a frustratingly small commission soon expanded into something very much bigger – a hundred tons of coins – but there was a snag. The Company was committed to Williams for the supply of a metal now in short supply and, in Boulton's eyes, he proved to be deliberately obstructive when he discovered that Soho had been awarded the coining contract. Eventually accommodation was reached with Williams and by December 1791 – in just over nine months – Boulton had struck over 17 million coins for Bombay in a variety of denominations from half-pice to half-anna [91].

14 Thomas Williams to Matthew Boulton, 31 October 1790 quoted in Hawker (1996), 32; Vice (1989), 6-7.

15 Matthew Boulton to Francis Swediaur, 7 February 1791, quoted in Doty (1998a), 45-46. Two years later Boulton even seems to have been thinking of disposing of his equipment to the United States: LC: Thomas Jefferson Papers, Th[omas] A[ttwood] Digges to Thomas Jefferson, 10 March 1793 and Digges to Thomas Pinckney, 6 April 1793. See also Elias and Finch (1982), 444 and 453.

119

92 Matthew Boulton: *cinq-sols médaille de confiance* for Monneron Frères, 1792.

It was a remarkable achievement not less so for the autumn of 1791 saw Boulton tackling several other overseas commissions. One, secured by Francis Swediaur who had acted as Boulton's clandestine go-between with the French government,[16] was for a series of weighty two- and five-sol tokens for the Parisian merchants Monneron Frères. This was a risky venture, vitiated initially by Williams's obstructive behaviour, and almost undone by the strain put upon Boulton's presses to cope with the force required to strike the massive five-sol pieces. The scheme, too, had no official endorsement but it was anticipated by the Monnerons that the tokens with their appropriately 'revolutionary' designs – the five-sol pieces were characterised by an obverse ellipse depicting the patriotic *Fête de la Fédération* adapted from Augustin Dupré's extremely popular medal for the occasion [92] – would be well-received in a country desperately short of a small-denomination currency. This seems to have been borne out by their ready circulation in Paris and other large cities and between October 1791 and August 1792 over seven million *monnerons* were produced and shipped over to France. But on 3 September 1792, in the midst of the political upheavals of that summer, the National Assembly banned the importation and issue of private tokens and the Monneron episode came to an untimely end. It was perhaps fortunate for Boulton's nascent machinery that it did but it proved to be a costly enterprise with unused copper having to be sold at a loss and redundant *monnerons* having to be recalled.[17]

Two colonial orders followed towards the end of 1792, one for silver dollars and copper pennies for the Sierra Leone Company, a trading venture in which Boulton was a shareholder, and the other for coppers for Bermuda. Although these were small commissions, overall 1791/92 proved to be a busy year for the Soho mint for Boulton had also now reconciled himself to the manufacture of provincial coins and had actively set about seeking contracts in this area (See **Table 1**). In the early summer of 1789 John Westwood had secured an order for provincial halfpennies from Walter Taylor, a Southampton ships' blockmaker and a major naval contractor with brewery interests [93], but the former's bankruptcy scotched the scheme, at any rate for a while, and by the time Westwood tried to renew it three months

93 Walter Taylor (1734-1803) holding the improved circular saw which he and his father had invented.

16 Francis Swediaur [*recte* Franz Xavier Schwediauer] (1748-1824) was an Austrian physician and chemist, an ardent revolutionary well-known in Parisian circles and a close friend of Danton. He was very much a 'cloak and dagger' individual who adopted the confusing expedient of writing in invisible ink in some of his correspondence with Boulton. Until they eventually quarrelled Swediaur was a useful European middleman for Boulton and was instrumental in securing the services of Noël-Alexandre Ponthon for Soho later in the year.

17 For the Monneron episode see Margolis (1988), 102-109; Doty (1998a), 308; Jones (2004), 187-203. See also Jones (1977), 8-9 for Dupré's medal.
It was not Boulton's only flirtation with Revolutionary France for he would go on to produces large quantities of buttons for the National Guard and cheap medalets depicting heroes of the Revolution for the Monnerons. He hedged his bets, however, by manufacturing *Fleur de Lys* buttons for the future Louis XVIII.

A MOST SATISFYING ADVENTURE

Table 1
Matthew Boulton's Provincial Coin Contracts

Date Struck	Issuer	Place of Issue	Approximate Quantity Struck	Pye Reference	D&H Reference[a]
1789	Associated Irish Mine Company	Cronebane and Dublin	20+ ton	——	Wicklow 3-31
1789-92	Parys Mine Company	Anglesey, London and Liverpool	30 ton (½d) 1 ton (1d)	Plate 3, 7 Plate 2, 5	Anglesey 357-364, 386-391 Anglesey 255
1790-95	John Wilkinson[b]	Willey, Snedshill, Bersham and Bradley	8+ ton	Plate 48, 7	War. 387-389, 393-394 and 420-421
1791	Cornish Metal Company	Truro	1+ ton	Plate 15, 2	Cornwall 2
1791	Gilbert Shearer & Company	Glasgow	6+ ton	Plate 21, 4	Lanarkshire 2
1791-92	Taylor, Moody & Company	Southampton	2+ ton	Plate 45, 2	Hants 89
1793	Henry Brownbill	Leeds	2+ ton	Plate 26, 3	Yorks. 30-41
1793-96	Mackintosh, Inglis & Wilson	Inverness	4+ ton	Plate 24, 1-2	Inverness 1-4
1794	Daniel Eccleston	Lancaster	1+ ton	Plate 26, 1	Lancs. 57-58
1795	Isaac Swainson	London	A few specimens	Plate 34, 10	Middx 907
1795	Christopher Ibberson	London	A few specimens	Plate 31, 1-2	Middx 339-42
1795	George Cotton	Hornchurch	2 cwt	Plate 23, 3	Essex 33-34
1795-96	William Croom	Dundee	10+ cwt	Plate 16, 10	Angus 12-13
1796	George Chapman George	Penryn	2+ cwt	Plate 41, 1	Cornwall 4
1796	Sir George Jackson	Bishop's Stortford	5 cwt	Plate 9, 5	Herts. 4
1801	Robert Woodcock	Enniscorthy	5+ ton	——	Wexford 1-4
1802	Davison & Hawksley	Arnold	4+ cwt	——	Notts. 1-4
1803-4	Viscount Charleville	Tullamore	4+ cwt	——	King's County 1-4

a The *D&H* references given here exclude trial pieces, patterns and proofs.

b Wilkinson's 'Ship' halfpence [Pye (1801), plate 48, 6; *D&H*: War. 336] have been excluded on the assumption that they were struck by Thomas Williams.

later, submitting specimen halfpennies engraved by Hancock [94], Walter Taylor had been persuaded by Boulton that Soho was on the brink of securing a regal coinage contract. Boulton's confidence was misplaced but he had succeeded in steering Taylor, an old business acquaintance, and Taylor's co-partner in the brewery concern, a local banker, Richard Vernon Moody, away from Westwood.[18] And a year

94 Westwood/Hancock: Southampton halfpenny for Taylor, Moody and Company, 1790: the pseudo-heraldic reverse reflecting the brewing and naval contracting interests of Walter Taylor and Richard Moody.

18 For Taylor, an inveterate inventor not only of improvements to ships' pulley blocks but also to pumps and baling equipment and an early proponent of high quality mass production (Woodcroft (1854) [1969], 561), see Pannell (1967), 51-72. Moody, mayor of Southampton in 1782, was a partner in the banking concern of Sadleir & Co. until his death in 1792: Dawes and Ward-Perkins (2000), II, 537-38.

COINAGE AND CURRENCY IN EIGHTEENTH-CENTURY BRITAIN

96   Boulton's suggestion of a silver token for Walter Taylor. Detail from a press copy of a letter from Matthew Boulton to Walter Taylor, 24 December 1789.

95   Matthew Boulton: Silver proof Southampton halfpenny for Taylor, Moody and Company, 1791.

later, when it had become abundantly clear that a government contract remained a chimera, Boulton had filched the Southampton project for himself. It was to be some months before Taylor and Moody saw their new tokens partly because of Boulton's involvement with his existing contracts and the indifferent health of Rambert Dumarest, the engraver charged with making the Southampton dies. The new tokens [95] differed from Westwood's in that the head of 'Sir' Bevois – now correctly knighted rather than canonised as he had been by Hancock – faced right not left and the pseudo-heraldic reverse of the earlier pieces had been replaced with a crowned Lancastrian rose, the traditional emblem of Hampshire. In all something approaching two hundred thousand halfpennies had been produced from one set of dies when the contract was completed in August 1792.[19] A hundred and more of these were presentation pieces struck in silver which interestingly calls to mind that in December 1789 when the subject of a Soho coinage for Southampton was being first broached Taylor had raised the possibility of a silver currency issue. The project came to nothing but Boulton did go so far as to design a prototype, discreetly marked '*90* Grains [5.83g] STANDA[d] Silver' [96]. No denominational

19   As with so many of Boulton's commissions the Southampton contract was dogged with problems. The initial batch of tokens when received by Taylor was found to be 'tarnished, nicked and scratched' and Taylor threatened to cancel the remainder of his order. Boulton assuaged Taylor, taking the offending tokens back, cleaning them and supplying complimentary specimens at his own cost. Even so a few of the tokens [*D&H*: Hants 89a] were struck on edged blanks intended for Anglesey pieces that were being struck on an adjacent press. For the Southampton token commission see Doty (1997a), 16-24.

122

A MOST SATISFYING ADVENTURE

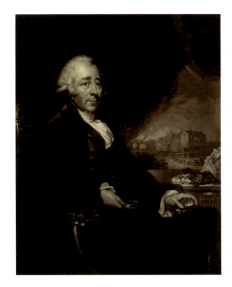

97 Mezzotint of Matthew Boulton after Carl von Breda, 1796. Boulton is portrayed as a gentleman connoisseur examining a medal, with minerals at his side and the Soho manufactory in the guise of a splendid country house in the background. The original portrait was painted in 1792.

value was expressed but the piece was presumably intended to pass for a shilling token at a weight slightly below the norm of 93 grains (6.03 g) for the regal coinage but a little more than the 87 grains of the reformed coinage of 1816.[20] Clearly Boulton's intention had been to produce something that would survive the speculator's melting pot without suffering public reproach.

But to return to the coppers for Southampton. Boulton was pleased with this first sortie into the manufacture of provincial coinage on his own account; he was no longer acting as the instrument of others but striking from his own blanks and from dies cut by his own engraver. And as the first specimens came off the presses he could boast to Taylor that 'Your Money will be the best Copper Coin that ever was made in this or any other Country the dies being very much to my satisfaction'. Boulton had taken full personal charge of his nascent mint and was determined that with so much hanging on a regal contract his private ventures into coining should brook no public criticism and that his tokens should capture the elegance and finish of the ormolu and silverware which graced the drawing rooms of notables throughout Europe. Dies were hardened and tempered 'with my own hand'.[21]

Agents were charged with seeking out the best engravers to satisfy his artistic instincts. Swediaur in Paris was instrumental in securing the unhappy Dumarest's successor, Ponthon, and well before the latter had left direct employment at Soho in 1795 Richard Chippindall – Boulton's long-suffering London agent who had failed to entice the engraver William Wilson [22] back to Soho in 1790 – had found Conrad Heinrich Küchler, a German refugee from the upheavals on the Continent. In the meantime Raspe [98], the ne'er-do-well German savant and anonymous author of *The Travels of Baron Munchausen*, who had attached himself to Boulton in Cornwall as Assay Master of the Cornish Metal Company, scoured the British Isles and the Continent although most of his prizes, the Irishman William Mossop, the Swedes Lars Grandel and Carl Enhörning, and Guillobé, a diffident amateur artist discovered in Edinburgh, among others, could not be tempted

98 Rudolph Erich Raspe (1737-94). Portrait Medallion by James Tassie, 1784.

20 And appreciably weightier than the standard of seventy-six sixpences to the troy pound proposed by Samuel Garbett: BAH: MS 3782/12/8/31, Matthew Boulton to Walter Taylor, 24 December 1789.

21 BAH: MS 3782/12/36, Matthew Boulton to Charles Dumergue, 19 August 1791.

22 History has treated William Wilson unfairly, Doty (1998a), 41, describing him as 'one of the most inept die-sinkers then working in the metropolis'. Boulton, however, regarded his former apprentice and chaser 'as an honest Man and a good engraver' although he was 'a bad Moddeler & not a good draughtsman': Matthew Boulton to R. E. Raspe, 30 March 1791 quoted in Hawker (1996), 37. He obviously had some faith in Wilson for he tried to re-engage him on at least two occasions; as he told Chippindall 'I had rather have an Englishman I know': Matthew Boulton to Richard Chippindall, 26 March 1790 quoted in Hawker (1996), 27.

123

99 Matthew Boulton: halfpenny for the Cornish Metal Company, 1791.

to Soho. He did score, however, with the modeller George Parbury [23] and with his greatest success of all, the Swedish painter Carl Fredrik von Breda, whose popularity as a portraitist in Britain owed much to Boulton and the Lunar circle and who provided Boulton with prototype drawings for some of Küchler's medals. Through Raspe's good offices a number of gifted artists and scholars came to Soho for a time and if only one or two made any impact on Boulton's business activities, others like Adam Afzelius, the distinguished Swedish botanist (and ally of Raspe in the search for Scandinavian engravers), added fulsomely to the reputation of Soho House, Boulton's self-styled *hôtel de l'amitié sur Handsworth Heath*, becoming a popular guest of the Lunar Society.[24] Raspe, too, through his association with James Tassie, supplied Boulton with casts of antique gems and medals and schemed to unite Tassie's artistry and Boulton's technical skill under his own numismatic direction. Perhaps if Boulton had trusted the German adventurer more the Soho mint might have reached even greater artistic heights than it did.[25]

Nevertheless, the Soho mint was about to enter its halcyon period in terms of token-making and under Boulton's meticulous stewardship his engravers produced some remarkable examples of provincial coinage, all of substantial weight and exceptional design. Dumarest, in the eleven months he was at Soho, engraved the dies for the Southampton tokens and halfpennies for Cornwall and Glasgow.[26] The Cornish tokens [99], struck for the Cornish Metal Company although they do not admit this origin, had been ordered by John Vivian [100], the ill-fated cartel's Deputy Governor.[27] Initially, a commission of 100 tons had tentatively been in Vivian's mind but in the event only a ton or so were struck for the days of the Cornish company were already numbered by the time that the first tokens had been delivered late in1791. The obverse of a druid's head was modelled by Dumarest on his rejected trial for Thomas Williams while the reverse depicted the traditional heraldic shield of Cornwall surmounted by a ducal coronet. Vivian's suggested reverse was simplified – to his own satisfaction – by omitting his proposed wreath and what he described as the 'foolish' Cornish motto of **ONE AND ALL** which he felt on reflection crowded the piece [101].[28]

100 John Vivian (d.1826).

23 Parbury modelled the figures of Liberty for the Monneron two-sol piece and the Sierra Leone lion: Gould (1972), 366, note 37. For Parbury, a metal-chaser as well as a modeller and portraitist in wax and clay, see the brief entry in Gunnis (1968), 290.

24 BAH: MS 3219/4/1, Matthew Boulton to James Watt, 7 February 1769.

25 For Raspe see Carswell (1950) and *ODNB*.

26 For transcriptions – not always strictly accurate – of Boulton's correspondence concerning these tokens see Hawker (1988) and (1989). Cf. also Doty (1997b), 11-19 and (1998b), 12-17.

27 John Vivian, a Cornish mine adventurer and Truro banker, had been instrumental in founding the Cornish Metal Company. He later moved into smelting and, establishing copper works in Swansea in 1809, became the second largest producer of copper in Britain.

28 John Vivian to Matthew Boulton, 10 May 1791 quoted in Hawker (1988), 227.

A MOST SATISFYING ADVENTURE

101 Vivian's original proposal for the reverse of the Cornish Halfpenny.

From start to finish the Cornish commission extended over the best part of two years. Delays were endemic in all Boulton's coinage projects, partly because he overextended himself – while the Cornish contract was in hand Boulton was also battling with his orders for Anglesey, the East India Company and Southampton – and partly because of the temperamental perfection of his die-sinkers. While Dumarest was struggling with the dies for the Cornish Metal Company's halfpenny he was working on another token, this time for Glasgow to be put out by the woollen and linen drapery business of Gilbert Shearer and Company of 19 Trongate [102/103].

102 Matthew Boulton: Glasgow halfpenny for Gilbert Shearer and Company, 1791.

103 The Trongate, Glasgow, in 1774. Gilbert Shearer's drapery business is said to have occupied the nearest of the low buildings adjacent to the Tron Church on the right of the sketch. Its projecting sign of a fleece can be dimly discerned.

A Shearer commission had originally been placed with John Westwood through Thomas Venables, a Birmingham merchant with Scottish connections, who had earlier secured for Westwood a contract for the tokens of the Edinburgh firm of Thomas and Alexander Hutchison. Knowing nothing of this Boulton had floated the idea of a municipal issue for Glasgow, Paisley and Greenock through Alexander Brown, a Glasgow merchant and friend of James Watt. With Brown's help and that of Watt's brother-in-law, Gilbert Hamilton, both influential in Glasgow's local government, Boulton was able in June 1791 to snatch the Shearer contract from Westwood to produce a town

104 Engraving (in reverse) of *La Naissance de la Reine* from Rubens' 'Marie de Médicis Cycle', depicting the river god of the Arno, the inspiration of the reverse design of the Glasgow halfpenny.

105 Reverse of Medal of the Emperor Ferdinand I (1551).

issue for Glasgow underwritten by the drapery firm.[29]

The result was Dumarest's finest production but its brilliantly executed reverse – 'done in one week', according to Boulton – owed its inspiration to Brown, a classical scholar and amateur artist, who was instrumental in suggesting the portrayal of the god of the river Arno which he had sketched from an engraving of one of the *tableaux* in the cycle of Rubens' paintings celebrating the life of Marie de Médicis in the Luxembourg palace, presumably the mirror-image engraving by Gaspard Duchange made familiar to a British audience from the album published many years earlier by the Nattier brothers [104].[30] Boulton, or more likely Dumarest, must have turned to another source, however, in finalising the design, perhaps to a fairly well-known sixteenth-century medal of the Emperor Ferdinand I [105], since the token unusually shows the Clyde river god holding a rudder as well as clutching an urn while the lion of the *tableau* has been omitted. Dumarest or perhaps Brown must have nodded over the accompanying legend NUNQUAM ARESCERE ('Never Run Dry') taken from Ovid's *Metamorphoses* but it was a textual blunder of no consequence.[31] The halfpenny more than lived up to the expectations of Gilbert Hamilton who had wanted 'a very handsome token so that it may be a pattern to any other Coinage which may be wanted for this Country'.[32] Struck at a standard of thirty-six to the lb it proved to be immensely popular; over six tons had been manufactured, when after the usual Soho delays, the order was eventually fulfilled towards the end of 1791. Hamilton's hopes were thus completed but not entirely in the way he had desired for, with regal copper being viewed with such suspicion in Scotland, the token's very success soon spawned a plethora of counterfeits.

By the time the contracts for Southampton, Cornwall and Glasgow had been completed Dumarest, intense, often unwell and always desperately homesick, had long left Soho to return to Paris. The search was on again for an engraver and, despite Boulton's outburst to Raspe that he was 'quite Sick of conceited French quacks', he nevertheless in the end appointed the young Parisian, Noël-Alexandre Ponthon. Enlisted by Swediaur on the recommendation of Dupré, Ponthon arrived at Soho with the peripatetic Austrian physician and spy in the

29 Alexander Brown was a former Edinburgh magistrate and Dean of Guild. He was described as 'a man of culture, a fine classical scholar, and a graceful artist. He was the inventor of the seals of several of the Glasgow corporations, and when Latin inscriptions were required on any occasion, they were invariably the production of his ready and correct pen'. Gilbert Hamilton was provost of Glasgow in 1792-94, a banker, and agent for the Carron Company.

30 Nattier (1710). Duchange's plate of Rubens' *La Naissance de la Reine* depicted the river god of the Arno – Marie de Médicis was born in Florence – in reverse. So popular were the engravings that they were snapped up as individual prints as they were published by an eager public that could not wait for the collected edition ['Avertissement']. The Marie de Médicis Cycle itself is now displayed in the Richelieu Wing of the Louvre.

31 *Recte* 'NUMQUAM ARESCERE': Ovid, *Metamorphoses*, Book 9, line 657.

32 BAH: MS 3782/12/36/105, Gilbert Hamilton to Matthew Boulton, 29 June 1791.

A MOST SATISFYING ADVENTURE

106 Matthew Boulton: penny for Bermuda, 1793.

107 Matthew Boulton: penny for the Sierra Leone Company, [1792].

108 Sketch submitted to Matthew Boulton for a proposed token coinage for Sir Richard Arkwright of Cromford, Derbyshire [enhanced to remove ink bleeding from the reverse of the page].

August of 1791.[33]

For his first eighteen months at Soho Ponthon was busied with the tokens for Monneron Frères and the coinages for Bermuda and the Sierra Leone Company. The Bermuda penny was concocted from a pattern 1788 halfpenny obverse die by Droz 'with the King's head on', for the use of which Treasury approval had been granted,[34] coupled with a new Ponthon reverse. Ponthon's die, dispatched to the West Indies in May 1793, was unremarkable, his engraving of a full-rigged merchantman ponderous and lacklustre [106]. His obverse for the Sierra Leone coinage [107], on the other hand, a crouching lion modelled by Parbury, was a dramatic evocation of the name of the old Portuguese trading post and his reverse, a clasping of hands, British and African, was telling in its understated symbolism of a Company territory now devised for the resettlement of freed slaves. Interestingly, this coinage, initially struck as a silver trading dollar and local copper penny towards the end of 1792, was, after a false start, remodelled a few months later on a decimal system from dollar to cent although this was in turn abandoned as savouring too much of Napoleonic metrication when the settlement became a crown colony in 1808.[35]

It was not for a lack of opportunities that Ponthon was unemployed on provincial coinage at this time. A number of overtures were made to Boulton but they proved abortive. In 1790 an approach had been made by Samuel More on behalf of the great Richard Arkwright for penny and halfpenny tokens avoiding 'all Appearance of Coin' to 'form as it were a Medal which may be taken in payment about his works [at Cromford in Derbyshire], and give no offence to anyone – somewhat in the Manner of John Wilkinson' [108].[36]

Nothing seems to have come of this proposal and the scheme was probably abandoned for the same reason that Boulton delayed the manufacture of Walter Taylor's Southampton tokens – his misplaced conviction that a government decision on a national copper coinage was imminent. By the time that it was clear eighteen months later that this was far from the case Arkwright had no doubt lost interest in the issue of his own tokens the copper content of which would in any case have far exceeded their face value. By August 1792 he was dead and it was left to his eldest son, also Richard, to issue the countermarked dollars that have put Cromford on the numismatic map [109].

In the spring of 1791 a projected coinage for Stirling had been summarily cancelled when, much to the embarrassment of the Birmingham agents who had steered the contract in the direction of Soho, the town's provost, Henry Jaffray, took fright from seeing in

---

33 Dumarest left Soho on 21 July 1791: Gould (1972), 313. Matthew Boulton to R. E. Raspe, 30 March 1791 quoted in Hawker (1996), 37. For Ponthon see Gould (1972).

34 BAH: MS 3782/12/40/94, Matthew Boulton to Robert Barclay, 15 March 1795; see p.136 below.

35 For the Sierra Leone coinage see Vice (1983), 19-35 and 131-45.

36 BAH: MBP 245/93, Samuel More to Matthew Boulton, 22 May 1790. The pennies were to weigh an ounce Troy and the halfpennies half an ounce both being proportionately broader in diameter than the corresponding Anglesey pieces.

127

109 Spanish silver dollar of Carlos IV (1803) countermarked for Cromford Mill, Derbyshire, c.1790s–1810.

110 Sketch submitted to Matthew Boulton for a proposed token coinage for Stirling.

'the News Pappers' [*sic*] that it was 'Expected that a New Coinage is to take place'. No patterns of these 'lost' tokens exist and were probably never made owing to delays on the part of Dumarest, but we do know what they might have looked like from sketches submitted to Soho.[37] Arkwright's tokens would have been an appropriate reflection of an archetypal self-made entrepreneur whose 'arrival' in society had been marked by a knighthood and armorial bearings; the Stirling halfpennies, an evocation of the mythical figure of 'Fingal', translated from Irish legend to Scotland and made popular by James Macpherson's Ossianic poems and Joseph Banks's 'discovery' of the eponymous cave on Staffa [110].[38]

Later, in the autumn of 1791, another approach, this time from a Stockport muslin manufacturer, Andrew Bury, also quickly went into limbo and it was not until the end of 1792 that Boulton was to resume his manufacture of provincial coins. This time for Samuel Birchall, a Quaker wool-stapler, on behalf of a Leeds syndicate, to produce a halfpenny emblematic of a town that was 'the heart of the Woollen Manufactory'. Birchall's suggestion that the token should portray the devices of a 'figure' on one side and Bishop Blaize, the patron saint of wool-combers, on the other, was quickly endorsed by Boulton who saw a way of profiting from the adaptation of existing dies. 'I think', he told his son, 'that a punch taken from the figure of Liberty which Ponthon has last done [for the Monneron two-sol *médaille de confiance* [111]], by taking away the little genius of france [the Gallic Cock] & substituting a Shield in lieu of a Book may answer for Birchills piece & take St Patrick from the Chronbane dye may Serve for Bishop Blazes head of which you may consult with Ponthon & Lawson'.[39]

In the event, while the obverse was reworked by Ponthon from one of Hancock's dies for the Cronebane halfpenny [88] with a somewhat simpler mitre and a wool-comb substituted for the original pastoral staff, the reverse with its skilful perspective view of the 'prodigiously extensive' Leeds Coloured Cloth Hall, was new, distinct and striking [112]. For once, too, the commission was completed in record time and by April 1793 perhaps 180,000 currency tokens had been struck, their edge reading, **PAYABLE AT H. BROWNBILL'S SILVERSMITH**, denoting the front man of the issuing consortium, Henry Brownbill, a local silversmith and watchmaker, well placed in Briggate, Leeds' main shopping street, to redeem the halfpennies if need arose.

It was a surprisingly small issue for a town the size of Leeds – rapidly becoming the fifth largest town in England – but Leeds was a place

37 BAH: MS 3782/12/36/61, Henry Jaffray to William and James Astbury (Birmingham factors who had acted as agents over the coinage), 6 April 1791. The sketches for Jaffray's halfpenny are enclosed with BAH: MBP 217/1, William and James Astbury to Matthew Boulton, 2 March 1791. See also BAH: MBP 217/2. There is a hint that the project may have been revived in the summer of 1791 but it came to nothing.

38 Banks's description of 'the cave of *Fhinn ... Fhinn Mac Coul*, whom the translator of *Ossian*'s works has called Fingal' was publicised by Pennant (1776), I, 302. 'How fortunate that in this cave we should meet with the remembrance of that chief, whose existence, as well as the whole *Epic* poem is almost doubted in *England*'.

39 BAH: MS 3782/13/36/94, Matthew Boulton to M. R. Boulton, 18 January 1793.

A MOST SATISFYING ADVENTURE

111   Obverse of a Monneron Frères *deux-sols médaille de confiance*, 1791.

where there was already a not unplentiful supply of small change – Westwood had produced five tons of halfpennies for Richard Paley, a local soap boiler turned speculative property developer, only two years earlier – and Birchall, a numismatic aficionado, was driven as much by the desire to promote an attractive monetary curiosity as to provide a reputable local currency; it was, after all, in character that he ordered a surprisingly large number of special strikings and was in the years ahead to prove a not backward customer in buying 'special editions' of other tokens and medals that Boulton produced during the early years of the Soho mint both to keep his workforce employed and to advertise his wares.

Sporadic as the work of Boulton's mint was it still excited close and eulogistic attention. The dubious American agent, Thomas Attwood Digges, penetrated Soho in March 1793 and reported back to Thomas Jefferson, the United States Secretary of State, that he had found 'a more excellent apparatus for Coining than any in Europe'.

> It cost him some thousands – The whole machine is moved by an improvd steam Engine which rolls the Copper, for half-pence <u>finer</u> than copper has before been rolld for the purpos's of money – It works the Coupoirs or screw press's for cutting the particular pieces of Copper, & coins both the faces & <u>edges</u> of money at the same time, with such superior excellence & cheapness of workmanship, as well as with marks of such powerful machinery as must totally prevent counterfeiting it.[40]

112   Matthew Boulton: Leeds halfpenny for Henry Brownbill, 1793

Ponthon's presence at Soho was erratic but he seems to have continued in Boulton's full-time employment until the summer of 1795. He had left the manufactory by the time of Küchler's arrival in the August of that year but remained in Birmingham until late 1795 or early 1796 and, his finances being always in a parlous state, he appears to have received occasional out-worker commissions from Boulton for some time after his departure from the manufactory. Over the whole period he was to engrave dies for another six tokens as well as those for the Monneron pieces, the Bermuda penny, the Sierra Leone coinage, some medals and other incidental work. Little of his work was to result in any quantity of provincial coinage other than his halfpennies for Daniel Eccleston, an eccentric Lancaster tradesman and lapsed Quaker, and William Croom, a Dundee draper, at least one commission being rejected because of Ponthon's negligent engraving.

Daniel Eccleston's 1794 halfpennies [113] are of interest because they were struck with a raised border incusely lettered – a precursor of Boulton's 1797 national coinage – and produced at a time when Boulton was experimenting with this novel feature to lessen coin wear and deter counterfeiting. Ponthon had already been working on a halfpenny for the Copper Company of Upper Canada incorporating this characteristic when Eccleston placed his order. At the time the raised rim must have appealed to Eccleston and although he subsequently changed his mind 'to have the Letters in <u>Relief</u>, like

---

40   LC: Thomas Jefferson Papers, Th[omas] A[ttwood] Digges to Thomas Jefferson, 10 March 1793. See also Elias and Finch (1982), 443.

129

COINAGE AND CURRENCY IN EIGHTEENTH-CENTURY BRITAIN

113   Matthew Boulton: Lancaster halfpenny for Daniel Eccleston, 1794.

114   Isaac Swainson (1746-1812).

115   Matthew Boulton: token for Isaac Swainson, [1795].

Mr. Wilkinsons instead of being <u>indented</u> as the Canada halfpenny is', the dies by then (10 July 1794) had been completed.[41] Evidently Eccleston, when faced with the costs and time taken up in engraving new dies, decided to accept the *status quo* and by 25 August a little over a ton of the halfpennies, struck in a lettered collar [PAYABLE . IN . LANCASTER . LIVERPOOL . MANCHESTER .] probably at the rate of 44 to the lb, with the type engraved in very low relief, had been dispatched from Soho. Eccleston's arrangement with Boulton had apparently been for two ton of tokens and a few weeks later Boulton intimated that he would 'give orders for what remains ... to be struck in relief, as you seem to prefer them executed in that manner'. New dies were prepared which resulted in a trial striking (*D&H*: Lancashire 56) but no commercial tokens resulted, the outstanding element of Eccleston's order most likely foundering because of his repeated procrastinations over payment of Boulton's original bill which was never ultimately honoured in its entirety.[42]

Eccleston's original obverse die was signed **PONTHON** (on the truncation of the bust's left shoulder). Another commission, for the quack doctor, Isaac Swainson [114], probably put in hand in February 1795, simply had the letter **P** in the exergue below the token's reverse image of Hygeia (the Goddess of Health) dropping herbs into a still [115]. Five hundredweight of these 'halfpennies' were ordered by Swainson, intended as advertising tickets for the sale of his patent medicine, 'Velnos' Vegetable Syrup', boldly inscribed on the reverse. Pye tells us that that the token order was cancelled because of the misspelling of his name – 'Jsaac Suainson' instead of 'Isaac Swainson' – and that only about twelve proof specimens were struck. Effective advertising, after all, was the life blood of quack cures and such a mistake would have been totally unacceptable to a man as promotion conscious as Swainson was. Interestingly, it seems that the negotiations between Swainson and Boulton were handled by a 'M[r]. Pearson', very probably Thomas Pearson, the Birmingham printer and stationer, who handled much of Soho's printing, and who, as was common with such tradesmen, could well have provided a local retail outlet for the nostrum.[43]

Swainson, born in Lancashire of a yeoman family and apparently of good education, made his way to London as a young man and it is said that after working for a time as a woollen draper, he became assistant to a Dr. Mercier in Frith Street, Soho, from whom, it is thought, he bought the rights to Velnos' Vegetable Syrup for £4,000. Swainson claimed in 1791 to be selling 20,000 bottles of the remedy each year and, according to the diarist Joseph Farington, he realized an average annual income of £5,000 from the mixture which is said to have sold for 13*s* a bottle. Although not medically qualified – though he is said, like a number of other quacks of the time, to have bought a Scottish

41   BAH: MS 3782/12/39/176, Daniel Eccleston to Matthew Boulton, 10 July 1794 and BAH: MS 3782/12/39/178, Matthew Boulton to Daniel Eccleston, 14 July 1794.

42   Soho was still trying unsuccessfully to recover the residue of Eccleston's debt in 1820.

43   Pye (1801), 14, Plate 34, no. 10. Sharp (1834), 72, no. 147 suggests that 'only a very few proofs were struck' and perhaps there were fewer than twelve original strikings. BAH: MBP 283/14, Matthew Robinson Boulton to Matthew Boulton, 9 February 1795.

A MOST SATISFYING ADVENTURE

MD – he won respect as a scientific botanist, especially in medicinal plants and from the proceeds of his nostrum bought a fine house at Twickenham where he laid out an extensive botanic garden.[44]

The origins of Velnos' Syrup are murky and the rights to its ownership a tangled web. Despite Swainson's claims to being 'sole proprietor of the genuine medicine' a version under that name had been patented as early as 1772 and well before the century's end a number of variants of the Syrup were being widely marketed with several practitioners claiming sole ownership of the genuine article. The Syrup seems to have begun as an antidote to consumption but it achieved its wide-spread popularity as a supposed curative for venereal diseases. For generations mercurial treatments had constituted the medically acceptable 'cure' for such diseases but their side effects and limited efficacy had spawned many non-mineral alternatives. The 1780s and '90s witnessed an extensive pamphlet war with advocates of vegetable cures attacking each other as much as they did the mercurial traditionalists of the medical profession. It was a war of words for profit as much as for science in which Swainson was well to the fore; a war, captured by Thomas Rowlandson in a famous caricature showing Swainson confronting a hostile phalanx of doctors urged on by a naked Mercury [116]. The actual composition of his Syrup remains a mystery to this day but Swainson's very secrecy – essential to his commercial success – never enabled him to shake off the accusation that the nostrum itself contained mercury despite his repeated protests to the contrary.

116 *Mercury and his Advocates defeated, or Vegetable Intrenchment* by Thomas Rowlandson, 1789.[45] Isaac Swainson promoting his Velnos' Syrup in the face of the opposition of regular practitioners advocating mercury.

44 Thompson (1928), 345; McAllister (1996), 89-92; Porter (2000), 58; Waters (1906), 53.
45 Engraving published 29 November 1789 by Samuel William Fores, 3 Piccadilly: George (1938), No. 7592.

131

Swainson earned a fulsome obituary in the *Gentleman's Magazine* in 1812 but, coupled as it was by an advertisement inserted by his nephew and successor, even in death he was pursued by the promotion he had so assiduously cultivated in life:

> The greater part of his life was devoted to the noblest of purposes (viz. an unremitting study, how he might most effectually remove or alleviate the sufferings of his fellow creatures) by preparing and administering the celebrated syrup of De Velnos, of which he was the sole proprietor. This important duty he discharged with fidelity and diligence, during a period of thirty years; and with a success which has hitherto been unequalled in the annals of medicine. [46]

Christopher Ibberson, proprietor of the coach office at the great Holborn inn, *The George and Blue Boar* [117],[47] stable-keeper and chapman,[48] seems to have had conversations with Boulton about the production of a token in the autumn of 1794 and finally confirmed a reduced initial order of half a ton on 20 December. Unfortunately, there was a hitch because the crest of the boar engraved on the original obverse die was thought to be too small but by 9 February the necessary changes were in hand with a larger crest and the engraver's name inscribed on the exergue line. Ten days had not passed, however, before Ibberson was rescinding the order, telling Boulton that 'in consequence of what appeared in the Gazette, a few evenings ago, there is not a doubt but the Circulation of the new Halfpence will be stopped'.[49]

---

46 *GM*, March 1812, 301.

47 *The George and Blue Boar*, which boasted 40 bedrooms, stabling for 52 horses and seven coach houses, stood on the south side of High Holborn, a few doors to the west of the junction with Red Lion Street (No. 270 on Richard Horwood's map of 1799). Originally The George it acquired its second name from The Blue Boar (immediately opposite) when the latter inn went out of business. It was famous as the place where the condemned drank on their way from Newgate to Tyburn promising to pay on their way back:
> As clever Tom Clinch, while the rabble was bawling,
> Rode stately through Holborn to die in his calling,
> He stopped at the 'George' for a bottle of sack,
> And promised to pay for it – when he came back…
>   Jonathan Swift, 1727.

48 Although often described as such it is by no means clear that Ibberson was actually landlord of the inn; when declared bankrupt with his co-partner son in 1799, he was described as a 'Stable-Keeper, Dealer, and Chapman' of High Holborn: *LG* No. 15103, 29 January 1799.

49 BAH: MBP 283/14, Matthew Robinson Boulton to Matthew Boulton, 9 February 1795; BAH: MS 3782/12/39/44 and MS 3782/12/40/69, Christopher Ibberson to Matthew Boulton, 20 December 1794 and 18 February 1795. The reference to the *Gazette* is unclear but it does not appear to refer to the *London Gazette*.

A MOST SATISFYING ADVENTURE

118 Matthew Boulton: 'Small Boar' and 'Large Boar' versions of the Holborn token for Christopher Ibberson, [1795].

117 A watercolour of the stable yard of *The George and Blue Boar*. Although a Victorian view little would have changed since Ibberson's time.

Although Ibberson's fears proved to be misplaced his order was never revived. Specimens of the 'small boar' variety [118] are extremely rare, Pye describing it as 'rrr' in 1801, noting that a specimen had sold for £2 12s 6d. He considered the 'large boar' variety [118] as common although, as Waters recognised in 1916, it is in fact quite a scarce token. Few of them entered the currency, most being marketed by Soho in their 'collectors' sets'. Surprisingly, since by now Boulton was abandoning such marking, the edges of legitimate Soho tokens were struck in a collar, inscribed **PAYABLE AT THE GEORGE & BLUE BOAR LONDON**.[50] Two anomalies are a mule obverse paired with an Enniscorthy reverse (*D&H*: Middx 340) presumably concocted at Soho post 1801 and an imitation piece (*D&H*: Middx 343 and 343 Bis) produced by William Taylor in the later nineteenth century when he acquired a cache of Soho dies.[51]

Boulton must have taken Ibberson's newspaper report seriously and concluded that a regal coinage contract was back in the offing for it is at this time that he hurriedly cobbled together the regal pattern halfpennies of 1795 with their incusely-lettered raised rims [119] and took the initiative himself in dissuading a friend from pursuing a token order with Soho. On 14 January 1795 George Bowser, the London agent of the Swansea copper smelters, Lockwood, Morris and Company [120], expressed an interest in ordering a ton of halfpence, very utilitarian in

119 Matthew Boulton: Pattern regal halfpenny, 1795.

50 Pye (1801), 13 (Plate 31, nos. 1 and 2); Pye [Waters] (1916), Plate No. 31.
51 DNW Auctions 67A, 29 September 2005, lot 1403 and T8, 6 October 2010, lot 276; Waters (1954), 14.

design, for the firm. John Morris of Clasemont, its principal and an old ally of Boulton, followed this up a month later with a further request for a coinage but rather 'more elegant' since it would then be more likely 'to get into general circulation, from which must arise the principal advantage'. The rumours of some embargo on provincial coinage and an imminent decision on a regal copper coinage that had assailed Ibberson persuaded Boulton to pour cold water on Morris's scheme. Morris, who was a not inconsiderable player in the copper trade and someone close to the ways of government, admitted that the suspension of private tokens had also occurred to him 'from the rumour of Government intending to do something effectual on this head'. He added:

> About ten years ago I had several conversations with M[r.] Rose on the subject & he then advis'd me to deliver in a memorial & terms of coining, which I did, & if they had then follow'd my plan when copper was so cheap, it would have been well on all sides; I shou'd like to renew my claim having a fair right to do so from my connexions with Government, & it wou'd give me particular pleasure to unite with you on the occasion, as the means probably of promoting our mutual interest...[52]

120   View of John Morris's Forest Copper Works, Swansea. From an engraving by Thomas Rothwell, 1791. Jabez Maud Fisher recorded in 1776 how the works 'vomit out vast Columns of thick Smoak, which curling as they rise, mount up into the Clouds, with which they mingle and are lost in the immensity of Space ... a most pleasing effect on the Landscape'. [53]

52   BAH: MS 3782/12/40/85, John Morris to Matthew Boulton, 1 March 1795. See also BAH: MS 3782/12/40/64, John Morris to Matthew Boulton, 16 February 1795.

53   Morgan (1992), 210. Fisher did recognise that the land surrounding the works although 'formerly crowded with the thickest Foliage' was 'now bereft of every Species of Verdure without the least appearance of Vegetation, so great is the effect of the Smoak from the Furnaces': Morgan (1992), 210-11. It is only since the 1960s that the devastated land has been reclaimed so that now there is little vestige of the industrial past of the area.

Whether Morris's ambitions were eventually fulfilled as a source of copper for the coinage of 1797 is not known. In the meantime, however, nothing came of his ideas for a provincial coinage.

Boulton is often accused of hypocrisy, on the one hand condemning trade tokens in his efforts to gain a government coining contract while simultaneously minting tokens himself. He had, it is true, few scruples about adopting often contradictory stances to suit such particular purposes as he had in mind but some correspondence with the Southwark brewer Robert Barclay at this time is worth quoting in some detail because of the light it throws on the complexity of Boulton's apparently variable attitude; balancing his concern that the general acceptance of tokens would persuade government to postpone serious consideration of a regal coinage with his anxiety to keep his new mint employed. On 14 March 1795 he wrote to Barclay:

> When the Anglesea Company first issued their Halfpence there was a great scarcity of Legal Copper Coin & as the intrinsick value of their Halfpenny was nearly equal to the nominal being 32 in the lb or 218¾ grain each; they were a convenience to the public without any apparent risk of much loss to the holders. Other Companies thought themselves likewise justified in issuing Halfpence & more desirous of profit they reduced theirs to 36 in the pound, others 40, 42 & 46 which latter is the size of the Kings Halfpenny, but the evil did not stop here. Some of the numerous Coiners not only coin'd Halfpence of 50 to 60 & 64 in the lb. but they counterfeited those of Anglesea & Jn°. Wilkinson and made them of about half the weight.
>
> I think I have seen at least twelve different Counterfeits of John Wilkinsons with his promissory inscription upon them. How these matters will be settled when the Day of reckinning [*sic*] comes I know not, as I fear Mr. Wilkinson will have some difficulty to discriminate his own Halfpence from those of others. The whole of this Business is illegal and counter to an Act Parliament expressly made to prevent the issuing of Copper Tokens and consequently the thing being illegal in itself the Counterfeiters are no more punishable than the original issuers. Hence it is evident that an honest legal [coin]age would answer your purpose better than any other particularly if made similar or superior to the Specimens I send you. But if our Government decline the Execution of a new legal Coinage and the Gentlemen at your intended Meeting on the 25th. Inst should agree to issue a Borough Token I must earnestly recommend that such Tokens be struck in collars like my specimen with every difficulty that can be devised to prevent Counterfeits.
>
> Each Halfpenny should weigh half an ounce, for the prevention of Counterfeits is an object of far greater consequence than any profit you can possibly desire from such a Coinage & I presume that by taking away the Temptation of great profits, and by superior Copper Rolling, Dies, apparatus, & workmanship in general the present mischiefs may be prevented in a great degree...

> When you have considered the Subject and come to any Resolution upon it, I should be happy to receive your Commands which I will execute more to your advantage than I think any other Person in this Country can do. Being minutely acquainted with the Copper Trade, concerned in Copper Mines, a Partner in two different Copper Smelting Works & possessing the best apparatus for that kind of Rolling & Coining in the World...[54]

The following day Boulton added:

> This line I write to your self <u>only</u> to say that I have not given any price in my other letter presently sent because I do not choose to have my Coinage put up by auction when I know that no Copper C[o]. or member of any C[o]. hath the power of makeing [sic] such Coin as you ought to have, if you have any, & what ever Price I may offer it at, it is probable they may offer at one farthing a pound less, but if you were to offer them 6[d] per lb more they could not make such Coin as mine; however in order that You may [be] qualifyd to speak upon that head I will tell you that my price for money made of fine Copper & fine Workmanship will be £140 a Ton deliverd at Birm[g]. The Car[g] by <u>Land</u> about £4 a Ton or by <u>Water</u> about one half...
>
> I was applyd to for half pence about a year ago for the Isle of Bermudas with the <u>King's head</u> on one Side but on that acc[t] I refused to make them; however the Merch[t]. applyd to the Treasury & obtain an order for <u>me</u> to make them & they were accordingly done. I must acknowledge that I wish you to have your Coin some how legalised by Gov[t]. for I have constantly set my face against the base tokens that are made & have thereby lost the makeing [sic] of many Hundreds of Tons. It is true I made a few for Anglesey & for Wilkinson which you may distinguish from all others by their being struck in Collers & those I did merely to try my apparatus when it was first made.[55]

Again, nothing came of Barclay's approach but a month later another overture was made to Boulton over a halfpenny for the Royal Liberty of Havering atte Bower (an ancient crown demesne enjoying chartered immunities and rights and comprising the Essex parishes of Havering, Romford and Hornchurch).[56]

On 4 April 1795 George Cotton, a corn factor of Romford – the capital of the Liberty –, wrote to Boulton. His letter does not appear to have survived but we do have copies of Boulton's reply of 8 April 1795. After quoting a cost of four guineas for a pair of dies Boulton continued:

---

54 BAH: MS 3782/12/40/92, Matthew Boulton to Robert Barclay, 14 March 1795.

55 BAH: MS 3782/12/40/94, Matthew Boulton to Robert Barclay, 15 March 1795.

56 The Liberty was established by charter in 1465 and continued until the nineteenth century. Under the Local Government Act of 1888 it was placed for administrative purposes under the newly formed Essex County Council. Little remained of the privileges of the Liberty except its separate criminal court, and in 1892 Havering was merged, by agreement, with the county.

A MOST SATISFYING ADVENTURE

> I ought in justice to suggest to you (in order to prevent you from falling into an error) that government is actually taking measures to put an entire Stop to the issuing of Tradesmen's Halfpence, and am theref[ore] led to suppose that you would judge it advisable to drop the Business at present.

In a slightly less positive sequel of the same date – worth quoting *in extenso* – he added:

> I have very little more to say to you upon the subject of Copper than what I have already said. My private opinion is, & I have some grounds for my opinion, that the only obstruction to a National Coinage arises from the Mint, for there can be no solid objection against issuing such a Coin as I can execute in conformity with the request of Mr. Pitt, who seemed very desirous of putting a stop to Counterfeiting. The Committee of Privy Counsell [*sic*] also approved my Specimens, & I was then flattered with the execution of 1500 Ton which I would undertake to execute in one third of the time that it can be done in the Mint & of such weight & workmanship as would produce the desired effect, & would undertake to put it into Circulation in England, Wales & Scotland, to pay for the Casks & every other Charge without putting govern[t]. to one farthing expense, except the sallereys [*sic*] of such persons as they may think proper to place over me as checks.
>
> I have lately seen a Collection of modern Tradesmen's Tokens consisting of 260 different sorts. Hence it is evident what confusion & mischief must arise from the present System of Copper Coinage.
>
> It is probable that the Minds & time of his Majestie's Ministers are at this time so absorbed by objects of far greater importance. Yet the time will shortly arive [*sic*] when the present Confusion of Coins must be put a Stop to & I know of no other mode of so effectually doing it as by making such a Coin as cannot be Counterfeited by any other Machinery than that which I possess & by taking away the Temptation of Profit by weight of Metal.[57]

But, unlike the overtures from Morris and Barclay which might have proved more profitable, this was not the end of the story. Cotton was unconvinced by Boulton's faith in government; he came to Soho and by June 1795 he had persuaded Boulton to produce the dies for what we know as the 'Hornchurch' halfpenny [121]. Initially, two hundred weight were ordered:

> to see how they would take as a substitute for Halfpence, as we are pestered with such paltry trash here, six of which will not weigh an ounce; if the People of our Liberty are satisfied with

121 Matthew Boulton: Hornchurch halfpenny for George Cotton, 1795.

---

57 BAH: MS 3782/12/40/112 and MS 3782/12/40/113, Matthew Boulton to George Cotton, 8 April 1795.

137

them [we] should want a considerable quantity, as I would risk Government interfering about the Business; having many Soldiers and Barrucks [sic] building here is the means of introducing such a large quantity of the small stampt Halfpence.[58]

Still Boulton must have prevaricated because more than three months were to elapse before we hear more about the halfpenny by which time it had become obvious that no embargo would be placed on provincial coins or that Soho would be given any coinage contract in the foreseeable future. Nevertheless, Cotton did not order the 'considerable quantity' he had hinted at and only the two hundredweight contemplated as a trial were finally struck. From the Soho Coinage ledgers we know exactly how many halfpennies were sent out to the day: 10,563 tokens made up in 125 rouleaux of 84 tokens with an additional short rouleau of 63 tokens, forwarded to Cotton via Richard Carpenter, an engraver and printer of 16, Aldgate High Street, on 2 October 1795.

The token is unpretentious in its design and lacks flair in its execution. The portrait bust of Edward IV is wooden while the reverse with its badge of the Liberty (taken from the seal of the Liberty with its representation of the former castellated royal palace at Havering) is pedestrian. No individual's name is inscribed on the halfpenny since Cotton had been acting not in his own interest but on behalf of the officers of the Liberty – its high bailiff and constables – and the reverse was considered as a sufficient promissory authority. More surprising, perhaps, is that the token is undated. This is unlikely to be an aberration on the part of Boulton; more likely it is deliberate and lies in the rumour of government action against provincial coins in the early part of the year and the increasingly hostile reaction against tokens in the public prints. With his eye primarily on a government contract concern over any involvement with provincial coin making might well have induced a degree of obfuscation on Boulton's part that the actual issuers could well have encouraged.

What the Matthew Boulton Papers do not tell us is the name of the die-sinker. Boulton's sensitivity over the leakage of information surrounding his operations meant that contemporary published information about Soho's token-making activities is thin. Pye's 1801 catalogue, the standard authority, is, therefore, not unnaturally silent. Traditionally the token has been ascribed to Ponthon, an attribution which, in published form, derives from Thomas Sharp who, while he was a contemporary Warwickshire collector with his ear close to the ground, was not faultless in his opinions.[59] Nevertheless, although Cotton was not sent his consignment until October 1795 by which time Ponthon had long left full time employment, the original dies had been sunk by the June of that year when he was still at the manufactory, and it seems reasonable to assume that they were completed by Ponthon in the ensuing months when he was still employed as an occasional outworker. It has been suggested that Küchler who had arrived at Soho in the August of 1795 may have been responsible for the dies – he had, after all, undertaken outwork for Boulton since 1793 though this had

---

58 BAH: MS 3782/12/40/189, George Cotton to Matthew Boulton, 20 June 1795.

59 Sharp (1834), 43.

A MOST SATISFYING ADVENTURE

122　Matthew Boulton: Dundee halfpenny for William Croom, 1795/96.

mainly been medallic in nature – but the Hornchurch halfpenny is completely lacking in Küchler's finesse and, if not by Ponthon, must be the product of a journeyman engraver.

Also undated and for much the same reason were the Dundee halfpennies [122] struck for William Croom, a wholesale draper with High Street retail premises in the town's Union Hall [123].[60] Croom was supplied with something approaching 53,000 tokens in two batches of December 1795 and February 1796 through the agency of the Birmingham factors Wilson and Smith.[61] Sharp, once more, tells us that the die-engraver was Ponthon who must again, if this information is correct, have undertaken the work as an occasional outworker. Although the reverse of the halfpenny is utilitarian – a mere recitation of Croom's retail stock [62] – the obverse depiction of the town arms and its supporters is very delicately executed; it is far superior to the heraldry of the Hornchurch halfpenny and one is left with more than a suspicion that on this occasion it might well be Küchler's handiwork.

123　The Union Hall (centre), High Street, Dundee. From a painting by George McGillivray, 1847.

60　For William Croom and his tokens, on which the following paragraphs are based, see Dykes (1998b).

61　Wilson and Smith were factors of St Paul's Square, Birmingham and acted as intermediaries between the Soho manufactory and Croom as did Tayler and Mander of Steelhouse Lane (and subsequently William and Alexander Walker of Sand Street) with the Inverness sail-cloth manufacturers, Mackintosh, Inglis and Wilson (*D&H*: Invernesshire 1-5). The use of such trading intermediaries presumably facilitated business where the customer was an unknown quantity to Soho or where he had existing commercial links with the intermediaries. The merchant, Thomas Venables of Newhall Street, similarly acted for John Westwood and had handled the latter's putative contract with Gilbert Shearer and Company, the Glasgow woollen drapers, before Boulton secured the manufacture of their tokens.

62　The spelling of 'WOOLEN' – now an Americanism – was not necessarily an error as is suggested by some modern authorities since it was a perfectly respectable eighteenth-century variant of the now standard British 'woollen'.

COINAGE AND CURRENCY IN EIGHTEENTH-CENTURY BRITAIN

124 Peter Kempson: Dundee 'Infirmary' halfpenny for William Croom, 1796.

The halfpennies must have served their purpose well in Dundee for in July Croom was seeking a further supply from Boulton but of a superior type.

> I Received [Croom writes] a few Copper pieces from Mess[rs] Wilson & Smith in Jan[y] & Feb[y] last which they had of you – be so good as write me in Course saying what you charge p[er] Cwt present money[.] I wish to have them well finished & if the additional expence be not verie [sic] considerable wou[ld] have the letters Sunk in [the] Same manner as 1/96 of a Rupee" done for the united East Indea Comp[y] or a Lancashire halfpenny of Daniel Ecclistone – I beg every information as to your terms, as if moderate more may be wanted afterwards besides this present intended order. [63]

The approach came to nothing. By return the Soho manufacturer replied personally to say that the cost of sheet copper was 'much raised' – it had, in fact, leapt to £126 per ton – and that his current price for 'coin struck in bright collers' was now £147 per ton ('15¾d per lb') 'to which must be added the cost of casks and car[g] [carriage]'.[64] Although no direct reply from Croom seems to have survived the matter was taken further through the agency of a friend, the Dundee numismatist and token promoter James Wright, junior. It appears that, nudged by Wright in his campaign to improve the design of provincial coins, what Croom had in mind by a 'well finished' token eventually took shape as the unnamed 'Infirmary' halfpenny [124] struck by Peter Kempson. As Wright was to explain, Boulton's terms for such a halfpenny 'bearing our Infirmary ... happening to be higher than he [Croom] was able to afford, Kempson of Birmingham was employed. Who, though he could not engrave so nicely as your superior artists, does work cheaper, & more adapted to such small undertakings'.[65]

Kempson's 'Infirmary' halfpennies are dated '1796' and were presumably manufactured towards the end of that year or early in 1797 for in the March of 1797 Wright presented a bronzed proof specimen to the Society of Antiquaries of Scotland. According to Pye Kempson struck ten hundredweights of the 'Infirmary' tokens (from dies by [Thomas] Wyon). These were of very good weight; existing specimens examined averaging out at 11.20 g, intimating a weight ratio of 40 pieces to the pound. The condition of surviving specimens suggests that the attraction of these pleasing pieces was essentially medallic although the prevalence of forgeries – lighter and cruder (*D&H*: Angusshire 16a) – does imply that they passed as small change in the town. Despite their anonymity the identity of their issuer

---

63 BAH: MS 3782/12/41/228, William Croom to Matthew Boulton, 27 July 1796. Croom is referring to Boulton's 1794 East India Company coinage for Madras (repeated in 1797 [132]) and his Lancaster halfpennies of Daniel Eccleston (*D&H*: Lancashire 57-8), precursors of the broad-rimmed, incuse-lettered 'cartwheel' coinage.

64 BAH: MS 3782/12/42/234, Matthew Boulton to William Croom, 1 August 1796.

65 BAH: MS 3782/12/42/215, James Wright to Matthew Boulton, 1 September 1797.

A MOST SATISFYING ADVENTURE

125   Francis Bassett, Baron de Dunstanville (1757-1835).

must have been well known in Dundee and Wright's Latin legend – bluntly translated by Miss Banks as 'We get our Money by Sea and Commerce' – must have struck a meaningful chord among Croom's fellow merchants.

No further instalment of 'named' tokens was struck by Boulton either but at some point the economically prudent Croom decided to employ Kempson to manufacture another supply, ten hundredweight, according to Pye, 'without collar' and from dies by [Thomas] Wyon. These are the tokens with 'rounded edge' listed by Dalton and Hamer as 'Angusshire 14 and 15' but misattributed by them to Boulton. Although they are of reasonable weight – the extant average examined is 9.65g – they do not compare in fabric or finish with the Boulton halfpennies and are simply a slavish copy of the original. Unhappily, unlike the Boulton archive, there are no surviving Kempson records to give us any insight into the latter's production costs or dates of manufacture. It is not unreasonable, though, to assume that the 'rounded edge' halfpence are post-July/August 1796; Croom was then still in contact with Boulton negotiating the abortive new issue which was eventually to appear from Kempson's coinery as the 'Infirmary' token. The 'rounded-edge' pieces are presumably subsequent to the latter too. The most likely scenario is that the hard-headed Croom, though seduced by Wright for a time into sponsoring the medallic 'Infirmary' halfpennies, decided that his business interests were better – and more cost-effectively – served by reverting to a re-issue of his more utilitarian shop ticket; and, having discovered in Kempson a cheaper manufacturer than Boulton, abandoned aesthetics for even greater commercial gain.

Another token, medallic in nature and with very finely engraved images was a piece commissioned in 1796 to commemorate the formation of the Penryn Volunteers two years before and celebrate the elevation that year of its commandant, Sir Francis Bassett of Tehidy [125], to the barony of de Dunstanville and full colonelcy of the corps [126]. Bassett was a rich Cornish landowner who enjoyed a princely copper mining income – he owned a fifth of all the ores in the county – and had been Governor of the Cornish Metal Company. In the early 1790s he had been a thorn in the flesh of Boulton and Watt with his support of Jonathan Hornblower in the battle for the steam engine patent, a stance taken up largely to 'disoblige' Watt's Pittite patron, Lord Falmouth, another great Cornish landowner with extensive

126   Matthew Boulton: Penryn Volunteers medallion, 1796.

141

127 Sir George Jackson (1725-1822). From a miniature by Richard Cosway.

mining interests. Boulton referred to him disparagingly as 'the little great man' while he struck James Boswell as a 'genteel, smart little man, well informed and lively' although his 'high Tory talk' was at variance with his parliamentary stance as a Foxite Whig.[66] Bassett was a patron of the arts and no doubt had considerable input into the design of the Penryn tokens although they were actually ordered by his second-in-command, George Chapman George, another Cornish acquaintance of Boulton's. Thomas Sharp names Ponthon as the engraver of these elegant tokens, and, although by the early summer of 1796 when they must have been in preparation – they were dispatched to George on 29 August – Ponthon was settled in London and might have undertaken the dies as an outworker, their level of artistry suggests that they were the work of his replacement Küchler.

Küchler had certainly been responsible a few months earlier in 1796 for the tokens struck for Sir George Jackson [127], promoter of the river Stort navigation in Hertfordshire, arguably the most handsome tokens ever produced at Soho. Cornish associations, too, may have played some part in their order for Jackson's contact with Boulton was initiated by John Knill, a London barrister of Gray's Inn but for many years a figure of some political and social significance in Cornwall and an old friend of Boulton.[67] Jackson himself had Cornish connections since, as a Government candidate with the support of Lord Falmouth, he had tried unsuccessfully to wrest the Parliamentary seat of Penryn from Francis Bassett, its sitting member, in the great election of 1784.[68] He was successively MP for Weymouth and for Colchester over the decade from 1786 to 1796 but made no great mark in Parliament. His real and abiding interest was the improvement of inland waterways and, from 1760 to 1769 'he employed his leisure hours in making the river

---

66 Rowe (1953), 82 et seqq; *ODNB*, s.v. de Dunstanville.
Francis Bassett had earned his baronetcy during the American war, as lieutenant-colonel of the North Devon militia, for marching the Cornish miners – many of them his own employees – to Plymouth to counter a Franco-Spanish landing and for strengthening the military defences there and at his harbour at Portreath. As a Portland Whig, now supporting the Pitt ministry, he was created baron de Dunstanville on 17 June 1796; he was promoted full colonel of the Volunteers on 24 December 1795.

67 John Knill (1734 (NS) -1811), Collector of Customs at St. Ives from 1762-82, was Mayor of the town in 1767; a pyramidal monument erected by him in 1782 and intended as his mausoleum still stands to the south-east of the town. Knill was later a Bencher (1804) and Treasurer (1805) of his Inn. He was described at the time of his death [29 March 1811] as 'a gentleman of rather singular character, though of great worth and probity ... [who] ... for many years past dined everyday at Dolly's chop-house, Paternoster Row'. He suggested Dolly's as a venue for a meeting between Boulton, Jackson, and himself to discuss the token scheme. See *GM*, April 1811, 401 and May 1811, 492.

68 Jackson had been Second Secretary of the Admiralty until dismissed on vindictive political grounds by Admiral Keppel, the First Lord, in 1782 (as Judge-Advocate of the Fleet Jackson had prosecuted Keppel at the latter's court martial in 1779). Jackson was a 'zealous friend and early patron' of Captain Cook whose father had been an employee of the Jackson family and who named Port Jackson, New South Wales (Sydney Harbour) and Point Jackson, New Zealand, after him. See *GM*, December 1822, 644 and *ODNB*, s.v. Duckett.

A MOST SATISFYING ADVENTURE

Stort navigable' from Bishop's Stortford to the Lea and the Thames.[69] Financially, as Jackson, its principal shareholder, later admitted, the scheme itself was not altogether the 'advantageous concern' he had envisaged but the canalisation of the Stort benefited the carriage of malted barley to London and helped save the local malting industry. No records exist of early tolls but it is known that in 1791, 19,000 sacks of flour and 97,000 quarters of malt were carried – the equivalent of 7,275 tons or 180 barge-loads of 40 tons.

The long, flat Stort barges, some almost 70ft in length and drawing about two feet of water, carried vast quantities of grain and malt weighing up to 60 tons and sometimes needed two horses to pull them along the towpath. The remarkable panoramic reverse of Jackson's token [128], portraying just such a barge rounding a bend in the Stort, was a *tour de force*. Jackson had originally opted for a much simpler design 'for being for use among the lower class it seems as if that production would soonest be admitted into their approbation'. Ears of barley would, he thought, strike the most immediate chord among the workers using the navigation but he was persuaded by Boulton that 'the Country people' would like a view of the Stort better and despite his reservations about 'Emblematical representations' being suited 'only to people of a rather higher rank' Jackson's sense of his own role in developing the scheme resulted in his coat of arms being used for the obverse. Jackson's expressed intention was 'solely to accommodate the neighbourhood' and to alleviate the difficulty 'the great traders' using the navigation had 'in getting circulation in Copper except in the meanest kind of halfpence'. But as he admitted he was 'childish about Conceits when once they have got possession of my noddle'.[70] Although there was a considerable delay on Boulton's part in dealing with the commission the hundredweight of halfpennies eventually produced in May 1796 (but dated 1795) proved so popular that Jackson increased his order to 5 cwt. Struck at 44 to the lb with the edge inscription **PAYABLE AT BISHOPS STORTFORD** (the last Soho tokens to employ a lettered edge) the final mintage came to 24,814 currency tokens together with proofs in copper, copper-gilt and silver. Commercial halfpennies they may have been but their elegance more than satisfied Jackson's 'conceit'. 'I esteem my curiosity in having had these halfpennies struck', he concluded to Boulton, 'as a fortunate event, as it has led to the pleasure of your acquaintance, which I hope I may be lucky enough to continue'.[71] It was a gesture that Boulton would have appreciated.

128 Matthew Boulton: Stort Navigation halfpenny for Sir George Jackson, 1795.

69 *GM*, December 1822, 644.

70 BAH: MS 3782/12/41/65, Matthew Boulton to Sir George Jackson, 18 February 1796; BAH: MS 3782/12/40/147, Sir George Jackson to John Knill, 4 and 26 May 1795. In 1797 Jackson inherited the estate of his second wife's uncle, Thomas Duckett, and took the name Duckett by royal licence, in accordance with his benefactor's will. The armorial bearings displayed on Jackson's halfpenny already contain an escutcheon of pretence charged with his heiress wife's arms including the Duckett saltire.

71 BAH: MS3782/12/41/205, Sir George Jackson to Matthew Boulton, 20 June 1795.

129   Matthew Boulton: Inverness halfpenny for Mackintosh, Inglis and Wilson, 1793.

130   Matthew Boulton: Inverness halfpenny for Mackintosh, Inglis and Wilson, 1794. The date has been transferred from the reverse stone to the obverse while the opportunity has been taken to identify the stone as the town's 'Stone of the Tubs' or Stone of Destiny.

Küchler had been appointed on a contract basis as a medallist while still living in London in 1793 and his first token commission had been for a family firm, Mackintosh, Inglis and Wilson, which operated a textile and sailcloth manufactory at Inverness. Overall it was to prove a much larger order than the majority of Boulton's token commissions and was to extend over more than three years. The initial order completed in the final months of 1793 and dated that year comprised something over a ton of copper probably struck at 42 tokens to the lb.[72] The reverse, displaying a cornucopia of flowers and fruit within the legend **CONCORDIA ET FIDELITAS** – the ancient burghal crest and motto of Inverness – floating unconnectedly above a stone bearing the date 1793, is clumsy in conception but the obverse of a rose and thistle tied together with a bow is more effective and betrays the engraver's medallic background [129]. A second order was placed by Mackintosh, Inglis and Wilson in the autumn of 1794 but the opportunity was taken to change the design slightly by moving the date (1794) to the obverse and replacing it on the stone with the Gaelic inscription **CLACH-NA-CUDDEN** (*recte* **CLACH-NA-CUDAINN**) [130]. This identified the previously obscure dated object below the cornucopia – the earliest token cataloguers ignored it – as the town's historic 'stone of tubs' where women returning from the river with their water pails paused for a rest and to which local fancy accorded an iconic status for the burgh's prosperity.[73] Just over a ton of tokens were struck again at a likely 42 halfpennies to the lb. Two further orders were to follow in 1795 and 1796, both of the 1794 type (other than changes of date) but sinking at the end to the distinctly lower standard of 46 halfpennies to the lb and using smaller quantities of copper.[74]

Over the four years 1793 to 1796 Soho produced more than 370,000 halfpennies for Mackintosh, Inglis and Wilson. Apart from the issues for Thomas Williams and John Wilkinson this was by far the largest token commission that came Boulton's way although for individual years it was exceeded by that for Taylor and Moody and more or less matched by those for the Cornish Metal Company and Daniel Eccleston. But 1796 was to mark the final year of Boulton's sortie into the manufacture of eighteenth-century provincial coinage. Soho received numerous proposals and orders for tokens in the meantime. John Morris's approach in 1795 has already been mentioned. A year later another copper entrepreneur, the great Cornish mine adventurer John Williams, wanted halfpenny tokens depicting 'a Fire Engine & Mine' on their obverse with 'a Cake of Copper, a Block of Tin and a

72   The arrangements for the order were handled by Tayler and Mander, factors of Steelhouse Lane, Birmingham, who also dealt with the second order of 1794.

73   Inverness's Stone of Destiny, originally in the street, was restored in 1900 after centuries of damage and vandalism and embedded in the plinth for the Merkat Cross outside the burgh's Town House where it is still to be seen.

74   William and Alexander Walker, merchants of Sand Street, Birmingham, handled the 1795 and 1796 orders of Mackintosh, Inglis and Wilson.

A MOST SATISFYING ADVENTURE

Fish' on the reverse. The order eventually came to nothing because of the impending issue of the Soho 'cartwheels' but the suggested designs were resurrected fifteen years later for Williams's 'Scorrier House' pennies so we have some idea of what might have been their appearance [131].

No more tokens were struck for currency by Soho until after the turn of the century for in June 1797 Boulton at last achieved his long cherished ambition of a government contract for the manufacture of a new regal coinage. But when his opportunity came it came suddenly and without warning just as Boulton was completing orders for the Gold Coast and for a second tranche of pieces for the Madras Presidency [132]. The early months of the year had been fraught with difficulty. The war with France was not going well and Britain was on the defence everywhere. Quoting Saint Paul, 'Without were fightings, within were fears', the *Annual Register* summed up a year 'more striking and alarming' than any other in the four decades of its existence.[75] An abortive French descent on Ireland in December 1796, frustrated by the weather, and an expeditionary landing of a motley force of 'very deplorable objects, without shoes or stockings, and scarce any other covering' at Fishguard in February 1797, farcical though it was, fuelled the febrile atmosphere of national insecurity. Despite Sir John Jervis's victory over a much more powerful Spanish fleet off Cape St. Vincent – a popular subject for token and medal manufacturers [133] – a very real fear of invasion intensified and people all over the country began to withdraw their guineas from the banks and conceal them in their houses or bury them in their gardens.[76] The run on the banks led to record transfers from the Bank of England's gold reserve already drained almost to exhaustion by mounting government borrowings

131 John Williams's 1811 'Scorrier House' penny with its images of 'a Fire Engine & Mine' and 'a Cake of Copper, a Block of Tin and a Fish' that he had hoped to depict on halfpenny tokens from Matthew Boulton in 1797.

133 Peter Kempson: Portsmouth halfpenny for Thomas Sharp with its Wyon design celebrating Sir John Jervis's naval victory off Cape St. Vincent, 1797.

132 Matthew Boulton: East India Company 1/48 rupee piece for the Madras Presidency, 1797.

75 *The Annual Register for the Year 1797* (1800), iv [The Second Epistle of Paul the Apostle to the Corinthians, vii, 5].

76 *The Times*, 3 March 1797. For the financial crisis and its aftermath see Feaveryear (1963), 179-87; Kelly (1976), 11-35; Ehrman (1996), 5-16; Dyer, G. P. (2002), 135-42.

145

for military expenditure and foreign subsidies;[77] by January its stock of bullion had fallen dramatically to less than £1.2 million. With banks everywhere stopping payment, government stock falling to a record low and the country's system of finance and credit facing collapse the nation was on the verge of bankruptcy. Cash payments by the Bank were therefore suspended at the end of February and the public encouraged to use banknotes instead of gold [134].[78] 'People have been struck mad with fright', Charlotte Matthews reported to Boulton from London, '& had not the severe remedy taken place respecting the Specie a general Bankruptcy must have been the Consequence – the People here receive the measure with great Cheerfullness & I wish the Country People may do the same'.[79]

As Charlotte Matthews had hoped banknotes, already a not unfamiliar means of exchange, quickly became the norm for day to day transactions as the Bank and then country banks and other local issuers in England and Wales were authorised to put out notes for less than £5, one of the first to take advantage of the new arrangements being John Wilkinson as we saw earlier (page 67 above). Within three years the circulation of Bank of England notes alone had risen from some £10 or £11 million in 1796 to nearly £16 million.[80] Financial confidence was soon restored but the episode was said by Lord Grenville years later to have been 'the most painful day' of Pitt's political life and although he decisively weathered the storm he could not escape the satirist's caustic pen:

> Of Augustus and Rome
> The poets still warble,
> How he found it of brick
> And left it of marble,
> So of Pitt and of England
> Men may say without vapour,
> That he found it of gold
> And left it of paper.[81]

---

77 In 1796 the Bank had also suffered a considerable drain of deposits back to France following the republic's restoration of the gold standard in the wake of the collapse of the *assignat*.

78 The stoppage of the redemption of the Bank's notes for gold was initially enjoined by Order in Council on 26 February. Despite Opposition denouncements that the action was a first step to national bankruptcy and that the notes would go the way of French *assignats* it was confirmed by Parliament in the Bank Restriction Act of 3 May 1797. What began as temporary suspension was to last for twenty-four years.

79 BAH: MS 3782/12/69/7, Charlotte Matthews to Matthew Boulton, 28 February 1797.

80 The new banknotes were authorised by 37 George III cap. 28, 37 George III cap. 32. By 37 George III cap 40 Scottish banks were empowered to issue notes of less than 20*s*. Feavearyear (1963), 192.

81 Hansard (1804-1820), XX (May-July 1811) (1812), 824; Stanhope (1862), III, 20.

A MOST SATISFYING ADVENTURE

134 *Bank-Notes, -- Paper-Money,-- French-Alarmists, ... ah! poor John-Bull!!!*
An etching of 1 March 1797 by James Gillray showing a yokelish John Bull trustingly accepting banknotes from Pitt as a Bank of England clerk despite the alarmist warnings of Stanhope, Sheridan and Fox in the guise of French revolutionaries.[82]

Despite the criticism Pitt's decisive measures restored confidence in the markets and rallied sentiment throughout the country. Banknotes became an accepted means of payment but they had their disadvantages. Local banknotes tended to enjoy only a limited geographical circulation while Bank of England notes did not normally stray far from the metropolis. Moreover, banknotes by themselves could not effectively meet the need for small change – flimsy, they were not practical as a rapidly circulating currency for small sums, occasionally as low as 3*s* 6*d* or even half-a-crown, and, often poorly engraved or printed, they were a godsend to the forger. It was, thus, with a belated recognition that there was a 'great want of Silver Coin ... particularly for the use of the lower Ranks of people'[83] that the government authorised the Bank on 3 March to issue from its reserves about half a million pounds' worth of Spanish dollars countermarked by the Mint with the king's head [35a and b]. The dollars were tariffed at 4*s* 9*d* each, a hasty readjustment from an original valuation of 4*s* 6*d* as the price of

---

82 George (1942), No. 8990.

83 Bank of England Archive: M695: 'Questions asked by the Privy Council's Committee on Coin on the 21st February 1798 and the answers given by the Bank', Q. 19. See also Kelly (1796), 134.

147

silver suddenly escalated.[84] Although at first they proved very popular – Parson Woodforde in rural Norfolk thought them commemorative of Jervis's 'great Victory over the Spanish Fleet'[85] – both the dollars themselves and the countermarks were quickly forged and the public began to fight shy of them. By the autumn only two-thirds of the issue had been taken up and in face of the rash of counterfeiting and a temporary fall in the price of silver even these were withdrawn to be replaced by 7*s* pieces in gold [36], the denomination the Bank had first petitioned for forty years before.[86]

It was against this background that Boulton was at last awarded his contract for a copper coinage. On 1 March the Commons asked the king to sanction the taking of measures 'for procuring an immediate supply of such Copper Coinage as may be best to the payment of the Laborious poor in the present Exigency'.[87] Two days later the matter was referred to a reconstituted Privy Council Committee on Coin. Immediately Liverpool alerted Boulton:

> In Consequence of the Difficulties which have occurred, in the present State of Affairs, to find a Circulating Medium for all Ranks of People and particularly those who are in less affluent Circumstances, it has been suggested, that it may be proper in such a Moment, to have a new Copper Coinage. There is no Man who can better judge of the Propriety of this Measure, and of the Plan that ought to be adopted, in issuing a Coinage of this Nature, than Yourself; and no one will execute it with more Accuracy, and more Expedition…[88]

In priming Boulton in this way Liverpool was living up to his reputation as a behind-the-scenes 'fixer' because, influential though he was in coinage matters, he was well aware that that there would be hurdles to overcome in the Committee's deliberations. And there were lengthy discussions. Nevertheless, driven by 'Jenky', the Committee moved swiftly, taking evidence from Thomas Williams on the availability of copper and receiving submissions from Boulton, young John Westwood and Charles Wyatt, the one-time manager of Williams's Birmingham mint as potential contractors. Sample specimens of their proposed coinages were submitted by the contenders, those of Westwood being his 'British Commercial' series [183] but before the

---

84   Thus inspiring the popular squib that 'Two kings' heads are not worth a crown'. Another satirical couplet was heard by Robert Southey (Cottle (1847), 210) as early as 25 April 1797 in the form:
     'To make Spanish dollars with Englishmen pass,
     Stamp the head of a fool, on the tail of an ass.'

85   Jameson (2005), 132.

86   Kelly (1976), 17-35 and Manville (2001), 3-4.
     Guineas continued to be minted for the Bank (primarily for the payment of its dividends) until 1799 after which the gold coinage was confined until 1813 to half guineas and the newly introduced 7*s* pieces.

87   Dyer and Gaspar (1992), 446.

88   BAH: MS 3782/12/42/34, Lord Liverpool to Matthew Boulton, 3 March 1797.

A MOST SATISFYING ADVENTURE

end of the month the Committee had submitted its report and on 9 June Boulton was awarded the contract he had striven for over so many years. In his letter to Boulton Liverpool had made it clear that the Committee would be looking for 'a Copper Coin, of the Value of Two Pence or Four Pence, so as to represent the Sixth, or the Third Part of a Shilling'.[89] In the end twopences and pence were decided upon, denominations never before struck in regal copper, the fear being, Liverpool later explained, that an issue of smaller coin would so discredit the old halfpennies, legal or counterfeit (tokens included among the latter), that they would be driven out of circulation faster than they could be replaced by Boulton's new coinage despite 'all his art and machinery'. As Boulton put it to a friend,

> a small Coinage of ½ pence ... would create Confusion in that Medium, rather than accommodation; & as it would take 2 Years to Coin a sufficient Quantity of halfpence to displace all the base Counterfeits now afloat, it was thought prudent to wave [*sic*] it at present, & Coin a moderate quantity of peny & two peny pieces; which will be a gentle introduction to a subsequent Coinage of ½ pence.[90]

But obviously even more in the mind of the Committee, as Liverpool's letter makes clear, was the consideration that, underpinning the Spanish dollars, this relatively high-value copper would go some way to providing a good-quality substitute for small silver, 'for the conveniency of change of the silver coin' as *The Times* put it.[91]

The new coins were to be struck on the traditional principle of full weight, the intrinsic value of their copper content plus the cost of fabrication being as far as was practicable equal to their face value. They were therefore massive and Boulton's steam presses had to be reinforced to withstand stresses far beyond those that had nearly been his undoing with the Monneron five-sol pieces six years before; for, at one ounce, even the new pennies were slightly heavier than the French *médailles de confiance* while the twopences weighed two ounces. The idea of linking the coins exactly to standard units of weight was Boulton's as was the notion that their diameters should serve as measures of length, eight of the latter, in line, originally intended to make one foot and seventeen pennies making two foot.[92] Although it was all very much touch-and-go by the end of April 1798 the contract

---

89   Liverpool recognised that the coin would be very bulky and heavy but he doubted whether 'this would be any Objection, to that Description of People, for whose Use the Coin is principally intended'.

90   Liverpool (1805), 195-96; BAH: MS 3782/12/42/84, Matthew Boulton to Sir George Shuckburgh-Evelyn. [Draft, endorsed in pencil 'March 1797'].

91   *The Times*, 9 March 1797.

92   In satisfying himself as to the exact coin diameters required Boulton procured a Standard foot from the Royal Society: Matthew Boulton to John Southern, 19 May and 28 May 1797 quoted in Prosser (1913), 379-80. The original linear measurement scheme was abandoned and, as actually struck, five twopences measured eight inches and five pennies seven inches: *Peck* (1960), 217.

149

for four hundred and eighty tons of pennies and twenty tons of twopenny pieces had been completed and over 17.5 million coins had been produced [135].[93]

They were distinctive not only in size and weight but also in design. A striking feature, which had been experimented with three years before on the much smaller platform of the Eccleston halfpennies and the East India coins for the Madras Presidency, was the broad raised and incusely inscribed rim of the coins that served to protect the low relief of the obverse and reverse images from too rapid a rate of wear. The dies were engraved by Küchler, the reverse figure of a Britannia emblematic of Britain's maritime power being taken from a sketch by the one-time Royal Academician and now Pittite MP for East Grinstead, Nathaniel Dance.[94] While not the most aesthetic of Boulton's productions or prime examples of Küchler's skill as a die-sinker these hefty coins – familiarly known as 'cartwheels' – were after all purely utilitarian in purpose and were far superior to anything that the Mint could have produced at the time. One unappreciative voice was that of the numismatically opinionated James Wright, junior, of Dundee who was at pains to make clear to Boulton his 'few strictures' on the coinage's design:

> [Is not] His **Majesty's head** ... considerably **too small** – & not **sufficiently raised**? Whether it would not have filled and pleased the eye more, & bore a better proportion to the **weight** and **massyness** of the surrounding circle – that the whole features & bust (keeping the present form) were expanded – so as **very nearly** to touch the extremities of the field both above & below... This enlargement would have enabled the artist to have cut deeper & given **more relief** in the higher parts of the cheek, curls of hair & shoulder, without straining the Die more in working. – No matter, though these more prominent parts had been raised a little higher than the broad circle – they might, no doubt suffer a little in circulation, but the circle without being higher than it is, would fully protect the profile & general outline, even in friction – and the great advantage & beauty of relief in all the pieces kept carefully is obvious...
>
> ... The **Flag** flying behind the distant ship is too large. Could not the whole figure of The Britannia have been **enlarged a little with advantage**.[95]

What Boulton's reactions were to Wright's criticisms can only be imagined. After all the king himself had approved the final designs of the coinage and had pronounced upon the size of his bust and the form of Britannia. Boulton would have been more cheered by the more

135   Matthew Boulton: Soho 'cartwheel penny', 1797.

---

93   Production of the twopenny pieces did not begin until January 1798.

94   Linecar (1977), 87-88. The Committee on Coin had wanted to go further in driving home Britain's naval prowess during the French war with references to the three battles of the Glorious 1st of June 1794, L'Orient 1795 and Cape St Vincent 1797.

95   BAH: MS 3782/12/42/215, James Wright, jnr. to Matthew Boulton, 1 September 1797.

general patriotic chord touched by the symbolism. As a correspondent put it with some enthusiasm to the *Monthly Review*:

> Küchler gave the figure of Britannia on the coinage new dignity and appropriateness; he brought back the Roman figure seated on a rock amidst the sea, among whose distant waves a line of battleships [*recte* one battleship] is sailing. In her left hand is the trident of her naval empery slanting above the shield that bears the Union Jack in right heraldic colours.[96]

A local poetaster was drawn to be even more eulogistic:

> WHEN Bacchus to Midas a patent bequeath'd
> (For so by the Poets we're told,)
> For turning, as long as on earth here he breath'd,
> Whatsoever he touch'd, into gold;
> No license he gave to the Phrygian Old Drone,
> On the bullion a STAMP to bestow;
> But the hoard a dead heap to the muckworm was grown,
> As no doit of it CURRENT would go.
> But had Bacchus to BOULTON imparted the power,
> To 'ply the philosopher's stone;
> That grant, though confin'd to the lapse of an hour,
> Had honor'd his Thyrsus and Throne! ...
> And yet if desert should be paid in due COIN;
> Modern works, which the ancients surpass,
> The Gods, in full synod, should lib'rally join,
> To applaud, though on COPPER or BRASS.
> And when, LIKE Celestials, with justice they aim,
> To discharge debts of honor below; –
> To give merit, but CURRENT and STERLING, its claim,
> 'Twine a wreath for the Man of SOHO'.[97]

Further contracts followed and by the time of their conclusion at the end of July 1799 Boulton's 'cartwheel' commitment had extended in total to 40 tons of twopences (722,180 coins) and 960 tons of pennies (43,969,204 coins). In the meantime the question of the manufacture of new halfpennies and farthings had repeatedly raised its head. These were the denominations – especially halfpennies – that were most wanted by the public and, as Liverpool understood, 'particularly from the Northern parts of the kingdom'. From Aberdeen Boulton heard from a customer, John Ewen, the silversmith and hardware man, that his 'Pennies, not [being] halfpennies, rendered them both less useful and acceptable ... [since] ... so many things are wanted in which a Half penny must be used' and from John Southern in Newcastle upon Tyne that 'Halfpence ... would be fully preferable and 2d pieces are not much liked'.[98] But there was a Gordian knot to be cut and that

---

96 *The Monthly Review* (1797), 119.

97 John Collins (1742-1808), 'EXTEMPORARY STANZAS, *On seeing the inimitable Copper coin of Mr. Boulton's Mint, at* Soho': quoted in Dent (1880), 188.

98 Liverpool (1805), 196; BAH: MBP 138/134, John Ewen to Matthew Boulton, 19 May 1798; BAH: MBP 343/33, John Southern to Matthew Boulton.

136 Matthew Boulton: Soho halfpenny, 1799.

was the opposition of the Mint to any further coining by Boulton: in Liverpool's words, 'the inferior Officers of the Mint contrived to raise objections, which suspended the execution of this measure' and it was not until the autumn of 1799, by which time the Soho mint had been reconstructed, that Boulton was awarded a contract for 550 tons of the smaller coins.[99] There had to be changes to Boulton's scheme of things, however, because the price of copper had gone up appreciably since 1797. The new halfpennies [136] and farthings were proportionately lighter than the two higher denominations and could not be used as half- and quarter-ounce weights as Boulton had planned. The raised rim and incuse lettering had gone too, to be replaced by a grained channel around the edge as a safeguard against counterfeiting.[100]

By the summer of 1800 the contract for the smaller currency had been completed and in the three years since the start of Boulton's operation some £275,000 in new copper coin had been manufactured at Soho. Boulton had taken the precaution of ensuring that an allowance had been made for distribution costs in his contract and he strove to deliver the new coin 'at every Mans Door in the two Kingdoms'.[101] In rural Hertfordshire a petty parish official was so struck by the new coins that he took the trouble to note their appearance in his diary[102] and the success of Boulton's undertaking meant that in many parts of the country the old counterfeit coinage and tokens were driven out of circulation and new issues stifled. In the Birmingham area tokens were quickly spurned in favour of the new 'cartwheels' and 'many persons, who had quantities of them received in the way of business, were at considerable loss by selling them for old metal at less than half their nominal value'.[103] But as we shall see later this was not everywhere; in more out of the way places not effectively covered by Boulton's distribution the old currency had a continuing acceptability. And, almost on cue with the appearance of the first Soho coins the price of copper began to escalate, the new weighty twopences and pennies disappeared into the melting pot and light-weight imitations quickly began to take their place. All Boulton's optimism that he had produced a coinage that was 'much more difficult to be Counterfeited than any Money ... in Europe' had proved to be misplaced.

What had been a fitful production of coin at Soho before June 1797 had since become an intensive endeavour to strike twenty tons of 'cartwheels' each week. But in 1798, in the midst of all this hectic activity, Boulton was able to meet an order for some fifteen tons of 'kepings' in traditional format for the East India factory at Bencoolen, and in the following year to strike a series of 'cartwheel' pennies and halfpennies for the Isle of Man, at the behest of its lord, the Duke of

99 Liverpool (1805), 196. On the reconstruction of the Soho mint, completed and running by May 1798, see Doty (1998a), 54-58.
100 Dyer and Gaspar (1992), 448; *Peck* (1960), 218.
101 PRO: BT6/118, ff.271-72, quoted in Dyer and Gaspar (1992), 448.
102 'New Halfpence this year [1800] and Last year, New penny piesses quoined in the year 1797': Johnson (1973), 54.
103 Gee (1798), 406-407.

Atholl, from dies by Küchler.

The few years after the completion of his regal contract in 1800 brought a period of respite to the Soho mint and Boulton returned to the manufacture of tokens; for a bank in recently ravaged County Wexford, in 1801, for a Nottinghamshire worsted mill in 1802 and for Viscount Charleville at Tullamore, King's County (County Offaly) in 1803 and 1804, and each issue was unusual in its own way.

Robert Woodcock's bank at Enniscorthy was registered on 14 September 1799 [104] as the town was beginning to recover from its devastation as the storm centre of the Irish Rebellion the previous year, an event implicit in the images of Woodcock's token [137]. Very likely engraved by Küchler the obverse was characterised by a sunken ellipse harking back to the five-sol *monnerons* of a decade earlier and framing a view of a beflagged Enniscorthy castle with the river Slaney flowing past. The flags with their saltire of St. Patrick rather than the harp of the rebels give some clue as to Woodcock's loyalist inclinations which are borne out again by the reverse of the token with its desolate prospect of Vinegar Hill crowned by its windmill – the eventual stronghold of the rebellion and site of its bloody suppression – beyond the blighted tree (a barren 'tree of liberty'?).[105] The token is very light in weight (averaging 7.8 g), struck at a standard even lower than the Mint's 52 Irish halfpennies to the lb, and takes a generous advantage of the Irish exchange rate of thirteen pence to the shilling. But the 655,304 pieces shipped to Woodcock must have enjoyed a fair degree of popularity judging by their general state of wear today.

The Arnold works, a worsted spinning factory about four miles north of Nottingham, had been established by Robert Davison (1751-1807) and John Hawksley (d. 1815) in 1791/92 after a fire had devastated an earlier mill of theirs on the river Leen in Nottingham itself.[106] The new five-storey complex at Arnot hill, on the road to Arnold, was said to have been the first steam-powered worsted mill in the area and by 1800 employed a thousand and more hands 'in house', at least half of whom were child poor-law 'apprentices' drafted in from London, Bristol and other large cities. Much criticism has been levelled at Davison and Hawksley for the alleged harsh treatment of their pauper apprentices but there is good evidence to suggest that they were responsible and enlightened employers and considerate to the people of Arnold – they also employed a thousand out-workers in and around the village – especially during the period of dearth in the autumn of 1800. They were at pains to declare that the apprentices would be 'well

137 Matthew Boulton: Enniscorthy token for Robert Woodcock, 1800.

---

104 Gilbart (1836), 23.

105 Woodcock is thought to have been a Quaker and would have had little sympathy with a rebellion which increasingly acquired the character of an anti-protestant cause and brought mayhem to Enniscorthy in the spring of 1798. His tokens were ordered through a Birmingham intermediary, the noted ivory turner Samuel Baker of the Bull Ring.

106 The original mill had been established on the banks of the Leen in 1788. Hawksley held two patents for combing wool (Patent Specifications 1956, 8 June 1793 and 2185, 4 July 1797: Woodcroft (1854) [1969], 257). His son was the distinguished civil engineer, Thomas Hawksley, FRS (1807-93).

138a Matthew Boulton: Arnold Works crown token for Davison and Hawksley, [1802].

clothed, lodged and boarded ... attend Church every Sabbath, and have proper masters appointed for their instruction' and there is little reason to doubt that these intentions were followed through although, in common with the practice at other mills, the juveniles worked long hours, day and night. Having said this, the mill did suffer from poor labour relations resulting probably from an ingrained local opposition to mechanisation – Davison and Hawksley introduced Cartwright's hated wool-combing machines into the mill in 1794 – and a reluctance on the part of hitherto-domestic workers to submit to the disciplines of the factory system, a situation exacerbated by the popular fury generated against Davison's pronounced radical views in the aftermath of the excesses of the French Revolution.[107]

Davison and Hawksley were well known to Soho. In 1797 the firm had apparently commissioned Boulton and Watt to convert their Newcomen engine to work on Watt's principles and to adapt it further the following year.[108] The token or 'pay tickets', dated 1791 presumably to commemorate the foundation of the factory, were produced in the summer of 1802. They are unusual in that although struck in 'mix'd metal' or copper they directly met the mill owners' need for silver coin for wages – some were even silver plated – put out in denominations

138b Davison and Hawksley's Arnold Works. Although dated 1822 the drawing, if authentic, must be based on a sketch or impression of at least a decade earlier before the mill was demolished.

107 Dickinson and Jenkins (1927), 312; *Nottingham Journal*, 20 December 1794; Burton (1923-24), 275-76; Chapman (1967), 179-96, 208-209 and passim; Chapman (2007), 117-130. The iniquities of child apprenticeship schemes and reactions to them are set out by George (1966), 250-53.

108 The Newcomen engine had been built by Francis Thompson, a Derbyshire engineer. Boulton and Watt's drawings for the altered engine are held by Birmingham Archives and Heritage Service [BAH MS 3147/Portfolio/149].

A MOST SATISFYING ADVENTURE

way above the norm for an eighteenth-century provincial coin as crowns, half crowns, shillings and sixpences [138a]. They are also distinctive in their symbolism for while the obverse fleece suspended from an abundant apple tree is conventional enough the reverse fasces crossed with a revolutionary spear and cap of liberty must have presented a provocative image in the febrile local politics of the time. Most specimens found today, especially in the higher values, are found only in moderate condition suggesting that they enjoyed a reasonable circulation in the locality even after the works closed down in 1810, which in itself is strange since the tokens are comparatively rare today.

The 'Tullamore' piece [139] – for the sum of **ONE SHILLING AND ONE PENNY**, an odd equivalence for thirteen pence Irish if that was what was intended – is often described as a truck ticket but it was occasioned by its promoter's recognition of 'the distress arising from our want of Silver currency' and that it circulated for small payments in the neighbourhood of the 20,000 acre Charleville estate is made clear by an official parliamentary submission in 1810.[109] Promissory, it was not payable on demand but, as its reverse made clear, only on the first Tuesday in the month! Although the order for the tokens was received in 1802 work was interrupted by a further order from the East India Company for Madras and problems in completing the dies. Eventually, although dated 1802, some ten thousand pieces were produced in two tranches in 1803 and 1804. Weighing nearly an ounce (28.35 g) they constituted what was one of Boulton's heaviest tokens and were the final sortie by Soho into British provincial coin making.[110] They also proved to be the last token commission of John Gregory Hancock, who, for a fleeting moment, now renewed an association with Boulton that had been broken a decade and more before. But more of Hancock and of Westwood in the next chapter.

For Boulton, while the steam engine business was the most lucrative of his adventures, it was the mint that seems to have given him most satisfaction as he turned his mind from products that depended on the 'Fashion, tast [*sic*], Caprice & Fancy of lords and ladies' to 'things usefull rather than ornamental'.[111] But by the time he had finally embarked on a regal copper coinage his health was beginning to decline and the direction of Soho was passing to a new generation. Boulton lived on until 1809 but for much of the new century he suffered severely from kidney problems and was for his last few years chair- and eventually bed-ridden. Johanna Schopenhauer, the German traveller, gives a charming vignette of him when, with her penchant for seeing industrial behemoths like the Bridgewater mines at Worsley and

139 Matthew Boulton: Tullamore token for Lord Charleville, [1803/1804].

109 Vice (1991b), 2-4; Gilbart (1836), 36.

110 'Tullamore' may not have marked the *absolute* end of token production at Soho. Tokens may have been occasionally struck in maintaining Soho's collection of old dies its museum of specimens and for the production of collectors' coin sets in the 1840s and perhaps later. For a valuable insight into the subject of Soho restrikes see Vice (1995).

111 Advice to his son referred to in a draft letter to E. G. Eckhardt, 1796 quoted in Jones (2008), 228.

155

the massive Walker ironworks at Masbrough, she called into Soho in 1805. She saw the manufactory steam engine at work and although the mint was not functioning that day experienced the master's delight in being able to explain to her personally the principles of its operation.[112]

> [W]e went to visit the establishment of Mr Boulton, the most remarkable sight of the region, called Soho. In the whole of England, perhaps in the whole of Europe, there is no more striking proof of what can be achieved by industry, diligence and continuous endeavour, than this friendly little place. We were heartily delighted to meet its creator, Matthew Boulton, now eighty years old [sic] and still in possession of all his mental faculties even though his body has long since been defeated by illness, age and relentless work. We found him incapacitated by severe pain... In the house he was carried by two sturdy servants, while out of doors he pushed himself about in a small comfortable carriage, invented in England to assist the lame and infirm who are so numerous there. His infirmity did not hinder him from showing us around personally... His dark eyes lit up with youthful fire when he told us how he had courageously fought and overcome the many difficulties he encountered. He explained and showed us everything in a most friendly manner.

---

112 Michaelis-Jena and Merson (1988), 16-17.

IV

A BIRMINGHAM TOKEN CONSORTIUM

AN INGENIOUS MECHANIC AND AN ADMIRED ARTIST

> You may recollect the name of Westwood. My Uncle, the late M[r] John W. was well known in Birm[m] as a general Manufacturer and maker of Medals & Coins. The original Copper Tokens made in the years 88 to 92 were wholly made by him and your Father. He was also the Inventor of the Copper Bolts for Shipping.
>
> John Westwood [Junior] to Matthew Robinson Boulton, 26 March 1821.[1]

The transfer of Thomas Williams's coining operations to Matthew Boulton in 1789 brought an end to John Westwood's long-standing association with the Anglesey entrepreneur. Westwood's direct involvement in the striking of coins for Williams had, one imagines, ceased soon after the appointment of Charles Wyatt as manager of the Great Charles Street warehouse but he no doubt had continued rolling copper and cutting blanks for the Anglesey mint. Now, however, even this business was closed to Westwood since Boulton had his own facilities at Soho. Westwood, though, had already decided to diversify into coin-making on his own account and as early as October 1787 he had acquired a press from Anthony Robinson, a Birmingham machine maker and smith.[2] The time now seemed ripe to him to embark on coining on a much larger scale. Boulton's, essentially self-serving advice, to buy Williams's redundant machinery – 'as I knew it would be injurious to Westwood to get new Presses made' – fell on deaf ears. Westwood, doubtless smarting over his abrupt loss of patronage, dismissed Williams's presses as the worst he had ever seen arguing that 'he could get new Presses twice as good at half the price' and promptly committed himself to the purchase of new equipment.[3]

---

[1] BAH: MBP 261/73.

[2] BAH: MS 3782/12/32/157, Thomas Greenhow to Matthew Boulton, 12 October 1787. Robinson's commitment to Westwood delayed his manufacture of a press for Boulton's East India Company Mint causing delays over the completion of the latter's Bencoolen contract.

[3] BAH: MS 3782/12/8/4, Matthew Boulton to Thomas Williams, 24 May 1789.

140 John Westwood's frontispiece to Myles Swinney's *British Museum or Universal Register*, 1771.

141 John Westwood: Medal celebrating the marriage of Christian VII of Denmark to Princess Caroline Matilda, the king's sister, 1768.

Westwood was now forty-five years old.[4] Little is known about his early life but there is good reason to believe that he had begun his career in Birmingham as a seal and copper-plate engraver and he is described as such in Sketchley's *Directory* for 1767, resident at the Bear and Ragged Staff in Bull Street. He is credited with a number of well-executed book illustrations [140] [5] and medals, including commemorative pieces for the visit of Christian VII of Denmark to England and his marriage to Princess Caroline Matilda, the king's sister [141], and for Garrick's Shakespeare Jubilee celebrations at Stratford in 1769 [142]. It has been plausibly argued, too, that he was also responsible for the *Resolution & Adventure* medal of 1772 [80], the Eyre Coote regimental medals two years' later and other, probably abortive, work for Boulton and Fothergill.[6]

Westwood issued his 'Shakespeare Jubilee' medal from Newhall Walk. Already die-sinking and metal-stamping may have been taking precedence over copper-plate engraving for by 1770, joined by his younger brother, Obadiah (c. 1746-1826), at 37 New Hall Street (the same address, for 'Street' and 'Walk' seem to have been indiscriminately used until 'Street' became the established usage), he could describe their business as that of 'Dye Sinkers and Coffin Furniture makers'.[7] Birmingham manufacture of coffin furniture – brass mountings, handles and ornaments – had been revolutionised by a die-stamping invention in 1769 and Obadiah had quickly taken advantage of this new development.[8] About this time, too, the brothers had embarked on the manufacture of coin scales and weights, a trade they continued for many years [48].[9]

By the late seventies, now removed around the corner to Great Charles Street, the brothers' paths had begun to diverge, Obadiah to concentrate on his coffin furniture, decorative stamped metal-work, button making and the production of popular medals, and John, in association with William Welch, the copper factor and Anglesey agent, to branch out into the merchandising of copper and brass, and, in due course, to gravitate into metal rolling at Witton, three miles north of the town.[10]

4 For Westwood and his association with John Gregory Hancock see Dykes (1999), 173-86.

5 Including plates for John Baskerville's folio Bible (1769-72), an engraving of a fractured leg in Tomlinson's *Medical Miscellany* (1769) and the frontispiece to Myles Swinney's ephemeral magazine, the *British Museum or Universal Register* (1771): Hill (1907), 77 note 80, 89 and 118.

6 Westwood (1926), 2-3; Smith (1985), 8, and 12; Vice (1998), 3-8. See also Symons (2006). Unfortunately *BHM* does not distinguish between the productions of the two John Westwoods but no medal after 1774 can be reasonably attributed to the uncle; the attribution of the unsigned *BHM* 149 (commemorating George Whitefield's death in 1770) to John Westwood, senior, is also very questionable.

7 Listed under 'Engravers and Chasers': Sketchley & Adams (1770).

8 The invention of John Pickering, a London gilt toy maker: Patent Specification 920, 7 March 1769: Woodcroft (1854) [1969], 442; Church and Smith (1966), 621.

9 Biggs (2004), 106; Withers and Withers (1993), 159-60 and *passim*. See p. 51 above.

10 Westwood is also said to have had mills at Saltley and King's Norton: Westwood (1926), 10. For a glimpse of Obadiah Westwood's medal making activities see Withers (1991), 29-33.

A BIRMINGHAM TOKEN CONSORTIUM

142 John Westwood: Medal for David Garrick's Shakespeare Jubilee celebrations at Stratford-upon-Avon, 1769.

Both brothers were inventive characters although some doubt has been cast on the originality of their inventions.[11] Obadiah was granted a patent in 1786 for a catch-all method of 'making trays, waiters, card-pans, caddies, dressing boxes, bottle-stands, ink-stands, coat, breast and other buttons, frames for picture and other things, mouldings, and ornaments for rooms and ceilings and for other purposes' by stamping treated textile pulps although the actual specification was restricted to button making and was suspiciously reminiscent of earlier patents awarded to Henry Clay, the Birmingham papier-mâché manufacturer.[12] A newspaper report in 1780 is said to have credited John Westwood with the invention of a new form of cannon which 'met with the highest approbation' of the Board of Ordnance[13] but this may simply have been based on some garbled reference to trials connected with John Wilkinson's famous patent of six years earlier. Westwood was, however, responsible for the patenting of a method of 'hardening and stiffening copper' by graduated cold rolling in 1783 but again the principles underlying the invention harked back to a patent granted almost two decades before to a Gloucestershire ironmaster.[14] Westwood's association with Welch had brought him into contact with Thomas Williams, and he now became even more closely linked with Williams who adopted Westwood's rolling methods at his Holywell manufactory. Westwood's invention, coupled, in some way, with a process for making copper bolts patented by William Collins,[15] paved the way for the Anglesey entrepreneur to gain a virtual European monopoly of copper sheathing for ships in the last decades of the eighteenth century.

The Williams and Collins connection led, in turn, to Westwood's becoming a key figure in the team involved in Williams's attempts to secure the contract for a regal coinage and in the production of the 'Copper King''s tokens. Although Pye's suggestion that Westwood minted the 'Monogram' Anglesey penny in 1786 [63] is by no means implausible Williams's actual production coinage was embarked upon at Holywell. From the gossip that intruded upon Boulton's sensitive ears it seems that Westwood, with Hancock, oversaw Williams's manufacture of 'Druid' coins both at Holywell and then initially at Birmingham when, after little more than a few weeks, the latter's coining operations were transferred to the Midlands. Shortly after the move to Birmingham and Wyatt's appointment to the Anglesey warehouse Westwood's supervision of Williams's mint must have come

---

11 Prosser (1881), 47 and 127.

12 Patent Specification 1576, 14 December 1786; cf. Patents 1180, 5 February 1778 and 1572, 9 November 1786 granted to Henry Clay: Woodcroft (1854) [1969], 606 and 110.

13 Westwood (1926), 10.

14 Patent Specification 1398, 15 November 1783: cf. Patent Specification 854, 31 July 1766 granted to John Purnell of Frampton-on-Severn: *Gloucester Journal*, 8 September 1766; Woodcroft (1856) [1969], 606 and 462.

15 Patent Specification 1388, 2 October 1783: Woodcroft (1856) [1969], 120.

159

to an end, a change that explains his decision in the autumn of 1787 to buy a press for himself and to turn to coining on his own account. No doubt this was on a small scale at first and bore no very close examination. It is likely, though, that he was responsible at this time for the striking of the pattern halfpennies [79a] that, based on a design by Samuel More and engraved by Hancock with more than a nod to Droz, were intended for submission to the Privy Council Committee on Coin in the spring of 1788, as samples, with Boulton's pieces [79c] and those of Pingo [79b], for a national coinage contract. They were probably put forward by Williams but that is a question that for the present must remain open.

As a copper roller Westwood's association with Williams was to continue for another year but the latter's decision to cut loose from the manufacture of coin and transfer this concern to Boulton in 1789 brought about a sudden and total reversal in Westwood's fortunes. He found himself under-employed in his copper-rolling business – in Birmingham and its vicinity there were already over half a dozen similar firms and Boulton with his own plant had no need for Westwood's services – and financially over-stretched just at a time when copper prices were wildly fluctuating. Moreover, his prodigality in commissioning additional coining presses in the late spring of 1789 was misplaced. By September Westwood was, financially, in a parlous state. No support came from Thomas Williams although the latter was now benefiting handsomely from his adoption of Westwood's rolling methods. By December Westwood had become bankrupt causing a number of respectable Birmingham backers including John Hurd to catch severe pecuniary colds.[16]

In the early months of the year Westwood had committed himself to the production of halfpennies for the Cheshire copper and brass manufacturers, the Macclesfield Copper Company (Roe and Company), and their associated mining firm at Cronebane in County Wicklow. But, as yet, he was still without the necessary machinery for large-scale coining, and with his affairs beginning to fall into increasing disarray he had, as we have seen, to subcontract his Cronebane commission to Boulton. An agreement to strike halfpennies for the Southampton partnership of Taylor, Moody and Company was called into question as a result of the bankruptcy after only a small run of specimen pieces had been completed [94] and the contract was eventually usurped by Boulton as was a tentative arrangement Westwood had made with the Glasgow woollen drapers, Gilbert Shearer and Company. We have no means of telling which of his enterprises forced him into a crisis of liquidity yet although Westwood was never able to discharge his debts both his coinery and metal-rolling business continued to function through the support of Hancock and his brother. And there is no doubt that even if by means of something of a sleight of hand others became the public face of his concerns Westwood still remained their

---

16   Westwood's bankruptcy as a 'Caster of Metals, Roller, Dealer and Chapman' was gazetted on 1 December 1789: *LG*, No. 13153, 28 November-1 December 1789, 753.

A BIRMINGHAM TOKEN CONSORTIUM

143   Westwood/Hancock: Macclesfield halfpenny for Roe and Company, 1790.

driving force. It was an arrangement that years later could allow John Westwood, junior, when approaching Matthew Robinson Boulton for a post in his proposed Calcutta mint for the East India Company, to maintain that the 'original Copper Tokens made in the years 88 to 92 were wholly made' by his uncle and Matthew Boulton.[17]

Perhaps through the helpful dilatoriness of Hancock in preparing the dies, Westwood was able, over Boulton's head, to retain the commission with the Macclesfield Copper Company for their own first halfpennies – the 'Beehive' tokens – although it was noised abroad that he had to have them struck in London. By the spring of 1790, however, his own presses were set up and running at his Great Charles Street premises and Westwood had struck another tranche of tokens [143] for the Macclesfield company and had undertaken to coin for Wilkinson. Although the new Macclesfield halfpennies paralleled Wilkinson's issues with their obverse portrait of Charles Roe, the company's founder, they did not project the arrogance of the ironmaster but rather the benignity of a kindly and shrewd man who had after all been dead for close on nine years. Roe's 'antique' bob wig, nevertheless, did attract some aesthetic censure from Joseph Moser who asserted that he had had several 'portrait' tokens rejected by shopkeepers in the Chester area on the grounds that 'we never take a wig halfpenny'.[18]

The Birmingham grapevine quickly alerted Boulton to the existence of Westwod's commissions as he told Garbett on 29 March:

> The Macclesfield Co have lately orderd of Jno Westwood an addition of 25 Tons to the 21 Ton lately issued by them (36 to the pound) & those of this last order have the Head of old Roe upon them... Mr Jno Wilkinson hath likewise orderd a certain number of Tons of his ½ pence with his own portrait upon them to be fabricated by Westwood.[19]

Boulton's seemingly casual comment to his old friend masked his outrage at the discovery that Wilkinson, already contracted to Soho,

---

17   Westwood, having heard that Boulton was planning a 'compleat (*sic*) Mint to go abroad', was offering his services in the capacity of a manager or engraver for, as he rather delicately put it, he was 'disengaged': BAH: MBP 261/73, 26 March 1821. Not for the first time had this talented artist fallen upon hard times and, now middle-aged, he had decided to give up his decaying business of engraving dies for medals and box lids. Westwood had, twenty years earlier (29 January 1800), tried to dispose of some of his dies to Boulton's father on the grounds that his business was then 'so very indifferent' : BAH: MS 3782/12/45/1800/32. His medallic work effectively came to an end in 1821 with his medal of Sir Robert Wilson (*BHM* 1168; *Eimer* 1156): there is no reason to associate *BHM* 928 (1816) or *BHM* 1317 (1827) with Westwood.

18   Moser (1798), 236 note †. The shopkeepers' reluctance to take 'Roe' halfpennies was probably less to do with any artistic sensibilities they might have possessed than with their suspicion of omnipresent counterfeits. Roe's portrait was again taken from his monument in Christ Church, Macclesfield.

19   BAH: MS 3782/12/62/83, Matthew Boulton to Samuel Garbett, 29 March 1790.

144   Westwood/Hancock: 'Vulcan' halfpenny for John Wilkinson, 1791.

145   'Vulcan', Plate X, no. 1 of Joseph Spence's *Polymetis*, 1747.

had engaged Westwood. To be fair to Wilkinson, always desperate for a speedy response to his orders, he had turned to Westwood in the face of Boulton's inveterate delays, since, as he later put it, 'a beefsteak to a man that is hungry will be preferred to venison, when waiting for it is a condition'.[20] Soho's production for the ironmaster was brought to an immediate halt but after nine months of stand-off Wilkinson found that Westwood's pretensions were no more valid than those of Soho – he could not meet a promised 17 cwt of halfpennies per week – and, chastened, Wilkinson had to abase himself to Boulton. '[W]hen I found', Boulton expostulated in return, venting 'a little bile from my own Stomach' … 'that you had pitted Westwood against me I stopped short as it w^d have been cowardly in me to have run against such a competitor. Splitting of ½ pence is the next thing to splitting of farthings. I do not love things in the ½ and ½ way'.[21] Profit came before pride, however, and, in the event, Boulton resumed striking for Wilkinson, producing several tons of 'Forge' halfpence over the years 1791 to 1793. Notwithstanding his accommodation with Boulton, 'the Salamander' continued to employ Westwood who struck some three ton of halfpennies, dated 1790 and 1791 [144]. These are distinguished on their reverse by a figure of Vulcan that Hancock is said to have modelled on the engraving of an antique cornelian in Joseph Spence's *Polymetis* [145] and a distinctive obverse bust with a more elaborately curled wig covering the ear.[22] Still, Dumarest's copy for Boulton of Hancock's original representation of Wilkinson – his 'resurrection' – and the 'old Forge' appealed more to the ironmaster than Hancock's new designs. Nevertheless, Wilkinson's discovery that the halfpennies in the first consignment from Soho were heavier than Westwood's tokens led to further argument with Boulton. 'Whatever Politicians and Statesmen may judge to be a proper Standard', Wilkinson grumbled, 'I shall incline (untill some regulation may prevent it) to oblige my Customers, particularly where it is so much to my own interest'.[23] As was the case with Wilkinson's 'Forge' halfpennies, and indeed all tokens of widespread circulation, the 'Vulcan' halfpennies were extensively counterfeited, genuine pieces always having the usual **WILLEY SNEDSHILL BERSHAM BRADLEY** as their edge inscription.

Surprisingly, neither Boulton's sharp-eyed watch over any semblance of encroachment on his nascent mint nor the claims of the younger Westwood, are borne out by Charles Pye in the quarto (1801) edition of his *Provincial Coins and Tokens*, traditionally regarded as the authoritative contemporary account of mainstream eighteenth-century token-making, at any rate as far as Birmingham is concerned.

20   John Wilkinson to Matthew Boulton, 11 October 1792 quoted in Chaloner (1948a), 308.

21   BAH: MBP 367/40, Matthew Boulton to John Wilkinson, October 1790.

22   Sharp (1834), 85; Spence (1747), 80 and Plate X, no. 1, derived from Leonardo Agostini. *Le gemme antiche figurate* (Rome 1657), I, Plate 118.

23   John Wilkinson to Matthew Boulton, 11 December 1790 quoted in Vice (1990), 4.

Here there is no mention of Westwood as the manufacturer of any Macclesfield or Wilkinson halfpennies. Indeed, Pye gives Westwood or his family scant recognition for token manufacture attributing to them a mere handful of tokens all of which fall outside the period specified by the nephew: to 'J. Westwood', the original [1786] 'Monogram' pattern for Thomas Williams's 'Druid Tokens' ([63]; Plate 1, 1); to 'O. Westwood', a halfpenny (1794) for James Lackington, the London bookseller ([226]; Plate 31, 4); and to 'Westwood' *simpliciter*, the Sherborne halfpenny (1793) of the banking firm of Pretor, Pew & Company ([176]; Plate 44, 7) and the 'Washington/Ship' Halfpenny (1793) ([163]; Plate 51, 10).[24]

If one were to believe Pye, therefore, John Westwood would have little place in the pantheon of eighteenth-century token manufacturers. Thomas Williams, Matthew Boulton and, from 1791, Peter Kempson, William Lutwyche and William Mainwaring all appear in his catalogue during the years 1788-1792.[25] The only other Birmingham token maker, and apart from Williams the most prolific, is 'Hancock' – John Gregory Hancock – who is credited with at least twelve series of provincial coins totalling many tons of copper, and, on the basis of Lutwyche's estimates, quoted by Thomas Sharp, a production of well over six and a half million tokens in a period of less than three years.[26]

Hancock's name had been linked with that of Westwood since their Holywell days. They were the Castor and Pollux of the earliest years of token making; to an agonised Boulton at that time 'the 2 best Die Engravers in England'.[27] And they were to be inseparably associated until Westwood's death in 1792. But Hancock, like Westwood, is an elusive character and little is actually known about him. Such information as we do have indicates that he was the son, likely the younger of two brothers, of a Robert Hancock (*c.* 1714-1792), also an engraver and long associated with the enterprises of the Boulton family.[28] Not unnaturally with such a background, both John Gregory, born about 1750, and his brother William were apprenticed for seven years to the hardware manufactory of Boulton and Fothergill in 1763,

---

24   Pye (1801) also refers to the younger Westwood's fraudulent copies – of the 'Monogram' Anglesey penny and the Southampton 'St Bevois' halfpenny, for instance – and his specious pennies, halfpennies and 'half-halfpennies' based on genuine tokens, but only to castigate them in his 'Advertisement' and the 'Observations' to his 'Index'.

25   William Mainwaring (d. 1794) may not have been a manufacturer as such; a token engraver he worked for Lutwyche who bought his dies after his death: cf. William Robert Hay quoted in Dykes (1997), 120.

26   Sharp (1834), ii; Sharp actually quotes Lutwyche's figure as 103,040 halfpence to the ton (the notional weight standard of Tower halfpence, i.e. 46 tokens to the lb avoirdupois).

27   BAH: MBP 148/97 (Matthew Boulton to Samuel Garbett, 22 April 1787); Matthew Boulton to J-P Droz (Draft), 12 June 1787 quoted in Hawker (1996), 10.

28   Robert Hancock's death was reported in *ABG* on 20 August 1792: 'Last week in his 79th. year, Mr. Robert Hancock, formerly of the Soho Manufactory, near this town'.

shortly after its establishment and the year before its move to Soho.[29] John Gregory Hancock is said to have continued at Soho for some time after the expiration of his indentures but by 1783 he had set up business on his own account in Birmingham as a die-sinker and had made his entry on the numismatic scene with the issue of his 'Joseph Priestley' medals to celebrate the scientist's fiftieth birthday [146].[30]

Surprisingly, in view of his later prominence as a coin engraver and medallist, the 'Priestley' medals seem to be Hancock's only authenticated numismatic productions until his involvement with the new provincial coinage of the Parys Mine Company four years later. By then he was regarded as a die-engraver of some distinction but no record of Hancock's other earlier work has come down to us. Hancock only really begins to emerge from the shadows in 1787 with his involvement with Thomas Williams. In that year, in addition to the Anglesey tokens, he is said to have engraved dies for a pattern guinea [31] and, in 1788, for the pattern halfpenny [79a] designed by More. There are, too, some unfinished uniface flans for the so-called trial 'halfpenny' of Samuel Garbett [38] which Matthew Young is said by Sharp to have attributed to Hancock.[32] The portrait is, certainly, redolent of the die-sinker's style. It seems unlikely, however, that these anomalous pieces predate the Anglesey issues as some have suggested. The more credible explanation is that they were produced by Hancock as trial specimens in the early 1790s and, rejected by Garbett whose attitude to tokens was, to say the least, guarded, remained in the die-sinker's possession for a few more years. Miss Banks, for instance,

146 John Gregory Hancock: Joseph Priestley medal in celebration of the scientist's fiftieth birthday with its two reverses showing different views of Priestley's scientific apparatus, 1783.

29 BAH: MBP 236/103: Articles of Agreement with Thomas Askey, 5 April 1764, varying the original indentures of 24 June 1763 which have not been traced.

30 *ABG*, 4 August 1783. By 1783 William Hancock had also gone into private business as a 'plater'. By 1797 he is described (in Pye's *Directory*) as a 'toyman', an activity that may have given rise to the erroneous notion that there had earlier been a family 'toy' business.

31 Forrer recorded a bronze uniface (obverse) pattern guinea of 'Spade type', signed 'HANCOCK', which would presumably date from *c.* 1787 and might be connected with Thomas Williams's campaign for a national coinage contract: Forrer (1902-1930), VII (1923), 414-415.

32 Sharp (1834), 121. Sharp thought Young's attribution somewhat questionable, although he considered that the work was respectable.

147 Hancock's view of the Crescent and Canal Basin. Detail from Plate G of Bisset's *Poetic Survey round Birmingham*, 1800.

148 John Gregory Hancock: Unfinished private token (uniface) portraying the artist's workshop.

did not acquire her specimen until 1798 and, bearing in mind her acquisitiveness and acquaintance with the individual portrayed, it would be surprising if she would not have obtained it very much earlier had it been available. Interestingly enough its first catalogue appearance is in Conder's *Arrangement* published in the same year.[33]

Hancock first appears in the Birmingham trade directories in 1785, described in that of Pye and presumably in the way of these things at his own instance, as a 'Modeller, Dye-sinker, and Chaser' in Bartholomew Row. Two years' later, now removed to 45 Edmund Street, he is shown, more simply, as an 'Artist'. This was to be his standard directory designation, though at a variety of addresses, until his final appearance in Chapman's volume for 1803, now resident in Hospital Street.[34] He was included among the fifteen Birmingham artists named on a plate (J) in Bisset's *Poetic Survey round Birmingham* (1800) to which he contributed several designs and copper-plate engravings [147] and it was as an 'artist', too, that he is described in the notice of his death at the age of 55 in *Aris's Birmingham Gazette* for 11 November 1805.[35] Five years earlier when he had essayed a private token or medal for himself it was an impression of an artist-engraver's studio that Hancock chose to portray [148]. According to Sharp it represented an interior view of Hancock's own workshop: 'To the workboard a vice is affixed, and near it an engraver's cushion; to the right of the window, in the distance, is seen a whole-length anatomical figure, and a female torso on a pedestal, with a large cast of a head resting against it, occupies the foreground'.[36]

Yet, although Hancock was seen, and saw himself, as an artist, a modeller and an engraver, his relationship with Westwood seems to have thrust him increasingly into a more general coining role. It is not without interest that when Boulton was drawn to make a note about the operation of Williams's Birmingham coin presses in 1788 it was Hancock that he mentioned: 'Hancox says he can work them so as to strike ½ pence with ¼ of 1 turn', while the following year, apropos of the Southampton commission that we know was initially awarded to Westwood, an alarmed Watt could report to his partner that 'H [Hancock] braggs that he can coin in your way, at half price that you can'.[37] Westwood clearly had an associate with a more than

---

33 Sharp (1834), 121. Miss Banks recorded the acquisition date of her Garbett 'halfpenny' as 26 February 1798 in her token catalogue: Banks MS Cat. VI (SSB 186-120); Conder (1798), 222.

34 The directories show Hancock, described as an 'artist', at Snowhill from 1791 to 1798, Summer Lane in 1800 and 1801, and, finally, Hospital Street in 1803.

35 *ABG*, 11 November 1805: 'Saturday, s'ennight [i.e. 2 November 1805], aged 55, sincerely lamented by all the friends and patrons of genius, that admired artist, Mr. J. G. Hancock, of this town'.

36 Sharp (1834), 29. Miss Banks states that this piece was 'intended by Hancock for his private token. such as it is there are only six': Banks MS Cat. VI (BM Reg. No.T.6334).

37 BAH: MBP Notebook 53 ('Coining Money', 1788), 89; BAH: MBP 351/154, James Watt to Matthew Boulton, 30 June 1789.

passing knowledge of the practical processes of minting, someone who had a talent for technical innovation [38] and who, when financial disaster struck in 1789, could help Westwood keep his new coinery afloat and, if it proved expedient to do so, assume its public image. That Hancock had some 'interest', whether pecuniary or otherwise, in the firm cannot be doubted – Obadiah Westwood publicly referred to such an arrangement shortly after John Westwood's death in 1792 – but Westwood remained in practical charge, a situation of which those in the know, like Boulton, were well aware; to other contemporaries, though, it may well have seemed that Hancock had taken charge of coining at Great Charles Street.

Hancock's apparent dominance at the coinery in Great Charles Street may have been little more than a convenient sham but it was one that was to be embedded for posterity by Charles Pye. By the time that he put out the plates for the quarto edition of his catalogue the Westwood's coin-making business had been defunct for more than five years and only Hancock was left as a ready witness of the Westwoods' activities. No doubt, in contributing to Pye's publication, Hancock would not have wished to underplay his own part in their token venture. And, captive to the evidence made available to him, Pye would have accepted the partial story that he was told which subsequent generations have, not unnaturally, accepted. Moreover, it was not only the cloud of bankruptcy that hung over Westwood. Both he and his brother had the reputation of being somewhat dubious characters, a factor of some significance in a town where business might be sharp but was dominated by some degree of rectitude at its higher levels which were all too conscious of 'Brummagem''s reputation in matters of coining. To Garbett Westwood was 'an ingenious Shabby Fellow, associated with Counterfeiters of Coin & Engraved Glasgow Bank Notes'.[39] It is not surprising, then, that Westwood's bankruptcy and fall from grace should be perceived as a just desert to a career of questionable integrity. There is more than a little inwardness in Pye's almost apologetic reference to him in his *Description of Modern Birmingham* where he 'considers it no more than an act of justice, to observe, that the manufacture of copper bolts, for fastening the timbers of ships together, was invented by Mr John Westwood, an inhabitant of this town'.[40] No reference to Westwood's major concern in copper rolling, no reference to his coining activities; no doubt reflections of his townsmen's wish to forget Westwood.

Unhappily, no business papers have survived to tell us anything

---

38   Hancock had presumably incorporated a 'fast thread' mechanism into Williams's presses. He was certainly of an inventive turn and was awarded patents for making parts for window frames(Patent Specification 2069, 15 October 1795), embossing paper (Patent Specification 2102, 6 April 1796) and for cutting and pressing metals (Patent Specification 2783, 14 September 1804): Woodcroft (1854) [1969], 246.

39   BAH: MS 3872/12/108/51, Notebook 3, 17 (26 March 1787). Although this comment appears in one of Boulton's notebooks it seems to be in Garbett's hand.

40   Pye (1823), 4.

A BIRMINGHAM TOKEN CONSORTIUM

concrete about Westwood's affairs but in fairness to him all those tokens attributed by Pye to Hancock as a manufacturer over these 'unknown' years, 1789-1792, should really be credited to Westwood or, at the very least, to Westwood and Hancock 'in concert'. And they were years of considerable activity during which something in the region of sixty-five tons of tokens were produced at the Great Charles Street coinery; all on traditional manually operated presses and representing only the visibly 'legal' tip of a sizeable and shady operation. Even in terms of authentic productions this meant the striking of well over 6.6 million tokens; a not unrespectable output in comparison with the much vaunted steam operation of Boulton that produced much the same quantity of provincial coins over the years 1789-92 although in these years, of course, it was also involved with large overseas commissions.

Although the Westwood/Hancock consortium continued making halfpennies for Wilkinson and the Macclesfield company into 1792 its order book took on a new dimension in 1790 when the firm began to add commercial customers to its staple of industrial concerns.

Taking them in date order the issuers of 'Westwood/Hancock' tokens, as described by Pye, are set out in **Table 2**:

Of the new commissions undertaken from 1791 only one was placed by a fully-fledged industrialist, John Morgan, a Carmarthen ironmaster and tinplate manufacturer [149] who, with his father,

149 John Morgan (1739-1805). From a miniature by Angelica Kauffmann.

Table 2
Westwood/Hancock Provincial Coin Contracts

Date	Issuer	Place of Issue	Quantity Struck (Pye 1801)	Pye Reference	D&H Reference [a]
1789-92	John Wilkinson[b]	Willey, Snedshill, Bersham and Bradley	6+ ton	Plate 48, 3,4,5,8,9 and 10	War. 424-430, 432-438 and 448-450
1789, 1790-92	Roe & Company	Macclesfield, Liverpool and Congleton	11 ton	Plate 36, 1,2 and 3	Ches. 9, 10-15 and 16-59
1790	Taylor, Moody & Co.	Southampton	A few specimens	Plate 45, 1	Hants 84
1790-92	T & A Hutchison	Edinburgh	10+ ton	Plate 18, 3	Lothian 23-30, 31-37 and 41-46
1791	Jonathan Garton & Co.	Hull	5 ton	Plate 23, 6	Yorks. 17-21
1791	Richard Paley	Leeds	5 ton	Plate 26, 3	Yorks. 43-51
1791	John Kershaw	Rochdale	2 ton	Plate 43, 1	Lancs. 140
1791-92	Thomas Clarke	Liverpool	10 ton	Plate 27, 4 and 5	Lancs. 61-78 and 95-99
1791-92	Thomas Worswick & Son	Lancaster	5 ton	Plate 26, 2	Lancs. 9-26 and 28
[1792]	John Morgan	Carmarthen	5 ton[c]	Plate 13, 5	Carmarthenshire 5-7
1792	Samuel Kingdon	Exeter	5 ton	Plate 19, 6	Devonshire 2-3
1792	William Absolon	Yarmouth	5 cwt	Plate 50, 1	Norf. 51-52

a The *D&H* references given here and in **Table 3** exclude trial pieces, patterns and proofs.

b It is difficult to disentangle the 'Hancock' pieces from those struck by Boulton and it is virtually certain that Wilkinson's 'Ship' halfpence and silver 3/6's [Plate 48, 6; *D&H*: War. 336-337] were struck by Thomas Williams.

c John Morgan's token is scarce today, even in the mediocre condition in which it is usually found, and the mintage figure given by Pye must be suspect.

150a Westwood/Hancock: Carmarthen Iron Works halfpenny for John Morgan [1792].

Robert, before him, did much to establish south-west Wales as the dominant region for the latter industry over the succeeding century and a half. Morgan had inherited a substantial business from his father in 1778 with four forges in Carmarthenshire (Kidwelly, Carmarthen, Whitland and Cwmdwyfran (the 'Valley of the Two Crows') and one in Pembrokeshire (Blackpool near Narberth) together with an iron and tinplate works in Carmarthen.[41] The enterprise, fully integrated from the manufacture of pig iron to the rolling of tin plate, continued to flourish under John Morgan – by 1800 possessing its own small fleet of sloops bringing tin from Cornwall and iron from the North-East – and with agents operative in Bristol, Liverpool and London, it achieved something of a European reputation. If the father is an elusive character even less is known of the son but John Morgan's status in Carmarthenshire society was recognised in 1782 with his appointment as the county's sheriff and by 1790 Morgan had added banking – the Carmarthen Furnace Bank – to his business interests.[42]

Morgan's remarkable token [150a], testifying to his 'delight in the iron trade', is one of the finest of the series and is a magnificent example of Hancock's work. The substantive issue is undated but from the evidence of a dated pattern (150b) it was presumably issued in 1792.[43] The obverse of the halfpenny convincingly conveys all the drama of the charcoal furnace at the **CARMARTHEN IRON WORKS** being tapped and the released molten metal being run into a casting bed. The engraving seems to have been based on a watercolour drawing by an unknown artist 'JCD' [150c] who also produced as a pendant an interior view of the **CWMDWYFRON IRON WORKS** which Hancock used for the reverse of the token. This depicts the operation of a water-powered tilt-hammer reminiscent of Hancock's 'Forge' scene for Wilkinson but is much more highly detailed.

The water-course flowing towards the furnace wheel at Carmarthen with the upper tin-mills in the foreground is depicted by the topographical artist Charles Norris (1779-1858) [151] in a painting of the turn of the century, which, though romantic in its setting, unfortunately adds little to our understanding of the scope of the undertaking.

150b Westwood/Hancock: Uniface pattern of the Carmarthen Iron Works halfpenny for John Morgan dated 1792.

41 For Robert and John Morgan see Green (1915), 245-56; Williams (1961), 440-49; James (1976), 31-54; Ince (1993), 28 and *ODNB*, s.v. 'Robert Morgan'.

At its height it is said that some 400 workers, 'girls and women as well as men', were employed in the iron and tin works at Carmarthen. By the turn of the century the works were, however, being dismissed as of 'old construction' and after Morgan's retirement from the business in 1800, dependent as they were on iron produced with charcoal and run by an incompetent management, they rapidly declined.

42 In 1810 the bank was acquired by David Morris and Sons who issued a silver shilling token the following year: Dalton (1922), 52 (Carmarthenshire 1-2). The Morris family took up partnerships in the ironworks business after John Morgan's retirement in 1800.

43 Miss Banks acquired her specimen of the substantive token in 1793: Banks MS Cat. VI, SSB 184-24-1.

A BIRMINGHAM TOKEN CONSORTIUM

150c Watercolour drawings of John Morgan's Carmarthen and Cwmdwyfron Ironworks by an unknown artist, 'JCD', c. 1790.

151 A view of the Carmarthen Tinworks by Charles Norris, c. 1800, looking along the leat to the arch leading to the furnace waterwheel.

Pye tells us that five tons of Morgan's tokens were struck. At a notional standard of 36 to the lb, which seems to be appropriate for the issue, this would imply some 400,000 pieces. They are, however, much scarcer today than such a figure would suggest and one is led to think that Pye either nodded or was misinformed. Perhaps only 'five cwt' (or some 20,000 halfpennies) was really intended, a more likely quantity for a token that although heavily used – it is rarely found in other than a worn state – was essentially local in its circulation, despite its edge-declaration to be payable in **LONDON BRISTOL AND CAERMARTHEN**. It is perhaps something of a paradox that what could have been a superb advertisement for Morgan's business should have been used purely for limited currency about his works. Maybe the cost of Hancock's delicate engraving militated against the production of more than a bare minimum of a set of dies (two obverses and one

169

152 Westwood/Hancock: A countermarked Yarmouth halfpenny for William Absolon, 1792.

153 Staffordshire stoneware jug decorated by William Absolon with the inscription 'A Trifle from Yarmouth', c. 1790.

reverse) which had resulted only after a series of trials and breakages.[44]

An equally small issue of halfpennies [152] was commissioned in the same year, 1792, by William Absolon (1751-1815), a Great Yarmouth china and glass dealer. Absolon, a local artist, decorated many of the wares he bought in and sold at his shop in the town's Market Row both to the order of local customers and to advertise the attractions of a trading and fishing port which was beginning to develop as a fashionable summer resort [153].[45] Although Absolon's tokens were intended as much for this same souvenir trade as for local currency they lacked the artistry of his now much sought after ceramics and glass. They were surprisingly pedestrian in their design reflecting, one imagines, the costs of the manufacturer rather than the aesthetics of the issuer: a full rigged sailing ship for the obverse and the arms of the town for the reverse, both becoming stock types for Birmingham-produced tokens of the period. Although Absolon was an adept at publicity – he produced 'skit' banknotes to publicise his business [46] – his tokens bear little comparison with the attractive shop pieces produced four years later for the Boulters, the Yarmouth museum keepers, by James Good [248]. According to Miss Banks Absolon had a fear of counterfeiting and impressed his legitimate halfpennies with a small rosette countermark (normally to the right of the reverse shield).[47] Countermarked tokens are much more common than unmarked ones but if the feared counterfeits do exist they must be exceedingly rare. On the other hand Absolon perhaps had reason to be suspicious for Hancock quickly adapted the reverse of his token to concoct the general circulation 'Washington/Ship' halfpenny [163].

The other commissions executed by the 'Westwood/Hancock consortium' were very much larger than those for Morgan and Absolon and met a desire on the part of their issuers or the syndicates that they fronted to provide a general, and profitable, petty-cash facility in the mushrooming conurbations, ebullient seaports and manufacturing towns they served; and, in some cases, just like John Wilkinson, selling on bulk quantities of their halfpennies to third-party issuers. According to Pye some ten ton of tokens were struck for the Edinburgh merchant house of Thomas and Alexander Hutchison over the years 1790, 1791 and 1792. As **Table 2** indicates these were joined during 1791 and 1792 by substantial issues for Liverpool – the third largest port in the country – (Thomas Clarke, a merchant with a speculative interest in the West Indian slave trade), Lancaster (Thomas

44 It seems likely that after the closure of the Westwood/Hancock coinery the token's dies came into the possession of Kempson who used them with his own flans to produce a number of collectors' pieces (e.g. D&H: Carmarthenshire 7d).

45 Absolon bought material in from manufacturers in a plain state which he then decorated. He was not a potter or glass-maker himself although he dignified his merchandise as 'Yarmouth Ware'. See Freeth (1909), 251-54.

46 Outing (2010), no. 4089.

47 Banks MS Cat. VI, SSB 195-174-2.

154 Westwood/Hancock: Rochdale halfpenny for John Kershaw, 1791

155 Westwood/Hancock: Edinburgh halfpenny for Thomas and Alexander Hutchison, 1791.

156 Westwood/Hancock: Hull halfpenny for Jonathan Garton and Company, 1791

Worswick and Son, merchants and bankers, again with shipping interests to the West Indies), Hull (the linen-drapery firm of Jonathan Garton and Company), Leeds (Richard Paley, soap boiler, cotton spinner, and local property developer), Rochdale (John Kershaw, a woollen merchant), and Exeter (Samuel Kingdon, a haberdasher and manufacturing ironmonger).

None of these tokens attained the imaginative artistry of Morgan's halfpenny although that of Kershaw is unusual in its rear-view representation of a weaver operating the reed of a loom [154]. Most, even if skilfully engraved, are fairly mundane in subject, boasting allegorical or historical figures pertinent to the place of issue coupled with the local coat-of-arms. Interestingly, too, while the 'industrial' tokens were boldly inscribed with their issuers' names, 'heads' or 'tails', the issuers of all the 'commercial' tokens were named only on the tokens' edges with a formulaic inscription: **PAYABLE AT THE WAREHOUSE OF THO^S & ALEX^R HUTCHISON .X.** [155], for instance, or **PAYABLE AT THE WAREHOUSE OF IONATHAN GARTON & CO. .X.** [156], and so on. It was a pattern of type and edge introduced by Westwood that, with variations, was to become a paradigm for the flood of individual shopkeepers' issues over the next few years and to permit too the combination of unassociated dies and edged blanks to create fabrications and 'rarities'.

A typical example was the halfpenny of Thomas Worswick with its romanticised bust of John of Gaunt as an obverse and the arms of Lancaster as a reverse [157]. Worswick, who lived during the heyday of Lancaster's prosperity as a West Indies trading port which he did much to promote, had risen from being a successful artisan craftsman – a watchmaker and silversmith – to become a leading local merchant and, unusually for a provincial silversmith, by 1781 Lancaster's first banker [158].[48] A decade later, like many other bankers in the great canal mania of 1789 to 1793, Worswick was deeply involved in the development of the Lancaster Canal. He had moved to Lancaster after his apprenticeship and, described as 'a watch movement maker', had been admitted a freeman of the town in 1754. Two years later he married the daughter of Robert Gillow, founder of the famous cabinet-making firm and, like Worswick himself, a member of an old Roman Catholic yeoman family from Great Singleton in the Fylde. Worswick is esteemed today for his long-case and bracket clocks many of the cases for which were supplied by the Gillows, a significant number being exported by Worswick with Gillow furniture, its drawers packed with watches and silverware, through a successful Atlantic shipping business operated jointly with

---

48 Thomas Chaldecott, who with Thomas Sharp issued tokens at Chichester and Portsmouth, was also a silversmith and a partner in a bank with branches in both towns: Dawes & Ward-Perkins (2000), 158-59 and 476.

157 Westwood/Hancock: Lancaster halfpenny for Thomas Worswick and Sons, 1792.

158 Thomas Worswick (*c*.1730-1804).

159 Westwood/Hancock: Exeter halfpenny for Samuel Kingdon, 1792.

the Gillows and Thomas Allman of St. Kitts.[49] Profits must have been affected during the American and French Revolutionary wars when the West Indian trade was particularly at risk, several of Worswick and Gillow's vessels being among the thirty or so local ships taken by enemy privateers.[50] Nevertheless, despite such war-time disruption, Worswick remained a significant figure in the commercial life of Lancaster until his death in 1804 – when he was described as a 'Gentleman Banker' – and he was fortunate not to experience the terminal decline of the town's West Indian trade and the economic depression after Waterloo that were to precipitate the failure of his bank in 1822.[51]

Worswick's halfpennies must have found considerable usage among the hives of workers in Lancaster's key industry, shipbuilding, and among the sail makers, block-makers and anchor smiths associated with it, as well as, from 1792, for the payment of wages of the 'navigators' cutting the Lancaster Canal. But they enjoyed a circulation well beyond the town and despite their declared promissory assurance – **PAYABLE AT THE WAREHOUSE OF THOS. WORSWICK & SONS .X.** – their very ubiquity rendered them as unredeemable as the regal copper. They consequently attracted the attention of the counterfeiting fraternity and copies, some remarkably good apart from their light weight, often much below the proper standard of 36 to the lb (12.6 g), proliferated on some scale.

Both the halfpennies of Samuel Kingdon (1745-1797) and Richard Paley (1746-1808) bore representations of Bishop Blaize, the patron saint of wool-combers, with the arms of Exeter and Leeds as their respective reverses. Kingdon, the son of established serge makers from Thorverton, near Exeter, took over a shop at the sign of the Golden Hammer in the city's Fore Street in 1768 where he sold 'all sorts of ironmongery and haberdashery goods, wholesale and retail'. Despite the theme of his token's obverse [159], reflecting his own background and Exeter's great trade in serges and other woollen goods, his main concern, as his shop-sign would suggest, was ironmongery and in 1787 he expanded this side of his business into a foundry, smith's shop and warehouse for the manufacture and sale of copper wares, fire-grates and cooking ranges.

Exeter's important serge market was in the eighteenth century surpassed only by that of Leeds but again although Richard Paley marked the importance of his own town's woollen manufacture in the symbolism of Bishop Blaize [160] his connection with the trade was through the ancillary business of soap boiling. Paley, the younger son of a small landowner near Settle and a cousin of the celebrated

---

49   For Worswick see Stuart (1999), 82-83; *ODNB*, s.v. 'Gillow family'; Hill (1954), 378-79; Dalziel (1993), 122; Pressnell (1956), 13, 274, 377. He is described as 'banker and silversmith' in *Bailey's Northern Directory ... for ... 1781*, s.v. 'Lancaster'.

50   Howson (2008), 33-34.

51   'Lancaster in all its distress never met with such a blow' as the failure of Thomas Worswick, Sons and Co. 'Many aged persons who had their hard earned savings vested there were brought to the verge of beggary and a great stagnation of trade was caused': Winstanley (1993), 146; Dawes & Ward-Perkins (2000), 2, 110; Hill (1958), 194.

theologian William Paley, had become a soap boiler in Leeds sometime before 1771 and using family capital [52] developed extensive soap works and malt kilns about the town. His interests were to extend far beyond soap boiling, though, and, while we have only fleeting glimpses of his activities, he played an important role in the early industrial history of the West Riding, building a flax mill and the town's first steam-powered cotton mills in Leeds, establishing a foundry in Wakefield and acquiring part ownership of the Bowling Iron Works in Bradford.[53]

Much more fully documented is Paley's involvement in the speculative development of high-density working-class housing in the east-end of Leeds.[54] From 1787 he invested heavily in land and housing and by 1800 was the second largest property owner in Leeds setting a pattern for the cheap speculative building in the east end of the town that later generations capitalised on; ugly, overcrowded, insanitary, back-to-back streets and courts cheek by jowl with steam-powered mills that characterised the Coketowns of Dickens's *Hard Times*. It was to be a deadly conjunction later castigated as 'the most unhealthy buildings which human perversity ever invented' but it did not come about in Paley's time.[55] He nevertheless led the way and given time he would no doubt have been as culpable as his successors but by 1803 he had been able to develop or sell off to others only a small proportion of his land holdings. And in that year his entrepreneurial ambitions came to an abrupt end for on 21 May he was declared bankrupt. As with Westwood we do not know which of his concerns gave rise to his downfall but, like too many today, Paley was overextended in the mortgage credit that sustained his property purchases and in the end it was his bankers in Huddersfield and Pontefract that brought him down. In 1805 he resigned from Leeds Corporation to which he had been elected in 1789 and for all his entrepreneurial prominence the 'Soap-Boiler, Dealer and Chapman', as he was described in his bankruptcy, quickly became a forgotten figure leaving no permanent name in the townscape he had done much to create. All that seems to have been rescued from Paley's ruin was his original soap-making business that continued to function under the direction of his son. The wheel had come full circle.[56]

We have touched in detail on only a few of the 'Westwood/Hancock' consortium's productions between 1791 and 1792. All were of good weight, struck at a notional 36 halfpennies to the lb (12.6 g) compared

160 Westwood/Hancock: Leeds halfpenny for Richard Paley, 1791.

---

52 Including loans from his father and the dowry of his wife said to be 'an agreeable lady with a fortune of £1,000': *Leeds Intelligencer*, 25 June 1771.

53 Paley's steam engines attracted James Watt, junior's attention in 1796 when he was in Leeds spying out patent violations.

54 For Paley, and particularly his career as a speculative housing developer, see Beresford (1974), 281-320 and the references cited therein.

55 *Leeds Mercury*, 20 November 1859. Some of Paley's housing was still occupied as late as 1955, over one hundred and fifty years after it was built and despite its condemnation of a century before: Beresford (1974), 287.

56 *LG*, No. 15591, 7-11 June 1803; Beresford (1974), 296. It was to be 1823 before all Paley's properties were disposed of and a final dividend paid to his creditors.

to the Tower standard of 46 halfpennies to the lb (10 g). But it was a considerable reduction on the weight of the pennies and halfpennies of the Parys Mine Company which had been struck to a standard of 16 pennies (or 32 halfpennies) to the lb (14.2g for the halfpennies) and was to continue as such through to 1792. It was Westwood who adopted the lower standard of 36 halfpennies to the lb when he embarked upon the coining of tokens with the Cronebane – though struck by Boulton the blanks had been produced by Westwood – and Macclesfield halfpennies in 1789. His own halfpennies for Wilkinson, begun in 1790, were also struck at this standard which evoked the ironmaster's complaint to Boulton mentioned earlier. Even so Wilkinson argued that Westwood's pieces 'were deem'd too heavy by people in general'.[57]

Wilkinson was describing the attitude of the 'secondary' issuers to whom he sold on his tokens in bulk and not the generality of users with whom they found a ready acceptance. In Liverpool, for instance, it was recorded in 1791 that the best copper coins in local circulation were 'Wilkinson's, Paris Mine. Co., Irish Company ['Cronebane'], Thos. Clarke, Chas Rowe, Geo. the 2nd'. They were detailed in weight order: [58]

Description	No. in 1 lb. weight
A Paris Mine Penny	16.19
A Paris Mine Half Penny	32.39
Thomas Clarke's Half Penny	35.83
Charles Rowe's Half Penny	36.41
Assoc. Irish Mine Company Half Penny	35.65
John Wilkinson anno. 1788 Half Penny	31.44
John Wilkinson anno. 1790 Half Penny	32.01
Colonel Mordaunt's Penny	25.61
A new Half Penny of Geo. 2nd	47.82
An Iron Nale[59]	—

All the tokens listed with the exception of Colonel Mordaunt's Halsall penny were extensively counterfeited.[60] This was the case too with most

---

57 BAH: MBP 367, John Wilkinson to Matthew Boulton, 11 December 1790 quoted in Chaloner (1948a), 307.

58 Anderson (1970), 88, note 1.

59 It seems strange that an 'iron Nale' should still be regarded as a form presumably of 'commodity currency' in a town like Liverpool as late as 1791 but it may hark back to the practice of factors furnishing nailers with materials and giving them credit with shopkeepers for bread, cheese and chandlery goods which they paid for in finished nails: comment by William Playfair in his edition (1805) of Adam Smith's *Wealth of Nations*, I, 36.

60 Some commentators (e.g. Redish (2000), 153) minimise the incidence of the counterfeiting of provincial coins on the basis of their proclaimed redeemability but their thesis can apply only to the post-1792 'localised' tokens and then only spasmodically. Of the large-scale issues only those of John Fielding, a Manchester grocer, seem to have escaped the attention of the counterfeiter.

of the halfpennies produced by the 'Westwood/Hancock' consortium. Only the halfpennies produced for John Morgan and William Absolon – despite his worries – seem to have escaped the attention of the forger although one of the Morgan tokens listed by Dalton and Hamer (Carmarthen 7*d*) is likely to be a copy by Kempson.[61]

John Westwood died on 9 March 1792.[62] His business ventures were taken over by his brother who ten days later placed an explanatory notice in *Aris's Birmingham Gazette* [161]. Westwood's debts had not been discharged – indeed, despite Obadiah's expressed intentions they were not to be settled for another year and then only on the basis of the payment of a very small dividend to his creditors.[63] For Obadiah the advertisement was a 'damage-limitation exercise' calculated to retain the confidence of his brother's remaining customers and the faith of his creditors. And, in association with Hancock, he continued the coining business that for all the family's vicissitudes had achieved a considerable success.

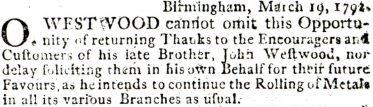

161 *Aris's Birmingham Gazette*, 19 March 1792.

A vivid insight into the concern is given a year later by Thomas Digges who had ferreted out a scheme to procure a contract for the coining of American cents in Birmingham. Though his informants were 'close & secret as to who the die sinker was, where coind &c[a]', he found out that these coins – the 'Washington/Eagle cents' ('... the President's head, not a bad likeness, & tolerably well executed') [162]

162 Obadiah Westwood's pattern cents, 1791

61 It is struck on a flan edged for Kempson's tokens for Bolingbroke, a Norwich haberdasher.

62 John Westwood's death was reported in *ABG* on 12 March 1792: 'On Friday night [9 March], Mr. John Westwood, a very ingenious mechanic of this town'.

63 For Westwood's coining debts in regard to Roe and Company see Vice (1991a), 5; Westwood's insolvency, though, did not merely relate to his coining debts.

COINAGE AND CURRENCY IN EIGHTEENTH-CENTURY BRITAIN

163 Obadiah Westwood/Hancock: 'Washington/Ship' halfpenny, 1793.

– had been manufactured, at the behest of William and Alexander Walker, Birmingham merchants with American trading interests, 'at Mr Obediah [sic] Westwoods (a considerable maker of these kinds of money, and that his die sinker Mr Jn° Gregory Hancock (one of the first in this place 'tho with the Character of a dissipated man)' – to Digges most Birmingham die-sinkers were drunken sots – 'and a prentice Lad Jn° Jordan, very Clever in that line, had executed them & still hold the dies'.[64]

The venture had been a 'speculation ... some hundred weight or so' of the coins having been 'sent to America & given to the President & other public Gentlemen; But that on the determination of Congress to mint their own money, thier (sic) scheme here had fallen thro''. Digges's exposure of the activities that Obadiah, and presumably his brother before him, were engaged in and his reference to 'these kinds of money' – copper currency and its token substitutes – suggests that the brothers' operation was on a comparatively large scale but that some of its endeavours did not bear too close an examination. Although much more research has to be done on the subject it is plain that, from the beginning, the counterfeits (or at any rate a high proportion of the more plausible ones) and the 'muled' pieces that dogged the consortium's large output of commercial tokens were actually struck in house; the Westwoods were, in fact, bypassing the legitimate 'proprietors' who had commissioned them and forging the latter's issues for their own direct profit.[65] A case in point is the 'general circulation' 'Washington/Ship' halfpenny [163] which Pye noted was struck from puncheons made by Hancock, the obverse die being that used for the 'Washington/Small Eagle' cent of 1791 [162] and the reverse an adaptation of that used for the Yarmouth halfpenny of the following year [152]. Pye said that although these concoctions 'were sold in small quantities to any person who would purchase them' they were common ('c') in his time.[66] This may be an overestimate because they are scarce today but that they were certainly popular and enjoyed a healthy circulation in their own day is borne out by the mediocre condition most of them are found in now.

It is hardly surprising that Obadiah's son, the younger John Westwood (1774-1850), brought up in such a counterfeiters' kitchen, should have devoted so much time to the specious fabrications that he foisted on a gullible public as token collecting took on the proportions of a mania; with his background such work was second nature to him. Hancock, himself, was evidently not above reproach and was already

---

64 LC: Thomas Jefferson Papers, Th[omas] A[ttwood] Digges to Thomas Jefferson, 10 March 1793 and LC: Pinckney Family Papers, Tho[ma]s A[ttwood] Digges to Thomas Pinckney, 12 March 1793. See also Elias and Finch (1982), 442-443 and 447; Taxay (1966), 53-54. The obstacles that Digges had had to overcome in tracking down Obadiah Westwood's coinery arose, in large measure, from the Walkers' suspicion of his being an American government agent and their awareness that Jefferson would have vetoed their scheme.

65 A practice by no means restricted to the Westwoods but indulged in by other coiners, especially Lutwyche and even the more respectable Kempson.

66 Pye (1801), 18.

involved in the counterfeiting of assignats, a not inconsiderable trade in Birmingham until it was disrupted by the declaration of war in February 1793. In his snooping about the town Digges discovered

> Assignats in quires, both stampd & signd, as well as in blank unstampd, with the proper paper and all the French words necessary in the Water marks, executed as I was told in London & sent hither for the Engravings printing & finishing strokes –The head of poor Louis however (which is done by a stamp the same as is on the Bills & notes here) appears now to be a want here, & a loss to these schemers; one of whom told me, cursing & execrating the war, that He should have been ten thousand pounds richer if the declaration had been delayd a month or two longer – Those assignats which I saw were all for ten, twenty, & two hundred Livres Each. [67]

While the Westwood/Hancock coinery might have been a flourishing business in 1793 some three years later when the collector William Robert Hay visited Birmingham, briskly sniffing out the town's token makers and grangerising his catalogues with the information he unearthed, he made no mention of Westwood and the workshop was defunct. 'Hancock', he laconically noted, 'had given up the Business as had Jourdan (*sic*) who had gone into a Manufactory for patent Window Frames'.[68] The stark truth was that the enterprise had been wound up almost two years before and Obadiah had gone the way of his brother into bankruptcy and numismatic oblivion in November 1794.[69] Again, it is impossible to distinguish the exact cause of Westwood's financial difficulties. Despite his declared intention in 1792 to continue his brother's copper-rolling business this seems to have faltered quickly in what was after all a time of great credit stringency and business failure and when he was gazetted it was in his old calling of 'Coffin Furniture Maker'. That he was able to re-establish himself rapidly in this trade is borne out by contemporary directories and he carried on well into the first decade of the new century, eventually retiring from Birmingham as a 'gentleman' and living into the 1820s.[70]

---

67   LC: Thomas Jefferson Papers, Th[omas] A[ttwood] Digges to Thomas Pinckney, 6 April 1793. See also Elias and Finch (1982), 455. In 1794 an employee of the Birmingham Assay Office was asked to cast some plates prior to repair by Hancock. The incident was reported to Garbett who informed Lord Hawkesbury: BAH: MBP 309/1481/2, Samuel Garbett to Matthew Boulton, 9 December 1794.

68   Dykes (1997), 120. During his visit to Birmingham in the September of 1796 Hay had discussions with a number of people intimately connected with the token scene including John Stubbs Jorden and Charles Pye.

69   *LG*, No. 13723, 15 -18 November 1794, 1139.

70   Trade directories show Obadiah Westwood continuing his coffin furniture business from Great Charles Street until he moved to Camphill about the turn of the century. He seems to have retired about 1808, subsequently moving to Sheffield (after 1811) and then to London (Chelsea) where he died in February 1826. Directory entries for 'Obadiah Westwood, die-sinker' at Camphill between 1808 and 1811 presumably relate to his son who subsequently became a Sheffield silversmith.

To what extent, if any, the coinery played a part in Obadiah's debacle is questionable but it is clear that at the time of his bankruptcy, or very soon after, the 'Westwood/Hancock' consortium went out of business, its final productions being the halfpennies for the Thames and Severn Canal Company and James Burton ('Foundling Fields') which were produced prior to May 1795.[71] Even if not directly a factor in the bankruptcy it is likely that the coinery had become increasingly unprofitable and a drain on scarce resources. For a sea-change was taking place in the nature of provincial coinage. The large-scale token production for industrial and commercial concerns that the Westwoods had depended upon was becoming a thing of the past. Increasingly the call was for comparatively low-volume issues to meet the needs of local shopkeepers which new thrusting manufacturers were better prepared to foster. Nevertheless, by and large, the consortium adhered to the old formula in its final two years, and, apart from the Burton halfpenny, continued to produce tokens in sizeable quantities (**Table 3**). What was now different, however, was that John Westwood's old weight standard of 36 halfpennies to the lb was abandoned. In line with the new manufacturers and with an eye to maximising profits, much lower yardsticks were adopted and even so were only notionally observed. The tokens of the Salop Woollen Manufactory and Sharp and Chaldecott seem to have been struck at about 44 halfpennies to the lb, those of Hawkins Bird and the Thames and Severn Canal Company at no more than 46 to the lb while Burton's tokens reached the nadir of 56 to the lb. The one exception to this decline was the halfpenny of Pretor, Pew and Whitty that seems to have been struck at a standard of 40 to the lb, no doubt exemplifying the rectitude of a country banker.

Two of the halfpennies, and those produced in the largest quantities, related to the trade and industry of the Severn. That of the Salop Woollen Manufactory, likely the flannel mill operated by the Shrewsbury firm of White Cooke, Sons, and Mason three miles upstream from the town 'at a place called the *Isle*', was a rather mundane token bearing the arms of

Table 3
Obadiah Westwood/Hancock Provincial Coin Contracts

Date	Issuer	Place of Issue	Quantity Struck (Pye 1801)	Pye Reference	D&H Reference
1793	Salop Woollen Manufactory	Shrewsbury	5 ton	Plate 44, 2	Shropshire 19-22
1793	Hawkins Bird	Bristol	1 ton	Plate 10, 4 & 5	Som. 88-89
1793	Pretor, Pew & Whitty	Sherborne	——[a]	Plate 44, 7	Dorset 7
1793	*Washington/Ship Halfpenny*	——	——	Plate 51, 10	Middx 1051
1794	Sharp & Chaldecott	Chichester & Portsmouth	1 ton	Plate 4, 3	Suss.19-20
1794	James Lackington [b]	London	3 cwt	Plate 31, 4	Middx 351]
1795	Thames & Severn Canal Co	Brimscombe Port	3 ton	Plate 10,2 & 3	Glos. 58; 59-61
1795	James Burton	London	3 cwt	Plate 29, 6 & 7	Middx 303-305

a Pye does not specify the mintage but the halfpennies are scarce.

b The Lackington halfpenny (*D&H*: Middx 351), although its manufacture was attributed by Pye to 'O. Westwood', was more likely to have been struck by Lutwyche (see page 185 below).

71 Both these pieces appear in Spence (1795), 19 (no. 126) and 45 (no. 304), published in May 1795.

164   Obadiah Westwood/Hancock: Shrewsbury halfpenny for White Cooke, Sons, and Mason, 1793.

165   Obadiah Westwood/Hancock: Thames and Severn Canal Company halfpenny, 1795.

Shrewsbury as its obverse device and a wool-pack for the reverse [164]. Unhappily, no attempt was made to depict the factory itself which to the traveller Arthur Aikin, who saw it in 1796, three years after it was built, was the 'greatest undertaking of the kind' in the area. '[A] vast series of machinery for spinning, fulling, and many other operations' was powered by a 'great water wheel' which had been successfully installed through the 'perseverance and great mechanical skill of Mr. Mason' despite the rapid flood of the river and silting of its bed.[72] The factory, combined with a corn mill, was still water-powered when it was put up for sale after the death of its then owner Edward Holt in 1824.[73]

On the basis of a notional striking of 44 halfpennies to the lb something in the region of 490,000 tokens would have been produced for the firm which would have used them not only to pay its mill workers but also the domestic weavers it employed in the surrounding area. The tokens judging by their average condition today were well received as a local currency and doubtless achieved a wider circulation because they were later copied.

The same was true of the halfpennies of the Thames and Severn Canal Company issued in part payment to the company's large labour force, from boatmen and wharfmen to lock-keepers and labourers, who, at the time of their issue, 1795, would have had earnings ranging from a decent 14s to as little as 5s a week. The tokens almost vie with John Morgan's tokens as the most celebrated of Hancock's productions. With their dramatic waterline view of a Severn trow bearing down on the observer and Hancock's meticulous portrayal of the eastern portal of the Sapperton Tunnel [165] they symbolised the company's twofold ambition to develop a riverine carrying trade from the upper Severn and Bristol through the Stroudwater navigation to its transhipment entrepôt at Brimscombe Port [166] and thence by canal barge to Lechlade and the Thames.[74]

The canal, largely sponsored by London merchants and Midlands industrial interests, opened in 1789. It proved to be moderately successful early on, facilitating the carriage to London of iron goods from Shropshire and considerably reducing the cost of coal from the Forest of Dean and Worcestershire as it reached the towns along its route: the price of coal at Cirencester, for instance, immediately fell from 24s to 18s a ton and at Lechlade from 32s or 33s a ton to 22s.[75] Over the years, however, competition from other canals, and navigational

---

72   Aikin (1797), 77-78. The partnership of White Cooke, Sons, and Mason was dissolved in 1798 to be succeeded by that of Holt and Mason. In 1802 Edward Holt took over sole operation of the mill.

73   *Salopian Journal*, 23 June 1824. An alternative issuer of the token might have been the firm of Powis and Hodges who built an integrated woollen factory in Coleham, Shrewsbury in 1790 at a cost of £10,000. The mill was one of the largest of its kind but the firm had gone bankrupt by 1795. Cf. Trinder (1996), 138-39.

74   For an early nineteenth-century description of Brimscombe Port see Brewer (1825) [2005], 183-84.

75   *GM*, February 1790, 110. 'How welcome such a sight must be in a country where fuel has been hitherto not only dear but scarce, may easily be imagined, and the inhabitants of Cirencester testified by public rejoicings their gladness on the occasion'': quoted in *Gloucestershire Notes and Queries*, 4 (1890), 445 from 'newspapers a hundred years ago'.

difficulties on the upper reaches of the Thames, limited the prospects of its being the Severn/London commercial link that had been hoped and the bulk of its trade became increasingly local, primarily serving the woollen mills of the Golden Valley between Stroud and Chalford.[76]

166 Detail of an oil painting of Brimscombe Port (*c.* 1790-1800), headquarters of the Severn and Thames Canal Company, showing a laden trow arriving from the west. Its cargo would be transferred to barges at Brimscombe for the remainder of the voyage east.

167 A Severn Trow. Detail from a view of Ham Court in Nash's *History of Worcestershire* (1799).

76 For the canal see Household (1969) and Paget-Tomlinson (1978), 229-30.

From the start the company built and operated its own fleet of boats, trows and smaller 'frigates' for the Severn and the Stroudwater and barges for the voyage from Brimscombe Port to the metropolis. The trow, an ancient Severn vessel, perhaps like the Humber keel derived from a Viking model and carrying a not dissimilar square-sail rig, was the maid of all work of the river operating from its upper stretches to the Bristol Channel. Virtually flat-bottomed, it ranged in burthen from 40 to 80 tons, most, like Hancock's depiction, having a single mast and topmast about eighty feet high. Some 16 to 20 feet wide and 60 feet long a new trow, when fitted out, cost in the region of £300 to £400.[77] Trows appear in a number of the engravings by James Ross in the Reverend Treadway Nash's *Collections for the History of Worcestershire* and one portrayal in particular, a bow quarter view of a trow under sail [167], might have provided some inspiration for Hancock's depiction although he omitted the bowsprit and, as a patriotic gesture in the opening year of war with revolutionary France, added an outsize union flag to the stern.[78]

To contemporaries the junction of the Severn and Thames was 'the grandest object ever attained by inland navigation' and the company's most daring engineering achievement was the passage 'through the bowels of the mountain' of Sapperton Hill, the highest part of the Cotswolds escarpment, 'bad rocky ground ... worse' than the engineer charged with surveying the route 'had ever seen'. The tunnel took five years to dig (mostly by hand though gunpowder was also used through the limestone sections) and was at the time the longest of its kind ever built (about 2¼ miles long with a bore of 15 feet). The work was difficult and hazardous and according to John Byng who visited the tunnel in July 1787 the labourers who 'come from the Derbyshire and Cornish mines, are in eternal danger and frequently perish by the falls of earth'. Byng, who was by nature a prophet of gloom, had explored the work in progress on

> a sledge cart ... drawn by two horses ... rumbling and jumbling thro mud, and over stones, with a small lighted candle in my hand, giving me a sight of the last horse, and sometimes of the arch: and "Serv'd only to discover sights of woe". – When the last peep of day light vanish'd, I was enveloped in thick smoke arising from the gunpowder of the miners, at whom, after passing by many labourers who work by small candles, I did at last arrive... My cart being reladen with stone, I was hoisted thereon ... and had a worse journey back, as I cou'd scarcely keep my seat. – The return of warmth, and happy day light I hail'd with pleasure, having journey'd a mile of darkness.[79]

---

77 *GM*, June 1758, 277; Harral (1824), I, 77.

78 Nash (1799), II, 444. The addition of the union flag may have reflected reports of the arrival of the first barge at Lechlade on 19 November 1789. 'She had an union flag at her mast head, and was saluted by 12 pieces of canon from Buscott [*sic*] Park, and by loud acclamations from thousands of spectators': *The Times*, 26 November 1789. See also *GM*, December 1789, 1139 for a description of the occasion.

79 Andrews (1934-38), I (1934), 260. 'Imagination boggles at the thought of men handling gunpowder by candlelight in the confined space of the headway, never more, and often less, than 4 ft wide and 6 ft high': Household (1969), 58.

He had entered the tunnel by its western Gothic-style Daneway access. More elaborate was the eastern Classical portal (restored in the 1970s [168]) and it was this that the canal company chose to depict on the reverse of its token. Hancock diligently detailed the blocks of rusticated stone used in the building, the flanking columns and the two niches, empty but undoubtedly intended for figures of Father Thames and Madam Sabrina to commemorate the canal's union of the two rivers; uncharacteristically, however, he omitted the vital right-hand pillar giving no support to the arch on that side.

168   The Eastern Portal to Sapperton Tunnel, 2001.

The Thames and Severn Canal Company's halfpennies were most likely struck at a standard of 46 to the lb. But at an even lower standard were the 'Foundling Fields' pieces, perhaps the swansong of the Westwood/Hancock consortium. Pye (1801) tells us that three cwt (or perhaps 18,500 pieces) were struck which although not inelegant in their simple design, were certainly puny, badly struck on very thin blanks at a likely standard of 56 to the lb (specimens, on average, weigh only about 8 g). At the initial striking the reverse die (*D&H*: Middx 303) broke, as did the second (*D&H*: Middx 304) [169a]. These versions are therefore quite rare, the first known from no more than two or three examples. It is only *D&H*: Middx 305 [169b] that was struck in any quantity and even that today is probably scarcer than some commentators suggest.[80]

169a

169b

169   Obadiah Westwood/Hancock: 'Foundling Fields' halfpennies for James Burton, 1795.

80   See Dykes (2010a).

A BIRMINGHAM TOKEN CONSORTIUM

170   William Hogarth's original pen and ink sketch for the Foundling Hospital's Coat of Arms, 1747.

All three versions share the same obverse die with its device of a lamb holding in its mouth a sprig of thyme, a representation of the crest on the arms of the Foundling Hospital [170] – designed by William Hogarth – which had been established in 1745 on Lamb's Conduit Fields, an extensive tract of open country in Bloomsbury.[81] The connection between the token and the Hospital was an indirect one, however. The fifty-six acre site that the Hospital had purchased was far bigger than that needed for its actual needs and as London expanded northward into the Bloomsbury area the Hospital decided in 1788, to embark upon its own 'improvement' plan. The scheme was put out to individual speculators who ranged from the small working journeyman to the larger capitalist but one developer soon began to tower above his fellows to dominate the construction of Bloomsbury for the next twenty years and become the most enterprising and successful London builder of his time.

This was the twenty-nine year old James Burton [171], already a successful architect and builder in south London who, within a decade, adding site to site until virtually all of the earmarked Foundling estate

---

81   Lamb's Conduit Fields was named after William Lamb, an Elizabethan philanthropist, who restored the local conduit from a tributary of the Thames to provide a public water supply in the area in 1577. For the Foundling Hospital and the development of its estate see McClure (1981) and Olsen (1964), 74-96.

development was in his hands at a cost to him of 'above £400,000 for the permanent benefit of the property of the Hospital'. As the surveyor to the foundation put it, 'Without such a man, possessed of very considerable talents, unwearied industry, and a capital of his own, the extraordinary success of the improvement of the Foundling estate could not have taken place'.[82] It was, though, but the beginning of an entrepreneurial career in the construction industry which saw him moving on to the adjacent Bedford and Skinners' Company estates in Bloomsbury, then to some of the Nash terraces around Regent's Park, a large part of Regent Street and finally Waterloo Place.[83] In the meantime Burton had undertaken the development of a big housing estate in Tunbridge Wells and finally the creation of the fashionable seaside resort of St Leonard's-on-Sea in Sussex – which by 1833, it was said, presented 'the most unique collection of elegant buildings of any watering place on the British coast'.[84]

171   James Burton (1761-1837). From an early nineteenth-century lithograph.

All this was in the future, however. In 1795 Burton was still actively developing that part of Bloomsbury bounded by the west side of Brunswick Square, Bernard Street, Great Coram Street and Woburn Place and it is this land to which the title 'Foundling Fields' was probably given, not an official Hospital designation but a popular shorthand for the area. And it is in this context that one must view the 'JB' halfpenny: as a genuinely redeemable token coin supplied by

---

82   Quoted in Olsen (1964), 79.

83   In most of his later developments Burton was assisted by his precocious tenth son who was to become the much more distinguished architect Decimus Burton (1800-1881) and who designed many of the father's projects including much of St Leonards.

84   For Burton's career see Colvin (1995), 199-200; *ODNB*; Summerson (1978), 169-92; Olsen (1964), 52-55 and *passim*; and Baines (1956), 13-19.

A BIRMINGHAM TOKEN CONSORTIUM

172 Obadiah Westwood/Hancock: Bristol halfpenny for Hawkins Bird, 1793.

173 Obadiah Westwood/Hancock: Chichester and Portsmouth halfpenny for Thomas Chaldecott and Thomas Sharp, 1794.

Burton to his subcontractors to help make up the wage bills of the workmen employed on this particular undertaking. Paltry the tokens may have been but there was no need for them to have been any heavier than they were since they must have been intended to be of only limited circulation in a restricted neighbourhood, probably venturing little further than the eponymous tavern in Lamb's Conduit Street which was the workers' nearest house of call. In such circumstances, too, there was no need to identify their issuer other than by his initials for recipients would have known that the tokens would have been readily honoured by someone who, canny Scot that he was, was an honest employer and immediately available at the centre of his hive of building activity.[85]

We have concentrated on the 'industrial' tokens produced by the Obadiah Westwood/Hancock consortium but they also ventured into the new field of shopkeeper tokens; for Hawkins Bird, a Bristol grocer and tea dealer [172], and for Thomas Chaldecott, a Chichester silversmith (issuing halfpennies jointly with Thomas Sharp, a Portsmouth mercer, in both towns) [173]. These tokens are dated respectively 1793 and 1794 and Pye as usual credits Hancock with their manufacture. He departs from this practice, however, over a James Lackington halfpenny [226] which uniquely he attributes to 'O. Westwood'. Pye specifies no die-sinker in this case and if the halfpenny was a consortium production one would have assumed this to have been Hancock who always seems to have been ready to press his claims to token production. The engraving does not measure up to Hancock's skills and, to confuse the situation further, in the 1795 edition of his catalogue Pye had named 'Wyon' in this role. More realistically, Thomas Sharp of Coventry, in his catalogue of the Chetwynd collection, suggested Roger Dixon, the engraver responsible for the main run of Lackington tokens. This series was made by Lutwyche and it seems much more plausible to transfer Pye's three hundredweight of this particular token from the consortium's *œuvre* to the other Lackington halfpennies emanating from the Lutwyche coinery.[86]

The Bird and the Sharp and Chaldecott Chichester halfpennies were struck in some quantity according to Pye: a ton (perhaps 105,000 pieces) in Bird's case and rather fewer in that of Sharp and Chaldecott. The latter tokens are of special interest because a virtually identical issue, also dated '1794' but with the reverse inscription **PORTSMOUTH AND CHICHESTER** and apparently struck by Kempson, was put out in the names of the two traders. This presumably reflects the demise of the Westwood consortium and the need for a continuing supply of halfpennies in the naval dockyard town which Sharp was to strive to meet again with a smallish issue also made by Kempson and appropriately celebrating Jervis's victory off Cape St. Vincent in

---

85 Much of this area, ravaged by bombing in the Second World War and subsequent redevelopment, has been replaced by the grotesquely modernist Brunswick Centre.

86 Pye (1801), 13; Pye (1795), ii; Sharp (1834), 64. It should be added that neither of the Wyon brothers or Dixon is known to have worked for the Westwoods.

174   Simon Pretor (1727-1804).

1797 [133]. Whether the issuers were connected in any way other than through their tokens we do not know. What we do know is that Chaldecott was partner in a Chichester bank, founded by his father, that operated in both towns; again, as in the instance of Worswick, an unusual example of a local silversmith turning to banking.[87]

One would not know from their tokens that Worswick or Chaldecott were bankers. Such reticence did not, however, apply to Pretor, Pew and Whitty the edge of whose halfpenny – **PAYABLE AT THE BANK IN SHERBORNE + DORSET +** – made no bones about the nature of the issuing authority. Theirs was the only genuine eighteenth-century provincial coin to have any overt claim to have been issued by a bank *sensu stricto* and even then Simon Pretor [174] operated a virtually inseparable grocery business in which the roots of the bank lay.[88] Pretor, originally from Lyme Regis, had set up his shop in Sherborne about 1750. While its nineteenth-century notes claimed that this was the date of the foundation of the bank this must have been wishful thinking about any *formalized* banking service although it might well have reflected an early venture into bill-discounting as a natural offshoot to a grocery concern that was as much wholesale as it was retail. Nothing is known, though, of any bank in Sherborne prior to Pretor's venture and at the time of his death in 1804 it was believed to have been the first of its kind in Dorset.[89]

Sherborne was a market town with a population of some three thousand souls including five attorneys, several silk and linen manufacturers and a multiplicity of substantial tradesmen. It was ripe for a 'banking shop' and there must have been many among Pretor's customers, people of substance extending to Yeovil, Ilchester, Wincanton and Castle Cary, who would have taken advantage of a facility non-existent in their own localities. A cryptic reference in one of Pretor's grocery advertisements of 1757 to 'other forms of business' being 'transacted on the most moderate Terms' is thus not without significance. Four years later Pretor was announcing, though still under his title of 'Grocer and Tea-man', that 'more than the current value of 36s. and 3l. 12s. pieces' would be 'immediately paid for in Guineas, Bank Notes or Bills of Exchange' for Portuguese money. It seems a strange inducement but, presumably, his nascent banking flair and eye to profit had identified a niche in the currency market which he could exploit by buying in the all too prevalent 'joes' and 'double joes' and then exporting them through his nephew, the Bristol merchant John Pinney, to the currency-starved West Indies where Portuguese specie was the dominant gold coinage.[90]

---

87 Griffiths, Chaldecott & Drew: Dawes & Ward-Perkins (2000), II, 158 and 476. The bank was founded in Chichester by John Chaldecott in 1774, the year he was appointed local receiver of diminished coin under the gold recoinage of 1773-76.

88 For Pretor and the Sherborne Bank tokens see Dykes (2005), 132-41.

89 *GM*, September 1804, 885. This is borne out by Dawes and Ward-Perkins (2000), II, 527.

90 *The Western Flying-Post; or Sherborne & Yeovil Mercury*, 5 July 1761. It will be recalled that James Woodforde paid 'Seven new guineas' for two 'double joes' in 1769: see p.49 above.

From Nevis Pinney kept his uncle's shop supplied with rum and sugar where an exotic spread of groceries and haberdashery – from eleven varieties of tea to coffee, chocolate, molasses, spices, rice, dried fruit, herrings, anchovies, wine, tobacco, turpentine, saltpetre, candles, gunpowder and shot, canary seed, gloves, laces and pins – were to be Pretor's prime preoccupation for much of the next thirty-eight years.[91] He bought from merchants in London, Bristol, Exeter, Devizes and Weymouth and often in quantities that stress his trade as a regional wholesaler as well as retail grocer. It was a prosperous concern, driven by a shrewd business sense, a total lack of sentiment and a fractious nature. By the last quarter of the eighteenth century he had also built up his banking arm to the extent that in 1774 he was encouraged to set up the separate banking house in Long Street, a stone's throw away from his grocery business near Sherborne's Conduit.[92]

Pretor never relinquished direct control of his grocery business, especially its wholesale side but by the 1790s he was aging and – with his sons-in-law, Richard Pew (1752-1834) and Samuel Whitty (1760-1833),[93] in his view, 'better pleased to be licking Honey of Thorns as Bankers than to be extracting the Sweets from the Sugar cane of the West Indies, the Rich fruit from the Mediterranean or the Aromatic Spices of the East Indies' – he decided to sell up.[94] When Pretor died, at the age of 76, he was described in the *Gentleman's Magazine* as 'a man of extensive knowledge, attained by a long life of observation... From his intimate acquaintance with commercial affairs, he was generally successful in his business, and consequently acquired a considerable fortune'.[95] His prudence served the bank well [175]. It survived the banking catastrophes of 1812 and 1825 and continued as a private bank, managed by Pretor's descendants, for another forty years until, in 1843, it merged with the National Provincial Bank of England.

The series of Sherborne halfpennies comprises three different types each of which in its own way presents the numismatist with something of a conundrum.

---

91   But not local produce such as butter, cheese and eggs that would have been bought at Sherborne's Tuesday, Thursday and Saturday markets.

92   DRO: Pretor Cashbook, 7 November 1774; Sherborne Estate, D/SHC – KG 1938, 10 March 1791.

93   Pew was a Shaftesbury surgeon and Whitty, a son of the inventor of the Axminster carpet, was the manager of the bank. The latter's elder brother, Thomas Whitty, was a partner in the Axminster bank of Hallett, Stevens and Whitty. Weinstock (1960), 79; DRO: Sherborne Parish Register (Marriages), 19 June 1786 and 27 April 1790; Dawes and Ward-Perkins (2000), II, 527.

94   DRO: Pretor Letter Book, Simon Pretor to W. P. Linnell, 8 February 1795.

95   *GM*, September 1804, 885.

COINAGE AND CURRENCY IN EIGHTEENTH-CENTURY BRITAIN

175 A Sherborne and Dorsetshire Bank note of 1792 in the name of Simon Pretor and Son, a year prior to Pretor's partnership with Richard Pew and Samuel Whitty. Pretor's son had died in 1790.

176 John Westwood, Jnr.: Sherborne halfpenny for Pretor, Pew and Whitty, [1796].

177 John Westwood, Jnr.: Sherborne halfpenny for Pretor, Pew and Whitty, 1796.

Although the first of the tokens – with the monogram *PP&W* as its obverse and the Pretor double-headed eagle as its reverse [176] – is dated 1793 it is not listed in any of the early catalogues of provincial coins until its inclusion in James Conder's *Arrangement* of 1798. Its absence from Samuel Birchall's *Descriptive List*, which was not published until the early part of 1796, is especially significant since, in addition to his own observations, Birchall had the benefit of information supplied by a number of enthusiastic collectors of provincial coins and by Matthew Young, a dealer with an encyclopaedic knowledge of the contemporary token scene. One of Birchall's correspondents was Miss Banks who although she was usually adept at securing pieces soon after they were struck, did not acquire her specimen until 2 January 1797.[96] It is of interest, too, that Pye attributed both the die-sinking and manufacture of this token to 'Westwood' in a context plainly pointing to the younger Westwood, Obadiah's son, John Westwood, junior, which in itself suggests a date post 1795. On balance it seems likely that the professed date of the token is a commemorative one, celebrating the formalisation of the banking partnership of Pretor, Pew and Whitty in 1793, and that the halfpenny was actually produced sometime in 1796, not too removed in time from the two other Sherborne Bank tokens. Although today the halfpenny is scarce in fine condition (i.e. EF or better), most specimens tend to exhibit appreciable wear which suggests that it circulated familiarly as small change in its neighbourhood over a not insignificant period uninhibited by the introduction of Boulton's 'cartwheel' coinage in 1797-99.

The date of the other two Sherborne tokens presents little difficulty but some mystery does surround the token bearing an image of the Long Street banking house [177]. In 1801 Pye judged both this piece and the halfpenny with a mis-spelled monogram *PW&P* [178] to have

---

96 Banks MS Cat. VI, SSB 194-143.

178 John Westwood, Jnr.: specious Sherborne halfpenny, 1796.

been 'made by Westwood *for sale*'; Both tokens are well struck and match the *PP&W* halfpenny in weight (11.2g or more) – the 'Bank House' token, on average, a healthy 12g at least – and both are very rare today. Miss Banks acquired her specimen of the 'Bank House' token on 13 July 1797 broadly confirming its expressed date of 1796.[97] The obverse image of the bank, allowing for the constrictions imposed on the die-sinker, is a not unfaithful representation of the original sixteenth/seventeenth century Long Street property as it would have appeared at the time and must have been copied from a contemporary engraving undertaken for the second edition of the Reverend John Hutchins' *History of Dorset* [179].[98]

179 *The Sherborne and Dorsetshire Bank.* From Hutchins, *The History and Antiquities of the County of Dorset* (2nd. Edition).

It is likely that the demand for the original Sherborne halfpennies was such that Pretor ordered the 'Bank House' token as replenishment but rejected the proofs because of the misspelling of his name on its reverse: **PRETER PEW & WHITTY BANKERS SHERBORNE DORSET 1796**. Pretor was a forthright character whose temper had not improved with age and whose pride would never have allowed him to accept a defective product that he would have deemed personally derogatory. Thus although intended to be a genuine commercial coin the halfpenny never passed the test of acceptability by its projector.

97 Banks MS Cat. VI, SSB 194-142.

98 Hutchins (1796-1815), IV (1815), 98. The original bank building – a grade II* listed structure with the canted oriel featured on the token and the engraving – still exists although in the early nineteenth century it was greatly altered, extended into an adjacent property and remodelled with a Gothic-Revival facade depicted on the firm's later bank notes.

180 John Westwood Jnr.: 'Liverpool Half Halfpenny', [*c*.1796].

181 John Westwood Jnr.: 'Macclesfield Penny', [*c*.1796].

182 John Westwood Jnr.: Perth halfpenny for David Peters, 1797.

Young Westwood on the other hand, ever mindful of his income, would not have failed to capitalise on his lost commission by using the spurned dies to produce a 'limited edition' token for the collectors' market as he did with the third bank halfpenny. This is again a well-struck token but the lettering of the obverse monogram is ordered wrongly and surely cannot be argued away as an unfortunate slip; one can only conclude that this piece was always intended to be specious and, as Pye said, was produced for sale and for the collector's market: no doubt Westwood was getting his own back on Pretor.

By now, with Obadiah Westwood's coin-making concern with Hancock long a thing of the past, young Westwood was concentrating on his 'limited edition' copies of earlier provincial coins and concocting 'half halfpenny' [180] and 'penny' novelties [181] for sale for which he was roundly castigated by Pye in the 'Advertisement' to his 1801 catalogue.[99] But Westwood's attempt to capitalise on what was a transient 'collecting' mania was soon over; his satirical 'Collectors' Halfpence' [281b and c] [100] proving to be a wry comment on a phenomenon that for all his artistry brought him little financial success.

Apart from the 'Sherborne Bank' halfpenny Pye attributed the engraving of only one other strictly commercial token to 'Westwood', a halfpenny issued by the Perth wine and spirit merchant, David Peters in 1797 that, interestingly, bears a double-headed eagle as its obverse rendering of the arms of Perth [182]. Again, the 'Westwood' here must be John Westwood, junior but what is intriguing about this piece is that Pye identified its manufacturer as Lutwyche, the only known association of young Westwood with this token maker. One must wonder on whose presses the other 'Westwood' pieces of the period 1795-1800 were actually struck. This is a conundrum that is heightened by Westwood's appearance among the contenders for the contract for a regal coinage in 1797. Undoubtedly the specimen coins he submitted to the Committee on Coin were the **BRITISH COMMERCIAL PENNY** and its two fractions [183] but how he envisaged striking them on the scale that would have been required had he won the contract remains a mystery.[101]

What happened to the other main protagonists in the consortium over the next year or so is unclear. Hancock continued as a die-sinker,

---

99 Pye (1801), 4.

100 Dalton and Hamer (Middx 298-99), credited these pieces to Denton (who was probably no more than a sales outlet) although Sharp (1834), 121 – and subsequently Samuel (1884), 435 – had attributed them to Westwood ; one version – a variety of the 'running asses' type – not insignificantly perhaps is struck on an unused 'Sherborne Bank' blank.

101 The 'British Commercial' series seems to have been first attributed to Westwood by the Rev. Henry Christmas in his rare and incomplete *Copper and Billon Coinage of the British Empire* (London 1868). *Peck* (1960), however, suggested that the die–sinker was Thomas Webb (page 237). That the coins were in fact produced by Westwood is conclusively demonstrated by his attempt to sell the dies and his remaining specimens to Boulton in 1800: BAH: MS 3782/12/45/1800/32. Some of the halfpennies are struck on old 'Cronebane' flans edged by John Westwood, senior (*D&H*: Middx 1006).

A BIRMINGHAM TOKEN CONSORTIUM

183 John Westwood Jnr.: 'British Commercial Penny', struck for submission to the Committee on Coin, 1797.

184 Thomas Dobbs: London halfpenny for Thomas and Robert Davidson, 1795.

185 'John Gregory Hancock, Jnr.': 'Sir Original' novelty token, 1800.

his final eighteenth-century provincial coin being a halfpenny for Thomas and Robert Davidson, London printers and pocket-book makers of Sise Lane in the City [184]. This was struck, according to Pye, by the Birmingham metal roller Thomas Dobbs, otherwise numismatically known, again through Pye, only for the 'Coventry Cross' version of Robert Reynolds's halfpennies dated 1794 and 1795 (D&H: War. 247-49 and 251). The 'Davidson' halfpenny had been produced by May 1795 and was most likely an order that the Westwood/Hancock consortium had been unable to complete. Apart from one final commission after the turn of the century for his old master Matthew Boulton – the Irish 'Tullamore' token [139] – all his other ventures were medallic commissions either directly for private patrons or for Peter Kempson.[102] But that was all over by 1803.[103] One suspects that his health had been questionable for some time. Digges thought him 'dissipated' as early as 1793, probably prone to drink as were so many of the die-sinkers that the American met. More sensitively, Sharp judged Hancock 'unfortunate and neglected', someone whose 'talents and genius' had been unfulfilled when he died, a broken man, in Birmingham in November 1805. No doubt his son (b. 24 June 1791), accounted an infant prodigy and credited in 1800 with the engraving of several private tokens and curiosities [185] at an age variously claimed to be seven or nine, had predeceased him to add to his woes.[104]

Young Westwood's fellow apprentice and exact contemporary, John Stubbs Jorden (b. 1774), persevered for twelve months or so, trying to continue token making in the old tradition.[105] Born at Wombourn, near Wolverhampton, Jorden was a member of a long-standing family of ironmasters but apart from his family background, sketchy in itself, virtually nothing is known about him until he first surfaces in a numismatic context in 1792. The collector, William Robert Hay, recorded, in his annotated copy of the *Virtuoso's Companion*, that the 'End of Pain. Rev. Pandora's Breeches' token was 'Executed as a Joke by Mess[rs]. Jourden & Hancock. The Head of Priestley by Hancock. The die on which Pandoras [sic] Breeches were sunk having broke after a few impressions were struck off, they executed an[r]. Rev.' [186a and b]. The token – probably the first of the political genre – was struck to commemorate an attempt to fire the House of Commons on 9 May 1792 and must have been put out within a few months of the incident because Miss Banks had acquired her specimen of 'Pandora's

---

102 See Dykes (1999), 179, note 23.

103 With the exception of the posthumously-reworked obverse of *BHM*: 613 no medals listed in *BHM* subsequent to *BHM* 550 (*Eimer* 946) [1803] can be attributed to Hancock.

104 Sharp (1834), v. Sharp, despite extensive enquiries, failed to find out anything about John Gregory Hancock, junior although George Barker, a supposed sponsor of young Hancock's work, was still very much alive.

105 For Jorden and his tokens see Dykes (2001).

191

186a

186b

186 John Gregory Hancock and John Stubbs Jorden: 'End of Pain' satirical tokens, [1792]. Hancock's characteristic profile of Joseph Priestley forms the head of the snake on the reverse of a.

Breeches' by 9 February 1793.[106]

According to Hay Jorden had 'learnt the Art' of die-sinking from Hancock. That he had been apprenticed to Hancock for some years, probably since 1788, is borne out by Digges who noted that 'This lad Jordan [sic], has two years of His time to serve, wishes much to go to America, but I suppose his time would be worth 200£'.[107] This was in the spring of 1793. But by September 1796, as Hay discovered, Jorden had given up die engraving for the manufacture of patent window frames. Jorden, it seems, had therefore worked as a die-sinker on his own account for little more than a year. This is a time-scale broadly supported by the exiguous nature of the token production credited to him by Pye (1801): six contracts in all – for 'Jorden, sen[ior]' (1795); the London scale-makers, Meymott and Son (1795); an unidentified London issuer, Peter Anderson (1795); an equally unknown John Webb of Newton, said by Conder to be one of the Warwickshire villages of that name (1796); the Coventry hatter and antiquary, Thomas Sharp (1797); and the London jewellers, Presbury and Son (not dated but likely to be very late, if, indeed, this last token was by Jorden).

None of Jorden's 1795 tokens is listed in the early catalogues put out by Hammond or Spence in the May of that year, but his 'Glamorgan Halfpenny' [187] does appear in one of Pye's octavo plates first published on 1 August 1795. It is reasonable to suppose, therefore, that this token was the first of Jorden's independent productions and was manufactured in the early summer of 1795. The obverse bust of Jestyn ap Gwrgan owes much to Hancock's influence and, interestingly, there exists a trial of its reverse die struck on a 'Thames and Severn' edged blank bearing on its other side an incuse impression of the Sapperton Tunnel (*D&H*: Glam. 2).[108] This, together with a 'Thames and Severn' halfpenny struck on a 'Glamorgan' edged blank (*D&H*: Glos. 60a) suggests some 'cross-over' in the production of the two issues. The 'Glamorgan' halfpenny was followed soon after by the 'Meymott' halfpenny which was first illustrated in a plate of the *Virtuoso's Companion* put out on 14 January 1796 and which shared for its obverse the same basic figure punch of 'Britannia' copied from a Droz or Küchler pattern halfpenny of 1790 or 1795.[109] Of Jorden's *oeuvre* only the 'Glamorgan' and the 'Meymott' halfpennies were, according to Pye, struck in any quantity: of the former a ton, perhaps 100,000 tokens – which may well be an overestimate because although the token was intended for circulation and, from the evidence of finds, clearly did circulate for some time in south Wales, it is relatively scarce today.[110]

The 'Glamorgan Halfpenny' is unique among eighteenth-century

---

106 Banks MS Cat. VI, SSB 194-156-1.

107 LC: Thomas Jefferson Papers, Th[omas A[ttwood] Digges to Thomas Jefferson, 10 March 1793. See also Elias and Finch (1982), 443.

108 [Peter Preston-Morley], DNW Auction T 6, 19 March 2009, lot 456.

109 See Dykes (2001), 128.

110 Pye (1801), 11.

A BIRMINGHAM TOKEN CONSORTIUM

187 John Stubbs Jorden: Glamorgan halfpenny probably struck for the Merthyr Tydfil iron-masters, William Taitt, Richard Crawshay and Samuel Homfray of Penydarren at the instance of William Jorden, 1795.

tokens in having its legends in the Welsh language: **JESTYN • AP • GWRGAN • TYWYSOG • MORGANWG • 1091** [Jestyn ap Gwrgan, Prince of Morganwg] and **Y • BRENHIN • AR • GYFRAITH** [The King and the Law].[111] What is of further special interest is that of the two distinct issues of the token, the substantive version – weighing on average something in excess of 10g – is struck in a four-segmented collar with a **raised** edge inscription: **GLAMORGAN HALFPENNY** with horizontally disposed leaves. Like his mentor Jorden was an innovative man.

There is a separate, quite rare, issue of the token [188] the obverse die of which broke resulting in the manufacture of only a few specimens; in Pye's day examples of the type were selling for as much as 10s 6d a piece.[112] This rare issue was struck in a plain collar, was much heavier, weighing an average 13.9 g, and must have been intended as a collector's piece although, strangely enough, while specimens of the ordinary version were made in silver, it was not struck in a precious metal. Both its obverse and reverse dies were those used for the substantive version but softened and reworked to create, *inter alia*, a more elaborate coronet for Jestyn ap Gwrgan and to refashion the reverse pedestal, removing the crown (but with vestiges of its cross still being apparent). This striking is not listed in any contemporary catalogue prior to Pye (1801). It did not find its way into James Conder's reasonably comprehensive *Arrangement* of 1798 while Miss Banks did not acquire her specimen until 14 November 1801.[113] The piece must therefore be quite late and distinct from the issue of the substantive halfpenny in 1795.

The circumstances of the issue of the substantive version have long been something of a mystery. There is, however, reliable contemporary evidence that it was struck for Jorden's father, a former Staffordshire ironmaster who settled in Swansea in the final years of the century, but there is also a traditional, if unsubstantiated, local belief that the token was made to the order of a group of ironmasters (William Taitt of Dowlais, Richard Crawshay of Cyfarthfa and Samuel Homfray of Penydarren) 'for necessary change' over thirty miles away in the Merthyr Tydfil area. The two leads may not be incompatible for we do know that William Jorden's family had previous business connections with the Homfrays and Jorden himself, it is thought, could well have come down to south Wales to help in the development of the Homfrays' vast new ironworks at Penydarren. In such a context it is not implausible to think of him as commissioning the 'Glamorgan Halfpenny' from his son for the Merthyr ironmasters, not only to meet the needs of their scores of workers – the Homfrays employed over nine hundred men, women and children at Penydarren [189] and Crawshay even more at

188 John Stubbs Jorden: Glamorgan halfpenny, special striking probably intended as a collector's piece, post 1795.

---

111 The Welsh of the reverse legend, *pace D&H*, Part XI: Anglesey and Wales (1915), xii, is correct because of the soft mutation of the initial 'C' of 'Cyfraith' to 'G' following 'ar' although the apostrophe between 'A' and 'R' [ac yr (and the) = a'r] has been omitted probably for aesthetic reasons.

112 Pye (1801), 11.

113 Banks MS Cat. VI, SSB 195-16-2.

193

189 The Penydarren Iron Works, c. 1811. From John George Wood's *The Principal Rivers of Wales Illustrated* (1813).

Cyfarthfa – but also of the labourers engaged on the digging of the new Glamorgan Canal serving the works. And although Crawshay, Taitt and Homfray were a fractious trio frequently at loggerheads with each other, they could occasionally try to act in concert as they had already done over the establishment – abortive, as it turned out – of an 'ironmasters' bank' at Merthyr in the spring of 1791.[114]

The 'Glamorgan Halfpenny' is usually found in a worn condition which suggests a circulation in industrial south Wales long after its nominal date of issue, comparatively late though this was, underlining, as with the Sherborne halfpenny, the continuing need for such a form of small change in areas not necessarily effectively covered by Boulton's 'cartwheel' coinage.

Jorden's 'Meymott' halfpenny [190] is one of his most attractive productions – Hay was moved to describe it as 'nearly the finest Executed of Tradesmens Tickets'.[115] Pye stated that not more than a hundredweight – perhaps some 5,000 pieces – were produced of the substantive version after a false start owing to the cracking of Jorden's first obverse die.[116] Weighing on average 10.33 g, it was struck for a London firm of scale-makers, Meymott and Son, with premises, as the token's edge inscription tells us, at 64 Bishopsgate Within on the corner of Wormwood Street. Clement

190 John Stubbs Jorden: London halfpenny for Clement Meymott and Son, 1795.

114 Richard Crawshay's son William and Samuel Homfray each later issued tokens of their own (Merthyr shilling, 1801 (Dalton (1922): Glamorganshire 1-7) and Tredegar Iron Company (TIC) penny, 1812 (Withers and Withers (1999), 178-79, nos. 1340-41)). Penydarren issued truck tickets, struck at Soho and in a variety of values, in 1800: Davis and Waters (1922), 338; Mason (ed.) (2009), 212.

115 Dykes (2001), 128.

116 Pye (1801), 14.

A BIRMINGHAM TOKEN CONSORTIUM

191a and b John Stubbs Jorden: London halfpennies for Peter Anderson, 1795

192 John Stubbs Jorden: Newton halfpenny for John Webb, 1796.

Meymott, the principal of the firm, was, appropriately enough, a member of the Blacksmiths' Company and, rather surprisingly, his son, Samuel, a member of the Vintners' Company by servitude; a reflection, perhaps, of a striving after status or of an early intention of entering another trade.[117]

With the exception of one rare variety of the first type, all were struck in a collar, the edge inscription (**CORNER OF WORMWOOD STREET BISHOPSGATE X**) where applicable being in raised letters. Versions were also struck in white metal, silver and gold – a unique proof said by Sharp to have been specially struck for Mr. [Clement] Meymott – as well as in copper.[118] Unfinished trials exist of the obverse die demonstrating clearly the basic figure punch that Jorden had copied from Droz or Küchler. Interestingly one of these is struck on a flan edged for Hancock's 'Davidson' halfpenny lending further weight to some continuing association with Hancock.

Production problems seem to have haunted Jorden's commissions. The heavy London City halfpennies produced for Peter Anderson in 1795, for instance, were attended with great difficulties. Anderson has never been positively identified but the edge legend – **PAYABLE AT THE HOUSE OF PETER ANDERSON** – suggests that he may have been associated with any one of a number of City mercantile firms of the period carrying his surname. Hamer assumed that, because of the very limited number of tokens struck, they were intended as a private issue. Their fine workmanship and their heavy weight (averaging 14.5 g) support this view although Pye (1801) makes the point that the dies broke during the second substantive striking limiting their production.[119]

Only one pair of dies was made. After trials in white metal and copper the obverse die was altered slightly and a few tokens having been made in the new format [191a] both dies were changed more materially. But as Pye tells us these then broke after eight new impressions were taken. The latter [191b] have what was intended to be London's City motto added above the obverse shield while the reverse monogram is ornamented, the improved design being unhappily marred by Jorden's apparent lack of familiarity with Latin or of precision in his engraving. Jorden departed from his previous edging practice with this issue for the legends were **impressed** on blanks that were subsequently struck in a bi-segmented collar and, for what it is worth, it is at least of passing interest in this context that, according to Waters, the contemporary collector Thomas Woodward attributed the token to Hancock in his annotated copy of Conder's *Arrangement*.[120]

Jorden's production problems were carried forward into his dies for the 1796 halfpennies of John Webb [192] which, according to Pye,

---

117 Guildhall Library MS 2885/1, 3 July 1766; MS 15212/2, 1 June 1785.

118 Sharp (1834), 66.

119 Hamer (1903/1904), I (1903/1904), 303; Pye (1801), 12.

120 Waters (1906), 13.

195

193 John Stubbs Jorden: Coventry halfpenny for Thomas Sharp, 1797.

broke after the striking of some four dozen pieces and the 'order was never completed, Mr. Jorden having about this time gone into another business'.[121] Conder's location of 'Newton' to Warwickshire was accepted by Sharp – himself a Warwickshire man – but has been challenged by modern authorities although no satisfactory alternative has been suggested.[122] Newtown in Powys is a possibility but attempts to associate the name Webb with this Welsh woollen manufacturing centre have so far been unavailing. But the halfpenny is anomalous on other grounds. It has the appearance of being a private token; it is heavy (14.3 g) and seems, prima facie, to have been struck in a plain collar. Close inspection of a number of specimens, however, suggests that the edge has been tooled to give that impression. The reverse is quite elegant but the obverse is clumsily designed. The halfpenny remains an enigma.

Jorden's 1797 halfpenny for Thomas Sharp (1770-1841), a Coventry hatter, local antiquarian and numismatist of some note, was clearly intended to be a private token.[123] From his youth Sharp had collected coins and had built up a respectable cabinet of provincial coins as they were issued and much of this was eventually to be absorbed into the token collection formed by Sir George Chetwynd of Grendon Hall, near Atherstone in Warwickshire. Sharp's catalogue for the Chetwynd collection was to be the work on which Sharp's numismatic reputation was to become largely based.

According to Pye four dozen specimens of the final version of Sharp's halfpenny [193] were struck, some in silver, but this was only after Jorden had struggled to achieve the correct perspective of his reverse depiction of Sharp's Coventry house. Pye's estimate of the number of the substantive issue struck was not challenged by Sharp but the tokens are very rare today and even in Pye's time were fetching 15s 6d.[124] It is the heaviest of Jorden's tokens and, weighing on average 15.75 g, is struck with **raised** edge lettering and interestingly its obverse harks back again to Hancock with the uncanny resemblance its composition bears to that of the latter's 'Davidson' halfpenny [184].

In 1792, together with two fellow townsmen (George Howlette and John Nickson), Sharp commissioned a series of views of all the buildings of interest in the county from a local drawing master, Henry Jeayes, and other artists for insertion in their copies of William Dugdale's *Antiquities of Warwickshire*. Nineteen of Jeayes' views were made available to Thomas Wyon for Kempson's series of Coventry tokens in 1797 and one of his sketches of the Free Grammar School formed the basis of Nickson's private halfpenny of 1799 [393].[125]

A Jeayes view of Sharp's house in Smithford Street – 'Peeping Tom's House' – with the King's Head coaching inn next door may have served as the original from which the street scene was taken but if it ever existed

---

121 Pye (1801), 15.
122 Conder (1798), 171; Sharp (1834), 98.
123 For Thomas Sharp, see *GM*, October 1841, 436-8; Fretton (1871), ix-xv; *ODNB*.
124 Pye (1801), 9 and Plate 15*, no. 2; Sharp (1834), 98.
125 Fretton (1871), x; Clarke (1992), 6-7.

A BIRMINGHAM TOKEN CONSORTIUM

it is now lost and our only clue to a prototype is an engraving of 1799 after Rowlandson showing a characteristically comic group of bystanders gawking in wonder at the first-floor effigy of 'Peeping Tom' [194]. Maybe it is Sharp himself who is peering out of his shop doorway aghast at an apprentice publicly flirting in his side entrance.

194   *Peeping Tom's House*, Coventry, 1799. From a tinted engraving after Thomas Rowlandson.

Why Sharp should employ Jorden for his token is a mystery. Adept as he was as a die-sinker the latter had no reputation for topographical engraving and bearing in mind Sharp's involvement with Wyon and Kempson over the Coventry 'Buildings' medalets it is surprising that he did not commission his own halfpenny from them. One can only think that Jorden's engagement predated the 'Buildings' series by some time – certainly before the summer of 1796 and his departure into the manufacture of patent window frames – and it must have been with some relief that, after a not altogether happy experience at Jorden's hands, Sharp turned to Wyon and Kempson for the production of what was after all a considerably larger commercial scheme.

The last token that has been credited to Jorden is that of Charles Presbury & Co. [195], a firm of manufacturing jewellers and hardwaremen at 9 New Street, Covent Garden and if Pye had not associated this trade ticket with Jorden it is virtually inconceivable that his name would have been attached to such a piece of shoddy workmanship.[126] The obverse die is a 'Wyon' production initially used by Kempson for the halfpennies of Dally and Son of Chichester dated 1794 and 1795 and subsequently used by him in the manufacture of an undated mule with the reverse of the 'Blofield Cavalry' halfpennies. These mules show the same 'tuning fork' flaw close to the 'E' of 'ELIZABETH' that developed during the initial 'Chichester' striking with,

195   John Stubbs Jorden: London halfpenny for Charles Presbury and Company [*c.*1796-98].

126   Pye (1801), 14.

197

additionally, a new blemish to the right of the queen's crown. Both defects are most pronounced in its new incarnation for 'Presbury' and make clear the order in which they were used. Finally, to muddy the waters still further the deteriorating die was used again for the production of a further poor quality instalment of 'Chichester' tokens. The substantive 'Blofield Cavalry' halfpenny is dated 1796 and is first catalogued in the *Virtuoso's Companion* in April 1797. The 'Presbury' halfpenny appears in no contemporary catalogue before Conder's *Arrangement* and its presumed date of production must thus lie sometime between late 1796 and the summer of 1798.[127]

If the obverse Kempson die suggests a cutting of corners to produce a cheap product the reverse makes this all too clear by the die-sinker's obvious reworking of a botched die of his own. Close examination of the reverse shows the vestiges of an original first line of the legend running obliquely underneath the sprig of leaves. It comes as little surprise to learn from Pye that Presbury countermanded his order after about three-dozen tokens were struck. All in all the halfpenny is hardly worthy of an engraver of the calibre of Jorden and one must ask whether it is, in fact, his production. What we know about its antecedents and subsequent history points to Kempson's workshop and this association is reinforced by its flan which, edged with an **impressed** London inscription (**PAYABLE IN LONDON + . + . + . x .**), is one used by Kempson elsewhere.

This, of course, leads us to the question as to whether Jorden actually *manufactured* the tokens attributed to him. Charles Pye is quite clear on this point; to him Jorden was responsible for the dies and *manufacture* of all six. Three of the tokens, those for Anderson, Webb and Sharp, bear out Pye's observation for they do not link with anything else and point to the operation of a small, discrete workshop. The 'Glamorgan' and the 'Meymott' halfpennies, on the other hand, have, as we have seen, some peculiar features that might suggest some continued relationship with his old mentor Hancock.[128] These are obviously aberrant pieces that are probably most easily explained away simply by Jorden's continued possession of some discarded 'Thames and Severn' flans and punches, but they might just indicate the striking of Jorden's only largish scale – and first – contract by his erstwhile employers before they closed down. The 'Presbury' halfpenny is the one real anomaly and links in with Kempson too closely for comfort. It is probably very late in the series, perhaps, as we have suggested, as late as 1798. It could well be a Kempson production but, if one believes Pye, it could be a comparatively trivial contract passed on by an overstretched manufacturer to an under-employed workshop with a suitably available obverse die.

---

127 Conder (1798), 94.

128 The later and separate use of an obverse 'Meymott' die (*D&H*: Middlesex 380-382) and a reverse die (*D&H*: Middlesex 385, 387-388) by William Williams has no bearing on this issue.

PRESENTATION OF THE COLOURS.

TO commemorate this Event, a MEDAL is struck from an approved Design (by BARBER) and dedicated to the Inhabitants of the Town of Birmingham, and in a more especial Manner to the LOYAL ASSOCIATIONS of CAVALRY and INFANTRY,

By the Public's obedient Servant,

J. S. JORDEN.

As the Public at large may be accommodated, the Medals are of Silver, Bronze, and Copper, either adapted as Regalias, or for the Cabinet; and by Permission, the Beadles of St. Philip's will attend with them on the Parade, in New-street, to deliver them to the Gentlemen of the Corps; and in the Field to those Ladies and Gentlemen who may be desirous of possessing them.

The Medals, in either Metal, may be had after this Day, at Messrs. Richards, High-street.

Mr. JORDEN has had the Honour to receive an Order for a Gold Medal for each of the LADIES who have worked the Colours, which are to be presented to them by the TOWN, and will be worn on the Occasion.

Birmingham, June 4, 1798.

196 Advertisement in *Aris's Birmingham Gazette* for Jorden's 'Loyal Associations' Medal, 4 June 1798.

The 'Presbury' halfpenny is the last token that can in any way be credited to Jorden but it was not his final numismatic venture of the century. On 4 June 1798 – the King's birthday – colours were presented to the Loyal Birmingham Light Horse Volunteers and the Birmingham Loyal Association on Birmingham Heath in the presence of a crowd of upward of fifty thousand enthusiastic onlookers who were remarkable for their 'peaceful, respectful and exemplary conduct' [196].[129] To mark the occasion Jorden was commissioned to strike a commemorative medal designed by Joseph Barber, a local artist and drawing master, and produced in white metal, copper, silver and copper-gilt. Its subscription, **JORDEN FECIT ET DEDICAVIT**, stresses Jorden's responsibility for the medal and its making [197]. It is a fine piece of work, 41 mm in diameter and again one must wonder whether Jorden himself had the capacity to strike as well as engrave it himself. This is certainly the inwardness of his advertisement in the local newspaper at the time but was the reality that he contracted the medal's manufacture out to someone like Kempson who was currently specializing in medallic work and moreover employing Hancock in this sphere. The problem of the 'Presbury' halfpenny gives one pause for thought.

Overall Jorden was singularly unsuccessful with his dies and produced only a handful of actual coins. But he was also, of course, unlucky in his generation. By the time he was able to venture out on his own the large-scale production of 'industrial' tokens had virtually run its course, while, within the year, the cut-throat competition for lesser provincial coin contracts, especially between the leading Birmingham manufacturers,

197 John Stubbs Jorden: 'Birmingham Loyal Associations' medal, 1798.

129 *ABG*, 11 June 1798.

Peter Kempson and William Lutwyche, was also beginning to peter out: as Charles Shephard, a keen observer of the token scene, recognised, by the early part of 1796 'the rage of coining was considerably abated'.[130] In any case, however short term Kempson's and Lutwyche's commanding positions might be, with established die-sinkers like Thomas Wyon and Roger Dixon contracted to them, there was little space for any new Birmingham engraver just out of apprenticeship. Despite his consummate skill, there were few crumbs for Jorden to pick up which doubtless explains why, after his immediate flush of work, his production of tokens was so limited and he was quickly persuaded to concentrate on another business.

By September 1796, as Hay noted, Jorden had 'gone into a Manufactory for patent Window Frames'. This might well have been as early as the autumn of 1795 and could well have involved Hancock who never seems to have been far from Jorden's side and significantly in the October of that year was awarded a patent for the construction of window 'uprights and crossbars'.[131] Local trade directories show that Jorden was to continue in various permutations of this business or as 'a metallic hot house manufacturer' for the best part of thirty years. Clearly of an inventive turn of mind like his mentors Hancock and the Westwoods Jorden obtained a clutch of patents for the glazing of horticultural buildings and, although he was forced into bankruptcy in 1819, he was able to continue in business as a 'metallic hot house maker' until he eventually disappeared from the directories in 1825 [198].[132]

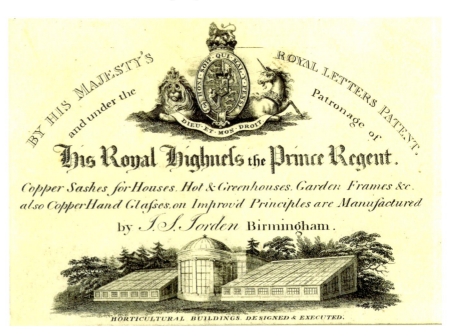

198   Trade Card of John Stubbs Jorden, 1814.

130   *GM*, February 1798, 120.
131   Patent Specification 2069, 15 October 1795: Woodcroft (1856) [1969], 246.
132   Patent Specifications 3478 and 3814, 20 August 1811 and 7 June 1814: Woodcroft (1856) [1969], 312; *LG*, No. 17500, 3 August 1819, 1375; Dykes (2001), 123.

What happened to him then is a mystery. One of Thomas Digges's typically questionable missions in Britain in the early 1790s had been the recruitment of expert workmen for the nascent industries of the United States; a dangerous and illegal practice punishable, as he was at pains to point out to Alexander Hamilton, by a stiff fine of '510£ & 12 months imprisonment' as well as 'very rough treatment'.[133] Much of his time in Birmingham had been spent in trying to inveigle suitable die-sinkers for the proposed United States mint. 'If the young man Jordan', he told Thomas Pinckney, the American minister in London, 'could be got I am of opinion He would answer better than any of those I have seen or spoken to here, for workmen in this line are very few, and often & [are] drunken & worthless in thier [sic] manners'.[134] If any inducement was offered to Jordan he certainly did not take it up at the time but whether he later fulfilled his youthful ambition to emigrate to the United States or follow an uncle who had set up an iron founding business in Canada is not known. Perhaps he went to Ireland since there is some tantalizing evidence that a 'J.S. Jorden' exhibited at a Dublin art exhibition in 1828. If he was still working as a medallist then it is difficult to believe that he had completely put aside medal making in the thirty years since the presentation of colours on Birmingham Heath and a critical examination of the many unsigned medals of the early nineteenth century, especially some of those still credited to Hancock after his death in 1805, might prove to be a productive exercise.

133 LC: Alexander Hamilton Papers, Tho[ma]s Digges to Alexander Hamilton, 6 April 1792. See also Elias and Finch (1982), 438. Samuel Garbett's Birmingham Commercial Committee was particularly concerned over the seduction of workers abroad at this time, offering a reward of 50 guineas for information that led to a successful conviction: *ABG* 2 February 1784, 31 January 1785 and 23 January 1786. See also Langford (1868), I, 318, 320 and 326).

134 LC: Pinckney Family Papers, Tho[ma]s A[ttwood] Digges to Thomas Pinckney, 12 March 1793: Elias and Finch (1982), 447.

V

THE NEW MEN

I stated to him [Walter Taylor of Southampton] the probability of Govt. Coining soon & suppressing all Counterfeits, & all provincial money with such other arguments as induced him to suspend his plan untill he sees what is likely to be done by Governmt. & if nothing is soon done I am perswaded that not only Mr Taylor but sundry other persons & Comps: in different parts of the Kingdom will issue their own half pence upon principles of Vanity as well as of profit. I have heard of several who intended it but have suspended their plans untill they see whether Governmt. take any measures before ye parlt. is dissolved.

Matthew Boulton to Samuel Garbett,
29 March 1790. [1]

From the want of a sufficient quantity of Mint Halfpence, a very base copper coin has been put into currency, to the amount of some thousand Tons, and to avoid a breach of the Law which has laid hold of many to their ruin, Coins have been made as promissory Notes for a Halfpenny, payable at particular Places specified upon the Pieces, more than $\frac{sixty}{forty}$ sorts have been made (some of which likewise have been counterfeited). These Practices have occasioned difficulty & distress to poor People, which will however increase, as Riders now Hawk about Patterns to procure Orders for new Coin.

Samuel Garbett to the Marquess of Lansdowne,
December 1794.[2]

In the summer of 1791 a group of midlands manufacturers and consumers of copper and brass floated a new company to combat the high prices set by the Cornish Metal Company/Anglesey cartel. By taking shares in a number of Cornish mines and setting up its own smelting works in the Swansea Valley the Birmingham Mining and Copper Company bid 'Defiance to the Paris Mountain and all the Confederates in Copper' and strove to put off the 'Shackles of Monopoly'.[3] The new co-operative proved to be a great success, it led to the establishment of similar companies in the town [4] and, by the

---

[1] BAH: MS 3782/12/62/83, Matthew Boulton to Samuel Garbett, 29 March 1790.

[2] BL: Lansdowne MSS: Shelburne 19, f. 87.

[3] *ABG*, 15 February 1790. For the company see Hamilton (1967), 231-35.

[4] The Rose (1793) and the Crown (1803) Copper Companies both of which issued copper tokens in the early nineteenth century.

199   Peter Kempson: Halfpenny for the Birmingham Mining and Copper Company, 1791.

turn of the century, had helped to secure Birmingham's place as the manufacturing core of the country's brass and copper industries.

But this was to be in the future. For the present and for our purposes, the interest of the company is that, in the wake of its foundation, it followed the practice of other industrial concerns and issued its own copper halfpennies; according to Charles Pye, one and a half tons in 1791 followed with about nine tons in 1792 [199].[5] They are attractive pieces with expertly engraved allegorical representations of 'Commerce' holding fasces expressing the unity of the shareholders and 'Prosperity' symbolized by a stork and a cornucopia. The edge inscription is unusual in that as well as listing the tokens' redemption centres, **BIRMINGHAM REDRUTH AND SWANSEA**, it incorporates the alchemical symbols for the seven planetary metals: gold, mercury, lead, silver, copper, tin and iron:

$$\odot \; \lozenge \; \hbar \; \mathcal{D} \; \varphi \; 4 \; \delta$$

Many of the 1791 pieces have a small '**W**' below the rock on which the obverse figure of 'Commerce' is sitting [200]. Most students have assumed the '**W**' to refer to the die-sinking workshop of the Wyon family since Pye gives 'Wyon' as the issue's engraver.[6] Pye also attributes their striking to Peter Kempson (1755-1824), a well-known local button-maker who was to play a significant role in the manufacture of provincial coins. Miss Banks, on the other hand, referring to the '**W**' piece in her collection, has a note in her manuscript catalogue that it was 'made by Mr. Whitmore of Birmingham'.[7] Her intervention must give some pause for thought for William Whitmore, as a substantial machine manufacturer [201] – including coining presses, 'one or two' of which he supplied to Thomas Williams when the latter set up his Great Charles Street coinery – would have been well placed to produce tokens for the Birmingham Company, and, as a large local consumer of copper, he had a strong personal interest in the Company as well.[8] On the other hand, while Pye's compendium cannot always be implicitly trusted in its detail, he and his collaborators are unlikely to have nodded too completely over

200   Enlargement of part of the obverse of William Whitmore's 1791 Birmingham Mining and Copper Company halfpenny showing the maker's initial '**W**' to the right above the exergue.

5   Pye (1801), 6.

6   The Wyons' modelling, chasing and die-engraving business was established by George Wyon about 1783 after he left Soho where he had been employed in the Silver, Plated and Ormolu department. His four sons were employed in the family firm which was taken over by Peter and Thomas Wyon after their father's death in 1797. Unless the Wyons' oeuvre is named (or initialled) one cannot be confident about attribution.

7   Banks MS Cat. VI, SSB 186-111.

8   BAH: MS 3782/12/73/83, Thomas Williams to Matthew Boulton, 8 June 1789. Bisset's *Directory* describes Whitmore as an 'Engineer and manufacturer of all Kinds of rolling and flatting Mills, Machines for weighing Barges, Boats, Waggons (*sic*), etc., Engines, Lathes, Stamps, Presses and Lancashire Watch-tools etc.'. Several examples of Whitmore's products are shown on the left and in the foreground of the engraving of his works reproduced from Plate U of Bisset's *Poetic Survey round Birmingham*, 1800 at p. 205 below. On Whitmore's involvement with the Birmingham Mining and Copper Company see *Copper Report* (1803), 655.

THE NEW MEN

201 View of William Whitmore's works. Detail from Plate U of Bisset's *Magnificent Directory of Birmingham*, 1800.

the identification of a Birmingham coiner. If Miss Banks's comment has validity, and there is no reason to doubt it, the likely solution to this apparent conflict of evidence must be that there was some division of manufacturing responsibility with Whitmore being responsible for the production of the 1791 'W' halfpennies and Kempson for the remainder, those without the initial and dated 1791 and 1792 which formed the bulk of the issue.[9]

Whatever the truth of their manufacture the Birmingham Company's halfpennies were among the last tokens to be struck in substantial quantities for a large-scale industrial concern and, typically, with their far flung circulation the '1792' issues were amply counterfeited, some almost certainly in the Kempson coinery itself. The Birmingham Company's tokens also heralded the arrival of newcomers to the token-making scene branching out from their traditional trades of button and toy making to profit from the new phenomenon; newcomers, of whom Kempson and his Birmingham neighbour William Lutwyche (*fl.* 1789-1801), were to be the most forward.

The problem facing the new men was that the industrial and commercial regions that had once clamoured for small change and had become the heartland of the early provincial coinages were now well served if not saturated with tokens so that finding much of a niche there for legitimate productions was difficult if not impossible. Even

---

9   Interestingly Pye omits the 'W' in his meticulous engraving of the halfpenny in the 1795 edition of his catalogue (Plate 12, no. 1) but includes it in that of 1801 (Plate 7, no. 3).

205

John Wilkinson could complain as early as November 1792 that there were 'so many private Coinages now on foot & so much interest used in circulating their different ½ pence that I cannot vend in my own Works one-fourth of what would have passed without trouble a year ago'.[10] Both Lutwyche – who, it is thought, was an old hand at counterfeiting Tower halfpence – and Kempson had cut their token-making teeth on the forging of popular issues and they now turned their attention increasingly to the speculative manufacture of non-attributable and hopelessly redeemable pieces which they produced in considerable quantities for 'general circulation'. At the same time, with the example of the Mint moneyers of the seventeenth-century before them, they began to exploit a localised custom for their product among the multitude of provincial shopkeepers – grocers ironmongers, drapers, booksellers, jewellers and the like – south and east of the country's Severn/Trent axial divide. In 1759 the Excise Office returned a total of 76,287 'regularly open' retail shops in this lowland zone (not counting those in London or inns and alehouses) and there must have been many more by the century's end.[11] While a considerable proportion would have been far too insignificant to have contemplated the issue of tokens the potential market must still have looked sufficiently lucrative to Kempson and Lutwyche to tempt them into mounting vigorous sales campaigns for a product tailored to the needs of particular communities. Token-making, in large part, thus became more supply- than demand-led and tokens, manufactured in comparatively modest quantities, a hawked rather than a commissioned commodity. The new men did not wait for customers to come to them but adopted the long-standing sales techniques of the Birmingham toy trade, systematically sending travelling salesmen or riders around the country armed with pattern books 'like so many wolves for orders' to drum up business and play upon potential clients' itch to make money and to 'obtain local notoriety by the issue of tokens', Boulton's 'principles of Vanity as well as of profit'.[12]

By the winter of 1794 when Samuel Garbett was inveighing against the practice, the evidence of the tokens themselves shows that Lutwyche had already carried out a concerted sales campaign in Kent and Sussex, securing orders in at least twenty towns and villages. Indeed, it is not too fanciful to trace his agent's route from Canterbury to Sandwich or Deal, along the coast to Hastings, and thence back through the Weald to Maidstone. A year or so before, in East Anglia, Kempson had anticipated Lutwyche by sending travellers out and, despite the latter's brisk competition, he had succeeded in building up a not unreasonable clientele in Essex, Suffolk and Norfolk. It was perhaps Kempson, too, who even

10   BAH: MS 3147/3/535/2, John Wilkinson to Matthew Boulton, 26 November 1792. See also Chaloner (1948a), 308.

11   Perhaps 90,000. The 1759 Excise Office returns are quoted in Mui & Mui (1989), 40 and 295-97. Even early in the century Defoe found he could not calculate the number of shopkeepers in the kingdom – 'we may as well count the stars': Defoe (1726), 399.

12   Robinson (1963-64), 43.

sought to penetrate the fastnesses of the Welsh borderland for a glimpse of this peddling is given in the misgivings expressed by a Flintshire magistrate about the activities of a 'rider' in the Chester area in 1794.

> A man came lately to a very respectable Tradesman, whom I know, and asked him if he wanted any pence, or halfpence coined; produced a card with forty or fifty different dies, and begged he would chuse such as would best answer the circulation of the place, and pay him by a draft for £60 at two months date; the payment of which might be stopped, if he did not furnish him with £100; in pence or halfpence in the course of one month – and toties quoties.
> Whether it proceeds from this, or other causes, I know not, but the Copper Coin of the Mint will not pass in this Country, so great is the Circulation and fair appearance of the Country Coinages, some of which, I am told, are only plated with Copper upon some less valuable Metal. [13]

Although Mr Thomas Griffith might urge the Treasury that it was a trade that ought to be checked his concerns were given short shrift by the officers of the Mint. Their advice to the Treasury, encapsulating half-a-century's hidebound attitude to the copper coinage, was a characteristically world-weary example of passing the buck. Admitting that 'the various private Copper pieces now passing in different parts of the Kingdom' were 'very numerous and much below the value they pretend to represent' they concluded:

> That the remedy, we conceive to be already with the Public, who can easily detect, as well the counterfeits as those spurious pieces; and who are fully authorized to refuse them both; and they have repeatedly found, on such occasions, that there has always appeared a sufficiency of genuine Copper Coin to answer every purpose of internal Commerce.
>
> That the sale and circulation of spurious Coins therefore, under any pretext whatever, we presume to be a serious and growing evil; but we are informed by our Sollicitor, that as yet there is no Law in this Country to prevent or punish for either. [14]

In the face of such a spiritless attitude and of an equally lymphatic stance on the part of government it was hardly surprising that, as Garbett recognised, token manufacturers should try to grasp whatever opportunities were presented to them to promote their product. All the same, the salesman working the shopkeepers of the north-east marches of Wales must have had a hopeless task. A year or so later a traveller making his way through the principality maintained that 'All

---

13 PRO MINT 1/14, ff. 243-44: Thomas Griffith 'of Rhual [Mold, Flintshire], near Chester' to the Treasury, 17 March 1794. Griffith (1740-1811) was High Sheriff of Flintshire in 1769-70 and 'for many years in the commission of the peace for that county': *Chester Chronicle*, 5 July 1811.

14 PRO MINT 1/14, ff. 244-45.

202   Peter Kempson: Specious 'Chester' halfpenny, [1794].

203   James Good: Maidstone halfpenny for James Smyth (Padsole Paper Mill), 1795.

the copper coin in Wales is heavy and good, three times more valuable than the trash circulated in London'; after all copper company tokens, including those of the Irish concerns, and Liverpool halfpennies were plentiful especially in the north-east of the country and the industrial south. Even as late as the autumn of 1796, the collector, Charles Shephard, could assert, that 'in Wales … the Anglesea pieces and a few others, of equal weight and value, had totally supplanted the copper currency of the kingdom'.[15] We do not know, of course, exactly what the Birmingham agent was touting, whether redeemable promissory halfpennies or unattributable specious issues to be circulated for pure profit. He does not seem to have had any luck at all with the former and if he did try to vend the latter, one possibility might have been the puzzling halfpennies supposedly put out by Roe and Company from Chester [202] and Macclesfield. Although undated these were probably initially made in 1794 and while they carry the **R & Co** monogram their light weight (just over 9 g) and the small quantities said by Pye (1801) to have been struck by Kempson (3 cwt and 5 cwt) must tell against any bona fide association with the copper company.[16]

Whatever Kempson or Lutwyche's expectations may have been, their sales drives must have proved something of an uphill struggle even in the supposed honey-pot of the south and east. In Maidstone, for example, an expanding town of 8,000 inhabitants with at least fifty eligible shopkeepers substantial enough to be listed in the directories, Kempson succeeded in capturing the paltry trade of only one customer but the likelihood is that he had been anticipated by a much larger local order secured by James Good, another Birmingham button-maker turned coiner, for the newly-built Padsole paper mill [203]. Hastings, half the size of Maidstone but with perhaps forty such shopkeepers, again produced only one customer – a local ironmonger – for Lutwyche; and, again, the order was similarly small, merely three cwt in each case according to Pye (1801).

Like Kempson, Lutwyche seems to have launched himself into token making in 1791 and over the next seven years produced more than sixty-five tons of legitimate provincial coins, mostly during 1794-1795. Yet while his output of authentic pieces made him Birmingham's largest token-maker during this period, it must have been outdone by his immense production of counterfeits, most of poor quality but some so good as to defy recognition, his mules and fabrications for the collectors' market, and the 'medleys' or evasions he put out between

15   Ferrar (1796) [2009], 4; *GM*, February 1798, 120. An indicative record (but one not attempting to be comprehensive) of eighteenth-century token finds in Wales maintained by the Department of Archaeology in NMW lists 52 tokens including 11 Anglesey, 6 Macclesfield, 5 Birmingham Mining & Copper Company and 4 Liverpool. My thanks are due to John Kenyon (for the reference to Ferrar) and to Edward Besly (for the list of finds).

16   Miss Banks acquired her specimens in 1794 (Chester: Banks MS Cat. VI, SSB 187-33) and 1795 (Macclesfield: Banks MS Cat. VI, SSB 193-60. Pye (1795) published them on 1 February 1795 and 1 May 1795 respectively. It is revealing that Pye (1801) does not list an issuer for either token.

THE NEW MEN

204 William Lutwyche: Warwickshire halfpenny for Joseph Farror, 1791.

205 Peter Kempson: Specious 'Lichfield' token, 1796.

1796 and 1798 as orders for tokens began to dry up.[17] His first venture – and its weight (on average approaching 13g or a standard of 36 to the lb) suggests that its expressed date of 1791 is reliable – was, although included in both of Pye's catalogues, a speculative non-promissory issue capitalising on the century's enthusiasm for Shakespeare as the country's 'national bard' [204]. According to Pye the halfpenny had been struck for 'Farror' who has been identified with Joseph Farror, a noteworthy Birmingham figure of the time, a local auctioneer, tea dealer and grocer, who is now best remembered as bequeathing the sum of 6d a week in perpetuity for the weekly cleaning of the town's projected statue of Lord Nelson.[18] Weighty though the piece was, in its very anonymity it exemplified the quick profits achievable by both manufacturer and issuer – often the same person – from the circulation of non-redemptive 'halfpennies' that could be absorbed into general currency; it was to be the first of many such tokens.[19]

Kempson, whose output of legitimate provincial coins was only a smidgen below that of Lutwyche, also indulged in the manufacture of 'general circulation' tokens and of counterfeits, many again of a high standard, and joined, too, in the fraud of producing mules, concoctions and falsely-edged tokens for the collectors' market. One such specious piece purporting to have been issued at Lichfield and bearing a naive bust of the city's most famous son, Samuel Johnson [205], was roundly condemned as being 'in all respects so unworthy of notice, as to be justly excluded from the Cabinet by every judicious collector'.[20] On the other hand his bona fide productions, engraved by Thomas Willetts – a relation – and the Wyons, especially Thomas Wyon, tended to be struck to a far higher standard and culminated in the remarkable series of Scottish pieces sponsored by the Dundee numismatist, James Wright, junior. As new commissions for provincial coins petered out in 1796-97 Kempson also turned to the manufacture of medalets featuring the public buildings of Birmingham [279a], Bath, Coventry and London and later to the production of high-quality private tokens and commemorative medals on which he employed the still-potent engraving skills of an ailing Hancock as well as of Thomas Wyon. In his public persona Kempson presented a somewhat more respectable front than Lutwyche or indeed some of his own coining activities would lead one to believe; a pillar of the Church (he was said by a fellow button-maker, a pious Methodist, to be a 'very rigid Establishment man'), he was substantial

---

17 Kent (1957) [1989], 891-904. For the work of Lutwyche and Kempson see Hawkins (1989), 68-69 and 35-42; and Mitchiner (1998), 1988-95 and 1978-87.

18 Pye (1801), 17; PRO: Prob/11/1506; Pye (1825), 63; [Samuel] (1880-89), 11 April 1883, 393; Langford (1868), II, 309. Farror (d. 1809) was also the Birmingham agent of the Phœnix Fire Office: Bisset (1808), plate 2. The Nelson statue by Richard Westmacott was unveiled on 25 October 1809 to coincide with the town's celebrations of the king's jubilee.

19 There are two versions of Farror's halfpenny, one struck in a collar. Of the other Pye suggests that ten tons were struck which seems an inordinately high production run for a token which is by no means common today: Pye (1801), 17.

20 Pitt (1817), II, 5.

206a John Gimblett: Silvered copper Birmingham Workhouse half crown (called down to 2*s* and countermarked W) for the Overseers of the Poor, 1788. Judging by the number of specimens in existence today it is likely that many more than the six dozen suggested by Pye (1801) were struck. Gimblett, who is otherwise unknown for the manufacture of tokens, may have been responsible for the issue of 'evasions' in the late 1790s but this is unproven.

206b William Luckcock Simmons: Wolverhampton shop ticket for Thomas Bevan, liquor merchant, *c*. 1797/98. According to Pye (1801) only six dozen specimens were struck before the dies broke and in his time specimens were fetching a guinea.

enough to serve as a Guardian of the Poor and, still in business, died a man of some means at his rural retreat in Moseley in 1824.[21]

Although Lutwyche and Kempson were very much at the spearhead of the shift into the new tokens and were to be by far their biggest manufacturers there were other smaller men coming on to the Birmingham token-making scene from 1792 onwards. Charles Pye lists the die-sinkers and token manufacturers known to him in 1801.[22] His schedule is the basis of **Table 4**, but it has been limited to the makers of 'provincial coins' *sensu stricto*,[23] and expanded to include the manufacturers' primary trades and addresses (as shown in his *Birmingham Directory* of 1791 and Chapman's *Birmingham Directory* of 1800), estimates of the number of their customers and output as represented in the 'INDEX' to Pye (1801) but modified by reference to Waters (1954), Bell (1963) and my own observations.[24]

In the period after 1792 there is firm evidence for the existence of thirteen or fourteen token-producing firms operative in Birmingham (fourteen if one includes William Mainwaring, a die-sinker and engraver who, except for his early medallic work, seems to have worked largely for Lutwyche who acquired Mainwaring's dies after the latter's death in 1794 and may have been responsible for the striking of Mainwaring's tokens).[25]

21 BAH: MS 218: Diary of Julius Hardy, 61. An annual rating of at least £20 was a necessary requirement for election to the Board of Guardians. Kempson's will was proved in the Prerogative Court of Canterbury on 1 July 1824: PRO: Prob 11/1688.

22 Pye (1801), [2].

23 Pye included in his catalogue private tokens and trade tickets. Some of these, especially the trade tickets, may well have found their way into the currency but that was not their primary purpose and they are not included here.

24 The Birmingham section of the *UBD* is a plagiarized version of Pye's 1791 directory. Pye (1801), 5-18. Strangely, Pye omits three manufacturers referred to in his 'Index to the Provincial Coins' that follows a few pages later: R B Morgan; William Simmons; and Obadiah Westwood. He also omits William Whitmore who has been added on the basis of Miss Banks's comment referred to above.

25 Gimblett, Morgan and Simmons are not included in this number because of the exiguous nature of their token production although each may have operated a 'coinery' of some sort. Surprisingly for such a substantial button maker, Gimblett's only known token is a Birmingham Workhouse half crown dated as early as 1788 [206a] of which only seventy-two specimens are said to have been struck (almost certainly too low an estimate) and was probably intended for some specific purpose of poor relief (Pye (1801), 7); Morgan's, a specious 'Northampton' piece credited to 'George Jobson Banker' and initially made for the collectors' market [280b]; and Simmons', a halfpenny for Thomas Bevan, a Wolverhampton liquor merchant [206b], an abortive production abandoned after the dies broke, again only seventy-two specimens having been struck according to Pye (1801), 18.

Table 4
Birmingham Manufacturers of Provincial Coins 1787-1804 [a]

Manufacturer [b]	Location [c]	Principal Trade	Customers [d]	Output [d] (Tons)
1787-1789: Thomas Williams	Holywell (Flintshire)/ Great Charles St.[e]	General	2	>300.00
1789-1795: Westwood/ Hancock Consortium [f]	Great Charles St.	Metal Roller/ Button & Coffin-furniture Maker/Die-sinker	18	>75.00
1789-1804: Matthew Boulton	Soho	General	16	>81.50 [g]
1791-1801: Peter Kempson (91-99)	Little Charles St.	Button Maker	49	>60.00
William Lutwyche (91-1801)	Temple Row/Saint Philip's Churchyard [h]	Toymaker	68	>65.00
William Whitmore (91)	Newhall St.	Engineer/Machine Manufacturer	1	≈1.00
1792-1798: William Mainwaring (92-94)	Temple Row	Buckle Maker	4	2.50*
Samuel Waring (93-95)	Bull St./Bradford St. [i]	Button Maker	3	4.25
Thomas Mynd (94-95)	Whittall St.	Buckle Maker	2	0.50*
Thomas Dobbs (94-95)	Livery St.	Metal Roller	2	1.50
Joseph Merry (95)	Cherry St.	Buckle Maker	1	0.075
James Good (95-97)	Lench St.	Button Maker	8	1.25*
John Stubbs Jorden (95-98) [j]	Great Charles St.	Die-sinker/Patent Window Frame Maker	1	0.25*
Joseph Kendrick (96-97)	Hill St.	Button Maker	3	0.75*
James Pitt (96-97)	Lancaster St.	Button/Toy maker	4	1.00*
Bonham Hammond (97) [Hammond, Turner & Dickenson]	Snow Hill	Button Maker	1	0.25*
Total			183	>595.00

a   A revised version of a table that appeared in Dykes (2004a), 170.

b   Gimblett (Button Maker, Snow Hill), Morgan, (Button Maker, Saint Paul's Square) and Simmons (Toy Maker, Saint Paul's Square) are omitted from the above list. See note 25 above.

c   Location – see [207] below for a map of Birmingham streets in 1795.

d   Customers are restricted to issuers of legitimate provincial coins.
    Those whose issues were aborted (e.g. Ibberson (Boulton) and Anderson, Presbury and Webb (Jorden)) are not included in the above list. Output is given in tons (decimalized) based on Pye (1801) except for Boulton (see g below). Where Pye has not quantified output a 'guestimate' marked * is given using 5 cwt as a basis for his description 'c' (common) – which may well be an underestimate in some cases – and ignoring his 's' (scarce) and 'r' (rare).

e   Williams had moved his coinery to Birmingham by the summer of 1787.

f   John Westwood, Snr. died on 29 March 1792 and the coinery business operated in conjunction with John Gregory Hancock was continued by Obadiah Hancock until the latter's bankruptcy in 1794.

g   Estimate based on evidence from BAH, Matthew Boulton Papers, Doty (1998) and Symons (2009).

h   Saint Philip's Churchyard from 1796.

i   Bradford St. from 1794.

j   Jorden had become a manufacturer of patent window frames by September 1796 after the closure of the Westwood/Hancock coinery the previous year.

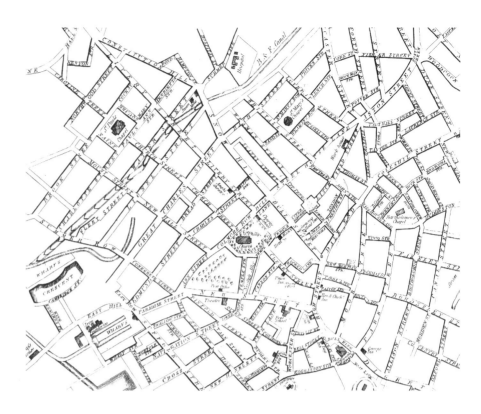

207 Birmingham Streets in 1795 (Detail from Pye's *Plan of Birmingham*, 11 September 1795). The map shows Birmingham's street system during its period of token production. Precise location of the coineries within the streets listed in Table 4 has not been attempted because of the lack of detailed site evidence.

What one sees from **Table 4** is that most of the post-1792 manufacturers are button makers or in closely associated trades although one should not be too dogmatic over the 'shorthand' definitions in contemporary directories. Over time there could be great flexibility in any one individual's occupation, reflecting both product development and personal career change, while a description like 'toy maker' could obscure a multitude of specialized trades. John Westwood is an example of a die-engraver moving to button making, to coining, the manufacture of weights and ultimately to metal rolling while the 'toy maker' Thomas Mynd actually specialized in the manufacture of high-class buckles.[26] Only Lutwyche, beginning as a toy maker, lists himself – from 1796 – as a provincial coin maker. Of the others one is described as a copper roller and dealer in metals (Dobbs), one as a 'general manufacturer' (Boulton), two as buckle makers (Mainwaring and Merry), six as button makers (Good, Hammond, Kendrick, Kempson and Waring) while one (Pitt) seems to have combined button and toy making with the trade of a locksmith and one (Obadiah Westwood), button-making with his speciality of manufacturing metal furniture for coffins. Jorden, still an apprentice in the Westwood coinery until 1795, does not appear in any directory until Pye's publication of February 1797 by which time he had transformed

26 Quickenden (1995), 354 ; Dykes (2000).

himself into a 'manufacturer of Iron Window-frames'.

Taking the period 1787 to 1798 as a whole, while something approaching 600 tons of authentic provincial coinage was produced, the bulk of this was actually struck before 1792 by Thomas Williams, Matthew Boulton and the John Westwood/Hancock consortium. For a variety of reasons one must not take the figures given for these three manufacturers as in any way definitive. They are underestimates as, almost certainly, are those given for Kempson and Lutwyche. But they give a reasonably trustworthy gauge of the volume of tokens produced and suggest that little more than 179 tons or so of authentic tokens were minted from 1792 onwards. As one can see from **Table 5**, Kempson and Lutwyche, together with the Westwood/Hancock consortium and Boulton, were responsible for most of this total. The remaining ten known token-making firms accounted for less than sixteen tons although Samuel Waring at least, like Lutwyche and Kempson, produced quantities of unprovenanced tokens for 'general circulation'. And while this means that these ten struck well over a million and a half legitimate provincial coins it was a total spread among some thirty-four customers and in a number of instances the individual output is quite minimal. It was, too, the result of a flurry of activity concentrated in a period of no more than three years for, with the exception of Mainwaring and Waring, these manufacturers do not appear on the scene until quite late on: Mynd and Dobbs in 1794 (Dobbs's entrance probably associated with the run-down of the Westwoods' business); Jorden, Merry and Good

Table 5
Birmingham Token Manufacturers and Provincial Coin Commissions 1792-1798

Manufacturer	Commissions							Total	Output (Tons)
	1792	1793	1794	1795	1796	1797	1798		
Matthew Boulton	3	3	2	4	4			16	≈12.25
Westwood/ Hancock Consortium	8	3	2	2	-	-	-	15	≈26.50
Peter Kempson	7	8	19	2	6	13	1	56	>60.00
William Lutwyche	4	3	37	15	5	4	1	69	>65.00
Total	22	17	60	23	15	17	2	156	>163.75
William Mainwaring	3	2	1	-	-	-	-	6	2.50
Samuel Waring		1		2				3	4.25
Thomas Mynd			1	1				2	1.50*
Thomas Dobbs			1	2				3	1.50
Joseph Merry				1				1	0.075
James Good				7	2	1		10	1.25*
John Stubbs Jorden				1				1	0.25*
Joseph Kendrick					2	1		3	2.25
James Pitt					1	3		4	1.00*
Bonham Hammond						1		1	1.00*
Total	3	3	3	14	5	6		34	15.575*

(who perhaps took over from Waring) in 1795; Kendrick and Pitt in 1796; and Hammond not until 1797 (and in that year only).[27]

What must give one pause for thought is that these button makers, toy makers and the like made up little more than six per cent of the total number of such Birmingham tradesmen recorded in the local directories of the time and the directories would not have included every eligible craftsman in the town. The likelihood is that the legitimate production of tokens was not a sufficiently attractive undertaking unless one was able to coin in some bulk and build up a significant customer base either through reputation or aggressive salesmanship. Copper, too, became increasingly scarce after 1792 and, although there were fluctuations, its price went up by leaps and bounds driven by the export demands of the East India Company and, after the declaration of war by revolutionary France in February 1793, by naval and military needs and the almost complete stoppage of ore and metal imports from an unsettled Europe.

The schedules of open market prices regularly published in the press and elsewhere demonstrate the inflationary trend in copper over the 1790s which shot up by 15% between 1793 and 1794 and continued to rise inexorably until the end of the decade (**Table 6**)[28]. It would be unwise, however, as some commentators have done, to put too much stress on these specific figures since they conceal the considerable fluctuations that could take place in any one year and more importantly as far as Birmingham's token makers are concerned, because other than exemplifying the rising market, they are by no means a clear-cut guide to the actual prices paid for manufactured copper in the town.

Table 6
Average Manufactured Copper Prices in £s per ton 1792-1799

1792	1793	1794	1795	1796	1797	1798	1799
100	100	115	120	125	135	135	145

If they had been, even fewer token makers would have entered the trade and those that did would have been quickly put out of business. In January 1795, for instance, a correspondent told the *Gentleman's Magazine* that the best sheet copper then stood at 14*d* per lb [£130 per ton] and added that it would come as a 'matter of wonder that the Birmingham workman, can afford the coins at 16*d* per lb [£150 per ton] which it is well known is about the usual price, when the expence of the die is paid by the person who orders them'.[29] On this basis the one

27 It might be added that it is probable that Morgan's specious 'Northampton' token for 'George Jobson' in its original plain-edged form was produced about the turn of the years 1794-95 and Simmons' Wolverhampton halfpenny for Bevan about 1797-98.

28 Based on *Copper Report* (1803), Appendix 9, 702. The above figures are averages for the years specified. At any point in a year the actual market price for manufactured copper might well be much higher or lower than the figure quoted.

29 *GM*, January 1795, 34.

THE NEW MEN

208 Joseph Merry: Bury St Edmunds halfpenny for Charles Guest, 1795.

and a half cwt of halfpennies produced that year by Joseph Merry for Charles Guest, the Bury St Edmunds auctioneer [208], light in weight at 48 to the lb, could have brought the buckle maker a *gross* gain – ignoring labour costs and overheads – of little more than £1 8s for the manufacture of 8,000 tokens. It seems an impossibly poor return for the effort involved even if the task had taken him no more than a day or two to complete bearing in mind that Guest stood to gain over £15 if none of the tokens was returned to him for redemption. Merry, of course, may have set his charges a little higher than the norm to compensate for such a small assignment but the truth was that, although Birmingham copper prices were certainly high and rising, this was not to the level of the market returns on which the writer to the *Gentleman's Magazine* relied. For despite the trauma of the times, the shortage of copper and the resulting inflation, the town's token makers did benefit to some degree from the cost savings that the Birmingham and the Rose companies were able to achieve in the purchase of copper as the instances in the following paragraphs suggest.[30] Boulton, moreover, through his own mining and smelting connections also had access to sources beyond the open market and both he and the Westwoods possessed the in-house manufacturing advantage of their own rolling plant as did Dobbs.

When he was snooping about Birmingham in the early months of 1793 Thomas Attwood Digges was told by Obadiah Westwood that his estimated cost of supplying a ton of cents at a weight standard of 29 pieces to the lb was £120 comprising a metal cost of about £90 and a coining charge of £30 (which covered the cost of engraving the dies, striking, lapping in paper and casking – but not, of course, delivery). For lower weight coins – involving greater numbers per lb and thus more work – Westwood's manufacturing charge would have been progressively higher so that for 40 pieces to the lb it would have risen to £42. His overall charge was calculated on the basis of a minimum order for twenty ton of coin and presumably allowed for a quantity discount and a *douceur* for future contracts from the American government. Boulton's prices, Digges added, were as 'equally cheap' as Westwood's 'notwithstanding the superior beauty & Excellence [of the former's coin] to any in England' although, as Digges noted, the price of copper was escalating.[31]

We know that later in 1793 Boulton was charging £102 per ton (11*d* per lb) for copper and £42 (4½*d* per lb) for coining his first order of Inverness halfpennies – with dies and packaging extra. Boulton's rates bear close comparison with those of Lutwyche, as retailed much later by Thomas Sharp.[32] Some time in the same year, 1793, Lutwyche had told

---

30 Hamilton (1967), 238 states that between 1793 and 1798 the difference between the Birmingham Company's copper buying price and its selling price did not on average exceed 7½%.

31 LC: Thomas Jefferson Papers, Th[omas] A[ttwood] Digges to Thomas Jefferson, 10 March 1793; see also Elias and Finch (1982), 445.

32 Sharp (1834), ii. Thomas Griffith, it will be remembered (p. 207 above), was told in early 1794 that £100 worth of tokens could be obtained for £60. At say 46 halfpennies to the lb this would equate to about £130 per ton.

215

a Birmingham dealer that his overall charge to a customer for a ton of tokens was £150. According to Sharp – and this information may not have come from Lutwyche's interlocutor – the price of 'tile copper' was then £105 per ton so that Lutwyche's manufacturing charge for striking tokens on a standard of 46 pieces to the lb (the Tower standard for regal halfpennies) was presumably in the region of £45. No mention was made of separate die or packaging costs which must have been subsumed in his overall price since Lutwyche calculated the issuer's profit on this figure. This would make Lutwyche's actual coining charge something in the region of £38 per ton or 4d per lb, a shade cheaper than Boulton's. What we do not know, of course, are what Lutwyche's or Boulton's coining *costs* were so we can only say that on the evidence we do have their *gross* profit (exclusive of labour, fuel costs (in the case of Boulton) and other overheads) must have been in the region of 35-40%.

Despite the rising market Boulton seems to have maintained his copper charges at a fairly consistent level and during 1795 he was even able to reduce his metal price slightly to £99 or £100 per ton.[33] But by the February of 1796 prices had hardened again and in the February of that year he was obliged to charge William Croom at the rate of £102 per ton for copper (plus his usual £42 per ton for coining) for the second tranche of his Dundee halfpennies. Boulton's invoices make straightforward reading but when Croom put out a feeler for a further order in the summer of 1796 Boulton replied in terms that are tantalizingly obfuscatory and difficult to interpret.[34] Explaining that the price of copper was then 'much raised', he continued:

> Sheet Copper is now 13½^d per lb [£126 per ton] of which it takes 3^{lb} to make 2^{lb} of coin & as the Scrap must be remelted it is worth 11^d only, & consequently the Blanks will cost in Copper 14¾^d per lb [£138 per ton].
>
> My price for Coin struck in bright Collers [*sic*] is 15¾^d [£147 per ton] to which must be added the Cost of Casks & Car^g.
>
> My General rule is to charge the Cost of the Dies & punchions wth. the Engraving which will be more or less according to the Device or work engraved & to deduct 2 guineas per Ton out of every Ton of Coin ordered therefrom.

Some light is thrown on Boulton's rather Daedalian thought processes by an equally convoluted letter he wrote to Thomas Lack, Lord Liverpool's secretary, three years later in the aftermath of recriminations between himself and Thomas Williams over allegations of profiteering. Drawing a comparison between Williams's charges and his own, he used

---

[33] Boulton quoted George Cotton £100 per ton for copper in April 1795 while he charged Mackintosh, Inglis and Wilson £99 per ton in the October and Croom £100 per ton in the December: BAH: MS 3782/12/40/112, Matthew Boulton to George Cotton, 8 April 1795; BAH: MBP 34/14, Mint Book 4, 1795-98, 24 October and 24 December 1795.

[34] BAH: MS 3782/12/42/215, Matthew Boulton to William Croom, 1 August 1796.

the same formula to explain that at the open market price [then 16*d* per lb] the 'Copper King' charged his 'Slaves' for 'sheet Copper hot rolled' it would cost 'more Money in Copper to make a Ton of coin without either Cutting-out, Milling, Annealing, Coining, Dies, &ca &ca &ca than I deliver the Coin [the 'cartwheel coinage'] for in every part of the Kingdom'. The almost unfathomable implication of Boulton's statement is that his charges to the government for copper were cheaper than Williams's metal price by 3*d* per lb.[35]

It seems likely that Boulton – unless he was indulging in one of his not infrequent exercises in disinformation – had adopted a similar approach in his letter to Croom since if one takes his figures at face value one can only construe that on an overall charge of 15¾*d* for a pound weight of coin his *gross* attainable profit would have amounted to merely one penny, a patent absurdity not least in the context of the accumulated mint losses he was desperately trying to reduce. It is more likely that the formula was used simply as an exemplification of market prices to justify the increase in his overall charge but that his actual price for copper would have been considerably lower. We know that Boulton's standard tariff for moneying was 4½*d* per lb, a rate that he usually maintained throughout the period.[36] If one deducts this figure from the overall charge of 15¾*d* per lb quoted to Croom Boulton's copper price would then be 11¼*d* per lb (£105 per ton).

However Boulton calculated his scissel wastage this is exactly the price he had charged Sir George Jackson two months earlier for the copper for his Bishop's Stortford tokens and that he was to bill George Chapman George for his Penryn halfpennies three weeks later. He was also able to reduce his coining charge to 4*d* (£37 per ton) for them, presumably as a special favour for customers he deemed influential, so that their overall accounts (exclusive of dies &c) amounted to 15¼*d* per lb or £142 per ton. But if Boulton had charged them his standard 4½*d* per lb for coining – this would have brought their total bills to £147 per ton which would, of course, have equated to the 15¾*d* per lb he quoted to Croom.

The increase Boulton sought of Croom over his previous order would have amounted to something like 30*s* for the likely 10 cwt that Croom might have ordered.[37] Such an increase does not seem inordinate at this time and one can only think from the disconcertingly complex nature of his letter that Boulton, despite his anxiety to keep his presses working, did not want to encourage Croom for some reason. At any rate his tactic – if that is what it was – was successful for, as we have seen, the frugal Scottish draper immediately took his business to Kempson 'who, though he could not engrave so nicely as your superior artists', James Wright

---

35 BAH: MS 3782/13/116, Matthew Boulton to Thomas Lack, 4 December 1799. What Boulton's formula clearly demonstrates is that one lb of copper did not make one lb of coin.

36 Cf. Dykes (1998b), 388. Boulton was still charging £42 per ton for coining Viscount Charleville's tokens in 1804, his copper price then being £144 per ton: Vice (1991b), 3.

37 This is roughly the quantity that Croom had earlier had from Boulton and that (according to Pye (1801), 9) he subsequently ordered from Kempson when he took his business to the latter's coinery.

subsequently told Boulton, 'does work cheaper, & more adapted to such small undertakings'.[38]

Reverting to our example of Merry and the intervention of the correspondent to the *Gentleman's Magazine*, Boulton in 1793, as we have seen, was charging 11*d* per lb for copper and 4½*d* for coining and, as Digges implied, his prices broadly reflected those generally current in Birmingham. On such a reading Merry's gross profit on Guest's halfpennies would have been nearer a much more plausible, if not very handsome, £3 5*s*. Even a figure like this suggests that coining for the smaller manufacturers was very much a sideline to their main business of button making or toy making. It must be remembered, too, that Kempson and Lutwyche had effectively cornered the market for provincial coins and enjoyed an economy of scale that the smaller men could not match. The suspicion must be that the smaller makers' contracts were the crumbs from the tables of the larger manufacturers when their order books were full; Mynd, Boulton's brother-in-law, may be a case in point and it is otherwise difficult to understand why a substantial button maker like Bonham Hammond should bother to mint only a single run of halfpennies – for Leith in 1797 (*D&H*: Lothian 60-61) – unless he was helping out someone like Kempson or Lutwyche.

As the price of copper rose so there was a compensatory reduction in the weight-ratio of tokens which over 1793 and 1794 came down sharply from the typical average of 36 to the lb set by the Westwoods to about 46 to the lb. This now became a standard which, while there were some startling exceptions such as the paltry halfpenny put out by William Mighell of Brightelmstone [Brighton] in 1796 at 72 to the lb [209], was broadly maintained for the remainder of the decade. Forty-six to forty-eight pieces to the lb reflected the weight-ratio of the old Tower halfpenny. At this standard, at any rate until 1796, the token-makers could more or less preserve their profit margin and, by broadly pegging their manufacturing prices, continue to afford their customers the opportunity of a substantial return on their investment. It was a standard, moreover, that was not completely unacceptable to the public for although it had plummeted over the decade it still provided an intrinsic metal value not markedly inferior to that of the earliest tokens. While Thomas Williams had encouraged people to believe from the start – and this became the public perception – that his Anglesey pennies contained nearly a penny's worth of copper this was never so. They and the halfpennies were intrinsically worth little more than three-fifths of their face value and on the whole this level of discrepancy seems to have been preserved throughout the production of provincial coinage, the progressive reductions in the weight of halfpenny tokens roughly balancing the increases in the cost of copper.[39]

While the standard remained stable, the remorseless rise in the price of copper led, by 1796, to a sharp reduction both in the quantity of tokens

209   William Lutwyche: Brightelmstone [Brighton] halfpenny for William Mighell, 1796.

---

38   See p. 140 above.

39   The contention that an Anglesey penny contained almost a penny's worth of copper was first put about, probably by Thomas Williams himself, in *The Daily Universal Register* of 28 March 1787: see p. 80 above. It was a myth perpetuated by Sharp (1834), i.

THE NEW MEN

210 A button maker operating a stamp with a capstan press in the background. From *The Book of Trades or Library of the Useful Arts*, 1806.

211a

211b Manually operated coin presses depicted on halfpenny tokens of William Lutwyche (a) and Thomas Spence (b).

produced – from about 22 ton in the previous year to some six ton in 1796 (and 1797) – and in the number of their issuers. Having said this it must be remembered that the date expressed on a token only indicates the likely year it was first struck and, in some instances, may well cloak a phasing of its production over an extended period.[40] Nevertheless, in general terms it seems clear that Birmingham token commissions, as **Table 5** indicates, had reached their high point in 1794 in very large measure because of the sales activities of Kempson and particularly Lutwyche. The following year, however, although the clutch of smaller manufacturers was momentarily boosted, the number of orders for legitimate provincial coins began to fall off; and dramatically so in 1796. Though beginning to be bolstered by the demand for Scottish issues orchestrated by James Wright it was to be cut back that year by more than two-thirds over its 1794 high, naturally petering out following the introduction of Boulton's 'cartwheel coinage' and leaving only Kempson and Lutwyche to produce a token each in 1798.[41]

Apart from the cost of copper none of the new manufacturers would have needed any appreciable degree of capital to set up their coining operations; all would have had access to hand-operated machine-tools adaptable for minting even if coining in some form had been foreign to their existing businesses [**210**]. After all, as we saw in chapter one, the ubiquity of such equipment in the Birmingham button and toy trades provided the rationale for 'Brummagem''s dire reputation for illicit coin making even though coining was rife elsewhere. Though presses, even by the 1750s, had become fairly refined, the equipment available to most petty manufacturers would have been fairly basic and restricted, at its best, to the manually operated presses of the types shown on Lutwyche's own tokens and those of Thomas Spence [**211a** and **b**].

What were certainly not available to these little men were steam-operated presses.[42] As far as is known only Boulton had such presses and he had succeeded in harnessing the new power only from the summer of 1789 when he began striking halfpennies for Cronebane. At Holywell Thomas Williams's rolling mills were turned by powerful water-wheels but as far as one can tell his coining presses were operated manually or by horse power as they must have been in Birmingham after his coining operation moved there in the summer of 1787.[43] Westwood and Thomas Dobbs, too, while they could rely on water power for their rolling mills at Witton and Lifford would have had to work their presses in Great Charles Street and Livery Street manually. The coining

40 Cf. Dyer, G. (1994) and Dyer (2001).

41 Table 5 extends only until 1798. Kempson, of course, went on to produce provincial coins until 1799, Lutwyche until 1801 and Boulton until after the turn of the century while other Birmingham token makers may have undertaken a dribble of repeat orders after 1798.

42 Or for that matter water-powered presses: points well developed by Selgin (2003), 478-509. On the problem of water-power in Birmingham which influenced Boulton's move to Soho see Pelham (1963), 64-91.

43 Harris (1964), 177-78. There is some evidence to suggest that wheel-operated presses were used at Holywell: Selgin (2003), 483.

219

212 *The Art of Coining.* An engraving from *The Universal Magazine*, 1750. The physicality needed to operate the press would have required more manpower than that shown. Cf. [213 below].

presses shown on Lutwyche's tokens may have been symbolic only but it is reasonable to assume that neither he nor Kempson had access to anything other than the types of manual screw presses illustrated there or in the *Universal Magazine* half a century earlier [212]. Lutwyche did contemplate buying a Boulton and Watt engine in 1796 but nothing came of it and we do not actually know what purpose Lutwyche had in mind for it.[44] One intriguing sidelight on the connection between steam and coinage was reported by *The Times*, when a forger was found operating coining equipment on a coal barge near Chelsea under the pretence of developing a scheme for steam navigation. As the newspaper put it instead of converting '*water* into *steam*' the 'artist' was turning '*lead*' into '*gold*' but even here steam was not obviously involved in the striking of coin.[45] We can, I think, be quite positive that except for Boulton's tokens from Cronebane onwards, every provincial coin between 1787 and 1797 was struck on a manually operated screw press, probably smaller, but no different in principle from those shown in Rudolph Ackermann's print of a stamping room at the Royal Mint in 1809 [213].

The large-output industrial and commercial tokens of the years 1787 to 1791 circulated as currency in many cases far from their expressed centres of redemption. Their very ubiquity meant that a high proportion of them naturally lost any claim they may have had to redeemability, and, like the regal currency before them, as they became embedded in the countrywide economy so they invited the attention of the counterfeiter. Indeed, it could be argued that they were a more attractive prey since counterfeits of tokens, just like the tokens they imitated, were, as the Mint Solicitor pointed out, beyond

44 BAH: MS 3782/12/41/207, William Lutwyche to Matthew Boulton, 21 June 1796.
45 *The Times*, 3 August 1790.

THE NEW MEN

213 Capstan Fly Presses (left) and Wheel Presses (right) at the Royal Mint. From Rudolph Ackermann's *Microcosm of London*, Vol. II, Plate 55 (1809).

the rigour of the admittedly ineffective laws framed against the forgery of regal copper. Wilkinson's halfpennies, the Macclesfield tokens of Roe and Company, especially those bearing the portrait of 'Old Roe', and the halfpennies of the Birmingham Mining and Copper Company, increasingly familiar across the country and with the authority of an established company behind them, all fell prey to the forger as did those of Worswick (Lancaster), Clarke (Liverpool), Reynolds (Coventry) and Hutchison (Edinburgh).[46]

The evidence of the tokens makes it clear that the very people who made the originals were among the chief culprits. Lutwyche was certainly involved in the business and even Kempson on a rather lesser scale; so were the Westwoods and Hancock. But there must have been others happily indulging in an activity that not only embraced direct forgeries but also tokens purporting to be put out by bogus firms like the 'Birmingham Coining & Copper Company' or spuriously aping familiar emblems such as 'druids' and monograms to fool the

46 And in Ireland a profusion of copies of the island's copper companies' halfpennies which seem to have outnumbered the originals.

221

214a

214b William Lutwyche: Manchester halfpennies for John Fielding, 1792 and 1793.

ignorant.[47] It was an extensive trade, and even if some contemporaries argued that the numbers of counterfeits were 'trifling in comparison with the Birmingham halfpence formerly in circulation' or that run of the mill fakes were relatively easy to detect because of the crudity of their engravings and their short weight – frequently a quarter to a third below that of the genuine article – there were still more than enough of them in circulation to be a 'considerable evil'.[48] The main thrust of the phenomenon seems to have been comparatively short lived, however, reaching its apogee by about 1792 before mutating into the equally profitable and more flexible production of anonymous pieces for 'general circulation' and the new phase of shopkeepers' tokens but it was sufficiently productive to be a major factor in bringing the whole edifice of provincial coinage into disrepute.

One series of tokens that did not engage the attention of the counterfeiter, surprisingly in view of the large quantities said to have been produced, was that struck by Lutwyche for John Fielding, a Manchester grocer. According to Pye (1801) twenty-one tons or well over two million halfpennies were produced in three varieties dated 1792 and 1793. In theory, Manchester, already the second largest provincial town in the country with a population rapidly approaching 75,000, would have been ripe for such a large issue which could have been readily absorbed locally or quickly dispersed to other parts of the country through its outlets to the Trent and Mersey Canal. Fielding's halfpennies should thus have been ideal candidates for forgery. Yet this did not happen and the only advantage taken of them was the later production by Lutwyche of some falsely-edged pieces for the collectors' market. The truth of the matter must be that Fielding's tokens were never produced in the vast numbers conceived by Pye.[49] The likelihood is that by 1792 Manchester had more than enough copper coin for its needs, not least in the quantities of tokens flooding out from Liverpool, Macclesfield and other nearby industrial and commercial centres – the Anglesey issues had early on become well established in the town – leaving little place for any new extensive issue. Fielding's tokens are certainly scarcer today than Pye's figures would lead one to suppose, the only halfpenny that is now manifestly not uncommon being that bearing the Duke of Bridgewater's arms and the legend **SUCCESS TO NAVIGATION**. Perhaps it should be separated from Fielding's other 'shopkeeper' tokens – unlike the latter it has no hint of Fielding's trades as a grocer or tea dealer – and, as some have suggested, it should perhaps be associated with the trade of Manchester's canal system. But such a notion can be no more than conjectural in the present stage of our knowledge for, unhappily, Fielding is one of too many token issuers who have disappeared into the limbo of history [214a and b].

47   Interestingly, the Parys Mine Company's pennies and halfpennies seem to have attracted few direct counterfeits.
48   *GM*, January 1795, 33-34.
49   Pye's figures for the three varieties are: *D&H*: Lancs. 127 – 10 tons; *D&H*: Lancs. 128-34 – 4 tons; and *D&H*: Lancs. 135 – 7 tons: Pye (1801), 15.

THE NEW MEN

Seventeen-ninety-two, the year of Fielding's first halfpenny, was the year that saw the start of the drive by Birmingham coiners to promote their product among provincial shopkeepers. Kempson directed his initial assault against Norwich where he succeeded in winning two speedy commissions not least one sponsored by John Harvey, a master-weaver and philanthropist of some consequence in a city that was to see eight other tradesmen issuing tokens over the next two years. In 1793 Kempson had garnered another eight contracts in the south and east of the country while Lutwyche, having completed his work for Fielding, probably in the following year concocted a halfpenny for Thomas Ball, a bankrupted Sleaford grocer, using a counterfeit Worswick obverse die and a reverse Fielding 'Bridgewater Arms' die.[50] It is a curious low-volume piece – according to Pye three hundredweight were produced – probably put out to take advantage of the building of the Sleaford Canal then under way and intended by Ball as a means of helping to repair his shaky finances. If this was Ball's motive it proved to be of little avail but the token's importance lies less in the Sleaford grocer's problems than in its confirmation of Lutwyche's role in the production of counterfeits.

Harvey's Norwich halfpenny [215] typifies the issues struck by Kempson and Lutwyche for country tradesmen at this time. While it prominently publicizes its locality of issue with a coat of arms, only through its edge inscription is the token's actual issuer, or more

215   Peter Kempson: Norwich halfpenny for John Harvey, 1792.

216   William Lutwyche: Goudhurst halfpenny for William Mynn, 1794, countermarked by the issuer.

accurately the individual formally answerable for its redemption, personalized. It may be that it was a formula – originating in a practice begun by the Westwoods with their commercial tokens, for Clarke and Worswick for example, – adopted to create the impression, truthfully or otherwise, that a token had the official imprimatur of the place named; that it may have been a 'town' halfpenny. This may perhaps have been the case, at least in some instances, although there is no positive evidence to support such a view. It is nevertheless of interest that John Harvey was mayor of Norwich at the time his token was issued. Confining the issuer's name to the edge, of course, allowed the same token design to be used indiscriminately for different tradesmen. This saving in cost happened in both Canterbury and in Goudhurst although in the latter town the issuers, William Mynn and William Fuggle, were eventually obliged to countermark their halfpennies with a bold 'F' or 'M' [216];

50   For some Ball tokens Lutwyche used edged blanks he had prepared for the 1794 halfpennies of John Simmons of Staplehurst (*D&H*: Kent 40).

223

217 Peter Kempson: Swansea halfpenny for John Voss, draper, printer and banker, 1796.

no doubt they were weary of repeatedly having to change each other's issues. Of course, confining the issuer's name to the edge also gave the manufacturer the opportunity of re-using spare edged-blanks with unrelated dies to create bogus tokens or 'rarities' for the collectors' market, a practice that both Lutwyche and Kempson indulged in without reserve; blanks inscribed for both Mynn ('**MYNS**' [sic]) and Fuggle ('**FRIGGLES**' or '**FUGGLES**' [sic]) were misused in this way, a '**FUGGLES**'-edged blank being used for a Lutwyche counterfeit of Boulton's Gilbert Shearer halfpenny, for instance.[51]

One other point should be made about edge names. We know, for instance, that in some cases the name cited did not represent the only tradesman concerned in a token's issue but only a 'front man' providing a focal redemption point for a group of townsmen acting in concert. The halfpennies in the name of Gilbert Shearer and Henry Brownbill are examples of this arrangement and it is not unreasonable to suppose that it may well have been so in other places that for their size are surprisingly represented by only one token issuer; Goldsmith & Son's Sudbury, for example, then a market town of at least three thousand souls with some two score tradesmen any of whom might have supported the tailoring firm in their venture.[52] But a cautionary note should be struck because there might have been good reasons for a town issue to be limited. Double the size of Sudbury was the thriving seaport and resort of Swansea – 'a nasty town' with 'some idle bathing company' according to John Byng – which again boasted only one issuer, the draper, printer and proto-banker John Voss, one of more than seventy eligible tradesmen in the town. According to Pye (1801) Voss put out only ten cwt of his elegant 'Wyon' designed halfpennies [217] but Swansea was rapidly developing into 'Copperopolis', the copper-smelting capital of the world, and with eight 'smoking' works just up-river – the Anglesey, Macclesfield and Birmingham companies among them – there was a plentiful supply of ready cash in the town [218].[53]

Little is really known about the circulation of shopkeepers' tokens and, outside the interest of collectors, there appear to be virtually no contemporary literary allusions to them other than the often hostile

---

51 *D&H*: Lanarkshire 4a, a token signed 'F A' (Francis Arnold). Lutwyche also used a '**FRIGGLES**'-edged blank for an Appledore halfpenny (*D&H*: Kent 3a) and a '**MYNS**' one for a Hastings halfpenny (*D&H*: Sussex 24a).

52 Cf. Dyer, G. P. (1994).

53 Andrews (1934-38), I (1934), 303. For Voss see Dykes (1952-54), 351.
    Between 1980 and 1992 the late Gerard Lahive and John Player discovered a sample of twenty tokens lost at Blackpill on the beach route taken by pedestrians from Swansea to Mumbles in the eighteenth century. They included four Anglesey pennies and a halfpenny, four Birmingham Mining and Copper Company halfpennies, three Macclesfield halfpennies with the bust of Roe, two Voss halfpennies, a Glamorgan and a Rochdale halfpenny. The tokens, which are only a small sample of such currency found by others on the sands of Swansea Bay but never recorded, were all discovered randomly intermingled with larger numbers of contemporary regal coinage emphasising their ready local interchangeability: Gerard Lahive, personal communication.

THE NEW MEN

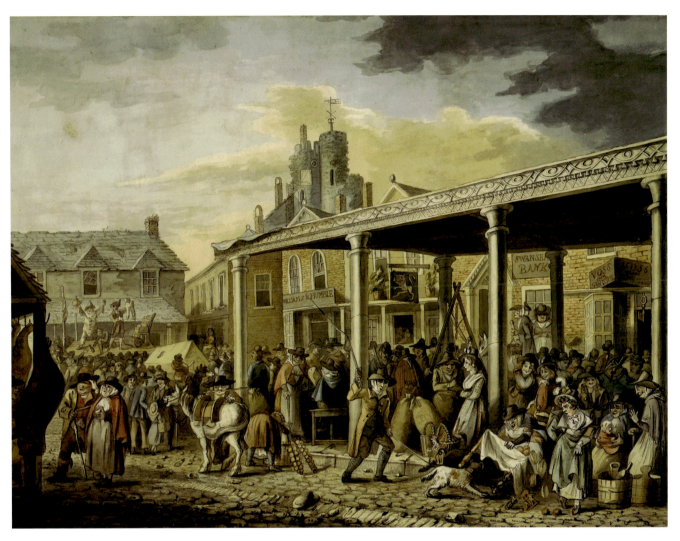

218 A 1793 watercolour drawing by John Nixon showing the Market Square, Swansea, with, to the right, John Voss's draper's shop at the sign of the Golden Key and the Swansea Bank of Walters and Voss next door.

remarks of contributors to the prints of the day most of whom had axes to grind anyway. The truth is that provided they passed reasonably readily in everyday commercial dealings tokens did not particularly disturb the lives of the middling sort of society who might have put pen to paper. While the age remained one predominantly of retail credit, even for smallish-scale purchases, cash was still needed for incidental payments, tips at inns, toll-gates and the like.[54] And tokens were just another element in the hotchpotch of copper currency the public had to put up with.[55]

The Reverend James Woodforde, rector of the Norfolk parish of Weston Longville, consistent and meticulous in recording his diurnal expenditure, even over his petty cash payments of a few pence or a shilling or two, never seemed to have been concerned about the state

54 In 1797 'R. Y.' accused 'tollmen at the turnpikes' of being 'a great means of circulating' tokens just as they had traditionally been of passing counterfeit coin : *GM*, April 1797, 269.

55 According to Joseph Moser the effect of tokens was apparently to reduce the value of 'Brummagems' by a half and even in places to drive them out of circulation: Moser (1798), 306.

225

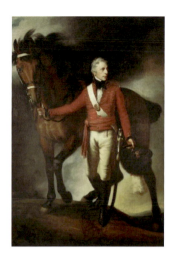

of the coinage nor to have had his payments refused because of its character or condition; nor for that matter, judging by his silence, did he ever seem to have found silver or copper hard to come by. One imagines that he must have used tokens on his not infrequent visits to Norwich – there must have been well over a million local issues alone in circulation about the city by 1796 – but he made no mention of them in his diary although he was something of a coin collector – always proud to show his 'small collection' off to visitors – and was a regular customer of the bookseller and token-issuer Richard Bacon [219].[56]

219 Peter Kempson: Norwich halfpenny for Richard Bacon, printer and bookseller, 1794.

Norwich, though long displaced by Bristol as the country's second city and now far outstripped by some of the great new industrial conurbations like Manchester, Liverpool and Birmingham, still boasted a population of more than 35,000 inhabitants and with its six thousand looms remained one of the country's most important manufacturing centres. With no fewer than 300 shops 'of established credit' including the businesses of nine token-issuers it must have been awash with copper coin; much of it not only of very dubious character but including a multitude of irredeemable 'foreign' and 'general currency' tokens that, like the ersatz regal copper before them, increasingly became a drug on the market, silting up shopkeepers' tills when they could not be offloaded. In 1795 one commentator claimed that he knew of a tradesman 'at this time who, though resident only in a market–town, and that not very populous, has upwards of 100 L. in copper halfpence'.[57] The situation must have been much worse in Norwich and it was for this sort of reason that a year later the principal tradesmen of the city decided to adopt a well-publicized measure of self-protection against the unknown and to accept only tokens

220 Three Norwich Token Issuers. (a) The Tory John Harvey (1755-1842), and the Whig brothers-in-law, (b) Nathaniel Bolingbroke (1757-1840) and (c) Sir John Harrison Yallop (1763-1835). All three were mayors of the city.

56 Winstanley and Jameson (1980-2007), *passim* and (2001), 265-66.
    Richard Bacon (1745-1812) was publisher of the weekly *Norwich Mercury*, a printer and also a grocer, auctioneer, appraiser and brandy merchant: Jewson (1975), 118; *ODNB*, s.v. Richard Mackenzie Bacon.

57 Beatriffe (1795), 74; Jewson (1975), 3; Corfield (1982), 183; *GM*, March 1795, 199.

issued by fellow townsmen.[58] Yet, all this seems to have passed James Woodforde by; he was obviously an exemplar of the inert majority who just had to use what was available.

Among the most attractive of the Norwich tokens were the halfpennies put out by the goldsmiths and tea dealers, Dunham and Yallop, especially their initial series of 1792 portraying their eighteenth-century shop front in the market place with its prominent sign of a golden eagle dangling a pearl from its beak [221].[59] Large numbers of tokens were issued by Yallop and, separately, by his brother-in-law, Nathaniel Bolingbroke, a silversmith and haberdasher (*D&H*: Norf. 14-16). Both, like John Harvey, were prominent Norwich citizens and both, like Harvey, were mayors of the city although of different political persuasions, Yallop being knighted in 1831 [220c].

221 William Mainwaring: Norwich halfpenny for Dunham and Yallop, goldsmiths and jewellers, 1792.

But lesser individuals in much smaller places than Norwich were persuaded to issue tokens as a result of the sales-drives of Kempson and Lutwyche in the east and south of England, villages as well as country towns; John Fuller [his token's edge is incorrectly inscribed '**FOLLER**'] and Elias Gilbert, for instance, in the little Sussex village of Northiam. In 1794 Lutwyche produced some 25,000 tokens for the two of them but how necessary these were in a village which numbered fewer than a thousand souls is problematic. In the same year and obviously as a result of his agent's slick patter in the area Lutwyche struck similar tokens, 10,000 at a time, for a clutch of even smaller villages over the border in Kent: Appledore, Brookland and Dymchurch. Most of Lutwyche's Kent and Sussex tokens are, in design terms, unimaginatively humdrum but one or two do stand out, William Peckham's Appledore halfpenny, for

---

58 *The Ipswich Journal*, 27 February 1796. I am grateful to Graham Dyer for this reference. Cf. the attitude of the tradesmen of the Liberty of Havering atte Bower evinced by George Cotton in his approach to Boulton for the Hornchurch halfpenny, a locally sponsored counter to the 'paltry trash' plaguing a part of Essex too close to the coining dens of London: see p. 137 above.

59 The shop sign appeared on its own as a reverse device on another Dunham and Yallop halfpenny dated 1793 [*D&H*: Norf. 31] but a view of the whole shop front was reinstated on their final issue of 1796 [*D&H*: Norf. 33].

COINAGE AND CURRENCY IN EIGHTEENTH-CENTURY BRITAIN

222 William Lutwyche: Appledore (Kent) halfpenny for William Peckham, shopkeeper, 1794.

223 James Good: Tenterden halfpenny for Isaac and Thankful Cloake, brewers, 1796.

224 Peter Kempson: Portsea halfpenny for Salmon, Courtney and Frost, innkeepers, 1796.

example, with its 'picturesque' reverse view of a 'smock' mill, a typical feature of the Kent of the time [222]. Equally attractive is the 'horse and dray' token produced by James Good for Isaac and Thankful Cloake's Tenterden brewery [223], both happy departures from the usual run of armorial bearings and issuers' ciphers however well engraved.

It is not without significance that the only token issuer in Tenterden, a Wealden market town of 3,000 inhabitants, was the local brewery. Strangely, however, bearing in mind what Evelyn said about the seventeenth-century series and its stronghold of the 'tavern and tippling house',[60] few tokens can be directly related to public houses or inns. And when they are, as with the attractive Portsea halfpenny of Salmon, Courtney and Frost [224] or the cryptic issue of Adam Little from Rupert Street in London's St. James's (*D&H*: Middx 472), it is only by an allusive iconography. Both these are urban issues, of course, as was the halfpenny of Taylor, Moody and Company [95] but, even in country areas, tokens would presumably have been readily passable in the local inns and alehouses that formed the largest cash trade in the country and the commonest interchange for small coin. And there must have been many rural shopkeepers in the south of England, describing themselves as drapers, grocers or even ironmongers on their tokens, who had much closer links with the beer trade than one realizes today.[61]

225 James Lackington (1746-1815).

60 Evelyn (1697), 16. And that the origin of the seventeenth-century tradesmen's tokens may have lain in the need of a tavern keeper near the Tower Mint for small change.

61 And not only in the south of England. The file-maker, Peter Stubs of Warrington, although not a token-issuer, was a prime example of a tradesman who kept an inn and associated brewery in addition to his main business: Ashton (1939).

228

THE NEW MEN

226 Obadiah Westwood/Hancock (but more likely William Lutwyche): London halfpenny for Lackington, Allen and Company, 1794.

The predominance of edge-named provincial coins is not to say that there were not tokens which much more boldly declared to the world the names and businesses of their issuers. Voss's halfpenny inscribed **JOHN VOSS DRAPER &c** and bearing his shop sign of a golden key is one instance of this. James Lackington [225], the nation's first large-scale bookseller, is another but a much bolder one. Lackington, whose shop, the 'Temple of the Muses' at the corner of Finsbury Square, became one of the sights of London, was the brashest of such issuers flooding the market with tokens that were both promissory and promotional.[62] He was one of the first of the 'ready money' tradesmen who, refusing credit, adopted the novel practice of selling for cash at fixed prices and made a fortune from the sale of cheap editions and remainders. Lackington's rags to riches progress, he claimed in his autobiography first published in 1791 when he was forty-five, had been of 'so much intrinsic merit, as would occasion it to be universally admired by all good judges, as a prodigious effort of human genius'.[63] Through this effort, he boasted, he had been 'highly instrumental in diffusing the general desire for reading, now so prevalent among the inferior orders of society'. Self-opinionated and vain, it was in character for Lackington to have himself portrayed on the obverse of his token with Fame blowing a trumpet on the reverse [226]. His firm was, after all, the **CHEAPEST BOOKSELLERS IN THE WORLD** as he proclaimed on his token and over the entrance to his shop.

A journeyman shoemaker, Lackington had been in the London book trade twenty years when he opened his vast emporium in Finsbury Square in 1794. His social pretensions were savagely ridiculed in the forty-seven stanzas of 'Peregrine Pindar''s *Ode to the Hero of Finsbury Square ... illustrative of his Genius as his own Biographer*. In John Nixon's caricature frontispiece to the poem [227] Lackington is shown climbing into his carriage up steps formed by Tillotson's *Sermons*, a Book of Common Prayer, and a Bible; protruding from a pocket are some papers, labelled 'PUFFS & LIES for my Book', and under his right arm he carries 'My Own Memoirs'; while a dog defecates on another copy of his autobiography much to the amusement of a jeering crowd congregated outside the 'Temple of the Muses'.

Lackington was by far the largest issuer of tokens in London and one of the first but, strangely, he never mentioned them in any of the later editions of his *Memoirs* and we have no knowledge of whether he readily redeemed them although they were said to be valid only in his shop. It may be that he caught a cold over their issue – perhaps many more than he ever envisaged came back for redemption – for 'Pindar' was quick to satirise them. Having lampooned Lackington's failure to have a statue of himself erected in Finsbury Square 'Pindar' turned his attention to the tokens and a five-guinea note that Lackington was also said to have issued:

---

62 Lutwyche is said to have manufactured seven tons of tokens for Lackington: Pye (1801), 13. This would have equated to almost 800,000 halfpennies.

63 Lackington (1827), xii.

COINAGE AND CURRENCY IN EIGHTEENTH-CENTURY BRITAIN

227 Lackington mounting his coach outside the 'Temple of the Muses' watched by a jeering crowd. Engraving by 'J N' [John Nixon], published 12 August 1795.

> But, tho' to Merit Envy's ever blind,
> (The Muse tells Truths – and who shall dare to stop her?)
> It could not check 'OUR HERO's' active Mind
> From sending forth his Miniature – in Copper:
> And MOORFIELDS Coin was hail'd with many a Grin,
> Till Hints came out, and then the Coin went in!
>
> As if Opposition made him thrive
> More eager still t'accommodate *the Nation* –
> Then came the Note, engrav'd – and GUINEAS FIVE
> Were sent about in gen'ral Circulation.
> But some Disaster marr'd this Undertaking,
> And Statue, Coin, and Notes, were all forsaken! [64]

64 'Pindar' (1795), 20, stanzas XXX and XXXI.

THE NEW MEN

228 William Lutwyche: London halfpenny for Lackington, Allen and Company, 1795.

Nothing is known about Lackington's paper currency but in a footnote to the *Ode* Pindar declared that Lackington

> anticipating the surprising Run his Halfpence would have, ordered to the Amount of £100, of them from a cheap Manufacturer at Birmingham; but when he understood that it would be safer to give up the Project, a Letter was dispatched to countermand the Order, when, very unfortunately for 'OUR HERO', the Tradesman sent Word that they were all struck off and ready, and that he must be paid for them; the Consequence was, they were sent up to Town by Waggon, and became a *dead Weight* upon 'OUR HERO'.[65]

If true, this story must have related to Lackington's final issue of tokens, struck by Lutwyche and dated 1795, the date of 'Pindar''s satire [228]. It is a pity that none of his tokens carries any impression of the 'Library' interior of the 'Temple of the Muses' with its half million volumes and grand central counter round which it was said a coach and four could be driven. Even a simplified view would, of course, have been too complex and expensive to produce in the small compass of a halfpenny. The scene, happily, is preserved for us on a contemporary trade card of Lackington's by John Walker and more famously elaborated in aquatint in Rudolph Ackermann's *The Microcosm of London* [229]. It was one of the sights of the town not to be missed; as a contemporary writer put it:

> The shop of Lackington may be deemed one of the curiosities of the metropolis, and deserves to be visited by every stranger, on account of the vast extent of the premises, and of the immense stock of books which are brought into one point of view.[66]

229 *The Temple of the Muses*. From Rudolph Ackermann's *Microcosm of London*, Vol. II, Plate 17 (1809).

65 'Pindar' (1795), 31.
66 Quoted in Longman (1916), 38.

231

COINAGE AND CURRENCY IN EIGHTEENTH-CENTURY BRITAIN

230 William Lutwyche: Warranty medalet for Basil Burchell, *c.* 1790s-1800s.

Of course not all shopkeepers' tokens were ever intended to serve as small change anyway and in the retailing cut and thrust of a large city – London stands out as the prime example – many were put out purely as advertising counters; in the module of a halfpenny but with no expression of value and merely giving the name and address of the issuer and the nature of his trade, occasionally at some length. The two functions, though, of money and publicity, were not necessarily distinct and more than a few tradesmen's tickets found their way into circulation as halfpenny substitutes and came back for redemption much to the dismay of the issuer.

A case in point was the ticket put out by the London dealer in quack nostrums, Basil Burchell (*c.* 1765-1838), from his shop at 79 Long Acre, at the sign of the 'Anodyne Necklace' [230], later versions of which, engraved by Arnold and manufactured by Lutwyche, he was obliged to have edged with the words **THIS IS NOT A COIN BUT A MEDAL** (*D&H*: Middx 274).[67] Although of no aesthetic pretension the ticket merits attention because of its singular role as a form of 'warranty' for Burchell's products as well as its being a means of advertising his business.

The Burchells had been established at 79 Long Acre as cutlers and toymen since the 1740s if not earlier – originally their sign was the 'Case of Knives' – but had quickly diversified into the sale of patent remedies, including, what became their specialty, wooden teething necklaces and sugar plums for worms, which they continued to market well into the nineteenth century.[68] It was a cut-throat trade and in the 1780s and 1790s Basil Burchell, grandson of the founder of the business, Matthew Burchell (d. 1777), was advertising his 'cures' vigorously in the press.[69] Hardly a week went by without a Burchell promotion in the *Times* or some other newspaper but in his campaign to keep his name and products constantly before the public he followed a family tradition, the emotional force of which had even caught Dr. Johnson's sardonic eye a generation and more earlier:

> The true pathos of advertisements must have sunk deep into the heart of every man that remembers the zeal shown by the seller of the anodyne necklace, for the ease and safety of 'poor toothing infants', and the affection with which he warned every mother, that 'she would never forgive herself', if her infant should perish without a necklace.[70]

---

67 This edge inscription was also used by Lutwyche on some of the halfpennies he produced for Michael Apsey of Bury St. Edmunds (*D&H*: Suffolk 28b).

68 Basil Burchell was still listed at 79 Long Acre as an 'Anodyne necklace-maker' in the *London Post Office Directory* for 1829 but probably retired about that year. He died at Bushey in 1838.

69 For an appraisal of the Burchells' promotion of their quack remedies see Doherty (1993), esp. 69-90.

70 Johnson (1761) [1963], 126.

232

THE NEW MEN

231 Woodcuts of (a) Basil Burchell shop signs of the 'Anodyne Necklace' and the 'Case of Knives' and (b) the warranty medal from his pamphlet *Anodyne Necklaces* (*c.* 1790-1800).

In the 1790s Burchell, describing himself as a jeweller and goldsmith, again in the footsteps of his grandfather put out an eight-page pamphlet, *Anodyne Necklaces* [231], claiming inherited secrets of manufacture and pseudo-medical properties for his products, and inveighing against the imitations sold by 'artful and unprincipled men'.[71] Burchell's tract was, in effect, a dressed-up elaboration of his newspaper advertisements, no more than a puff for his preparations which he sold at an expensive 5*s* 5*d* for each necklace (or 54*s* per dozen to sell again) and 2*s* 8*d* for three dozen sugar plums in a box (or 1*s* 1½*d* for one dozen). 'To merchants, country dealers, and charitable persons to give away', the price of the sugar plums was reduced to 10*s* per gross.

The necklaces, probably comprising peony-wood beads 'artificially prepared, small, like barley-corns', were said when warmed to give off 'a vast swarm of Subtle Effluvia, from the prodigious Quantity of *Alcalious Anodyne Sulphur*, and *Spirits*' with which they were impregnated, 'and Wandering about the Mouth of the Child, are presently DRAWN into the Ailing Gums by the violent Suction the Swell'd Gums are Endowed with'. No doubt the child also chewed on the beads to ease its pain but, for whatever reason, perhaps they did really work for 'Antiquity' Smith recounted how:

> Being frequently thrown into my cradle by the servant, as a cross little brat, the care of my tender mother induced her to purchase one of Mr. Burchell's Anodyne Necklaces ... and it was agreed by most of my mother's gossiping friends, that the effluvia arising from it when warm acted in so friendly a manner, that my fevered gums were considerably relieved.[72]

Burchell's sugar plums, a type of boiled lozenge, were described as 'the best Physic in the world for children, and all persons who are averse to quantities of Apothecary's draughts, bolusses, pills, &c. which are generally very difficult to take, disagreeable in taste, and unfriendly to the stomach'. The properties of the medicine were, truly amazing! If three doses were taken twice a year 'either by grown persons or children', Burchell claimed, 'they entirely free the body from foul humours, purify the blood, completely cleanse the stomach, bowels and glands producing a perfect state of health'. They were proved, he asserted, to have had 'the most surprising success' in the treatment of an extraordinary range of complaints from worms to colic, rheumatism, 'thickness of hearing', colds, whooping cough which 'too frequently baffles the skill of the most eminent physicians' and even small pox and measles. But this remarkable restorative, 'the best and cheapest family physic extant', was simply a strong purgative made up as a sweet palatable preparation perhaps not too different from the worm

---

71 Hodgkin (1884), 132; The Wellcome Library: Bur. Suppl. P. Mathew Burchell's four page promotion had appeared *c.* 1750 (BL: RB.31.b.137/53). These two pamphlets and that referred to in note 75 below appear to be the only ones extant.

72 Smith (1905), 8.

233

lozenges of the Cheapside apothecary John Ching that contained jalap and some element of mercury.[73] Whatever the constituents of the sugar plums may have been, they, the anodyne necklaces and the gold and silver lockets and pap spoons that Burchell sold with them for his 'carriage trade' provided Burchell with a handsome income allowing him to end his days comfortably as a country gentleman in Hertfordshire.

In his pamphlet Burchell stressed, with the benefit of an illustrative woodcut, that as a protection against counterfeits customers should ensure that there was 'a medal made of a metal nearly resembling silver, the same as is given with this book, fixed on the outside of each Necklace, and one formed of fine copper, attached to the outside of each box and packet of Sugar Plums'. This use of Burchell's 'medals' as guarantees of authenticity, of course, explains why so many specimens are found punched with a hole usually at the same point in the field. As Miss Banks noted, 'Those that are put up with the medicines, have each a hole for the convenience of fixing to the packet'.[74] Burchell's 'medals' probably spanned the best part of a decade at least. We do not know the exact date of his first pamphlet but Miss Banks recorded one of her specimens of the 'medal' as having been issued 'before 1795' while a later version of Burchell's pamphlet, said to have been published after 1801, repeated his earlier caution, again with an exemplary woodcut of the 'medal'.[75]

Samuel dismissed Burchell's 'medal' as a 'miserable ticket' that was 'wretched' in design.[76] Perhaps he was being unfair but it has to be admitted that most tradesmen's tickets were far more imaginative in conception. They were, after all, promotional instruments and in an age

232 Pidcock's Menagerie, Exeter Change, viewed from the Strand, *c.* 1810. An arcade ran along the ground floor mainly occupied by 'boutique' toy shops. The menagerie was housed in a series of confined dens and cages on the first floor.

73 Ching, who patented his lozenges in 1796 (Patent Specification 2121, 28 June 1796: Woodcroft (1856) [1969], 104)), also issued a tradesman ticket (*D&H*: Middx 282).

74 Banks MS Cat. VI, SSB 191-68-3.

75 Banks MS Cat. VI, SSB 191-68-3. The Wellcome Library: 6137/P.

76 Samuel (1880-1889), 7 June 1882, 608-609.

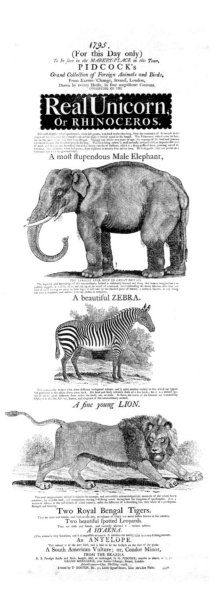

233 Show bill for Pidcock's Menagerie, embellished with Bewick woodcuts and designed to be displayed wherever the show was appearing. Although dated '1795' in manuscript the bill must have been published in 1799.

when advertising tended to consist only of press notices and handbills, they provided, as Professor Mathias has put it, an ideal medium where 'persuasive – even aggressive – advertising could flourish'.[77]

Simple in form but very attractive in their imagery are the tickets put out by Gilbert Pidcock (d. 1810) to advertise his Grand Menagerie at Exeter Change in the Strand (a site now occupied by Burleigh House and the Strand Palace Hotel). Nothing is known of Pidcock's early life but by 1779 he was operating a travelling show of exotic animals and, if the story is true, by 1783 had sufficient means to lend the eminent surgeon, John Hunter (1728-93), £500 in cash to enable him to buy the corpse of the Irish giant, Charles Byrne.[78] A decade later the 'Modern Noah' had established his 'wonderful Ark' at Exeter Change [232] as the only permanent show of its kind in London and, no doubt partly because of its vigorous advertising, it became one of the city's most celebrated institutions, and a fashionable venue for polite society including members of the Royal family.[79]

Specimens were taken around the London fairs and during the summer months the exhibition continued to tour the provinces [233]. And it was during such a visit of the show to Newcastle upon Tyne that the engraver Thomas Bewick made a number of sketches of Pidcock's beasts that he later made into woodcuts.[80]

What was featured as the 'largest collection of the Animal and Feathered Creation ever Exhibited to the Public' was augmented in 1793 by the addition of a 'Most Stupendous Male Elephant', a 'Solomon of Beasts', landed from the East Indiaman *Rose* on 4 September. In the early hours of the following morning 'Antiquity' Smith, on one of his nocturnal perambulations about the City, met up with the sagacious animal on its way from Tower Wharf to the menagerie, trudging on 'with strict obedience to his keepers'. Later Smith 'had the honour ... of partaking of a pot of Barclay's Entire with this same elephant' having been 'assured by the elephant's keeper that if he would offer the beast a shilling, he would see the noble animal nod his head and drink a pot of porter'.

> The elephant no sooner had taken the shilling ... than he gave it to the keeper, and eagerly watched his return with the beer. The elephant then, after placing his proboscis to the top of the tankard, drew up nearly the whole of the then good beverage.[81]

77 Mathias (1962), 36.

78 Altick (1978), 38-39. Byrne's skeleton remains in the Hunterian Museum at the Royal College of Surgeons of England.

79 Altick (1978), 307-308.

80 It still appeared at Bartholomew Fair in the early nineteenth century where it is captured in an aquatint plate in Rudolph Ackermann's *The Microcosm of London* (Volume I, 1808). It was likely Pidcock's 'Great Shew of Wild beast, A Large Elefont and Lyons &c &c', too, that the Hertfordshire farmer, John Carrington, gazed at in wonder in the county town on 20 September 1800: Johnson (1973), 52.

81 Smith (1905), 107; cf. Bingley (1820), 150-51. This elephant, which died in 1803, was not the famous 'Chunee' which was not acquired by the menagerie until 1810 and after Pidcock's time.

COINAGE AND CURRENCY IN EIGHTEENTH-CENTURY BRITAIN

234 Pidcock's two-headed heifer engraved by Thomas Bewick.

235 William Lutwyche: 'Elephant and Heifer' advertising ticket for Gilbert Pidcock.

236a Silver *denarius* (obverse) of Julius Caesar, 49-48 BC.

236b William Lutwyche: 'Elephant' (obverse) farthing-size advertising ticket for Gilbert Pidcock.

The elephant was engraved for Pidcock by Bewick and, with his cuts of a zebra and a lion, took its place in a show bill that while it was a costly production could be used generally to publicize any venue the menagerie visited. Bewick's engraving of Pidcock's celebrated two-headed heifer was also included as an embellishment to Garner's 1800 *Brief Description* of the exhibition [234].[82] These were all used by Charles James as the basis for his dies for Pidcock's tickets. The elephant and heifer [235][83] were, of course, the stars of Pidcock's menagerie at this time and James's portrayal of the former beast caught the imagination of no less a medallic connoisseur than James Wright. It was, he ventured, 'at least as well represented as the same animal is by old Roman artists, upon *denarii*, of the family *Cæcilia*, or upon those of *Julius*, and of *Augustus*' [236a and b].[84]

Pidcock's tokens, purposefully a vehicle for popularizing his show, were given in change to customers and thus in theory could have passed into the currency.[85] Some obviously did so but it is more than likely that most were kept as mementos by visitors or acquired by collectors intrigued by their exotic images; after all, the majority of Pidcock's tickets that have survived tend to be found in extremely fine condition today and their popularity as collectors' pieces is underlined by the number of varieties that were concocted through the interchange of the series' dies, a practice of which Pidcock himself may not have been unaware.

Apart from his two general 'Birds and Beasts' tickets (*D&H*: Middx 414 [237] and 415) all Pidcock's substantive tokens up to the end of the century have **PIDCOCK'S EXHIBITION**[86] as their obverse inscription and **EXETER CHANGE STRAND LONDON** on the reverse, the obverses featuring the elephant, an antelope and a nylghau – that, according to Thomas Sharp, replaced the antelope when that die failed – with the heifer, rhinoceros (right-facing), an ostrich and a cockatoo ('farthing' only) as reverse images. The 'Elephant'/'Rhinoceros' 'halfpenny' is that depicted on plate 26 of Denton and Prattent's *Virtuoso's Companion* [238] but the rhinoceros – copied by James from Buffon's *Histoire Naturelle* – must have been advertised by Pidcock at this time more in hope than as an expression of fact for the only rhinoceros in Pidcock's collection in 1795 was a stuffed one.

---

82 Garner (1800), 29.

83 The geologist, Robert Jameson, recounted how, as a nineteen year old, he had seen the heifer at Exeter Change on 24 August 1793; it 'eats only with one head, but when food is thrown to it the other head imitates it in all its motions; [it] was 14 years old': Sweet (1965), 84-85.

84 *The Edinburgh Magazine*, February 1796, 133-34 and reprinted in essence in *The Monthly Magazine*, December 1796, 869.

85 Sharp (1834), 209. In 1793 Jameson paid '1s. & 3d. to see the collection'– probably reduced because of summer touring – at Exeter Change; 'the 3d. was to the Keeper': Sweet (1965), 85.

86 The 'Antelope' obverse has the legend **PIDCOCK'S EXHIBITION ALIVE** with the date 1795 in the exergue.

THE NEW MEN

237 William Lutwyche: 'Birds and Beast' advertising ticket for Gilbert Pidcock.

238 Prattent's depiction of Pidcock's 'Elephant'/'Rhinoceros' 'Halfpenny' (*D&H*: Middx 416, 416a or b), *The Virtuoso's Companion*, Plate 26, 12 October 1795.

239 William Lutwyche: 'Rhinoceros' advertising ticket for Gilbert Pidcock, *c.* 1799.

Rhinoceros or 'unicorns' were excessively rare in eighteenth-century Britain, only four surviving the voyage from India to London between 1684 and 1799. Pidcock's original animal – the subject of an iconic painting by George Stubbs [87] – was the third and is known to have been at the Exeter Change by 1790. Pidcock acquired the rhinoceros when he bought the original Exeter Change collection from its original owner, Thomas Clark, in February 1793. Unhappily the animal died on tour at Cosham, near Portsmouth, in the summer of 1793, but nothing daunted Pidcock had it recreated in stuffed form for continued exhibition.[88] According to the prolific author, the Reverend William Bingley,

> This animal exhibited no symptoms of a ferocious propensity and would even allow himself to be patted on the back and sides by strangers. His docility was about equal to that of a tolerably tractable Pig: ... He usually ate, every day, twenty-eight pounds weight of clover, besides about the same weight of ship biscuit, and a great quantity of greens. He was allowed also five pails of water twice or thrice a day; and he was fond of sweet wines, of which he would often drink three or four bottles in the course of a few hours. His voice was not much unlike the bleating of a calf. This was usually exerted when he observed any person with fruit or other favourite food in his hand; and in such cases, it seems to have been a mark of his anxiety to have food given him...[89]

Pidcock was not able to acquire a replacement for another four years. At last, in great excitement in the September of 1799, he alerted Bewick to the news that he had 'purchased a fine Rhinocerous [*sic*]' adding 'I think I shall want a Cut for that'.[90] The engraving was duly supplied to be included in Garner's 1800 guide and to be used as the basis for a new die of a left-facing rhinoceros [239]. Whether this animal was less tractable than its wine-bibbing predecessor is not known but perhaps significantly it was depicted both by Bewick and Pidcock's die engraver with a chain halter and was sold by Pidcock after only a month or two to the Holy Roman Emperor, Francis II. Unfortunately, it died in a Drury Lane stable in November 1799 while awaiting passage to the war-torn continent.[91]

Pidcock's tokens can be divided into two distinct groups; those struck in 1795-96 and probably for some time afterwards and those that were manufactured from 1799 onwards, though the dies of the

---

87 Probably painted *c.* 1790-91, acquired by John Hunter by 1793 and since the early nineteenth century in the Hunterian Museum at the Royal College of Surgeons.

88 Clarke (1986), 70-75; Bingley (1820), I, 127. Bingley mistakenly refers to 'Corsham near Portsmouth' and has been followed by many commentators since. Robert Jameson reported seeing the stuffed rhinoceros at Bartholomew Fair on 6 September 1793, it having died 'a short time before ... which loss I much regretted': Sweet (1965), 91-92.

89 Bingley (1820), I, 126.

90 Gilbert Pidcock to Thomas Bewick, 21 September 1799, quoted in Uglow (2006), 268.

91 Bingley (1820), I, 127.

COINAGE AND CURRENCY IN EIGHTEENTH-CENTURY BRITAIN

240 Skidmore: 'Royal Male Tiger' (obverse) advertising ticket for Gilbert Pidcock.

first were intermixed with the second. According to Pye (1801) the dies of the first series were cut by James – who was responsible for most of Thomas Spence's dies – and who is also said by Pye to have *struck* some of the resultant Pidcock tokens although others were attributed to Lutwyche's coinery. One cannot be certain, however, that James ever had a significant, or indeed any, manufacturing capacity himself. [92] A strong case can be made for most of his dies being coined by Skidmore who is thought to have been striking at least some Spence dies even before he acquired ownership of the bulk of them from the radical bookseller in the winter of 1796/97.[93] Unhappily, far too little is known about the relationship between die sinkers and manufacturers at this time but it could well be that while James was the principal employed to make both Pidcock's and Spence's tokens he farmed their actual coining out, in the case of the Exeter Change pieces alternating between the Lutwyche and Skidmore workshops as need arose. This would explain the existence of the anomalous 'Royal Male Tiger 1796' dies associated with a variety of Pidcock's animal dies, both obverse and reverse [240]. All these 'Tiger' 'halfpennies' were struck on **SPENCE X**-edged flans [94] and one's presumption must be that they were concocted in the workshop that was responsible for the manufacture of Spence's pieces, a consideration by no means weakened by the combination of the 'Tiger' die with James's 'John Thelwall' die for Thomas Spence (*D&H*: Middx 870) or the use of his 'Louis XVI' die with a 'Nylghau' die (*D&H*: Middx 446).[95]

While one cannot absolutely rule out the possibility that these anomalous pieces were struck by James himself it would seem more likely that they were products of the Skidmore coinery although, apart from the two exceptions noted above, they are self-contained within the Pidcock series and otherwise never muled with supposed Skidmore pieces. Such a suggestion poses other difficulties however. None of these freak concoctions appear in any publication before Conder's *Arrangement*. There is, therefore, a putative gap between Birchall's *Descriptive List* in the early spring of 1796 and the autumn of 1798 when these tokens – although dated '1796' – could have seen the light of day and at some point towards the end of period – we do not know when – the Skidmore coinery closed down. To muddy the waters still further two of the dies used in the 'Tiger' series – the 'Elephant' and the 'Rhinoceros' – had, according to Pye, been employed by Lutwyche to make Pidcock's early 'Elephant'/'Heifer'

---

92 Cf. Boon (1983), 121; Hawkins (1989), 24-25.

93 Cf. Thompson (1969), 143-44.

94 *D&H*: Middx 344, 418, 436, 441, 442, 443 and 870; 416 also has the SPENCE X edge.

95 The original pairing of the 'Louis XVI' die was presumably with a 'fleurs-de-lis' die (*D&H*: Middx 1003) which was also combined with a Minerva' die (*D&H*: Middx 516); in turn the last was also combined with a 'Reverse 2' of Skidmore's 'Churches and Gates' series (*D&H*: Middx 515).

THE NEW MEN

241 Skidmore: 'The Wanderow' [lion-tailed macaque] (obverse) advertising ticket for Gilbert Pidcock, 1801.

and his 'Elephant'/'Rhinoceros' 'halfpennies'.[96] Lutwyche must also have been responsible for muling 'Elephant' and 'Heifer' dies with those depicting the 'Royal Arms' and a 'Toucan' (D&H: Middx 455, 426 and 454), Dixon dies, that he had used for a specious **LONDON AND MIDDLESEX** halfpenny (D&H: Middx 952) and a trade ticket for the London taxidermist, Thomas Hall [244]. We cannot tell when these latter mulings took place but, again, they are first noticed only by Conder in 1798. For the present the truth of the making of Pidcock's tickets or the 'Tiger' series cannot be established but it does seem that if Skidmore did manufacture some of the tokens there must at some point have been a cross-over between his coinery and that of Lutwyche and it cannot be beyond the bounds of possibility that Lutwyche bought up Skidmore's residual blanks when the latter's coining operation came to an end.

At the turn of the century a further series of Pidcock tokens was produced adding a kangaroo with its young, a zebra, a crane, a lion-tailed macaque [241] and a lion with its cub-substitute puppy to the menagerie. These 'new' tokens were presumably all made by Lutwyche. There was by then, though, no 'Pye' to guide collectors. But as with the earlier Pidcock dies – and now including them, too – the new dies, in true Lutwyche fashion, were 'mixed *together* ... to make a number of varieties'.[97] Even these later tickets present another problem, however, for Sharp asserts that the dies for this series – other than the anonymous and anomalous 'Lion and Dog' tokens (D&H: Middx 427-431) – were struck by Jacobs.[98] Although usually meticulous in his identification of die sinkers Sharp must have been mistaken. None of the new dies was signed – the kangaroo die does sport a 'J' – and Sharp, one imagines, must have meant James who, after all, signed the 'Elephant', 'Antelope', 'Nylghau' and 'Ostrich' dies in the earlier series. Perhaps one day further research will allow all the conundrums to be unravelled.

When Pidcock's original rhinoceros died at Portsmouth in 1793 it was hastily buried on the order of the mayor because of the offensive state of its remains but it was later resurrected during the night and preserved by the London taxidermist, Thomas Hall, who advertised his handiwork in a token of 1795, depicting the rhinoceros, a kangaroo and an armadillo, all three of which been on show at the Exeter Change [243].[99] Presiding over 'The Curiosity House' in City Road, close to Finsbury Square, the site of Lackington's bookshop, 'The First Artist in Europe for Preserving Birds Beasts &c' was very much the showman and exhibited his collection of exotica at fairs about London using the old-wig seller 'Sir Jeffrey Dunstan' as a

---

96 Pye also attributed to Lutwyche the manufacture of the James-engraved 'Elephant'/'Cockatoo' and 'Elephant'/'Heifer' 'farthings' and a specious 'Aylesbury' halfpenny (D&H: Bucks. 7).

97 Pye (1801), 14.

98 Sharp (1834), 209.

99 This paragraph owes much to Brooke (2000), 10-15.

COINAGE AND CURRENCY IN EIGHTEENTH-CENTURY BRITAIN

242 Thomas Hall. Line engraving, 1790s.

huckster to advertise his displays and including the 'white negress', Mrs Newsham, in his show; both appeared on his tokens as did a stuffed toucan [244] which figured prominently in an engraving of Hall also produced for advertising purposes at around this time [242]. By the 1820s his 'grand zoonecrophylacium' was said to contain two thousand specimens of 'birds, beasts, fish, reptiles and insects from all parts of the known world', a special attraction being

240

THE NEW MEN

243 William Lutwyche: Advertising ticket for Thomas Hall, 1795.

244 William Lutwyche: 'Toucan' Advertising ticket for Thomas Hall, [1795].

an automaton of 'a grand group of stuffed singing birds singing their wild notes as natural as life'.

Hall was very much in evidence at King's sale of the contents of Parkinson's Leverian Museum in 1806 with two other dealers in curiosities, Robert Heslop and Peter Ratley, both of whom issued trade tokens. Heslop, with a shop in nearby Chiswell Street, sold a rag-bag of curios, coins, paintings and artists' colours. For some reason, obscure to us now, he portrayed the seventeenth-century contortionist, Joseph Clark, on his token, a likeness taken from a contemporary print (*D&H*: Middx 336). Ratley, of Duke's Court, off St Martin's Lane, seems to have been a somewhat more discriminating dealer. Specializing in pictures and prints he was responsible for a very fine Kempson token engraved in the Wyon workshop [245]. It was presumably intended for presentation to his more favoured customers, catching their eye with the token's obverse rendition of a popular and fitting mezzotint 'droll' of the day by Philip Dawe after a Henry Morland 'candle-light' scene [246] but not failing to advertise on the reverse the other diverse lines of Ratley's business – shells, ores and minerals. Coins are not mentioned among the curios he sold but we do know that Miss Banks was one of the customers who frequented his shop. Henry Morland exhibited the original painting several times at the Free Society of Artists, publishing a description in 1775: 'An Italian Connoisseur and tired boy. The connoisseur is an admirer of no pictures but Italian, therefore his taste is greatly affronted on being shown a Dutch picture; nevertheless his attention is engaged by some effect he sees in the landscape – has forgot the boy, who is tired with holding the picture in a heavy frame, which he is just ready to drop'.[100]

Ratley is known to us today little more than from his token. Much the same is true of Richard Summers, a purveyor of the exotic in Old Cavendish Street, just off Oxford Street. His 'card of address', was especially arresting because of its glaring, bare-teethed image of 'A **WILD MAN'S HEAD FROM THE LAND OF JESSO**' [247]. Who or what the wild man was has never been explained. 'Jesso' or Ezo was a former name for Japan's second island, Hokkaido, still a land of

245 Peter Kempson: London shop ticket for Peter Ratley of Duke's Court, St Martin's Lane, 1795.

---

100 Dawe's mezzotint of Morland's *Connoisseur and Tired Boy* was published by Robert Sayer on 1 November 1773. Philip Dawe (*c.*1745-*c.*1809) had been a pupil of Henry Morland, became his principal engraver and was a close friend of Morland's artist son George.

241

COINAGE AND CURRENCY IN EIGHTEENTH-CENTURY BRITAIN

246 Philip Dawe's mezzotint of Henry Morland's *Connoisseur and Tired Boy*, 1773.

247 Manufacturer unknown: London shop ticket for Richard Summers, Old Cavendish Street, 1797.

mystery, and what was presumably merely an ape's head embellished by an enthusiastic taxidermist must have been intended to represent a 'hairy Ainu', one of the island's aboriginal Caucasoid inhabitants, 'savage men', as a traveller's hearsay report described them in 1565, 'clothed in beast-skins, rough bodied with huge beards and monstrous mustaches, which they hold up with little forks as they drink'; a bogus exhibit but a prize draw for Summers' 'museum'.[101]

When considering the tokens of these vendors of the curious mention must be made of the Boulter family of Great Yarmouth who for nearly thirty years ran an 'Exhibition of Natural and Artificial Curiosities' – including 'the hand of a woman supposed to have been a criminal' – in conjunction with a shop selling jewellery, haberdashery and patent medicines. The *Museum Boulterianum*, puffed by an elegant advertisement piece struck by James Good [248], typified the commercial museum-cum-shop that flourished, especially in spa

---

101 Cooper (1965), 294; see also Cooper (1965), 289-90 and Brooke (1998), 35. The Ainu people, who are still to be found on Hokkaido, were recognized by the Japanese diet as 'an indigenous people with a distinct language, religion and culture' in 2008. The observation about the Ainu's use of the 'little forks' was apparently substantially correct.

242

THE NEW MEN

towns, in the eighteenth century.[102] More celebrated than the Boulters was James Bisset (1761-1832) who, for several years at the turn of the century, ran an 'elegant shop in the fancy line and in petrifaction ornaments' combined with a cabinet of curiosities in Birmingham's New Street [249] before moving to Leamington Spa.[103] Bisset's trade ticket [250], engraved by 'Wyon' and struck by Lutwyche in 1795, bears the obverse legend **BISSET^S MUSEUM & FANCY PICTURE MANUFACTORY** surrounding a colonnaded object – Birchall describes it as a 'temple' so it may have masonic overtones – with miniatures disposed around it.[104] The reverse shows 'curiosities of spar' – urns and obelisks, some apparently pierced for clock dials – with the inscription **ALABASTER SPAR AND PETRIFACTION WAREHOUSE**.

Bisset was a versatile character: a miniaturist, a writer and poetaster, a businessman, a manufacturer of artistic novelties, and something of a connoisseur of paintings. Early on he had been a collector of curiosities and, like Daniel Boulter, reflecting the fascination of the time in the

248   James Good: Great Yarmouth shop ticket for Joseph, Daniel and John Boulter, 1796.

250   William Lutwyche: Birmingham shop ticket for James Bisset, [1795].

discoveries of the South Seas, built up a collection of a wide range of artefacts from 'savage nations' in Africa and the Pacific to tickle the fancy of seekers after the unusual and the exotic. As he confided to his 'Memoir':

> When the celebrated Navigator Captain Cook returned from his voyage round the world, & I had seen various designs & curious pieces of workmanship from Otahetta & other isles, I began to collect every thing of the kind I could lay my hands on, and having collected many coins & a few antiques, I began to form a kind of cabinet, which in a few years attracted the attention of my friends & acquaintance,

249   Bisset's Museum shown on the left of Plate C of Bisset's *Magnificent Directory of Birmingham*, 1800.

102   The contents of the Boulters' Museum – including 'British, Roman, Saxon and English coins and medals in gold, silver and copper' were detailed in Beatriffe (1795), 14, the shop being described as 'a neat magazine of modern niceties'. For the Boulters' museum see Brooke (1997b).

103   For Bisset see WRO: CR1563/246, MS 'Memoir of James Bisset' (1818); Dudley (1904); *ODNB*; *GM*, Supplement 1832, 648-50; Langford (1868), II, 119-122; Walker (1934), 23-28; Berg (1998), 28-37.

104   The ticket is first listed in *The Virtuoso's Companion*, Plate 25, 12 October 1795. See also Birchall (1796), 11 (no. 39). A rare and presumably early version (*D&H*: War. 119) omits the miniatures.

243

and as I had a vast number of rather extraordinary designs of my own doing they cut a pretty good show, which I was happy to exhibit gratis to any who honored me at my lodgings with a call.[105]

Bisset eventually expanded his cabinet of curiosities into the New Street 'Modern Museum' and 'Imperial Picture and Petrifaction Warehouse' that is shown in one of Francis Eginton's engravings for Bisset's *Magnificent Directory of Birmingham*. Perhaps it is Bisset himself standing at the door to gauge visitors' reactions to his displays of 'Fancy Miniature and Imperial' pictures, most of his own creation,[106] 'Alabaster, Spar, and Petrifaction Chimney Ornaments, original Marmatinto ['marble dust'] Drawings, Paintings in Oil and Water Colours, Curious Transparencies' and 'Models in Wax'. As he versified the scene:

> Eight hours every day my Museum I tend
> To wait on each Traveller, Stranger or Friend.
> To design Works of Fancy, and Sketches to make,
> You'll allow in each day a few moments will take.
> Some scores of young Artists, with hearts full of joy
> If trade's brisk or dull, thus have constant employ.
> And ev'ry day teems with some works rare and new
> Which, Gratis to all, I exhibit to view.[107]

There may well have been coins and medals among the 'works rare and new' but it was to be a few more years before Bisset branched out into the publication of his own medals, not least his popular mementos of Pitt, Fox and Nelson – who had visited his shop in September 1802 and taken a bumper of wine with him, much to the delight of the assembled throng – and his celebratory medals of George III's jubilee. He catered for 'every branch of the Royal Family' for was he not – as he claimed in his *Memoir* – 'medallist to their Majesties'.[108]

Bisset's facility in composing amusing and grandiloquent verses on the topics of the day brought him a considerable profit and his chief claim to fame today rests not with his artistic creations or his museum but with his *Poetic Survey round Birmingham* and his *Ramble of the Gods through Birmingham*, topographical surveys written in heroic verse and intended as a 'grand tour' of the 'works of genius' of a town that was a 'seat of arts'. The poetry was coupled with a practical and '*Magnificent Directory, with the names and professions, &c. superbly engraved in emblematic plates*'; the whole publication being, as

---

105 WRO: CR1563/246, MS 'Memoir of James Bisset' (1818). Parts of the memoir, but not this passage, are reproduced in Dudley (1904).

106 Bisset's 'Imperial Pictures' were 'a very curious & novel kind of painting on the inside of convex glasses, which I called "Imperial" in consequence of having an order for designing some of them from the Russian ambassador's original sketches for the then celebrated empress Catherine': WRO: CR1563/246, MS 'Memoir of James Bisset' (1818).

107 Quoted in Brooke (1997a), 43.

108 Dudley (1904), 84-85. For Bisset's medals, engraved by Peter Wyon and published in 1805, 1806 and 1809, see *BHM* 579, 608, 617, 651, 652 and 667; *GM*, March 1809, 252 and 348. For Nelson's visit to Birmingham see Langford (1868), II, 206-207.

THE NEW MEN

251 William Lutwyche: Celebratory token for John Freeth, 'The Birmingham Poet', *c*. 1796.

Maxine Berg puts it, 'a public exhibition of the new manufacturing town ... a celebration of industrial expansion' and a vivid evocation in classical mode of Birmingham's underlying artistry and invention. The plates, themselves combining the useful and the artistic, Bisset hoped, would 'probably, in Time, from the Novelty of the Design, and the Eccentricity of such Concatenation, find a Place in the Cabinets of the Cognoscenti, or the Libraries of the Literati'.[109]

Bisset was an active Freemason and a radical Whig who had acted as deputy chairman of the ill-starred revolution dinner at the Royal Hotel that had sparked the Birmingham riots in July 1791. A gregarious man, he was a leading member of a number of local debating societies including a convivial group of like minds – middling tradesmen and professionals, including the equally resourceful James Sketchley, fellow Mason and token issuer (*D&H*: Middx 369-72)[110] – that met at the Leicester Arms, the Bell Street tavern kept by John Freeth, 'The Birmingham Poet' [251], to discuss the issues of the day.[111] The Freeth Coffee House circle, dubbed by its political opponents as the 'Apostles' or the 'Jacobin Club', was captured in a composite portrait commissioned from a young Prussian artist Johannes Eckstein for fifty guineas in 1792 [252]. Freeth, in his characteristic tricorne hat, Bisset and Sketchley all appeared in the genial group, whose portraits, Bisset later wrote,

> were admirably executed after the manner of Hogarth's celebrated group of the Modern Midnight Conversation, and hung up in the tavern, there to remain as a tontine, till claimed by the survivor of the twelve, whose property it is then to be.[112] The house was kept by a very worthy tagger of rhymes, known by the name of 'Poet Freeth'; no tavern in the town was held in higher repute or better frequented, and many thousands of visitors have been drawn to the room to see the painting, as the generosity of the gentlemen whose portraits were drawn were well-known, being rather of eccentric habits, and all of them excellent boon companions and most social friends, though composed of High Churchmen and inveterate Whigs, and differing in their religious creeds as much or perhaps more than any dozen of men that ever met in society.[113]

109 Berg (1998), 33; Walker (1934), 23-26. The *Directory* was first published in 1800 with a second edition, *Bisset's Magnificent Guide, or, Grand Copperplate Directory for the Town of Birmingham*, in 1808. According to Bisset the copperplate engravings cost him 500 guineas and he lost £200 on the whole venture: Dudley (1904), 80.

110 Sketchley (d. 1801 at Pekipsy, near New York) was the proprietor of a register office, partner in a variety of newspaper and magazine ventures in Bristol and Bath as well as Birmingham, publisher of the earliest of Birmingham's trade directories, and an auctioneer. For Sketchley see Walker (1934), 2-14; Money (1977), 137-39; *ABG*, 28 September 1801 and *GM*, December 1801, 1153.

111 For John Freeth (1731-1808), the topical balladeer to whom Bisset saw himself as heir, see Horden (1993) and *GM*, October 1808, 955. Cf. also Money (1977), 103-104 and *passim*.

112 Under the terms of the tontine the portrait became Bisset's property only five months before his own death at Leamington Spa in August 1832. He had moved to Leamington in 1813 where he had opened a museum, newsroom, and picture gallery the previous year.

113 *GM*, March 1829, 281.

245

252   *John Freeth and his Circle*, an oil painting by Johannes Eckstein (1762-1802), 1792. Freeth is third from the left, the dandified James Bisset fourth from the right with James Sketchley in the background behind him.[114]

One cannot tell from Francis Eginton's emblematic engraving in the *Magnificent Directory* [249] what objects adorned the window of Bisset's shop-cum-museum although no doubt, as one of his rhymes suggests, the miniatures, 'fancy pictures' and 'chimney ornaments' depicted on his token were numbered among them, since:

> Successive crowds of Strangers in amaze
> (With mouths wide open) thro' the windows gaze.
> Perhaps the Spars or Grottos court attraction
> Whilst Paintings some prefer to Petrifaction.[106]

Nor can we tell what the interior was like. For such a glimpse, though, we can perhaps turn to the London halfpenny of Thomas Salter [253]. Salter and his partners had opened a branch of their hatter's business at 47 Charing Cross in 1793 – the address shown on the halfpenny – but they had other established outlets in the East

---

114   Forty years on Bisset, apropos his own exquisite appearance in the portrait, rather shamefacedly concluded that:
> Some probably at ruffles may, and neat laced neckcloth stare;
> Whilst others might remark work'd vest, green coat, and powdered hair...
>   (Quoted in Dudley (1904), 62).
Of Sketchley, a passionate Freemason, Bisset commented:,
> In the background of all, behold where there stands
> A man – who if Masonry e're was the theme,
> His bosom with rapture would glow and expand.
> No man ever known was more proud of the name.
>   (Quoted in Walker (1934), 13).

THE NEW MEN

253 Skidmore: London shop ticket for Thomas Salter, hatter, Charing Cross, [1794-95].

254 Peter Kempson: Birmingham penny token for Benjamin Jacob, ironmonger and auctioneer, 1798.

255a Skidmore: Birmingham shop ticket for William Hallan, china and glass dealer, [1795].

255b Peter Kempson: Norwich halfpenny for Robert Campin, haberdasher, 1794.

255c William Lutwyche: Norwich halfpenny for Joseph Clarke, hosier, 1794.

255d William Lutwyche: Bury St. Edmunds halfpenny for Michael Apsey, ironmonger, [1795].

End too and again specialised in the cheaper end of their market. Advertising their emporium in Charing Cross as **THE CHEAPEST HAT WAREHOUSE IN THE WORLD** they presented its façade as a typical bay-windowed shop-front with large 'modern' plate-glass panes – not unlike that still to be seen in Artillery Lane, Spitalfields.

It is the activity inside the shop that grips our attention, however: three men working felt in a side room while a fourth blocks a hat on a mould in the display area and the manager, holding up the finished article, entices the viewer in, a potential customer, to view the rest of his stock. A more static vision of a shop is provided by Benjamin Jacob, a Birmingham ironmonger, engraver and auctioneer. Jacob's ironmongery business, recently opened in Bull Street by the Welch Cross, is featured on the obverse of his 1798 penny where a welcoming shopman stands behind his counter surrounded by a stack of goods ranging from a fire grate to a parasol or umbrella [254].[115]

Boots, shoes, gloves, crockery and cutlery as well as stoves and grates proliferated on shopkeepers' tokens [255] but perhaps the most graphic and comprehensive display of their goods was that of Jasper Augustus and Simon Alexander Kelly, a prominent firm of saddle and harness-makers who introduced a horse and its jockey on to the obverse of their halfpenny. Saddles, bridle-bits, spurs, riding crops and umbrellas were **SOLD CHEAP AT THEIR MANUFACTORY STRAND LONDON** all of which were portrayed on the reverse of the token [256]. Jasper Kelly was obviously of an inventive turn of mind and had two patents granted to him in the 1790s but despite his ingenuity and the firm's warrant as saddle makers to the Prince of Wales the Kellys were declared bankrupt in 1813.[116]

Cheapness was again the theme of one of the most novel of eighteenth-century promissory tokens. Its issuer this time was a serial bankrupt, James Niblock, a linen draper who for some years had been in partnership with a William Hunter in Liverpool. They were declared bankrupt in August 1791 and subsequently moved to Bristol but in May 1795 their partnership was dissolved shortly after they had issued a token, manufactured by Waring, describing their business as a **GENERAL COMMISSION & PUBLIC SALE ROOM** at Bridge Street and portraying a figure of 'Justice' rather ludicrously holding an auctioneer's hammer as well as her usual set of scales. This was a business that Niblock continued in tandem with his linen drapery after the break-up of the partnership and it was as an auctioneer that Niblock described himself in the *Bristol Directory* for 1795. Nevertheless, a new token that he issued in his sole name later that year clearly related to

256 William Lutwyche: London halfpenny for Jasper and Simon Kelly, saddlery and harness makers, [1794].

---

115 Jacob is first known as a chaser and engraver in Birmingham in 1785 but in 1791 moved out to the Hockley Road eventually returning to the town seven years later: Powell (1977), 172-73.

116 Patent Specifications 1810, 28 May 1791 and 2082, 19 January 1796: Woodcroft (1856) [1969], 317; *UBD*; *LG*, No. 16705, 20 February 1813. Jasper Kelly seems to have turned his hand to the construction of 'arches and other erections and buildings' about the time of his bankruptcy: Patent Specification 3516, 15 January 1812: Woodcroft (1856) [1969], 317.

THE NEW MEN

257 James Good: Bristol token for James Niblock, draper and auctioneer, 1795.

258 James Good: Lowestoft token for Richard Powles, artist and merchant, 1795.

his drapery concern. It is a fascinating halfpenny, the obverse a novel conversation piece with one man telling another: 'I want to buy some cheap bargains' and the other replying: 'Then go to Niblock's in Bridge Street' [257]. By 1798 and perhaps a year or so earlier Niblock had joined forces with a George Burgess in another partnership, running both a linen drapery and operating as a firm of 'Commercial Brokers, Auctioneers, Repository & General Job Warehouse' but he continued to be dogged by misfortune or incapacity and in 1800 he and Burgess were both declared bankrupt. Within three years, however, the irrepressible Niblock, having dissolved his partnership with Burgess, was back in business as James Niblock & Company, 'Wholesale and Retail Linen & Woollen Drapers, Hosiers & Job Warehouse', but by 1817 he and his then partner, Richard Stanley Latham, had become bankrupt once more. Niblock finally disappears from the record in the eighteen-twenties still being pursued by creditors and still apparently running a drapery business but now in Bath.[117]

The Niblock token was one of a handful engraved by William Davies for James Good, a Birmingham button maker specialising in gilded wares who seems to have taken over Samuel Waring's coining business. Davies, who had worked for Waring and engraved the Niblock and Hunter halfpenny, was an adept die-cutter and most of his small, mainly pictorial or scenic, output was executed to a high standard. It included both the Cloakes' Tenterden brewery token [223] and that for the Boulters at Yarmouth [248] but his most engaging handiwork was for the rival East Anglian port of Lowestoft, just ten miles south in Suffolk. With its fascinating views of bathing machines on its fine beach and a herring drifter at work, the Lowestoft halfpenny of 1795 encapsulated the duality of a town that was both a rising watering place 'much resorted to in the bathing season by the nobility and gentry' and an established fishing port [258]. The scenes depicted are clearly based on informed sketches [259], probably 'drawn from the life' by Richard Powles (1763-1807), a talented local artist who was celebrated for his views of Lowestoft and whose initials **R P** appear in a roundel below the obverse beach scene. Although by the time the token was issued Powles had embarked on a mercantile career in London he continued to maintain a close connection with Lowestoft and may well have had a hand in the token's issue as well as being its originating artist.[118]

As in other towns it could have been the case that a group of tradesmen was involved, perhaps with municipal support, and it would be a nice conceit to think that among them was the ebullient Scrivener Capon, landlord of the Crown Inn, who introduced bathing machines to Lowestoft in 1768 'from a model procured from Margate' [262] and did

117 *LG*, No. 13331, 2 August 1791; No. 13782, 26 May 1795; No.15308, 4 November 1800; No. 15510, 28 August 1802; No. 17211, 21 January 1817; No. 17958, 16 September 1823; and other Gazette entries; Matthews (1795, 1798, 1801 and 1803).

118 For Powles see Godden (1985), 159-60. Something of a child prodigy Powles was employed as an artist at the Lowestoft china factory from about the age of eight until he was 'grown up'. He had strong family connections with Denmark where he spent some time and was responsible for the preparation of Admiralty charts for the sea area around Elsinore.

249

much to popularize the town as a genteel seaside resort.[119] It is, after all, medicinal sea bathing rather than the local fishery that gets pride of place on the token. The notion, first voiced by Charles Golding on the basis of the obverse initials, that the token was put out by a 'Robert Peach [sic] ... a wealthy fish merchant', is surely untenable. Although the Peaches were a fishery family of some consequence in Lowestoft and had been since at least the early 1750s there is no evidence that a *Robert* Peach ever existed; as the token's issuer he must have been a pure invention.[120]

259 The Low Lighthouse at Lowestoft. Watercolour drawing by Richard Powles, 1784. Dredgers of the type depicted on the Lowestoft Halfpenny are shown under repair near the Light while to the left, is a group of bathing machines first introduced to the town in 1768.

Only one other token promoted the attractions of a seaside resort, Eastbourne, and this time we can be certain of the issuer: Frederick George Fisher, a local bookseller and stationer [260]. Fisher's token was really nothing more than a device to puff the advantages of Eastbourne in the needle competition between resorts for custom. It is, nonetheless, of great interest because it portrays the façade of the circulating library [261] he set up in 1790 adjacent to 'Mrs. Webb's Warm Sea Water Baths', both essential constituents of a watering place claiming to be 'much frequented by the nobility and gentry for sea-bathing'. The token, dated 1796 and again struck by Good and engraved by either Davies or perhaps Francis Arnold, stresses the nature of the clientele such a resort aspired to and depended upon – **PROSPERITY TO THE GENTRY WHO VISIT EASTBOURN** – while the advantages of the town are expressed on its edge: **CELEBRATED FOR PURE AIR AND SEA BATHING**.

119 Gillingwater ([1790]), 51. Capon has a minor place in numismatic history over his swallowing a crown piece 'in a moment of hilarity and frolic'; an incident and its consequences recounted in some detail in *GM*, December 1799, 1043-44.

120 Golding (1868), 85. It would, surely, have been extraordinary for a fish merchant to have issued a token that elevated the sea bathing attractions of Lowestoft above a depiction of his livelihood.

THE NEW MEN

The circulating library was more than a repository of books, cheap and frivolous, if not unwholesome, novels to while away the leaden hours between shopping in the morning, visiting in the afternoon and bathing. It was central to the experience of being on holiday, a hub of social activity where reading, even of the newspapers, was only one among a variety of attractions.[121] The Eastbourne library and lounge no doubt echoed, if perhaps on a smaller scale, the establishment Fisher also operated in Brighton where to tempt the visiting 'nobility and gentry' he kept 'constantly on sale an elegant assortment of Jewelry, Stationary [sic], Tunbridge Ware, Perfumery, Gloves, Parasols, useful and entertaining Books, Patent Medicines &c. &c. &c., with the largest collection in Brighton of Grand and Small Piano Fortes for hire, by the best makers, and a great variety of new Music'. But he also ran an afternoon and evening lottery. 'It is thus that I have spent every day almost since I have been here', noted the thirteen year old Charlotte Francis in her journal of a summer holiday in Brighton in 1799, 'shopping of a morning rafles [sic] in the evening. I really can find time for nothing or little else'.[122] For Jane Austen, the library in the 'young & rising Bathing-place' of 'Sanditon' was a Mecca of meeting and gossip with 'Drawers of rings & Broches [sic]', trifles, souvenirs and knick-knacks for sale – 'all the useless things in the World that c^d not be done without … among so many pretty Temptations'. Fisher's Brighton enterprise maintained a subscription book where 'if you pay a

260 James Good: Eastbourne shop ticket for Frederick George Fisher, library and shop keeper, 1796.

261 The Eastbourne Library, *c*. 1819, after improvements by Robert Heatherly. From a contemporary engraving.

121   There were over a thousand circulating libraries in Britain by 1800.

122   [Fisher] (1800), after 92; BL Egerton MSS 3706A, Vol. 36, ff. 18-18b. Charlotte Francis's manuscript 'Journal of what passed in an excursion to Brighton 1799' [16 August-23 September], gives some fascinating glimpses of a contemporary sea-side holiday and of the importance of Fisher's Brighton library as a focal point of social activity with gambling seemingly being a primary function.

Fisher's Eastbourne library was acquired by Robert Heatherly in 1815 and continued under a succession of different owners until 1913. It was still hiring out pianos at the beginning of the twentieth century. The building, little changed, was eventually demolished in 1948.

crown you may write your name ... & your address & your friends find you out'. No doubt he had one at Eastbourne, too, and as at 'Sanditon' visitors quizzed it just to discover the *ton* of the place. The Francis family certainly consulted his Brighton 'book' on a number of occasions to see who was in town.[123]

Fisher, who was also Brighton's postmaster, was declared bankrupt in December 1803 but although he was forced to give up his Brighton library and eventually dispose of the stock (including 4000 books) the Eastbourne business continued to be managed by his family and within a year Fisher himself was back in business in Brighton running an auction room and newspaper lounge.[124]

262 *Summer Amusement at Margate* by Thomas Rowlandson, 1815, showing bathing machines of the type introduced to Lowestoft and a Circulating Library with a Bathing Establishment in the background.

Both the Lowestoft and the Eastbourne halfpennies are admirable examples of how provincial coins could reflect 'in their exquisite designs' the 'rich diversity of interests and aspirations' of contemporary society.[125] But tokens, too, made something of the 'surge of energy' that was such a feature of the age and was to lead to Britain's becoming the most important developing economy in the world by the century's

123 Chapman (1954), 368 and 390; BL: Egerton MSS 3706A, Vol. 36, f.15.
124 Longman (1916), 67-68; *LG*, No.15679, 28 February 1804.
125 Klingender (1943), 41.

THE NEW MEN

263a Peter Kempson: Gloucester token for the Gloucester and Berkeley Canal Company, 1797.

end. They mirrored the drive for 'Improvement' that pervaded the air: the promotion of commerce through the construction of better quays and warehouses; of transport through the cutting of canals, the building of bridges, the making of turnpikes, and the development of the mail coach; of agriculture through better methods of farming; urban development through street improvements, new civic buildings and the creation of public gardens; and the betterment of the poor through the provision of schools and hospitals [263].[126]

Nevertheless, it is surprising, bearing in mind the circumstances of their genesis, that they illustrate so little of the revolutionary technological and industrial changes that were stirring in the country at the time and caught the attention of contemporaries; those 'discoveries and improvements' that 'diffuse a glory over this country unattainable by conquest or dominion' as the *Encyclopædia Britannica* put it.[127] The large industrial companies – Anglesey, Roe and Company, the Birmingham Mining and Copper Company – chose allegorical allusion and classical symbolism rather than any realistic representation of their mines and works. The nearest one comes to this is Wilkinson's view of a smithy – the 'old Forge' that pleased him better than 'Vulcan' – and even this is more figurative than graphic as indeed is the solitary horse whim of the west Cumberland Low Hall Colliery token [265].[128] Even the Ketley Inclined Plane, lauded as the last word in lifting machinery since it actually worked, was based on an age-old principle [263f]. With John Morgan's halfpenny we do get a feel for the activity of a small iron works through Hancock's meticulous recreation. Yet it was the old world of agriculture and cottage industry that captured the imagination of token makers and issuers. There is no hint of Arkwright's giant spinning factories; indeed the only reference to cotton – Britain's fastest growing 'new' industry – is by way of Mordaunt's factory near Ormskirk [60] or Thomas Scott's mill at Gatehouse of Fleet [267], and no hint of the new power of steam or of the 'dark Satanic mills' that were beginning to transform Lancashire towns like Manchester into industrial wens.[129]

The emphasis is on the old national staple of wool, rooted for generations in the countryside and the market town and embodied on tokens nation-wide by its patron saint Bishop Blaize, a woolsack or the Golden Fleece. And while the occasional rural spinning factory, Moggridge and Joyce's Dunkirk water-mill at Freshford, for example [268], might be depicted it is the weaver's hand-loom [215 and 270a] that has pride of place, reflecting the traditionally domestic character of the industry even though it was now increasingly monopolized by large-scale merchant clothiers or hosiers who owned the cottage implements

---

126 Cf. Girouard (1990), 86.

127 George (1953), 107.

128 For Low Hall Colliery see Finlay (2006), 31-32.

129 As we saw earlier (pp. 127-28 above) Arkwright did toy with the idea of issuing tokens himself but the scheme came to nothing and it may be that the porter shown on Fielding's Manchester halfpenny (*D&H*: Lancs.135) is carrying bales of cotton.

253

COINAGE AND CURRENCY IN EIGHTEENTH-CENTURY BRITAIN

263b Peter Kempson: Dundee halfpenny for Alexander Molison, merchant, 1795.

263c Peter Kempson: Dundee penny for Thomas Webster, Jnr., rope and sailcloth maker, 1797.

263d Thomas Mynd: Presentation Basingstoke Canal 'Shilling' for John Pinkerton, canal builder, [1794].

263e Skidmore(?): Specious Sunderland token, [1797].

263f Peter Kempson: Coalbrookdale and Ketley halfpenny for William Reynolds, ironmaster, 1792.

263g William Lutwyche: 'Walcot Turnpike Token' for Francis Heath, ironmonger, Bath, 1796.

263h Thomas Mynd: 'Mail Coach Halfpenny' supportive of John Palmer, dismissed comptroller general of the Post Office, perhaps sponsored by the engraver James Fittler, 1794/95.

263i John Milton: Wroxham threepenny token for the Reverend Daniel Collyer of Wroxham Hall, Norfolk, 1797.

THE NEW MEN

264 *The Mail Coach.* An engraving by James Fittler, dedicated to John Palmer, after an oil painting of the Bath Mail by George Robertson, 1803

265 Peter Kempson: Low Hall Colliery halfpenny for Sir Wilfrid Lawson of Isell, Cumberland, 1797.

and raw material and paid the craftsmen a wage; men such as John Harvey whom we met in Norwich or the Nottingham master-hosier Walter Merrey who had such problems in making up his wage packets.

Lace-making was another cottage industry that was organized in much this way and a halfpenny by Kempson put out by a controlling City firm of haberdashers and lace merchants, Chambers, Langston, Hall & Company, portrays a girl working lace under the shade of a tree. It is an idyllic scene that belies the unremitting toil of ten to twelve hours a day that was the harsh reality demanded of a domestic craft too often productive of debilitating disease [269]. Passing through the

266 Coal Mine near Neath, Glamorgan, showing a horse working a whim. From a hand-coloured aquatint by John Hassell, 1798.

255

COINAGE AND CURRENCY IN EIGHTEENTH-CENTURY BRITAIN

267 Samuel Waring: Gatehouse halfpenny for Thomas Scott and Company, cotton spinners, Gatehouse-of-Fleet, Kirkcudbrightshire, 1793.

268 William Lutwyche: Dunkirk halfpenny for Moggridge and Joyce, clothiers, Freshford, Somerset, 1795.

269 Peter Kempson: Leighton Buzzard halfpenny for Chambers, Langston and Hall, haberdashers and lace merchants, 1794.

270a Peter Kempson: Haverhill halfpenny for John Fincham, clothier, 1794.

270b Peter Kempson: Ipswich halfpenny for Robert Manning, [1793].

271 William Lutwyche: Hereford halfpenny for Charles Honiatt, mercer, 1794.

256

THE NEW MEN

272 Medallion of James Wright, Jnr. (1768-1798) after William Tassie, 1800.

273 Peter Kempson: 'Penny of Scotland', celebratory medalet of Adam Smith for James Wright, Jnr., 1797.

Home Counties at the time Thomas Pennant noted that there was 'scarcely a door to be seen, during summer, in most towns, but what is occupied by some industrious pale faced lass; their sedentary trade forbidding the rose to bloom in their sickly cheeks'.[130]

Such symbolism and the apposite legends of some tokens – **SUCCESS TO THE PLOUGH & FLEECE, SUCCESS TO THE PLOUGH AND SHUTTLE** and **GOD PRESERVE THE PLOUGH & SAIL** [270a and b]] – while they may appear to represent a nostalgic yearning for a happier pre-industrial age in fact convey the reality of the hand-operated manufactures and agricultural economy of the areas where they circulated: bay and say cloth in Colchester [349], worsted in Norwich, sailcloth in Plymouth and even cider in Hereford [271]. Most contemporaries, especially south-east of the Severn-Trent divide where the majority of the 'pictorial' and 'shopkeeper' or 'retail' tokens were issued, while they might enthuse about specific 'improvements' seemed barely conscious of the full import of the economic changes that were taking place, often almost imperceptibly slowly and in, to them, remote areas of the country.

James Wright ('Civis' of the periodicals and contributor of the 'Preface' to Conder's *Arrangement*) [272],[131] a man conspicuously aware of these changes and wedded to memorialising them on coinage, looked forward to

> the magnificent iron arch over the Wear at Sunderland, which immortalizes the name of Burdon; the rocky entrance to the Duke of Bridgewater's astonishing subterraneous navigation at Worsley; Eddystone lights, docks at Liverpool and Hull; some of the largest steam-engines, cranes, locks, drawbridges, &c. throughout the kingdom ... [having] the Numismatic honours paid to him [sic] which their magnitude and usefulness render due! And it is to be lamented that among the few coins struck for Scotland, not one comes under this description. How ornamental and honourable would it be for some of them to bear the figures, and perpetuate the dates of the erection of the greatest foundery [sic] in the world at Carron; the north bridge at Edinburgh; the elegant bridges at Perth and Glasgow; the great quay at Aberdeen; or the vast and useful aqueduct over the Kelvin, supporting, at a stupendous elevation, one of the greatest canals [the Forth and Clyde Canal] in Europe.[132]

But even he failed wholly to live up to these dictates when it came to the tokens he inspired and persuaded local tradesmen to finance. His actual approach to the 'striking emblems of that spirit of industry and

---

130 Pennant (1811), 460. The image of a rural lace-maker is repeated on Moore's Great Portland Street token (*D&H*: Middx 389) which is also engraved by 'Wyon' for Kempson.

131 For James Wright see Dykes (1996a), 195-99.

132 *The Monthly Magazine and British Register*, December 1796, 868. Both the Wear Bridge [263e] and the Eddystone Lighthouse (*Davis*: Devon 21) were eventually (1797 and 1801 respectively) commemorated on tokens.

257

274   Peter Kempson: Perth halfpenny for John Ferrier, hosier, 1797.

275   Peter Kempson: Perth halfpenny for John Ferrier, hosier, 1797.

commerce, which characterizes the present times, and especially the British nation' is epitomised in the reverse of his 'Penny of Scotland' with its time-honoured symbols of trade and agriculture [273]. He does portray the Dundee Glass Works and Smeaton's Tay Bridge at Perth [274] – 'the finest in Britain, next to the three at London' – but otherwise he gives us few 'representations of the great and useful undertakings of the present times' that he yearned to see on tokens. Carron ultimately escapes his attention and when he exemplifies the 'many large Water-Machines' in the Perth area, emphasising that 'nowhere in Europe are there [so many] in the same place', what he in fact shows us is a tiny rural water-mill à la picturesque [275].[133] The Tay salmon fishing, 'perhaps the richest in the world', is typified by the traditional scene of a solitary fisherman hauling on a small net with his coble lying alongside [274], no reference being made to the newly adopted industrial-scale stake-net fishing that was already causing so much contention on the river.

Perhaps had he not died prematurely in April 1798 Wright would have included some striking representations of industry and commerce in the 'sett [*sic*] of *Scottish Medalets* ... of interesting national objects' that he was projecting with Kempson at the time. But this was not to be and the industries that Wright knew at first hand – he was a member of an affluent Dundee linen-merchant family [276a] – and did depict on his tokens were still very much embedded in time-honoured practices; most

276a   Peter Kempson: Dundee farthing for James Wright, Jnr., 1796.

276b   Peter Kempson: Dundee halfpenny for Thomas Webster, Jnr., rope and sailcloth maker, 1797.

276c   Peter Kempson: Perth farthing for John Ferrier, hosier, 1798.

133   *The Monthly Magazine and British Register*, December 1796, 868; NMS: SAS Letter Books, MS letter, James Wright, Jnr. to Alexander Smellie, 11 December 1797.

THE NEW MEN

of the processes required for textile manufacture, for flax-heckling [276b] and bleaching [276c], were still domestic and hand operated while the mills of the area would remain water-driven for a generation and more. Steam, which would bring great manufacturing prosperity to Perth and Dundee in the nineteenth century, lay very much in the future.

Wright, a Fellow of the Society of Antiquaries of Scotland, was as imbued with the history and architecture of his country as he was with its economic development. '*Fac-similes* of remarkable buildings', both ancient and modern, he maintained, also deserved to be 'signalized' on coinage; an opinion he carried through to his tokens, often pairing the old with the new, making use of engravings in Robert Small's *Statistical Account of Dundee* but largely relying on his own drawings – since he was no mean artist – which he preserved in a still-surviving sketchbook [277].[134]

277 Some of James Wright's 'Original DESIGNS for COINS and MEDALS'. From his Drawing Book, 1783-*c*.1797. No. 3, 'COWGATE PORT – THE LAST REMAINS OF OUR ANCIENT WALLS', the reverse of the halfpenny for the Dundee retailers Alexander Swap & Company *(D&H:* Angus 21-22), reflects Wright's anxiety to preserve images of ancient buildings as well as to celebrate the modern.

What strikes one about Wright's tokens is the optimism that underlies his images and, even more, his cramped and naïve over-use of 'political arithmetic' to emphasise the progress that he was anxious to portray [278]. It was an optimism that, despite the strains of war

278 Peter Kempson: Dundee penny, celebratory medalet of Admiral Duncan for James Wright, Jnr., 1798.

134 *The Monthly Magazine and British Register*, December 1796, 868; NMS: SAS Letter Books, MS letter, James Wright, Jnr. to Alexander Smellie 21 December 1797; Small (*c*.1793). Wright's Drawing Book was acquired some years ago by the National Library of Scotland (Acc. 11596).

259

and the economic distress of the mid-1790s, was a general feature of the tradesmen's tokens of the period. Richard Bacon's Norwich halfpenny, for example, with its luxuriant golden fleece and confident legend that **GOOD TIMES WILL COME** [219] gives no hint of the imminent decline of the East Anglian worsted trade in the face of cheaper competition from Yorkshire.[135]

When Wright died in 1798, not yet thirty years of age but harassed by severe financial problems and deep personal misfortune, his enthusiasm for quality token and medallic design was undiminished and he still had many schemes in the offing. His death was not only a personal tragedy but, as Charles Shephard put it, was 'a considerable loss to the lovers of medals as no person interested himself more in their improvement'.[136] But his career as a numismatic impresario had been a short one. It had not been until 1795 that his first token, for Alexander Molison, a Dundee merchant,[137] had appeared [263b] and, by the following year when he had fully embarked on his token-making ventures with Kempson, provincial coinage, even in Scotland with its ingrained antipathy to regal copper, was rapidly on the decline. At the same time the collecting of tokens had reached manic proportions and it was to meet the cravings of this market that Kempson had already turned to the production of superior medalets – his initial series instancing Birmingham buildings had been an inspiration to Wright – and it was to the collecting fraternity that the diminishing band of token manufacturers now turned their attention [279].

279a

279

Peter Kempson: Birmingham 'Building' medalet depicting the Soho Manufactory, c. 1796, James Wright's 'Penny' Medallions celebrating the attempted escape of Mary, Queen of Scots from Loch Leven Castle, 1797, and the restoration of Paisley Abbey Church, [1798].

279b

279c

135 For an excellent discussion of numismatic representations of the golden fleece see Thompson (2009),199-212.

136 Dykes (1996a), 198; Shephard (1798), 742.

137 Molison, who died in 1798, was by 1796 severely financially embarrassed, the fate, it seems, of a number of token issuers: Dundee City Archives, Howff Burial Registers, 12 February 1798; Trust Disposition, 30 April 1796.

VI

COLLECTORS, DEALERS AND RADICALS

> The superior workmanship of the *Anglesey* Pennies and Halfpence, and other early Tokens, induced a few coin collectors to preserve specimens of them; and after a time, as the number of these pieces increased, and the desire of obtaining choice impressions became more general, a few individuals (whose proximity to the manufacturers at Birmingham gave them frequent and ready means of access,) began to watch the completion of new dies, and not only to procure first impressions, but frequently proofs in an unfinished state, as well as other varieties and specimens, the preservation of which may, perhaps, be entirely ascribed to their vigilance [*sic*].
>
> The desire of collecting Provincial Tokens rapidly increased, until at length it absolutely became a mania.
>
> Thomas Sharp, *A Catalogue of Provincial Copper Coins … in the collection of Sir George Chetwynd …* (1834) iii.

The original Anglesey pennies, the *Daily Universal Register* reported, had been snapped up 'with great avidity' by London collectors struck by the beauty of this pioneer series. And as tokens grew in number and variety so, as Thomas Sharp tells us, a natural urge to collect them mushroomed. Perhaps with the example of the novelty-seeking Byng in mind the late Charles Wilson Peck long ago pictured 'the interest and excitement of some traveller journeying up and down the country and turning out his pockets each night to examine any new varieties of halfpenny tokens received in change during the day'.[1] But the pursuit quickly matured from being one dependent on serendipitously finding the odd unfamiliar specimen in one's change. As Peck pointed out the fact that so many tokens are found today showing little sign of wear is witness to their being 'collected' from the start, and collected and sought out in a systematic manner.

In their hunt for choice pieces collectors – and here Miss Banks comes very much to mind – went out of their way, in Sharp's words, 'to procure first impressions' direct from the manufacturers and frequently even 'proofs in an unfinished state, as well as other varieties and specimens'. This scramble for provincial coins was a lesson not lost on manufacturers. The aesthetics and the subject-topicality of their product – the driving forces of the increasingly fashionable

---

[1] Peck (1947), 345.

280a William Lutwyche: Mule halfpenny concocted from a Leeds (Paley) obverse [160] and a Dunkirk (Moggridge and Joyce) obverse [268].

pastime – were immediately appreciated and turned to account by the sale of specimen tokens direct to collectors and to dealers, themselves a phenomenon of the new enthusiasm. Matthew Boulton, for one, was not behindhand in this. Early on, as we have seen, he had provided favoured friends with choice pieces but by 1793, if not before, he was further exploiting the potential of his coinery by regularly supplying specimen sets of coins and tokens on a commercial basis to personal customers such as Samuel Birchall and urging his agents to promote their sale to metropolitan toymen and coin dealers like the Youngs.[2]

The early collectors, as one will appreciate from **Table 5**, had only a limited number of tokens to seek out but as the enthusiasm for collecting provincial coins took hold manufacturers met the growing demand not simply through the sale of their authentic issues but by the concoction of spurious 'varieties', striking 'genuine' tokens on unrelated or falsely-edged blanks. This was, in a sense, a not unnatural extension of the existing unscrupulous practice of using legitimate dies with plain-edged or milled blanks to foist unattributable and thus unredeemable currency issues on the public, but now it was calculatingly aimed at the collectors' market by the creation of apparently rare pieces that could command inflated prices. By the early part of 1795 a new trick had emerged of combining dies not intended to be used together to create artificial rarities; 'vulgarly called "*Bastard*s"' as Hammond referred to them in the August of that year, but, according to Sharp, quickly becoming known by 'the very appropriate term "Mule" … the manufacturing of which in London was carried to an almost incredible extent, and all for the purpose of sale'.[3] Both Kempson and Lutwyche happily indulged in these practices, Lutwyche, to take just one example for instance, pairing an old Westwood/Hancock obverse die for Paley of Leeds with the obverse of one of his own 'Dunkirk' dies [**280a**]. It was not only the token-makers who were at fault, however, for mules were sponsored by token-issuing collectors themselves. Lacan Lambe and John Jelly of Bath, for instance, were castigated by Charles Pye for contributing 'in no small degree to the number of mules, by an extravagant combination

280b Robert Brickdale Morgan: Fictitious 'Northampton' halfpenny for 'George Jobson, Banker', 1794/95.

280c Skidmore (?): Fictitious (?) 'Beverley' hafpenny for 'Green, Pawnbroker', 1797 overstruck on a Middlesex halfpenny for Jonathan Dennis, 1794.

2   The sale of specimen sets seems to have ceased being a regular feature of Soho business about 1805 and was not resumed until the time of M. P. W. Boulton and then only on a limited basis. Cf. Vice (1995).

3   Hammond (1795), '*To the Public*'; Sharp (1834), iv. For the dating of the term 'mule' see Thompson (1969) 156-58.

COLLECTORS, DEALERS AND RADICALS

280d Skidmore: Specious Dunmow halfpenny, [1794-95].

281a Matthew Denton's 'Blockheads' Farthing' and 281b and 281c John Westwood's lampoons on token collectors published during the collecting mania.

of their own dies'[4] while Thomas Spence advanced the practice to a sophisticated degree for his own eccentric political purposes until his dies were acquired by Skidmore to be used on a profligate scale purely as a profit-making exercise. Sharp tells us that

> the encouragement too generally given by collectors to this species of fraud, naturally led to a still further utterance of them…
>
> Such was the extent of unblushing effrontery to which this trade was carried, that coins holding up the collectors themselves to ridicule (certainly but too well deserved) were struck by these very dealers; witness Denton's Farthing, 'We three Blockheads be' [281a],[5] and more especially the 'Token Collector's Halfpenny', which they employed *Westwood* [6] to manufacture for them, wherein the reckless passion for collecting was pungently ridiculed in the reverse, 'Asses running for halfpence' [281b], whilst the encouragement given to the creation of new varieties by combining obverse and reverse dies that had no real connection, was admirably designated in the other reverse, of an ass and mule saluting each other, having for the legend, 'Be assured, friend mule, you shall never want my protection' [281c].[7]

Token collecting had much of the character of a virtuoso pursuit but at the same time, even more than that of the contemporary print, it could be eminently affordable; it savoured of classical taste and refinement but it had none of the expense or complexity of the quest of the antique. Moreover, tokens reflected the immediacy of modern commerce and industry and in many instances were admirable examples of design and workmanship. As such they were very much an interest of the snug middling sort, people involved in urban trade or operating on its professional fringes who in some instances issued their own tokens: attorneys (John Jelly of Bath, George Barker and Thomas Welch of Birmingham, Robert Reeve

281c

281b

4   Pye (1801), 'Advertisement', 3 note.

5   Miss Banks (Banks MS Cat. VI, SSB,191.84) tells us that the 'Blockheads' farthing was engraved by one 'Phillips' while according to Waters ((1906), 58) Thomas Woodward, another contemporary collector, noted in his copy of Conder's *Arrangement* that it was by an equally unknown 'Russell'.

6   The younger John Westwood. The 'Token Collector's Halfpennies' (*D&H*: Middx 298 and 299) are presumably attributed by Dalton and Hamer to 'Denton' as the dealer who commissioned and issued them.

7   Sharp (1834), iii-iv.

263

282a William Lutwyche: Bath farthing for Lacon Lander Lambe, grocer and tea dealer, 1795.

282b Skidmore (?): London halfpenny for Robert Orchard, grocer and tea dealer, 1795.

of Lowestoft, and Charles Shephard of Lincolns Inn), a schoolmaster and spa proprietor (David Arnot of Holt near Bradford-on-Avon), an engraver and publicist (Charles Pye of Birmingham), an antiquarian hatter (Thomas Sharp of Coventry), a Quaker woolstapler (Samuel Birchall of Leeds), a silk-mercer and amateur engraver (Frederick Atkinson of York), a draper (James Conder of Ipswich), grocers and tea-dealers (the twenty-one year old Lacan Lander Lambe of Bath [282a],[8] the obsessively self-centred Londoner Robert Orchard [282b], and Samuel Prentice of Bungay), a Scottish textile merchant (James Wright of Dundee) and a Staffordshire calico printer who encouraged his local vicar into the hobby (John Harding and the Reverend Francis Blick of Tamworth).[9]

The list might be extended. The collectors who helped Birchall with his *Descriptive List* included among their number a York lace-weaver (William Ellis), a watchmaker (James Carlill), and an accountant and schoolmaster (John Rippon). Admittedly, there were some social exceptions. Thomas Woodward, who also assisted Birchall and collaborated with James Conder in his *Arrangement of Provincial Coins*, was an East Anglian landowner and magistrate;[10] George Chetwynd, the son of a baronet; William Robert Hay (the promoter, with William Orme (a drawing master) and Thomas Tomlinson (a surgeon), of the Buxton token [283]), a scion of the aristocracy and a barrister – haplessly as it turned out – before he turned to the Church; and, of course, the redoubtable Sarah Banks.

In the final years of provincial coinage some of these collectors commissioned their own personal tokens. The first of such pieces was said to have been struck by John Milton, for a City merchant, David Alves Rebello, in 1795 [284]. It was an example taken up by other collectors over the next few years, especially those with ready access to Birmingham or London die-sinkers and manufacturers. Thanks to the influence of Thomas Welch and George Barker – both issuers of such pieces [384 and 285], as was Charles Pye himself [382] – great care was taken to illustrate the bulk of them in the 1801 edition of the

283 Peter Kempson: Buxton halfpenny for William Robert Hay, William Orme and Thomas Tomlinson, 1796.

284 John Milton: Private Hackney token for David Alves Rebello, 1795. Said to have been the first private token.

8 Sydney Sydenham identified 'Mr Lambe' as the twenty-one year old Bath grocer Lacon Lander Lambe, thus explaining the interlaced 'L's on his 1795 farthings: Sydenham (1907-1908), columns 10670-71.

9 Harding's collection of tokens was acquired by Sir George Chetwynd. Blick's 'numismatological library' and his collection of coins and tokens were sold at Sotheby's in June and July 1843: Manville and Robertson (1986), 84; Manville (2009), 30.

10 Woodward (1745-1820) was also a distinguished botanist and fellow of the Linnean Society: *ODNB*.

COLLECTORS, DEALERS AND RADICALS

285 Peter Kempson: Private Birmingham halfpenny for George Barker, 1797.

latter's *Provincial Coins and Tokens*. Indeed, the 'private token' as a distinct category of provincial coin was first publicised as such in Pye's work, deliberately intermingled with the genuine trade tokens and 'cards of address' or 'shop-tickets' that it primarily set out to depict and no doubt included to encourage sponsorship of the catalogue.

Often fine examples of the die-sinkers' art, expertly struck and costly in production, these private tokens were, as a rule, minted in strictly limited numbers, from a handful to a few dozen, either as a singular indulgence in egotism or, more rationally, for exchange with fellow enthusiasts for like pieces. Thomas Thompson, the radical Whig MP, for one, was adamant that he would part with a specimen of his 'Evesham' penny [286] only in return for the rarities he needed 'to perfect his collection'; even the blandishments of Sarah Banks failed to break this resolve, her initial offerings being dismissed as 'very inconsiderable for Scarcity'.[11] It seems likely that it was Thompson who bound in to a copy of Conder's *Arrangement* a list of at least some of the exchanges he made. Miss Banks eventually settled with a Birmingham Workhouse token but Thomas Welch who never reciprocated was dismissed, with not untypical contempt, as 'a mere fraud'.[12] Thompson's token, dated JUNE · 6 · 1796, commemorated his re-election to the Commons that year and, in this particular sense, is on a par with Milton's Herefordshire 'halfpenny' for Robert Biddulph, another radical Whig [334].

Seventeen-ninety-five saw the collecting mania reaching its high point but as it peaked so the market for provincial coins as currency began to crumble. Within a twelvemonth manufacturers – reduced by now mainly to Kempson [287], Lutwyche and the London coiners Skidmore and Williams – were finding that they had to diversify and find other outlets for their coining equipment.

Lutwyche pursued the dubious in the production of evasions or

287 Peter Kempson: Private Warwickshire penny token bearing Peter Kempson's cypher, 1796.

286 Skidmore: Private Evesham penny for Thomas Thompson, 1796.

11 Banks MSS: Thomas Thompson to Sarah Sophia Banks, 23 December 1796. Miss Banks did eventually acquire two specimens of Thompson's penny: Banks MS Cat. VI, SSB 9-52-1 and 9-52 -2 (bronze).

12 Guildhall Library: S737. Cf. Welch (2010), 29-32.
Thomas Thompson (1767-1818) was said to be the natural son of 'Levi the Jew, well known in the City and on the Exchange'. In France during the peace of 1802-1803 Thompson was arrested by Napoleon on the resumption of hostilities and not released until 1815: Thorne (1986), V, 367-68.

265

'medleys' on an ever increasing scale, Kempson began to develop a more medallic approach to tokens which bore fruit in his various 'buildings' series while Skidmore tried both to ape Kempson, if more shoddily, and, more deceitfully, to juggle with a plethora of mules and fabrications to dupe his unwary metropolitan patrons. By now tokens had outrun their early claim to being something of a respectable alternative coinage; their making, at its most innocent if calculatedly profitable level, had become a 'speculation', a salve for the collector's insatiable itch or the shopkeeper's need for advertisement, and, at its most sophisticated, an insidious political weapon carried to its apogee in the hands of a Thomas Spence.

The token mania provided a heyday for the established coin dealers and spawned a mushroom growth of the dubious and the fly-by-night who sought to take advantage of the new medium. The few professional numismatists that functioned in London had already been castigated by the Scottish antiquary John Pinkerton [288] with his usual 'controversial asperity' in the second edition (1789) of his *Essay on Medals*:

288   John Pinkerton (1758-1826).

> If any man of common sense and honesty were to take up the trade of selling coins in London, he would make a fortune in a short time. This profitable business is now in the hands of one or two dealers, who ruin their own interest by making an elegant study a trade of knavery and imposition. If they buy 300 coins for 10s. they will ask 3s. for one of the worst of them! nay, sell forged coins as true to the ignorant! The simpletons complain of want of business. A knave is always a fool.[13]

Pinkerton's petulant outburst which he removed from the third edition (1808) of his *Essay* had already drawn forth from his fellow countryman, James Wright, the riposte that, while indeed most London dealers were 'knaves and fools' 'an honourable exception' had to be made of 'Henry Young of Ludgate Street, whom I have experienced to be candid, honest, & greatly superior to the imputation of imposing false coins as true; though not to be remarked for much taste or liberal education – he has considerable practical knowledge of coins, of which he makes fair use'.[14]

Henry Young (c.1738-1811), by the standards of the time, was certainly no knave. A goldsmith and jeweller – on some of his trade cards he adds the callings of 'Hardware & Toyman' – he had been established at 9 Fleet Street for a decade or more before moving east to the sign of the 'Star and Garter' at 18 Ludgate Street about the year 1779. This was just down the hill from St Paul's Cathedral, the west front of which featured on the obverse of a shop ticket he issued in both copper and silver in 1794 [289].

13   Pinkerton (1789), II, 189, footnote *.
14   NLS: Pinkerton Papers, MS. 1709, ff. 55 (5), 54 (4), James Wright, Jnr. to John Pinkerton, 24 June 1795.

COLLECTORS, DEALERS AND RADICALS

289 Peter Kempson: London shop ticket (Silver Proof) for Henry Young, 1794.

290a Henry Young's Trade Card, *c.* 1779-1784.

For reasons that are still obscure he deserted Ludgate Street in 1796 for 10 Tavistock Street, Covent Garden, but within a couple of years he was back in Ludgate Street, two doors down from his former shop in what appear from the street atlases of the time to be larger premises at no. 16 and where his son Matthew was now to play the dominant role.[15]

At an early stage he had branched out into the sale of ancient and modern coins and, judging from contemporary trade directories, by 1784 this had become a significant part of his business.[16] A decade later, perhaps increasingly under the influence of his son, coins and medals had eclipsed the other activities of the firm – a compliment slip of the mid-1790s and his metallic shop ticket would suggest this – and advantage was being taken of the token 'mania' and a new breed of collector.

290b Henry Young's Compliment Slip, *c.* 1794.

15 *GM*, March 1811, 296; Contemporary London trade directories; Hawkins (1989), 880-83.

16 London directories between 1769 and 1781 describe Young as a 'Goldsmith and Toyman' but from 1784 onwards as a 'Goldsmith and Dealer in Coins and Medals'.

267

Together with his notably more cultivated neighbour in Tavistock Street, Richard Miles, who, in terms of tokens concentrated more on the seventeenth-century series,[17] Young dominated the respectable end of the professional London coin scene and enjoyed a considerable business rapport with numismatists throughout the country and overseas. He was closely involved in the publication of Birchall's *Descriptive List* and was one of those who provided Charles Pye with information about London tokens for his *Provincial Coins and Tokens* of 1801.

After Henry Young's retirement in 1804 the business was continued and enhanced by his son until the latter's death as the doyen of the trade in 1838.[18] Matthew Young [291] not only dealt in coins and medals but he had restrikes made from Milton's 'Fullarton' dies for the collectors' market, and about the same time – 1828 – also had struck a number of specimen patterns from original Roettier Jacobite dies that had come into his possession. He also ventured more directly than his father into publishing, issuing Pye's plates of Jean Dassier's *Medals* in 1797, a reprint of Pye's 1801 catalogue in 1819 and a collected edition of Snelling's works in 1823. In 1798 while still in partnership with his father and, perhaps to mark their return to Ludgate Street, he issued a penny-sized shop ticket engraved by Milton with a broad rim in the style of Boulton [292]. Following his father's retirement he removed his business to 46 High Holborn and finally, about 1827, back to Tavistock Street at no. 41 where, shortly before his death, he engaged W. J. Taylor to produce a 'halfpenny' shop ticket the dies for which, after a false start, could not be completed before his untimely death at the age of 68. His library, vast stock of coins, medals and tokens and his personal numismatic collection was sold at Sotheby's over the four years, 1838 to 1841 for a total of nearly £10,000.[19]

291 Matthew Young (1771-1838).

---

17 For Richard Miles (1740-1819) see Richard Sainthill's obituary in *GM*, February 1820, 179-182, reprinted in Sainthill (1844), 13-21.

18 *The Gentleman's Magazine* recalled that Matthew Young was highly esteemed by the most eminent collectors 'and will be sincerely regretted for his quiet, amiable manners, his honourable dealings, and his willingness and skill to assist them in their pleasing pursuits'. He was also said to have frequently assisted Sothebys in cataloguing coins assigned to them for auction: *GM*, July 1838, 107.

19 For the 'after life' of this token see Hamer (1903-4), 315-17.
Details of the sales of Young's collections are given by Manville and Robertson (1986), 75, 76, 80, 81, 82, 83 [portion of numismatic collection reserved by Young's niece], 84 [non-numismatic items]; Manville (2009), 327.

COLLECTORS, DEALERS AND RADICALS

292   John Milton: Private London penny shop ticket for Matthew Young, 1798.

Charles Shephard, an antiquary with a ready pen, tells us in his series of 'Essays on the Provincial Half-Pennies' that the principal London token dealers in 1798 were 'Young, Hancock, Skidmore, Hammond, Spence, and Denton', company that, one suspects, Young would rather have done without.[20] John Hammond, the printer-dealer (*fl.* 1794-1810), we met at the beginning of this book. Little is known about him other than at the time of the issue of his catalogue he was also the publisher of a short-lived monthly magazine, *The Bouquet or Blossoms of Fancy*. As an inducement to prospective purchasers and contributors Hammond promised an 'ELEGANT SILVER MEDAL GRATIS … to the Author of the best Essay, or best Answer to the Prize Enigma' [293]. No examples of this are known to exist today and the magazine itself had only a short existence, as far as we can tell not surviving beyond 1796.[21] Hammond was someone who only too clearly appreciated the harvest to be reaped from the new collecting craze. As a dealer his credentials were dubious and he had a reputation for charging inflated prices but he was the first to produce a catalogue to assist collectors in the 'augmentation and arrangement' of their cabinets. What he did not do was issue his own token and in this he differed from the other four dealers listed by Shephard.

John Hancock of Leather Lane, Holborn, an umbrella maker who increasingly found coin dealing as profitable an enterprise as vending protection against the weather, went so far as to issue two substantive varieties of shop-ticket between 1796 and 1798 although probably not in any great number. Pye tells us that these were manufactured by Skidmore from dies produced by Jacobs, an obscure London engraver who specialised in topographical subjects and was responsible for the

293   Advertisement for Hammond's periodical *The Bouquet or Blossoms of Fancy*.

---

20   Shephard (1798), 120 footnote *.

21   A copy of parts of *The Bouquet* for 1796 (Volume II) exists with the additional title-page imprint of the radical bookseller H. D. Symonds as a distributor of the periodical: BL: P.P.5251.gb. Symonds was also a publisher of the *Continuation* of Denton and Prattent's *Virtuoso's Companion*.

269

COINAGE AND CURRENCY IN EIGHTEENTH-CENTURY BRITAIN

294 Skidmore: London shop ticket for John Hancock, umbrella maker and coin dealer, 1796.

295 Skidmore: London shop ticket for John Hancock, umbrella maker and coin dealer, 1798.

building medalets put out by Skidmore and by Prattent.[22]

As with many of his dies Jacobs' initial obverse for Hancock – an open umbrella displayed above a contemporary shop front [294] – was engraved on inferior steel and broke after only a few specimens were struck. The cracked die was quickly replaced with another bearing the image of an open umbrella only but paired with the original reverse. The resulting token is quite scarce and was followed in 1798 by an even rarer variety, now described as a **HALFPENNY** and bearing on its obverse a facetious armorial shield of three umbrellas and on its reverse a small boy putting coins in a precariously upright tray [295].

'Skidmore', publicly berated by Shephard as 'one of the most reprehensible dealers' of the time for his 'multiplication of obverses and reverses',[23] can be identified with a family of London iron founders and furnishing ironmongers. Originally from what was to become the Black Country around Dudley, John Skidmore (d. 1823) had established a foundry in Coppice Row, Clerkenwell about 1784 and had subsequently set up shop premises or an 'extensive Warehouse' for the 'Nobility, Gentry, and others' not far away to the west in High Holborn in 1789.[24] Four years later he had taken his eldest son, Meremoth, into partnership and early in 1795 or perhaps even late in 1794 they issued a token that though payable at the Skidmores' furnishing 'repository' was probably intended to be as much a shop ticket as a commercial halfpenny.

The obverse of the token depicts a fire-grate of the type that contemporaries labelled a 'register' stove [25] while the reverse portrays

22 Pye (1801), 10, listed Jacobs as 'B. Jacobs' and described him as a London die-sinker in his 'List of Die-Sinkers and Manufacturers'. He has been identified by some with the Birmingham ironmonger and engraver Benjamin Jacob who issued a penny token in 1798 [254] but this seems implausible since the latter was still in business in Birmingham at the relevant time. See p. 247 above and Powell (1977), 172-73.

23 Shephard (1798), 121.

24 *The Times*, 19 November 1789, 1. For the Skidmores and their tokens see Dykes (2007), 246-63 and (2010b), 200.
'Warehouse' like 'repository' was then a fashionably genteel euphemism for a shop, especially one catering for both the retail and wholesale trade A correspondent to the *London Chronicle* commented in 1765 on the affectation: 'Have we now any shops? Are they not all turned into Warehouses?'.

25 A 'register stove' was a domestic fire-grate with a 'register' or damper, a metal plate in the chimney flue used to regulate the draught and combustion of the fire. Representations of a 'register stove' also appear on the halfpennies issued by Clark and Harris (*D&H*: Middx 283-84) and William Parker (*D&H*: Dublin 351-53), respectively London and Dublin furnishing ironmongers, while earlier 'Bath Stoves' (a type of hob grate) appear on the tokens of Schooling and Son (*D&H*: Middx 474) and Michael Apsey of Bury St. Edmunds [255d], also furnishing ironmongers.

270

COLLECTORS, DEALERS AND RADICALS

296 Skidmore: London halfpenny token/trade ticket, 1795.

a traditional forge scene [296].[26] According to Pye the token was engraved by 'Wyon' and manufactured by Skidmore.[27] Although it is evident from their later muling that at some juncture the dies had come into Skidmore's possession, doubts have been expressed as to whether this initial token was actually struck by him and the suggestion has been made on grounds of style that it was minted in Birmingham. This might point to Kempson as its manufacturer and there is a 'crossover' link with Skidmore in the use of '**COVENTRY TOKEN**'-edged blanks for a tranche of the latter's buildings medalets. But this is a later development which might well be a consequence of the demise of the Skidmore coinery and the dispersal of its dies. There is no real reason to question Skidmore's being the *manufacturer* of his own halfpenny in 1794/95. In the nature of his business he would, at the very least, have had equipment that could easily have been adapted for the striking of coin while it must be remembered, too, that the token was very much a personal advertising tool which would explain why its initial standard – which lies more in its 'Wyon' design than its execution – is superior to so much of Skidmore's later slipshod production.[28]

While the 'Register Stove' obverse of his 'commercial' halfpenny gives some clue as to the main thrust of Skidmore's primary business – he boasted that he was 'Stove Grate-maker to His Majesty's Honourable Board of Ordnance' – its naturally constricted compass does less than justice to the wide variety of products he marketed, some of which were displayed in an engraved trade card that he put out at the turn of the century [297]. Here a whole emporium of tempting merchandise was illustrated: an 'improved' register stove 'on Count Rumford's plan';[29] a hall lantern; a box of 'warranted' cutlery; a patent bell-hanging system; a range 'with or without ovens and boilers &c'; a smoke jack ('greatly improved') for powering a roasting spit; and, for the carriage trade, an 'everlasting metallic nave' or wheel hub for which Skidmore had obtained a patent in August 1799, though whether it would have endured 'to the end of time' as he claimed, bearing in mind the brittleness of the cast iron of its components, must

26 The reverse quickly developed a flaw between two and four o' clock. The edge is usually diagonally milled although there are rare specimens with a plain edge while examples of the normal issue are also known in brass, with early proofs in silver which do not exhibit the flaw.

27 Pye (1801), 14 and plate XXXIV, no. 6. Skidmore's token was first listed in John Hammond's 'Christopher Williams' catalogue published by 7 May 1795 if not earlier: Williams (1795), 15, no. 147. Miss Banks, however, did not acquire a specimen until 14 October 1795: Banks MS Cat. VI, SSB 195-17.

28 Bell (1963), 121. Pye's vagueness over the quantity of pieces manufactured is also a telling point against a Birmingham provenance.

29 A 'Rumford Stove' was the recent invention of Sir Benjamin Thompson, Count von Rumford, devised to reduce downdraughts and increase the radiant heat of the fire. It had not been patented and was often copied so that Skidmore's offering may have been just such a plagiarised version.

be doubted.[30] Most of these articles would have been produced in the Clerkenwell foundry but some, the 'warranted' cutlery, for instance, would have been drawn down from a specialist cutler in Sheffield and other stock from West Midlands connections.

297   Skidmore and Son's Trade Card issued sometime between 1799 and 1801.

Utilitarian as much of Skidmore's output was he was nevertheless always alive to the demands of the affluent end of his market and did not neglect the production of highly ornamented articles to satisfy the latest decorative fashion. An innovative character, as we have seen, he had already, in 1786, been granted a patent for a process of embellishing a considerable range of merchandise, including stove grates, fenders, shovels, tongs and pokers, with 'foil stones, Bristol stones, paste, and all sorts of pinched glass, lapped glass, and every other stone, glass, and composition used in or applicable to the jewellery trade', translating the functional into showy luxuries for clients in easy circumstances.[31]

Skidmore was well placed to profit from the opportunities arising from the need to furnish and decorate the houses springing up in the Bloomsbury area in these years and despite the temporary decrease in such building that followed the outbreak of the war with France in 1793 he is unlikely to have lacked advantage from his military connections during the spate of barrack construction that was a feature of the time. In 1809 John Skidmore retired to the rural tranquillity of Nun Green

---

30   Patent Specification 2337, 8 August 1799, granted jointly to John Skidmore and George Dodson, cabinetmaker of Blackfriars Road: Woodcroft (1854) [1969], 165 and 520; the invented nave was promoted as something that 'must endure for many generations, nay, it may be supposed, to the end of time'.

31   Patent Specification 1552, 5 August 1786: Woodcroft (1854) [1969], 520.
     Patents, in themselves, were a form of advertisement, 'a sign of modernity and technical ingenuity ... displaying the patent holder's place in enlightened society as a creator of novelties, as making advances based on scientific principles, as part of the world of the arts': Berg (2005), 179.

COLLECTORS, DEALERS AND RADICALS

298a Skidmore: Specious Worcestershire penny token for Meremoth Skidmore, [1796].

298b Skidmore: Specious 'Hyde Park halfpenny' for Gamaliel Skidmore, [1796].

in Peckham and what was clearly an established business was taken over by Meremoth who a few months later entered into a new joint partnership with a younger brother, Gamaliel [298a and b].

Although the Skidmores' coinery was subsidiary to the main focus of their business, for two or three years in the mid-seventeen-nineties it proved to be the most prolific of London token manufactories, calculated to reap some economic advantage from the token collecting 'mania' that was reaching its peak by the beginning of the year 1795.[32] One can be fairly positive that it was actually operating commercially at the time of the production of the 'commercial halfpenny' or at least very soon afterwards. Unhappily, in trying to date the earliest Skidmore tokens more precisely one is handicapped by the absence of any published catalogue prior to the spring of 1795. We do know, however, that in the March of that year Miss Banks bought a specimen of Salter's shop ticket [253]. While Pye did not specify a manufacturer for this token he did credit the die-cutting to Jacobs and it is a reasonable presumption, therefore, that it was produced in the Skidmore foundry.[33] By the May of 1795 when Hammond's and Spence's initial catalogues had come out it is apparent that Skidmore was well entrenched in the manufacture of tokens.[34] It is likely that Skidmore had started the coining business during the winter with the intention of manufacturing commercial tokens or shop tickets. Coming relatively late on the token-making scene, however, he was able to attract few commissions of this kind – those of Price (Hendon), Henderson ('Filtering Stone Warehouse'), James Spittle ('Blackfriars') [299], Salter and of course his own were among the earliest [35] – and he was quickly making specious tokens for general sale; for instance the 'Dudley' and 'Brighton' halfpennies put out respectively, according to Miss Banks, by the engraver Charles James [300] and by Benjamin

---

32 Shephard (1798), 120, states that the 'enthusiasm' for collecting tokens was the 'most prevalent and regular in the latter part of the year 1794'.

33 Banks MS Cat. VI, SSB, 192.75; Pye (1801), 14; Waters (1906), 34. On 17 March 1795 Miss Banks also acquired a Spence 'Odd Fellows' ('Pitt & Fox') halfpenny, a token that can plausibly be attributed to Skidmore's coinery: Banks MS 'List of coins ...'.

34 Between them they described at least twenty-one tokens that can be plausibly attributed to Skidmore's manufactory in addition to his 'commercial halfpenny': see Dykes (2007), 251-53.

35 To this list Hammond's *Virtuoso's Guide* (July) adds Edinburgh, Campbell (*D&H*: Lothian 13) and London, Schooling (*D&H*: Middx 474); and Spence's *Supplement* (August 1795), Birmingham 'William Allan' (*sic – recte* 'Hallan') (*D&H*: War. 131) also. While Pye (1801) accepts all three as genuine commercial tokens there must be considerable doubt about the last.

Miss Banks identified 'Henderson, the corner of Rupert street' as the issuer of the 'Filtering Stone' halfpenny and 'James Spittle' as that of 'Blackfriars': Banks MS Cat. VI, SSB 191-165 ('Filtering Stone') and SSB192-99 ('Blackfriars'). She acquired the latter in May 1795.

273

Deverell, an orange merchant in Fleet Market [301].[36]

Skidmore must also have been striking Spence's political pieces at this time but it was not until considerably later in 1795 that he began to imitate the latter's technique of intermixing dies. On 14 December a whole plate of Denton and Prattent's *Virtuoso's Companion* [301] was devoted to the 'Brighton' halfpenny and its mules (including the Spence 'Heart in Hand' reverse (*D&H*: Sussex 6-9)). And by the turn of the year, judging from Birchall's *Descriptive List*, Skidmore was interchanging dies extensively, including some of Spence's long before the latter gave up business. When eventually Spence sold the bulk of his dies to Skidmore the latter proceeded to produce even more varietal mules for collectors although few of them captured the political purpose or wry wit of the radical's bizarre extravaganza and some of them made a nonsense of the original message intended; they were simply a 'jobbing' enterprise to gull collectors through the creation of freak and costly varieties.[37]

299   Skidmore: London shop ticket for James Spittle, cheesemonger, Blackfriars, [1794-95].

300   Skidmore: Specious 'Dudley Token' for Charles James, die engraver, [1794-95].

36   Banks MS Cat. VI, SSB 188-8 and SSB 186-167 acquired respectively in June and May 1795. Pye (1795), 'Advertisement', note *, tells us that neither token was known to be in circulation in the towns named on them.
The 'Shepherd' reverse of the 'Dudley' halfpenny, which would have had personal resonance with Skidmore, was also used as the reverse of Spence's 'Deserted Village' token often with its false date of '1790' partially effaced [313]: see p. 280 below. The scene is said to have been taken from an engraving by W. Hawkins in *The Works* (1794 edition) of William Shenstone, the Staffordshire landscape gardener and poet.

37   *D&P*, Plate 45; Birchall (1796), 12 (no. 50), 73 (no. 172), 122 (no. 37) and 128 (no. 200). Birchall's catalogue is dated by its prefatorial subscription, 'January 30 1796'.

301 Benjamin Deverell's 'Brighton' halfpenny (top) and its mules. *The Virtuoso's Companion*, Plate 45, 14 December 1795.

How the coinery was organised is far from clear but most of its medallic productions came to be identified by the monogram '*PSC°*' or the name '**P. SKIDMORE**'. Since the mid-nineteenth century these designations have been associated with a 'Peter' Skidmore said to have been the 'Son' of 'Skidmore and Son' (in reality, of course, this was Meremoth Skidmore). It is now known thanks to Miss Banks that they refer in fact to Skidmore's second son Paul.[38] Little is known about Paul Skidmore other than his birth in December 1775 and his apprenticeship to a member of the Tylers' Company in 1789. This

---

38   See Dykes (2007) and Banks MS Cat. VI, SSB,191.9-1, listing an undated 'Clerkenwell – St. Martin Ludgate' 'halfpenny' medalet (*D&H*: Middx 612) acquired on 12 April 1796.

302 Skidmore: Specious 'Kidderminster Halfpenny' for 'T. Santer', [1795].

303 Skidmore: 'London Churches and Gates' series medalet of St John's Gate, 1797.

never seems to have been completed perhaps because of the start-up of the coinery which must have taken place when he could have been no more than nineteen. He is not mentioned in John Skidmore's will of 22 August 1822 and had presumably died by then. Indeed, the fact that he never became a partner in the family ironmongery firm might suggest that he had died many years before.

It was probably about the autumn of 1795 that Paul Skidmore began to take a more prominent part in an already established enterprise and perhaps to turn some artistic talent to practical effect, a progression exemplified with the issue of the 'Kidderminster' halfpenny [302] and leading in the winter to the launch of the *PSC°* 'Buildings' 'halfpennies' [303].[39] These, starting with the undated issues, were to continue into 1797 when penny module pieces – the 'Clerkenwell' [304] and the 'Globe' series – were added to the coinery's architectural portfolio. To what extent the designations '*PSC°*' or the name '**P. Skidmore**' distinguished an entity separate from the ironmongery concern cannot be established but it is unrealistic to believe that John Skidmore, even if influenced by his son, did not fund the undertaking as an opportunistic facet of his main business. Contemporaries invariably referred to the coinery and the coin dealership under the name 'Skidmore' or 'Skidmore, an ironmonger of Holborn' implying that for all practical purposes they saw the undertakings as run by John Skidmore himself.

These medallic tokens were intended as collectors' items even if, compared to the similar pieces of Kempson, they were struck from dies of inferior steel indifferently engraved. But alongside this medallic output, the firm remained active in intermixing the dies of its other tokens a practice that became more extensive with the transfer of most of Spence's dies into Skidmore's ownership in the winter of 1796/97.[40] Over the next twelve months the coinery was at its busiest but collectors were already beginning to react against the multiplicity of mules, their artificially contrived scarcity and their cost. Interest in the

304 Skidmore 'Clerkenwell' series medalet of the Small Pox Hospital, St Pancras, [1797].

39 Interestingly Thomas Sharp identified 'P. Skidmore' as a die-sinker, attributing to him among other tokens some of the 'Clerkenwell' dies not signed by Jacobs: see Dykes (2007), 260-61.

40 One cannot posit a precise date for Skidmore's acquisition of the Spence dies because of the vagueness of the available evidence provided by 'R. Y.' (1797), 471 and Shephard (1798), 122.

COLLECTORS, DEALERS AND RADICALS

'Buildings' pieces was also beginning to wane and by February 1798 Shephard was noting that new tokens were becoming fewer. Already, however, the Skidmore coinery was running down and towards the end of 1797 it effectively ceased production of new issues.

The thrust of Skidmore's coining activities was directed to the collectors' market and it is more than likely that he was one of the backers of the *Virtuoso's Companion* (1795-97) which, according to Hay, was supported by the 'inferior manufacturers and jobbers in provincial Tokens ... in order to induce hasty collectors to buy the trash they circulated'.[41] As well as striking for Spence Skidmore certainly produced at least some of the shoddy pieces engraved by or for Matthew Denton, a printer and engraver of Hospital Gate and then St. John Street, West Smithfield, and for Thomas Prattent of near-by Cloth Fair.

305 Prattent's engraving of the Albion Flour Mill, Blackfriars. From the *European Magazine*, May 1787.

41   Hay quoted in [Preston]-Morley (1971-74), (1971), 4.

COINAGE AND CURRENCY IN EIGHTEENTH-CENTURY BRITAIN

306   Skidmore or William Williams: 'London and Westminster' series medalet for Thomas Prattent: Albion Flour Mill, 1797.

Prattent (*fl.* 1787-1819), himself an engraver and printseller well known for his topographical plates in the magazines of the period [305], was responsible for the 'London and Westminster' series of 'Buildings' medalets [306] and a number of specious issues [307] although he seems to have relied on William Williams, the St. Martin's Lane button maker, for the manufacture of at least part of his output. He was the 'proprietor' of the *Virtuoso's Companion* and undertook all the engravings for the catalogue while Denton, until the spring of 1797 when he moved away from the area to Mead Row in Lambeth, was its publisher. With Denton, a possible relation of Thomas Denton, the Holborn bookseller and silver-plater hanged for coining in 1789, we are certainly plumbing the depths of the trade.[42] Denton combined the sale of tokens with his printing and engraving business. His own crude productions left a great deal to be desired in both design and execution but they could occasionally be humorous. Although he admitted it to his 1801 catalogue Pye thought Denton's 'Blockheads' farthing [281a] 'execrable'.[43] Nevertheless, the obverse image seems to have proved sufficiently popular for Denton to recycle it to advertise the bloodletting and dental expertise of a neighbouring Smithfield barber [308].[44]

Surprisingly, Denton is said to have been responsible for a specious 'North Shields Halfpenny' [309] which is far superior to the general run of either his own or Prattent's output. The attribution, based on the use of the centre of the token's obverse die with those for a Smithfield and a Lambeth farthing put out by Denton, is, however, a shaky one. It is likely that the latter concoctions – and that using Prattent's 'Loyal Britons Lodge' [307] – result not from Denton's enterprise but from the coinery he employed. The finger naturally points to the Skidmores and the issue serves to punctuate the murky and complex relationship that existed between the Skidmores, Prattent, Denton and Spence, a relationship that in the present state of our knowledge is virtually impossible to unravel.

307   Skidmore: Specious 'London Commercial Token' obverse with 'Loyal Britons Lodge' reverse for Thomas Prattent, 1796

308   Skidmore: Matthew Denton's farthing for Harrison, barber of West Smithfield, 1797.

42   *Proceedings of the Old Bailey*, 3 June 1789; *The Times*, 2 July 1789, 3

43   Whether Denton engraved his own dies is unclear. See note 5, p. 263 above.

44   Pye (1801), 12. The suggestion by Samuel (1880-89), 25 October 1882, 448, that Harrison was in reality a brewer seems to arise from his confusing Long Lane, West Smithfield with the similarly-named street in Southwark.

COLLECTORS, DEALERS AND RADICALS

309   Skidmore: Specious 'North Shields Halfpenny', 1795.

310   Thomas Spence (1750-1814). From an engraving by Thomas Bewick, 1810.

The driving force of most of this coterie was the profit that might be gained from the naivety of collectors. For Thomas Spence [310], though, the promotion of tokens was only incidentally a money-making concern.[45] A poor schoolmaster from Newcastle upon Tyne, self-educated and imbued with millenarian ideas and notions about the natural rights and equality of men, personal setbacks and hostility to his advanced views on the collective ownership of land – his 'Plan'– caused him to move to London towards the end of the 1780s. By 1792 he had set up a stall at the corner of Chancery Lane and Holborn selling radical tracts and pamphlets (many of his own composition), promoting his 'Plan', and involving himself in the progressive politics of the heady days following the French Revolution.[46] His passionate propaganda and extremist associations led to his arrest on a number of occasions and, self-appointed as 'the unfee'd Advocate of the disinherited seed of Adam',[47] he became regarded by the government as a 'violent democrat' although Pitt himself is said to have seen him as a harmless Utopian crank of little consequence. By the early part of 1793 he had moved to new premises, the 'Hive of Liberty' – 'a dirty house' – in Little Turnstile, a narrow passage off Holborn, where he kept up his unremitting literary output [311].[48] But Spence was always on the brink of penury and to keep himself afloat he added coins and tokens to the tracts and pamphlets he had for sale. No doubt he had an eye to the income that might be generated from the burgeoning collectors' market but, as with his handbills and prints and the graffiti he chalked on walls, he was quick to appreciate the value tokens might have as a 'short-hand' means of disseminating his ideas among working people who would not necessarily be reached by his lengthier publications. Thus by the spring of 1795 when he brought out his *Coin Collector's Companion* he had embarked on the production

311   Skidmore: 'Little Turnstile Halfpenny' for Thomas Spence, 1796.

---

45   For Spence see *ODNB*; Rudkin (1966); Ashraf (1983); Wood (1994), esp. 64-89. For Spence's tokens see Waters (1917), esp. 9-11; Thompson (1969), 126-62; (1971), 136-38 and (1976), 671-79.

46   He also sold saloop, a hot drink of milk, sugar and powdered sassafras.

47   Quoted in Rudkin (1966), 114.

48   McCalman (1988), 66; Brown (1918), 135.

279

COINAGE AND CURRENCY IN EIGHTEENTH-CENTURY BRITAIN

312 Skidmore: 'Cain and Abel' agrarian reform token for Thomas Spence, [1795].

313 Skidmore: 'Deserted Village' agrarian reform token for Thomas Spence, 1795.

of his own political pieces to add to the wide-ranging literary armoury he used to broadcast his views.

As Eneas Mackenzie, an early Spence biographer, put it, 'one of the singular plans he adopted of attracting public attention to his plan was the striking of a variety of copper coins' which 'he frequently distributed by jerking them from his window' to any passer-by.[49] But Spence's tokens went far beyond his 'Plan' as 'R.Y.', almost certainly the collector William Robert Hay and a man of decidedly conservative inclinations, shrewdly intimated to the *Gentleman's Magazine*. He recalled visiting Spence's shop where he saw 'many thousands of different tokens lying in heaps…These, therefore, could not be considered as struck for a limited sale. I confess, considering the number I saw struck, and what the subjects of them were, I thought myself justified in supposing that it was the intention to circulate them very widely'.[50] To Mackenzie some of Spence's tokens were 'extremely curious'. They were, in fact, often quite brilliant satirical productions, based on popular imagery, folklore and aphorism the meaning of which virtually any beholder, however uneducated, would be able to grasp, with dies that were designed to be combined in different pairings to drive home a variety of messages. As Hay, annotating his copy of the *Virtuoso's Companion*, realised, Spence's dies 'tho not apparently mischievous in themselves, were capable of making a strong impression when mixed with others … [W]ithout arrangement of them, one could scarcely conceive how industrious and ingenious these jacobins were, in the instance of medals, to poison the minds of the Community'.[51]

It was natural that Spence should use his tokens to express his sentiments on agrarian reform and with his 'Cain and Abel'/'Bonfire' combination he did so quite dramatically; landlord oppression began with the first murder and such tyranny would end only when all the deeds embodying the ownership of land were surrendered and burnt [312]. A grim vista of rural decay resulting from enclosures with the legend **ONLY ONE MASTER GRASPS THE WHOLE DOMAIN**, the latter scene being derived from a Bewick illustration to Goldsmith's *Deserted Village* from which the quotation is taken [313], was often coupled with the more placid prospect of a shepherd reclining in a pastoral landscape – the reverse of James's 'Dudley' halfpenny with its false original date frequently partially obliterated [300] – to emphasise the happy consequence of the adoption of Spence's 'Plan'.[52] The underlying theme of the advantage taken of a docile populace was brought into play again in Spence's animal imagery; an ass, for example, overladen with the double burdens of rents and taxes is contrasted with a free North American Indian brave declaring **IF RENTS I ONCE CONSENT TO PAY MY LIBERTY IS PASSED AWAY**. Even more effective is a

---

49 Mackenzie (1827), I, 401.

50 'R.Y.' (1797), 269; Dykes (1997), 122.

51 [Preston]-Morley (1971-74), (1971), 109.

52 See p. 279 above.

COLLECTORS, DEALERS AND RADICALS

314 Skidmore: 'Freedom and Servitude' satirical token for Thomas Spence, 1796.

sly satire that at first sight might seem to be pure entertainment where an independent London alley cat [53] stares fixedly at the onlooker with the legend **MY FREEDOM I + AMONG SLAVES ENJOY +** and is contrasted with an eager-to-please dog, stick in mouth, and the legend **MUCH GRATITUDE . BRINGS SERVITUDE** [314]. Here, as Robert Thompson demonstrated in his seminal studies of Spence's dies, Spence could on occasion rise to the level of the universal and offer 'a profound insight into the nature of society'.[54]

Spence's tokens with their striking images and pithy, slogan-like legends must have reached further than many of his often bewildering literary outpourings but how effective they were in disseminating his message will never be known. They probably unnerved establishment figures like Hay more than they excited the working people they were aimed at. As Robert Thompson has pointed out, while they were intended to circulate, few of Spence's pieces show signs of much wear and were probably picked up as curiosities more than anything else. Nevertheless, their propaganda purpose was clear and they were sometimes tied in with equally accessible prints or etchings. His 'over-burdened ass' 'halfpenny' was, for instance, adapted as a broadside just as his 'farthing' token of a man walking on all fours was mirrored in his son's caricature of *The Civil Citizen*. The latter image coupled on some tokens with that of a padlock and the word **MUM** conveyed an instantly recognisable thrust against the government's 'Gagging Acts' of December 1795 [315a and b].

315 (a) Spence's farthing token of a man walking on all fours, inscribed IF THE LAW REQUIRES IT WE WILL WALK THUS (enlarged) based on (b) the caricature print, THE CIVIL CITIZEN 1796, etched by his son William Spence (d.c. 1797)

53   Mackenzie said that Spence regarded the figure of the cat as his personal symbol because like the cat 'he could be stroked down, but he would not suffer himself to be rubbed against the grain': Mackenzie (1827), I, 401. The token was one of Spence's favourites and was buried with him at his request.

54   Thompson (1976), 671.

316 Skidmore: Anti-Pitt halfpenny token for Thomas Spence, [1796].

317 Skidmore: Anti-Pitt farthing token for Thomas Spence, 1796.

It was Spence's aggressively revolutionary tokens that were to make the most impact on contemporaries and to bring down upon him the opprobrium expressed in the *Gentleman's Magazine*. Spence's most virulent satire was reserved for Pitt, associated with the Devil, Janus-like, on his **EVEN FELLOWS** 'farthing' and with the prime minister's severed head set atop a pole surrounded by a group of exulting yokels on his **TREE OF LIBERTY** 'halfpenny' [316]. On his **END OF PIT** token Spence goes even further showing Pitt hanging from a gallows with the 'I' of Pitt's name represented by the all-seeing and approving eye of God; to drive home the motif more directly the legend **SUCH IS THE REWARD OF TYRANTS 1796** backs on to some farthing versions of the image [317].

Spence's attacks on Pitt had already been a feature of his penny weekly *One Penny Worth of Pig's Meat: Lessons for the Swinish Multitude* that he produced between 1793 and 1795 and later reprinted in volume form [318].

318 Frontispiece to *Pig's Meat*.

It was the cheapest of all the radical periodicals of the time, comprising a medley of his own poems and articles and with extracts from other writers that Spence had fastened upon to support his schemes for reform and his commitment to revolution.[55] Spence repeatedly advertised *Pig's Meat* on tokens showing a pig trampling on emblems of church and state, a device taken from the frontispiece to the bound volumes of the journal and capitalising on Edmund Burke's [319] fear, expressed in his *Reflections*, that learning under the Revolution in France would be destroyed and 'trodden down under

319 John Westwood, Jnr.: Specious 'Malton Penny' in commemoration of Edmund Burke, 1798.

55 Cf. Rudkin (1966), 16-20.

COLLECTORS, DEALERS AND RADICALS

320 Skidmore: 'Pigs Meat' farthing token for Thomas Spence, [1795].

321 Thomas Spence's Handbill of *New Coins*, 1796/97.

the hoofs of a swinish multitude'.[56] Some versions of this device, in both halfpenny and farthing sizes, are complemented with his self-advertising 'Bewick' portrait and reference to his imprisonment for treasonable practices in 1794 [320].

Though Spence was to remain active as a polemicist pursuing 'his earnest desire to benefit mankind' for the best part of another two decades his token-making days were soon over. In the winter of 1796/97 he produced a handbill of *New Coins* [321].[57] Although this circular provides documentary evidence of the extent of Spence's muling some of the intended combinations were never produced and the advertisement must have been Spence's swan song for about this time, it seems, he gave up dealing in tokens and sold his dies 'principally, if not entirely' to Skidmore. Even if profit had never been his chief concern his token venture had been a commercial failure – he probably never attracted many actual buyers except among collectors, most of his tokens being given away as free publicity – and according to Shephard 'Spence experienced the punishment of his dishonesty, and became a bankrupt'. His financial state, always precarious, was probably also the cause of his departure from Little Turnstile to 9 Oxford Street where he had set up a small shop by March 1797.[58]

Spence, of course, was following in a more sophisticated and imaginative fashion an age-old practice of simplifying complex ideas for popular consumption, a practice adopted only a few years earlier over Paine's *The Rights of Man* the 'cream and substance' of which was made much more accessible to people in the form of chap books, broadsides and medals than through the lengthy pamphlet itself. Examples of the medals, far cruder than anything Spence would have contemplated until he embarked, much later, on countermarking coins, are two lead pieces which Miss Banks tells us 'were distributed at Dundee instead of Tom Paine's Book … now hardly to be seen having been stopped by the leading People'.[59] The obverse legend of [322a], **THE NATION IS ESSENTIALLY THE SOURCE OF ALL SOVEREIGNTY,**

56 Burke (1790) [1989], 130: 'Along with its natural protectors and guardians, learning will be cast into the mire, and trodden down under the hoofs of a swinish multitude'. Although Burke clearly directed the phrase 'swinish multitude' at the revolutionaries in France it cost Burke dear being endlessly taken out of context and presented to mean that he regarded the common people of Britain as swine.
The 'pig' emblem may have originated in a Bewick woodcut. Miss Rudkin noted that it bore 'a striking resemblance to the picture of a wonderful performing pig in the *Newcastle Chronicle*, July 27, 1787': Rudkin (1966), 16.

57 Miss Banks had two copies of the handbill bound in with her *Supplements* to the *Coin Collector's Companion*: RM Library.

58 'R. Y.' (1797), 471; Shephard (1798), 122; Thompson (1969), 128. Spence's removal from Holborn also seems to have coincided with the death of his son perhaps from smallpox: Rudkin (1966), 94-95.

59 Banks MS Cat. VI, 'Seditious Tokens, &c.', 5. They were probably also the pieces 'with inscriptions expressive of liberty and equality' reported in 1792 to have been 'in circulation among the commonalty': Meikle (1912), 95.

283

322a

322b

322 Seditious lead medals (BHM: 501 and 502) made and distributed in Scotland in 1792.

is the first clause of article III of the *Declaration of the Rights of Man* while that of [322b] is Lafayette's maxim, **FOR A NATION TO BE FREE IT IS SUFFICIENT THAT IT WILLS IT**. Both statements would have been perfectly familiar to readers of Part I of Paine's work and no doubt they were commonly reiterated slogans but, to bring the message home, references to impress warrants, equal representation and just taxation were added to the agenda.[60] Struck by James Bell, a Leith tinman, the medals, 'bearing inscriptions of a seditious tendency ... obviously calculated to stir up a spirit of insurrection and opposition to the established government', achieved more than a passing notoriety as part of the evidence cited in one of the earliest Scottish treason trials in January 1793.[61]

Thomas Spence was not the only bookseller involved in the advanced radical movements of the 1790s or to be incarcerated in 'black Newgate' because of his activities as fears of Jacobin-inspired domestic upheaval gripped the country in the face of war with France. But only one other issued his own token. Like Spence, a member of the London Corresponding Society, Daniel Isaac Eaton [323] was at the centre of the controversy surrounding Paine's *The Rights of Man* and was twice arraigned for publishing libellous pamphlets in 1793.[62] Later that year he set up his own printing press and began publishing *Hog's Wash* – later retitled *Politics for the People, or a Salmagundy for Swine*. Like Spence's *Pig's Meat* it was a satirical weekly designed to spread political enlightenment among the masses and, again, like *Pig's Meat* it was a mixture of original articles, excerpts from other authors, ballads and verses. When, in its eighth issue, Eaton published a satire by John Thelwall traducing the King as a game-cock, 'a haughty sanguinary tyrant of the farmyard', he was again prosecuted for seditious libel but once more acquitted, an event triumphantly celebrated by a medal struck by the London Corresponding Society. Engraved by Florimond Goddard, a clock and watchmaker of 8 Rathbone Place, fourteen silver versions were struck for presentation to the defence counsel and jurymen concerned in the trial.[63] Based on the theme of Thelwall's allegory it depicted a 'Bantum Cock' on its obverse with the names of

60 Paine (1791) [1994], 80 and 91.
    An impress warrant, countersigned by a chief magistrate or his deputy, was the necessary legal authority to allow a press-gang to operate in a particular locality.
61 Howell & Howell (1817), 30-31.
62 For Eaton see *ODNB*; Wood (1994), 89-93; and Longman (1916), 29-33.
63 Goddard was a member of the Corresponding Society. Copper and white metal versions of the medal (the latter for sale to members of the Society at 6*d* each) were also produced but a dispute having arisen between Goddard and the Society over the price of his die and the sale of the copper medals, the medals were handed over to Thomas Hardy, the founder and secretary of the Society, and were impounded when he was arrested on 12 May 1794: Thale (1983) 117,123, 154, 260, 268, 274 and 276.

COLLECTORS, DEALERS AND RADICALS

323 Daniel Isaac Eaton (*c*.1753-1814).

324 Manufacturer unknown: London Corresponding Society medal celebrating the acquittal of Daniel Eaton, 1794.

the jurymen on the reverse [324].[64]

Although dated 14 March 1794 the medals were seized before they could be issued and it was not until July 1795 that they were returned to the Society and distributed to the recipients. In the meantime Eaton had issued his own medalet based on a design made for the frontispiece of the first number of *Hog's Wash* by another member of the Society, William Worship, a printseller and engraver of Ball Court, Lombard Street. Worship's original drawing represented 'Swine feeding out of *a trough*, and a *Cock* upon some paling in the back Ground, on one Side an Oak tree on the other the Tree of Liberty'. Combined with an obverse profile portrait of Eaton this was simplified for the medalet that according to Pye was engraved by William Davies and struck by Good [325].[65] As 'The Cock and Swine' the device was also adopted by Eaton as the sign for his premises at 74 Newgate Street.

325 James Good: Celebratory medalet for the acquittal of Daniel Eaton, 1795.

Eaton was just one of a number of extreme radical propagandists to be arrested for political activities during the Pitt government's so-called 'Reign of Terror', an 'Aera when', as James Wright put it, 'British-Men, like the ill-fated Romans during the detestible [*sic*] Spy-system under the legislation of Tib[erius] – are liable to imprisonment, banishment & mulct, for speaking & publishing abstract opinions!'.[66] Daniel Holt, a Newark printer, two London booksellers, James Ridgway and Henry Delahay Symonds – a publisher, incidentally, of the *Continuation* of Denton and Prattent's *Virtuoso's Companion* – and William Winterbotham, a Baptist minister from Plymouth and friend of Robert Southey, all ended up in the State Side of Newgate Prison for propagating seditious views, their confinement commemorated on a 'halfpenny' token, said by Pye to have been engraved for Kempson by one of the Wyons [326]. Unlike Eaton only their names are inscribed on the token but we can form a fairly accurate idea of the

---

64 Thale (1983), 117. Originally the silver medals were to be given to the jurymen and it was only at a later stage that the two barristers (Felix Vaughan and John Gurney) were added to the proposed recipients. This is why they are not referred to on the medal.

65 Thale (1983), 169; Pye (1801), 13.

66 NLS: Pinkerton Papers MS 1709: James Wright, Jnr. to John Pinkerton, postscript to letter of 13 August 1795, f.59.

COINAGE AND CURRENCY IN EIGHTEENTH-CENTURY BRITAIN

326 Peter Kempson: 'Newgate' 'halfpenny' commemorating the imprisonment of Symonds, Winterbotham, Ridgway and Holt, 1795.

appearance of Holt, Ridgway and Symonds from some fascinating portrait caricatures by Richard Newton (1777-1798), the precocious young cartoonist who worked for the radically minded publisher, William Holland, imprisoned in Newgate at the same time. Two of Newton's caricatures, *Soulagement en Prison or Comfort in Prison* [327] and *Promenade in the State Side of Newgate* [328], show how the prison's political inmates could, in Francis Place's words, be 'comfortably accommodated, well provided for as to food' and able to have their friends 'not only to visit them but sometimes to dine with them'.[67] But such advantages were gratified only at a price and the State Side was crowded with felons who could also pay for the privilege of being housed there,[68] so crowded, in fact, that shortly after the caricatures

327 *Soulagement en Prison or Comfort in Prison*. Watercolour drawing for an etching by Richard Newton, August 1793. Included in this group of prisoners and visitors dining in the State Side of Newgate in August 1793 are Lord George Gordon (extreme left), William Holland (below Gordon), Thomas Townley Macan (3rd from the left on the near side of the table), James Ridgway (4th from the left and facing Macan) and Henry Delahay Symonds (to the right of Ridgway and holding the tankard). On the far side of the table are Daniel Holt (above and to the right of Ridgway), next to him Daniel Isaac Eaton (immediately above the bottle to the left of Ridgway) with Joseph Gerald facing Gordon, glass in hand. The young man standing full face to the observer and next to the servant, Mrs Moore, is almost certainly the seventeen-year-old Newton himself.[69]

67 Francis Place (BL: Additional MSS. 27808, f. 95) quoted in George (1942), No. 8339.

68 Cf. Eaton's *Extortions and Abuses of Newgate* (1813), quoted in Waters (1906), 18.

69 I am grateful to Susan Walker of the Lewis Walpole Library for the above identification. It differs from those of George (1942), No. 8339 and Alexander (1998), 120-21, which were based on a photograph of a completed but divergent etching.

COLLECTORS, DEALERS AND RADICALS

were drawn it was ravaged by gaol fever. Lord George Gordon – in Newgate for a libel of Marie Antoinette since 1788 and the subject of a Spence halfpenny [329] – and Thomas Townley Macan – imprisoned for attempting to blow up the King's Bench Prison – both died of the disease in November 1793 while soon after his release in 1797 Holt died of consumption brought on by his four-year confinement.

328 Detail from *Promenade in the State Side of Newgate*, 5 October 1793. Included in this etching by Richard Newton are John Horne Tooke (3rd from left), Lord George Gordon (centre), behind him to the right Henry Delahay Symonds, then James Ridgway and Daniel Isaac Eaton (the small man in the tricorne hat) with Daniel Holt at the extreme right of the group.[70]

329 Skidmore: Lord George Gordon (1751-93), the obverse of a token for Thomas Spence, [1795].

Most of the individuals depicted in the cartoons were prominent members of the London Corresponding Society (LCS), the most influential of all the radical societies of the period.[71] It had been established in January 1792 during the early enthusiasm generated by events in France and inspired by Tom Paine's *Rights of Man* to promote the cause of parliamentary reform and form links with groups of similar persuasion throughout the country. The Society's founder, Thomas Hardy, was a Piccadilly shoemaker and although some of its leading lights were broadly from 'the middling sort', attorneys, medical men, writers, booksellers and printers, most of its membership was drawn from the politically conscious and articulate artisan population of London, 'tradesmen, mechanicks and shopkeepers' and

70 George (1942), No. 8342; Alexander (1998), 37-38.
71 For the LCS see Brown (1918); Collins (1954) and Thale (1983).

287

'journeymen of all kinds'. With its low weekly subscription (1*d*) and campaign for annual parliaments and universal manhood suffrage the Society was designed to appeal to 'men beyond the political pale'. Yet, although popular, the LCS was never a proletarian society and while it certainly contained rabble-rousers eager to murder Pitt and guillotine the King its active membership was drawn from the more skilled and sober ranks of the working population, hardly 'the very lowest order of society ... filthy & ragged ... wretched looking blackguards' that many detractors made out.[72]

In its early hopeful days the Society's energies were directed to mobilizing support for its ideas through readings and debates at its meetings and the publication and widespread distribution of pamphlets and tracts across the country. Though its expressed emphasis had been on political change through constitutional means, its championship of Paine's writings and its questioning of the existing property order coupled with its countrywide networking, cellular organization and moves towards establishing a national convention on the French model thoroughly alarmed an establishment which, in Burke's words, saw the Society increasingly as a subversive and clandestine 'Mother of all Mischief'.[73] By 1793, impelled by the drift to extremism in France, fear of invasion and of revolutionary conspiracy at home, the government decided to take action against the LCS and the older, more prestigious Society for Constitutional Information (SCI) and to strike against some of their leaders including Hardy, John Thelwall and John Horne Tooke on charges of high treason.[74] Hardy's acquittal in November 1794, followed by those of Tooke and Thelwall and the dropping of charges against the other accused, was greeted with jubilation 'expressed without restraint' [75] and led to a flood of medals and tokens celebrating the events and the brilliant advocacy of Thomas Erskine and Vicary Gibbs, the defence barristers [330].

Although the treason prosecutions had frightened away many members of the Society the acquittals quickly restored its credit and in the dire economic conditions of 1795 – commonly attributed to the war with France – numbers began to pick up again. Amid cries of 'Bread' and 'No War' support for the Society was drummed up through mass open air meetings and it was probably as part of this proselyting effort in the autumn of that year that a medalet was widely distributed to publicise the Society [331].

With the rallying cry of **UNITED FOR A REFORM OF PARLIAMENT** it stressed the peaceful intentions of the Society, called for an end to the war with France and for unity in the face

330 Skidmore: Medalet celebrating the failure of the 1794 treason trials and the advocacy of Erskine and Gibbs, the defence lawyers, 1794.

---

72 Thale (1983), xix.

73 Weinstein (2002), 37.

74 Although Tooke, a leading light of the SCI and regarded by Pitt as the 'heart of the reform movement' (Brown (1918), 52), was never formally a member of the LCS he was very much its mentor.

75 *Annual Register*, 1794, 279. For the trials see Brown (1918).

COLLECTORS, DEALERS AND RADICALS

331 William Lutwyche (?): Medalet publicising the London Corresponding Society, 1795.

of repression. Its obverse image was taken from an engraving of Aesop's fable of the ploughman's quarrelsome sons,[76] sponsored by John Williams, a Leicester Square wine merchant, which had been adopted the previous year for the Society's membership tickets. Representing unity through strength it depicted the allegory of an old man instructing his sons how to break a bundle of sticks 'by pulling one at a time & thus destroying that Body which could not be broke when tied together'.[77] Perhaps by analogy with the 'Erskine/Gibbs' medalets the token is said to have been engraved by one of the Wyons and although there is nothing concrete to substantiate this some of the mules that resulted from the use of the obverse must have emanated from the Lutwyche workshop; others though suggest a London provenance, pointing to Williams or more likely Skidmore.[78] At the same time, while there is no positive evidence that the medalet was actually issued by the LCS itself, a request addressed to the Society by a radical Edinburgh bookseller in July 1796, for its publications, and 'more especially medals like half-pence, for which there was a demand', might well suggest that this was so.[79]

The revival of the LCS was short-lived for Pitt's two 'Gagging Acts' of December 1795 (The Treasonable Practices Act and the Seditious Meetings Act) effectively destroyed the Society as an organization with a broad popular membership. By 1798 all that was left was an alienated rump of activists who, driven deeply underground and rejecting the peaceful campaigning methods of its earlier leadership, had adopted the conspiratorial and treasonable character so grimly depicted in the 'grotesque, satanic enormity' of a frightening cartoon by James Gillray [332].[80] By July 1799 the Society had been suppressed.

---

76 See Temple and Temple (1998), 68

77 Thale (1983), 197-98, quoting the Government spy John Groves' report of the LCS General Committee meeting, 10 July 1794.

78 Cf. Waters (1906), 17 and (1954), 13. Sharp (1834), 157, specifies no die-sinker for this token.

79 Meikle (1912), 185.

80 Brewer (1986), 40.

COINAGE AND CURRENCY IN EIGHTEENTH-CENTURY BRITAIN

332 *London Corresponding Society, Alarm'd, – Vide Guilty Conscience.* Aquatint by James Gillray, published 20 April 1798.[81] A highly tendentious caricature reflecting the conspiratorial underground nature of the Society after 1795. Among the simian-looking grotesques are a butcher and a barber.

333 William Robert Hay (1761-1839) in later life. Mezzotint after a portrait by James Lonsdale (1820), 1837.

81 George (1942), No. 9202

COLLECTORS, DEALERS AND RADICALS

It was the existence of the political tokens that was at the heart of the controversy between 'Civis' (James Wright) and 'R. Y.' (William Robert Hay) [333] in the *Gentleman's Magazine* in 1796-97. Diametrically opposed to each other in their politics, Wright, a radical Whig,[82] and Hay, a die-hard Tory, the political tokens were for the latter 'clumsy and paltry productions ... hourly issuing from every dirty alley in London or Birmingham, for the purposes of imposition; in some instances for purposes of a more serious and premeditated ill-tendency; much less to the encouragement of a very extensive circulation of base coinage'.[83] They came from 'the very ditch of this dirty traffic'.[84] Even the 'Trial-tokens', when seen together would appear what they really were, 'trash', 'with a very few exceptions, beneath the notice of any friend of the Arts. By classing the political pieces together he will observe better how little merit is to be found in them. For the most part, they are despicable in their designs, and most clumsily struck on the basest metal'.[85]

While agreeing with 'R.Y.' that 'a very large proportion of these pieces ... from their mean execution and designs ... [were] unworthy of the patronage of any person of good taste and good sense', the latter's 'very peevish humour' was too much for 'CIVIS':

> ... the trifling political jettons of Spence and others, sedition pieces (improperly put into Birchall's List, p. 3) &c. ... can produce no effect more important than that of licentious caricatures, which excite laughter or excite contempt... [S]urely R.Y. does not 'do well to be angry,' and ascribe a grovelling taste for dirty ditch-water to such of his brother collectors as may be disposed to set apart a cell or two in a miscellaneous drawer for such *lusae monetae*. The enlightened medallist is of no party.[86]

The potential of tokens for political propaganda was of course no new phenomenon. There had been a rash of medalets at the height of the Wilksite commotions in the 1760s and '70s, during the Regency crisis of 1789 and to celebrate the King's recovery from illness. Loyalists were certainly not behind hand in harnessing the token to their cause, the halfpenny of Thomas and Robert Davidson, the City printers, being just one example [184], but their productions tended to the pedestrian. They rarely achieved anything like the subtlety of Spence or the drama of Milton's frustrated Hereford bull trampling on Tory chains on the medalet issued to commemorate the victory of the radical Whig, Robert Biddulph – 'the Friend of Peace and Liberty'

---

82 Wright's advanced political views, instanced by his promotion of a cheap edition of Thomas Paine's *Rights of Man*, is said to have caused him to be the object of political surveillance: Dykes (1996a), 198.

83 'R. Y.' (1796), 753.

84 'R. Y.' (1796), 754.

85 'R. Y.' (1797), 267.

86 'Civis' (1797), 34, 31, 32.

334 John Milton: An original celebratory election medalet for Robert Biddulph, 1796.

– as second member in the Herefordshire election of June, 1796 [**334**]. Milton's engraving was modelled on a plate in Joseph Spence's *Polymetis* although the original had no chains [**335**]. In the words of the reforming polemicist, George Dyer (1755–1841), the scene represented 'the independent conduct of the Herefordshire yeomanry' in Biddulph's return. Whatever the medalet's message and Dyer's gloss – the growing unpopularity of the French war and the high price of corn certainly played their part in the election – traditional aristocratic interest had nevertheless not been without its importance (Biddulph was a nominee of the Foxite duke of Norfolk), and opponents were quick to dismiss the bull as a reflection of Biddulph's earlier 'nabob' career as a contractor in bullocks in Bengal.[87]

Loyalists, on the other hand, could descend to the macabre and Hancock and his associates were to the forefront in capitalizing on anti-radical fervour in the revolutionary years. Hancock himself, it seems, had been responsible for the grotesque but popular medallion marking the Birmingham riots of July 1791 [**336**] and a year later, with John Stubbs Jorden, he produced an anti-Paine token [**186a and b**] (which Spence used as the model for his hanging effigy of Pitt [**317**]

335 'Taurus' from Plate XXV of Joseph Spence's Polymetis, 1747.

336 Westwood/Hancock (?): Hancock's anti-sedition medalet commemorating the Birmingham riots of July 1791.

337 John Westwood, Jnr. (?): Unofficial 'Birmingham Loyal Associations' medalet, 1798.

87 See *The Monthly Magazine and British Register*, June 1797, 441; January 1798, 26-27; July Supplement, 542-545; and Dykes (forthcoming).
Two substantive versions of the medalet were produced, the dies of the first [**334**] (according to Pye (1801), 11) breaking after 'a few specimens' were struck. Of the second (unsigned but also attributed to Milton) Pye tells us that 2,076 specimens were struck, 'intended for halfpence, but found too expensive'.
For Biddulph, later Myddleton Biddulph, (1761-1814) see Thorne (1986), III, 205-206.

COLLECTORS, DEALERS AND RADICALS

338 John Westwood, Jnr.: Anti-Jacobin 'Greatheads' medalet, 1797.

and Skidmore was to copy (*D&H*: Middx 827-828 and 834-835)). Reminiscent of this is the 'unofficial' and even more gruesome medalet struck to celebrate the presentation of colours to the Loyal Birmingham Light Horse Volunteers and the Birmingham Loyal Association on 4 June 1798 [337]. The reverse line of gibbets with Priestley first in the row implies the hand of Hancock who had given Priestley's head to the snake on the reverse of the 'Pandora's Breeches' version of his anti-Paine token [186a] but the date of the piece is more likely to suggest the involvement of the younger Westwood who had already engraved the anti-Jacobin 'Greatheads' medalet the year before [338].[88]

Political tokens, Hay's 'trash', 'general circulation' halfpennies, mules and concoctions directed at the collectors' market were bringing the whole structure of the provincial coin into disrepute and no-one was being more gulled than the collector who had, in one sense at least, started the downward process. Charles Pye, who had brought his first catalogue to a premature end because of the 'prodigious' increase in inferior pieces and false tokens for 'the sole purpose of furnishing the collectors', joined in the debate in the *Gentleman's Magazine* but by then the end was already coming into sight.

> So long as they [provincial coins] were manufactured with reputation, it was to me a pleasing study; but, when they were counterfeited for the worst of purposes, to impose upon the publick, the obverses and reverses mixed on purpose to make variety, and the inscription on the edges varied for the same purpose, it became a matter of surprize to me that the collectors would suffer themselves to be duped in this manner... The manufacturing of this rubbish, or, as it may properly be called, wasting of copper, has been systematically brought forward; and collectors have purchased without considering that they were manufactured for no other purpose than to impose on them.[89]

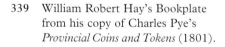

339 William Robert Hay's Bookplate from his copy of Charles Pye's *Provincial Coins and Tokens* (1801).

88 Davis (1895), 8 (no. 46) confuses this 'Volunteers halfpenny' with Jorden's official medal [199]. Davis attributed the engraving of the 'Greatheads Penny' to Westwood and its manufacture to Kempson. The similar 'Loggerheads Penny' was presumably intended as a pendant: Davis (1895), 11-12 (nos. 61-65).

89 Pye (1795), 'ADVERTISEMENT'; Pye (1796), 991-92.

VII

LAST THINGS

> Posterity will look with astonishment at the number and variety of provincial coins struck by various descriptions of men in the present century, and so far exceeding in design and workmanship the little towns-pieces and tokens issued about 100 years ago as a temporary supply to the circulation of copper money. These like those have lived but a short time; and, for want of the sanction of public and legal authority, are sinking fast into neglect, except in the cabinets of our Virtuosi who, it should seem, ... have been finely imposed on... A collection of them was handsomely engraved by Mr. Pye, of Birmingham, who seems to have left off just before the inundation of spurious fictitious ones overspread the town; for John Bull must be duped; and, if he cannot get spurious antiques from Italy, must be amused with collecting spurious works of modern art at home.
>
> *The Gentleman's Magazine*, December 1797, 1034-35.

By the time that Matthew Boulton's dream of a regal coinage contract was at long last fulfilled in June 1797 the eighteenth-century token, introduced a decade earlier as a 'temporary supply to the circulation of copper money' and seen by many as a nostrum for the problem of small change, had degenerated into a gallimaufry of notionally promissory tokens accompanied by a welter of counterfeits, anonymous pieces struck for 'general circulation' and a plenitude of non-convertible shop tickets, medalets, collectors' 'rarities' and political pieces. While reasonable standards had been maintained not the barest of criticism percolated through to the public prints of the day; but, though provincial coinage probably impinged little on the everyday lives of readers of periodicals like the *Gentleman's Magazine*, by 1794 it had become the subject of some debate as it was perceived to be dominated by low-weight and debased issues of questionable provenance and redemption, little better than the long-standing bugbear of counterfeit regal copper.[1] As early as April 1794 – for some reason his letter was not published until the December – a correspondent from Manchester was drawn to protest to the magazine that

---

[1] This *GM* correspondence was short-lived extending only from December 1794 to March 1795. When tokens next became a subject of discussion in the magazine in September 1796 the debate had moved from practical concern with the currency to collecting and the arrangement of a token cabinet. It was this latter dialogue that was marked by the controversy between 'R. Y.' and 'Civis' largely over political pieces.

> Whilst the laws are too lax to restrain the present licentious increase of private MINTS, the great profit they afford must continually hold forth an almost irresistible temptation... So that almost every new piece of copper, which has been issued under the name of a halfpenny, has been progressively more worthless in every point of view: and, though the ingenuity of the artist may have conciliated an indulgence to some, others have made their appearance without any kind of merit to palliate their obtrusion upon the publick.[2]

It was a theme quickly taken up by another contributor:

> The wretchedly debased state of our copper coinage, and the quantity of counterfeit half-pence, that are so plentifully poured upon the publick, have long and loudly demanded the strictest notice and interference of the Legislature ... and it is obvious that, until Government takes upon it to give us some redress, the evil will go on continually increasing, to the great decline of the Arts, and the infamy and degradation of our national character.[3]

Both writers – as indeed many others, for instance John Pinkerton[4] – did not distinguish between provincial coins and counterfeits and lumped them all together. Others were more discriminating. No complaint could be made against 'the first tokens', those of Thomas Williams and John Wilkinson, and 'all of which have been struck by Mr Bolton [*sic*]', qualified one writer in January 1795; but while the problem of forgery might have been 'trifling in comparison with the Birmingham halfpence' even he had to admit that the 'great influx of counterfeits' had by then 'become a considerable evil'.[5] It was, though, not simply the light-weight or the 'spurious fictitious ones' that were the subject of censure. The whole nature of 'promissory' tokens and the accountability of outwardly bona fide issuers were also matters of concern for the notion of what a 'promissory' token coinage implied was interpreted loosely by many tradesmen. Much has been made by some recent commentators of the professed convertibility of tokens, assuming from this a readiness on the part of their issuers to change them for coin of the realm.[6] Even at the time one correspondent to the *Gentleman's Magazine* could rather naively say, 'Where a tradesman has a die cut for his own use, and puts his name on the token, nobody can be injured, as he will for his credit's sake receive them whenever brought; and, in this case, whether they weigh more or less is of little consequence to the publick'.[7] In practice, this could turn out to be far from the case. There were too many shopkeepers like the one known to 'Obadiah'

---

2 *GM*, December 1794, 1082.

3 *GM*, January 1795, 14.

4 Pinkerton (1789), II, 85. See p. 58 above.

5 *GM*, January 1795, 33-34.

6 Redish (2000), 153; Sargent and Velde (2003), 271, 292 and 303.

7 *GM*, January 1795, 34.

LAST THINGS

writing from an unidentified 'Sha'. 'The only tradesman in this part of the kingdom, who has issued tokens', he complained, 'refuses to give current coin for them, and will take them only in payment of goods at his own shop ... the poor are considerable sufferers'.[8] 'S. E.', in his turn, questioned whether a tradesman was 'by law compellable to exchange those [provincial coins] which he has really issued'. He thought the situation 'tolerably clear if it be considered that these tokens are in fact promissory notes'.[9]

But they were not and there was no *legal* compulsion on a tradesman to redeem his tokens however much he might declare them to be promissory. In practice redemption depended on the whim of the issuer, his conscience and no doubt some degree of public constraint within the local community. It was all too easy for a tradesman to take tokens back only in payment for further goods, to refuse them altogether or to deny membership of a recognized token-issuing association which someone else fronted. And in what was a hard-headed age there must have been a number of promoters who saw their venture as no more than a means of 'speculative gain' and who would have been happy never to see their halfpennies again once they had been released upon the public. It was after all the principle on which Lutwyche promoted his tokens and trumpeted the profit that might be made from them.

Professor Redish has suggested that the fact that tokens 'were carefully stamped' rendered them less susceptible to counterfeiting.[10] This was far from the case for it was the best and weightiest tokens that predominantly fell a prey to the forger. Sold on to other issuers, as they became more generalized in their circulation and remote from their professed centres of redemption so their very ubiquity rendered them as non-redeemable as the regal copper and as prone to counterfeiting. It was the shopkeepers' tokens that had a considerable degree of protection from the attention of the counterfeiter and this was very largely because they circulated in a limited geographical milieu where forgeries would have been more readily identifiable.[11] But the localism that set these later tokens apart from the 'industrial' and 'mercantile' issues also presented difficulties. In their nature they were subject to the same problems that had beset their predecessors in the seventeenth century for as Albert Jouvin had noted in 1672 the new promissory halfpence did not have any great degree of acceptability outside their own immediate areas. Joseph Moser, the London Magistrate and controversialist [340], – no devotee of tokens, it has to be admitted – commented that, during an extended tour of the northern parts of the country, he had found that the token no longer had 'that unlimited circulation which it had while a novelty: you cannot now pass at Barnet nor even at Doncaster, a Provincial halfpenny which you

340   Joseph Moser (1748-1819).

---

8   *GM*, March 1795, 199-200.

9   *GM*, February 1795, 130.

10 Redish (2000), 153.

11 But not from their own manufacturers who mixed their edges and created mules for the collectors' market.

took at York'; even change he had 'received at one turnpike gate was very frequently refused at the next'.[12]

> The Provincial halfpence, which were in one town of general currency, were in another scrupulously examined, and perhaps half of them rejected; or only deemed passable at a diminished valuation. I remarked the operation of this capricious system in many places, particularly in markets, and saw that it was productive of considerable contention, and consequently hindrance of business; of fraud in the original promulgators, and loss and inconvenience to the poor.

This was in the early months of 1798, when following the issue of Boulton's 'cartwheel' coins there was a mounting fear that tokens might be suppressed, but Moser's encounters with toll keepers and shopkeepers could have been experienced by any traveller as early as 1794. Tradesmen had a legitimate excuse to be wary of the spreading shoals of a provincial coinage increasingly dominated by low-weight and debased issues of questionable provenance. We have seen how those of Norwich had adopted a policy of accepting only local tokens, motivated, like George Cotton and his fellow townsmen in Romford, by a concern to counter the 'paltry trash' that was plaguing their communities. Those of Ipswich quickly followed suit. 'Most assuredly a very judicious regulation', commented the *Ipswich Journal*, 'as we are well informed a vast quantity [of tokens] have lately been brought to this place, consigned to persons who make a traffic of selling them, at the rate of 15d. for a shilling... [I]n case a speedy stop be not put to the circulation of such halfpence here, they will become a very great nuisance to the retail trader, who will be so burthened with them, as to be unable to make his regular payments, without allowing a discount to turn them into cash, as was really the case with the light halfpence about ten years since'.[13]

Provincial coins, even those of good weight, were abused in another way. The *Gentleman's Magazine*'s Manchester correspondent, for instance, maintained that 'if the legal copper of the kingdom were applied only according to the original intention, merely for necessary change, and not for paying half the wages of many artisans and others, there is little doubt but it would be found sufficient'.[14] His argument reflected the long-standing complaint of copper being used to bulk up pay packets and now provincial coins were subjected to similar opprobrium. They were, insisted Joseph Moser, 'an imposition upon the public in general, and the lower class of society in particular'.

> Persons in considerable business, and of great opulence, either as manufacturers, tradesmen, shopkeepers, or those engaged

---

12   Moser (1798), 307.

13   *The Ipswich Journal*, 27 February 1796. See pp. 226-27 above. One may instance Moser's experience in Chester where he 'offered *three* genuine Tower halfpence for half an ounce of snuff. The shopkeeper refused them, saying, that he must have *six* of those, or *three* of the Provincial': Moser (1798), 306, footnote.

14   *GM*, December 1794, 1083.

in public works, where a number of men are employed ... who have in the existing scarcity of silver a pretence, though not an excuse, either make or contract for large quantities of these Provincial halfpence ... and ... disperse them to their workmen and labourers, in the proportion of five shillings in silver, and five shillings *worth* of copper: though it frequently happens that these poor mechanics, and the labourers that are, in particular, employed in canals, in which branch of visionary industry there is *even* now considerable speculations, are paid their ten shillings per week wholly in these kind of tokens.

And as he enlarged in a footnote:

These Provincial halfpence are packed up in five shilling papers, for the convenience of payment. Two of the said papers are the remuneration for a *week's* labour in the neighbourhood of Chester, and in many parts of the North. I have frequently observed large piles of them in the offices for aquatic speculations, and have more than once been present at their distribution.[15]

Whether such a practice as Moser so graphically described was as widespread as many have come to believe is open to question. Copper coin was included in wage packets because it was essential for petty retail transactions and tokens were thus a useful adjunct to the daily-living facilities that had to be set up by employers for isolated industrial communities and for the omnipresent camps of canal navvies; not unrelated to 'truck' but not necessarily unpaternal. While there must certainly have been abuses, overall tokens were probably no more than a makeweight in the average worker's pay; welcome both to the employer and the employee, especially in the early days of their production and where copper coinage was not otherwise available. But wages tended generally to range anywhere in the region of 10*s* to 15*s* per week; figures that might be much higher for skilled workers, especially in the good times before 1793 and in areas with a high-wage economy. Silver, therefore, defective and diminished as it was, still played a critical role in the actual payment of wages which is why so many employers spent such efforts in hunting it down and paying premiums for it and why the Committee on Coin did not completely have its head in the sand when it pontificated in 1798 that 'Silver Coin is the Coin which the Poor principally use'.[16] There is, too, a great deal of evidence to show that the majority of employers still embraced other, more established, means of overcoming their need for cash than tokens – through credit notes, part payment in kind, delayed wages or group payments in large denomination notes or coin. Credit, in particular, took the place of cash as it had done everywhere for

---

15   Moser (1798), 306 and footnote.
16   PRO: BT 6/127, 10 February 1798.

centuries even for the most trivial of transactions.[17]

So how important were tokens in the economy of the time? Were they so vital to the success of the Industrial Revolution that without them the developments of the time might have been seriously disrupted as some have argued or have 'slowed' down almost to 'a snail's pace' as one economic historian has rather more cautiously put it?[18] The truth of such a contention is debatable for the real significance of tokens in relation to the Industrial Revolution was less in the actual payment of industrial wages, although this was the beginning of their story and seems to underlie the premise, than in providing ready money with which working people could meet their everyday needs. They could do this increasingly only through retail outlets – 'standing' shops – and to understand eighteenth-century tokens – as indeed their predecessors of a hundred years before – one must look beyond industrialization, important though this was, to the broader development of urban life and the commercialization of society. Such factors were what in essence underlay the token phenomenon, spurred on Kempson and Lutwyche to promote their products in market towns, and led to the dominance of shopkeepers as token issuers.

By the time they had run their course something in the region of six hundred tons of copper had been converted into perhaps forty million provincial coins. These figures are, of course, largely based on what Charles Pye gleaned from willing manufacturers and informed collectors but, incomplete as they are, they give us as reliable a scenario as we are ever likely to get.[19] What the figures make clear is that over the decade or so of their production genuine provincial coins came to total almost half of the legitimate regal copper struck in fits and starts over the preceding century.[20] But what must be stressed is that the bulk of the production was over by 1792, Thomas Williams alone having been responsible for more than 250 tons of copper – in the region of 13 million coins - between1787 and 1789. What we do not know is how long these early tokens remained in circulation or the extent to which, as they wandered far from their putative centres of redemption [21] and the price of copper rose, they were melted down to be replaced by lighter weight pieces. One certainly has a feeling from the critiques of the time that even by 1794 the original 'full weight' and 'honest' halfpennies had become things of the past.

When James Wright, with typical hyperbole, was moved to say that

17   Cf. Hoppit (1986), 64-78; Brewer (1989), 186-87. 'Tick' in a tavern is an obvious example of petty credit and one, of course, that could be readily exploited.

18   Selgin (2008), 2.

19   See Table 4, p. 211 above.
     Pye has no figures for the ever-secretive Boulton, which have to be established from the Soho archive, for Thomas Mynd, Boulton's brother-in-law, James Good, William Mainwaring or for most of tokens struck in London.

20   Between 1694 and 1775 over 1388 tons of regal copper coin had been struck: Challis (1992b), 376 and 379; Dyer and Gaspar (1992), 435 and 436.

21   Interestingly the Hutchisons' Edinburgh halfpennies were 'in general circulation' in Glasgow almost as soon as they were issued, 'generally one or two in changing 6ᵈ': BAH: MS 3782/12/66/19: James Lawson to Matthew Boulton, 5 September 1791.

provincial coins had 'almost totally supplanted the present very barbarous national copper currency' there were areas of the country where, if a Newcastle correspondent to the *Monthly Magazine* is to be believed, they had not yet even touched.[22] Where they did circulate, by the mid-nineties and well before, except for localized and reputable shopkeepers' issues, they had in general become submerged as just one more non-convertible element in the general mishmash of copper, preponderantly counterfeit, that passed for small change.

Having said this, for all the public agonising about tokens in the mid-1790s there can be little doubt that they would have continued to run their course if it had not been for the financial crisis of 1797 and the suspension of cash payments. It was the consequent disappearance of guineas and half guineas from circulation and the need for a fractional currency below the lowest paper denomination of £1 that precipitated the decisions to issue countermarked dollars and to award a coinage contract to Matthew Boulton.[23] Although Moser might fulminate against provincial coins being 'instruments of fraud and oppression' that should be suppressed forthwith – even as he was writing Boulton's 'cartwheel' coppers were already reaching out through the country – they were far from uppermost in the government's mind in instituting the new copper coinage. They were never declared illegal in 1797.[24] Indeed, the initial restriction of the new coinage to pennies – with twopenny pieces following in January 1798 – was the result of a conscious decision to prevent the old halfpenny-based coinage of whatever kind being driven out of circulation and causing 'a great confusion among the lower ranks of people'.[25]

Yet, despite this concern not to 'displace all the base Counterfeits now afloat', in those places where the new coinage did appear it quickly tended to stifle the circulation of tokens, if only for a time. Not so much because it was popular as currency – it was not; it was too heavy and 'inconvenient to carry far' and halfpennies were what people were used to and wanted – but because of a fear that the old would be suppressed which the government did nothing to dispel.[26] In the Birmingham area as early as July 1797, almost as soon as the first 'cartwheel' pennies were issued, while there was a recrudescence of 'good lawful old halfpence … which had been laid by in expectation of what had happened', tokens were being spurned and 'many persons, who had quantities of them received in the way of business, were at considerable

22 'Civis' (1796), 867; *The Monthly Magazine*, May 1797, 351: this observation was probably based on personal experience since no genuine tokens were issued in Northumberland. Sharp (1834), [i] said that tokens 'almost superseded the national currency' but he was including in his observation the early nineteenth-century series and particularly the silver shillings and sixpences which seem to have dominated the country's retail trade by 1812.

23 See pages pp. 145-50 above.

24 Cf. Bell (1963), 10 and 59.

25 Liverpool (1805), 196.

26 Liverpool (1805), 195-96; BAH: MS 3782/12/42/84, Matthew Boulton to Sir George Shuckburgh-Evelyn [Draft, endorsed in pencil 'March 1797']; PRO: BT6/118, ff. 271-72; Gee (1798), 407. See also p. 151 above.

loss by selling them for old metal at less than half their nominal value'. According to Moser, many poor people were left with 'large quantities by them, or have been obliged to sell to the tinker, for the merest trifle, that trash which they had been weak enough to receive as the reward of industry and ingenuity'.[27] And it was not just the dross that was being rejected. In September John Sherwin, a Burslem iron merchant, contacted Peter Stubbs, the Warrington file maker: 'I should be glad to send you some Macclesfield and Anglesey halfpence if they pass with you because they are stopt with us'.[28] In Bath by the beginning of 1799, it may be added, an enterprising tradesman was offering to relieve prospective customers of any 'bad halfpence they had on hand' but at the same time was adamant that he would not take 'promissory' tokens.[29]

On the other hand, the evidence of some tokens, circulating in more out of the way places that Boulton's 'cartwheels' did not reach effectively despite his overarching ambition of delivering the coin 'at every Mans Door in the two Kingdoms' or where they were not sufficiently favoured, even after the introduction of halfpennies and farthings in 1799, strongly suggests that on the basis of 'needs must' a small proportion of provincial coins had a continued acceptability. The wear exhibited by many 'Glamorgan' halfpennies, for instance, implies a circulation in industrial south Wales long after their nominal date of issue of 1795 and the same is true of tokens in other areas. Graham Dyer has shown us quite convincingly that although dated '1793' the Sudbury tokens of Thomas Goldsmith were produced in batches up to 1796 and that specimens of his final group show signs of years of usage.[30] And certainly the vogue for tokens in parts of Scotland did not really reach its apogee until 1797 although, admittedly, this was due mainly to the fostering activities of James Wright of Dundee.

Moreover, almost on cue with the appearance of the Soho coins the price of copper escalated appreciably and the old cycle began again. As in the 1770s the new heavy coins disappeared into the counterfeiters' melting pots to be replaced by light-weight imitations and by the early 1800s complaints of shortages of good copper coin had resurrected themselves: it was a scenario in which tokens found a new lease of life and, even after the large Boulton copper issues of 1806/1807 largely

---

27 Moser (1798), 307. Moser's disparagement of wage-earners is, of course, totally unjustified. As Professor Mathias pithily put it 'it needed a bold workman to present tokens to his master and demand their face value in coins of the realm': Mathias (1962), 21 and (1979), 200.

28 Gee (1798), 406-7; Ashton (1939), 121.

29 *Bath Journal*, 21 January 1799, transcribed in the Sydenham Collection, City of Bath Reference Library, 897.

30 Dyer, G. P. (1994) and (2000).

put a stop to them,[31] they – and their nineteenth-century successors – although technically banned in 1817, did not effectively disappear from circulation until the new copper coinages of George IV had become established throughout the country. And even then some of them took an unconscionably long time dying.[32]

There remains one puzzle. It cannot be stressed too much that the fundamental currency problem facing the country in the eighteenth century was a shortage of good silver coin. Why then did the token makers not turn their attention to producing shillings and sixpences, as they were to do less than a generation later? Samuel Garbett had consistently urged on Boulton the production of silver coin rather than copper and silver coin of a lower weight standard than that traditionally struck by the Royal Mint; that is a token coinage. After all what passed as regal silver was little more than *token* itself. A major and recurrent drawback, as we have seen, was the scarcity of the metal and the price it commanded in the market. Yet silver tokens had certainly not been dismissed out of hand. When there had been a fleeting easing in the price of the metal towards the end of the 1780s John Wilkinson had tentatively embarked on such a project, issuing 'Fine Silver' tokens with an initial circulating value of 3s 6d [74]. And he seems to have been thinking of reviving the idea of a silver coinage by the end of 1789 when Boulton himself was flirting with Walter Taylor's scheme to strike silver pieces [96].[33]

It is said that neither Wilkinson nor Boulton took their schemes any further primarily because of a general belief that the private striking of any sort of silver coin would be regarded as an infringement of the royal prerogative. This was certainly a consideration for James Wright when, in the closing years of the century following the restoration of confidence after the financial crisis of the early part of 1797, there was again a temporary fall in the price of silver.[34] Wright toyed with the idea of putting out a silver shilling in Dundee celebrating his supposed Highland descent but he quickly thought better of it and replaced it with a shilling 'medal' instead [341a and b]. As he explained to Joseph Planta, then under-librarian of the British Museum, when sending him a specimen, 'as I began to be a little uneasy at the boldness of

---

31 In February 1808 Sir Joseph Banks, rather over sanguinely, said that a 'complete stop' had been 'put to that nefarious practice [of counterfeiting and provincial coin making] by the new copper tokens... Ever since Mr. Boulton's coin has been fairly in circulation no other coin has been seen in circulation in the country to the north of Stamford': BT 6/119, 22 February 1808, quoted in Mathias (2004), 82.

32 It might be thought that the eighteenth-century token would have completely disappeared with the introduction of the smaller module bronze coinage in 1860. Nevertheless, the writer recalls the odd token occurring in small change in 1940s Swansea and Nicholas Mayhew tells us that Wilkinson halfpennies could be found circulating in Birmingham even in the 1960s: Mayhew (1999), 104.

33 See pp. 86-87 and 122-23 above.

34 The easing of the price of silver in the latter part of 1797 prompted a consortium of London bankers to promote a regal coinage of shillings and sixpences – the 'Dorrien & Magens' shilling of 1798 – but the scheme was halted by the government: see p. 39 above.

341a Peter Kempson: Dundee shilling (copper proof) for James Wright, Jnr., 1797.

341b Peter Kempson: Dundee 'Silver Medal' (copper proof) for James Wright, Jnr., 1797.

342 John Milton: Troon Canal Company halfpenny (silver proof) for William Fullarton, 1797.

attempting to circulate <u>silver</u> coin, a prerogative of the Crown alone, I soon determined to issue none for circulation in that form as '<u>Payable</u>', so that only <u>6 Doz.</u> were struck – & no more of these I think ever shall be struck'.[35] The perceived strictures surrounding the private striking of a silver coinage did not, however, inhibit a fellow Scot taking such a scheme much further.

Colonel William Fullarton (1754-1808), an improving Ayrshire landowner, former diplomat and soldier,[36] had for some years been engaged in promoting the construction of a canal from the Kilmarnock coalfield to a projected new harbour at Troon when in 1797, with the prospect of the canal becoming a reality, he decided to embark on a currency to meet the needs of the workforce involved. Through the agency of Matthew Young Fullarton had dies for a halfpenny token cut by the former Mint engraver John Milton.[37] Bearing a romanticised bust of William Wallace, the 'Scottish Hero' supposedly of local antecedents, and a female figure emblematic of Scotland with the motto **SCOTIA REDIVIVA**, the token [342] was ranked by Wright, with his typical exuberance, as being 'high among the best productions of modern art'. The small number struck – according to Pye, five hundred and seventy-six pieces – might suggest that the tokens were designed simply as a promotional exercise in connection with the bill that Fullarton, as an MP for Ayrshire, was attempting to steer through the Commons in the summer of that year. But since at least five hundred of the pieces were struck without a collar it seems more likely that they were intended as the first instalment of a more utilitarian and extensive issue brought to a premature end by the canal bill's failure to pass the Lords in July 1797.[38]

Despite his setback Fullarton continued to press ahead with his canal scheme and within eighteen months, with greater political success in prospect, he had set about the production of a second coinage, again engraved by Milton. By now, however, he seems to have moved away from the idea of restricting himself to copper. His new piece, with its neo-classical portrait of Adam Smith, *à la Brutus* [343], based on a medallion by James Tassie [344a], and its reverse of a female figure in

35   NHM: DTC XI, 163, James Wright, Jnr. to Joseph Planta, 22 May 1797 [Extract of part of an enclosure to Sir Joseph Banks]. Wright explained that the shilling was 'of good silver, and very highly finished, indeed the very best work of the Artist [Wyon] was ordered, the dies cost me <u>£3-13-6</u>'.

36   Fullarton was author of a *General View of the Agriculture of the County of Ayr* (1793). He was well acquainted with Robert Burns who, sending Fullarton verse and songs, wrote to him on 3 October 1791: 'I am ambitious, covetously ambitious of being known to a gentleman whom I am proud to call my Countryman: a gentleman who was a Foreign Embassador [*sic*] as soon as he was a Man; & a Leader of Armies as soon as he was a Soldier; & that with an eclat unknown to the usual minions of a Court': Ferguson and Roy (1985), 115. Burns also complimented Fullarton in his poem *The Vision*, Duan I, stanza 22.
     For Fullarton see *ODNB* and for his token coinages see Dykes (2002), 149-163.

37   For Milton see Stainton (1983), 133-59.

38   Conder (1798), 'Preface', note (*g*); Pye (1801), 6 and plate 4, no. 7.

LAST THINGS

343   John Milton: Troon Canal Company 'Adam Smith' shilling (copper proof) for William Fullarton, 1798.

classical pose grieving over a military defeat, was intended for a shilling but it never got beyond the stage of being an unfinished essay and according to Pye only 'a few proofs' – or rather patterns - were made in copper and silver.[39]

The derivation of the reverse image has been open to a number of interpretations. In fact it can be shown to derive once more from Tassie; this time from one of the reproductions of ancient and modern gems for which he was perhaps more widely known at the time than for his portrait medallions [344b]. They were much in vogue among London jewellers and would have been familiar objects to both Young and the aesthetic Milton. The impression in question copied a neo-

344   (a) Portrait Medallion of Adam Smith in his 64th Year by James Tassie, 1787; and (b) Plaster impression by Tassie of a neo-classical gem ('A Conquered Province') by Giovanni Pichler.

classical sardonyx by the celebrated gem-engraver Giovanni Pichler (1734-91) in the collection of Kenneth Mackenzie, Lord Fortrose, which Fullarton himself could well have seen in Naples in 1770 when on the Grand Tour [345].[40]

Milton seems to have had problems with the striking of the dies and in January 1799 Fullarton cancelled the project telling Matthew Young that he intended to embark on another token venture. By now

39   Pye (1801), 6 and plate 4, no. 8.

40   Dykes (2002), 152. A glimpse of Fullarton's Grand Tour is given by his travelling companion Robert Brydone in the latter's *A tour through Sicily and Malta…* (1773).
Kenneth Mackenzie (1744-1781) was a grandson of the attainted fifth Earl of Seaforth. Created Viscount Fortrose in 1766 he was elevated to the earldom of Seaforth (a new creation in the Irish peerage) in 1771. He raised a regiment of foot in 1778 (later becoming a constituent of the Seaforth Highlanders) but sailing with them to the East Indies he died at sea in 1781.

COINAGE AND CURRENCY IN EIGHTEENTH-CENTURY BRITAIN

345 Colonel Fullarton (the seated figure in the background) in the Naples apartment of Lord Fortrose (standing centre) in 1770 when on the Grand Tour. A *scène de genre* by Pietro Fabris.

Fullarton had secured the ear of the Prince of Wales and, so he said, the latter's approval to have his 'Profile, – Emblems & Arms, impressed on such Tokens as the Troon Company, may have occasion to Circulate'. Matthew Young was asked 'to get M^r. Milton without delay to execute a die for a shilling coin' [346a] based very closely on the existing silver coinage and cautioned that 'as there will be others required for Half Crowns, Sixpences and Halfpence' [346b] great care should be taken to maintain strict secrecy about the affair.[41] An extensive coinage was in the wind and news of it was something that Young was unable to keep to himself. Within the month he had either bragged about it or confessed his concern to Miss Banks who, of course, immediately told her brother.

Sir Joseph Banks, a member of the recently reconstituted Privy Council committee on coin, straightway warned Milton off the project, unnerving him with the prospect of the dire consequences he would

41 The 'one-and-sixpenny' pieces listed by Davis (1904), 199-200 are halfpenny patterns.

346a John Milton: Troon Canal Company pattern shilling (original, thin flan) for William Fullarton, 1799.

346b John Milton: Troon Canal Company halfpenny (original, with unbroken label of difference on impaled Scottish arms) for William Fullarton, 1799.

be likely to face for coining in a precious metal.[42] With the powerful backing of Lord Liverpool – still a leading figure in coinage matters though now ageing and unwell – he eventually succeeded in persuading Fullarton himself to drop a scheme for an 'imaginary coinage' so like the real thing as to confound the unwary and encourage fraud and, moreover, an infringement of a royal prerogative that the Prince of Wales had no authority to assume. Fullarton, although he gave in, did so with an ill grace and a variety of specious arguments. Fundamentally he could not see that he was breaking any law by producing coin that did not actually *copy* the regal currency and here he was probably on stronger ground than he realized for it was a view that the government law officers were also inclined to. As Liverpool ruefully – and privately – admitted to Banks, the Attorney General was minded that 'anyone may issue coins, even of silver, provided they call them tokens, and that they do not exhibit any imitations or resemblances of his Majesty's current coin'.[43] Fullarton's sin was that his tokens *did* bear too great a similarity to the regal coinage. Had he been made aware of the Attorney General's opinion he might have pressed ahead with his coinage in a somewhat different form. He certainly did not intend to give it up but, in the event, the canal project was abandoned and with it any need for a token currency.

Fullarton and Wilkinson – and James Wright – were unfortunately before their time. For just over a decade into the new century and in the midst of another financial crisis with 'a scarcity of small coin' that was said to be 'an evil of the greatest magnitude' tokens again began to make their appearance; and this time with large numbers of silver pieces.[44] What had changed attitudes over the decade or so since the Troon canal episode was that in 1804 the Bank of England had issued its own 'five shilling dollars', Spanish pieces-of-eight (worth 4*s* 9*d*) completely overstruck by Boulton to a design by Küchler [347]; not current coin of the realm, the Treasury hastened to tell a protesting Mint, but *tokens* 'issued by the Bank of England for the convenience of the public'.[45] Government had, in fact, itself exploited the loophole in the law identified by the Attorney General in 1799 and, with the issue of 3*s*

---

42 'Coining in Gold or Silver', Banks told Milton, in whom he seems to have had a paternalistic interest, 'I find is considered by the common Law of England as a special prerogative of the Crown; & any subject therefore who coins, or who is accessary [*sic*] to Coining in those metals, is guilty of one of the highest misdemeanors [*sic*] a subject is capable of committing; of course liable to fine & imprisonment of more than ordinary severity': NHM: DTC XI, 194, Sir Joseph Banks to John Milton, 11 February 1799. Milton, who, two years earlier, had been dismissed from a post at the Mint for rather naively supplying dies for the counterfeiting of foreign gold and only just escaped prosecution, would, of course, have been considerably affected by Banks's argument.

43 NHM: DTC XI, 227-228, Lord Liverpool to Sir Joseph Banks, 26 May 1799.

44 *The Times*, 9 April 1811, 2.

45 Kelly (1976), 55. The Committee on Coin had wanted the reverse inscription on the 'regenerated dollars' to be 'Bank of England Dollar, a Token for Five Shillings' but time did not permit the dies to be so engraved: Kelly (1976), 57.

COINAGE AND CURRENCY IN EIGHTEENTH-CENTURY BRITAIN

347 Matthew Boulton: Bank of England dollar overstruck on Spanish dollar, 1804.

and 1s 6d Bank tokens when the new currency crisis came in 1811, set a precedent that encouraged not merely a resurgence of copper tokens but also a flood of silver shillings and sixpences. 'Since Ministers have transferred to the Bank of England one of the prerogatives of the Crown, that of coining' commented a contemporary, 'every other Bank, Banker, Agent, Merchant and Shopkeeper, has taken it for granted that an equal right of assuming a royal prerogative is the privilege of all'.[46] And it was not only redeemable silver issues put out by respectable bankers and tradesmen that now appeared but, as the phenomenon gathered momentum, an attendant rash of speculative and fraudulent light-weight pieces that were quickly to bring the whole series into disrepute for the same reasons that had operated against the copper tokens of the 1790s. Nevertheless the tokens served a necessary purpose in the virtual absence of an official silver currency and due to public pressure it was to take three years to bring their issue to a close.[47] In the meantime agitation began to mount for a reform of the silver coinage and with a public now accustomed to a token currency, especially through the Bank tokens of which it could never get enough, the way was opened for the introduction of a non-intrinsic silver currency in 1816/17 and for the dead hand of John Locke to be at long last laid to rest.[48]

Although this was all to be in the future the story of Colonel Fullarton's coinage did not end in 1799. Milton was allowed to finish his dies provided he kept them in his own possession with the hint that he might be able to strike 'medals' from them, presumably as non-currency collectors' pieces. It seems likely, however, that apart from a few original 'thin' shillings and an equally limited number of copper halfpennies Milton did not take advantage of this arrangement and scrupulously restricted his strikings to 'soft metal' or tin pieces. Miss Banks kept in touch with him until his death in 1805 and bearing in mind her acquisitiveness and her brother's interest in the Fullarton affair it is significant that apart from a 'thin' shilling there are no silver pieces in her collection although these are well known today in all the proposed denominations.[49] There is evidence that, after the main protagonists had departed the scene

---

46 Quoted in Phillips (1900), 26.

47 The circulation of silver tokens, with the exception of those of the Bank of England and the Bank of Ireland, was eventually banned in 1814 but copper tokens lingered on for another four years, those of the Birmingham Workhouse and the Sheffield Overseers being continued respectively until 1820 and 1823.

48 The Coinage Act of 1816 incorporated many of Lord Liverpool's proposals. Gold was formalised as the only standard, silver becoming a representative coinage and, with a legal tender restricted to two guineas, henceforward being struck at the ratio of 5s 6d to the troy ounce rather than 5s 2d. Copper, however, was untouched and with the country still assimilating the vast quantities of Boulton's 1806/1807 coinage new copper was not to be introduced until the 1820s.

49 Miss Banks's collection contained a silver shilling (SSB 202.46, acquired 11 February 1799), a copper halfpenny (SSB 202.49, acquired 15 August 1799), and a half-crown, shilling and sixpence in tin (SSB 202.45, SSB 202.47 and SSB 202.48, all acquired 20 November 1799).

LAST THINGS

348a W. J Taylor (?): Restrike 'Troon Canal Company' half-crown for Matthew Young, late 1820s–1830s.

348b W. J Taylor: Restrike 'Troon Canal Company' aluminium sixpence, *c.* 1850s-60s

and the old-type silver coinage had been demonetized, Matthew Young quietly produced silver specimens 'of beautiful workmanship' for sale to collectors at some point in the late 1820s or early '30s [348a].[50] It may be that these Young restrikes were made by William Joseph Taylor (1802-85) who certainly went on decades later to produce more 'Fullarton' patterns from original and newly-struck dies in a variety of metals including gold and the new and comparatively rare aluminum. And it is these Taylor re-strikes and concoctions [348b] that make up the bulk of the Fullarton pieces available to collectors today. Taylor also came into possession of a large number of Soho dies in the 1860s which explains the mules of a 'Fullarton' 'Prince of Wales' halfpenny obverse (*Davis*: Ayrshire 12) and a shilling obverse with a Boulton 'Swainson' reverse (*D&H*: Ayrshire 8).[51]

Many years ago Professor Mathias subtitled his elegant survey of the trade token 'The Industrial Revolution Illustrated'.[52] Such a rubric, though, was justified only by the inclusion in his superb plates of examples of early nineteenth-century tokens with their graphic images of blast furnaces, steam engines, lead works and smelteries. For as we suggested earlier the tokens of the last decade of the eighteenth century tell us less about the industrial changes that were then still only in their infancy than about age-old techniques and processes: the hand-looms, horse whims and water-mills of a proto-industrial society. Nor were the tokens themselves the product of new industrial methods. Only Boulton – and only after 1789 – had the facility of striking tokens by means of steam; all the other manufacturers, in Holywell, in Birmingham and in London were, as far as we can tell, dependent on traditional manually operated screw presses and remained so throughout the period of eighteenth-century token making. Outside Soho, such innovations as there were – Hancock's for example – were adaptations of established techniques. By far the majority of tokens were thus produced not using new technologies as Sargent and Velde have suggested [53] but in the old way as exemplified in John Bluck's aquatint of the Royal Mint before its modernization by Boulton [213]. Eighteenth-century tokens, then, cannot truly be described as a 'monument to the Industrial Revolution' either in their manufacture or in the 'industrial' images they portrayed. What they did display, with a 'combination of intellectual vigour, social consciousness and imaginative design' was the life and times of contemporary society, its activities, fashions and political impulses.[54]

---

50 Boyne (1866), 25. Purvey (1972), 129 suggested that this was 'about 1828' but I have found no corroborative evidence to support his statement. Fullarton died in 1808, Miss Banks in 1818 and Sir Joseph in 1820. The old silver coinage was declared illegal on 1 March 1817.

51 Dykes (2002), 158; Cf. Vice (1995).

52 Mathias (1962).

53 Sargent and Velde (2003), 271.

54 Klingender (1943), 46.

In doing so the artistry of many tokens could hardly be bettered, especially when Hancock at his best or young, up-and-coming engravers of the calibre of the Wyon brothers or Francis Arnold had a hand in their production. Even Joseph Moser, a skilled artist himself, while condemning tokens for 'the evils that accrue' had to admit, echoing James Wright, that 'perhaps there may, among the immense number, be found some that are, in point of workmanship, nearly equal to those of the independent states of Greece, and superior to many of the Roman medals, particularly those of the lower empire'.[55]

Perhaps the last word should be with Charles Shephard, as he strained to give the token some meaning for future generations:

> They form a valuable conservatory of antiquities for posterity: they bear valuable representations, in proportion as the originals of these representations are valuable, of various buildings, of political, historical, and biographical memoirs, of national sentiments and national inclinations, of customs, dress, and manners, of commerce, trade, and manufactures, of industrious occupations, and of the arts and sciences: they are almost all valuable, as they will here afterwards show the trades that were carried on, the forms of various instruments and utensils, of animals and animated creatures, of natural and artificial curiosities.[56]

---

55   Moser (1798), 305.

56   Shephard (1799), 207. Charles Shephard's series of six essays in the *Gentleman's Magazine* between January 1798 and March 1799 cast a valuable light on the contemporary token scene. It is not clear who he actually was. He did not disclose his surname until his last essay and until then simply used the initials 'C. SH.'. In the issues of the magazine for March and September 1798 he gave his address as 'Grays Inn' and he is recorded in the records of the Inn as a tenant of chambers at 14 Grays Inn Square. It is very likely that he was the 'Charles Shepherd [*sic*], eldest son of Charles Shepherd, late of Hoxton Square Middlesex gentleman, deceased,' who was admitted to membership of the Inn on 26 April 1798. There is no record of his subsequent Call to the Bar but it could well be that he was an attorney renting rooms in the Inn.

APPENDIX I

Schedule of Provincial Coins Issued between 1791 and 1798

This list comprises only those provincial coins that, as far as one can gauge, were intended to serve the purposes of coinage although many of the urban tokens may well, in their nature, have functioned as shop tickets. Shop tickets *sensu stricto* (i.e. metallic 'cards of address' with no stated value or pledge of redemption) have, however, been omitted as have political tokens although there are many instances of both finding their way into circulation. Tokens which were produced for 'general circulation' and have no indication of any redeeming authority (including, for example, the 'Chester' halfpenny, its 'Macclesfield' counterpart and the 'London & Middlesex' and 'Warwickshire' halfpennies said by Pye (1801) to have been put out by 'W. Sheward' and 'Farror') have been excluded too as have the plethora of counterfeits, and the concoctions, private tokens and medalets produced for the collectors' market. Aborted issues, such as the Sherborne 'Bank House' halfpenny of 1796 and Boulton's 'Ibberson' token [1795], have also been omitted.

The starting point – and fundamental authority – for the compilation has been Pye (1801) but account has been taken of the manuscript observations of Miss Banks (BM, Department of Coins and Medals), James Wright, Jnr. (SAS) and other contemporary writings. Reference has also been made to Waters (1954), Samuel (1880-1889) – and hence Bell (1963, 1966 and 1968) – and Sydenham (1904 and 1908).

The tokens are dated according to their inscription except where they are known to have been produced in another year (e.g. Bishop's Stortford (Sir George Jackson) and Swansea (John Voss). Where no date is specified on a token an estimate (asterisked*) is given based on the known date of an acquisition by Miss Banks, the evidence of the Boulton Archive or on *termini* suggested by contemporary catalogues. It should be stressed that in a number of cases tokens continued to be produced in batches in years subsequent to their published date and in the case of Matthew Boulton sets of specimens were made available to collectors at least until 1805 and probably again later in the nineteenth century.

Where there is doubt as to the name of an issuer, manufacturer or die-sinker the name is italicized. Where no issuer's name is given on a token but it is known from other sources it is shown in square brackets. In the case of multiple places of issue normally only the first location is listed. Where there is no place of issue specified this is shown in square brackets.

1791

Halfpennies

County	Place	Issuer	Manufacturer	Die Sinker
Anglesey	Anglesey	P M Co [Parys Mine Company]	Boulton	Dumarest
		P M Co [Parys Mine Company]	Wm Williams	Wm Wilson
Cheshire	Macclesfield	[Roe & Company]	Westwood/Hancock	Hancock
Cornwall	[Truro]	[Cornish Metal Company]	Boulton	Dumarest
Hampshire	Southampton	Taylor, Moody & Company	Boulton	Dumarest
Lanarkshire	Glasgow	Gilbert Shearer & Company	Boulton	Dumarest
Lancashire	Lancaster	Thomas Worswick & Sons	Westwood/Hancock	Hancock
	Liverpool	Thomas Clarke	Westwood/Hancock	Hancock
	Rochdale	John Kershaw	Westwood/Hancock	Hancock
Lothian	Edinburgh	Thomas & Alexander Hutchison	Westwood/Hancock	Hancock
Shropshire	Willey	John Wilkinson	Westwood/Hancock	Hancock
Yorkshire	Hull	Jonathan Garton & Company	Westwood/Hancock	Hancock
	Leeds	Richard Paley	Westwood/Hancock	Hancock
Warwickshire	Birmingham	Birmingham Mining & Copper Company	Kempson	Wyon
		Birmingham Mining & Copper Company	Whitmore	Wyon

Farthings

County	Place	Issuer		
Lanarkshire	Glasgow	Alexander Hamilton	—	—

1792

Pennies

County	Place	Issuer	Manufacturer	Die Sinker
Anglesey	Anglesey	P M Co [Parys Mine Company]	Boulton	Hancock

Halfpennies

County	Place	Issuer	Manufacturer	Die Sinker
Carmarthenshire	Carmarthen	John Morgan	Westwood/Hancock	Hancock
Devon	Exeter	Samuel Kingdon	Westwood/Hancock	Hancock
Cheshire	Macclesfield	Roe & Company	Westwood/Hancock	Hancock

APPENDIX I

County Dublin	Dublin & Ballymurtagh	H M Co [Hibernian Mine Company]	——	——
Hampshire	Newport (Isle of Wight)	Robert Bird Wilkins	Mainwaring	Mainwaring
	Southampton	Taylor, Moody & Company	Boulton	Dumarest
Lancashire	Lancaster	Thomas Worswick & Sons	Westwood/ Hancock	Hancock
	Liverpool	Thomas Clarke	Westwood/ Hancock	Hancock
	Manchester	John Fielding	Lutwyche	Mainwaring
	Rochdale	John Kershaw	Kempson	Wyon
Lothian	Edinburgh	Thomas & Alexander Hutchison	Westwood/ Hancock	Hancock
Norfolk	Norwich	Dunham & Yallop	Mainwaring	Mainwaring
		Nathaniel Bolingbroke	Kempson	Wyon
		John Harvey	Kempson	Wyon
	Yarmouth	William Absolon	Westwood/ Hancock	Hancock
Nottinghamshire	Nottingham	William Donald & Company	Kempson	Wyon
Shropshire	Coalbrookdale & Ketley	[William Reynolds]	Kempson	Wyon
	Willey	John Wilkinson	Westwood/ Hancock	Hancock
		John Wilkinson	Boulton	Dumarest (Hancock)
Warwickshire	Birmingham	Henry Biggs	——	Patrick
		Henry Biggs*	——	Patrick
		Birmingham Mining & Copper Company	Kempson	Wyon
		William Donald & Company	Kempson	Wyon
		Henry Hickman	Mainwaring	Mainwaring
	Birmingham (Westminster)	Henry Hickman	Lutwyche	Mainwaring
	Coventry	Robert Reynolds & Company	Lutwyche	Mainwaring
Yorkshire	Huddersfield	John Downing	Lutwyche	Mainwaring

313

1793

Halfpennies

County Dublin	Dublin & Ballymurtagh	H M Co [Hibernian Mine Company]	——	Mossop
Gloucestershire	Bristol	Hawkins Bird	Westwood/Hancock	Hancock
Hampshire	Emsworth	John Stride	Kempson	Wyon
	Petersfield	Eames, Holland & Andrews	Kempson	Wyon
Invernesshire	Inverness	Mackintosh, Inglis & Wilson	Boulton	Küchler
Kircudbrightshire	Gatehouse of Fleet	Scott & Company	Waring	Davies
Lancashire	Manchester	John Fielding	Lutwyche	Arnold
		John Fielding	Lutwyche	Dixon
	Wainfleet	Wright & Palmer	Kempson	Wyon
Norfolk	Norwich	Robert Campin	Kempson (& another)	——
		Dunham & Yallop	Mainwaring	Mainwaring
		Dunham & Yallop	Mainwaring	Mainwaring
Shropshire	Shrewsbury	Salop Woollen Manufactory	Westwood/Hancock	Hancock
	Willey	John Wilkinson	Boulton	Dumarest (Hancock)
Staffordshire	Leek	[Phillips & Ford]	Kempson	Wyon
Suffolk	Bury St Edmunds	Philip Deck*	Kempson	Wyon
	Ipswich	Robert Manning*	Kempson	Wyon
	Sudbury	Goldsmith & Sons	Kempson	Wyon
Yorkshire	Huddersfield	John Downing	Lutwyche	Mainwaring
	Leeds	Henry Brownbill	Boulton	Ponthon
	Sheffield	John Hands	Hands	Hands

314

APPENDIX I

349 Peter Kempson: Colchester halfpenny for Charles Heath, bay maker, 1794.

1794
Pennies

Suffolk	Bury St Edmunds	Philip Deck	Mainwaring	Mainwaring

Halfpennies

Bedfordshire	Leighton Buzzard	Chambers, Langston, Hall & Company	Kempson	Wyon
County Dublin	Dublin & Ballymurtagh	H M Co [Hibernian Mine Company]	——	Mossop
	Dublin	Talbort Fyan	Lutwyche	Arnold
		William Parker	Lutwyche	Arnold
		L & R [Lloyd & Ridley]	——	Mossop
		L & R [Lloyd & Ridley]	——	Mossop
		MFW	——	Mossop
Essex	Braintree & Bocking	William Goldsmith	Kempson	Wyon
	Chelmsford	William Clacher & Company	Kempson	Wyon
	Colchester	Charles Heath [349]	Kempson	Wyon
Hampshire	Emsworth	John Stride	Kempson	Wyon
	Gosport	John Jordan	Kempson	Wyon
	Portsea	Edward Sargeant	Kempson	Wyon
	Portsmouth & Chichester	Sharp & Chaldecott	Kempson	Wyon
Herefordshire	Hereford	Charles Honiatt	Lutwyche	Arnold
Invernesshire	Inverness	Mackintosh, Inglis & Wilson	Boulton	Küchler
Kent	Appledore	William Peckham	Lutwyche	Wyon
	Benenden	Thomas Reeves	Lutwyche	Wyon
	Brookland	Thomas King	Lutwyche	Arnold
	Canterbury	John Matthews/James Robinson	Lutwyche	Dixon
	Deal	Richard Long	Lutwyche	Wyon
	Dover	John Horn	Lutwyche	Dixon
	Dymchurch	William Parris	Lutwyche	Wyon
	Faversham	John Crow	Lutwyche	Dixon
	Goudhurst	William Fuggle/William Mynn	Lutwyche	Arnold
	Hawkhurst	Charles Hider	Lutwyche	Arnold
	Hythe	Richard Shipdem	Lutwyche	Arnold
	Lamberhurst	Thomas Foster	Lutwyche	Wyon

315

COINAGE AND CURRENCY IN EIGHTEENTH-CENTURY BRITAIN

350 Thomas Mynd: London halfpenny for John Fowler, oil man, Long Acre, 1794.

351 Manufacturer unknown: London 'Franklin Press' token for John Watt, printer, Lincoln Inn Fields, 1794.

		John Gibbs	Lutwyche	Wyon
	New Romney	John Sawyer	Lutwyche	Wyon
	Sandwich	Thomas Bundock*	Lutwyche	Dixon
	Staplehurst	John Simmons	Lutwyche	Arnold
Lancashire	Lancaster	Daniel Eccleston	Boulton	Ponthon
Lincolnshire	Spalding	Thomas Jennings	Kempson	Wyon
Middlesex	London	John Bebbington*	——	——
		John Fowler [350]	Mynd	Wyon
		The Franklin Press [351][1]	——	——
		J & S Kelly*	Lutwyche	Dixon
		James Lackington & Company	Westwood/ Hancock or Lutwyche	Hancock or Dixon
		Lackington, Allen & Company	Lutwyche	Dixon
		B Price	Skidmore	James
		Francis Shackleton	Lutwyche	Dixon
		'The Black Horse', Tower Hill (Masonic)*	Lutwyche	Dixon
Norfolk	Norwich	Richard Bacon	Kempson	Wyon
		Bullen & Martin	Kempson	Wyon
		Robert Campin	Kempson (& another)	——
		Joseph Clarke	Lutwyche	Arnold
		Richard Dinmore & Son*	Kempson	Wyon
Somerset	Bath	William Gye	Lutwyche	Wyon
		Francis Heath	Lutwyche	Wyon
		Mary Lambe & Son [352]	Lutwyche	Arnold
	Bridgwater	John Holloway & Son	Kempson	Wyon
Suffolk	Blything	Sir John Rous	Kempson	Hancock
	Bungay	Samuel Prentice	Lutwyche	Arnold
	Bury St Edmunds	James Goer*	Kempson	Wyon
	Haverhill	John Fincham	Kempson	Wyon
	Ipswich	James Conder	Kempson	Wyon

1 The status of this piece as a commercial token is debatable and may be political in intent. It is said to have been issued by the printing firm of John Watt of Wild's Court, Lincoln's Inn Fields where Benjamin Franklin worked as a journeyman printer during 1725-26: Blades (1883), 120; Waters (1906), 20-21; Longman (1916), 33-34.

APPENDIX I

352 William Lutwyche: Bath penny token for Mary Lambe and Son, grocers and tea dealers, 1794.

Sussex	Chichester	Richard Dally & Son	Kempson	Wyon
	Chichester & Portsmouth	Sharp & Chaldecott	Westwood/ Hancock	Hancock
	Frant	George Ring	Lutwyche	Wyon
	Hastings	James Tebay	Lutwyche	Wyon
	Northiam	John Foller	Lutwyche	Wyon
		Elias Gilbert	Lutwyche	Wyon
	Winchelsea	Richard Maplesden	Lutwyche	Wyon
		Richard Maplesden	Lutwyche	Wyon
Warwickshire	Birmingham	James Sketchley	Lutwyche	Dixon
	Coventry	Robert Reynolds & Company	Dobbs	——
Yorkshire	Sheffield	John Hands	Hands	Hands

Farthings

Somerset	Bath	Francis Heath	Lutwyche	Wyon
		Lacon Lambe	Lutwyche	Arnold

1795
Halfpennies

353 Thomas Mynd 'Kent Halfpenny' for Thomas Haycraft, ironmonger, Deptford, 1795.

Angus	Dundee	Alexander Molison	Kempson	Wyon
Buckinghamshire	Chesham	Adam Simpson	Lutwyche	Dixon
Dorset	Poole	James Bayly	Lutwyche	Arnold
County Dublin	Dublin	John Ord*	——	Mossop
		William Parker	Lutwyche	Arnold
Essex	Hornchurch	George Cotton	Boulton	Ponthon
	Maldon	William Draper*	Good	Davies
Glamorgan	Glamorgan	William Jorden	Jorden	Jorden
	Swansea	John Voss	Kempson	Wyon
Gloucestershire	Brimscombe Port	Thames & Severn Canal Co	Westwood/ Hancock	Hancock
	Bristol	Niblock & Hunter	Waring	Davies
		Niblock & Hunter	Good	Davies
Invernesshire	Inverness	Mackintosh, Inglis & Wilson	Boulton	Küchler
Kent	Canterbury	Edward Pillow	Waring	Dixon
	Deptford	Thomas Haycraft [353]	Mynd	——
	Maidstone	Henry Oliver	Lutwyche	Dixon
		James Smyth	Good	Davies
Lincolnshire	Sleaford	Thomas Ball*	Lutwyche	----/(Dixon)

317

COINAGE AND CURRENCY IN EIGHTEENTH-CENTURY BRITAIN

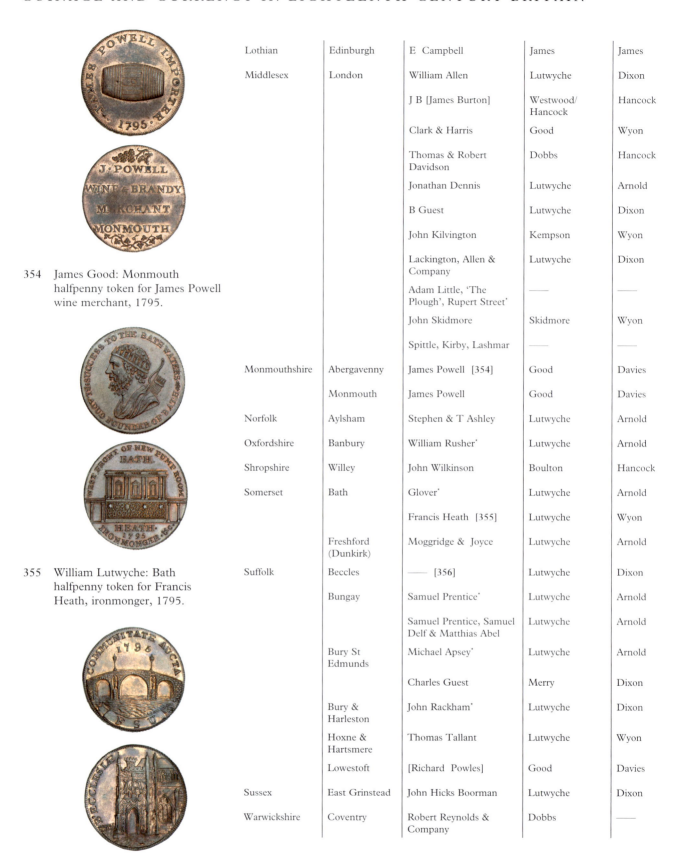

Lothian	Edinburgh	E Campbell	James	James
Middlesex	London	William Allen	Lutwyche	Dixon
		J B [James Burton]	Westwood/ Hancock	Hancock
		Clark & Harris	Good	Wyon
		Thomas & Robert Davidson	Dobbs	Hancock
		Jonathan Dennis	Lutwyche	Arnold
		B Guest	Lutwyche	Dixon
		John Kilvington	Kempson	Wyon
		Lackington, Allen & Company	Lutwyche	Dixon
		Adam Little, 'The Plough', Rupert Street'	—	—
		John Skidmore	Skidmore	Wyon
		Spittle, Kirby, Lashmar	—	—
Monmouthshire	Abergavenny	James Powell [354]	Good	Davies
	Monmouth	James Powell	Good	Davies
Norfolk	Aylsham	Stephen & T Ashley	Lutwyche	Arnold
Oxfordshire	Banbury	William Rusher'	Lutwyche	Arnold
Shropshire	Willey	John Wilkinson	Boulton	Hancock
Somerset	Bath	Glover'	Lutwyche	Arnold
		Francis Heath [355]	Lutwyche	Wyon
	Freshford (Dunkirk)	Moggridge & Joyce	Lutwyche	Arnold
Suffolk	Beccles	—— [356]	Lutwyche	Dixon
	Bungay	Samuel Prentice'	Lutwyche	Arnold
		Samuel Prentice, Samuel Delf & Matthias Abel	Lutwyche	Arnold
	Bury St Edmunds	Michael Apsey'	Lutwyche	Arnold
		Charles Guest	Merry	Dixon
	Bury & Harleston	John Rackham'	Lutwyche	Dixon
	Hoxne & Hartsmere	Thomas Tallant	Lutwyche	Wyon
	Lowestoft	[Richard Powles]	Good	Davies
Sussex	East Grinstead	John Hicks Boorman	Lutwyche	Dixon
Warwickshire	Coventry	Robert Reynolds & Company	Dobbs	—

354 James Good: Monmouth halfpenny token for James Powell wine merchant, 1795.

355 William Lutwyche: Bath halfpenny token for Francis Heath, ironmonger, 1795.

356 William Lutwyche: Beccles halfpenny token, perhaps a 'town' issue, 1795.

APPENDIX I

357 Peter Kempson: Newent halfpenny token for John Nourse Morse, mercer and fruit tree dealer, 1796.

358 Skidmore: Edinburgh halfpenny token for E. Campbell, tobacconist, 1796.

Farthings

Dorset	Poole	James Bayly	Lutwyche	Arnold
Somerset	Bath	Francis Heath	Lutwyche	Wyon
		Mary Lambe & Son	Lutwyche	Wyon

1796

Halfpennies

Angus	Dundee	William Croom*	Boulton	Ponthon
		William Croom*	Kempson	Wyon
		[William Croom]	Kempson	Wyon
	Montrose	James Bisset	Good	Davies
Cornwall	Penryn	George Chapman George	Boulton	Küchler
Devon	Plymouth	Shepheard, Dove, Hammett & Company	Lutwyche	Arnold
Dorset	Sherborne	Pretor, Pew & Whitty	Westwood/Hancock	Westwood, Jnr
Gloucestershire	Newent	John Morse [357]	Kempson	Wyon
Hampshire	Gosport & Sheerness	Benjamin & John Jones	Pitt	—
	Portsea	Samuel Salmon, John Courtney & Edward Frost	Kempson	Willetts
Hertfordshire	Bishop's Stortford	Sir George Jackson	Boulton	Küchler
Invernesshire	Inverness	Mackintosh, Inglis & Wilson	Boulton	Küchler
Kent	Tenterden	Isaac & Thankful Cloake	Good	Davies
Lothian	Edinburgh	E Campbell [358]	Skidmore	James
		Henry Harrison	—	—
	Leith	John White	Kendrick	—
Norfolk	Norwich	Dunham & Yallop	Lutwyche	Arnold
Suffolk	Bungay	Samuel Prentice	Lutwyche	Arnold
Sussex	Brighton	William Mighell	Lutwyche	Wyon
Wiltshire	Devizes	Joseph Baster	Lutwyche	Arnold
	Salisbury	J & T Sharpe	Kempson	Wyon

Farthings

Angus	Dundee	J M & Co	Kempson	Willetts
		James Wright, Jnr	Kempson	Wyon

319

COINAGE AND CURRENCY IN EIGHTEENTH-CENTURY BRITAIN

1797

Pennies

| Angus | Dundee | Thomas Webster, Jnr | Kempson | Wyon |

Halfpennies

Angus	Dundee	John Pilmer	Kempson	Wyon
		Alexander Swap & Company	Kempson	Wyon
		[Thomas Webster, Jnr]	Kempson	Wyon
	Forfar	John Steele [359]	Kempson	Willetts
	Montrose	James Bisset	Good	Davies
Devon	Puddington	W[illiam] Waller [360][2]	----	----
Fife	Burntisland	Burntisland Vitriol Company	Lutwyche	Dixon
Gloucestershire	Gloucester	Gloucester & Berkeley Canal Company	Kempson	Wyon
Hampshire	Portsmouth	Robinson, Mooney & Carter	Pitt	Wyon
		Thomas Sharp*	Kempson	Wyon
	Portsmouth & Portsea	Joseph Brent*	Pitt	——
Lothian	Edinburgh	Anderson, Leslie & Company	Kempson	Wyon
	Leith	——	Hammond	——
Middlesex	London	Michael & Henry Oppenheim	Lutwyche	Arnold
Perthshire	Perth	John Ferrier	Kempson	Willetts
		John Ferrier	Kempson	Willetts
		Patrick Maxwell	Kendrick	——
		David Peters	Lutwyche	Westwood
Somerset	Crewkerne	Sparks & Gidley	Pitt	Wyon
	Yeovil	Brett & Cayme	Lutwyche	Arnold
Surrey	Croyden	Daniel Garraway [361]	Kendrick	----
Staffordshire	Stafford	William Horton & Company	Kempson	Willetts

Farthings

| Angus | Dundee | James Wright, Jnr | Kempson | Wyon |
| | | James Wright, Jnr | Kempson | Wyon |

359 Peter Kempson: Forfar halfpenny token for John Steele, draper, 1797.

360 Manufacturer unknown: Puddington (Devon) halfpenny token for William Waller, ironmonger, 1797.

2   Dickinson (2008), 127-46.

APPENDIX I

1798
Halfpennies

Hampshire	West Cowes (Isle of Wight)	Thomas Ayrton & Company	Lutwyche	Arnold (Hancock)

Farthings

Perthshire	Perth	[John Ferrier]	Kempson	Willetts

361 Joseph Kendrick: Croydon halfpenny for Daniel Garraway, tea dealer, 1797.

DISTRIBUTION MAP OF EIGHTEENTH-CENTURY PROVINCIAL COINS 1787-1804

(Based on R. C. Bell's Commercial Coins 1787-1804 (1963), 15)

The line marks the Severn-Trent Divide

321

APPENDIX II

Biographical Notes on Artists, Engravers and Die Sinkers[1]

Francis Arnold (1772-1829) – Birmingham. An accomplished engraver, Arnold was, after the Wyons, the most prolific of Birmingham die-sinkers. He began as a die-sinker for William Lutwyche in 1793 and took over as the latter's main engraver on William Mainwaring's death the following year. Arnold was responsible for the dies of at least 31 provincial coins, together with a large number of trade tickets and tokens made for sale and an unknown quantity of Lutwyche counterfeits. Apart from a trade ticket engraved for James Good (*D&H*: Wiltshire 4) he seems to have worked solely for Lutwyche.

William Davies (*fl.*1795-1813) – Birmingham. Again a skilful engraver who produced attractive dies mainly for James Good (8) but also for Samuel Waring (2) and may have engraved the dies for several early nineteenth-century silver tokens. Pye (1797) recorded his address as Great Charles Street.

Roger Dixon (*c.*1755-1827) – Birmingham. A die sinker associated mainly with William Lutwyche for whom he created dies for 20 tokens (and one reverse), for medalets and, it is suspected, counterfeits. He also engraved dies for the single tokens struck by Joseph Merry (*D&H*: Suffolk 30) and Samuel Waring (*D&H*: Kent 8-10) in 1795 and, in the early nineteenth century, is said to have worked with Thomas Halliday (1771-1844).[2] In 1791(*UBD*) his address was listed as Temple Row, Birmingham, but by 1797 (Pye (1797)) he had moved to St. Philip's Churchyard.

Jean-Pierre Droz (1746-1823)[3] – Soho. See Chapter II. A Parisian engraver of Swiss extraction employed by Boulton between 1788 and 1790 for his technical inventiveness and artistic talent. Droz did not live up to Boulton's expectations, their relationship proved to be an unhappy one and Boulton was left with little to show for his money or his trials other than some first-class patterns and Soho's medal celebrating the king's recovery from illness in 1789. To Boulton Droz was 'the most ungrateful, most ungenerous, & basest man I ever had any concern with';[4] nevertheless, apart from his difficult time at Soho, Droz's career

---

1 Based on Pye (1801), *UBD*, Pye (1797), Sharp (1834), Forrer (1902-1930) [a magnificently encyclopaedic work but now dated and to be treated with care], *ODNB* and authorities cited in the footnotes below. Unless otherwise stated the quantities of tokens given relate to authentic provincial coins.

2 Halliday was not a token manufacturer as is traditionally thought but a die-sinker and medallist most of whose work was struck by his fellow former Soho apprentice Edward Thomason (*c.* 1769-1849).

3 Pollard (1968); Doty (1999), 26-45.

4 MS 3782/13/36/48: Matthew Boulton to Matthew Robinson Boulton, 30 August 1790.

was a distinguished one culminating in his appointment by Napoleon as General Administrator of the Coins and Medals of France.

Rambert Dumarest (1760-1806) –Soho. See Chapter III. A French engraver, succeeding Droz in August 1790, Dumarest worked at Soho until June 1791 during which time he engraved the dies for three tokens. Returning to France he was active as a medallist and in 1803 Boulton engaged Dumarest to engrave the reverse of his 'Medallic Scale' medal as a rebuttal of Droz's claims of responsibility for the coining improvements achieved at Soho.

John Gregory Hancock (*c*.1750-1805) – Birmingham. See Chapter IV.

John Gregory Hancock, Junior (bap. 1792) – Birmingham. Allegedly a child prodigy who was credited with the dies for some private tokens and novelties in 1800 at ages variously stated to be seven, eight or nine. He presumably died young for Sharp found no trace of his existence in 1834 although George Barker, one of his supposed sponsors, was then still very much alive.[5]

B[enjamin] Jacobs (*fl*. 1790s) – London. An obscure engraver employed by Skidmore, Jacobs, who specialised in topographical subjects, was responsible for the building medalets put out by Skidmore and by Prattent.

Charles James (*fl*. 1795-1801) – London. The identification of James with a chaser and die-sinker of this name active in Birmingham in the later 1780s [6] is by no means proven. Whether or not he was originally active in Birmingham James was established in London by the mid-1790s at 6, Martlett Court, Bow Street, an address from which he issued advertisement pieces *c*. 1796. He was responsible for the dies for Thomas Spence's tokens and for tokens issued by Robert Orchard, Campbell of Edinburgh and Gilbert Pidcock. Although Pye (1801) cited James as a manufacturer it seems unlikely that he had any such capacity but relied on the Skidmore coinery.

John Stubbs Jorden (1774-) – Birmingham. See Chapter IV.

Conrad Heinrich Küchler (*c*.1740-1810)[7] – Soho. See Chapter III. Born in Flanders of probable German extraction Küchler was employed at Soho from 1793 until his death. The best-known of Boulton's mint engravers Küchler enjoyed an international standing. A designer as well as die-cutter, Küchler was responsible for two or possibly three tokens

---

[5] Sharp (1834), v.

[6] Hawkins (1989), 24. Hawkins qualifies his identification by referring to the possibility of the Jameses being only namesakes.

[7] Pollard (1970).

and, more notably, for the Soho regal coinages and the 1804 Bank of England dollar but his reputation rests mainly on the outstanding medals he engraved for Boulton.

William Mainwaring (1768-1794) – Birmingham. Mainwaring was in business as a plated button-maker in 1791 (*UBD*), with premises in Temple Row. He produced token dies for Lutwyche from 1791 until his death in December 1794 (5) but Pye (1801) also credited him with the manufacture as well as the engraving of other tokens between 1792 and 1794 (6). Although doubts have been expressed about Pye's claims the quantities involved would not have been beyond the capacity of a well set-up button-maker.

John Milton (1759-1805)[8] – London. A medallist and gem-engraver of considerable talent, whom Sharp (1834) described as 'powerful and skilful',[9] Milton was a protégé of Sir Joseph Banks – interestingly his first privately commissioned medal was for the Lincolnshire Society of Industry in 1785, the first year he was to exhibit at the Royal Academy. He was appointed an assistant engraver at the Royal Mint in 1787 but, supplementing his income with private commissions, he was dismissed a decade later for engraving dies for the counterfeiting of foreign gold. His private token work included the dies for the original Parys Mine Company patterns struck by John Westwood in 1786, the 'Marle Pit' threepence for the Reverend Daniel Collyer of Wroxham Hall, Norfolk, in 1797, the patterns engraved for Colonel Fullarton's Troon Canal project and private pieces for David Alves Rebello, James Conder and Matthew Young. Milton was elected a fellow of the Society of Antiquaries in 1792.

William Mossop (1751-1805)[10] – Dublin. Irish medallist and wax modeller and appreciably the best medallist working in Ireland in the late eighteenth century. Resident as a general engraver at 13 Essex Quay from 1783, he worked for Camac, Kyan, and Camac of Dublin between 1792 and 1797 engraving the dies for their Hibernian Mine Company tokens (dated 1792, 1793 and 1794) and, it is said, superintending the issue of the coinage. The financial failure of the firm in 1797 obliged Mossop to return to private medallic work and seal engraving. In 1794 he had engraved dies for two other token issuers and maybe more. A versatile craftsman, he worked with a variety of metals as well as wax, ivory, and precious stones.

Benjamin Patrick (*fl.* 1784-1812)[11] – Birmingham. Little is known about this engraver who made the dies for only three tokens; two struck

---

8   Stainton (1983).

9   iv.

10 *Dictionary of Irish Biography*.

11 Symons (2006), 298; Withers and Withers (1999), 20 and 139.

for Henry Biggs of Birmingham by an unlisted manufacturer (1792) and an anonymous 'North Wales' halfpenny (1794) produced, according to Pye (1801), by Samuel Waring. Patrick is also said to have engraved the dies for a number of early nineteenth-century tokens including the penny issued in 1811 by William Booth, the forger. He may have been related to the die-sinker James Patrick of 20 Upper Priory whose business he apparently took over in the mid-1780s but he is absent from directories after this period until the early nineteenth century when he is listed as a die-sinker in Bath Street.

Spencer Perry (*c*. 1753-1835) – Birmingham. Known only for the crudely nondescript tokens issued by William Hallan. Pye (1801) does not list the manufacturer but this may well have been Skidmore.

John Phillp (1778-1815) – Soho. A talented artist, Phillp worked at the Soho manufactory from 1793, initially as an apprentice and then as a designer and engraver. In coinage and medallic work he assisted and eventually took over from Küchler and was responsible, it is said, for the dies of the 1809 Boulton Funeral Medal [*BHM* 662; *Eimer* 1003].[12] Brought to Soho from Cornwall, Phillp was thought, both in his lifetime and since, to have been a natural son of Matthew Boulton but there is no conclusive proof of this.

------- **Phillips** (*fl*. 1790s) – London. Said by Miss Banks to have engraved the dies for the 'Blockheads' farthing. Perhaps the 'I. PHILLIPS' who signed a medal commemorating the rebuilding of St. James's Church, Clerkenwell, 1788-92 (*BHM* 290).

Noel Alexandre Ponthon (*c*. 1770-1835)[13] - Soho. See Chapter III. Ponthon was employed intermittently at Soho between August 1791 and September 1795 and subsequently on out-working commissions. He engraved dies for seven of Soho's British tokens and, among Boulton's overseas work, the Monneron pieces and the Sierra Leone coinage. In addition to undertaking medallic work for Boulton Ponthon also engraved the dies for Lutwyche's trade tickets and, on stylistic grounds it has been suggested, that he may possibly have been responsible for those for Lutwyche's penny token for the 'Birmingham Poet', John Freeth.

------- **Russell** (*fl*. 1790) – London. According to Waters (1906) the contemporary collector, Thomas Woodward, noted in his copy of Conder's *Arrangement* that an otherwise unknown 'Russell' engraved the dies for the 'Blockheads' farthing.[14]

---

12 Dickinson (1937), 193.

13 Gould (1972).

14 58.

------- **Smith** (*fl.* 1795) – London. Pye (1801) stated that Smith cut dies for William Williams, the St Martin's Lane manufacturer. Otherwise nothing is known about Smith whom Forrer confused with the later modeller and medallist, Thomas Smith.

Thomas Webb (*c.* 1760-1843) – Birmingham. A first class medallist Webb is said to have been employed as an engraver at Soho. Pye (1797) records his address as Cannon Street which suggests that he was in private business by the time of the directory. He cut the dies for the private 'Birmingham Halfpennies' for Barker and Pye (1797) and has been erroneously credited with the 1797 British Commercial Penny and its fractions (now known to have been executed by the younger John Westwood). Webb is best known for his early nineteenth-century medallic work for Edward Thomason.

John Westwood, Senior (1744-1792) – Birmingham. See Chapter IV.

John Westwood, Junior (1774-1850) – Birmingham. See Chapter IV. The son of Obadiah Westwood and nephew of John Westwood, senior, he worked as an engraver for his father and then, perhaps, on his own account, moving to Sheffield at the turn of the century and subsequently London. Apart from the '1793' (probably 1796) Sherborne token and Peters' Perth halfpenny of 1797, he mostly resorted to fabricating tokens for sale to collectors. The 'Token Collector's' halfpennies, said to have been commissioned by 'the dealers',[15] are attributed to Westwood.

Obadiah Westwood (1747-1826) – Birmingham. See Chapter IV.

Thomas Willetts (*fl.* 1797-1820) – Birmingham. Willetts was employed by Kempson, a relation, on a variety of commissions between 1796 and 1801, possibly for some of the 'Buildings' medalets and in particular for the Scottish tokens designed by James Wright. Pye (1797) records his address as Great Charles Street. Sharp (1834) tells us that Willetts was responsible for the dies of the Birmingham Workhouse sixpence and threepence pieces (1813).[16]

William Wilson[17] – London. See Chapter III. A former Soho apprentice and journeyman diesinker and chaser, Wilson left the manufactory in 1782 to set up a die-sinking business in London. Boulton, who regarded him 'an honest Man and a good engraver', tried unsuccessfully to lure him back to Soho in 1790 on the departure of Droz but was told that Wilson was too favourably employed to contemplate a move. As far as is known his token involvement was comparatively small comprising the Parys Mine Company halfpenny dated 1791 (signed W) together with some patterns and copies of the Anglesey series.

---

15   Sharp (1834), iii-iv.
16   189-190.
17   Quickenden (1995), 356; Quickenden (2007), 56-57.

George (*c.* 1740 -1797), **Thomas** (1767-1830) and **Peter Wyon** (1767-1822) – Birmingham. **George Wyon** was employed as a designer and modeller at the Soho manufactory from 1775 until about 1782[18] or later. In the 1780s he established his own business in Birmingham as a modeller, chaser and die-sinker and was joined in the business by his four sons all of whom became die-engravers. Wyon's workshop, which was taken over by the eldest twin sons on their father's death in 1797, was responsible for the dies of a large proportion of the tokens put out in the 1790s but, except for those signed by **Thomas Wyon**, there can be no absolute certainty of who actually engraved what. Thomas Wyon, however, is the only member of the family listed in Pye (1801) and Sharp (1834) – who had a direct hand in the promotion of the Coventry 'Buildings' tokens – asserts that 'Most of the Tokens and Medalets produced at Kempson's manufactory, as well as several of the former denomination struck by Lutwyche, were engraved by him, and his series of Bath, Birmingham, Coventry, Gloucester, and London buildings, discover considerable merit in that particular style of workmanship; some of them, more especially a part of the Coventry series, approach to a very high degree of excellence'.[19]

The Wyon workshop was based at various addresses in Birmingham, for much of the time in Temple Street (*UBD*), but had been established in Lionel Street by the time of George Wyon's death (Pye (1797)). In 1800 Thomas Wyon moved to London where he continued engraving dies for medals and tokens and in 1816 became Chief Engraver of His Majesty's Seals. **Peter Wyon** continued in business in Birmingham, producing tokens and medals, including the large medal of Boulton after a model by Roux (1809). The Birmingham business ended with Peter Wyon's death in 1822 but that based in London continued until the 1930s.

362 Peter Kempson: Private penny token for Thomas Wyon, 1796.

---

18 Quickenden (1995), 356.

19 Sharp (1834), v.

APPENDIX III

THE CONTEMPORARY CATALOGUES

From the time of the first Anglesey pennies tokens had been prized as *curiosities* and by 1794/95 a fashionable collecting hobby was developing into something of a mania. Tokens were struck as 'collectors' pieces' created specifically for this virtuoso market, many produced merely to rook the besotted - artificial rarities, concocted from otherwise common pieces by mixing obverses and reverses - or tendentious political pieces to advance the ideologies of polemicists such as Thomas Spence, the radical bookseller.

Between 1795 and 1801 a number of catalogues were published which both fostered and fed upon the new craze. Some were simply letter-press pamphlets, little more than lists of a dealer's stock or puffs for new issues; others were illustrated with copperplate engravings of varying skill and accuracy, one of the earliest being of especial elegance.

By the close of 1794 Charles Shephard, writing in the *Gentleman's Magazine*, said that the 'token mania' had reached its height:

> [T]he number of [provincial] coins in existence already amounted to three or four hundred; the collectors were perplexed in making new acquisitions and in arranging their cabinets; much confusion ensued; and so great was the desire of the curious to collect all the modern provincial pieces, that it was found indispensably necessary, for the means of augmentation and arrangement, to obtain assistance from a printed list of them.[1]

1. JOHN HAMMOND (*fl.* 1794-1810):

This need was first met by John Hammond, a master printer at the Charing Cross end of St Martin's Lane, London, known to have been in business there over the period 1794 to 1810.[2] Hammond was the publisher of a short-lived monthly magazine, *The Bouquet or Blossoms of Fancy* (1795-96?), which promised to award an 'ELEGANT SILVER MEDAL GRATIS ... to the Author of the best Essay, or best Answer to the Prize Enigma' contributed to the periodical. Otherwise, little is

---

[1] Shephard (1798), 120. Although Shephard dated the 'most prevalent and regular' collecting enthusiasm to the latter part of 1794 the catalogue evidence would suggest that it did not really begin to reach its peak until 1795, by the May of that year, according to Spence, having become a 'universal rage' (p. 332 below).

[2] Todd (1972), 88.

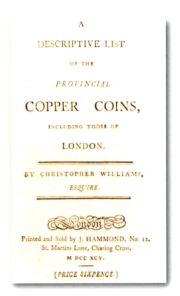

363 Title Page of John Hammond's first Catalogue, 1795.

known about him except that at the time of the issue of his catalogue he was also a coin dealer of dubious credentials with a reputation for charging inflated prices.

His token catalogue, *A DESCRIPTIVE LIST OF THE PROVINCIAL COPPER COINS*, issued at sixpence, was a duodecimo pamphlet of thirty letterpress pages (including the title page) with the typographic heading 'A DESCRIPTIVE LIST, &c,' at page 3 (the first page of the list proper), the whole being originally bound in marbled card. 341 tokens are listed in no particular order and without illustration.

The catalogue is excessively rare today, only three copies being known to exist: two originating from Miss Banks's library (one in the Royal Mint Library and the second (from that Library) now in a private collection); and a third also in a private collection.[3]

Shephard implies that Hammond's catalogue was published 'in the latter part of the year 1794'. But his memory was probably at fault for the title page is dated 1795 while both of Miss Banks's copies are personally inscribed with her date of acquisition – 'May 7.1795'. And bearing in mind her great enthusiasm for tokens it is reasonable to suppose that Miss Banks acquired her copies very shortly after publication.

All that we know of Hammond in terms of his coin dealing comes from Shephard. He castigates Hammond for his 'notoriously bad ... practice in the sale of coins and ... self-interested ... views'. While stressing the shortcomings of Hammond's publication, however, he accords him the honour of being the first to produce a list of tokens:

> This list was very useful at its first promulgation, but it was only temporary; it contains short descriptions of about three hundred coins, promiscuously arranged; it was in consequence rather difficult to find the description of any particular coin, and, the collection being very imperfect, it was uncertain whether it actually contained that description.[4]

The title page tells us that the *List* was 'printed and sold' by Hammond, but credits its authorship to 'Christopher Williams, Esquire', an identity that has plagued numismatists down the generations. Shephard had heard that the catalogue had been 'edited by Mr. Birchall of Leeds [see 4 below], and it might have been suggested by that gentleman' but, he admitted that 'of this I have not any accurate information'. This may just have been gossip, and the name simply a device, a 'respectable cover' for Hammond to create the illusion that his catalogue had been independently edited by a gentleman-collector, and something other than a mere trade list. Be that as it may, there can be little doubt that 'Christopher Williams' was a nom de plume and Miss Banks, ever persistent in her search for the

---

3   The two privately owned copies were auctioned respectively by Spink & Son Ltd. (Sale 47, 10 October 1985, lot 1320) and DNW (Sale T9, 6 October, 2010, lot 4290); and Glendining & Co. (Sale 5/1992, 4 June 1992, lot 369).

4   Shephard (1798), 212-13.

APPENDIX III

truth, and well aware of Hammond's ways, took care to note in her library list - 'Christopher Williams (a fictitious name)'.[5]

[Manville (2005), No. 237].

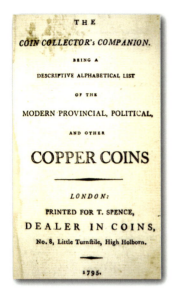

364 Title Page of Thomas Spence's Catalogue, 1795.

2. THOMAS SPENCE (1750-1814):

Hammond's initial list was quickly followed by Thomas Spence's *COIN COLLECTOR's COMPANION*. Again without illustrations, Spence's catalogue, octavo (in half sheets), was published, according to Shephard, 'in the beginning of 1795' and, selling at the same price of sixpence, 'immediately eclipsed' Hammond's. Miss Banks records her purchase of 'Mr. Spence's publication on tokens' on 16 May 1795, and it is likely that it was published only days before this date.[6] 'The whole work', Shephard tells us, 'contained descriptions of about five hundred coins ... [and] ... had three advantages over the preceding list; the account of nearly two hundred additional half-pennies, the alphabetical arrangement, and the copiousness of its descriptions'.[7]

There appear to have been two issues bound originally in marbled card or blue wrappers, each dated 1795 – the second version published in the August of that year – with the same title page and, again, duodecimo in size. Each was published from 8 Little Turnstile, a narrow lane off High Holborn, from a shop that Spence characteristically called the 'Hive of Liberty'. Since contemporary owners bound in additional material provided by Spence, it is not easy to establish the exact content of these issues on publication. But they seem to conform to the following basic format, although there are minor printing variations.

(a) The first issue of May 1795 comprises fifty letterpress pages (thirteen of which are blank) listing, in alphabetical sections, 352 tokens together with a single page '*ADDENDA*' of nine coins 'having been by accident omitted in their proper Places'. Some copies – but they are very rare – incorporate a two-page notice '**TO THE PUBLIC**' which may originally have been published as a separate 'flyer' and subsequently bound in.

(b) The second issue of August 1795 again comprises fifty letterpress pages but now lists 356 tokens with a revised pagination. The first forty-eight pages are identical to those in the first issue but the original pages 49 and 50 have been replaced by amended versions adding four new entries to the list. In addition there is a six page '**SUPPLEMENT TO SPENCE's LIST OF COINS**' (paginated in Roman numerals,

---

5   Royal Mint Museum: Miss Banks's MS Numismatic Library Catalogue. In the British Museum's version of this list (appended to Volume VII (Medals) of her MS Catalogue, BM: Department of Coins and Medals, Arc R19) 'Christopher Williams' is referred to as 'a feigned Name'.

6   Banks MS 'List of Coins ...'.

7   Shephard (1798), 213.

331

i-vi) adding a further 64 tokens, and replacing the '*ADDENDA*' of the First Issue. The numbering of page ii of the **SUPPLEMENT** is inverted in early printings but is later corrected although the contents of the page remain the same. It is evident that the '**SUPPLEMENT**' (printed together with revised pages 49 and 50) was also produced as a separate pamphlet for those collectors who wished simply to augment their copies of the First Issue. This is borne out by the existence of a discrete copy once owned by Miss Banks (now in the Royal Mint Library) and inscribed by her 'August 14. 1795', and must be what Shephard referred to as an 'appendix' selling at one penny.[8]

In his notice '*TO THE PUBLIC*' Spence asks, rather disingenuously, what had occasioned the 'universal rage of collecting Coins?' In answer to which he responds:

> There is no other way to preserve them from Oblivion. Again, some of them, on account of Device, some for neatness of Workmanship, and all on account of their great Variety, may, nay will, claim the attention of the Curious in after-ages. These considerations incite the judicious to make Collections, especially of the best Impressions, while they are yet cheap and easily to be met with, well knowing that they will never be of less value, nor their Beauty encreased by Wear.

But Spence was not appealing to the 'investor collector'. His catalogue was less a genuine listing of existing tokens – though it was his business to sell tokens of all kinds – than a 'puff' for his own products; and a 'puff' not so much for profit, as for political ends, which Shephard argued had 'done more harm to the coinage than any other persons in the aggregate'.[9] Some copies have Spence's handbill of *New Coins* (see page 283 above) added to the volume.

To his old friend, Thomas Bewick, who engraved his portrait, he 'was one of the warmest philanthropists in the world. The happiness of mankind seemed with him to absorb every other consideration'. Spence's junior contemporary, the radical reformer Francis Place, recalled him as being

> a very simple, very honest, single minded man, querulous in his disposition odd in his manners, he was remarkably irritable. He was perfectly sincere, unpractised in the ways of the world, to an extent few could imagine in a man who had been pushed about in it as he had been, yet what is more remarkable this character never changed, and he died as much of a child in some respects as he was when he arrived at the usual age of manhood.[10]

[Manville (2005), No. 236].

---

[8] Shephard (1798), 213.

[9] Shephard (1798), 122.

[10] Bewick (1862), 71-72; BL: Francis Place MSS, Additional MS 27808, f. 152.

APPENDIX III

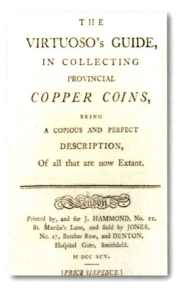

365 Title Page of John Hammond's second Catalogue, 1795.

3. JOHN HAMMOND (*fl.* 1794-1810):

The success of Spence's publication persuaded Hammond, 'by way of retaliation', to issue, later in 1795, 'a second edition of his catalogue, in alphabetical arrangement also, in that manner taking advantage of his antagonist's improvement'.[11] Miss Banks records the purchase of Hammond's new *VIRTUOSO's GUIDE, IN COLLECTING PROVINCIAL COPPER COINS*, once more priced at sixpence, on 2 July 1795.[12] Characteristically, she must have acquired more than one copy since that now in the Royal Mint library is inscribed by her with the date 'Aug: 15. 1795', the day after she acquired the Spence 'Supplement'.

Octavo, bound in marbled card, and without illustrations, the letterpress catalogue comprises a title page, a preliminary two-page explanatory notice '*To the Public*', followed by forty-six pages (including a single page '**ADDENDA**') describing 428 tokens. In his introductory notice Hammond justifies his new work:

> AFTER Two Publications that bear a Similarity to this, have been presented to the Public, a Third at first Sight may appear superfluous and unnecessary; but when the Reader reflects on the Incorrectness of the preceding Lists, he will see the necessity of a complete and correct one, which has been long wanting, and which the Compiler flatters himself this will be found to be: And as he has taken great pains and trouble by strictly scrutinizing some very extensive and valuable Collections, the Public may rest assured, that all here have been seen, and are actually in being. On the other hand, there are none mentioned twice over, by referring the Reader from one place to another, which so frequently occurred in the course of the last List that was Published.

To Shephard the new publication 'was a valuable improvement on the former; it was alphabetically arranged and contained a very copious, though far from a compleat [*sic*], account of nearly the whole of the provincial coins that were at that time promulgated'.[13]

This time no editor's name appears on the title page but it is of interest to note that Hammond has extended his sales-outlets to '**JONES, No.17, Butcher Row, and Denton of Hospital Gate, Smithfield**'. More will be said about Denton later whose numismatic connections with Hammond seem to have been close. Jones cannot be identified from contemporary directories unless he is the James Jones, a Butcher Row cheesemonger listed in the *Universal British Directory* (if this is the correct identification, selling coin catalogues seems an intriguing sideline to vending cheese). The association of Denton and Jones as selling agents for Hammond's catalogue does raise the question of whether they had any links with the bookseller, inventor

---

11 Shephard (1798), 120.

12 Banks MS 'List of Coins ...'.

13 Shephard (1798, 213.

and forger Thomas Denton, and an accomplice, John Jones, who were hanged at Newgate in 1789 for possessing coining implements. Time will perhaps tell.

[Manville (2005), No. 233].

4. SAMUEL BIRCHALL (1761-1814):

The lists published by Hammond and Spence were, Shephard observed, 'all capable of receiving very great enlargement; as they contained only partial descriptions of the provincial half-pennies, and paid very little attention to the various dates and superscriptions, and readings on the edges'. In 1796 they were superseded by another 'verbal' list, *A DESCRIPTIVE LIST OF THE PROVINCIAL COPPER COINS OR TOKENS*, published on 30 January by the Samuel Birchall who had been rumoured to have had a hand in Hammond's first list, that supposedly edited by 'Christopher Williams'.

'Mr. Birchall', Shephard tells us, 'industrious as a collector and vigilant as a compiler' published his catalogue 'at eighteen pence or two shillings each copy'.

> This catalogue [he goes on] was a valuable acquisition; for, exclusive of the original list, it contains a very copious appendix. The coins, at least the greater part, are arranged in the alphabetical order of the places where they were coined, or of which they are memorials. - Though considerable merit is due to Mr. Birchall, when we reflect on the complex nature of the work, and the confusion so very prevalent at the time of its promulgation, yet he might have made his descriptive list far more compleat [sic], and his plan of arrangement more easy and accurate.[14]

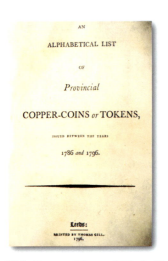

366 Title Pages of Samuel Birchall's Catalogue, 1796.

Charles Pye [see 5 and 7 below], too, found Birchall's catalogue wanting for though Birchall had obviously 'taken a great deal of pains … and his collection must have cost him many pounds' he had included some pieces 'that were not intended either as coins and tokens when issued' and had omitted other legitimate ones. His main criticism was directed, however, at Birchall's taking in a 'great mass' of mules intended '*to impose upon the publick*'. Pye remained suspicious of Birchall and was later to accuse him of promoting the extensive series of falsely-edged versions of his private token that exist although this deception may well have carried out by the manufacturer of the tokens as a private speculation rather than on the instructions of Birchall himself.[15]

The octavo catalogue, bound again in marbled boards, comprises a tipped-in engraved title-page by Christopher Livesey, a local Leeds engraver and copper-plate printer, carrying a vignette of the halfpenny

---

14 Shephard (1798), 213.

15 Pye (1796), 991; Pye (1801), 12.

APPENDIX III

367 Peter Kempson: 'Leeds Commercial Halfpenny' for Samuel Birchall, 1795

token Birchall issued in 1795 [367] and announcing that the catalogue was sold by Henry Young, the London jeweller and coin dealer, a letterpress title page, giving the name of the printer, Thomas Gill of Leeds, and a preface, 'TO THE COLLECTORS of PROVINCIAL COINS'. Then follow 141 numbered pages including a substantial 'APPENDIX' (pages 109-140) and an additional 'ERRATA' page. Eighteen pages are left blank for notes and additions.

Birchall seems to have intended to produce a second edition of his catalogue because a copy exists, with his bookplate, containing additional entries and a much-extended list of errata, but it was never published.[16]

Birchall was a Quaker, a rich Leeds woolstapler who, we are told by a nineteenth-century biographer, was 'an ardent lover of everything connected with natural history, and other scientific and antiquarian pursuits. He formed valuable collections of stuffed birds and beasts, of mineralogy, of gold and silver coins, and of copper tokens - especially of those that were chiefly issued between 1786 and 1796 ... [and] ... kept up an extensive acquaintance with men of letters of similar pursuits in other parts of the country'.[17] Birchall was also a customer of Matthew Boulton, and bought one of James Watt's copying presses from Soho. He was a regular purchaser of 'toys', and sets of coins from the firm, and was the intermediary for a consortium that promoted a halfpenny token issued in the name of Henry Brownbill, a Leeds watchmaker and silversmith.[18]

[Manville, No. 239].

5. CHARLES PYE (1749-1830):

The catalogues so far described were 'confined to meer verbal description' but, 'a taste for encouraging the arts' had led in the summer of 1794, as Shephard tells us, 'to the publication of engravings ... containing accurate delineations of the original coins'.[19] The first series of such engravings, *PROVINCIAL COPPER COINS*, was published on subscription by Charles Pye of Birmingham in twelve octavo numbers, three plates in each, at half-a-crown per number. Proofs of the plates on large paper were also published at 5s per number.

First issued in August 1794, each set of plates, bound in blue wrappers with a distinctively hand-numbered engraved 'putto' label, was avidly awaited by collectors, for the 'ingenious Mr Pye['s] ... plates' were 'executed in a very masterly manner, the resemblances of the coins are exact and finely finished, and his specimens are derived from the most authentic sources'.[20]

16 John Drury, Catalogue 12 (1973), 336.
17 Taylor (1865), 253.
18 Vice (1992), 2-6.
19 Shephard (1798), 213-14.
20 Shephard (1798), 214.

COINAGE AND CURRENCY IN EIGHTEENTH-CENTURY BRITAIN

370   Plate 3 of Charles Pye's *Provincial Copper Coins*, 1 June 1795.

Proposals for this Work.

I. THAT the Plates be engraved in an uniform Manner, each Plate to contain five Coins.

II. That three Plates constitute a Number, Price 2s. 6d. each Number.

III. That fifty Proofs, only, be taken on large Paper, at 5s. each Number: — The Money to be paid on Delivery.

IV. That a Number be published, the first of each Month, (if possible) until the Series is gone through, which, in all Probability, will extend to eight Numbers.

V. That when the Work is complete, the Price will be raised to 3s. each Number, or 1s. every Plate; therefore those who subscribe will have a decided Preference, not only in the Prints, but in the Price.

N. B. Very few Proofs remain unsubscribed for, therefore, those who prefer them are requested to be early in their Applications to *Mr. Nichols*, Red Lion Passage, Fleet-Street; *Mr. Baldwin*, Paternoster-Row; *Messrs. Egerton's*, Charing-Cross; *Mr. Debrett*, Piccadilly; *Mr. Richardson*, Royal Exchange, London; *Mr. Swinney*, *Mr. Pearson*, or C. Pye, Engraver, Birmingham, where the former Numbers may be had.

368   Flyer for Charles Pye's *Provincial Copper Coins*, 1794

369   Pye's 'putto' label for the wrapper of an original three-plate issue of his *Provincial Copper Coins* No. 2, 1 September 1794.

Even the hard-headed Birmingham industrialist Samuel Garbett, by no means a devotee of trade tokens, was captivated and in December he was anxiously reminding his friend Matthew Boulton not to forget to bring him the latest instalment of 'Pye's prints of halfpence'.[21]

Yet the very elegance and meticulous execution of Pye's engravings militated against the economic success of the enterprise. Pye also found it increasingly difficult to find reputable specimens to include in his plates and with the publication of the eleventh set in July 1795 he decided to give the venture up. Already, he had decided to advance the price of each ordinary set to three shillings [371] and the flood of tokens that had appeared over the previous months – 'many of them', complained Pye, 'so infamous that ... they are a disgrace to the age we live in' – was making the scrupulous representation Pye had embarked on, unmanageable.[22]

21   BAH: MBP 309/148, Samuel Garbett to Matthew Boulton, 9 December 1794.
22   Pye (1795), 'ADVERTISEMENT'.

APPENDIX III

> ### Provincial Copper Coins or Tokens.
>
> C. PYE respectfully informs those who approve of this Publication, that the Contents of his Cabinet is now nearly Exhibited before them, and is desirous of informing them that he has heard of several different Sorts that he has not been able to procure; therefore requests those who issue them, or any Person who can accommodate him with any Tokens not at present described, that they will have the Goodness to send one of them free of Expence, before the First of May, either to Mr. JOHN NICHOLS, Red Lion Passage, Fleet Street, London; or to him at Birmingham; and what are consistent with the Plan already adopted, shall in due Course be engraved.
>
> N. B. The Price is intended to be advanced to THREE SHILLINGS each Number, on the First of August next.
>
> BIRMINGHAM, 25th March, 1795.

371 Pye's announcement of the increase in the price of his plates from 2s 6d to 3s each number.

> THE Promoters of this Publication are requested to observe, that the TWELFTH NUMBER will so far exhaust my Cabinet, that I have not a sufficient Quantity to make another; therefore, on the First of September, No. 12 is intended to be published, with a Title Page for the Work, and an Alphabetical Index to the Tokens described.
>
> Those who have not purchased their Numbers regularly, are requested to be early in their Application for them, as none will be sold after the Month of September under One Shilling for every Plate.
>
> Charles Pye.

372 Pye's announcement of the cessation of his *Provincial Copper Coins*.

In September 1795, to wind up the project [372] Pye, produced an engraved title page [373], a letterpress 'ADVERTISEMENT' or preface (dated '*Birmingham, Sept. 1, 1795*') and a three-page letterpress index to enable subscribers to bind the thirty-six plates so far published as a single octavo or imperial octavo (large paper) volume, *PROVINCIAL COPPER COINS OR TOKENS, ISSUED BETWEEN THE YEARS 1787 AND 1796, ENGRAVED BY CHARLES PYE, OF BIRMINGHAM FROM THE ORIGINALS IN HIS OWN POSSESSION.*

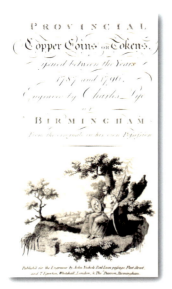

373 Title Page of Pye's *Provincial Copper Coins or Tokens*, 1795, with his vignette of Britannia seated under a tree contemplating a portrait of George III.

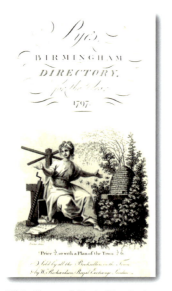

374 Title Page of *Pye's Birmingham Directory*, 1797.

The Dictionary of National Biography tells us that Pye, in the expectation of succeeding to a fortune, had seen no need to practise any trade, but that when his prospects were destroyed as the result of a lawsuit, he was obliged to maintain his family by writing works on local history and antiquities – subjects he had already explored as a gentleman amateur.[23] The truth, however, appears to be rather more prosaic. In reality, Charles Pye seems originally to have been a Birmingham watchmaker and engraver. About 1780 he gave his business up to become a wine merchant. Undercapitalised, he applied for, and obtained, a collectorship of window and hearth taxes but treated the duties he collected as a 'perquisite' to fund his private wine business. Even for the relaxed eighteenth century this behaviour was regarded as wholly improper, and by the time that Pye had discharged his debts to the Crown and to the multitude of private creditors who hounded him as soon as the scandal broke he was left penniless. To make a living Pye turned back to engraving, and, from 1785, to the new venture of compiling directories of Birmingham.

Over the next fifteen years he produced a number of editions, each with a plan of the town, and from 1787 charged 2s for a directory or 2s 6d for one with the plan. As time wore on, however, his attitude to the compilation of entries became more and more casual. Originally his directories were based on a personal canvass of the town, with free insertions, but by the turn of the century he had given up this approach, advertising for entries with an insertion charge of sixpence each. Not surprisingly, this method of proceeding proved to be unsuccessful and after 1800 Pye published no more directories.[24] He had a ready and versatile pen, however, and over the succeeding years produced a number of books ranging from *The New Chemical Nomenclature* (1802), *A New Dictionary of Ancient Geography* (1803), and *A Description of Modern Birmingham* (1820) republished in 1825 and subsequent years as *The Stranger's Guide to Modern Birmingham*. They all helped to re-establish his reputation but his life had been 'a troublesome' one as his obituarist recollected when Pye died on 30 March 1830 in his eighty-first year.[25]

[Manville (2005), 230].

23 *ODNB*, s.v. Pye, John (1782-1874).

24 Walker (1934), 18-21. No copies of the advertised plan of Birmingham are known to exist in extant copies of Pye's directories for 1787, 1788, 1791 or 1797. The only recorded copy of his final edition of 1800 [Bodleian Library] contains a plan separately published by Pye in 1795 and adapted from one originally engraved by him in 1792.

25 *ABG*, 5 April 1830.

APPENDIX III

6. MATTHEW DENTON (fl. late 18th Century) & **THOMAS PRATTENT** (fl. 1787-1819):

Before Pye had abandoned his octavo sets of plates in the summer of 1795 another engraving venture had been embarked upon, but one that made no attempt to capture the delicacy and accuracy of Pye's draughtsmanship. As Shephard observed, it 'lacked the taste, the perfection and the liberality of [Pye's work] ... [and] ... was also unattended with that expence'.[26]

The large duodecimo *VIRTUOSO'S COMPANION AND COIN COLLECTOR'S GUIDE* appeared in periodic parts collected into eight volumes between 1795 and 1797.

Initially published by Matthew Denton, a petty coin dealer, printer and engraver, at first from Hospital Gate, West Smithfield (Volumes 1–4, 10 July 1795 to 1 September 1796) and then from nearby St John's Street (Volumes 5–6, 12 September 1796 to 11 February 1797) it was completed by Thomas Prattent of Cloth Fair, West Smithfield (Volumes 7 and 8, from 22 April 1797) who was responsible for the engraving throughout. The 'proprietor' of the project, mentioned in the 'Preface', is not named on the title page of the initial volume, but on that of the '**CONTINUATION**' (preceding Volume 5) it is said to be Prattent which is what Miss Banks understood. Both Denton and Prattent produced tokens, Denton's tending to the satirical, and Prattent concentrating on views of public buildings, or specious issues. Miss Banks believed that when the catalogue first came out it was intended to embellish Hammond's *Virtuoso's Guide* therefore taking almost the same name.[27] The main thrust of Denton and Prattent's catalogue, however, was to push their own productions and those of other London token manufacturers, including the Skidmores who bought up Spence's dies in the winter of 1796/1797, and interchanged them even more mercilessly than the propagandist himself.

Hay noted in his own copy of *The Virtuoso's Companion* that:

> Denton was an engraver & printer, but a man of no eminence in his art; and was intimate with all the inferior manufacturers and jobbers in provincial Tokens - indeed it is probable that the work was supported by them in order to induce hasty collectors to buy the trash they circulated. Thus we may account for many of the disgraceful dies here represented, as well as the infinite interchange and pirating of dies.[28]

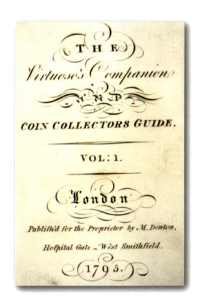

375 Title Page of Volume I of *The Virtuoso's Companion*, 1795.

Hay added that 'The publicat^n. was principally supported by the Jobbers in Medals. All Spence's trash was introduced - and the interchange of dies, a mere jobbing trick, were [*sic*] here inserted in a way that no respectable author or tradesman would have ventured to have done'.

26   Shephard (1798), 214.

27   Banks MS 'List of Coins ...'.

28   Quoted in Dykes (1997), 120.

339

376 Plate 17 of *The Virtuoso's Companion* illustrating three of the Skidmores' Tokens.

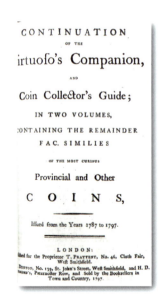

377 Title Page of the *Continuation* of *The Virtuoso's Companion*, 1797.

The compilation appeared in three-plate parts put out at ten-day to fortnightly intervals and costing 6*d* per part, eventually comprising 240 interleaved plates divided into eight volumes, ten parts to each volume with four coins to each plate. Initially the work was to have been completed in four volumes with 120 plates but this was extended to six volumes of 180 plates in September 1796 'in consequence of the great number of new coins that have made their appearance during the publication of this work', and finally to eight volumes in December 1796. Volume 5 was prefaced with a supplementary title page, 'CONTINUATION OF THE Virtuoso's Companion', dated 1797.

It is of interest that, as well as naming Prattent as its proprietor, the 'CONTINUATION' title page pairs the London bookseller, H. D. Symonds of Paternoster Row, with Denton as a publisher of *The Virtuoso's Companion*. Henry Delahay Symonds (*c*.1741-1816), whose name also appeared on the wrappers in which each set was issued, had, in the early 1790s, been deeply involved in radical politics and in 1793 had achieved notoriety with the publication of a series of tracts, including the second part of Thomas Paine's *Rights of Man*. This had resulted in his being fined and imprisoned in Newgate for seditious libel [327] and [328].[29] It was an imprisonment, with other radicals, that was commemorated with the issue of the series of 'Newgate' tokens or medalets in 1794 and 1795 [326] and by the time *The Virtuoso's Companion* was first issued he had only recently been released.

Engraved and numbered title pages were issued for each of the eight volumes, as was an overall, unnumbered title page dated 1797, and indexes were provided at the conclusion of volumes 4, 6 and 8. Each volume of ten numbers, wrapped in a blue paper cover with an expanded imprint and with the terms or 'CONDITIONS' of publication on its lower face, was reissued as it was completed for 5*s*.[30]

Complete sets of the catalogue are very rare, and perfect issues of the last two volumes are extremely difficult to obtain probably because many of the original subscribers had allowed their subscriptions to lapse by the time they were published. Since binding of the compendium was a private matter bindings vary considerably both in what they contain and in the ordering of their contents. As finally bound up, for instance, the first volume should contain a frontispiece, '**History protecting Medals from the Ravages of Time**' (engraved by Prattent from a drawing by Joseph Bowring and dated 1796), a single-page '**PREFACE**' setting out the objects of the enterprise, and a four-page essay, '**OBSERVATIONS ON COINS**'. This was contributed by the Scottish collector and token promoter, James Wright, Jnr. of Dundee, and was an essay that had already appeared in substantially the same form in *The Edinburgh Magazine* for February 1796.

The cheapness of the catalogue, compared to Pye's editions, is striking. The paper is inferior and the printing seems to have been

---

29 See pp. 285-87 above.

30 A note to the 'CONDITIONS' recommended the work to 'Hair-Workers, Jewellers, &c. &c. from the many curious and useful emblematical Figures and Devices'.

APPENDIX III

378 Titled paper cover for volume 5 of *The Virtuoso's Companion*.

carried out in a somewhat cavalier fashion for there are discrepancies in pagination which vary between copies. The Prattent engravings are indifferent throughout, and deteriorate considerably after Denton's departure from Smithfield to Lambeth in the spring of 1797. As Miss Banks noted 'since Denton went away, Prattent has been very careless' and he soon became even more casual and even dropped the 'month' imprint from the plate dates after the number for 13 May 1797.[31] This is surprising, since Prattent was a skilful, if not very inspiring, engraver, who not only contributed the elegant frontispiece to the catalogue, but was well known for his topographical etchings in the magazines of the period. The obverse of the 'Albion Mill' penny in the London and Westminster series of medalets he produced in 1797 [306], for instance, was taken from an engraving he had done for the *European Magazine* of May 1787 [305].[32] Prattent's engraving does not seem to have been a profitable pursuit, however, because by 1804 he was languishing in the Marshalsea Prison, arrested for debt.[33]

[Manville (2005), Nos. 238-238b].

379 Frontispiece to *The Virtuoso's Companion* engraved by Thomas Prattent, 1796.

7. CHARLES PYE (1749-1830):

As we have seen, after his first and unremunerative sortie, into the publication of quality engravings of provincial coins, Pye returned to his other, equally profitless, pursuit of producing Birmingham directories. In 1801, however, he was persuaded to engrave – though in a much less ambitious outline format – a new and enlarged quarto edition of his catalogue.

Pye's 1795 work 'being incomplete ... and great numbers of genuine tokens having been issued since, I was induced to think that a certain guide to *discriminate* true from counterfeit tokens, would be highly useful to collectors, and not unentertaining to the general reader'.[34] Initially the fifty five plates (1-52, 15★, 18★ and 35★) he completed, assisted by his younger son John (1782-1874) who was in time to become a far more famous engraver, were issued in four-part monthly numbers priced at two shillings and sixpence each. On conclusion of the series a detailed 18 page '**INDEX**' listing die-sinkers, manufacturers, proprietors, quantities issued and '**OBSERVATIONS**', with a two-page explanatory introduction or '**ADVERTISEMENT**', were published for binding into an overall volume.

PROVINCIAL COINS AND TOKENS, ISSUED FROM THE YEAR 1787 TO THE YEAR 1801 was an attempt to sort out for the collector what Pye defined in his '**ADVERTISEMENT**' as 'genuine tokens'.

---

31 Royal Mint Museum: Note by Miss Banks inside the back cover of her two-volume copy of *The Virtuoso's Companion*.

32 See pp. 277-78 above.

33 *LG*, 31 July, 934 and successive issues.

34 Pye (1801), [3].

He included, though, not only redeemable tokens 'actually made for the purpose of circulation' but also 'shop-bills' and private issues, and a few unprovenanced pieces made for currency The private pieces were, no doubt, included to encourage sponsorship and Pye produced his own token [382] specifically to encourage exchanges for insertion.

The information provided in the index was supplied to Pye, as the professed editor, by a number of collectors and other authorities. Although it has to be treated with caution and can be faulted on a few fronts, some of the assertions about mintage figures, for instance, being questionable, the new catalogue remains the best contemporary authority for any study of the regular eighteenth century token series. The actual editor of the catalogue was said to be not Pye but the Birmingham attorney, Thomas Welch [384], who wrote the '**ADVERTISEMENT**' (although signed by Pye) and who, together with a fellow Birmingham attorney George Barker and another collector (probably Thomas Sharp of Coventry), supplied many of the tokens that Pye illustrated and most of the information given in the '**INDEX**'. Miss Banks, who was in a position to know, thought that Welch had advanced money on the publication as well.[35]

380   Flyer for Charles Pye's *Provincial Coins and Tokens*, 1801.

381   Title Page of Charles Pye's *Provincial Coins and Tokens*, 1801.

382   Peter Kempson: Private 'Birmingham Halfpenny' for Charles Pye, 1797.

384   Peter Kempson: Private penny token for Thomas Welch, Birmingham, 1800.

35   Royal Mint Museum: Note by Miss Banks on a letter cover slipped into Pye's *Provincial Coins and Tokens* (1801): 'This Cat: made by M[r]. Welch supposed to be M[r]. Pyes [sic] Collection. Probably M[r]. Welch had advanced money upon it. April 25. 1801'.

APPENDIX III

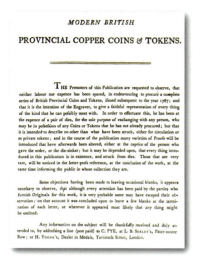

383 Supplementary Notice for Charles Pye's *Provincial Coins and Tokens*, 1801.

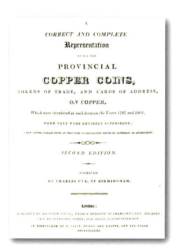

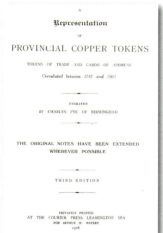

386 Title Pages of the editions of Pye's *Provincial Coins and Tokens* published by (a) Matthew Young (1819) and (b) Arthur W. Waters (1916).

385 Plate 21 of Pye's *Provincial Coins and Tokens*, 1801.

There are two later quarto editions of Pye's work which should be briefly mentioned for completeness.

The first, entitled *A CORRECT AND COMPLETE REPRESENTATION OF ALL THE PROVINCIAL COPPER COINS, TOKENS OF TRADE, AND CARDS OF ADDRESS, ON COPPER WHICH WERE CIRCULATED AS SUCH BETWEEN THE YEARS 1787 AND 1800*, was produced in his lifetime, and presumably with his approval, from the original plates by Matthew Young, the London coin dealer and son of Henry Young who had been involved in Birchall's *Descriptive List*. Although undated this was in 1819, judging by a notice in *The Monthly Magazine* published on 1 January 1820. There is said, too, to be a further printing of this edition put out in the 1830s prior to Young's death in 1838, with plates 25, 35, 41 and 49 watermarked '1831' but otherwise identical to the 1819 edition.[36]

Almost a century later Arthur William Waters, the Leamington Spa bookseller and coin dealer (1869-1962), published a third quarto edition. This 1916 edition, *A REPRESENTATION OF*

---

36 *The Monthly Magazine or British Register*, Vol. 48 (1819), 542. ('New Books PUBLISHED IN DECEMBER [1819]'); Manville (2005), No. 281.

343

387 James Conder. A lithograph by George Rowe, 1821.

388 John Milton: Private penny token for James Conder, 1796.

PROVINCIAL COPPER TOKENS TOKENS OF TRADE AND CARDS OF ADDRESS CIRCULATED BETWEEN 1787 AND 1801, was limited to 23 copies, each signed and numbered by Waters. It reproduces most of Pye's engravings from his original plates – nine plates were missing and Waters reproduced them in facsimile (in fact he reproduced ten: 5, 9, 11, 13, 15, 17, 18★, 24, 34 and 52) to complete the set – but the scholarly value of the work is considerably reduced because Waters revised Pye's notes without distinguishing his later revisions from the original statements.

Waters included in the preliminaries of his edition a portrait frontispiece of Thomas Sharp, reprints of the title pages of the first and the second (Young's) editions, Pye's 'NAMES OF DIE-SINKERS AND MANUFACTURERS' and original 'ADVERTISEMENT' together with a reprint of the priced catalogue of the Thomas Welch sale of tokens on 17-19 September 1801, 'the first Token Sale of Note'.

[Manville (2005), Nos. 255, 281 and 763].

8. JAMES CONDER (1763-1823):

In describing Charles Pye's 1801 *Provincial Coins and Tokens*, we have leapt forward somewhat in time, for the last token catalogue to be published in the eighteenth century was actually James Conder's *ARRANGEMENT OF PROVINCIAL COINS, TOKENS, AND MEDALETS* and it was to remain the standard popular token catalogue for most of the nineteenth century.

James Conder, said to be 'a gentleman of respectable abilities, liberal in his views, modest in his pretensions', was the youngest son of an eminent nonconformist divine, born at Mile End, London, and educated at the dissenters' school at Ware. For many years he was a linen draper and haberdasher in Ipswich and published several tokens advertising his drapery business. Conder also readily took advantage of the collectors' market by creating 'rarities' through the creation of mules and of limited 'editions' of his own tokens [388]. Conder's extensive numismatic collection, especially the token element, which during his lifetime was said to be unrivalled, was eventually auctioned at Sotheby's in 1855.[37]

Conder's catalogue was initially published at Ipswich in 1798 in a single- or two-volume small octavo letterpress edition, bound in boards, with three plates, engraved by Isaac Taylor of Colchester, father of the author of the nursery rhyme, 'Twinkle, Twinkle, Little Star'. This first 'edition' or printing extends to 331 pages (including an 'Appendix' (pp.309-322), an index (pp.323-330) and an errata page). The catalogue proper is preceded by an '**Address to the Public**' by Conder dated 1 August 1798, and a fourteen page '**PREFACE** BY THE LATE *James Wright, Esq. of Dundee*' dated 30 December 1797,

---

[37] For Conder see *GM*, June (Supplement) 1823, 648-50 and *ODNB*.

APPENDIX III

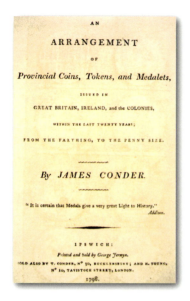

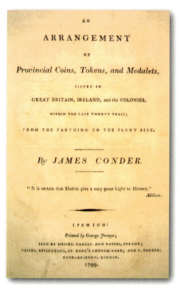

389 Title Pages of Conder's *Arrangement*, 1798 and 1799.

an essay 'elegantly written, abounding with information, and enriched with original and interesting observation'. Wright, who had also provided the introductory essay to Denton and Prattent's *Virtuoso's Companion*, died in April 1798, and thus never saw the work published, delayed because Conder sustained 'a severe corporeal affliction that would not permit him to attend to his favourite employment'. Despite his illness Shephard, who devoted a whole essay to the catalogue, concluded that Conder had

> persevered in his perplexing occupation with unwearied diligence, has explored every source of information, and has exerted every endeavour [*sic*], to render his arrangement useful, elegant, and accurate. It is no extravagant commendation of the present work, to say, that it has far surpassed all preceding attempts, and fully answered its intended purposes.[38]

390 Plate I of Conder's' *Arrangement* illustrating *inter alia* Conder's Private Ipswich token commemorating Cardinal Wolsey.

38 Shephard (1798), 741-745.

345

391 Sir George Chetwynd. Obverse of the 'Grendon Halfpenny', 1842.

A second 'edition' of the *Arrangement*, although it was not dignified with this name, was published in 1799. Its title page is virtually identical with that of the 1798 issue apart from the 'publication' imprint at its foot and the contents are unchanged although some versions incorporate two additional plates by Taylor.

Small quarto versions of both 'editions' were also published, the text mostly printed on the recto pages only, and in 1800 and 1804 separate revised Appendices were printed. The latter are both excessively rare, according to Miss Banks only twelve copies of that of 1800 being printed.[39]

Conder's only real claim to fame was his catalogue. Although its illustrated material was meagre, it remained the critical popular aid to token collecting until the publication of James Atkins' work almost a century later.[40] And through it Conder's name was perpetuated by its adoption by American collectors as a popular name for eighteenth-century tokens which has lasted to this day.

[Manville (2005), Nos. 248, 250-51 and 259A].

392 Thomas Sharp. From an etching by Dawson Turner after a drawing by John Sell Cotman, 1823.

8. THOMAS SHARP (1770-1841):

The final catalogue in this survey is included because, although it was not published until 1834 its editor, Thomas Sharp, and the owner of the collection it listed, Sir George Chetwynd (1783-1850) [391], were both contemporary collectors of the eighteenth-century series who were personally able to throw a great deal of light on many of the issues.

Sharp, born in Leamington Spa, was a Coventry hatter who from a very early age had immersed himself in local antiquities and was a frequent contributor to the *Gentleman's Magazine*.[41] As noted above (page 196) in 1798 Sharp, with two fellow local antiquaries, George Howlette and George Nickson [393], commissioned views of all the buildings of interest in Warwickshire, to be engraved and inserted in their copies of William Dugdale's county history. Retiring from his retail business in 1804 Sharp devoted his additional leisure to antiquarian research, producing a series of pamphlets and articles, and in 1824 a *Guide to Coventry*. His chief work, *A dissertation on the pageants, or dramatic mysteries, anciently performed at Coventry by the trading companies of that City* (1825), was praised by Sir Walter Scott for its 'carefulness and extent of research' and remains indispensable, especially because of the loss by enemy action in 1940 of the guild records which Sharp had used to provide the plays with a context. Part of Sharp's library was sold by Sotheby's in 1858 and, unhappily, the bulk of his collections of

---

39 Both Appendices are listed in Miss Bank's Library catalogue but her copies do not seem to have survived: Banks MS 'List of Coins ...'.

40 Atkins(1892).

41 For Sharp see *GM*, October 1841, 436-38; Fretton (1871) in Sharp (1871), ix-xv; *ODNB*.

APPENDIX III

393 Peter Kempson: Private 'Coventry Halfpenny' for John Nickson, leather manufacturer, 1799.

394 Title Page of Sharp's 'Chetwynd' Catalogue, 1834.

Warwickshire manuscripts was destroyed in a fire at the Birmingham Reference Library in 1879. Annotated copies of his *Dissertation on the Dramatic Mysteries* and of a volume of his Coventry tracts, however, survive in the British Library.

A keen numismatist from his youth he had a large collection of Roman and English coins including a gold 'half-florin' or 'leopard' of Edward III now in the British Museum and of which he was said to be 'the casual and fortunate purchaser'.[42] His collection was sold to the Reverend William Woolston (1780-1817) of Adderbury, Oxfordshire in the early years of the nineteenth century. In addition to publishing his private Coventry halfpenny in 1797 [193], he made available some of the views of Coventry that he, Howlette and Nickson had commissioned to Thomas Wyon for Kempson's 'Coventry Buildings' series.

Sharp's *A Catalogue of Provincial Copper Coins, Tokens, Tickets and Medalets … in the Collection of Sir George Chetwynd, Baronet*, printed, for private distribution, by J.B. Nichols & Son of 25, Parliament Street, London, contains the first account of nineteenth-century tokens, and, with the 1801 edition of Pye's work, is one of the primary sources of information about the eighteenth-century series.

In large quarto format the catalogue comprises 280 pages with an important 'INTRODUCTION' (pages i-ix.) and an 'INDEX' (pages xiii-xxi) as preliminaries. Pages xi and xii were never printed. There are vignettes of Chetwynd's token on the title page and of Grendon Hall (demolished in 1933) as a colophon on the verso of the last printed page (page 280).

There is some doubt as to how many copies of the catalogue were printed but most authorities agree on fifty-two, some copies having only 228 pages,[43] omitting Parts V to IX (Ireland; the Colonies; Tickets and Medalets). Six copies were printed on fine paper and at least one copy was interleaved.

Sir George Chetwynd, the second baronet, of Grendon Hall, near Atherstone, Warwickshire, had started to collect tokens at the time of their issue but in 1830, after a break in collecting, he set out to perfect his collection. He bought many valuable specimens direct from Matthew Young and from the saleroom, and acquired the tokens of John Harding of Tamworth. The 'celebrated and valuable' Chetwynd collection was auctioned at Christie's in August 1872.

[Manville (2005), No. 300].

---

42 *GM*, October 1800, 945; *GM*, October 1841, 437.
    Four specimens of the 'leopard' – now classified as a 'florin' – are known today, two of which are in the British Museum and one in the Ashmolean Museum.

43 E. I. Carlyle's original biography of Sharp in *DNB* (1897) states that sixty copies were printed, a claim omitted from *ODNB*.
    For a list of presentation copies of Sharp's *Catalogue* up to 1847 'taken from the fly-leaf of Sir George Chetwynd's own copy of the work' see Yeates (1917), cols. 363-64. The present writer's own copy was presented to 'M[r]. [William] Morris Chester' on 19 April 1859 by the third baronet, also Sir George Chetwynd (1808-69).
    According to Yeates the publishers (J. B. Nichols and Son) were paid £50 on account on 10 January 1834 and £120 balance on 16 December 1834.

395   Grendon Hall (demolished 1933), an engraved vignette from Sharp's 'Chetwynd' Catalogue, 1834.

BIBLIOGRAPHY

Manuscript Primary Sources

Bank of England Archive:
   M695: 'Questions asked by the Privy Council's Committee on Coin on the 21st February 1798 and the Answers given by the Bank.

Birmingham Central Library (Archives and Heritage Service):
   MS 3147: Boulton and Watt Collection.
   MS 3219: James Watt & Family Papers.
   MS 3782: Matthew Boulton Papers.
   MS 218: Diary of Julius Hardy, 1788-93.

British Library:
   Additional MSS 10113: Collection of papers formed by Sir Julius Caesar, relating to the Mint and Mint affairs.
   Additional MS 27808: Francis Place MSS.
   Additional MSS 38421-2: Papers of the 1st Earl of Liverpool relating to the Mint, coinage and kindred subjects.
   Additional MSS 48020 (Yelverton MS. 21): Miscellaneous tracts and papers, mostly relating to trade, coinage, etc.
   Lansdowne MSS B11: f.188v, Samuel Garbett to Lord Lansdowne, 16 April 1786.
   Lansdowne MSS (Shelburne) 19: f. 87, Samuel Garbett to Lord Lansdowne, December 1794.
   Egerton MSS 3706 A: Barrett Collection: Charlotte Barrett, 'Journal of what passed in an excursion to Brighton'.

British Museum (Department of Coins and Medals):
   Banks, Sarah Sophia, MS 'List of coins &c., presents to me, & of do that I have bought'.
   -------, MS Catalogue of Coins, Medals and Tokens, 8 volumes: Arc R19.

Cornwall Record Office:
   AD/1583/2-4, Boulton and Watt Collection: Thomas Wilson Correspondence.

Dorset Record Office:
   Pretor Papers.
   Sherborne Estate Papers.

Goldsmith's Library, University of London:
   Haynes, Hopton (1700), MS 'Brief Memoires Relating to the Silver & Gold Coins of England: With an Account of the Corruption of the Hammered Moneys; And of the Reform by the Late Grand Coynage At the Tower & the five Country Mints, In the Years 1696. 1697. 1698. & 1699'.

Library of Congress:
Thomas Jefferson Papers: Digges Correspondence.

Natural History Museum (Botany Library):
Dawson Turner Copies (DTC): Banks Correspondence.

National Library of Scotland:
Pinkerton Papers.
James Wright's Drawing Book: Acc. 11596.

National Museum of Scotland:
Society of Antiquaries of Scotland Letter Books: MSS letters of James Wright, Jnr. to Alexander Smellie.

Public Record Office:
BT 6: Board of Trade Papers relating to the Committee on Coin and other coinage matters.
MINT 1: Royal Mint Record Books.
MINT 8: Records relating to copper coinage.
PROB11: Will probates proved before the Prerogative Court of Canterbury.
SP 37/27/427-28: MS 'Copy of M^r. Chamberlayne's Letter to Lord Shelburne with observations on Messrs. Garbett's Report'.
SP 35/28109: *THE OLD TURN-P [TURNIP] MAN'S HUE-AND-CRY After More MONEY, OR Two Bunches of TURNIPS for a Penny* (London, 1721).

Royal Mint Museum:
[Banks, Sarah Sophia], MS list of her 'Numismatic Library: Provincial Tokens &c'.
Miss Banks's annotated copies of contemporary token catalogues and other coinage ephemera.

Society of Antiquaries of London:
Minute Book.

Warwickshire County Record Office:
CR 1563/246: MS 'Memoir of James Bisset' (1818).

Wellcome Library:
Bur. Suppl. P: Burchell, Basil (*c.* 1790-1800) *Anodyne Necklaces.*
6137/P: Burchell, Basil (post 1800) *Anodyne Necklaces.*

Miscellaneous:
Notes on the contemporary token scene by William Robert Hay in his copies of Pye (1795) and the *Virtuoso's Companion* (1795-97), now in the possession, respectively, of the writer and Robert Thompson. The notes in the *Virtuoso's Companion* have been transcribed by [Preston]-Morley (1971-74).

BIBLIOGRAPHY

Printed Primary Sources[1]

Newspapers and Magazines:
The Annual Register.
Aris's Birmingham Gazette.
Chester Chronicle.
The Daily Universal Register (January 1785-December 1787, thereafter *The Times*).
The European Magazine.
The General Magazine and Impartial Review.
The Gentleman's Magazine.
The Gloucester Journal.
The Ipswich Journal.
The London Gazette.
The Monthly Review.
The New London Magazine.
The Salopian Journal.
The Times (January 1788 -).
The Western Flying-Post; or Sherborne & Yeovil Mercury.

Other Printed Sources

Ackermann, Rudolph (1808-1810), *The Microcosm of London* (3 volumes, London).

Aikin, Arthur (1797), *Journal of a Tour through North Wales and Part of Shropshire* (London).

Andrews, C. Bruyn (ed.) (1934-38), *The Torrington Diaries* (4 volumes, London).

Anonymous (1644), *A Remedie against the losse of the Subject by Farthing-Tokens: Discovering the great abuses of them heretofore: and the Prevention of the like hereafter: ...* (London).

Anonymous (1753), *Some Cautions concerning the Copper Coin; with proposals for preventing the illegal practice of coining ...* (2nd. Edition, London).

Anonymous (1771), *A Letter to the Members of Parliament on the Present state of the Coinage with Proposals for the better Regulation thereof* (London).

Archenholz, Johann Wilhelm von (1789), *A Picture of England: containing a description of the laws, customs, and manners of England...* (2 volumes, London).

Aspinall, A (ed.) (1967), *The Later Correspondence of George III, Volume 3* (Cambridge).

Austen-Leigh, R. A. (ed.) (1942), *Austen Papers 1704-1856* ([Colchester]).

Barnard, F. P. (1915), 'Petition 'For the Restoring of Farthing Tokens', *BNJ*, Vol. 11, 169-81.

Beatriffe, Richard (1795), *The Norfolk Tour: or, Traveller's Pocket Companion* (Norwich).

---

[1] The contemporary catalogues described in Appendix III are not listed in this Bibliography.

Beer, E. S. de (1955), *The Diary of John Evelyn* (6 volumes, Oxford).

Bewick, Thomas (1862), *A Memoir of Thomas Bewick, Written by Himself* (Newcastle-on-Tyne and London).

Bingley, W. (1820), *Animal Biography, or, Popular Zoology* (4 volumes, 5th. Edition, London).

Bisset, James (1800), *A Poetic Survey Round Birmingham, with a brief description of the different curiosities and manufactures of the place, accompanied with a magnificent directory, with the names and professions, &c. superbly engraved in emblematic plates* (Birmingham).

—— (1808), *Bisset's Magnificent Guide, or, Grand Copperplate Directory for the Town of Birmingham* (Birmingham).

Boswell, James (1799) [1934], *Boswell's Life of Samuel Johnson … Volume 2* (ed. George Birkbeck Hill, and L.F. Powell), (Oxford).

Brewer, J. N. (1825) [2005], *Delineations of Gloucestershire: Views of the Principal Seats of Nobility & Gentry* (Stroud).

Burke, Edmund (1790) [1989], *Reflections on the Revolution in France* (ed. L. G. Mitchell) in Paul Langford (ed.), *The Writings and Speeches of Edmund Burke, Volume 8: The French Revolution 1790-1794* (Oxford).

—— (1854-56), *The Works of the Right Honourable Edmund Burke, Volume 2: Political Miscellanies …* (London).

Calendar of State Papers, Domestic Series, 1651, ed. Mary Anne Everett Green (1877, London).

——, *Domestic Series, 1651-1652*, ed. Mary Anne Everett Green (1877, London).

——, *Charles II, 1661-1662*, ed. Mary Anne Everett Green (1861, London).

Calendar of State Papers and Manuscripts … Venice Vol. 2, 1509-1519, ed. Rawdon Brown (1867, London).

Chapman, R. W. (ed.) (1954), *The Works of Jane Austen, Volume 6, Minor Works* (London).

[Chapman, Thomas] (1800), *Birmingham Directory* (Birmingham).

'Civis' [James Wright, Junior, of Dundee] (1796), [Letter to the Editor], *The Monthly Magazine*, No. XI (December), 867-70.

—— (1797), [Letter to the Editor], *GM*, Vol. 67 (January), 31-4; (April), 270-71.

Cobbett, William [and after 1812 Hansard, Thomas Curson] (ed.) (1806-20), *Parliamentary History of England: from the Norman Conquest in 1066 to the year 1803* (36 volumes, London).

[Colquhoun, Patrick] (1795), *Facts and Observations relative to Coinage and Circulation of Counterfeit or Base Money …* (London).

—— (1796), *A Treatise on the Police of the Metropolis …* (2nd. Edition, London).

Colquhoun, P. (1800), *A Treatise on the Police of the Metropolis …* (6th. Edition, London).

Conduitt, John (1774) [1967], *Observations upon the Present State of our Gold and Silver Coins, 1730* (London), reprinted in Shaw (1967), 185-214.

Copper Report (1803) – *House of Commons Report on the State of the Copper Trade and Copper Mines …, 1799* printed in *Reports from committees of the House of Commons*, Vol. 10, *Miscellaneous subjects 1785-1801* (London), 653 *et seqq*.

Darwin, Erasmus (1795), *The Botanic Garden. A Poem, in Two Parts. Part I. Containing the Economy of Vegetation. Part II. The Loves of the Plants. With Philosophical Notes* (3rd. Edition, London).

Davis, Herbert (ed.) (1955), *Irish Tracts 1728-1733: The Prose Works of Jonathan Swift, Volume the Twelfth* (Oxford).

Defoe, Daniel (1726), *The Complete English Tradesman* (London).

Dobrée, Bonamy (1932), *The Letters of Philip Dormer Stanhope, 4th Earl of Chesterfield* (6 volumes, London).

Dudley, T. B. (ed.) (1904), *Memoir of James Bisset* (Leamington Spa).

Eland, G. (ed.) (1931), *Purefoy Letters 1735-1753* (London).

Elias, Robert H. and Finch, Eugene D. (eds.) (1982), *Letters of Thomas Attwood Digges (1742-1821)* (Columbia, SC).

Erasmus, Desidarius (1533), *Adagiorum Opus* (Basel).

Evelyn, J. (1697), *Numismata, A Discourse of Medals, Antient and Modern* (London).

Eyre, Adam (1877), 'A Dyurnall, or Catalogue of all my Accions and Expences from the 1st January, 1646-[7]', ed. H. J. Morehouse, in *Yorkshire Diaries and Autobiographies in the Seventeenth and Eighteenth Centuries*, Surtees Society, Vol. 67, 1-118 and 351-57 (Durham).

[Farrer, Baroness (Katherine Euphemia)] (ed.) (1903), *Letters of Josiah Wedgwood 1762-1780*, 2 volumes (London).

Fennor, William (1617) [1930], *The Compter's Commonwealth or a Voyage made to an Infernal Island …* (London) reprinted in Judges (1930), 423-87.

Ferguson, J. De Lancey (ed.) (1985), *The Letters of Robert Burns, Volume II, 1790-1796* (2nd. Edition, ed. G. Ross Roy, Oxford).

Ferrar, John (1796) [2009], *A Tour from Dublin to London in 1795; through the Isle of Anglesea, Bangor, Conway and Kensington* (Dublin).

[Fisher, Frederick George] (1800), *Brighton New Guide; or, a Description of Brighthelmston* (2nd. Edition, London).

Folkes, Martin (1763), *Tables of English Silver and Gold Coins* (London).

Furnivall, F. J. (ed.) (1870), *The first Boke of the Introduction of Knowledge made by Andrew Borde of Physicke Doctor* in *Andrew Borde's Introduction of Knowledge and Dyetary of Helth* [before 1542], EETS, Extra Series, Vol. 10, 111-222.

Garbett, Samuel and Garbett, Francis (1837), *Report on the Mint, 1782* in *Report from the Select Committee on the Royal Mint* (Parliamentary Papers, London), Appendix 34, 215-23.

Garner, T. (1800), *A Brief Description of the Principal Foreign Animals and Birds now exhibited at the Grand Menagerie over Exeter Exchange, The Property of Mr Gilbert Pidcock* (London).

Gee, James (1798), [Letter to the Editor], *The European Magazine*, Vol. 33 (June), 406-407.

Gillingwater, Edmund ([1790]), *An Historical Account of the Ancient Town of Lowestoft in the County of Suffolk* (London).

Green, Mary Anne Everett (ed.) (1856), *Diary of John Rous, Incumbent of Santon Downham, Suffolk, from 1625-1642*, Camden Society, Vol. 66 (London).

Grose, Francis (1796) [1931]), *A Classical Dictionary of the Vulgar Tongue* (3rd. Edition, ed. Eric Partridge, London).

—— and Astle, Thomas (eds.) (1807-1809), *The Antiquarian Repertory* (4 volumes, London).

Hamer, S. H. (1902/1903), 'Notes on Some Interesting Token Books and their Original Owner', *SNC*, Vol. 11 (June 1903), columns 6048-56.

Hansard, T. C. (ed.) (1804-1820), *The Parliamentary Debates from the Year 1803 to the present time*, Volume 20 (1811, London).

Harral, Thomas (1824), *Picturesque Views of the River Severn: with Historical and Topographical Descriptions* (2 volumes, London).

Harris, Joseph (1757), *An Essay upon Money and Coins: Part I - The Theories of Commerce, Money, and Exchanges* (London).

—— 1758 [1856], *An Essay upon Money and Coins: Part II* (London) reprinted in [McCulloch] (1856), 432-512.

[Hill, John] (1751), *The Adventures of Mr George Edwards, a Creole* (London).

Historical Manuscripts Commission (1894), *Fourteenth Report, Appendix, Part 4: The Manuscripts of Lord Kenyon* (London).

—— (1895), *Fourteenth Report, Appendix, Part 8: The Manuscripts of Lincoln … &c* (London).

—— (1896), *Fifteenth Report, Appendix, Part 1: The Manuscripts of the Earl of Dartmouth*, Vol. 3 (London).

Hughes, Paul L. and Larkin, James F. (eds.) (1964-69), *Tudor Royal Proclamations 1485-1603*, 3 volumes (New Haven, Conn.).

Hutchins, John (1796-1815), *The History and Antiquities of the County of Dorset* (2nd. Edition, 4 volumes, London).

Jameson, Peter (ed.) (2005), *The Diary of James Woodforde, Volume 15, 1796-1797* (n. p., Parson Woodforde Society).

Johnson, Samuel (1761) [1963], *The Idler, Number 41, Saturday, 27 January 1759 (The Yale Edition of the Works of Samuel Johnson, Volume 2*, ed. W. J. Bate, John M. Bullitt and L. F. Powell, New Haven Conn.).

Johnson, W. Branch (1973), *'Memorandoms For …'. The Diary between 1798 and 1810 of John Carrington. Farmer, Chief Constable, Tax Assessor, Surveyor of Highways and Overseer of the Poor, of Bramfield in Hertfordshire* (London).

Judges, A. V. (ed.) (1930), *The Elizabethan Underworld* (London).

Keir, James (1809) [1947], *Memoir of Matthew Boulton* (Birmingham).

Keiser, Rut (1968), Thomas Platter d. J., *Beschreibung der Reisen durch Frankreich, Spanien, England und die Niederlande, 1595-1600* (Basel).

Kelly, Patrick Hyde (ed.) (1991), *Locke on Money* (2 volumes, Oxford).

Lackington, James (1827), *Memoirs of the Forty-Five First Years of the Life of James Lackington* (London).

Lamond, Elizabeth (ed.) (1893), *A Discourse of the Common Weal of this Realm of England* (Cambridge).

Larkin, James F. (ed.) (1983), *Stuart Royal Proclamations: Volume 2 Royal Proclamations of King Charles I 1625-1646* (Oxford).

Larkin, James F. and Hughes, Paul L. (eds.) (1973), *Stuart royal proclamations: Volume 1 Royal Proclamations of King James I 1603-1625* (Oxford).

Latham, Robert and Matthews, William (eds.) (1970-83), *The Diary of Samuel Pepys* (11 volumes, London).

[Layton, Henry] (1697), *Observations concerning Money and Coin and especially those of England* (London).

[Leake, Stephen Martin] (1726), *Nummi Britannici Historia: or an Historical Account of English Money ...* (London).

Leake, Stephen Martin (1745), *An Historical Account of English Money ...* (2nd. Edition, London).

—— (1793), *An Historical Account of English Money ...* (3rd. Edition, London).

[Leslie, Charles] (1739), *On the Scarcity of the Copper Coin. A Satyr.* ([Edinburgh]).

Lewis, W. S. and Wallace, A. Dayle (eds.) (1952), *Horace Walpole's Correspondence with Thomas Chatterton ...* (The Yale edition of Horace Walpole's correspondence, Volume 16 (London).

—— —— (eds.) (1965), *Horace Walpole's Correspondence with the Countess of Upper Ossory, II,* (The Yale edition of Horace Walpole's correspondence, Volume 33 (London).

Liverpool, Charles [Jenkinson], Earl of (1805), *A Treatise on the Coins of the Realm in a letter to the King* (Oxford).

Lowndes, William (1695) [1856], *A Report containing an Essay for the amendment of the Silver Coins*, reprinted in [McCulloch] (1856), 169-258.

[McCulloch, John Ramsay] (ed.) (1856), *A Select Collection of Scarce and Valuable Tracts on Money* (London).

Mare, Margaret L. and Quarrel, W. H. (1938), *Lichtenberg's Visits to England as described in his Letters and Diaries* (Oxford).

Marshall, J. D. (ed.) (1967), *The Autobiography of William Stout of Lancaster 1665-1752* (Manchester and New York).

Merrey, Walter (1789), *Remarks on the Coinage of England* (Nottingham).

Michaelis-Jena, Ruth and Merson, Willy (1988), *A Lady Travels: Journeys in England and Scotland from the Diaries of Johanna Schopenhauer* (London).

Morgan, Kenneth (ed.) (1992), *An American Quaker in the British Isles. The Travel Journals of Jabez Maud Fisher, 1775-1779* (Oxford).

Moritz, Karl Philipp (1795) [1924], *Travels of Carl Philipp Moritz in England in 1782. A reprint of The English Translation of 1795* (London).

[Morris, Corbyn] (1757), *A Letter balancing the Causes of the present Scarcity of our Silver Coin and the Means of immediate Remedy, and future Prevention of this Evil* (London).

Moser, Joseph (1798), 'Thoughts on the Provincial Copper Coins', *The European Magazine*, Vol. 33 (March), 153-56; (April), 232-37; (May), 303-308.

Myers, A. R. (ed.) (1969), *English Historical Documents, Vol. 4, 1327-1485* (London).

Nares, Robert (1822), *A Glossary; or, Collection of Words, Phrases, Names, and Allusions to Customs, Proverbs, &c....* (London).

[Nash, Treadway Russell] (1799), *Collections for the History of Worcestershire* (2 volumes, 2nd. Edition, London).

Nattier, Jean-Baptiste and Nattier, Jean-Marc (1710), La *Gallerie du Palais du Luxembourg peinte par Rubens ...* (Paris).

Newton, Isaac (1701-25) [1967], *Mint Reports* reprinted in Shaw (New York, 1967), 135-79.

Paine, Thomas (1791) [1994], *Rights of Man* (London).

Pennant, Thomas (1776), *A Tour in Scotland and Voyage to the Hebrides* (2 Parts, 2nd. Edition, London).

—— (1810), *Tours in Wales* (3 volumes, London).

—— (1811), *The Journey from Chester to London* (London).

Petty, Sir William (1695) [1856], *Quantulumcunque concerning Money. To the Lord Marquess of Halyfax, Anno 1682*, reprinted in [McCulloch] (1856), 157-167.

'Pindar, Peregrine' (1795), *Ode to the Hero of Finsbury Square* (London).

Pinkerton, John (1789), *An Essay on Medals* (2 volumes, 2nd. Edition, London).

—— (1808), *An Essay on Medals* (2 volumes, 3rd. Edition, London).

Pitt, William (1817), *A Topographical History of Staffordshire ...* (2 volumes, Newcastle under Lyme).

Pottle, Frederick A. (1951), *Boswell's London Journal 1762-1763* (London).

[Preston]-Morley, Peter (1971-74), 'An Annotated Copy of "Virtuoso's Companion"', *Token Corresponding Society Bulletin*, Vol. 1, Parts 1-12: 2-6, 37-38, 46-48, 73-78, 106-10, 126-28, 151-55, 174-76, 200-203, 235-36, 260, 272-76; Vol. 2, Parts 13-17: 16-20, 37-40, 55-57, 71-73, 99-104.

[Pye, Charles] (1791), *Pye's Birmingham Directory* (Birmingham).

Pye, Charles (1796), [Letter to the Editor], *GM*, Vol.66 (December), 991-92.

—— (1797), *Pye's Birmingham Directory For ... 1797...* (Birmingham).

—— (1825), *The Stranger's Guide to Modern Birmingham ...* (Birmingham).

Rannie, D. W. (ed.) (1898), *Remarks and Collections of Thomas Hearne, Volume 4* (Oxford).

Raspe, Rudolph Erich (1791), *A descriptive catalogue of a general collection of ancient and modern engraved gems, cameos as well as intaglios ...* (London).

Raven, Jon (1977), *The Urban & Industrial Songs of the Black Country and Birmingham* (Wolverhampton).

Razzell, Peter (ed.) (1995), *The Journals of Two Travellers in Elizabethan and early Stuart England: Thomas Platter and Horatio Busino* (London).

Razzell, P. E. and Wainwright, R. W. (1973), *The Victorian Working Class: Selections from Letters to the Morning Chronicle* (London).

Rollins, Hyder Edward (1931), *The Pepys Ballads, Volume 7, 1693-1702* (Cambridge, Mass).

Rowlands, Henry (1766), *Mona Antiqua Restaurata, an archæological discourse on the antiquities, natural and historical, of the Isle of Anglesey...* (2nd. Edition, London).

Ruding, Rogers (1799), *A Proposal for Restoring the Antient Constitution of the Mint* (London).

'R. Y.' [William Robert Hay] (1796), [Letter to the Editor], *GM*, Vol.66 (September), 752-54'; (October), 837-38.

―― (1797), [Letter to the Editor], *GM*, Vol.67 (April), 267-70. (June), 471-72.

Sancho, Ignatius (1803), *Letters of the late Ignatius Sancho, An African* (London).

Shaw, Stebbing (1798-1801), *The History and Antiquities of Staffordshire* (2 volumes, London).

Shaw, Wm. A. (1967), *Select Tracts and Documents Illustrative of English Monetary History 1626-1730* (New York).

Shephard, Ch[arles] (1798/99), 'Essays on the Provincial Halfpennies', *GM*, Vol. 68 (January), 10-13; (February), 118-22; (March), 212-15; (September), 741-5; (October), 829-32; Vol. 69 (March), 206-209.

[Sketchley, James] (1767), *Sketchley's Birmingham, Wolverhampton & Walsall Directory ... Third Edition ...* ([Birmingham]).

―― (1770), *Sketchley & Adams's Tradesman's True Guide : or an Universal Directory for ... Birmingham, Wolverhampton, Walsall, Dudley & the Villages in the Neighbourhood ...* (Birmingham).

Small, Robert (*c.*1793), *A Statistical Account of the Parish and Town of Dundee in the Year XDCCXCII* (Dundee).

Smith, Adam (1789) [1994]), *The Wealth of Nations* (5th. Edition, ed. Edwin Cannan, New York).

Smith, John Thomas (1905), A *Book for a Rainy Day or Recollections of the events of the years 1766-1833* (ed. Wilfred Whitten, London).

Smollett, Tobias (1748) [1995], *Roderick Random* (London).

Snelling, Thomas (1762), *A View of the Silver Coin and coinage of England* (London).

―― (1763), *A View of the Gold Coin and Coinage of England* (London).

―― (1766a), *A View of the Copper Coin and Coinage of England* (London).

―― (1766b), *A View of the Coins at this Time current throughout Europe* (London).

―― (1766c), *The Doctrine of Gold and Silver Computations* (London).

―― (1769), *A View of the Origin, Nature, and Use of Jettons or Counters* (London).

[Southey, Robert] (1807), *Letters from England: by Don Manuel Alvarez Espriella* (3 volumes, London).

Spence, [Joseph] (1747), *Polymetis: or an Enquiry concerning the Agreement between the works of the Roman Poets and the remains of the Ancient Artists ...* (London).

Sterne, Laurence (1768) [1984], *A Sentimental Journey* (Oxford).

Stukeley, William (1740), *Stonehenge: a Temple restor'd to the British*

Druids (London).

Sweet, Jessie M. (1963), 'Robert Jameson in London, 1793', *Annals of Science*, Vol. 19, 81-116.

[Swinney, Myles] (1773), *Swinney's Birmingham Directory: or Gentleman's & Tradesman's Complete Guide* (Birmingham).

Thale, Mary (ed.) (1983), *Selections from the Papers of the London Corresponding Society 1792-1799* (Cambridge).

Thicknesse, Philip, (1777), *A Year's Journey through France and part of Spain* (2 volumes, Dublin).

Thirsk, Joan and Cooper, J. P. (eds.) (1972), *Seventeenth-Century Economic Documents* (Oxford).

Thomas, Edward (1903), *The Poems of John Dyer* (London).

[Barfoot, Peter and Wilkes, John] (1790-98), *The Universal British Directory* (5 volumes, London).

Vallavine, Peter (1742), *Observations on the Present Condition of the Current Coins of this Kingdom ...* (London).

Vaughan, Rice (1675) [1856], *A Discourse of Coin and Coinage ...* reprinted in [McCulloch] (1856), 1-119.

Ward, Charles E. (ed.) (1942), *The Letters of John Dryden: with Letters addressed to Him* (Durham, NC).

Watt, James (1809) [1943], *Memoir of Matthew Boulton* (Birmingham).

[Whatley, George] (1762), *Reflections on Coin in General; on the Coins of Gold and Silver in Great Britain in particular ...* (London).

White, Gilbert (1813), *The Natural History and Antiquities of Selborne in the County of Southampton* (London).

Williams, C. H. (ed.) (1967), *English Historical Documents*, Vol. 5, *1485-1558* (London).

Williams, Clare (1937), *Thomas Platter's Travels in England 1599* (London).

Winstanley, R. L. (ed.) (1986), *The Ansford Diary of James Woodforde, Volume 4: 1769-1771* (n. p., Parson Woodforde Society).

—— and Jameson, Peter (2001), *The Diary of James Woodforde, Volume 12: 1788-1790* (n. p., Parson Woodforde Society).

Secondary Sources

Alexander, David (1998), *Richard Newton and English caricature in the 1790s* (Manchester).

Allen, G. C. (1923), 'An Eighteenth-Century Combination in the Copper-Mining Industry', *The Economic Journal*, Vol. 33, 74-85.

Allen, Martin (2004), 'The English Currency and the Commercialization of England before the Black Death' in Wood (ed.) (2004), 31-50.

Altick, Richard D (1978), *The Shows of London* (Cambridge, Mass.)

Anderson, B. L. (1970), 'Money and the Structure of Credit in the Eighteenth Century', *Business History*, Vol. 12, 85-101.

Appleby, Joyce Oldham (1978), *Economic Thought and Ideology in Seventeenth-Century England* (Princeton, NJ).

Archer, Angela (2000), *The Making of Brewin Dolphin* (Newport, Essex).

Archibald, M. M. and Cowell, M. R. (eds.) (1993), *Metallurgy in Numismatics, Volume 3* (London).

Ashraf, P M. [Kemp-] (1983), *The Life and Times of Thomas Spence* (Newcastle upon Tyne).

Ashton, T. S. (1939), *An Eighteenth-Century Industrialist: Peter Stubs of Warrington 1756-1806* (Manchester).

—— (1948), *The Industrial Revolution 1760-1830* (London).

—— (1953), 'The Bill of Exchange and Private Banks in Lancashire, 1790-1830' in Ashton and Sayers (1953), 37-49.

—— (1955), *An Economic History of England: The 18th Century* (London).

—— (1963), *Iron and Steel in the Industrial Revolution* (Manchester).

—— and Sayers, R. S. (eds.) (1953), *Papers in English Monetary History* (Oxford),

—— and Sykes, Joseph (1929), *The Coal Industry of the Eighteenth Century* (Manchester).

Atkins, James (1892), *The Tradesmen's Tokens of the Eighteenth Century* (London).

Attwood, Philip (2003), *Italian Medals c. 1530-1600 in British Public Collections* (2 volumes, London).

Baines, J. Manwaring (1956), *Burton's St. Leonards* (Hastings).

Barnard, F. P. (1916), *The Casting-Counter and the Counting-Board: a chapter in the history of numismatics and early arithmetic* (Oxford).

—— (1921), 'Some Unrecorded Tokens', *NC*, Fifth Series, Vol. 1, 152-55.

—— (1926), 'Forgery of English Copper Money in the Eighteenth Century', *NC*, Fifth Series, Vol. 6, 341-60.

Bell, R. C. (1963), *Commercial Coins 1787-1804* (Newcastle upon Tyne).

—— (1966), *Tradesmen's Tickets and Private Tokens 1785-1819* (Newcastle upon Tyne).

—— (1968), *Specious Tokens and those struck for General Circulation 1784-1804* (Newcastle upon Tyne).

—— (1987), *Political and Commemorative Pieces simulating Tradesmen's Tokens 1770-1802* (Felixstowe).

Beloff, Max (1938), *Public Order and Popular Disturbances 1660-1714* (London).

Beresford, Maurice (1974), 'The Making of a Townscape: Richard Paley in the east end of Leeds', in Chalklin and Havinden (1974), 281-320.

Berg, Maxine (1985), *The Age of Manufactures: Industry, innovation and work in Britain 1700-1820* (London).

—— (1998), 'Inventors of the World of Goods' in Bruland and O'Brien (1998), 21-50.

—— (2005), *Luxury and Pleasure in Eighteenth-Century Britain* (Oxford).

Berry, George (1974), *Medieval English Jetons* (London).

Besly, Edward (1995), 'Short Cross and other medieval coins from Llanfaes, Anglesey', *BNJ*, Vol.65, 46-82.

Biggs, Norman (2004), 'Provincial Coin-Weights in the Eighteenth Century', *BNJ*, Vol. 74, 102-20

Bindman, David (1989), *The Shadow of the Guillotine: Britain and the French Revolution* (London).

Bird, N. du Quesne (1998), 'The Bristol Civic Tokens of the 16th Century', *SNC*, Vol. 106 (July), 262-63.

Blades, William (1883), *Numismata Typographica; or the Medallic History of Printing* (London).

Boon, George C. (1973), *Welsh Tokens of the Seventeenth Century* (Cardiff).

—— (1983), 'Medals of the Anglesey Druidical Society and their place in Romantic Druidical Iconography', *Archaeologia Cambrensis*, Vol. 132, 116-25.

Borrow, George (1857), *The Romany Rye* (2 volumes, London).

Bowring, John (1843), *Memoirs of Jeremy Bentham* (Edinburgh).

Boyne, William (1866), *The Silver Tokens of Great Britain and Ireland …* (London).

Brewer, John (1982), 'Commercialization and Politics', Part II of McKendrick *et al.* (1982), 197-264.

—— (1986), *The Common People and Politics 1750-1790s* (Cambridge).

—— (1989), *The Sinews of Power: War, Money and the English State, 1688-1783* (London).

—— and Plumb, J. H. (eds.), *The Birth of a Consumer Society: The Commercialization of Eighteenth-century England* (London).

—— and Styles, John (1980), *An Ungovernable People: The English and their Law in the Seventeenth and Eighteenth Centuries* (London).

Brooke, David S. (1997a), 'James Bisset's Museum', *CTCN*, Vol. 2, No. 1, 42-46.

—— (1997b),'Boulter's Museum (1778-1802)', *CTCN*, Vol. 2, No. 2, 34-36.

—— (1998), 'Pure Air, Sea Bathing and Flimsy Novels', *CTCJ*, Vol. 3, No. 3, 21-25.

—— (2000), 'Where Stuffed Birds Sing', *CTCJ*, Vol. 5, No. 4, 10-15.

Brown, Laurence (1980), *British Historical Medals 1760-1960, Volume I, The Accession of George III to the Death of William IV* (London).

Brown, Philip Anthony (1918), *The French Revolution in English History* (London).

Bruland, Kristine and O'Brien, Patrick (eds.) (1998), *From Family Firms to Corporate Capitalism, Essays in Business and Industrial History in Honour of Peter Mathias* (Oxford).

Burn, Jacob Henry (1855), *A Descriptive Catalogue of the London Traders, Tavern, and Coffee-House Tokens current in the Seventeenth Century; presented to the Corporation Library by Henry Benjamin Hanbury Beaufoy* (London).

Burton, F. E. (1923-24), 'Arnold Village Tokens', *BNJ*, Vol.17, 275-76.

Caldecott, J. B. (1943), 'Issue of Halfpenny and Farthing Tokens by Norwich, 1580', *NC*, Sixth Series, Vol. 3, 105-106.

—— and Yates, G. C. (1907), 'Leaden Tokens', *BNJ*, Vol. 4, 317-26.

Carlile, William Warrand (1901), *The Evolution of Modern Money* (London).

Carswell, John (1950), *The Prospector* (London).

Carter, Harold B. (1988), *Sir Joseph Banks 1743-1820* (London).

Chalklin, C. W. and Havinden, M. A. (1974), *Rural Change and Urban Growth 1500-1800* (London).

Challis, C. E. (1978), *The Tudor Coinage* (Manchester).

—— (1989), *Currency and the Economy in Tudor and early Stuart England* (London).

—— (ed.) (1992a), *A New History of the Royal Mint* (Cambridge).

—— (1992b), 'Lord Hastings to the Great Silver Recoinage' in Challis (1992a), 179-397.

Chaloner, W. H. (1948a), 'New Light on John Wilkinson's Token Coinage', *SCMB*, No. 362 (July), 306-308.

—— (1948b), 'John Wilkinson as Note Issuer and Banker', *SCMB*, No. 367 (December), 550-53.

—— (1953 and 1954), 'Charles Roe of Macclesfield (1715-81): An Eighteenth-Century Industrialist', *Transactions of the Lancashire and Cheshire Antiquarian Society*, Vol. LXII (1953), 133-56; Vol. LXIII (1954), 52-86. [Reprinted in Ward (1992), 51-101].

—— (1972), 'The Problem of "Colonel Mordaunt's Penny" 1783-1791', *SCMB*, No.650 (October), 402-3.

Chapman, Stanley D. (1967), *The Early Factory Masters: The Transition to the Factory System in the Midlands Textile Industry* (Newton Abbot).

—— (2007), 'Davison & Hawksley, Worsted Spinners of Arnold, Nottinghamshire, 1787-1810: Political Idealism and Economic Reality', *Transactions of the Thoroton Society*, Vol. 111, 117-30.

Christmas, Henry (1868), *The Copper and Billon Coinage of the British Empire* [London].

Church, R. A. and Smith, Barbara M. D. (1966), 'Competition and Monopoly in the Coffin Furniture Industry, 1870-1915', *EconHR*, 2nd. Series, Vol. 19, 621-41.

Cipolla, Carlo M. (1956), *Money, Prices, and Civilization in the Mediterranean World* (Princeton, NJ).

Clapham, John (1944), *The Bank of England: A History* (2 volumes, Cambridge).

Clarke, T. H., (1986), *The Rhinoceros from Dürer to Stubbs 1515-1799* (London).

Clarke, Ronald Aquilla (1992), *Illustrating a City: Edward Rudge and Art in Coventry, c.1760-1830* (Coventry).

Collins, Henry (1954), 'The London Corresponding Society' in Saville (1954), 103-134.

Colvin, Howard (1995), *A Biographical Dictionary of British Architects 1600-1840* (3rd. edition, New Haven, Conn.).

Cook, B. J. (1999), 'Foreign Coins in Medieval England' in Travaini (1999), 231-84.

Cooper, Denis R. (1988), *The Art and Craft of Coinmaking: a History of Minting Technology* (London).

Cooper, Michael (1965), *They came to Japan: An Anthology of European Reports on Japan, 1543-1640* (London).

Corfield, P. J. (1982), *The Impact of English Towns 1700-1800* (Oxford).

Cossons, A. (1959), 'Wilkinson Token Error Perpetuated', *SCMB*, No.492 (May), 127.

Cottle, Joseph (1847), *Reminiscences of Samuel Taylor Coleridge and Robert Southey* (London).

Court, W. H. B. (1938), *The Rise of the Midland Industries 1600-1838* (London).

Courtenay, William J. (1972-73), 'Token Coinage and the Administration of Poor Relief during the late Middle Ages', *Journal of Interdisciplinary History*, Vol. 3, 275-95.

Craig, Sir John (1946), *Newton at the Mint* (Cambridge).

—— (1953), *The Mint: A History of the London Mint From AD 287 to 1948* (Cambridge).

Crook, Malcolm, Doyle, William and Forrest, Alan (eds.) (2004), *Enlightenment and Revolution, Essays in Honour of Norman Hampson* (Aldershot).

Crouzet, François (1985), *The First Industrialists: The problem of origins* (Cambridge).

Cule, J. E. (1940), 'Finance and Industry in the Eighteenth Century: The Firm of Boulton and Watt', *Economic History*, Vol. 4, 319-25.

Dalton, R. (1922), *The Silver Token-Coinage mainly issued between 1811 and 1812* (Leamington Spa).

—— and Hamer, S. H. (1910-1918), *The Provincial Token-Coinage of the Eighteenth Century* (3 volumes, London). [Revised reprint in 1 volume, ed. Alan Davisson (1990 and 2004, Cold Spring, MN)].

Dalziel, Nigel (1993), 'Trade and Transition, 1690-1815' in White (1993), 91-144.

Davies, Glyn (1994), *A History of Money: From Ancient Times to the Present Day* (Cardiff).

Davis, W. J. (1895), *The Token Coinage of Warwickshire with Descriptive and Historical Notes* (Birmingham).

Davis, W. J. (1904), *The Nineteenth Century Token Coinage of Great Britain* …(London).

—— and Waters, A. W. (1922), *Tickets and Passes of Great Britain and Ireland* … (Leamington Spa).

Dawes, Margaret and Ward-Perkins, C. N. (2000), *Country Banks of England and Wales: Private Provincial Banks and Bankers, 1688-1953* (2 volumes, Canterbury).

Delieb, Eric (1971), *The Great Silver Manufactory: Matthew Boulton and the Birmingham Silversmiths, 1760-1790* (London).

Dent, Robert K. (1880), *Old and New Birmingham. A history of the Town and its People* (Birmingham).

Dickinson, H. W. (1914), *John Wilkinson, Ironmaster* (Ulverston).

—— (1936), *James Watt, Craftsman and Engineer* (Cambridge).

—— (1937), *Matthew Boulton* (Cambridge).

—— and Jenkins, Rhys (1927), *James Watt and the Steam Engine* (Oxford).

—— and Vowles, H. P. (1943), *James Watt and the Industrial Revolution* (London).

Dickinson, Michael (1986), *Seventeenth Century Tokens of the British Isles and their Values* (London).

—— (2008), 'Puddington bared, W. Waller revealed', *TCSB*, Vol.9 (2007-10), No. 4, 127-46. [Reprinted in *CTCJ*, Vol.13, No. 4 (2008-2009), 10-25].

Dodd, A. H. (1951), *The Industrial Revolution in North Wales* (Cardiff).

Doherty, Francis (1993), *A Study in Eighteenth-Century Advertising Methods : the Anodyne Necklace* (Lewiston, NY).

Dolan, Brian (2004), *Josiah Wedgwood, Entrepreneur to the Enlightenment* (London).

Dolley, Michael and Hocking, Anthony (1963), '"Plumbei Angliae": A Find of Sixteenth-Century (?) Lead Tokens from Huntingdon', *SNC*, Vol. 71 (October), 206-207.

Dolley, Michael and Seaby, W. A. (1971), 'A Find of Thirteenth-Century Pewter tokens from the National Museum Excavations at Winetavern Street, Dublin', *SNC*, Vol. 79 (December), 446-48.

Doty, Richard (1997a), 'Matthew Boulton's Tokens for Southampton', *CTCN*, Vol. 2, No. 1, 16-24.

—— (1997b), 'Matthew Boulton's Cornish Token', *CTCN*, Vol. 2, No. 2, 11-19.

—— (1998a), *The Soho Mint & the Industrialization of Money* (London).

—— (1998b), 'Matthew Boulton's Token for Glasgow', *CTCJ*, Vol. 3, No. 1, 12-17.

Dyer, Christopher (1994), *Everyday Life in Medieval England* (London).

—— (1997), 'Peasants and Coins: The Uses of Money in the Middle Ages', *BNJ*, Vol. 67, 30-47.

—— (1998), *Standards of Living in the later Middle Ages: Social Change in England c. 1200-1520* (Cambridge).

—— (2002), *Making a Living in the Middle Ages: The People of Britain 850-1520* (New Haven, Conn.).

—— (2005), *An Age of Transition? Economy and Society in England in the Later Middle Ages* (Oxford).

Dyer, Graham (1994), 'Sudbury Tokens' (unpublished BANS Congress Lecture, April).

—— (1996), 'Thomas Graham's Copper Survey of 1857', *BNJ*, Vol. 66, 60-66.

—— (1997), 'Quarter-sovereigns and other small gold patterns of the mid-Victorian period', *BNJ*, Vol. 67, 73-83.

—— (2001), 'Further Thoughts on Sudbury Halfpennies of 1793' (unpublished Token Congress Lecture, November).

—— (2002) 'The Currency Crisis of 1797', *BNJ*, Vol. 72, 135-42.

Dyer, G. P. and Gaspar, P. P. (1982), 'The Dorrien & Magens Shilling of 1798', *BNJ*, Vol. 52, 198-214.

—— —— (1992), 'Reform, The New Technology and Tower Hill' in Challis (ed.) (1992a), 398-606.

Dykes, D. W. (1952-54), 'Some Local Tokens and their Issuers in early nineteenth-century Swansea', *BNJ*, Vol. 27, 345-53.

—— (1961), 'Seventeenth Century Tradesmen's Tokens of Swansea: Mathew Davies and Isaac After of Swansea', *Gower*, Vol. 14, 62-66.

—— (1996a), 'James Wright, Junior (1768-98): The Radical Numismatist of Dundee', *SNC*, Vol. 104 (July/August), 195-99.

—— (1996b), 'A Royal Washerwoman Unmasked: The Loch Leven Penny', *SNC*, Vol. 104 (November), 406-407.

—— (1997), 'Who was R.Y.: Searching for an Identity', *BNJ*, Vol. 67, 115-22.

—— (1998a), 'The Myth of Mr. Dawes's Monogram', *SNC*, Vol. 106 (October), 352-355.

—— (1998b), 'Mr Croom's Halfpennies', *SNC*, Vol. 106 (November), 386-89.

—— (1999), 'John Gregory Hancock and the Westwood Brothers: An Eighteenth-Century Token Consortium', *BNJ*, Vol. 69, 173-86.

—— (2000), 'The Tokens of Thomas Mynd', *BNJ*, Vol. 70, 90-102.

—— (2001), 'John Stubbs Jorden, Die-Sinker and Medallist', *BNJ*, Vol. 71, 119-35.

—— (2002), 'The Token Coinage of William Fullarton', *BNJ*, Vol. 72, 149-63.

—— (2003), 'The Eighteenth and early Nineteenth-Century Token', *BNJ*, Vol. 73, 169-74.

—— (2004a), 'Some Reflections on Provincial Coinage, 1787-1797', *BNJ*, Vol. 74, 160-74.

—— (2004b), 'The "Dunkirk" Halfpenny', *BNJ*, Vol. 74, 190-97.

—— (2005a), 'Mr. Garbett's "Sixpence"', *SNC*, Vol. 113 (June), 169-72 and 'An Addendum' (August), 246.

—— (2005b), 'The Sherborne Bank Tokens', *BNJ*, Vol. 75, 132-41.

—— (2007), '"Peter" Skidmore: the man who never was', *BNJ*, Vol. 77, 246-63.

—— (2010a), '"J B" of "Foundling Fields"', *BNJ*, Vol. 80, 166-75.

—— (2010b), '"Peter" Skidmore: the man who never was. An Addendum', *BNJ*, Vol. 80, 201.

—— (forthcoming) 'Robert Biddulph and his Bull'.

Eimer, Christopher (2010), *British Commemorative Medals and their Values* (London).

Erhman, John (1996), *The Younger Pitt, The Consuming Struggle* (London).

Eustace, Katherine (2006), 'Britannia: some high points in the history of the iconography on British coinage', *BNJ*, Vol. 76, 323-36.

Everitt, A. M. (1967), 'The Marketing of Agricultural Produce' in Thirsk (ed.) (1967), 466-592.

Everson, Tim (2007), *The Galata Guide to the Farthing Tokens of James I & Charles I* (Lanfyllin).

Fay, C. R. (1933), 'Locke versus Lowndes', *Cambridge Historical Journal*, Vol. 4, 143-55.

Feavearyear, Sir Albert (1963), *The Pound Sterling: A History of English Money* (2nd. Edition revised by E. Victor Morgan, Oxford).

Fell, Alfred (1908), *The Early Iron Industry of Furness and District: an historical and descriptive account from earliest times to the end of the 18th century* (Ulverston).

Finlay, Michael (2006), *The Mining and related Tokens of West Cumberland* ([Carlisle]).

Fisher, H. E. S. (1971), *The Portugal Trade: A Study of Anglo-Portuguese Commerce 1700-1770* (London, 1971).

Fitton, R. S. and Wadsworth, A. P. (1958), *The Strutts and the Arkwrights 1758-1830: A Study of the early Factory System* (Manchester).

Fitzmaurice, Lord (1912), *Life of William, Earl of Shelburne, afterwards first Marquess of Lansdowne* (2 volumes, London).

Flinn, M.W. (1962), *Men of Iron: The Crowleys in the Early Iron Industry* (Edinburgh).

Forrer, L. (1902-1930), *Biographical Dictionary of Medallists* (8 volumes, London) [*Index* compiled by J. S. Martin (2004) (London].

Freeth, Frank (1909), 'Absolon of Yarmouth', *The Connoisseur*, Vol. 23, 251-54.

Fretton, William George (1871), 'Memoir of Thomas Sharp', in Sharp (1871), ix-xv.

Gaskill, Malcolm (2000), *Crime and Mentalities in Early Modern England* (Cambridge).

Gascoigne, John (1994), *Joseph Banks and the English Enlightenment: Useful Knowledge and Polite Culture* (Cambridge).

Gash, Norman (1984), *Lord Liverpool* (London).

George, Mary Dorothy (1938), *Catalogue of Political and Personal Satires preserved in the Department of Prints and Drawings in the British Museum, Vol. 6, 1784-1792* (London).

—— (1942), *Catalogue of Political and Personal Satires preserved in the Department of Prints and Drawings in the British Museum, Vol. 7, 1793-1800* (London).

—— (1947), *Catalogue of Political and Personal Satires preserved in the Department of Prints and Drawings in the British Museum, Vol.8, 1801-1810* (London).

—— (1953), *England in Transition* ([Harmondsworth]).

—— (1992), *London Life in the Eighteenth Century* (Harmondsworth).

Gilbart, James William (1836), *The History of Banking in Ireland* (London).

Gilboy, Elizabeth W. (1934), *Wages in Eighteenth Century England* (Cambridge, Mass.).

Gill, Conrad (1952), *History of Birmingham, Volume 1: Manor and Borough to 1865* (London).

Girouard, Mark (1990), *The English Town* (New Haven, Conn.).

Godden, Geoffrey A. (1985), *Lowestoft Porcelains* (Woodbridge).

Golding, Charles (1868), *The Coinage of Suffolk ...* (London).

Goodison, Nicholas (2002), *Matthew Boulton: Ormolu* (London).

Gould, Brian M. (1969), 'Matthew Boulton's East India Mint in London, 1786-88', *SCMB*, No. 612 (August), 270-77.

—— (1972), 'Noël-Alexandre Ponthon, Medallist and Miniaturist (1769/70-1835)', *SCMB*, No. 648 (August), 312-19 and No. 649

(September), 361-67.

Green, Francis (1915), 'Carmarthen Tinworks and its Founder', *West Wales Historical Records*, Vol. 5, 245-70.

Grierson, P[hilip] (1971), 'The Monetary Pattern of Sixteenth-Century Coinage', *TRHS*, Fifth Series, Vol. 21, 45-60.

—— (1972), 'Notes on Early Tudor Coinage – 2. Erasmus's Lead Tokens', *BNJ*, Vol. 41, 85-87.

—— (1975), *Numismatics* (London).

Griffiths, Antony and Williams, Reginald (1987), *The Department of Prints & Drawings in the British Museum* (London).

Grinsell, L. V. (1962), *A Brief Numismatic History of Bristol* (Bristol).

—— (1972), *The Bristol Mint: An Historical Outline* (Bristol).

Grinsell, L.V., Blunt, C. E. and Dolley, R. H. M. (1973), *Sylloge of Coins of the British Isles, Vol. 19, Bristol and Gloucester Museums* (London).

Gunnis, Rupert (1968), *Dictionary of British sculptors 1660-1851* (London).

Hamer, S. H. (1903/1904-1906), 'Notes on the Private Tokens, their Issuers and Die-Sinkers', *BNJ*, Vol. 1 (1903/4), 299-332; Vol.2 (1905), 369-96; Vol. 3 (1906), 271-79.

Hamilton, Henry (1967), *The English Brass and Copper Industries to 1800* (2nd. Edition, London).

Hancox, E. R. H. (1908), 'Finds of Mediaeval cut Halfpence and Farthings at Dunwich', *BNJ*, Vol. V, 123-34.

Harris, J. R. (1950), 'Michael Hughes of Sutton: The Influence of Welsh Copper on Lancashire Business, 1780-1815', *Transactions of the Historic Society of Lancashire and Cheshire*, Vol. 101, 139-167.

—— (1964), *The Copper King: a biography of Thomas Williams of Llanidan* (Liverpool).

—— (1966), 'Copper and Shipping in the Eighteenth Century', *EconHR*, 2nd. Series, Vol. 19, 550-68.

—— (1967), 'The Employment of Steam Power in the Eighteenth Century', *History*, Vol. 52, 133-148.

Hawker, C. R. (1988), 'Eighteenth-Century Token Notes from Matthew Boulton's Letters: The Cornish and Glasgow Halfpennies', *SCMB*, No. 833 (September), 199-204 and No.834 (October), 227-30.

—— (1989), 'Eighteenth-Century Token Notes from Matthew Boulton's Letters: The Glasgow Halfpenny', *SCMB*, No. 843 (September), 200-202 and No.844 (October), 227-30.

—— (1996), *Druid Tokens: Eighteenth Century Token Notes from Matthew Boulton's Letters: The Anglesey Series* (Studley).

Hawkins, R. N. (1989), *A Dictionary of British metallic tickets, checks, medalets, tallies, and counters* (London).

Heal, Ambrose (1928), 'A XVII Century MS. List of Tokens', *N&Q*, Vol. 154 (7 January), 3-5; (14 January), 25-27; (21 January), 41-43; (28 January), 58-61; (4 February), 78-81; (11 February), 96-99; (18 February), 113-14; (25 February), 129-32.

Heinze, Rudolph W. (1969), 'The Pricing of Meat: A Study in the

Use of Royal Proclamations in the Reign of Henry VIII', *The Historical Journal*, Vol. 12, 583-95.

Hewitt, V. H. and Keyworth, J. M. (1987), *As Good as Gold: 300 years of British Bank Note Design* (London).

Hill, Joseph (1907), *The Book Makers of Old Birmingham* (Birmingham).

Hill, Tom (1958), 'The Worswick Tokens of Lancaster', *SCMB*, No. 480 (May 1958), 194.

Hilton, George W. (1960), *The Truck System: including a history of the British Truck Acts, 1465-1960* (Cambridge).

Hodgkin, J. Eliot (1884), 'Anodyne Necklace ...', *N&Q*, 6th. Series, Vol. 9 (16 February), 132.

Hopkins, Eric (1998), *The Rise of the Manufacturing Town: Birmingham and the Industrial Revolution* (Stroud).

Hoppit, Julian (1986), 'The use and abuse of credit in eighteenth-century England' in McKendrick and Outhwaite (1986), 64-78.

Horden, John (1993), *John Freeth (1731-1808), Political Ballad-Writer and Innkeeper* (Oxford).

Horsefield, J. Keith (1960), *British Monetary Experiments 1650-1710* (London).

—— (1982), 'Copper v. Tin Coins in Seventeenth-Century', *BNJ*, Vol. 52, 161-80.

Household, Humphrey (1969), *The Thames & Severn Canal* (Newton Abbot).

Howell, T. B. and Howell, T. J. (eds.) (1817), *Cobbett's Complete Collection of State Trials ... Volume 23* (London).

Howson, George (2008), *The Making of Lancaster: People, Places and War, 1789-1815* (Lancaster).

James, Terrence (1976), 'Carmarthen Tinplate Works 1800-1821', *The Carmarthenshire Antiquary*, Vol. 12, 31-54.

Jewson C. B. (1975), *The Jacobin City: a Portrait of Norwich in its Reaction to the French Revolution 1788-1802* (Glasgow).

John, A. H. (1950), *The Industrial Development of South Wales* (Cardiff).

Jones, Mark (1977), *Medals of the French Revolution* (London).

Jones, Peter M. (2004), '"England Expects ...": Trading in Liberty in the Age of Trafalgar' in Crook, Doyle and Forrest (2004), 187-203.

—— (2008), *Industrial Enlightenment: Science, Technology and Culture in Birmingham and the West Midlands, 1760-1820* (Manchester).

Kelly, E. M. (1976), *Spanish Dollars and Silver Tokens: An Account of the issues of the Bank of England 1797-1816* (London).

Kennett, Bill, (n.d.) 'West Cumberland Carriers' Tokens – Part 1, The Earliest', *TCSB*, Vol. 6, 247-51.

K[ent], G. C. (1912), *British Metallic Coins and Tradesmen's Tokens with their Value from 1600-1912* (Chichester); Supplementary Title and Index (1913) (Chichester).

Kent, J. P. C. (1957) [1989], 'Forgery in the reign of George III: the problem of medley halfpence' (unpublished British Numismatic Society Lecture, May): an abstract of the paper is printed in Hawkins (1989), 893-904.

—— (1969), 'Three Seventeenth- and Eighteenth-Century Finds: Westmacote (Bredon), Worcs., Treasure Trove', *BNJ*, Vol.38, 166.

—— (1985), 'The Circulation of Portuguese Coins in Great Britain', *Actas Do III Congresso Nacional de Numismática* (Lisbon), 389-405.

—— (2005), *Coinage and Currency in London from the London and Middlesex Records and other sources: from Roman times to the Victorians* (London).

Kenyon, George T. (1873), *The Life of Lloyd, First Lord Kenyon, Lord Chief Justice of England* (London).

Kenyon, Robert Lloyd (1884), *The Gold Coins of England* (London).

Klingender, Francis D[onald] (1943), 'Eighteenth Century Pence and Ha'pence, *Architectural Review*, Vol. 93 (February 1943), 40-46 and (March 1943), xli-xlii.

------ (1972), *Art and the Industrial Revolution* (Revised edition by Arthur Elton, London).

Langford, J. A. (1868), *A Century of Birmingham Life: a Chronicle of Local Events, 1741- 1841* (2 volumes, Birmingham).

Latimer, John (1908), *Sixteenth-Century Bristol* (Bristol)

Linecar, H. W. A. (1977), *British Coin Designs and Designers* (London).

Llwyd, Angharad (1833) *A history of the Island of Mona or Anglesey…* (Ruthin).

Longman, William (1916), *Tokens of the Eighteenth Century connected with Booksellers & Bookmakers* (London).

Lord, John (1923), *Capital and Steam-Power 1750-1800* (London).

McAllister, Marie E. (1996), 'John Burrows and the Vegetable Wars' in Merians (1996), 85-102.

Macaulay, Thomas Babington (1849-61), *The History of England from the Accession of James II*, Vol. 4 (1855) (London).

McCalman, Iain (1988), *Radical Underworld: Prophets, Revolutionaries and Pornographers in London, 1795-1840* (Cambridge).

McKendrick, Neil, Brewer, John and Plumb, J. H. (eds.) (1982), *The Birth of a Consumer Society: The Commercialization of Eighteenth-century England* (London).

McKendrick, Neil and Outhwaite, R. B. (eds.) (1986), *Business Life and Public Policy, Essays in Honour of D. C. Coleman* (Cambridge).

Mackenzie, E. (1827), *A Descriptive and Historical Account of the Town and County of Newcastle upon Tyne …* (2 volumes, Newcastle upon Tyne).

McClure, Ruth K. (1981), *Coram's Children. The London Foundling Hospital in the Eighteenth Century* (New Haven, Conn. and London).

Macquoid, Percy and Edwards, Ralph (1954), *The Dictionary of English Furniture: from the Middle Ages to the late Georgian Period* (3 volumes, London).

Malcolm, L. W. G. (1925), 'On a Hoard of Silver Coins found at Welsh Back, Bristol', *NC*, Fifth Series, Vol. 5, 236-64 and 402.

Mantoux, Paul (1948), *The Industrial Revolution in the Eighteenth Century* (London).

Manville, Harrington. E. (2001), *Tokens of the Industrial Revolution: Foreign Silver Coins countermarked for use in Great Britain, c.1787-1828* (London).

—— (2005), *Numismatic Guide to British and Irish Printed Books 1600-2004, Encyclopædia of British Numismatics, Volume III* (London).

—— (2009), *Biographical Dictionary of British and Irish Numismatics, Encyclopædia of British Numismatics, Volume IV* (London).

—— and Robertson, Terence J. (1986), *British Numismatic Auction Catalogues 1710-1984, Encyclopædia of British Numismatics, Volume I* (London).

Margolis, Richard (1988), 'Matthew Boulton's French Ventures of 1791 and 1792: Tokens for the Monneron Frères of Paris and Isle de France', *BNJ*, Vol. 58, 102-109.

Marsh, John (1971), *Clip a Bright Guinea: The Yorkshire Coiners of the Eighteenth Century* (London).

Mason, Shena (2005), *The Hardware Man's Daughter: Matthew Boulton and his 'Dear Girl'* (Chichester).

—— (ed.) (2009), *Matthew Boulton: Selling what all the World Desires* (Birmingham).

Mathias, Peter (1962), *English Trade Tokens: The Industrial Revolution Illustrated* (London).

—— (1979), 'The People's Money in the Eighteenth Century: the Royal Mint, Trade Tokens and the Economy' in *The Transformation of England* (London), 190-208. [An annotated version of the 'Introduction' to *English Trade Tokens*].

—— (2004), 'Official and Unofficial Money in the Eighteenth Century: The Evolving Uses of Currency', *BNJ*, Vol. 74, 68-83.

Matthew, H. C. G. and Harrison, Sir Brian (eds.) (2004), *Oxford Dictionary of National Biography* (Oxford). [Also available in online edition].

Matthews, William (1935), 'The Lincolnshire Dialect in the Eighteenth Century', *N&Q*, Vol. 169 (7 December), 398–404.

Mayhew, N. J. (ed.) (1977), *Edwardian Monetary Affairs (1279-1344)* (Oxford).

—— (1999), *Sterling: the rise and fall of a currency* (London).

Meikle, Henry W (1912), *Scotland and the French Revolution* (Glasgow).

Merians, Linda E. (ed.) (1996), *The Secret Malady, Venereal Disease in Eighteenth-Century Britain and France* (Lexington, Ky.).

Milne, J. G. (ed.) (1935), *Catalogue of Oxfordshire Seventeenth-Century Tokens* (Oxford).

—— (1949-51), 'Seventeenth Century Tokens: The Browne Willis Cabinet', *BNJ*, Vol. 26, 333-338.

Mitchiner, Michael (1998), *Jetons, Medalets and Tokens, Volume 3, British Isles, circa 1558 to 1830* (London).

—— and Skinner, Anne (1983), 'English Tokens, *c*.1200 to 1425', *BNJ*, Vol. 53, 29-77.

—— —— (1986) 'Contemporary forgeries of late seventeenth-Century English tin coins: the implications for the study of leaden tokens', *NC*, Vol. 146,178-84.

Money, John (1977), *Experience and Identity: Birmingham and the West Midlands 1760-1800* (Manchester).

Mui, Hoh-cheung and Mui, Lorna H. (1989), *Shops and Shopkeeping in Eighteenth-Century England* (London).

Muldrew, Craig (1998), *The Economy of Obligation: The culture of credit and social relations in early modern England* (Basingstoke).

—— (2001) '"Hard Food for Midas": Cash and Its Social Value in Early Modern England', *Past and Present*, No. 170, 78-120.

Murray, David (1885), *A Note on some Glasgow and other Provincial Coins and Tokens* (Glasgow).

Norris, D. M. (1947-48), 'Some Birmingham Medallists', *Birmingham Archaeological Society Transactions and Proceedings*, Vol. 6, 71-75.

Norris, J. M. (1958), 'Samuel Garbett and the early development of Industrial Lobbying in Great Britain', *EconHR*, Vol. 10, 450-60.

—— (1963), *Shelburne and Reform* (London).

Olsen, Donald J. (1964), *Town Planning in London. The Eighteenth & Nineteenth Centuries* (New Haven, Conn.).

Oman, Charles (1931), *The Coinage of England* (Oxford).

Outing, Roger (2010), *The Standard Catalogue of the Provincial Banknotes of England and Wales* (Honiton).

Owen, Felicity (1994), 'John Thomas ("Antiquity") Smith: A Renaissance man for the Georgian age', *Apollo*, Vol. 140, 34-36.

Paget-Tomlinson, Edward W. (1978), *The Complete Book of Canal & River Navigations* (Albrighton, Wolverhampton).

Palmer, Alfred Neobard (1899), 'John Wilkinson and the Old Bersham Iron Works', *Trans Cymmr, 1897-98*, 23-64.

Palmer, N. J. and Mayhew, N. J. (1977), 'Medieval Coins and Jetons from Oxford Excavations' in Mayhew (ed.) (1977), 81-95.

Pannell, J. P. M. (1967), *Old Southampton Shores* (Newton Abbot).

Pawson, Eric (1979), *The Early Industrial Revolution: Britain in the Eighteenth Century* (London).

Peck, C. W. (1947), 'Eighteenth Century Tradesmen's Tokens: An Introduction to the Series', *SCMB*, No.352 (September), 344-48. [Reprinted in Seaby and Seaby (1949), 86-90].

—— (1960), *English Copper, Tin and Bronze Coins in the British Museum 1558-1958* (London).

Pelham, R. A. (1963), 'The Water-Power Crisis in Birmingham in the Eighteenth Century', *University of Birmingham Historical Journal*, Vol. 9, 64-91.

Philips, C. H. (1961), *The East India Company 1784-1834* (Manchester).

Phillips, Maberly (1894), *A History of Banks, Bankers, & Banking in Northumberland, Durham, and North Yorkshire ...* (London).

—— (1900), *The Token Money of the Bank of England, 1797 to 1816* (London).

Pierson, William Harvey, Jr. (1949), 'Notes on Early Industrial Architecture in England', *The Journal of the Society of Architectural Historians*, Vol. 8, No. 1/2 (Jan. – Jun.), 1-32.

Pollard, J. G. (1968), 'Matthew Boulton and J.-P. Droz', *NC*, Seventh Series, Vol. 8, 241-65.

—— (1970), 'Matthew Boulton and Conrad Heinrich Küchler',

NC, Seventh Series, Vol. 10, 259-318.

Porteous, John (1969), *Coins in History: a survey of coinage from the Reform of Diocletian to the Latin Monetary Union* (London).

Porter, Roy (2000), *Quacks: Fakers & Charlatans in English Medicine* (Stroud).

Powell, John S. (1977), 'Benjamin Jacob, His Token', *SCMB*, No. 705 (May), 172-73.

Pressnell, L. S. (1956), *Country Banking in the Industrial Revolution* (Oxford).

Pridmore, F. (1975), *The Coins of the British Commonwealth of Nations: Part 4. India, Volume 1, East India Company Presidency Series c.1642-1835* (London).

Pritchard, John E. (1899), 'Bristol Tokens of the Sixteenth and Seventeenth Centuries', *NC*, Third Series, Vol. 19, 350-61.

—— (1902), 'Bristol Tokens of the Sixteenth and Seventeenth Centuries' ['Miscellanea'], *NC*, Fourth Series, Vol. 2, 385-87.

Prosser, Richard B. (1881), *Birmingham Inventors and Inventors* (Birmingham).

Quickenden, Kenneth (1980), 'Boulton and Fothergill Silver: Business plans and Miscalculations', *Art History*, Vol. 3, 274-94.

—— (1995), 'Boulton and Fothergill's Silversmiths', *Silver Society Journal*, No. 7, 342-56.

—— (2007), 'Richard Chippindall and the Boultons', *Silver Studies, The Journal of the Silver Society*, No. 22, 51-65.

Randall, John (1917), *Our coal and iron industries, and the men who have wrought in connection with them: the Wilkinsons* (Madeley, Salop).

Redish, Angela (2000), *Bimetallism: An Economic and Historical Analysis* (Cambridge).

Roberts, Jane (ed.) (2004), *George III & Queen Charlotte: Patronage, Collecting and Court Taste* (London).

Robinson, Eric (1953), 'Matthew Boulton, Patron of the Arts', *Annals of Science*, Vol. 9, 368-376.

—— (1957), 'Matthew Boulton's Birthplace and his Home at Snow Hill: A Problem in Detection', *Transactions of the Birmingham and Warwickshire Archaeological Society*, Vol. 75, 85-89.

—— (1962-63), 'The Lunar Society: its Membership and Organisation', *Transactions of the Newcomen Society*, Vol. 35, 153-77.

—— (1963-64), 'Eighteenth-Century Commerce and Fashion: Matthew Boulton's Marketing Techniques', *EconHR*, 2nd. Series, Vol. 16, 39-60.

Robinson, John Martin (1979), *The Wyatts, an architectural dynasty* (Oxford).

Robinson, P. H. (1971), 'The Eighteenth-Century Coin Hoard from Pillaton Hall, Staffs.', *BNJ*, Vol. 40, 124-35.

—— (1972), 'The Dunchurch and Stafford Finds of Eighteenth-Century Halfpence and Counterfeits', *BNJ*, Vol. 41, 147-58.

Rogers, D. J. de S. (1995), *Views of Small Change before 1613* (London).

Roll, Eric (1968), *An Early Experiment in Industrial Organisation:*

Being a History of the Firm of Boulton and Watt, 1775-1805 (London).

Roth, H. Ling (1906), *The Yorkshire Coiners 1767-1783, and Notes of Old and Prehistoric Halifax* (Halifax).

Rowe, C. M. (1966), *Salisbury's Local Coinage* (Salisbury).

Rowe, John (1953), *Cornwall in the Age of the Industrial Revolution* (Liverpool).

Rowlands, John (1966), *Copper Mountain* (Llangefni).

Ruding, Rogers (1817), *Annals of the Coinage of Great Britain and its Dependencies* (1st. Edition, 3 volumes, London).

—— (1840), *Annals of the Coinage of Great Britain and its Dependencies* (3rd. Edition, 3 volumes, London).

Rudkin, Olive D. (1966), *Thomas Spence and his Connections* (New York).

Rule, John (1992a), *Albion's People: English Society, 1714-1815* (London).

—— (1992b), *The Vital Century: England's Developing Economy, 1714-1815* (London).

Sainthill, Richard (1844), *An Olla Podrida; or, Scraps, Numismatic, Antiquarian, and Literary* (London).

—— (1853), *An Olla Podrida; or, Scraps, Numismatic, Antiquarian, and Literary. Volume the Second* (London).

[Samuel, Richard Thomas] (1880-1889), 'Provincial Copper Coins and Tokens (Eighteenth and Nineteenth Centuries)', *The Bazaar, Exchange and Mart and Journal of the Household*, passim. [Reprinted in 1 volume, ed. Alan Davisson (1996, Cold Spring, MN)].

Sargent, Thomas J and Velde, François R (2003), *The Big Problem of small Change* (2nd. Edition, Princeton, NJ).

Scarfe, Norman (1995), *Innocent Espionage: The La Rochefoucauld Brothers' Tour of England in 1785* (Woodbridge).

Schofield, Robert E. (1957), 'The Industrial Orientation of Science in the Lunar Society of Birmingham', *Isis*, Vol. 48, 408-15

—— (1963), *The Lunar Society of Birmingham: A Social History of Provincial Science and Industry in Eighteenth-Century England* (Oxford).

Seaby, Herbert Allen and Seaby, Peter John (1949), *A Catalogue of the Copper coins and Tokens of the British Isles* (London).

Seaman, R. (1972), 'A Further Find of Coins from Dunwich', *BNJ*, Vol. 41, 27-33.

Selgin, George (2003), 'Steam, hot air, and small change: Matthew Boulton and the reform of Britain's coinage', *EconHR*, Vol. 56, 478-509.

—— (2005), 'Charles Wyatt, manager of the Parys Mine mint: a study in ingratitude', *BNJ*, Vol. 75, 113-20.

—— (2008), *Good Money* (Ann Arbor, Mich.).

Sharp, Thomas (1871), *Illustrative Papers on the History and Antiquities of the city of Coventry ...* (Birmingham).

Sharpe, Kevin (1979), *Sir Robert Cotton 1586-1631: History and Politics in early Modern England* (Oxford).

Shaw, W. A. (1896), *The History of Currency 1252-1896* (2nd. Edition, London).

Skipp, Victor (1980), *A History of Greater Birmingham – down to 1830* (Birmingham).

Smiles, Samuel (1865), *Lives of Boulton and Watt. Principally from the original Soho MSS.* (London).

Smith, Edward (1911), *The Life of Sir Joseph Banks* (London).

Smith, L. Richard (1985), *The Resolution & Adventure Medal* (Sydney).

Solkin, David H. (1982), *Richard Wilson, The Landscape of Reaction* (London).

Spufford, Peter (1963), 'Continental Coins in late medieval England', *BNJ*, Vol. 32, 127-39.

—— (1988), *Money and its Use in Medieval Europe* (Cambridge).

Stainton, T. (1983), 'John Milton, Medallist, 1759-1805', *BNJ*, Vol. 53, 133-59.

Stanope, Earl (1862), *Life of the Right Honourable William Pitt* (2nd. Edition, 4 volumes, London).

Stockdale, James (1872), *Annales Caermoelenses or Annals of Cartmel* (Ulverston).

Stuart, Susan E. (1999), *Biographical List of Clockmakers: North Lancashire and South Westmorland 1680-1900* (Lancaster).

Styles, John (1980), '"Our traitorous money makers": the Yorkshire coiners and the law, 1760-83' in Brewer and Styles (1980), 172-249 and 342-71.

Summerson, John (1978), *Georgian London* (3rd. Edition, London).

Supple, B. E. (1957), 'Currency and Commerce in the Early Seventeenth Century', *EconHR*, New Series, Vol. 10, 239-55.

Sutherland, Lucy Stuart (1933), *A London Merchant 1695-1774* (London).

Sydenham, S. (1903-1904), 'Bath Token Issues of the 18th Century', *SNC*, Vol.12, columns 7371-76; 7438-44; 7511-16.

—— (1907-1908), 'Bath Token Issues', *SNC*, Vol. 16, columns 10670-72.

Symons, David (2006), 'A Pass for the 'Birmingham Theatre', 1774', *BNJ*, Vol. 76, 312-22.

Tann, Jennifer (1970), *The Development of the Factory* (London).

—— (1993), *Birmingham Assay Office 1773-1993* (Birmingham).

Taxay, Don (1966), *The U. S. Mint and Coinage: An Illustrated History from 1776 to the Present* (New York).

Taylor, R. V. (1865), *The Biographia Leodiensis; or Biographical Sketches of the Worthies of Leeds and Neighbourhood* (London).

Thirsk, Joan (ed.) (1967), *The Agrarian History of England and Wales, Volume 4, 1500-1640* (Cambridge).

Thomason, Sir Edward (1845), *Memoirs during Half a Century* (2 volumes, London).

Thompson, C. J. S. (1928), *The Quacks of Old London* (London).

Thompson, R. H. (1969), 'The Dies of Thomas Spence (1750-1814)', *BNJ*, Vol. 38, 126-62.

—— (1971), 'The Dies of Thomas Spence (1750-1814): Additions and Corrections', *BNJ*, Vol. 40, 136-38.

—— (1976), 'Jacobin Grotesques: the Deliberate Muling of Dies in Late Eighteenth-century England', *Actes du 8ème Congrès International de Numismatique, 1973* (Paris), 671-79.

—— (1981), 'French assignats current in Britain: the parliamentary debates', *BNJ*, Vol. 51, 200-203.

—— (1988), *Sylloge of Coins of the British Isles, Vol. 38, The Norweb Collection, Part 2, Dorset, Durham, Essex and Gloucestershire* (London).

—— (1989) 'Central or Local Production of Seventeenth-Century Tokens', *BNJ*, Vol. 59, 198-211.

—— (1993), 'Mechanisation at the 17th-century London mint: the testimony of tokens' in Archibald and Cowell (eds.), 143-53.

—— (1999), 'The Petty Coinage: Sir William Petty's Tokens and his Views on Small Change' in Thompson and Dickinson (1999), xi-xviii.

—— (2000), 'Edward Nourse and a Farthing's Worth of Copper', *BNJ*, Vol. 70, 147-50.

—— (2003), 'Tokens and Paranumismatics to 1700', *BNJ*, Vol. 7, 161-68.

—— (2007), 'Contemporary References to Tokens, the Downfall of Coffee-Pence, and the Sultaness' in Thompson and Dickinson (2007), xi-xvii.

—— (2009), 'The Golden Fleece in Britain', *BNJ*, Vol. 79, 199-212.

Thompson, R. H. and Dickinson, M. J. (1999), *Sylloge of Coins of the British Isles, Vol. 49, The Norweb Collection, Part 6, Wiltshire to Yorkshire, Ireland to Wales* (London).

—— —— (2007), *Sylloge of Coins of the British Isles, Vol. 59, The Norweb Collection, Part 7, City of London* (London).

Thorne, R. G. (1986), *The History of Parliament. The House of Commons 1790-1820*, 5 volumes (London).

Todd, William B. (1972), *A Directory of Printers and others in Allied Trades: London and Vicinity 1800-1840* (London).

Travaini, L. (ed.) (1999), *Local Coins, Foreign Coins: Italy and Europe 11th-15th Centuries* (Milan).

Trinder, Barrie (1996), *The Industrial Archaeology of Shropshire* (Chichester).

Uglow, Jenny (2002), *The Lunar Men: The Friends who made the Future, 1730-1810* (London).

—— (2006), *Nature's Engraver: a Life of Thomas Bewick* (London).

Unwin, George (1968), *Samuel Oldknow and the Arkwrights: the Industrial Revolution at Stockport and Marple* (Manchester).

Vice, David (1983), *The Coinage of British West Africa and St. Helena 1648-1958* (Birmingham).

—— (1988), 'The *Resolution* and *Adventure* Medal', *Format*, No. 36 (March), 2-4.

—— (1989), 'The Soho Mint & the Anglesey Tokens of the Parys Mine Company', *Format*, No. 38 (April), 2-9.

—— (1990), 'The Tokens of John Wilkinson', *Format*, No. 40 (March), 2-8.

—— (1991a), 'The Cronebane Token of the Associated Irish Mine Company', *Format*, No. 42 (January), 2-6.

—— (1991b), 'The Tullamore Token of Viscount Charleville', *Format*, No. 43 (May), 2-4.

—— (1995), 'A Fresh Insight into Soho Mint Restrikes and those responsible for their Manufacture', *Format*, No. 52 (September), 3-14.

—— (1997), [Letter to the Editor], *CTCN*, Vol. 1, No. 4, 41-45.

—— (1998), 'Medals and Medallions struck at Boulton and Fothergill's Soho Manufactory', *Format*, No. 57, 3-9.

Vilar, Pierre (1984), *A History of Gold and Money 1450-1920* (Translated by Judith White, London).

Wadsworth, Alfred P. and Mann, Julia de Lacy (1931), *The Cotton Trade and Industrial Lancashire 1600-1780* (Manchester).

Walker, Benjamin (1934), 'Birmingham Directories', *Birmingham Archaeological Society Transactions and Proceedings*, Vol. 58, 1-36.

Ward, W. R. (ed.) (1992), *Palatinate Studies* (Manchester).

Waters, Arthur William (1906), *Notes gleaned from Contemporary Literature, &c. respecting the Issuers of the Eighteenth Century Tokens struck for the County of Middlesex ...* (Leamington Spa).

—— (1917), *The Trial of Thomas Spence in 1801* (Leamington Spa).

—— (1954), *Notes on Eighteenth Century Tokens* (London).

Weinstein, Benjamin (2002), 'Popular Constitutionalism and the London Corresponding Society', *Albion*, Vol. 34, 37-57.

Weinstock, Maureen (1953), *Studies in Dorset History* (Dorchester).

—— (1960), *More Dorset Studies* (Dorchester).

Welch, Harold (2010), 'A Curmudgeon's Copy of *Conder's Arrangement*', *CTCJ*, Vol. 15, No. 2, 29-32.

Westwood, Arthur (1926), *Matthew Boulton's 'Otaheite' Medal* (Birmingham).

White, Andrew (ed.) (1993), *A History of Lancaster 1193-1993* (Keele).

White, D. P. (1977), 'The Birmingham Button Industry', *Post-Medieval Archaeology*, Vol. 11, 67-79.

Willan, T. S. (1976), *The Inland Trade: Studies in English internal trade in the Sixteenth and Seventeenth Centuries* (Manchester).

Williams, L. J. (1961), 'The Welsh Tinplate Trade in the Mid-Eighteenth Century', *EconHR*, New Series, Vol. 13, 440-49.

Williamson, George C. (1967), *Trade Tokens issued in the Seventeenth Century in England, Wales, and Ireland*, 3 volumes (London) [Reprint of 1st. edition in 2 volumes (1889-1891)].

Winstanley, Michael (1993), 'The Town Transformed, 1815-1914' in White, *A History of Lancaster 1193-1993* (Keele), 145-198.

Withers, Paul (1991), 'A Medallic Feud', *The Medal*, No.18, 29-33.

—— and Withers, Bente R. (1993), *British Coin-Weights* (Llanfyllin).

—— —— (1999), *British Copper Tokens 1811-1820* (Llanfyllin).

—— —— (2001), *The Farthings and Halfpennies of Edward I and II* (Llanfyllin).

—— —— (2010), *The Token Book, 17th, 18th & 19th Century Tokens and their Values* (Llanfyllin).

Wood, Diana (ed.) (2004), *Medieval Money Matters* (Oxford).

Wood, Marcus (1994), *Radical Satire and Print Culture 1790-1822*

(Oxford).

Woodcroft, Bennet (1854) [1969], *Alphabetical Index of Patentees of Inventions* (Kelly Reprint with an introduction and appendix of additions and corrections, New York).

Wrigley, E. A. and Schofield, R.S. (1989), *The Population History of England 1541-1871: A Reconstruction* (Cambridge).

Wright, Thomas (1873), *The Works of James Gillray, the Caricaturist; with the History of his Life and Times* (London).

—— and Evans, R. H. (1851), *Historical and Descriptive Account of the Caricatures of James Gillray* (London).

Yeates, F. Willson (1917), 'Sharp's Catalogue of the Chetwynd Collection', *SNC*, cols. 363-64 (July/August 1917).

Theses and Dissertations

Bebbington, P.S. (1938), 'Samuel Garbett, 1717-1803: a Birmingham Pioneer', M. Comm. thesis, University of Birmingham.

Cule, J. E. (1935), 'The Financial History of Matthew Boulton 1759-1800', M. Comm. thesis, University of Birmingham.

Powell, John S. (1977), 'The Birmingham Coiners 1780-1816', M. A. thesis, University of Sussex.

Quickenden, Kenneth (1989), 'Boulton and Fothergill Silver', Ph. D. thesis, University of London (Westfield College).

Wager, Andrew J. (1977), 'Birmingham and the Nation's Copper Coinage 1750-1820: a Study in Local Initiative', B. A. dissertation, University of Birmingham.

INDEX

Page references in italics refer to illustrations and captions
Images of coins and tokens are not ordinarily included in the Index
nor are entries in the Tables or Appendix I

Abbott, Lemuel Francis, *84*
Absolon, William, Great Yarmouth, 170, *170*
Ackermann, Rudolph, 220, *221*, 231, *231*, 235 n. 80
Aesop ('The Ploughman's Quarrelsome Sons'), 289
Aikin, Arthur, 179
Anderson, Peter, 195
Anglesey tokens, 76-84, 115, 118-19, 135-36, 159, 174, 218, 261, 300, 302
Annual Register, The, 145
Anodyne Necklaces, 232-33, *233*
Arkwright, Richard, 70 n. 124, 127
Arnold, Francis, 224 n. 51, 250, 310, 323
Arnold Works, Nottingham, 153-55, *154*
Ashton, T. S., 39-40, 64, 65-66
Assignats, 67, 177
Associated Irish Mine Company, Cronebane, 116-18, 160, 174
Associated Smelters, 74, 97
Austen, Jane, 251
Bacon, Richard, Norwich, 226, 260
Ball, Nicholas, Chudleigh, 11
Ball. Thomas, Sleaford, 223
Ballard, Richard, 17, *18*
Bank of England, 38, 46-48, 145-48, *147*
Banks, Sarah Sophia, 1-5, *3*, 79, 141, 165, 170, 188, 191-93, 204, 234, 241, 264-65, 273, 283, 306, 308, 326, 330-32, 339, 341, 346
Banks, Sir Joseph, 1, 4, 98, 105, 128, 307, 325
Barber, Joseph, Birmingham, 199
Barclay, Robert, 135-36
Barker, George, Birmingham, 191 n. 104, 263, 324
Barnard, Sir John, 42
Barrington, Daines, 79
Bassett, Sir Francis, Bart, Baron de Dunstanville and 1st Baron Bassett, 141-42
Bath, 302
Bayley, Thomas Butterworth, Manchester, 84
Bayly, Sir Nicholas, 72
Bell, James, 284

Bencoolen (Sumatra) coinage, 105-6, 152
Bentham, Jeremy, 74
Berg, Maxine, 245
Bermuda penny, 120, 127, 129, 136
Bewick, Thomas, 235-37, *235*, *236*, *279*, 280, 283, 332
Biddulph, Robert, 265, 291-92
Bingley, William, 237
Birchall, Samuel, Leeds, 86, 128, 188, 262, 334-35
Bird, Hawkins, Bristol, 178, 185
Birmingham ('Brummagem'), 65, 78, 82-84, 88, 219, 226, 309
'Birmingham ('Brummagem') Halfpennies', 55
'Birmingham Coining & Copper Company', 221
Birmingham Loyal Associations medals, 199, *199*, 293
Birmingham Mining & Copper Company, 203-5
Bisset, James, Birmingham, 91, 93, 165, 243-45, *243*, 246
Bloomsbury, 183-84
Bluck, John, *221*, 309
Bolingbroke, Nathaniel, Norwich, *226*, 227
Bombay presidency coinage, 119
Boon, George, 21-22, 23, 77
Boswell, James, 96, 142
Boulter, Joseph, Daniel and John, Great Yarmouth, 170, 242-43, 249
Boulton, Matthew, 1 n. 2, 44, 56, 58, 65, 69, 75-76, 79-81, 83, 85, 87-114, *88*, 115-56, *123*, 161-63, 165, 203, 212-13, 215-18, 262, 301-3, 307, 309, 323, 325-27, 335
Boulton, Matthew, Snr, 88
Boulton & Fothergill, 158, 163
Bouquet or Blossoms of Fancy, The, 269, *269*, 329
Breda, Carl Fredrik von, *123*, 124
Brighton (Bright[h]elmstone), 218, 251-52
Brimscombe Port, 179, *180*, 181
Bristol tokens, 11, 16, 20
'British Commercial' coinage, 148, 190
Brtiish Druid, A, 65, *65*
Brown, Alexander, Glasgow, 125-26

Brown, John, Bristol, 11
Brownbill, Henry, Leeds, 128, 224, 335
Building medalets, 209, 276-77
Bumpstead, Christopher, 9-10
Burchell, Basil, 232-35
Burchell, Matthew, 232
Burke, Edmund, 100 n. 95, 282-83, *282*, 288
Burton, James, 178, 182-85, *184*
Bury, Andrew, Stockport, 128
Buxton, 117
Byng, John (later 5th Viscount Torrington), 51, 58, 117-18, 181, 224
Cape St Vincent, battle of, 145, 148, 185-86
Capon, Scrivener, Lowestoft, 249-50
Carey, George Saville, 84
Carmarthen Iron Works, 168-69, *169*, 253
Carpenter, Richard, 138
Carrington, John, Hertfordshire, 235 n. 80, 152
'Cartwheel' coinage, 149-52, 188, 301-2
Chaldecott, Thomas, Chichester and Portsmouth, 178, 185-86
Chamberlayne, William, Mint solicitor (later solicitor to the Treasury), 43, 51
Chambers, Langston, Hall & Company, 255
Charleville, Charles William Bury, 1st Viscount (later Earl of), 153, 155
Chester, 207, 208
Chetwynd, Sir George, 196, 264, 346-47, *346*
Ching, John, 234
Chippindall, Richard, 123
Circulating libraries, 251-52, *251*, *252*
Civil Citizen, The, 281, *281*
Clarke, Thomas, Liverpool, 170, 174
Clay, Henry, Birmingham, 159
Cloake, Isaac & Thankful, Tenterden, 228, 249
Coal mine near Neath, Glamorgan, 255
Coining equipment, 78, 157, 219-20, *219*, *220*, *221*, 309-10
Coin weights, 51, *51*
'Collectors' Halfpence', 190, 263
Collins, William, 74, 76, 77, 105, 159
Colquhoun, Patrick, 50, 56-58, *56*
Committee on Coin, Privy Council, 1 n. 2, 39, 44, 67-68, 105, 108-110, 137, 148-49, 160, 299
Conder, James, 188, 196, 198, 344-46, *344*
Conduitt, John, 37, 42, 45
Coote, Sir Eyre, regimental medals, 105, 158

Copper Company of Upper Canada, 129-30
Copper prices, 214-19
Cornish Metal Company, 75, 97, 113, 119, 123-25, 141, 144, 203
Cornwall, 96-97
Cosway, Richard, *142*
Cotton, George, Romford, 136-38, 298
Cotton, Sir Robert, 12, *12*
Counterfeit regal copper, 54-61, 67-69
Counterfeit tokens, 220-22
Courtney, John, Portsea, 228
Craig, Sir John, 10, 36, 59, 109
Crawshay, Richard, Cyfarthfa, 193-94
Credit, 8, 299-300
Criticism of tokens, 20-21, 295-99
Cromford, 127
Cronebane. *See* Associated Irish Mine Company
Croom, William, 129, 139-41, 216-18
Crowley, Sir Ambrose, 66
Crowleys, 64
Curwens, 69
Daily Universal Register, The, 40, 71, 80-81, 261
Dance, Nathaniel, 150
Dartmouth, William Legge, 2nd Earl of, 98
Darwin, Erasmus, 89 n. 58, 93, 96,
Davidson, Thomas & Robert, 191, 291
Davies, William, 249-50, 285, 323
Davison & Hawksley. *See* Arnold Works.
Dawe, Philip, 241, *242*
Dawes, John, 72-74, *72*, 81, 103
Day, Thomas, 95
Denton, Matthew, 263, 277-78, 333, 339-41
Denton & Prattent, 236, 274, *275*, 277, 339-41, 345
Deverell, Benjamin, 274, *275*
Digges, Thomas Attwood, 55, 129, 175-76, *177*, 191, 192, 201, 215
Dixon, Roger, 185, 200, 323
Dobbs, Thomas, 191, 212-13, 215, 219
Dollars, Bank of England, 308
Dollars, countermarked, 39, 147-49, 301
Doty, Richard, 116
Droz, Jean-Pierre, 76, 103-7, *108*, 118, 160, 323-24, 327
Dryden, John, 28
Duchange, Gaspard, 126, *126*
Dumarest, Rambert, 118, 122, 124-26, 162, 324
Dundee, 139, *139*, 258-60, 283
Dunham & Yallop, Norwich, 227
Dupré, Augustin, 120, 126
Dyer, George, 292
Dyer, Graham, 302

INDEX

East India Company, 74, 85, 105-6, 119, 140, 214
Eastbourne, 250-52, *251*
Eaton, Daniel Isaac, 284-86, *286*, *287*
Eccleston, Daniel, Lancaster, 129-30, 140, 144
Eckstein, Johannes, 245, *246*
Effingham, Thomas Howard, 3rd Earl of, 75, 103, 109, *109*
Eginton, Francis, *90*, *243*, 244, *246*
Elizabeth I, 9, 12
Elizabeth, Princess, 2
Encyclopædia Britannica, 253
'End of Pain' tokens, 191-92, 293
Enniscorthy, 153
Erasmus, Desidarius, 8
Erskine, Thomas, 288
Evelyn, John, 16, 21, 27, 32, 228
Ewen, John, Aberdeen, 151
Eyre, Adam, Yorkshire, 27-28
Falmouth, George Evelyn Boscawen, 3rd Viscount, 141-42
Farington, Joseph, 130
Farror, Joseph, Birmingham, 209
Favri, Nicolo di, 8, 10
Feavearyear, Sir Albert, 59
Ferdinand I, Holy Roman Emperor, medal, 126
Ferrar, John, 207-8
Fielding, John, Manchester, 222
'Fingal', 128
Fisher, Frederick George, Eastbourne, 250-52
Fisher, Jabez Maud, 91, 94, 134
Fittler, James, *255*
Folkes, Martin, 28
Ford, Sir Edward, 21
Ford, Richard, Birmingham, 80
Foreign coin as currency, 6-7, 10, 12, 40, 59
Forest Copper Works, Swansea (Lockwood, Morris & Company), *134*
Fortrose, Kenneth Mackenzie, Viscount (later Earl of Seaforth), 305-6, *306*
Fothergill, John, 90, 98-99
'Foundling Fields'. *See* Burton, James
Francis, Charlotte, 251-52
Freeth, John, 'The Birmingham Poet', 66-67, 245, *246*
Frost, Edward, Portsea, 228
Fuggle, William, Goudhurst, 223-24
Fullarton, Colonel William, 304-9, *306*
Fuller, John, Northiam, 227
Furness ironmasters, 65
Galey-Halpeny, 6-7
Garbett, Francis, 43
Garbett, Samuel, 43, *43*, 44, 79-81, 86, 88, 95, 99-101, 110-12, 161, 164, 166, 202 n. 133, 203, 206, 303, 336
Garner, T., 236-37, *236*
Garton & Company, Jonathan, Hull, 171
General Magazine, The, 84,
Gentleman's Magazine, The, v, 81-82, *82*, 86, 187, 214, 280, 282, 291, 293, 295-97, 298
George and Blue Boar, The, 132-33, *133*
George III, 80, 109, 150
George, George Chapman, 142, 217
George, Prince of Wales (later George IV), 306-7
Gibbs, Vicary, 288
Gillow family, furniture makers, 171-72
Gillray, James, 3, *3*, *147*, 289, *290*
'Glamorgan Halfpenny', 192-94, 302
Glasgow, 125-26, *125*
Goddard, Florimond, 284
Golding, Charles, 250
Goldsmith & Son, Sudbury, 224, 302
Good, James, 170, 208, 212-13, 228, 242, 249-50, 285, 323
Gordon, Lord George, 286-87, *286*, *287*
Grendon Hall, 196, 347-48, *348*
Griffith, Thomas, Rhual, 207
Guest, Charles, Bury St Edmunds, 215, 218
Guinea, 27, 36, 51-52
Hall, Thomas, 239-41, *240*
Halliday, Thomas, 323
Halsall Mill, Ormskirk, 70, 174
Hamilton, Gilbert, Glasgow, 125-26
Hammond, Bonham, 212, 214, 218
Hammond, John, 1,192, 262, 269, *269*, 329-31, 333-34, 339
Hancock, John, 270
Hancock, John Gregory, 78, 80-81, 84-86, 104, 113, 115-18, 122, 155, 159-86, *165*, 190-92, 199-201, 209, 292, 310
Hancock, John Gregory, Jnr, 191, 324
Hancock, Robert, 163
Hancock, William, 163-64
Hardy, Thomas, 287-88
Harington, John, 1st Baron Harington of Exton, 13
Harris, Joseph, v-vi, 45, *46*
Harvey, John, Norwich, 223, 226-27, *226*, 255
Havering atte Bower, Liberty of, 136-39
Hawkesbury. *See* Liverpool, Charles Jenkinson, 1st Earl of
Hay, William Robert ('R. Y.'), 76, *77*, 177, 191-92, 194, 200, 277, 280, *290*, 291, *293*, 339
Haynes, Hopton, 28
Heslop, Robert, 241
Hogarth, William, *49*, 183, *183*

379

Hog's Wash, 284-85
Holywell, 80-83, 104, 159-60, 219, 309
Homfray, Samuel, Penydarren, 193-94
Hornchurch. *See* Havering atte Bower
Howlette, George, Coventry, 196
Hughes, Edward, 72, *72*, 73
Hurd, John, Birmingham, 116-17, 160
Hutchison, Thomas & Alexander, 125, 170-71, 300 n. 21
Ibberson, Christopher, 132-33, *133*
'Improvement', 253
Inns, issuing tokens, 16, 228
Ipswich, 298
Ipswich Journal, The, 227 n. 58, 298
Jacob, Benjamin, Birmingham, 248
Jacobs, B[enjamin], 270, 273, 324
Jackson (later Duckett), Sir George, 1st baronet, 142-43, *142*, 217
Jaffray, Henry, Stirling, 127-28, *128*
James I, 12-13, 22
James, Charles, 236, 238-39, 273-74, 280, 324
Jeayes, Henry, Coventry, 196
Jervis, Sir John (later Earl of St. Vincent), 145, 148
'Jesso' (Ezo -- Hokkaido), 241-42
Jestyn ap Gwrgan, 192-93
Johnson, Samuel, v, 209, 232
Jorden, John Stubbs, 176-77, 191-201, *200*, 212-13, 292
Jorden, William, 193
Jouvin, Albert, 20
Kauffmann, Angelica, *167*
Keir, James, 89, 94, 98
Kelly, Jasper & Simon, 248
Kempson, Peter, 140, 163, 197, 199-200, 204-10, 212-13, 217-21, 223, 241, 255, 260, 262, 265-66, 271, 276, 285, 300, 328
Kendrick, Joseph, 212, 214
Kershaw, John, Rochdale, 171
Kingdon, Samuel, Exeter, 171-72
King's Head tavern, Tower Street, 15
Knill, John, 142
Küchler, Conrad Heinrich, 123, 129, 138-39, 142, 144, 150-51, 153, 307, 324-25, 326
La Naissance de la Reine, 126
Lack, Thomas, 216
Lackington, James, 163, 185, *228*, 229-31, *230*, *231*
Lahive, Gerard, 224 n. 53
Lansdowne, William Petty, [*formerly* Fitzmaurice], 1st Marquess of (earlier 2nd Earl of Shelburne), 43, 60, 88, 100, *100*
Lawrence, Sir Thomas, *71*
Leake, Stephen Martin, 24
Leeds, 128-29, 172-73

Leslie, Charles, 35
Lichtenberg, Georg Christoph, 96
Little, Adam, *The Plough*, Rupert Street, 228
Liverpool, 70, 170, 174, 226
Liverpool, Charles Jenkinson, 1st Earl of (earlier 1st Baron Hawkesbury), 1 n. 2, 41, 44, *44*, 45, 47, 50, 58-59, 62-63, 102, 105, 109-10, 114, 148-49, 151-52, 307
Livesey, Christopher, Leeds, 334
Locke, John, 30-31, *30*
Lockwood, Morris & Company, 133-34
London Corresponding Society, 284, 287-90, *290*
Lonsdale, James, *290*
Lowestoft, 249-50, *250*
Lowndes, William, 28-30
Lowther collieries, 70
Lunar Society, 89, 124
Lutwyche, William, 163, 200, 205-6, 208-10, 212-13, 215-16, 219-24, 227, 231, 238-39, 262, 265-66, 300, 323, 325, 326, 328
Macclesfield Copper Company (Roe & Company), 72, 75, 114-18, 160-61, 174
Macclesfield, Roe monument, 117, *117*

Mackenzie, Eneas, 280
Mackintosh, Inglis & Wilson, 144
Madras presidency coinage, 140 n. 63, 145, 150, 155
Mail Coach, The, 255
Mainwaring, William, 163, 210, 212-13, 323, 325
Malcolm, Sarah, 49, *49*
Manchester, 51, 84, 222, 226, 295
Margate, 249, *252*
'Marie de Médicis Cycle', Luxembourg palace (now in the Louvre), 126
Marindin, John Philip, Birmingham, 103
Mathias, Peter, 61, 309
Matthews, Charlotte, 146
Matthews, William, 96
Mercury, 131, *131*, 234
Merrey, Walter, 46, 48, 52, 62, 68, 255
Merry, Joseph, 212-13, 215, 218, 323
Meymott & Son, 194-95
Mighell, William, Brighton, 218
Miles, Richard, 268
Milton, John, 264, 291-92, 304-9, 325
Molison, Alexander, Dundee, 260
Mona Mine Company, 71, 75
Monneron Frères, 120, 128-29, 149
Monthly Magazine, The, 301, 343
Monthly Review, The, 151
Moody, Richard Vernon, Southampton, 122

INDEX

Moon, John, Halsall mill superintendent, 70 n. 124
Mordaunt, Colonel Charles, 70, 174
More, Samuel, 104-5, 127, 160
Morgan, John, Carmarthen, 167-70, *167*
Morland, Henry, 241, *242*
Morris, John (later Sir John Morris, Bart.), 134-35
Moser, Joseph, 161, 297-99, *297*, 301-2, 310
Mossop, William, 123, 325
Motteux, John, 85, 105, 119
'Mules', 262
Murdock, William, 97-98
Museum Boulterianum, 242
Mynd, Thomas, 212, 218
Mynn, William, Goudhurst, 223-24
Mynydd Parys (Parys Mountain), 72-73, *73*, 75
Nares, Robert, v
Nattier brothers, 126, *126*
Newcastle upon Tyne, 64, 69, 301
Newgate prison, 284, 285-87, *286*, *287*, 340
Newton, Sir Isaac, 36
Newton, Richard, 286, *286*, *287*
Niblock, James, Bristol, 248-49
Nickson, John, Coventry, 196
Nixon, John, *225*, 229, *230*
Norris, Charles, *169*
North, Frederick ([*known as* Lord North], later 2nd earl of Guilford), 50, 98
Norwich, 11, 223, 226-27, 255
Oldknow, Samuel. 63-65, *63*, 67, 94
'Otaheite' medal, 105, 158
Paineite Medals, 283-84
Paley, Richard, Leeds, 129, 171-73, 262
Paper money, 66-67, 146-47, *147*
Parbury, George, 124, 127
Parys Mine Company, 70-71, 76, 78
Patrick, Benjamin, 325-26
'Peach[e], Robert', Lowestoft, 250
Peck, Charles Wilson, 261
Peckham, William, Appledore (Kent), 227-28
'Peeping Tom's House', Coventry, 196-97, *197*
Pennant, Thomas, 72-73, 257
Penryn Volunteers 'halfpenny', 141, 217
Penydarren Iron Works, 193-94, *194*
Perry, Spencer, 326
Peters, David, Perth, 190
Petty, Sir William, 21, 26
Pew, Richard, [Shaftesbury], 187
Philip, John, 326
Phillips, ----, 326
Pichler, Giovanni, 305, *305*

Pidcock, Gilbert, 235-39
Pidcock's Menagerie, Exeter Change, *234*, 235
Pig's Meat, 282-84, *282*
'Pindar, Peregrine', 229-31, *230*
Pingo, Lewis, *24*, 104, 159
Pinkerton, John, 58, 266, *266*
Pinto, Isaac de, 49
Pitt, James, 212, 214
Pitt, William, 44, 45, 83, 98, 100-3, 105, 109-10, 137, 146-47, *147*, 282, 288-89, 292
Place, Francis, 286, 332
Platter, Thomas, 10
Player, John, 224 n. 53
Pollard, Graham, 107
Polymetis. *See* Spence, Joseph
Ponthon, Noël-Alexandre, 123, 126-29, 130, 138-39, 142, 326
Portuguese coin as currency, 47-50, *48*, *50*
Powis & Hodges, Shrewsbury. *See* Salop Woollen Manufactory
Powles, Richard, 249-50, *250*
Prattent, Thomas, 270, 277-78, *277*, 324, 339-41, *341*
Pre-industrial symbolism, 253, 255, 257
Presbury & Company, Charles, 197-99
Pretor, Pew & Whitty, bankers, 163, 178, 186, *189*
Pretor, Simon, Sherborne, 186-90, *186*
Priestley, Joseph, 89 n. 58, 164, *164*, 293
Private tokens, 264-65
Pye, Charles, 78, 86-87, 116-18, 138, 140. 162-63, 166-67, 176, 185, 190-98, 208-10, 212, 222, 224, 238, 262, 264-65, 271, 273, 285, 293, 295, 300, 325-28, 334-38, 341-44
Plan of Birmingham, 212
Ramage, David, 22-23
Raspe, Rudolph Erich, 56, 123-24, *123*, 126
Ratley, Peter, 241
Recoinages: Gold, 50-52; Silver, 31-33
Redish, Angela, 297
Regal coinage, state of: Copper, 26-27, 52-61; Gold, 45-52; Silver, 27-33, 35-45
Reynolds, Sir Joshua, *100*
Rights of Man, The, 283-84, 287, 291 n. 82, 340
Robinson, Anthony, Birmingham, 157
Roe & Company. *See* Macclesfield Copper Company
Roettier, John, 26
Roll, Eric, 94-95
Romford. *See* Havering atte Bower
Rose, George, 43 n. 31, 134

Rouse, Rowland, Market Harborough, 41
Rowlandson, Thomas, 131, *131*, 197, *197*, *252*
Royal Mint, 15, 22-23, 59, 220, *221*, 303, 309
Rubens, Peter Paul, 126, *126*
Ruding, Rogers, 53
Rule, John, 64
Russell, -----, 326
St Eustatius medal, 105
St Leonard's-on-Sea, 184
Salmon, Samuel, Portsea, 228
Salop Woollen Manufactory, Shrewsbury, 178-79
Salter, Thomas, 246-48, 273
Samuel, Richard Thomas, 234
Sapperton Tunnel, 179, 181-82, *182*
Scale, John, 95, 105-6, 108
Schaak, J. S. C., *88*
Schopenhauer, Johanna, 155-56
Scottish base coin, 6, 9, 12
Shakespeare Jubilee medal, 158
Sharp, Thomas, 138, 142, 164-65, 185, 191, 195-97, 215-16, 236, 239, 261-63, 324-25, 328, 344, 346-48, *346*
Sharp, Thomas (Chichester and Portsmouth), 145, 178, 185-86
Shearer & Company, Gilbert, 125, 160, 224
Shelburne. *See* Lansdowne, William Petty, [*formerly* Fitzmaurice], 1st Marquess of
Shephard, Charles, 200, 208, 260, 269-70, 283, 310, 329, 330-45
Sherborne, 17, 186
Sherborne & Dorsetshire Bank, 186-90, *188*, *189*
Sherwin, John, Burslem, 302
Sierra Leone Company coinage, 120, 127, 129
Silver tokens, 122-23, 303-308
Sketchley, James, 245, *246*
Skidmore, John, 238-39, 263, 266, 270-77, *272*, 283, 289, 293, 324
Skidmore, Gamaliel, 273
Skidmore, Meremoth, 273, 275
Skidmore, Paul, 275-76
Small, Robert, 259
Smith, Adam, 7, 42-43, 45, 305, *305*
Smith, John Thomas ('Antiquity'), 2-4, 233, 235
Smith, -----, 327
Smollett, Tobias, 49
Snelling, Thomas, 1, 13, 24-25, *24*, *25*, *48*, 58
Soho: House, *90*, 91; Manufactory, 90-95, *92*, 156; Mint, 108
Solitude, 77-78, *78*

Southern, John, 151-52
Spence, Joseph, 162, *162*, 292, *292*
Spence, Thomas, 219, 238, 263, 266, 274, 276, 279-83, *279*, 287, 293, 331-32
Spence, William, 281, *281*, 283 n. 58
'Steam' barge, 220
Steam power, 96, 106, 219, 309
Sterne, Laurence, 41
Stockport, 84, 128
Stort navigation, 142-43
Stout, William, Lancaster, 27-29
Stubbs, George, 237
Stubbs, Peter, Warrington, 302
Stukeley, William, 77, *77*
Summers, Richard, 241
Sugar Plums, 233-34
Suspension of cash payments, 146-47, *147*, 301
Swainson, Isaac, 130-32, *130*, *131*
Swansea ('Copperopolis'), vi, 193, 224, *225*
Swediaur, Francis, 120, 123, 126
Swift, Jonathan, 66
Symonds, Henry Delahay, 285-86, *286*, *287*, 340
Taitt, William, Dowlais, 193-94
Tassie, James, *123*, 124, 305, *305*
Tassie, William, *257*
Taylor & Lloyd, Birmingham bankers, 66, 99
Taylor & Mander, 139 n. 61
Taylor, Isaac, Colchester, 344-45
Taylor, John, 88
Taylor, Moody & Company, Southampton, 119, 122, 144, 160, 228
Taylor, Walter, Southampton, 120-23, *120*, 303
Taylor, William Joseph, 133, 269, 309
Temple of the Muses, The, Finsbury Square, 229, *230*, 231, *231*
Thames & Severn Canal Company, The, 178-82
Thelwall, John, 284
Thicknesse, Philip, 51-52
Thompson, Robert, 22, 25, 281
Thompson, Thomas, 265
Thomson, James, 77
Thoresby, Ralph, 24
Times, The, 59, *108*, 109, 149, 181 n. 78, 220, 232
'Tin Man', London, 60
Token collectors, 261-65
Token weight standards, 173-74, 178, 218
Tokens, early: Medieval, 5-8; Tudor, 8-12; Royal farthing, 12-14; Seventeenth-Century, 15-23, 25

INDEX

Tollgate keepers, 58-59, *59*
Troon Canal Company, 304-7
Trow, Severn, 179, *180*, 181
Tullamore. See Charleville, Charles William Bury, 1st Viscount (later Earl of)
Turnip Man, The, 36
Tyery, Nicholas, 8-9,
Uxbridge, Henry William Paget [*formerly* Bayly], 1st Earl of (later 1st Marquess of Anglesey), 75
Vallavine, Peter, 39, 41, 48-49
Vaughan, Rice, 35
Velnos' Vegetable Syrup, 130-31, *131*
Venables, Thomas, Birmingham, 125, 139 n. 61
Vernon, John, Mint solicitor, 69
Vice, David, 118
Violet, Thomas, 15
Vivian, John, 84, 124, *124*
Voss, John, Swansea, vi, 224, *225*, 229
Walker, William & Alexander, 139 n. 61, 176
Wallace, William, 304
Walpole, Horace, 60
Waring, Samuel, 212-14, 249, 323, 326
'Washington/Eagle cents', 175-76
'Washington/Ship' halfpenny, 163, 176
Waters, Arthur William, 195, 326, 343-44
Watt, James, 75, 89 n. 58, 96, 99, 106-7, 115, 125, 165, 335
Webb, John, Newton, 195-96
Webb, Thomas, 190 n. 101, 327
Wedgwood, Josiah, 89, 92
Welch, Thomas, Birmingham, 263, 265, 342, *342*, 344
Welch, William, Birmingham, 76, 158
Westwood/Hancock consortium, 165-85, 191, 221, 223
Westwood, John, vi, 51, *51*, 74-76, 78, 80, 83, 87, 103-5, 113-17, 129, 157-75, *157*, 212, 219, 325
Westwood, John, Jnr, 148, 157, 161, 176, 188-90, 219, 263, 293, 327
Westwood, Obadiah, 51, *51*, 158, 166, 175-78, *175*, 212, 215
Whatley, George, 36-37
White Cooke, Sons, & Mason, Shrewsbury. See Salop Woollen Manufactory
Whitmore, William, 83, 204-5, *205*
Whitty, Samuel, Sherborne, 187
Whore's Curse, 46
Wilkinson, John, 66-67, 80, 83-87, *84*, 135, 161-62, 174, 206, 303
Willetts, Thomas, 209, 327
'Williams, Christopher', 330-31
Williams, John (Scorrier House), 144-45
Williams, John (London Corresponding Society), 289
Williams, Thomas, vi, 71-87, *71*, 97, 99, 103-5, 112-14, 124, 148, 157, 159-60, 204, 213, 216-19, 300
Williams, William, 113, 117, 266, 278, 289, 327
Willis, Browne, 15, 24
Wilson & Smith, Birmingham, 139-40
Wilson, Richard, 77-78, *78*
Wilson, Thomas, 97, 108, 113
Wilson, William, 113, 123, 327
Wood's Halfpence, 59
Woodcock, Robert, 153
Woodforde, James, 49, 148, 225-26, 227
Woodward, Thomas, 195, 326
Woollett, William, 77, *78*
Worship, William, 285
Worswick, Thomas, 171-72, *172*, 186
Wright, James, Jnr ('Civis'), 140-41, 150, 209, 217-19, 236, 257-60, *257*, 266, 285, 291, 300-4, 310, 345
  Drawing Book, 259, *259*
Wyatt, Charles, 83, 115, 118, 148, 157
Wyon, [Thomas], 140-41, 197, 200, 209, 328
Wyon workshop, 204, 224, 241, 271, 286, 289, 310, 328
Yallop, Sir John Harrison, Norwich, 226, 227
Young, Henry, 266-68, *267*, *268*, 334-35
Young, Matthew, 164, 268-69, *268*, 304, 306, 309, 343, 347